MARRIAGES OF EARLY EDGECOMBE COUNTY NORTH CAROLINA 1733-1868

By
Ruth Smith Williams
and
Margarette Glenn Griffin

Published by

DIXIE LETTER SERVICE

Rocky Mount, North Carolina

1958

This volume was reproduced from
An 1958 edition located in the
Publisher's private library,
Greenville, South Carolina

All rights reserved. No part of this publication may be reproduced,
stored in a retrieval system, transmitted in any form, posted
on to the web in any form or by any means without the
prior written permission of the publisher.

Please direct all correspondence and orders to:

www.southernhistoricalpress.com
or
SOUTHERN HISTORICAL PRESS, Inc.
PO BOX 1267
375 West Broad Street
Greenville, SC 29601
southernhistoricalpress@gmail.com

Originally published: Rocky Mount, NC 1958
Reprinted 2018 by:
Southern Historical Press, Inc.
ISBN #0-89308-946-X
All rights Reserved.
Printed in the United States of America

Dedicated

to

the brides and grooms of early Edgecombe and their descendants, pioneers all, who carved out of the wilderness, a center of farming, industry, religion and culture, of which present and future generations may well feel proud.

OLD MARRIAGE RECORDS

National Society D. A. R. Magazine, March, 1955

Copied by permission

Marriage records of long ago,
Interesting? I find them so.
Young people these in a nation new,
Who lived and loved and married, too.
Much more to me these records state,
Than name of bride, of groom, and wedding date.
Young builders these of the pioneer home,
Where the principles of freedom were rooted and grown.
A nation young but growing fast,
Asks much of its youth—so great its task.
They met the challenge. Well the part they played,
Our nation rests on the foundation they laid.
Our fullness of life, our freedoms, we know,
In a country new were not always so.
Our traditions, our heritage, life, the American way,
Had their beginnings with the youth of that day.
They met the challenge in the spirit of their time.
Can we do as much? It's yours now, and mine.
The spirit of our time? America's task.
The answer was given before the question was asked.
Turn to the records of long, long ago.
The blood of their veins is the same, you know,
That flows through ours. But, oh, let us pray
For the faith of our fathers. How we need it today!

      Lelia Paul Chase (Mrs. Houston)
      Member, John Sevier Chapter, Tennessee

FOREWORD

Immediately following the publication of our "Abstracts of Wills of Edgecombe County, 1733-1856," we were besieged with requests to publish the marriage records of early Edgecombe.

Co-incidentally, Mr. William Perry Johnson, editor of The North Carolinian, a genealogical quarterly magazine published in Raleigh, featured an article pertaining to the marriage records on file in the counties of North Carolina. We quote his statement concerning Edgecombe County marriage records:

> "There are 157 Marriage Bonds preserved for the 1760--1773 period. The Marriage Bonds for 1741-1759 are missing, as well as for 1774-1798. About 4000 of the original Marriage Bonds are in the Archives in Raleigh, with the exception of one file box in the Court House, dated 1761-1799.
> The Marriage Register in the Court House begins in 1851. Also in the Court House is a file of Marriage Bonds or licenses dating from 1829, but incomplete prior to 1868."

With the realization of the loss of our early records, we were determined to supplement those on file with all available authentic marriage records.

When our project became public knowledge, many old Bibles and family registers were opened to us. In fact, the response was so generous and the accumulation of fine records so great that the "Marriage, Birth and Death Records of Early Edgecombe" became two volumes: "Marriage Records of Early Edgecombe," and "Bible and Tombstone Records of Early Edgecombe," these two complementing our "Abstracts of Wills of Edgecombe County."

It is gratifying to us that we can offer this trilogy of valuable data.

As in all early records, spelling of proper names was varied. However, our aim has been to make a true copy of all available records.

                        Ruth Smith Williams
                        Margarette Glenn Griffin

January 15, 1958

ACKNOWLEDGEMENTS

We acknowledge with deep appreciation the cordial assistance of Miss Mace Edmondson, Edgecombe County Registrar of Deeds, Tarboro, North Carolina, and her staff, who were most helpful.

We are indebted to Mr. Hugh B. Johnston, Jr. for his gracious assistance and continued interest in our publications.

We are grateful to all of our contributors whose help has been so valuable in assembling this data.

INTRODUCTION

The territory covered by these marriage records has been altered considerably since the days of the earliest settlements. When Edgecombe County was first outlined in 1732, it occupied a tremendous and sparsely populated area south of the Virginia line, southwest of the Roanoke River, northwest of the Beaufort County line, and northeast of sprawling Craven County. In 1746 a new line was drawn to separate on the west what was to become on subsequent dates the modern Counties of Warren, Franklin, Vance, and Granville, with corners of Durham, Person, and perhaps even Caswell Counties.

In 1758 the thickly populated area north of Fishing Creek and the western side of the present Martin County were formed into Halifax County. In 1777 the western half of Edgecombe County was sliced off to create Nash County, and in 1855 its southern end was removed to make a considerable part of Wilson County. Excepting a few minor variations, these changes resulted in the boundaries of the Edgecombe County of today.

From 1669 to 1740 in the Colony of North Carolina, although the ideal marriage was performed by an Episcopal Minister, it was so difficult to locate ecclesiastical services that a law remained in effect whereby a couple could take two or three witnesses before the Governor or any member of his Council and obtain a lawful certificate of marriage. This was naturally a great hardship in the outlying communities, and marriages of the non-conformist (and sometimes the common-law) variety were quite common. Comparatively few marriages of that period may be proven except by deeds of gift, bequests in wills, and the records of Quaker Meetings.

With the rapid increase in population and the continuing shortage of official Episcopal Ministers, a new law was passed in 1741 with the idea of making it easier for people to get married legally. In the absence of a clergyman, any Justice of the Peace could perform the ceremony after the proper preliminary steps had been taken. The Clerk of the Court received £0.20.0 for the Governor and issued a License for an additional fee of £0.5.0, requiring a bond of £50.0.0 in Proclamation Money as a guarantee of the eligibility of the contracting parties. Finally, the Minister received £0.10.0 or the Justice of the Peace £0.5.0 for his services.

A cheaper alternative was to pay the Minister or Reader of the local Episcopal Church £0.1.6 to Publish the Banns publicly three times and supply a Certificate that could take the place of the County License. Penalties were provided by the law for the violation of either requirement, and against the intermarriage of whites, blacks, and Indians, which was described as "that abominable Mixture and spurious issue."

In 1766 the Marriage Act was amended so that weddings conducted by Presbyterian Ministers were legal after the payment of all the proper fees for a License, but a resident Episcopal clergyman could still demand the fee for the ceremony, whether or not he actually officiated. The Act of 1778 was more radical, for it allowed any Justice of the Peace or any ordained Minister of the Gospel to marry couples, for £0.20.0 North Carolina money if by license, and for £0.10.0 if by Publication. The Clerk of the Court of the County in which the bride resided could charge only £0.16.0 for issuing a License, but the amount of the bond was now increased to £500. The Quakers were privileged to continue their manner of marriage, while the Readers or Ministers of other denominations could Publish the Banns on three separate Sundays and then issue a Certificate to any Minister or Justice of the Peace for a fee of £0.4.0.

In Edgecombe County, no Marriage Bond prior to 1760 has survived, or from the period of 1774 to 1798. About 150 bonds dating from 1760 to 1773 are in the State Archives, along with some 4,000 from 1799 to 1850, when a new State Law required the keeping of a Marriage Register. (The present system of licensing has been in effect since 1868.) There has also been a considerable loss of records, even in the years listed, and it has been estimated that the bonds never reflected more than one-third of all the marriages actually performed. Consequently, those that survive are of great genealogical value, for hundreds of people married who never deeded an acre of land or owned enough personal property to feel the necessity for making a will.

Realizing the defects of the collection of Marriage Bonds and Certificates preserved in our State Archives, the joint authors of this work have endeavored to supplement their compilation by the addition of all marriages that could be inferred or proven by the wills of Edgecombe County during that period, while the present writer and several other friends have contributed many additional marriages derived from large personal collections of Bible records and of the abstracts of deeds and divisions of estates.

It is to be regretted that all surviving Family Bibles in Edgecombe County cannot be discovered and copied, and that the main body of deeds and divisions cannot be examined before this book reaches the press. Although it would be ideal for all known sources of marriage data associated with Edgecombe County to be included here, as the work will hardly be reprinted in our generation, we should understand the limitations of time and convenience under which the compilers have worked.

This volume will join their **Abstracts of The Wills of Edgecombe County, 1733 - 1856,** as an invaluable contribution to Edgecombe County genealogy.

HUGH BUCKNER JOHNSTON

Wilson, North Carolina
July 31, 1957

MINISTERS AND JUSTICES

A few of the justices and ministers who performed marriage ceremonies in Edgecombe County in its earlier years:

Capt. William J. Armstrong, Esq., 1845-1856.
Elder Joshua Barnes, 1780-1816.
Joshua Barnes, Esq., last of the ante-bellum period.
Capt. Nathan Barnes, Esq., 1759-1777.
Col. William W. Batts, Esq., last of the ante-bellum period.
Willie J. Batts, Esq. last of the ante-bellum period.
Elder Benjamin Bynum, last of the ante-bellum period.
Elder John Henry Daniel, 1837-1866.
John Dew, Esq., 1802-1811.
Capt. John Dew, Esq., 1744-1760.
Larry Dew, Esq., 1834-1862.
Joseph Farmer, Esq., 1789-1795.
Elder Nathan Gilbert, 1795-1808.
Elder Robert D. Hart, 1857-1866.
Elder Reuben Hayes, 1788-1802.
Col. Henry Horn, Esq., prior to 1785.
John Horn, Esq., 1808-1833.
Maj. Amos Johnston, Esq., 1778-1816.
Col. Jonas Johnston, Esq., 1778-1779.
Randal Johnston, Esq., 1808-1816.
Elder Joshua Lawrence, 1801-1843.
Elder Ichabod Moore, 1821-1857.
Elder John Moore, Jr., after 1775.
Elder John Moore, Sr., after 1757.
Elder Bennett P. Pitt, end of ante-bellum period.
Joab P. Pitt, Esq., 1834-1854.
Elder William Robbins, Jr., 1817-1824.
Elder William Robbins, Sr., 1817-1824.
Elder Miles Scarborough, 1780-1783.
Elder Jordan Sherrod, 1800-1842.
Elnathan Tart, Esq., to 1795.
Enos Tart, Esq., 1806-1817.
Elder Elza Taylor, Jr., after 1852.
Elder Elza Taylor, Sr., 1828-1853.
Elder Hilliard Taylor, after 1855.
Ichabod Thomas, Esq., 1804-1826.

Elder John Thomas, Jr., 1775-1782.
Elder John Thomas, Sr., Esq., 1749-1788.
Elder John R. Thomas, Esq., 1820-1826.
Elder Jonathan Thomas, 1758-1775.
Joseph Thomas, Esq., 1937-1743.
Capt. Micajah Thomas, Esq., 1760-1769.
Maj. Theophilus Thomas, Esq., 1775-1803.
Elder Thomas Wells, after 1857.
Elder William B. Williams, 1853-1866.
Elder Francis Winstead, after 1803.
James B. Woodard, Esq., 1834-1855.

From the column of The Old Reporter, in the Evening Telegram, by Mr. Hugh B. Johnston, Jr.

CLERKS OF THE SUPERIOR COURT

of

Edgecombe County, North Carolina
1760 - 1958

James Hall	1760 - 1772
Edward Hall	1772 - 1819
Michael Hearn	1820 - 1837
Joseph Bell	1837 - 1849
John Norfleet	1849 - 1855
M. A. Jones	1856 - 1864
Irvin Thigpen	1864 - 1868
John Norfleet	1868 - 1874
H. L. Staton, Jr.	1874 - 1878
W. A. Duggin	1878 - 1882
J. J. Atkinson	1882 - 1882
H. L. Staton	1883 - 1886
B. J. Keech	1886 - 1890
Ed Pennington	1890 - 1906
A. T. Walston	1906 - 1945
W. S. Babcock	1946 - 1955
Don Gilliam, Jr.	1955 - 19___

PART I

MARRIAGE RECORDS ON FILE
IN EDGECOMBE COUNTY COURT HOUSE
MARRIAGE BONDS TO 1867

The original marriage bonds of Edgecombe County, North Carolina are in possession of the North Carolina Historical Commission, Raleigh. They are filed alphabetically in boxes and may be consulted by the public.

Some of the bonds were copied by Mrs. Julia C. Maconnahay and Mrs. William S. West of the staff of the Historical Commission, and the remainder by a group of youths of Wake County, North Carolina working on a National Youth Administration project. All were alphabetized and checked by either Mrs. Maconnahay or Mrs. West.

The above compilation was typed and the index of brides was made under the supervision of the Genealogical Society of Utah, 80 North Main Street, Salt Lake City, Utah.

Edgecombe County was formed in 1732 from Bertie County, North Carolina.

Marriage Bonds are listed alphabetically under name of the groom. Bride's name appears in the index. Name which precedes the witness (w) is that of the bondsman.

MARRIAGE RECORDS
TAKEN FROM THE REGISTER FOR 1867 - 1868

A

Abingdon, Hardaman - Elizabeth Biggs, 5 Feb. 1830, Dempsey Pittman, (w) Ml. Hearn.

————, Aron - Zany Braswell, 10 May 1866, R. B. Bassett, (w) Irvin Thigpen.

Abram, Arder - Elizabeth Deal, 4 Mar. 1839, Ivey Warren.

Abram, Arder - Sarah Deal, 2 Sept. 1846, William Abram, (w) John Norfleet.

Abram, Elisha - Mary F. Dupree, 22 Aug. 1848, Jesse W. Leigh, (w) John Norfleet.

Abram, William - Polly Mayo, 18 Aug. 1846, John J. Wilson, (w) John Norfleet, Clk.

Adams, Alexander - Kiddy Wells, 4 Aug. 1836, Micajah Rose, (w) T. C. Hearn.

Adams, Hopewell - Polly Evans, 5 Oct. 1816, John Price, (w) Ml. Hearn.

Adams, James - Nancy Williams, 16 May 1835, Zachariah Weaver, (w) T. C. Hearn.

Adams, James H. - Evilina Harris, 24 Dec. 1866, m. 27 Dec. 1866 by W. W. Parker, J. P., (w) William Biggs, D. C.

Adams, Jesse St. - Martha A. Tart, 17 Dec. 1843, John Wilkinson, (w) John Norfleet, Clk.

Adams, John J. - Susan C. Ellis, 5 Nov. 1858, m. 7 Nov. 1858 by Thomas Atkinson, J. P., E. H. Joyner, (w) J. H. Dozier.

Adams, Lott - Chairty Moody, 3 Feb. 1848, Blake Williford, James Williams, (w) John Norfleet.

Adams, William - Arcady Winstead, 9 Oct. 1833, William Adams, Sr., (w) T. C. Hearn.

Adams, Willie - Louisa Braswell, 19 Aug. 1848, (w) John Norfleet.

Adkins, John - Penelope Staton, 24 Jan. 1835, Joseph Knight, (w) Ml. Hearn.

Adkins, Joseph - Delphia A. Bradley, 10 Nov. 1861, m. 22 Nov. 1866 by L. R. Cherry, J. P., Cornelius Bradley, (w) Irvin Thigpen, Clk.

Adkins, William H. - Jane Harper, 1 Feb. 1866, m. 1 Feb. 1866 by Thos. R. Owens, V. D. M., F. M. Bradley, (w) Irvin Thigpen, Clk.

Admon, Willie - Lavina Braswell, 2 July 1840, Joel D. Braswell.

Aiken, C. E. - Betty R. Dunn, 22 Feb. 1865, m. 22 Feb. 1865, Thomas R. Owens, M. G., Robert Whitehurst, (w) Irvin Thigpen.

Alford, Edmund — see Olford.

Alford, Jesse - Della Ann Downing, 4 Oct. 1859, m. 6 Oct. 1859 by John Stamper, M. G., Edmund Alford, (w) W. A. Jones, Clk.

Allen, John H. - Laura Beel, 24 Oct. 1861, m. 24 Oct. 1861 by J. B. Bobbitt, J. J. Hussey, (w) J. W. Hussey.

Allen, Richard - Betha Rud, 30 Jan. 1841, David Harrell, (w) John Norfleet, Clk.

Allen, Robert - Mary Walston, 1 Jan. 1860, m. 13 Jan. 1861 by B. P. Pitt, J. P., James Langley, (w) W. A. Jones.

Allen, Warren S. - Lettisha Sikes, 11 Sept. 1854, m. 22 Sept. 1854 by William Ellis, J. P., N. O. Owens.

Allsbrook, Jesse - Mary Ann Carlile, 3 Mar. 1856, m. 4 Mar. 1856 by R. H. Pender, J. P. (w) W. S. Pitt.

Allsbrook, Newsom - Mrs. James A. Parker, 20 June 1855, m. 20 June 1855 by Elisha Cromwell, J. P., Elisha Cromwell, (w) W. S. Pitt, Clk.

Allsbrook, James - Phebe Wall, 20 Mar. 1764, William May, (w) Thos. Cavenah.

Allsbrook, Lewis - Elizabeth Dixon, 6 Mar. 1848, James K. Harper, (w) W. L. Dozier.

Alsobrook, James - Charlotte Hanes, 21 Apr. 1837, John Taylor, (w) Ml. Hearn.

Alsobrook, William - Penelope Ellinor, 20 July 1827, Ely Porter, (w) Ml. Hearn.

Amason, David W. - Elizabeth Hays, 21 Jan. 1846, Benjamin Rogers.

Amason, Enos - Elizabeth Woodard, 28 Feb. 1831, James Woodard, (w) Ml. Hearn.

Amason, Isaac N. - M. Barnes, 23 Feb. 1839, Benjamin Rogers.

Amason, John - Elizabeth Barnes, 9 Nov. 1824, Elisha Amason, (w) Ml. Hearn.

Amason, John Jr. - Dorcas Bateman, 5 Mar. 1823, William Barnes, Robert Joyner, (w) Ml. Hearn.

Amason, Levi - Judith Woodard, 17 Mar. 1825, Elizah Price, Blake Little, (w) Ml. Hearn.

Amason, Loderick - Matilda Byrum, 21 May 1847, W. M. Staton.

Amason, Thomas - Sally Barnes, 24 Jan. 1833, (w) Ml. Hearn.

Amason, Thomas - Martha Bailey, 24 Aug. 1846, Larry D. Farmer, (w) John Norfleet, C. C.

Amason, William - Nancy Kail, 31 Aug. 1831, John Andrews, (w) Ml. Hearn.

Amis, Doner, (s. Jim Amis) - Jane Savage, 18 Apr. 1868, m. 18 Apr. 1868 by John S. Dancy, J. P. (w) Irvin Thigpen.

Anderson, George - Polly Patterson, 31 July 1824, B. Wilkinson, (w) N. Matthewson.

Anderson, George W. - Elizabeth Fountain, 27 May 1845, Jno. Manning.

Anderson, Henry - Lovey Staton, ——— 1799, George Anderson, (w) S. Wren.

Anderson, Henry - Martha Brake, 18 Feb. 1840, James Lewis, (w) Jo. Bell, C. C. C.

Anderson, Henry J. - Priscilla Wells, 26 June 1851. m. 26 June 1851 by William F. Mercer, J. P., J. H. Bullock, (w) John Norfleet, Clk.

Anderson, James - Tabitha Peal, 30 Aug. 1832, David Pittman, (w) Ml. Hearn.

Anderson, James - Martha A. J. Watkins, 22 Dec. 1832, Gilbert Mares, (w) Ml. Hearn.

Anderson, James - Frances Warbritton, 18 Feb. 1862, m. 20 Feb. 1862 by C. B. Killebrew, J. P., John Hide, (w) W. A. Jones.

Anderson, John - Nancy Taylor, 10 Sept. 1823, George Anderson, (w) Ml. Hearn, C. C. C.

Anderson, John - Sarah H. Pittman, 8 Mar. 1866, m. 15 Mar. 1866 by L. R. Cherry, J. P., James M. Mayo, (w) Irvin Thigpen, Clk.

Anderson, Joshua - Catharine Bradley, 25 Dec. 1828, Micajah Anderson, James Alsobrook, (w) Ml. Hearn.

Anderson, Josiah - Eliza H. Freeman, 3 Dec. 1829, John Lloyd, (w) Ml. Hearn.

Anderson, Micajah - Nancy Newsom, 8 Nov. 1823, John Booth, (w) Ml. Hearn.

Anderson, Micaja - Asola Denton, 22 Jan. 1861, m. 5 Feb. 1861 by John W. Johnson, J. P., (w) W. A. Jones.

Anderson, Micajah - Harriet Faithful, 10 May 1843, Joseph Pittman, (w) John Norfleet.

Anderson, Micajah - Elizabeth Ann Edwards, 27 Dec. 1850, Wesley Pittman.

Anderson, Mikajah - Eliza Fountain, 16 Mar. 1864, m. 17 Mar. 1864 by L. R. Cherry, J. P., William H. Austin, (w) T. W. Hussey.

Anderson, Nathan - Penellopy Jernigan, 19 Dec. 1845, Washington Barnes.

Anderson, Thomas - Malissa Weeks, 3 Mar. 1851, m. 4 Mar. 1851 by Lunsford R. Cherry, J. P., Henry Newsom, (w) John Norfleet.

Anderson, Thomas - Susan Weeks, 1 Apr. 1857, m. 2 Apr. 1857 by W. F. Louis, J. P., William L. Hart, (w) J. H. Dozier.

Anderson, Thomas - Rosa Gray, 21 Apr. 1866, P. J. Fugua, (w) Irvin Thigpen.

Anderson, William - Ann McDonald, 2 Nov. 1762, James McDonald, (w) John Spendelow.

Anderson, William - Mourning Price, 21 July 1763, Jonathan Coleman, (w) John Spendelow.

Anderson, Zadock - Jackey Butler, 6 Mar. 1828, (w) Ml. Hearn.

Andleton (Anderson?), Austin - Synthia Sparkman, 12 Oct. 1822, Thos. Amason, (w) N. Mathewson.

Andrews, James W. - Susan M. Howell, 3 Feb. 1861, m. 5 Feb. 1861 by William J. Long, J. P., Isaac Batts, (w) W. A. Jones Clk.

Andrews, Micajah - Elizabeth Jamerson, 26 Jan. 1763, Thomas Williams, (w) James Hall.

Andrews, Ned. - Penny Knight, 24 Dec. 1866, m. 1 Jan. 1867 by James R. Thigpen, J. P., (w) Irvin Thigpen, Clk.

Andrews, Samuel A. - C. C. Andrews, 10 Jan. 1856, m. 14 Jan. 1856 by Jesse Harrell, J. P., Randolph Wichard, (w) W. S. Pitt, Clk.

Andrews, Sherrod - Julia Bond, 14 Jan. 1866, m. 14 Jan. 1866 by Jos. Blount Cheshire, Epis. Min., J. B. Hyatt, (w) Irvin Thigpen, Clk.

Andrews, William W. - Nancy E. Taylor, 11 Dec. 1865, m. 14 Dec. 1865 by William Harvell (Harrell?) J. P., W. D. Andrews, (w) Irvin Thigpen, Clk.

Angier, Oakes - Amelia Smith, 3 June 1824, Job Felton, (w) Ml. Hearn.

Anthony, J. J. - Caroline E. Gatlin, 30 May 1854, m. 30 May 1854 by Thomas R. Owen, M. G., T. W. Ward, (w) W. S. Pitt, Clk.

Applewhite, Council - Sarah Bynum, 22 Feb. 1841, Jacob Barnes, (w) John Norfleet.

Archer, William - Polly Ann Reed, 8 July 1859, m. 10 July 1859 by Benet P. Pitt, J. P., Jonas Walston.

Armstrong, B. B. - Neomey E. Baker, 10 Apr. 1854, Amos J. Armstrong.

Armstrong, Columbus - Mary Boon, 2 Nov. 1859, m. 3 Nov. 1859 by Hilliard S. Taylor, A. B. M. G., William G. Billips, (w) J. H. Dozier.

Armstrong, Fred - Caroline Whitney, 22 June 1866, R. A. Watson, (w) Irvin Thigpen.

Armstrong, Gray - Margaret Brake, 19 Jan. 1859, m. 20 Jan. 1859 by C. B. Killebrew, J. P., Spencer L. Hart, (w) J. H. Dozier.

Armstrong, Henry - Catherine Harris, 10 May 1849, William Clark, (w) John Norfleet.

Armstrong, James H. - Emely Land, 21 Dec. 1831, Henry Austin, (w) Ml. Hearn.

Armstrong, John - Margaret S. Cawsy (Causey) 16 Jan. 1854, m. 17 Jan. 1854 by J. C. Knight, J. P., William W. Armstrong, (w) W. S. Pitt, Clk.

Armstrong, Lawrence T. - Malissa A. Pittman, 12 Dec. 1859, m. 22 Dec. 1859 by John W. Johnson, J. P., William W. Armstrong, (w) W. A. Jones.

Armstrong, Micajah - Treacy Wilkinson, 16 Mar. 1835, Gray Armstrong, (w) T. C. Hearn.

Armstrong, Robert - William Ann Peel, 11 Sept. 1858, m. 16 Sept. 1858 by C. B. Killebrew, J. P., John Peel, (w) W. A. Jones.

Armstrong, Robert H. - Luvenia F. Lancaster, 17 Nov. 1866, m. 20 Nov. 1866 by Hilyard S. Taylor, A. B. M. G. George W. Armstrong, (w) John Norfleet.

Armstrong, Thomas - Celia Taylor, 11 Oct. 1823, Orren Bullock, John Clark, (w) Ml. Hearn.

Armstrong, Thomas W. - Nancy Williams, Jan. 25, 1841, E. G. Armstrong, (w) John Norfleet.

Armstrong, William C. - Elizabeth Wells, 12 Jan. 1852, m. 13 Jan. 1852 by C. B. Killebrew, J. P., William Armstrong, (w) John Norfleet.

Armstrong, William J. - Elizabeth Braswell, 3 Jan. 1832, Henry Austin, (w) T. C. Hearn.

Armstrong, William J. - Catherine Baker, 2 Feb. 1846, G. E. Armstrong, (w) John Norfleet.

Arrington, Archibald H. - Catherine Elizabeth Wimberly, 14 Mar. 1855, m. 14 Mar. 1855 by Thomas R. Owens, M. G., T. M. Arrington, (w) W. S. Pitt, Clk.

Arrington, Arthur - Elizabeth Irwin, 7 Dec. 1830, Godwin Cotten, (w) Ml. Hearn.

Arrington, James H. - Mary W. B. Spruill, 5 Mar. 1822, John S. Thompkins, (w) Ml. Hearn.

Artis, Micajah - Rilly Eatman, 14 Apr. 1826, Hilliard Horn, (w) H. Blount, C. C. C.

Atkins, David - Martha Lane, 5 Jan. 1843, Everitt Mills, (w) John Norfleet.

Atkins, James - Emily Pope, 19 Apr. 1842, William F. Bull, (w) R. Norfleet.

Atkins, John - Lucy Portis, 6 Sept. 1834, Joshua L. Anderson, (w) T. C. Hearn.

Atkins, John - Mary Parker, 27 June 1836, John Davidson, (w) Theo. C. Hearn.

Atkins, Lawrence - Sarah Philips, 3 Sept. 1866, m. 4 Sept. 1866 by W. F. Lewis, J. P., J. A. Philips, Irvin Thigpen, Clk.

Atkins, William - Charlotte Peel, 16 Apr. 1833, Stephen Harper, (w) T. C. Hearn, D. C.

Atkinson, Alvin H. - Mary A. Ellis, 17 Aug. 1848, Lewis Ellis, (w) John Norfleet.

Atkinson, Drsury (Drury?) - Celia Vick, 16 Dec. 1827, James Jackson, (w) Ml. Hearn.

Atkinson, John A. - Esther J. Tyson, 22 Nov. 1830, James J. Horne, (w) L. H. Hearn.

Atkinson, Robert A. - Bethelda P. Biggs, 11 Sept. 1848, Bat. Weathersbee, (w) John Norfleet, Clk.

Atkinson, Theophilus - Sally Bridgers, 19 Dec. 1831, Aaron Atkinson, (w) Ml. Hearn.

Atkinson, William - Mary Pitt, 3 Oct. 1866, m. 6 Oct. 1866 by Allen Warren, J. P., Frank Wa ston, (w) Irvin Thigpen, Clk.

Atkinson, Willie - Sarah Wilkinson, 3 Jan. 1829, Thomas Gattis, (w) Ml. Hearn.

Austin, Robert H. - Delha Dancy Foreman, 16 Oct. 1860, m. 16 Oct. 1860 by Thomas R. Owens, M. G., John Norfleet, (w) W. A. Jones, Clk.

Avent, Thomas V. (s. of T. W. Avent) - Emily Spencer Hart, (dau. of Franklin Hart) 14 Apr. 1868, m. 15 Apr. 1868 by Jos. Blount Cheshire, Epis. Min., (w) Irvin Thigpen.

B

Bagley, Alvin - Elizabeth Applewhite, 21 Jan. 1852, m. 5 Feb. 1852 by Nathan Anderson, M. G., W. Thompson, (w) John Norfleet.

Bailey, Barry - Martha Williams, 21 Oct. 1841, John Williams, (w) John Norfleet.

Bailey, Birt - Mahala F. Braswell, 27 Dec. 1848, William T. Braswell, (w) Benjamin Norfleet.

Bailey, Henry - Louisa Brown, 15 Nov. 1833, William Knight, (w) T. C. Hearn.

Bailey, Richard - Charity Byrum, 25 Aug. 1847, Cofield Ellis, (w) John Norfleet.

Baker, Blake - Nancy Barnes, 17 Jan. 1825, James Barnes, (w) Ml. Hearn.

Baker, Daniel - Mary Sharpe, 20 Jan. 1857, m. 20 Jan. 1857 by Theol. Atkinson, J. P., Noah Wiggins, (w) J. H. Dozier.

Baker, David G. - Catherine Williams, 23 Jan. 1834, Moses Baker, (w) Ml. Hearn.

Baker, Evans - Catherine Dixon, 28 May 1849, Henry Dixon, (w) John Norfleet.

Baker, George - Lurana Wilson, 10 Mar. 1849, Simmons Jones, (w) John Norfleet.

Baker, James - Cherry Smith, 8 May 1832, Reddick Barnes, (w) T. C. Hearn.

Baker, James - Tempe Ellis, 21 Jan. 1846, William Varnold, (w) John Norfleet.

Baker, John - Nancy Walston, 2 June 1850, Littleton Walston, (w) John Norfleet.

Baker, Joseph H. - Susan Foxhall, 14 May 1855, m. 15 May 1855 by Jos. Blount Cheshire, Epis. Min., John A. Williams, (w) W. S. Pitt.

Baker, Richard - Nancy Bumpass, 27 Nov. 1849, Lunsford R. Cherry

Baker, Thomas - Penelopy Williams, 12 Jan. 1763, Aaron Baker.

Baker, William J. - Sally R. Powell, 8 July 1848, J. L. Bryen, (w) Benjamin Norfleet.

Baker, William S.. - Julia Shurley, 8 Jan. 1831, John Pitt, (w) L. H. Hearn.

Ballard, Joseph - Frances Dicken, 25 Feb. 1823, Barthl. Bowers, (w) Ml. Hearn.

Baly, Bennet - Ginsey Pitman, 27 Oct. 1825, Josiah Williams, (w) Ml. Hearn.
Banes, John E. - Edith Evans, 27 Aug. 1851, m. 7 Sept. 1851 by James W. Barnes, J. P., (w) John Norfleet.
Banks, Thomas - Patsey Cone, 15 Jan. 1828, Noah Leggett, (w) Ml. Hearn.
Bardin, B. H. of Wayne County - Nancy Rountree, 12 June 1854, m. 15 June 1854 by Nathan Anderson, John W. Farrow.
Barefoot, Farmer - Peggy Ellis, 1 Feb. 1842, Larry Dew.
Barefoot, Rufus - Polly Mayo, 1 Jan. 1842, Larry Dew.
Barfield, Blount - Lydia Drew, 9 June 1834, Henry Savidge, (w) Ml. Hearn.
Barfield, Bynum - Sally Drew, 24 Aug. 1829, John Gaiter. (w) Ml. Hearn.
Barfield, Ephraim - Lavina Gater, 31 Oct. 1822, John Gaitor, Fred Bell, (w) Ml. Hearn.
Barfield, Ephraim - Frances Vick. 22 May 1866, (?) m. 24 May 1811 by J. W. Howard, J. P., George W. Ward, (w) Irvin Thigpen.
Barfield, Etherington - Penelope Gaitor, 2 Sept. 1828, John Barfield, Sr., (w) Ml. Hearn.
Barfield, Ethenton - Margaret Bell, 20 Sept. 1831, Jesse Price, (w) L. H. Hearn.
Barfield. H. E. - Mary Howard, 3 Feb. 1857, m. 5 Feb. 1857 by William L. Long, J. P., Robert Howard.
Barfield, Henry - Liza Ann Downin, 14 Jan. 1854 m. 16 Feb. 1854 by R. H. Pender, J. P., Kinchen Harrell, (w) W. S. Pitt.
Barfield, John - Nancy Savedge, 19 Aug. 1833, William Garrett, (w) Ml. Hearn.
Barfield, Lewis - Sally Gaiter, 18 Mar. 1828, John Barfield, (w) Ml. Hearn.
Barker, John J. - Drucilla Rix (Ricks), 21 Dec. 1833, Alsley Bevers, (w) T. C. Hearn.
Barlow, David - Peninah Surley (Shurley?), 21 Jan. 1834, (w) T. C. Hearn.
Barlow, Miles - Cherry Staton, 27 Dec. 1865, m. 31 Dec. 1865 by Thomas R. Owen, B. D. M., J. B. Coffield, (w) Irvin Thigpen.
Barnes, Arthur - Joana Mainor, 18 Feb. 1860, m. 22 Feb. 1860 by A. H. Goddin, M. G., George Howard, Jr.
Barnes, Balum (s. of Medy Batts) - Ellen Williams (dau. of Dancy Williams), 7 Apr. 1868, m. 12 Apr. 1868 by J. W. Jenkins, M. G., (w) Irvin Thigpen.

Barnes, Benjamin - Penelope Pittman, 28 Aug. 1866, m. 1 Sept. 1866 by L. R. Cherry, B. G. Pittman, (w) M. L. Hussey.

Barnes, Bennit - Martha Eason, 22 June 1852, m. 23 June 1852 by W. Y. Moore, J P., (w) John Norfleet, Clk.

Barnes, Bryan Jr. - Sally Farmer, 22 Mar. 1823, Henry Shurley, (w) Ml. Hearn.

Barnes, Burrell W. - Francis Ruffin, 30 Dec. 1857, m. 3 Jan. 1858 by Hilliard Taylor, J. P., O. J. Proctor.

Barnes, Dempsey - Priscilla Farmer, 29 Dec. 1828, Jesse Barnes, Jr., (w) Ml. Hearn.

Barnes, Dempsey (s. of Jesse) - Judida Pitt, 25 Mar. 1836, Samuel P. Jenkins, (w) Ml. Hearn.

Barnes, Dempsey - Harriet Dew, 4 Aug. 1836, Willie Braswell, (w) T. C. Hearn.

Barnes, Dempsey - Margaret Thorn, 24 Nov. 1840.

Barnes, Edwin -Olivia Vines, 23 June 1866, m. 26 June 1866 by Erwin A. Yates, M. G., J. J. Atkinson, (w) Irvin Thigpen.

Barnes, Elias - Mahala Sharpe, 16 Feb. 1830, Orren Bullock, (w) Ml. Hearn.

Barnes, Elisha - Teresa Barnes, 30 Nov. 1846, Solo. Pender Jr., (w) E. D. Macnair.

Barnes, Francis U. - Sussannah Daws, 6 Feb. 1856, m. 7 Feb. 1856 by Theo Thomas, J. P., Miles Daws, (w) W. S. Pitt, Clk.

Barnes, Hardy - Tempe Drake, 23 May 1848, William Lodge, (w) John Norfleet.

Barnes, Hardy F. - Unity Ellis, 27 Feb. 1826, Jesse Winstead, (w) Ml. Hearn.

Barnes, Jacob H. - Aney Ann Skinner, 4 Oct. 1841, William D. Petway.

Barnes, James - Tempy Parker, 1 July 1812, Drewrey Pender, (w) N. Mathewson.

Barnes, James - Sally Barnes, 1 June 1825, Frederick F. Robbins, (w) Ml. Hearn.

Barnes, James - Elizabeth J. Robbins, 13 Apr. 1844, W. D. Thorn, (w) John Norfleet.

Barnes, James - Louisa Ellis, 27 Nov. 1849, Benjamin Norfleet.

Barnes, James A. - Sally Daniel, 12 Nov. 1836, (w) Ml. Hearn.

Barnes, James W. - Mary Ann Bridgers, 29 Sept. 1851, m. 14 Oct. 1851 by M. Williams, J. P., Thomas H. Bridgers, (w) ―――――.

Barnes, Jesse - Orpah Fort, 2 Feb. 1761, George Fort, (w) Jams. Hall.
Barnes, Jesse - Treacy Rountree, 11 Oct. 1833, Orren Bullock, (w) T. C. Hearn.
Barnes, Jesse Jr. - Sarah Rountree, 25 Feb. 1834, Joshua Barnes, (w) T. C. Hearn.
Barnes, John - Prissey Coleman, 15 July 1822, John Horn, (w) Ml. Hearn.
Barnes, Jno. R. - Margaret Ruffin, 10 Jan. 1831, Benjamin Boykin, Michael Hearn.
Barnes, Joseph J. - Elizabeth Exum, 3 Dec. 1850, Pomeroy Clark.
Barnes, Joseph J. M. - Obedience Robbins, 28 June 1837, Reddick B. Bridgers, (w) Ml. Hearn.
Barnes, Joshua - Matilda Bynum, 8 May 1843, William Barnes, Jr.
Barnes, Malachi - Ony Tisdale, 22 Feb. 1800, James Horne, (w) J. H. Hall.
Barnes, Reddick - Patsey Simms, 20 Dec. 1799, Lawrence Page, (w) S. Wren.
Barnes, Reddick Jr. - Mary Baker, 13 Jan. 1825, John Webb, (w) Ml. Hearn.
Barnes, Robert - Mary Cahoon, 29 Oct. 1819, Gray Armstrong, (w) Michl. Hearn.
Barnes, Stephen - Mary Skinner, 4 Jan. 1825, Arthur Robbins, (w) Ml. Hearn.
Barnes, Thomas - Sally Worrell, 27 Dec. 1825, William D. Farmer, (w) Ml. Hearn.
Barnes, Thomas - Louisa Ward, 3 Oct. 1854, m. 3 Oct. 1854 by John Dew, J. P., Jonathan T. Dew, (w) John Dew, Willie J. Pettway.
Barnes, Warren B. - Margaret Thomas, 26 Apr. 1830, Thomas Amason, (w) Ml. Hearn.
Barnes, Washington - Mary E. Thomas, 29 Sept. 1838, D. C. Bell, (w) Jo. Bell.
Barnes, Willi - Sindarilla Farmer, 20 Sept. 1833; Burrell Lane, (w) Ml. Hearn.
Barnes, William - Jane Wilkins, 29 Nov. 1833, Ml. Hearn.
Barnes, William - Sarah Ellis, 28 May 1839, (w) Jo. Bell, C. C.
Barnes, William R. - Betsey Worrell, 25 May 1837, James G. H. Worrell, (w) T. C. Hearn.
Barnes, William W. - Polly Eure, 7 Jan. 1845, James S. Barnes, (w) William Norfleet.

Barnes, Willie - Obedience Flowers, 25 Nov. 1825, H. Auston, (w) Ml. Hearn.
Barnes, Willie G. - Mary E. Armstrong, 8 Nov. 1850, James W. Barnes, (w) John Norfleet.
Barns, David W. - Elizabeth Thorn, 17 Dec. 1833, Jordan Robbins, (w) T. C. Hearn.
Barns, Jacob - Sarah Wester, 10 Dec. 1762, John Jones, (w) John Spendelow.
Barrett, William - Ann Carter, 3 Mar. 1767, John King.
Barron, Bolin B. - Mary E. Amanda Thomas, 8 July 1851, m. 9 July 1851 by Mark Bennett, V. D. M., Siley E. Faircloth, (w) Benjamin Norfleet.
Barron, John - Avery Pitman, 5 Nov. 1799, Jesse Pitman, (w) S. Wren.
Barron, Thomas - Elsey Morgan, 11 Aug. 1828, Benjamin Sharp. (w) Ml. Hearn.
Barron, William F. - Sally A. Boon, 26 Sept. 1844, James E. Kelly, (w) John Norfleet.
Barrow, James - Celia Cherry, 10 May 1844, William Cobb, (w) John Norfleet.
Bass, James - Eliza Daniel, 25 Nov. 1833, James A. Barnes, (w) T. C. Hearn.
Bass, John - Milisha Mabry, 29 Dec. 1827, Wilkinson Mabry (w) Ml. Hearn.
Bass, Theophilus - Winney Bass, 6 June 1843, John Norfleet.
Bass, Thomas W. - Elizabeth Barnes, 29 Nov. 1852, m. 2 Dec. 1852 by Nathan Anderson, Willie Simms, (w) Jacob S. Barnes.
Bass, Turner - Susan Dicken, 29 Dec. 1826, Coffield King, (w) Ml. Hearn.
Bass, Turner - Rebecca Mabry of Halifax, 7 Sept. 1829, Whitmell K. Bullock, (w) Ml. Hearn.
Bassett, R. B. - Mary Jane Wilson, 16 Sept. 1862, m. 17 Sept. 1862 by Charles P. Simpson, M. G., M. R. Long, (w) T. W. Hussey.
Battle, Amos - Margaret Parker, 1 Jan. 1830, (w) Ml. Hearn.
Battle, Benjamin - Henrietta Parker, 5 Oct. 1832, Amos J. Battle, (w) T. C. Hearn.
Battle, J. J. - Susan Philips, 16 Feb. 1861, m. 19 Feb. 1861 by Jos. Blount Cheshire, Epis. Min., (w) F. D. Foxhall.
Battle, Jack - Mary D. Battle, 1 Feb. 1866, m. 15 Feb. 1866 by G. H. Griffin, J. P., R. A. Watson, (w) Irvin Thigpen.
Battle, James P. - Catherine R. Horne, 11 Jan. 1858, m. 12 Jan. 1858 by Joel W. Tucker, M. G., Marcus J. Battle, (w) W. A. Jones, Clk.

Battle, Jordan - Peggy Ann Battle, 16 Aug. 1866. J. F. Allison, (w) Irvin Thigpen.

Battle, Joseph S. - Mary A. Horn, 2 Dec. 1826, Etheldred Gray, John H. Mathewson, (w) Ml. Hearn.

Battle, Kemp P. - Martha A. Battle, 24 Nov. 1855, m. 28 Nov. 1855 by Jos. Blount Cheshire, M. G., W. H. Johnston, (w) W. S. Pitt, Clk.

Battle, William S. - Elizabeth Dancy, 17 June 1845, John L. Bridgers, (w) John Norfleet.

Batts, Benjamin - Lucy Bryan, 25 May 1824, Henry Bryan (w) Ml. Hearn.

Batts, Benjamin B. - Matilda Gardner, 1 June 1848, Henry D. Hunter. John Norfleet, Clk.

Batts, Benjamin B. - Lucy Pittman, wid., 9 Nov. 1848, J. B. Hyatt, (w) John Norfleet.

Batts, David - Sally Wilkinson, 1 May 1846, Albert Farmer, (w) John Norfleet.

Batts, David W. - Pennina Gill, 6 Mar. 1855, m. 8 Mar. 1855 by Alexander Gatlin, E. H. Harriss, (w) W. S. Pitt.

Batts, James B. - Lucretia Land, 15 Mar. 1842, William J. Armstrong, (w) John Norfleet.

Batts, Jeremiah - Harriet Joyner, 14 Feb. 1839, Willie Batts.

Batts, Jeremiah - Winnaford Long, 28 July 1864, m. 31 July 1864 by L. C. Pender, J. P., Turner Peel, (w) T. W. Hussey.

Batts, John B. - Margaret Sharpe, 26 Dec. 1848, William W. Batts, (w) John Norfleet.

Batts, John - Elizabeth Farmer, 19 May 1828, David Williams, (w) Ml. Hearn.

Batts, John - Pheraby Reed, 11 Dec. 1828, Charles Mabry, (w) Ml. Hearn.

Batts, Redmond - Lucretia Gardner, 20 Jan. 1829, William Gardner, (w) Ml. Hearn.

Batts, William - Patsey Woodard, 12 Nov. 1822, (w) Ml. Hearn.

Batts, W. W. - Margaret P. Woodard, 27 Nov. 1853, Jos. R. Thorn, (w) W. S. Pitt.

Batts, William - Mary Winstead, 27 May 1839, Nathan Morris, (w) Jo. Bell, C. C. C.

Batts, William - Gatsy Thomas, 2 Aug. 1844, Willie J. Batts, (w) John Norfleet.

Batts, William B. - Martha A. Strickland, 17 May 1854, m. 18 May 1854 by L. S. Dunn, J. P., Baker W. Mabry, (w) W. S. Pitt, Clk.

Batts, Willie J. - Ann Eliza Poland, 5 Nov. 1851, m. 5 Nov. 1851 by D. W. Barnes, J. P., Calvin Moore, (w) John Norfleet.

Battley, William F. - Mary Eliza Jenkins, 15 July 1839, Weldon S. Hunter, (w) Jo. Bell.

Bealand, John - Penny Williams, 21 Oct. 1835, John Bealand, (w) T. C. Hearn.

Bealand, Josiah - Betsev Williams, 20 Oct. 1833, Benjamin Thornell, (w) T. C. Hearn.

Beardsley, Lambert P. - Nancy R. Wilkins, 20 Mar. 1860, m, 27 Mar. 1860 by Elder Benjamin Bynum, Lemuel Deberry, (w) W. A. Jones.

Bedford, John - Sally Harris, 22 June 1840, James Ellinor, (w) Jn. Norfleet.

Bedford, Thomas - Emily Williams, 30 Aug. 1836, Jos. B. Braddy, (w) L. H. Hearn.

Beech, Henry - Mary Dilliard, 26 Dec. 1837, Robert R. Braswell.

Beeland, David - Polly Pelt, 24 Oct. 1825, John Beeland, (w) Ml. Hearn.

Beeland, James - Elizabeth Jordan, 17 Aug. 1842, Frederick Jordan, (w) John Norfleet.

Beeman, Ivey - Katherine Owens, 23 July 1841, James B. Broome.

Beeman, Ivy - Tallitha Eason, 10 Dec. 1844, Benjamin Dilda, (w) John Norfleet.

Beeman, Jo. - Harriet Braswell, 2 May 1859, m. 4 May 1859 by Hilyard S. Taylor, A. B. M. G., James Mullen, (w) W. A. Jones.

Beeman, Miles - Asenith Rodgers, 23 Oct. 1843, Ashly Gay, (w) John Norfleet.

Beland, Duncan - Louisana Braswell, 22 June 1854, m. 22 June 1854 by Jno. Dancy, J. P., L. W. Vick, (w) W. S. Pitt.

Beland, Powell - Mary Griffin, 9 Feb. 1828, Jetty Griffin, (w) Ml. Hearn.

Beland, Willie - Jane Wells, 7 Mar. 1866, m. 9 Mar. 1866 by H. S. Taylor, A. B. M. G., Hilliard Davis, (w) Irvin Thigpen.

Belcher, Benjamin - Alvana Wilkerson, 16 Nov. 1859, m. 17 Nov. 1859 by George Joyner, George Belcher, (w) James H. Dozier.

Belcher, Cesar - Jane Sharpe, 1 Jan. 1866, James H. Exum, (w) Irvin Thigpen.

Belcher, Henry - Martha Shurly, 18 Apr. 1844, James Dupree, (w) John Norfleet.

Belcher, Lewis - Rebecca Pitts, 25 July 1843, A. J. Cotten, (w) John Norfleet.
Belcher, Robert - Emily Cotten, 4 Feb. 1837, Geraldus Shurley, (w) T. C. Hearn.
Belcher, Robert - Mary Mayo, 21 Dec. 1853, m. 21 Dec. 1853 by W. Y. Moore, J. P., Henry Belcher, (w) W. S. Pitt.
Belcher, Willie - Martha Cotten, 29 Dec. 1842, J. J. Porter.
Bell, Benjamin - Lewsey Amey, 20 Nov. (1768), Epathraditus Killbee.
Bell, Bennett - Matilda Webb, 26 Dec. 1865, John B. Cobb, (w) Irvin Thigpen.
Bell, Bennett B. - Susan Turner, 10 Oct. 1832, Henry S. Hyman, (w) L. H. Hearn.
Bell, David B. - Margaret S. Petway, 12 Aug. 1848, Henry Hyman, (w) John Norfleet.
Bell, Henry - Rachel Bellamy, 29 June 1866, m. 29 June 1866 by ―――――, J. B. Coffield, (w) Irvin Thigpen.
Bell, Henry E. - Aggy Jonston, 3 June 1852, m. 3 June 1852 by John W. Farmer, J. P., G. B. Sharpe, (w) John W. Farmer, J. P.
Bell, James - Lucinda Evans, 15 Feb. 1851, m. 15 Feb. 1851 by Joshua Barnes, J.P., James W. Price, (w) John Norfleet.
Bell, Joshua - Margaret Varb, 29 Oct. 1846, Simmons B. Staton, (w) John Norfleet.
Bell, L. D. - Julia Bell, 4 June 1840, McG. G. W. Bell.
Bell, Marmaduke N. Jr. - Mary Landon, 23 Feb. 1826, (w) Ml. Hearn.
Bell, Marmaduke Sr. - Mary Barfield, 10 Oct. 1844, (w) John Norfleet.
Bell, Newsom - S. A. Batts, 19 Apr. 1838, Stephen Bradley, (w) Jo. Bell, C. C.
Bell, Ricca - Tempy Anderson, 7 May 1840, Samuel Gaitor.
Bell, Richard - Sally Jones, 18 Aug. 1836, William Drew, (w) T. C. Hearn.
Bell, Robert - Betsey Walston, 16 Dec. 1823, Littleton Walston, (w) Ml. Hearn.
Bell, Thomas - Nancy Dixon, 7 Feb. 1827, Solomon Pender, (w) Ml. Hearn.
Bell, William - Elizabeth Bell, 12 Oct. 1839, Henry Hyman, (w) Jo. Bell.
Bell, William B. - Martha Savage, 10 Feb. 1852, m. 12 Feb. 1852 by Blount Cooper, Bythie Howell, (w) John Norfleet.

Bell, William H. - Laura Jones, 15 Oct. 1866, m. 16 Oct. 1866 by William F. Bell, M. G., M. L. Bell, (w) Irvin Thigpen.

Bellamy, Alexander - Sarah Boykin, 14 Dec. 1829, William Foxhall, (w) L. H. Hearn.

Bellamy, John F. - Sarah Coffield, 21 Mar. 1836, William Bellamy, (w) Ml. Hearn.

Bellamy, William E. - Mary L. Howell, 11 Mar. 1857, m. 12 Mar. 1857 by Orren Williams, J. P., J N. Edwards, (w) J. H. Dozier.

Bellamy, William Jr.   Evelina B. Benton, 8 Nov. 1828, Robert Joyner, (w) Ml. Hearn.

Bembrey, Kenneth - Mary W. Mayo, 14 Aug. 1822, Laurence Mayo, (w) N. Mathewson.

Bennet, Philomen - Lucretia Pope, 2 May 1837, (w) Ml. Hearn.

Bennett, Charles E. - Emily B. Pallomountain, 24 Apr. 1860, m. 26 Apr. 1860 by Thomas R. Owen, M. G., W. B. Smith, (w) W. A. Jones.

Bennett, Stephen - Elizabeth Bell, 10 Oct. 1829, Dempsey Bryan, (w) Ml. Hearn.

Bennett, Mark H. - Elizabeth Bridgers, 14 Sept. 1824, Dempsey Bryan, (w) Ml. Hearn.

Benson, Thomas - Martha King, 22 May 1832, Elias Bryan, (w) Ml. Hearn.

Benthall, Azal - Mary Carter, 24 Dec. 1764, Kindred Carter, (w) J. Hall.

Bergeron, Elisha - Sally Sims, 25 Feb. (1826), Nathan Eason (w) Ml. Hearn.

Best, Robert - Harriet Staton, 18 May 1841, Benjamin C. Mayo, (w) John Norfleet.

Biggs, William - Eliza Parker, 31 July 1822, Lemuel L. Parker. (w) N. Mathewson.

Bilberry, Dewell - Nancy Spicer, 24 Feb. 1823, George W. Killebrew, William D. Jenkins, (w) Ml. Hearn.

Bilberry, James - Annie H. Bradley, 20 Feb. 1823, Willis Bradley, (w) Ml. Hearn.

Bilbrowe, James - Magret Kelly, 19 Feb. 1766, Thomas Harris, (w) James Hall.

Bilbry, James - Ann Waller, 4 Dec. 1830, Ml. Hearn.

Bilbry, Nathaniel - Nancy Coffield, 31 Jan. 1824, Joshua Sasnett, (w) N. Mathewson.

Billips, William - Elizabeth Ellinor, 20 June 1833, Henry Austin, (w) T. C. Hearn.

Billups, Richard N. - Mahala Fountain, 16 Aug. 1820 (1826?), Joshua Warren, (w) John H. Mathewson.

Bird, John - Marinah Stalling, 2 Apr. 1833, John Farmer, (w) Ml. Hearn.

Bishop, Edmund - Annis Marks, 11 Jan. 1831, James Coker. (w) L. H. Hearn.

Bishup, James R. - Rovenia Proctor. 1 Dec. 1860. m. 4 Dec. 1860 by Hilyard S. Taylor, A. B. M. G., L. Harrell.

Blackburn, John - Patsey Harrison. 25 Oct. 1817, Allen Blackburn, William Edmund, (w) Ml. Hearn.

Blackburn, Turner - Mary Jackson, 6 May 1829, Richard Edmonds, (w) Ml. Hearn.

Blackburn, William - Absala Anderson, 5 Jan. 1823, Benjamin Anderson, (w) Ml. Hearn.

Blakely, John - Martha Griffis, 28 Apr. 1829, John Fort, (w) Ml. Hearn.

Blakely, Thomas J. - Nancy Stafford, 13 Oct. 1828, John Fort, (w) Ml. Hearn.

Bland, William - Abby Evans, 24 Dec. 1862, Jarrett Cross, (w) Irvin Thigpen.

Blocker, Charles - Sallie A. Cromwell. 12 May 1863, m. 12 May 1863 by J. H. Daniel, Coffield King, (w) Irvin Thigpen.

Blount, John G. - Susan A. Andrews. 12 July 1866, m. 22 July 1866 by William Harrell, J. P., John Harris, (w) Irvin Thigpen.

Blount, Rigdan - Milly Dupree, 28 Dec. 1866, m. 28 Dec 1866 by John S. Dancy, J. P., Snorwood Edwards, (w) Irvin Thigpen.

Blount, Wiggins - Levi Blount. 6 May 1839, (w) Jo Bell.

Boazman, James - Mary Ruffin, 7 Nov. 1838, Harmon Stallings, (w) Jo. Bell, C. C.

Bolton, Richard - Sarah Langston, 1 Jan. 1770, Leonard Langston.

Bond, Francis L. - Martha E. Dancy, 20 Nov. 1849, Will. Geo. Thomas, (w) John Norfleet, Clk.

Bond, Lewis - Mary Norman, 20 June 1833, Henry Johnston, (w) T. C. Hearn.

Bond, Richard - Jean Allen, 25 Nov. 1763, James Ellinor.

Bond, William - Rosy Hancy, 2 July 1852, m. 6 July 1852 by Theo. Thomas, J. P., James B. Thomas, (w) John Norfleet.

Bonner, Charles C. - Caroline Gray, 20 Nov. 1850, Edward C. Pasteur, (w) John Norfleet.

Bonner, Henry G. - William Ann Tedder, 23 Oct. 1858, m. 24 Oct. 1858 by W. Closs, M. G., E. A. Sherman, (w) W. A. Jones.

Boon, Eli - Nancy Johnston, 30 Nov. 1837, Benjamin Sharpe, (w) Jo. Bell, C. C. C.

Boon, James - Piety Wells, 4 Jan. 1825, Dempsey Jenkins, (w) Ml. Hearn.

Boon, Joshua L. - Easter Gay, 23 Oct. 1837, Bennett Braswell, (w) Jo. Bell, C. C. C.

Boon, Laynard (Maynard?) - Emeliza Brake, 24 Apr. 1832, Daniel Brake, (w) Ml. Hearn.

Boon, William - Mary Barnes, 22 July 1851, m. 24 July 1851 by Elisha Barnes, J. P., Henry Barnes, (w) John W Farmer.

Boone, Bolin J. - James C. Guion, 1 Apr. 1824, James Brenan, (w) N. Mathewson.

Booth, James - Mary Pender, 16 Sept. 1824, David Barnes, (w) Ml. Hearn.

Booth, John - Salvent Spell, 24 Dec. 1799, John W. Peyton, (w) J. Wren.

Borden, Arnold - Maria A. Brownrigg, 8 Aug. 1824, John A. Irwin, Jr., (w) Ml. Hearn.

Boseman, Isaac - Margarett Belberry, 30 Aug. 1860, m. 30 Aug. 1860 by E. D. Macnair, J. P., William Pender.

Boseman, John H. - Sally Hammond, 26 Dec. 1843, John Skinner, (w) John Norfleet.

Boseman, Moses - Cilla Armstrong, 13 Aug. 1866, m. 26 Aug. 1866 by W. W. Parker, R. A. Watson, (w) Irvin Thigpen.

Bossell, Ephraim - Delaney Daniel, 16 Jan. 1824, Levi Daniel, (w) N. Mathewson.

Bourne, Henry C. - Florence Dicken, 7 Oct. 1863, m. 8 Oct. 1863 by Thomas R. Owen, M. G., J. W. Wimbely, (w) T. W. Hussey.

Bowers, Franklin - Martha Mayo, 27 Dec. 1828, Christopher Harrell, Jr., (w) Ml. Hearn.

Bowers, George - Jennet Southerland, 16 Nov. 1824, David Barnes.

Boyce, Richard - Martha Bruce, 11 July 1853, m. 12 July 1853 by ─────, Kenneth Pippen, (w) John Norfleet.

Boykin, Edward - Esther Williams, 2 Apr. 1799, (w) S. Wren.

Boykin, John G. - Peninah Landing, 19 Nov. 1855, m. 22 Nov. 1855 by Thos. L. Maner, J. P., James H. Savedge, (w) W. S. Pitt, Clk.

Boys (Boice?), John - Eliza Hays, 23 Jan. 1855, m. 23 Jan. 1855 by Nathan Anderson, William A. Gay, (w) W. S. Pitt.

Braddy, Josephus - Sally A. F. C. Fleming, 28 Aug. 1855, m. 4 Sept. 1855 by Bennett P. Pitt, F. D. S. Fleming, (w) W. S. Pitt.

Braddy. Marmaduke - Lavinah Biggs, 17 Dec. (1812), Lemuel L. Parker, (w) Ml. Hearn.

Braddy, William J. - Elizabeth Andrews, 2 June 1849, John R. Morning, (w) Ml. Hearn.

Bradely (Bradley) Willie - Fanny Kite, 28 Mar. 1844, Joseph Kane, (w) John Norfleet.

Bradley, Benbury - Lydia Edmondson, 26 Nov. 1843, Micajah E. Bradley, (w) John Norfleet, Clk.

Bradley, Bennett - Sabra Griffin, 19 Mar. 1827, Benjamin Wilkinson (w) Ml. Hearn.

Bradley, Cornelius - Martha Bradley, 19 May 1868, m. 21 May 1868 by S. L. Hart, J. P., (w) Irvin Thigpen.

Bradley, David Jr. - Mourning Barnes, 2 Dec. 1810, Bennett Barrow, (w) Ml. Hearn.

Bradley, Elias - Mary E. Bradley, 22 June 1836, Willis Bradley, (w) Ml. Hearn.

Bradley, Francis M. - Lucy A. Atkins, 22 Nov. 1865, m. 23 Nov. 1865 by John W. Johnson, J. P., James J. Price, (w) Irvin Thigpen.

Bradley, Henry - Lucy Weeks, 15 Mar. 1853, m. 16 Mar. 1853 by Lunsford R. Cherry, J. P., Elias Bradley, (w) John Norfleet.

Bradley, John - Elizabeth Guy (Gay?), 16 May 1850, William Long, (w) John Norfleet.

Bradley, Little Berry - Winnefred Edmondson, 25 Jan. 1834, Alexander Bradley, (w) Ml. Hearn.

Bradley, Micajah E. - Senderilla Parker, 25 Mar. 1828, James Belberry, (w) Ml. Hearn.

Bradley, William E. - Caroline E. Proctor, 26 July 1860, m. 26 July 1860 by Hilyard S. Taylor, A. B. M. G., William Worsley, (w) Jas. H. Dozier.

Bradley, Willie - Nancy Linch, 21 Jan. 1828, (w) Ml. Hearn.

Bradley, Willis - Mary Bell, 14 June 1830, Richard Britt, (w) L. H. Hearn.

Bradley, Alexander - Elizabeth Edmondson, 25 Jan. 1834, Little Berry Bradley, (w) Ml. Hearn.

Bradly, John - Nancy Hales, 19 Dec. 1844, Richard Pond, (w) John Norfleet.

Bradly, Joseph John - Martha E. Leggett, 20 Dec. 1853, Elias Bradley, (w) W. S. Pitt.

Bradly, Stephen - Winifred Bradley, 25 Jan. 1853, m. 1 Feb. 1853 by William F. Lewis, J. P., David Neel, (w) John Norfleet.

Bradly, William D. - Elizabeth Bradly, 10 Mar. 1851, M. E. Bradly, (w) John Norfleet, C. C.

Bradly, William H. - Bethelda Bradley, 19 Sept. 1865, m. 19 Sept. 1865 by John W. Johnson, Jordan W. Johnson, (w) T. W. Hussey.

Bradly, Willis - Susan Bradly, 13 Mar. 1857, Elias Bradley.

Brake, Amos - Suzanna Harper, 24 Jan. 1846, James F. Clark, (w) John Norfleet.

Brake, Doris - Margaret Griffin, 20 Feb. 1832, William W. Armstrong, (w) T. C. Hearn.

Brake, John - Margaret Jane Bell, 22 July 1848, W. E. Spicer, (w) W. L. Dozier, D. C.

Brake, Josiah - Sally T. Brand, 13 Mar. 1848, William Brake, (w) John Norfleet.

Brake, Nathan - Phebe Luper, 20 Apr. 1826, Darris Brake, (w) Ml. Hearn.

Brake, William - Catherine Griffin, 15 Dec. 1841, William Griffin, (w) John Norfleet, Clk.

Brake, Willie - Catherine Trevathan, 25 Feb. 1824, Jesse Brake, (w) Ml. Hearn.

Brantley, Jacob - Rachel Rawls, 28 Feb. (1830?), Jacob S. Barnes, (w) Ml. Hearn.

Brantley, Johnston - Penelope Porter, 4 Jan. 1823, Thomas W. King, Coffield King, (w) Ml. Hearn.

Brantly, John - Elizabeth Barnes, 17 Feb. 1800, Benjamin Dickinson, (w) S. Wren.

Brasswell, Bythel - Elizabeth Griffin, 1 Sept. 1836, Benjamin Daws, John L. Peele, (w) W. L. Hearn.

Brasswell, Richard - Tabitha Alsobrook, 8 May 1832, James Ellinor, (w) L. H. Hearn.

Brasswell, Zadock R. - Evalina Gardner, 6 Mar. 1834 (1854), m. 14 Mar. 1854 by C. C. Bonner, J. P., Theophilus Moore, (w) W. S. Pitt.

Braswell, Alexander - Tempy Simpson, 29 June 1833, Bythel Braswell, (w) T. C. Hearn.

Braswell, Archelus - Margaret A. Cutchins, 24 Feb. 1848, Richard A. Savage, (w) John Norfleet.

Braswell, Baker W. - Elizabeth Harper, 10 Jan. 1859, m. 12 Jan. 1860 by John W. Johnson, Lawrence Burges, (w) W. A. Jones.

Braswell, Benjamin G. - Mary E. Hargroves, 9 Jan. 1851, m. 25 Jan. 1851 by William H. Hines, J. P., B. Williams, (w) John Norfleet.
Braswell, Bennet - Patsey Haney, 17 Apr. 1839, Nathan H. Sessums, (w) Jo. Bell.
Braswell, Bythal - Eliza Gay, 23 Feb. 1841, Willie Braswell, Young Proctor, (w) John Norfleet.
Braswell, Cally S. - Martha Ann Trevathan, 5 June 1855, T. P. Braswell, (w) W. S. Pitt, Clk.
Braswell, Caman - Winney Braswell, 29 Dec. 1866, Gray Armstrong, (w) Irvin Thigpen.
Braswell, David - Nancy Ratterford, 14 Sept. 1762, Robert Allen, (w) J. Hall.
Braswell, David - Elizabeth Taylor, 29 Jan. 1827, John Braswell. Joseph Lancaster, (w) Ml. Hearn.
Braswell, Elijah - Dicey Bradley, 12 June 1866, m. 13 June 1866 by W. F. Lewis, J. P., A. Braswell, (w) Irvin Thigpen.
Braswell, Frank - Dellah Braswell, 10 Nov. 1866, m. 13 Nov. 1866 by W. F. Lewis, J. P., Mills Speight, (w) Irvin Thigpen.
Braswell, Hardy - Indiana Hart, 12 June 1866, m. 28 June 1866 by W. F. Lewis, J. P., A Braswell, (w) Irvin Thigpen.
Braswell, Isaac - Elizabeth Moore, 2 May 1861, m. 3 May 1861 by R. W. Gatlin, J. P., J. B. Hyatt, (w) J. W. Hussey.
Braswell, James - Lucinda Proctor, 7 June 1844, Robert R. Braswell, (w) John Norfleet, Clk.
Braswell, Joel D. - Lousana Robbins, 29 Dec. 1846, Thomas J. Braswell, (w) W. L. Dozier.
Braswell, John - Rebecca Clark, 16 Dec. 1835, John P. Stewart, (w) John Norfleet.
Braswell, Lewelling - Penny Moore, 9 Sept. 1844, Moses Moore, (w) John Norfleet.
Braswell, Robert - Martha Lancaster, 12 Mar. 1850, Cally S. Braswell, (w) John Norfleet.
Braswell, Robert R. - Ansey Wilkinson, 4 Dec. 1823, Benjamin Braswell, (w) Ml. Hearn.
Braswell, Robert S. - Martha Hargrove, 30 Mar. 1858, m. 1 Apr. 1858 by Wm. R. Mercer, J. P., J. H. Draughn.
Braswell, Samuel - Mary Williams, 30 Nov. 1762, David Braswell, (w) John Spendelow.
Braswell, Sampson - ———— Moore, 31 May 1762, (Edward Moore), (w) Thomas Hall.

Braswell, Simon - Mary Turner, 25 Feb. 1764, James Braswell, (w) Thomas Hall.
Braswell, Solomon - Rachel Bird, 24 Dec. 1765, Wms. Sharrod.
Braswell, Thomas J. - Elizabeth Robbins, 19 Jan. 1846, Elza Taylor, (w) John Norfleet.
Braswell, Thomas P. - Emily Stalings, 10 Dec. 1860, m. 11 Dec. 1860 by Bennett P. Pitt, J. P., Bennett P. Jenkins, (w) J. H. Dozier.
Braswell, Wilie - Bytha Perry, 31 July 1839, Willie P. Weaver, (w) Jo. Bell, C. C.
Braswell, William H. - Emeliza Knight, 9 Dec. 1856, m. 20 Dec. 1856 by K. Thigpen, J. P., James U. Savage, (w) W. A. Jones.
Braswell, William T. - Elizabeth J. Cutchen, 30 May 1855, m. 31 May 1855 by W. F. Lewis, J. P., Allen C. Taylor, (w) W. S. Pitt.
Braswell, Willie - Mary Bullock, 13 July 1829, Orren Bullock, (w) Ml. Hearn.
Braswell. Willie C. - Mary Moonyham, 27 May 1856, m. 3 June 1856 by Wm. F. Mercer, J. P., B. W. Braswell, (w)———.
Braswell, Zadoc - Sally Howell, 27 Jan. 1800, Morriss Proctor, (w) S. Wren.
Brewer, James M. - Elizabeth A. Sparks, 8 Dec. 1847, F. L. Bond, (w) John Norfleet.
Bridgers, Allen - Liley Jones, 20 Feb. 1866, m. 25 Feb. 1866 by J. F. Batts, J. P., E. G. Worsley, (w) Irvin Thigpen.
Bridgers, Briton - Pernetta Pitt, 7 Mar. 1827, John Bridgers, (w) Ml. Hearn.
Bridgers, Edwin B. - Mary Atkinson, 15 Mar. 1851, m. 20 Mar. 1851 by Mark Bennett, V. D. M., Perry Pitt, (w) John Norfleet.
Bridgers, James - Milley Freeman, 13 Jan. 1825, Henry Austin, (w) Ml. Hearn.
Bridgers, James W. - Elizabeth Gardner, 30 Dec. 1852, m. 4 Jan. 1853 by William H. Hines, J. P., T. H. Bridgers, (w) John Norfleet.
Bridgers, William - Hester Jane Flora, 22 Aug. 1849, Spencer Stokes, (w) Benjamin Norfleet.
Bridgers, Ralph - Rhoda A. U. Atkinson, 16 Aug. 1852, m. 19 Aug. 1852 by Mark Bennett, Charles H. Jenkins, (w) John Norfleet.
Bridges, Reddin - Mary Thomas, 18 Feb. 1855, m. 20 Feb. 1855 by Theo. Atkinson, Joshua Barnes, (w) W. S. Pitt, Clk.

Bridges, Robert R. - Margaret E. Johnston, 11 Dec. 1849, John L. Bridges, (w) John Norfleet.

Briley, Allen - Susan Roberson, 9 Jan. 1847, Allen Mayo, (w) J. Norfleet.

Brinkley, Dempsey - Priscilla Price, 28 Nov. 1806, Asa Price, (w) Ml. Hearn.

Brinkley, Jackson W. - Martha Farmer, 21 Jan. 1853, m. 21 Jan. 1853 by Joshua Barnes, J. P., W. W. Flowers, (w) John Norfleet.

Brinkly, David - Gilly Brinkly, 11 Jan. 1840, David Walston, James Barnes, (w) Jo. Bell, Clk.

Brinn, Isaac - Elizabeth Clark, 15 July 1862, m. 17 July 1862 by C. B. Killebrew, J. P., William Clark, (w) Irvin Thigpen.

Brinn, Isaac M. - Catherine Morgan, 20 July 1855, m. 24 July 1855 by L. C. Pender, J. P., Braswell Brinn, (w) W. A. Jones.

Britt, Alexander - Susana Harper, 22 Dec. 1857, T. H. Lane.

Britt, David - Susan Savage, 13 Feb. 1860, m. 14 Feb. 1860 by C. B. Killebrew, J. P., Isaac W. Bryum, ? (w).

Britt, William - Sally Jones, 5 Jan. 1825, Weeks Parker, (w) Ml. Hearn.

Brooks, A. G. - Patience Simms, 23 Dec. 1851, m. 23 Dec. 1851 by J. B. Jackson, J. H. Barnes, (w) Joseph S. Holt.

Brooks, Guilford - Dicy James, 6 Aug. 1823, Willis Weathersbee, (w) Ml. Hearn.

Brown, Baker S. - Delphia A. Williams, 25 May, 1852, m. 26 May 1852 by Wm. F. Mercer, J. P., Bythal G. Brown, (w) John Norfleet.

Brown, Bythal - Catherine Moore, 31 Aug. 1847, Moses Moore, (w) John Norfleet, Clk.

Brown, Denson - Polly Thorne, 5 Feb. 1823, Peoples Hill, (w) Ml. Hearn.

Brown, Denson - Sally Hinton, 21 Jan. 1824, Jo. P. Pitt, (w) Ml. Hearn.

Brown, Denson - Temperance Hardy, 16 June 1827, Nathan Lewis, (w) Ml. Hearn.

Brown, Edwin - Margaret Vick, 29 May 1817, David Alsobrook, (w) John Norfleet.

Brown, Gray J. - Sally Ann Long, 27 May 1851, m. 27 May 1851 by William H. Hines, J. P., John I. Killebrew, (w) Benjamin Norfleet.

Brown, Henry - Rachel Ruffin, 30 June 1824, Zachariah Dew.

Brown, Joseph - Martha A. Leigh, 15 Mar. 1855, m. 15 Mar. 1855 by Jesse Harrell, J. P., William Harrell, (w) W. S. Pitt.

Brown, Joseph John - Martha Ann Taylor, 3 May 1847, Jonas Brown, (w) W. L. Dozier, (w) D. P. Clark.

Brown, Lunsford R. - Matilda Pippen, 4 Mar. 1834, Samuel Hyman, (w) Theos. C. Hearn.

Brown, Robert C. - Mary L. Daniel, 4 Dec. 1860, m. 4 Dec. 1860 by David Cobb, J. P., Rueben Cobb.

Brown, Robert C. - A. E. Daniel, 5 May 1866, m. 6 May, 1866 by C. B. Hassell, John W. Pippen, (w) Irvin Thigpen.

Brown, Theo. - Margaret Warren, 14 Apr. 1860, m. 15 Apr. 1860 by William Harrell, J. P., James R. Warren, L. B. Brown, (w) W. A. Jones.

Brown, Theophilus - Sarah Harrell, 18 Feb. 1822, John Williams, Lemmon Brown, (w) Ml. Hearn.

Brown, William - Ellen A. Hyman, 4 Dec. 1835, Lunsford Brown, (w) T. C. Hearn.

Brown, William - Betsy Hinton, 18 Dec. 1840, Denson Brown, (w) John Norfleet.

Brown, William H. - Henretta Dunford, 8 May 1866, m. 10 May 1866 by R. J. Johnson, J. P., J. E. Brown, (w) Irvin Thigpen.

Bruer, Samuel S. B. - Sally Cobb, 4 Jan. 1849, George Drake, (w) Benjamin Norfleet.

Bryan, Arthur - Rodah Hobbey, 4 Jan. 1766, David Turner, (w) T. Cavenah.

Bryan, Bartholomew - Jenny Spain, 2 Jan. 1815, Joshua Lawrence, (w) Ml. Hearn.

Bryan, Battle - Rachel Britt, 25 Aug. 1828, Marmaduke D. Braddy, (w) Ml. Hearn.

Bryan, Blake - Penelope Edmondson, 21 Dec. 1831, Weeks Harper, (w) Ml. Hearn.

Bryan, Blount - Margaret Cherry, 15 Dec. 1847, C. G. Wilkinson, (w) John Norfleet.

Bryan, Blount - Elisabeth Sherod, 11 Oct. 1864, m. 11 Oct. 1864 by John A. Stamper, Gray Bryan, (w) Irvin Thigpen.

Bryan, Drew S. - Mary E. Lawrence, 3 June 1852, m. 3 June 1852 by L. S. Dunn, J. P., D. B. Bell, (w) John Norfleet.

Bryan, Henry - Mary P. Bell, 10 Dec. 1827, Robert Joyner, (w) Ml. Hearn.

Bryan, Henry Jr. - Lucy Savage, 11 Dec. 1844, Charles Mabry, (w) John Norfleet.

Bryan, Isaac - Lucinda Lloyd, 4 Nov. 1866, Theo. Dickens, (w) I. Thigpen.

Bryan, Isaac R. - Eliza Brake, 21 Mar. 186—, W. T. Bryan, (w) I. Thigpen.

Bryan, J. C. - W. A. Staton, 4 Apr. 1866, m. 5 Apr. 1866 by Thos. T. Owen, V. D. M., W. A. Jones, (w) Irvin Thigpen.

Bryan, John - Sarah Hobby, 1 July 1766, David Turner, (w) James Hall.

Bryan, John - Martha Davis, 7 Oct. 1829, Bythel Staton, Sen., (w) Ml. Hearn.

Bryan, Joseph J. - Nancy Bryan, 18 Oct. 1866, m. 18 Oct. 1866 by W. P. Lloyd, J. P., James S. Strickland, (w) Irvin Thigpen.

Bryan, William D. - Margaret C. Benton, 11 Aug. 1835, Lemuel W. Lawrence, (w) T. C. Hearn.

Bryan, William T. - Lucy Taylor, 21 Dec. 1843, Henry Foxhall, (w) John Norfleet.

Bryant, Alexander - Sally Bryan, 14 July 1841, Martin Gardner, (w) John Norfleet.

Bryant, Battle - Sarah F. Johnson, 15 Oct. 1856, m. 16 Oct. 1856 by W. F. Lewis, J. P., Spencer Hart, (w) J. H. Dozier.

Bryant, Dempsey D. - Martha C. Johnson, 18 Sept. 1856, m. 18 Sept. 1856 by L. C. Pender, J. P., Benjamin T. Hart, (w) J. H. Dozier.

Bryant, Jacob - Inda Hargroves, 29 Jan. 1800, William Cahoon, (w) S. Wren.

Bryant, Joseph - Martha Harper, 13 July, 1854, m. 13 July 1854 by Joshua Barnes, J. P., J. W. Farrar, J. T. Dew.

Bryant, W. L. - Emiliza Bryan, 10 May 1841, John Fort.

Bryant, William - Amanda Stallings, 24 Jan. 1849, Braswell Britt, (w) John Norfleet.

Bullock, Edwin - Barsha Edwards, 3 Jan. 1828, Thomas Gatlin, (w) Ml. Hearn.

Bullock, Jesse B. - Lezina Worsley, 13 Aug. 1847, Henry R. Johnson, (w) John Norfleet.

Bullock, Jonathan - Elizabeth Bryan, 23 Mar. 1818, William Pender, (w) Michl. Hearn.

Bullock, Jonathan N. - Martha Lancaster, 24 Oct. 1851, m. 29 Oct. 1851 by W. E. Spain, J. P., J. R. Williams, (w) Benjamin Norfleet.

Bullock, Lorenzo D. B. - Jane Williams, 22 Aug. 1850, Levi L. Lancaster, (w) John Norfleet.

Bullock. Ned - Vestia Walker, 13 May 1865, m. 18 May 1865, Thos. R. Owen, M. G., Irvin Thigpen, (w) Irvin Thigpen.
Bullock, Orren - Edie Barnes, 3 May 1824, Whitmell K. Bullock, (w) N. Mathewson.
Bullock, Orren - Dolly Killebrew, 30 Aug. 1835, Thomas J. Bullock, (w) T. C. Hearn.
Bullock, Stephen - Winny Roberson, 24 Mar. 1800, Jesse Robinson, Thomas B. Jenkins, (w) J. H. Hall.
Bulluck, Bennett - Martha Barnes, 2 Oct. 1832, Willie H. Braswell, (w) Theos. C. Hearn.
Bulluck, Blount - Mary Farmer, 12 Nov. 1832, Willie H. Braswell, (w) T. C. Hearn.
Bulluck, Thomas - Sarah Taylor, 5 Feb. 1855, m. 8 Feb. 1855 by John L. Michaux, (w) W. S. Pitt.
Bulluck, William J. - Jane Thorn, 19 Apr. 1859, m. 19 Apr. 1859 by C. B. Killebrew, J. P., C. B. Killebrew, (w) W. A. Jones.
Bunn, David - Elizabeth Thomas, 29 June 1831, Joab Horne, (w) L. H. Hearn.
Bunn, Lewis - Hasty Batts, 19 May 1866, m. 20 May 1866 by J. F. Batts, J. P., Jerry Mabry, (w) Irvin Thigpen.
Bunn, Redmon - Mary H. Bryan, 12 Mar. 1832, Charles Harrison, (w) Ml. Hearn.
Bunting, Gary - Blaney Taylor, 30 Dec. 1852 by Jesse Harrell, J. P.
Bunting, Gray - Lucy Meeks, 27 Aug. 1850, Lewelling Harrell, (w) Benjamin Norfleet.
Bunting, John - Lucretia Pippen, 17 May 1806, Daniel Bunting, (w) E. Hall.
Bunting, William - Rebecca Louisa Brown, 31 Aug. 1853, William Harrell, (w) W. S. Pitt.
Buntyn, Daniel - Lydia Mayo, 24 Feb. 1825, William Hopkins, (w) Ml. Hearn.
Buntyn, Lawrence - Mary Crisp, 3 July 1828, Gideon C. Spellings, (w) Ml. Hearn.
Buntyn, Richard - Elizabeth May, 29 Oct. 1822, Lawrence Buntyn, Pitman Worsley, (w) Ml. Hearn.
Burges, George - Fatha Ann Mears, 18 Oct. 1865, m. 22 Oct. 1865 by John W. Johnson, J. P., William T. Dunn, (w) Irvin Thigpen.
Burnett, Benjamin - Elizabeth T. Powell, 6 Oct. 1849, Jas. M. Redmond, (w) Benjamin Norfleet.
Burnett, Silus - Fereby Watson, 19 Apr. (1799), Joel Bryan.

Burass, Hardy - Dicey Owens, 21 Jan. 1836, Benjamin Gay, (w) T. C. Hearn.

Burgess, Harrison - Mary Bunn, 3 Aug. 1835, Braswell Britt, (w) T. C. Hearn.

Burras, Thos. L. (s. of James) - Louisa Tyler (dau. of William). 2 Apr. 1868, m. 2 Apr. 1868 by Thos. R. Owen, V. D. M., (w) Irvin Thigpen, Clk.

Burras, Seth - Sally Loyd, 12 Apr. 1830, John Burras, James Burras, William D. Petway, (w) Ml. Hearn.

Burriss. Bennett - Martha Eason, 22 June 1852, m. 23 July 1852 by W. Y. Moore, J. P., John Thigpen, (w) John Norfleet, Clk.

Burris, Willie - Jinny Marley, 10 Feb. 1829, Nathan Marley, (w) Ml. Hearn.

Burriss, Isaac - Zoan Owens, 18 Apr. 1850, John Thigpen, (w) Benjamin Norfleet.

Burrows, John - Elizabeth Moore, 2 Mar. 1831, William D. Petway, (w) Ml. Hearn.

Burton, C. W. - L. R. Pender, 9 Oct. 1855, m. 9 Oct. 1855 by Thomas R. Owens, M. G., David Neil, (w) W. S. Pitt, Clk.

Butler, Edmund - Rebecca Odom, 18 Nov. 1835, John Lloyd, (w) Ml. Hearn.

Butts, Caleb - Viney Boykin, 28 Sept. 1835, James Etheredge, (w) Ml. Hearn.

Bynum, Benjamin - Katey Hines, 18 Nov. 1815, Turner Bynum, (w) N. Mathewson.

Bynum, Richard - Mary E. Cobb, 13 Feb. 1857, m. 17 Feb. 1857 by S. H. Daniel, M. G., Thomas D. Gray.

Bynum, Reubin - Spicy Ellis, 25 Feb. 1834, Benjamin Bynum, (w) T. C. Hearn.

Byrum, Jacob - Nancy Felton, 9 Jan. 1827, Joab Felton, (w) Ml. Hearn.

Byrum, John - Treacy Barnes, 17 Jan. 1832, David Webb, Jonas J. Bell, (w) Ml. Hearn.

Byrum, John - Amanda Owens, 9 Nov. 1858, m. 11 Nov. 1858 by R. J. Johnson, J. P., Brittain Edwards, (w) W. A. Jones.

Byrum, Patrick - Jane Felts, 16 Oct. 1854, m. 19 Oct. 1854 by W. Y. Moore, Jacob Byrum, (w) W. S. Pitt, Clk.

Byrum, Thomas - Treacy Webb, 6 June 1835, John Byrum, (w) Ml. Hearn.

Byrum, Turner - Patsey Barron, 26 Nov. 1858, m. 30 Nov. 1858 by J. R. Pitt, J. P., J. L. Bridges, (w) W. A. Jones.

C

Cabe, Josiah - Darkey Ann Nowell, 26 May 1828, John Thigpen, (w) Ml. Hearn.

Cahoon, Charles - Elisa Joiner, 20 Aug. 1866, Dowd Norfleet, (w) Irvin Thigpen.

Cahoon. Owen - Mary Braswell, 24 Mar. 1827, Moses Spicer, (w) Ml. Hearn.

Calhoon, Andrew A. - Nancy Barnes, 30 Nov. 1836, Thomas Williford, (w) Ml. Hearn.

Callaghan, John O. - Peninah Thomas, 9 Aug. 1851, m. 14 Aug. 1851 by Elisha Barnes, J. P., E. Isiah Farmer, (w) John Norfleet, Clk.

Camp, Humphrey S. - Nancy Bishop, 28 Dec. 1822, Drew Braswell, (w) Ml. Hearn.

Camper, Trim - Abba Cotton, 3 Apr. 1866, m. 7 Apr. 1866 by James F. Jenkins, J. P., Richard H. Garrett, (w) Irvin Thigpen.

Canady, John - Milly Fleming, 4 Feb. 1854, m. 7 Feb. 1854 by J. C. Knight, James Stallings, (w) W. S. Pitt, Clk.

Cannady, Samuel - Elizabeth Allen, 18 Jan. 1783, John Darman.

Capps, William - Elizabeth Revis, 23 Mar. 1853, m. 28 Mar. 1853 by R. H. Pender, J. P., Dickerson Ruffin, (w) John Norfleet.

Carlile, James - Drucilla Mayo, 26 Mar. 1836, Frederick Jones, William Smith, (w) Ml. Hearn.

Carlile, Robert - Sarah Coleman, 5 Jan. 1763, Kadar Coleman, (w) James Hall, (w) Thomas H. Hall.

Carlile, Robert Henry - Elizabeth Wyatt, 27 Oct. 1854, Green Bell, (w) M. A. Jones.

Carlisle, Bennett - Frances Cherry, 10 Dec. 1851, m. 12 Dec. 1851 by Henry T. Clark, J. P., George Lawrence Winborn, (w) John Norfleet, Clk.

Carnack, Samuel B. - Polly G. Davis, 27 May 1840, Wyatt Mayo, (w) John Norfleet.

Carney, Henry - Sabra Cherry, 1 Dec. 1823, John W. Cherry, (w) Ml. Hearn.

Carney, James - Mary A. Hopkins, 15 Jan. 1850, Right Carney, (w) John Norfleet.

Carney, Wright - Elizabeth Whitehurst, 19 Mar. 1850, Benjamin Staton, (w) John Norfleet.

Carr, David - Penina Carter, 18 Jan. 1854, m. 19 Jan. 1854 by Theo. Atkinson, J. P., Kinchen Varnell, (w) T. M. Arrington.

Carr, David - Ann Gardner, 28 Aug. 1866, m. 28 Aug. 1866 by B. P. Pitt, J. P., Phesenton Walston, (w) M. L. Hussey.

Carson, Obediah - Albena Nelson, 27 July 1829, Frederick Taylor, Wilie Council, (w) Ml. Hearn.

Carson, Sam - Sarah Freeman, 26 Nov. 1841, Samuel Carson Philip A. R. C. Cohoon.

Carthy, Green - Susan Thompson, 29 Aug. 1849, Robert H Pender.

Carter, Isaac - Georgiana Pittman, 6 Dec. 1866, m. 6 Dec. 1866 by W. P. Lloyd, J. P., Patrick Bynum, (w) Irvin Thigpen, Clk.

Carter, John - Nancy Dunford, 29 Jan. 1825, Thomas Mewborn, (w) Ml. Hearn.

Carter, John - Martha Robbins, 28 Mar. 1836, Zachariah Carter, (w) Ml. Hearn.

Carter, Lewis - Priscilla Dunford, 1 Aug. 1835, John R. Pitts, (w) Ml. Hearn.

Carter, Moore - Millicent Ellis, 15 June 1829, John Ritter, (w) Ml. Hearn.

Carter, Zachariah - Sally Ward, 6 Jan. 1836, Joab Johnston, (w) T. C. Hearn.

Causey, Cullen - Dolly Lodge, 2 Jan. 1823, Edmund Edwards, (w) Ml. Hearn, Henry Austin.

Causey, Franklin - Margaret Armstrong, 11 Jan. 1855, m. 11 Jan. 1855 by L. C. Pender, J. P., Joseph Stallings, (w) W. S. Pitt, Clk.

Causey, Greenberry - Vicey Lodge, 17 Mar. 1825, Edmund Edwards, Allen Nettles, (w) Ml. Hearn.

Causey, Leavin - Nancy McDuell, 18 Oct. 1816, Philip Causey, Thomas Harriss, (w) N. Mathewson.

Cavalier, Charles N. - Myra Lee (Daughter of Col. Richard B. Lee of Va.), 23 Aug. 1864, m. 23 Aug. 1864 by Henry T. Clark, J. P., Charles H. Snead, (w) T. W. Hussey.

Chamberlain, Spencer W. - Olivia L. Hart, 21 Nov. 1866. m. 21 Nov. 1866 by Jos. Blount Cheshire, M. G., E. E. Blake, (w) Irvin Thigpen.

Chapman, James Henry - Helen B. Gray, 5 Oct. 1858, m. 6 Oct. 1858 by Jos. Blount Cheshire, Epis. Min., K. H. Dicker, (w) William A. Jones, Clk.

Charles, Francis M. - Augusta S. Jones, 17 Apr. 1866, m. 1 May 1866 by Jos. Blount Cheshire, Epis. Min., William R. Chesson, (w) Irvin Thigpen.

Cherry, Cader - Mary Bell, 14 Nov. 1828, Coffield King, (w) Ml. Hearn.

Cherry, David - Sally Taylor, 3 Nov. 1829, Edward Cobb, (w) L. H. Hearn.

Cherry, Dawson - Nisey Edmundson, 26 Feb. 1829, Eli Howell, (w) Ml. Hearn.

Cherry, Eli - Mary E. Dupree, 10 Dec. 1847, Kenneth Thigpen, (w) John Norfleet.

Cherry, Elisha - Frankey Taylor, 2 Mar. 1837, James Deal, (w) Ml. Hearn.

Cherry, Henry C. - Mary Ann Jones, 14 Mar. 1861, m. 14 Mar. 1861 by J. B. Bobbitt, Charles B. Bennett, (w) W. A. Jones.

Cherry, Jesse - Milly Robinson, 10 Apr. 1847, Leaster S. Cobb.

Cherry, Jesse B. - Sishey Cummings, 23 Dec. 1845, William Warren, (w) John Norfleet.

Cherry, Jesse B. - Marinda Webb, 25 Nov. 1852, m. 25 Nov. 1852 by J. R. Pitt, J. P., James Barron, (w) John Norfleet, Clk.

Cherry, John E. - Henrietta Howell, 1 Dec. 1863, m. 1 Dec. 1863 by J. H. Daniel, Sr., Charles P. Jenkins, (w) J. H. Hussey.

Cherry, Lunsford R. - Milly Pittman, 31 Mar. 1826, Reddin Pittman, (w) Ml. Hearn.

Cherry, Lunsford R. - Mary George, 4 July, 1832, Charles W. Knight, (w) Ml. Hearn.

Cherry, S. T. - Margaret Killebrew, 12 Dec. 1860, m. 12 Dec. 1860 by K. Thigpen, J. P., Thomas W. Hussey, (w) W. A. Jones, Clk.

Cherry, Stephen - Malzina Sharpe, 23 Jan. 1848, Levi Cherry, (w) John Norfleet.

Cherry, Thomas B. - Emily Bell, 2 Mar. 1830, Whitmell K. Bulluck, (w) Ml. Hearn.

Cherry, Thomas F. - Emily Batts, 30 Mar. 1863, m. 31 Mar. 1863 by J. H. Daniel, Sr., J. H. Daniel, Sr., (w) Irvin Thigpen, Clk.

Cherry, William R. - Frances Savage, 21 Apr. 1857, m. 22 Apr. 1857 by K. Thigpen, J. P., Jesse Savage, (w) W. A. Jones.

Chesson, William - Laura Jones, 5 May 1866, m. 5 May 1866 by J. G. Batts, J. P., L. A. Williams, (w) Irvin Thigpen.

Chistie (Christy?), Thomas H. - Martha H. Barfield, 25 Jan. 1859, Laurence Billips, (w) W. A. Jones.

Cheshire, Joseph Blount - Elizabeth T. Parker, 8 Feb. Russell Chapman, (w) John Norfleet, Clk.

Chester, John - Patsy May, 30 Jan. 1833, Robert Owens, (w) T. C. Hearn.

Churchwell, Leroy - Polly Bunting, 5 Nov. 1847, Henry Ford, (w) John Norfleet.

Clark, Drury - Abra Holland, 8 Oct. 1799, James Holland, (w) S. Wren.

Clark, Edwin G. - Martha Barnes, 11 Oct. 1847, William Tomilson, (w) John Norfleet.

Clark, Franklin - Lucinda Armstrong, 8 Jan. 1850, William Clark, (w) John Norfleet.

Clark, Henry - Louisa Peel, 22 Apr. 1851, m. 22 Apr. 1851 by J. C. Knight, J. P., Henry R. Johnson, (w) John Norfleet.

Clark, James - Pennina Beake (Brake?), 1 Oct. 1844, William Griffin.

Clark, John - Nancy Flowers, 27 Nov. 1856, m. 27 Nov. 1856 by Lunsford R. Cherry, J. P., Thomas Tomlinson, (w) J. H. Dozier.

Clark, Francis - Lovey Savage, 2 Aug. 1831, Levi Wilkinson, (w) L. H. Hearn.

Cloman, William - Rebecca E. Mabrey, 19 Nov. 1851, m. 20 Nov. 1851 by Blount Cooper, Robert H. Austin, (w) John Norfleet.

Cobb, A. B. - Susan J. Wilkerson, 12 May 1857, m. 12 May, 1857 by Thomas Norfleet, J. P., John H. Leigh, (w) J. H. Dozier.

Cobb, David - Elizabeth Pippen, 27 Mar. 1850, Irvin Thigpen, (w) John Norfleet.

Cobb, Eaton - Mary Thigpen, 10 July 1822, John Cobb, (w) Ml. Hearn.

Cobb, Edward - Sally Cherry, 7 June 1819, John Cobb, (w) Ml. Hearn.

Cobb, Edward - Mary Belcher, 3 Dec. 1834, John Newton, Jr., (w) T. C. Hearn.

Cobb, Ephraim E. - Emily Harrill, 13 Jan. 1849, Stephen B. Cobb, (w) John Norfleet.

Cobb, Frederick W. - Celia Owens, 16 July 1828, Redding White, (w) Ml. Hearn.

Cobb, Gray - Winnifred Wootten, 7 Jan. 1825, Jonathan Gay, (w) Ml. Hearn.

Cobb, Gray - Martha Flora, 17 Mar. 1846, Benjamin Thornell, (w) John Norfleet.

Cobb, Gray - Martha Little, 16 July 1856, m. 16 July 1856 by Elisha Cromwell, J. P., Elisha Cromwell, (w) J. H. Dozier.

Cobb, Hardy - Rebecca Batts, 5 Nov. 1850, Willie J. Batts, (w) John Norfleet, Clk.

Cobb, Hines - Harriett Wells, 23 Oct. 1843, (w) John Norfleet, Clk.

Cobb, James - Elvy Bartee, 28 Nov. 1826, Blake Little, (w) Ml. Hearn.

Cobb, John Exum - Pennina Mumford, 19 May 1845, William D. Thorp, (w) John Norfleet.

Cobb, Jonas G. - Martha Ann Shelton, 18 Dec. 1849, David M. Cobb. (w) John Norfleet.

Cobb, Jonas G. - Elizabeth Owen, 7 May 1855, m. 8 May 1855 by W. Y. Moore, J. P., Levi E. Cobb, (w) W. S. Pitt, Clk.

Cobb, Joseph - Sally Kearney, 30 Mar. 1843, William Norfleet.

Cobb, Leaster S. - Margaret Braswell, 19 June 1847, Joseph Stallings, (w) John Norfleet.

Cobb, Micajah - Sally Wells, 1 Feb. 1831, William J. Armstrong, (w) John Norfleet.

Cobb, Peter - Delah Battle, 17 Feb. 1866, m. 18 Feb. 1866 by E. D. McNair, J. P., Elias Grimmer, (w) Irvin Thigpen.

Cobb, Richard - Susan Mosely, 23 Dec. 1847, Elias Sumland, (w) James H. Dozier.

Cobb, Stephen - Polly Mann, 18 Aug. 1826, Nathan Mathewson, (w) Ml. Hearn.

Cobb, Thomas - Delphis Reasons, 12 Jan. 1848, George Drake, (w) John Norfleet, Clk.

Cobb, Thomas - Mary Harris, 15 Nov. 1852, m. 15 Nov. 1852 by John F. Hughes, J. P., James Keel, (w) John Norfleet, Quincy Lawrence.

Cobb, William T. - Laura M. Worsley, 12 Dec. 1865, m. 13 Dec. 1865 by Thomas R. Owen, M. G., John A. Davis, (w) Irvin Thigpen.

Coffield, Joseph B. - Elizabeth P. Pender, 12 Sept. 1865, m. 20 Sept. 1865 by Thomas R. Owen, M. G., Donald Williams, (w) Irvin Thigpen.

Coggins, John - Margaret Bedford, 14 Sept. 1830, Solomon Pippen, (w) L. H. Hearn.

Coggins, Kenneth - Martha Morris, 19 Sept. 1847, A. R. Barlow, (w) John Norfleet.

Coggins, William - Lucinda Mayo, 25 Apr. 1843, Asa Brown, (w) John Norfleet.

Cohoon, Philip A. R. C. - Martha E. Sutton (widow), 18 Feb. 1841, Pengrine P. Clemants.

Coker, Henry - Emelissa Pittman, 4 Jan. 1860, m. 5 Jan. 1860 by Lunsford R. Cherry, J. P., Harris Pope, (w) J. H. Dozier.

Coker, John - Louisa Teat, 24 Feb. 1831, James Coker, (w) Ml. Hearn.

Coker, John - Mary Talbert, 3 Dec. 1841.

Coker, John -- Elizabeth Fountain, 4 Dec. 1858, Spear Coker, (w) W. A. Jones.

Coker, William - Charlotte Neal, 19 June 1837, Stephen Coker, (w) T. C. Hearn.

Coker, William - Penninah Denton, 26 July 1855, James Deal, (w) W. S. Pitt, Clk.

Coleman, Aaron H. - Honor Bradley, 21 Nov. 1822, Benjamin Anderson, (w) Ml. Hearn.

Coleman, John - Rebecca Dancy, 7 June 1799, James Dancy, (w) Samuel Wren.

Coleman, John - Sally Jordan, 6 Feb. 1826, Henry Taylor, (w) Ml. Hearn.

Coleman, Jonathan - Keziah Price, 4 Jan. 1763, William Anderson, (w) John Spendelow.

Coleman, Kadar - Susannah Stephenson, 5 Apr. 1764, Stephen Coleman, (w) Thomas Cavanah.

Coleman, Robert - Sarah Story (widow), 13 Aug. 1762, (w) James Hall.

Coleman, William - Agatha Hedgepeth, 14 Nov. 1820, William Barnes, (w) N. Mathewson.

Collins, David - Mary Cherry, 19 Aug. 1863, m. 20 Aug. 1863 by W. N. Pepper, J. P., J. B. Hyatt, (w) Irvin Thigpen.

Conyers, L. M. - Margaret Hart, 21 Oct. 1856, m. 22 Oct. 1856 by Thomas R. Owen, M. G., B. H. Gatlin, (w) J. H. Dozier, D. C.

Cook, F. M. - Ann Terrell, 15 Feb. 1859, W. T. Mac Nair.

Cook, Mathias - Charity Welch, 13 Apr. 1763, Josiah Swearingen, (w) James Hall.

Cook, William - Elizabeth Amazon, 12 Aug. 1844, Abram Stallings, (w) John Norfleet.

Cooper, Benton - Phillis Battle, 24 Dec. 1866, m. 25 Dec. 1866 by W. W. Parker, J. P., (w) Irvin Thigpen.

Cooper, Bynum - Jennett L. Howard, 27 Apr. 1858, m. 29 Apr. 1858 by William S. Long, J. P., Thos. W. Howard, (w) W. A. Jones.

Cooper, Eaton D. - Sarah Leggett, 4 Apr. 1827, Levin Leggett, (w) Ml. Hearn.

Corbett, Redmond - Chloe Hattaway, 29 Apr. 1835, Gray Edwards, (w) Ml. Hearn.

Corbitt, Allen - Tamsy Harris, 4 May 1846, Jackson Corbitt, (w) John Norfleet.

Corbitt, Allen - Sally Abrams, 11 Mar. 1858, Adam Corbett, (w) W. H. Jones.
Corbitt, Jesse - Delphia Felton, 21 Jan. 1851, Jacob Bynum, (w) John Norfleet.
Corbitt, Reading - Vina Wootten, 22 Jan. 1823, Clemon Shivers, H. Willeford, (w) Ml. Hearn.
Corbitt, Samuel - Ansy Ritter, 6 July 1836, Enos Harrell, (w) T. C. Hearn.
Corbitt, Shadrach - Harriett Howard, 1 July 1835, John Mayo, (w) Ml. Hearn.
Corbit, Washington - Jacksie Louisa Edwards, 8 Aug. 1841, Ashley H. Edwards.
Cornish, John - Temperance Barnes, 20 Nov. 1828, Levi Worrell, (w) Ml. Hearn.
Cornish, William - Louisa Stallings, 9 Nov. 1834, John Cornish, (w) Tho. C. Hearn.
Cotten, Alex S. - Martha Wilkins, Jan. 1814, Spencer Cotten, (w) Ml. Hearn.
Cotten, Amos, - Zilpha Wimberly, 23 Oct. 1760, Joseph Cotten, (w) James Hall.
Cotten, Andrew - Elizabeth Belcher, 1 Jan. 1844, James Dupree.
Cotten, Andrew J. - Mary E. Jenkins, 11 Aug. 1856, m. 12 Aug. 1856 by R. J. Carson, M. G., Jesse Mercer, (w) J. H. Dozier.
Cotten, Arthur S. - Louisa Mayo, 8 May 1827, Kenneth C. Staton, (w) Ml. Hearn.
Cotten, Edward S. - Penny Hawkins, 15 Mar. 1847, Elias Bradley, (w) John Norfleet.
Cotten, Frederick R. - Elizabeth W. Coffield, 23 Sept. 1846, John Norfleet.
Cotton, John L. - Emily Savage, 4 Feb. 1836, Noah Leggett, (w) T. C. Hearn.
Cotton, John W. - Laura P. Clark, 19 Dec. 1832, Albert B. Stith, (w) Theodore C. Hearn.
Cotton, Robert - Abselle Cotton, 7 Oct. 1763, Joseph Cotton, (w) E. J. Hall.
Council, Josiah - Charlotte Taylor, 31 Oct. 1838, Willie Council, (w) Jo. Bell, C. C.
Council, Willie - Julia Purviss, 14 Sept. 1836, Joshua Pender, (w) T. C. Hearn.
Cowans, Noah C. - Malinda Lewis, 8 July 1824, Lewis D. Wilson.

Cox, William - Penelope B. Battle, 25 Nov. 1856, m. 27 Nov. 1856 by Jos. Blount Cheshire, M. G., John L. Bridgers, (w) W. A. Jones.

Craft, Thomas - Matilda Bynum, 24 Nov. 1846, Abner Eason, (w) John Norfleet.

Crawford, James L. - Sally Ann Andrews. 14 Jan. 1858, m. 14 Jan. 1858 by David Cobb, J. P., W. J. Andrews, (w) J. H. Dozier.

Crawford, William T. - Martha C. Biggs, 19 Dec. 1865, m. 20 Dec. 1865 by C. B. Hassell, J. B. Coffield, (w) Irvin Thigpen.

Crenshaw, William M. - Catherine Austin, 12 Feb. 1839, W. A. Jeffreys, (w) Jo. Bell.

Crickmon, Sion - Winaford Burras, 9 Jan. 1866, m. 10 Jan. 1866 by J. G. Barkley, B. M., Willie Burras, (w) Irvin Thigpen.

Crisp, Ashley - Rosina Eagles, ————, Ezekial Crisp, (w) John Norfleet.

Crisp, Benjamin - Charlotte House, 10 Aug. 1835, Guilford M. Mooring, (w) T. C. Hearn.

Crisp, Eason - Zoa Ann Edwards, 11 Feb. 1837, Ezekiel Crisp, (w) Ml. Hearn.

Crisp, Ezekial - Louisa Cobb, 25 ——— 1835, Abner C. Wilkinson, (w) Ml. Hearn.

Crisp, G. W. - Nancy Carson, 26 Dec. 1840, Lewelling Staton.

Crisp, Jesse - Nancy Crisp, 8 Aug. 1838, Lawrence Buntyn, (w) Jo. Bell.

Crisp, Jesse Jr. - Liza Barnhill, 10 Nov. 1827, R. Cherry, (w) Ml. Hearn.

Crisp, John W. - Jennett Crisp, 20 Nov. 1832, Gray Andrews, (w) Ml. Hearn.

Crisp, Levi - Lucinda Cobb, 30 Jan. 1841, Ezekiel Crisp, (w) John Norfleet.

Crisp, Silas E. - Sally E. Edwards, 7 Jan. 1857, m. 8 Jan. 1857 by W. Y. Moore, J. P., James Johnson, (w) J. H. Dozier.

Crisp, Theophilus - Elizabeth Wright, 31 Mar..1849, Laurence Buntyn, (w) John Norfleet.

Crisp, William S. - Cindarilla Edwards, 16 Feb. 1856, m. 21 Feb. 1856 by W. Y. Moore, J. P., Silas E. Crisp, (w) W. S. Pitt, Clk.

Crofton, Norman - Sarah L. Philips, 1 Sept. 1846, D. Barlow.

Cromwell, Elisha - Margaret Cromwell, 1 Feb. 1848, Kenneth Thigpen, (w) John Norfleet, Clk.

Cromwell, Lewis - Anna Hargrove, 30 June 1866, m. 30 June 1866 by J. B. Coffield, (w) Irvin Thigpen.

Cromwell, Newsom - Martha McDowell, 28 Dec. 1829, Job Thigpen, (w) Ml. Hearn.

Cromwell, Patrick S. - Peninah Little, 14 Aug. 1826, William D. Petway, (w) S. W. Sugg.

Crone, John - Edith Gay, 25 Oct. 1854, m. 26 Oct. 1854 by C. C. Bonner, J. P., W. B. Crone, M. Wester, W. B. Turner, (w) W. S. Pitt.

Cross, Stephen - Polly Neill, 17 Apr. 1799, R. Cathen, (w) Samuel Wrenn.

Crowley, H. C. - Priscilla Pettitt, 31 Oct. 1866, m. 31 Oct. 1866 by E. D. McNaire, J. P., E. S. Thigpen, (w) Irvin Thigpen.

Crudup, George - Priscilla Thomas, 2 May 1761, Samuel Edwards, (w) James ———

Crudup, Josiah - Elizabeth Battle, 28 Nov. 1767, Elisha Battle, (w) Edward Hall.

Culpepper, Erasmus - Chloe Whitehead, 17 Aug. 1765, Thomas Whitehead, (w) J. Hall.

Culpepper, Robert A. - Milly Braswell, 8 Jan. 1855, Francis M. B. Curl, (w) W. S. Pitt, Clk.

Cummings, David - Elizabeth Dunn, 7 Jan. 1847, John Dunn, (w) John Norfleet.

Cummings, David - Mary Dunn, 21 Mar. 1848, John Dunn, (w) John Norfleet, Clk.

Cummings, Joshua - Rebecca Ann Dupree, 3 Apr. 1858, m. 4 Apr. 1858 by Bennett P. Pitt, J. P., Staten Cummings, (w) W. A. Jones.

Curry, James - Sally Hopkins, 9 Apr. 1844, Benberry Bradley, (w) William Norfleet.

Cutchen, Eli - Sally Ann Odom, 29 Sept. 1852, m. 31 Sept. 1852 by Thomas L. Maner, J. P., Henry E. Odom, (w) John Norfleet.

Cutchen, Elijah - Conzada Parker, 23 Dec. 1848, Weeks Harper, (w) John Norfleet.

Cutchen, Harry - Henretta Cherry, 15 Oct. 1866, m. 21 Oct. 1866 by L. R. Cherry, J. P., J. M. Cutchin, (w) Irvin Thigpen.

Cutchen, Joseph H. - Ellen Hart, 24 Nov. 1858, A. Braswell.

Cutchin, Eli - Harriett Horn, 19 Nov. 1829, Josiah Cutchins, (w) W. S. Pitt.

Cutchin, Josiah - Sally Best, 8 Dec. 1825, Willie R. Howard, (w) Ml. Hearn.

Cutchin, Norfleet - Peggy Ann Bradley, 5 May 1853, m. 10 May 1853 by R. Pittman, J. P.. Jos. Cutchin, (w) Benjamin Norfleet.

Cutchin, Thomas - Mary Best, 21 June 1824, (w) Ml. Hearn.

Cutchin, Thomas H. - Hester Ann M. L. Linch, 15 Aug. 1835, Henry Johnston, (w) T. C. Hearn.

Cutchin, William - Mary A. Barfield, 9 Jan. 1855, m. 11 Jan. 1855 by W. F. Lewis, J. P., Thomas F. Cherry, (w) W. S Pitt, Clk.

D

Dancy, Cicero - Indiana Dancy, 1 Mar. 1866, m. 1 Mar. 1866 by Jos. Blount Cheshire, M. G., James E. Simonson, (w) Irvin Thigpen.

Dancy, John Sol. - Cornelia V. Battle, 11 Dec. 1843, William F. Martin, (w) John Norfleet.

Dancy, John S. - Ann E. Hyman, 10 Nov. 1858, m. 11 Nov. 1858 by Jos. Blount Cheshire, M. G., F. D. Foxhall, (w) W. A. Jones, Clk.

Dancy, Leander - Mary Ann Glover, 3 Aug. 1866, m. 3 Aug. 1866 by J. F. Batts, J. P., Henry Sparrow, (w) Irvin Thigpen.

Dancy, William - Agnes Little, 20 Aug. 1765, Robert Gray, (w) James Hall.

Dancy, William F. - Mary Eliza Battle, 14 Jan. 1858, m. 14 Jan. 1858 by Jos. Blount Cheshire, M. G., John S. Dancy, (w) W. A. Jones, Clk.

Daniel, Enos - Martha Bateman, 20 Dec. 1844. Ruffin Daniel, (w) John Norfleet.

Daniel, Isaac - Nancy Parker, 24 Aug. 1829, Frederick F. Robbins, (w) Ml. Hearn.

Daniel, Jacob - Sally Barnes, 31 Dec. 1823, Stephen Barnes Jr., (w) N. Mathewson.

Daniel, James - Eliza Purvis, 20 Dec. 1851, m. 23 Dec. 1851 by William Hyman, M. G., Ander J. Purvis, (w) John Norfleet, Clk.

Daniel, James R. - Catherine Wiggins, 2 July 1849, Orrin P. Daniel, (w) John Norfleet.

Daniel, John H. - Miniza Long, 26 Dec. 1825, Nathan Woodard, (w) Ml. Hearn.

Daniel, John J. - Sally Ann Donaldson, 28 Dec. 1831, David Williams, (w) Ml. Hearn.

Daniel, John T. - Polly Wiggins, 22 July 1850, Justice H. Daniel, (w) John Norfleet.

Daniel, Justice G. - Julia A. Bynum, 7 June 1848, William S. Daniel, (w) John Norfleet.
Daniel, Robert L. - Emily Purvis, 13 Oct. 1849, John A. Purvis, John Norfleet, Clk.
Daniel, Dempsey - Lydia Knight, 15 Apr. 1824, Willis Knight, (w) Ml. Hearn.
Daniel, Thomas - Sally Barnes, 4 July 1831, Canady Morgan, (w) L. H. Hearn.
Daniel, William B. - Amanda W. Williford, 9 Dec. 1845, John G. Williford, (w) John Norfleet.
Daniel, William B. - Penina Williford, 12 Apr. 1855, m. 14 Apr. 1855 by Alex Gattis, Pharoah Farmer, (w) W. S. Pitt, Clk.
Daniel, Willie - Eliza Rountree, 25 Jan. 1847, Joshua Barnes.
Daughtridge, Alfred   Polly Griffin, 22 Jan. 1851, William M. Daughtridge, (w) John Norfleet.
Daughtridge, Eli - Charity Ruffin, 5 Dec. 1863, m. 8 Dec. 1863 by Hilyard S. Taylor, A. B. M. G., (w) Irvin Thigpen.
Daughtridge, Redmond, Eveline Davis, 22 Jan. 1862, m. 23 Jan. 1862 by Hilyard S. Taylor, A. B. M. G., Nathan Lewis, (w) T. W. Hussey.
Daughtridge, Richard H. - Harriett L. A. Minor, 30 Oct. 1866, m. 1 Nov. 1866 by Hilyard S Taylor, A. B. M. G., Redmond Daughtridge, (w) Irvin Thigpen.
Daughtry, Jeremiah - Peggy Davis, 17 July 1828, James Jackson, (w) Ml. Hearn.
Daughtry, Reddin - Priscilla Ford, 11 Oct. 1837, Wm. A. Pope, (w) T. C. Hearn.
Daughtry, William - Priscilla Dahaughtry, 21 July 1824, Hardy Flowers.
See Dortridge.
Daughtry, William H. - Mary E. Braswell, 1 July 1853, m. 16 July 1853 by William H. Hines, J. P., Birt Bailey, (w) John Norfleet.
Dautridge, William - Elizabeth Proctor, 23 Dec. 1851, m. 28 Dec. 1851 by Theo. Thomas, J. P., Joshua L. Bond, (w) John Norfleet.
Dautridge, Willie - Sophy Braswell, 3 Nov. 1847, John W. Robbins, (w) John Norfleet.
Davenport, George - Mary Ann Taylor, 4 March 1845, William Taylor, (w) William Norfleet
Davis, Benjamin - Elizabeth Wootten, 1 Jan. 1833, Robert Davis. (w) Ml. Hearn.

Davis, Henry - Patsey Price, 30 Mar. 1825, Bythel Straton, (w) Ml. Hearn.

Davis, James - Louiza Barfield, 9 Jan. 1849, Marcus C. Davis, (w) John Norfleet.

Davis, Jesse - Milbury Morris, 1 July 1822, John Horn, (w) Ml. Hearn.

Davis, John A. - Jennie E. Worsley, 2 Oct. 1815, (1865?), m. 30 Oct. 1865 by Thos. R. Owen, W. L. Cobb, (w) Irvin Thigpen.

Davis, Miles - Harriet Barnes, 13 Mar. 1855, m. 15 Mar. 1855 by Theo. Thomas, J. P., B. W. Barnes, (w) W. L. Pitt, Clk.

Davis, Robert - Russia Ann Nettle, 11 Jan. 1841, John Walston.

Davis, Stephen D. C. - Nancy Gray, 13 Feb. 1838, John H. Ricks, (w) Jo. Bell, C. C.

Davis, Thomas - Sarah Colwell, 28 Feb. 1764, Joshua Johnson, (w) Edward Hall.

Davis, Thomas - Anne King, 25 Dec. 1769, John King.

Davis, Willoughby J. - Temperance Stallings, 25 Mar. 1850, John W. Davis, (w) John Norfleet.

Daws, Benjamin - Nancy Braswell, 18 Dec. 1827, John Daws, (w) Ml. Hearn.

Daws, Ephrem - Nancy Adams, 21 Mar. 1837, Wm. Adams, (w) T. C. Hearn.

Daws, John - Nancy Robbins, 18 Feb. 1826, Jacob Robbins, (w) Ml. Hearn.

Daws, Martin - Nelly Edwards, 5 Feb. 1835, Isaac Robins, (w) Ml. Hearn.

Daws, Nathan - Mary Farmer, 30 Sept. 1829, Burrel Land, (w) Ml. Hearn.

Daws, Reddin - Sarah Sharpe, 2 Oct. 1860, m. 5 Oct. 1860 by Hilyard S. Taylor, M. G., Hilliard Daws, (w) W. A. Jones.

Day, John - Margaret Mitchell, 11 Feb. 1832, Thos. D. Gatlin, (w) Ml. Hearn.

Deal, John - Sally Lucinda Edwards, 15 Dec. 1858, m. 19 Dec. 1858 by Benit P. Pitt, J. P., John T. Brown, (w) W. A. Jones, Clk.

Deale, James - Emily Lawrence, 14 Feb. 1839, Ivey Warren, (w) Jo. Bell.

Deans, Benjamin - Obedience Barnes, 27 Nov. 1832, William Barnes, Jesse Barnes, Jr., (w) Ml. Hearn.

Deans, Dempsey - Delphia Farmer, 11 Sept. 1843, Jacob Taylor, (w) John Norfleet.

Deans, James - Penny Barnes, 15 Dec. 1830, James Barnes, (w) L. H. Hearn.

Deans, Willie - Martha Simms, 27 Oct. 1840, William Woodard.

Deberry, Lemuel - Elizabeth Stanton, 7 Jan. 1828, Nathan N. Rountree, (w) Ml. Hearn.

Deloach, James - Emily Ponds, 17 Apr. 1861, m. 21 Apr. 1861 by J. B. Bobbit, Jesse C. Little, (w) W. A. Jones, Clk.

Deloach, Jess - Penelope Ruffin, 8 Mar. 1768, William Deloach, (w) Edward Hall.

Denton, Benjamin - Mary L. Womack, 1 June 1855, E. C. McDowell, (w) W. S. Pitt, Clk.

Denton, Exum F. - Susan Anderson, 29 July 1845, Micajah E. Bradley, (w) John Norfleet, Clk.

Denton, James - Julia Ann Lilly, 25 Nov. 1859, m. 25 Nov. 1859 by William R. Cherry, J. P., R. A. Savage, (w) W. A. Jones, Clk.

Denton, John - Sally Lee, 25 Oct. 1832, James Ellinor (w) Ml. Hearn.

Denton, Thomas H. - Celestia Tyler, 2 Apr. 1863, m. 2 Apr. 1863 by W. F. Lewis, J. P., William F. Lewis, (w) Irvin Thigpen.

Denton, William Henry - Ona Ruffin, 1 Nov. 1858, m. 8 Nov. 1858 by Lunsford R. Cherry, J. P., Jordan Philips, (w) J. H. Dozier.

Denton, Willie - Eliza Shirley, 15 Oct. 1860, m. 15 Oct. 1869 by W. F. Lewis, J. P., Jordan Philips, (w) W. A. Jones.

Devanport, Frederick - Harriett Manning, 9 Oct. 1825, Delaney Whitehurst, (w) John H. Mathewson.

Dew, Abraham - Elizabeth Hickman, 2 Dec. 1763, Nathaniel Hickman, (w) John Spendelow.

Dew, George - Nancy Lawrence, 7 Mar. 1844, John Garrett, (w) John Norfleet, Clk.

Dew, John - Martha Simms, 26 Feb. 1844, Larry D. Farmer.

Dew, Jonathan T. - Martha Ann Ellis, 2 May 1853, m. 10 May 1853 by W. Edmundson, J. P., Jos. Barbee, J. P. Edwards, (w) John Norfleet, Clk.

Dew, Lewis - Sally Causeway, 6 Aug. 1842, Gray Lodge, (w) John Norfleet, Clk.

Dicken, George - Amanda Sherod, 13 Mar. 1866, m. 15 Mar. 1866 by J. F. Batts, J. P., E. M. Bryan, (w) Irvin Thigpen.

Dicken, Henry - Sarah Savage, 7 Feb. 1845, William H. Savage, (w) John Norfleet, Clk.
Dicken, Jacob - Lucy Swanner, 3 Mar. 1866, Dolphin Dickens, (w) Irvin Thigpen.
Dicken. Matthew H. - Claranda Dixon, 4 Apr. 1831, Isaac Tolbot, (w) Ml. Hearn.
Dicken, William H. - Lucy Thurston, 15 Mar. 1834, Benjamin Boykin, (w) T. C. Hearn.
Dickens, George - Amy Hargrove, 19 June 1866, m. 21 June 1866 by W. F. Lewis, J. P., H. L. Leggett, (w) Irvin Thigpen.
Dickens, James - Milly Cobb, 11 May 1866, m. 12 May 1866 by William Harrell, J. P., J. B. Coffield, (w) Irvin Thigpen.
Dickens, Lewis - Susan Mabrey, 8 Oct. 1823, William Savage, (w) N. Mathewson.
Dickens, Peter - Arie Mabrey, 21 Feb. 1866, m. 15 Apr. 1866 by J. F. Batts, J. P., Bythul Mabrey, (w) Irvin Thigpen.
Dickens, William N. - Delah Fountain, 21 Aug. 1861, m. 25 Aug. 1864 by W. F. Lewis, J. P., R. J. Lane, (w) Irvin Thigpen.
Dickinson, Jacob - Mourning Thomas, 19 Nov. 1770, George Wimberly, (w) William Hall.
Dickson, Randall - Louisa Harriss, 4 Mar. 1828, Augustin Farmer, (w) Ml. Hearn.
Dildy, Benjamin - Absly Howard, 27 Apr. 1841, James R. Broome, (w) John Norfleet, Clk.
Dildy, Benjamin - Matilda Cobb, 28 May 1847, Lewis Dildy, (w) John Norfleet.
Dilliard, Henry - Maria Braswell, 8 July 1834, Thomas Dickinson, (w) L. H. Hearn.
Dilliard, Henry N. - Polly Hill, 22 Dec. 1830, Allen Jones, (w) Ml. Hearn.
Dilliard, James - Elizabeth Long, 19 Dec. 1831, Benjamin Wilkinson, (w) Ml. Hearn.
Dilliard, James - Delitha Jones, 7 Feb. 1854, m. 14 Feb. 1854 by C. W. Speers, R. S. Petway, (w) W. S. Pitt, Clk.
Dilliard, John - Mary Moore, 31 Mar. 1762, Robert Roberts.
Dilliard, John - Margarett Taylor, 3 Feb. 1866, m. 4 Feb. 1866 by Hilyard Taylor, M. G., R. A. Watson, (w) Irvin Thigpen.
Dilliard, Orren - Mary Warbbleton, 10 Feb. 1846, Henry B. Johnson, (w) John Norfleet.
Dilliard, Orren - Mary Watkins, 6 Jan. 1852, m. 6 Jan. 1852 by W. E. Spicer, J. P., Henry R. Johnson, (w) John Norfleet, Clk.

Dixon, Green - Betsey Robbins, 4 Oct. 1831, Joseph Winstead, (w) L. H. Hearn.

Dixon, Green - Elizabeth Bradley, 12 Nov. 1799, David Bradley, (w) S. Wren.

Dixon, Hardy C. - Martha Armstrong, 15 Mar. 1849, Henry Dixon, (w) John Norfleet.

Dixon, Henry - Susan Moore, 20 Oct. 1834, Burrell Moore, (w) T. C. Hearn.

Dixon, Henry Q. - Mary L. Bradley, 6 Jan. 1866, m. 7 Jan. 1866 by L. R. Cherry, J. P., James W. House, (w) Irvin Thigpen.

Dixon, Jesse - Elizabeth Barnes, 1 Mar. 1853, m. 17 Mar. 1853 by William H. Hines, J. P., W. W. Batts, (w) Benjamin Norfleet.

Dixon, John R. - Hulda L. Daniel, 4 Sept. 1865, m. 7 Sept. 1865 by Go. Joyner, M. G., R. C. Brown, (w) Irvin Thigpen.

Dixon, Miller - Elizabeth Wilson, 4 Oct. 1864, m. 5 Oct. 1864 by W. R. Jordan, J. P., Robert Whitehurst, (w) Irvin Thigpen.

Dixon, Nicholas - Catherine Dew, 18 Dec. 1815, Elijah Robbins, (w) Ml. Hearn.

Dixon, Orran - Nancy Pitman, 27 —— 1838, Stephen Coker, John Coker, (w) Jo. Bell, C. C. C.

Dixon, Randall - Jane Griffin, 4 Apr. 1850, Baker B. Armstrong.

Dixon, Thomas - Sarah Sellers, 15 June 1763, Thomas Pridgeon.

Dixon, William - Pennina Barnes, 30 Jan. 1849, Randall Dixon, (w) John Norfleet.

Doil, Edmond - Priscilla Wember (Wemberley?), 18 Feb. 1832, Bennett H. Bell, Edwin Doyel, (w) T. C. Hearn.

Dordan, Cornelius - Rhoda Grimes, 25 Aug. 1813, John Rakestraw.

Dorman, Edwin - Susan Weeks, 4 Jan. 1836, Samuel Proctor, (w) Ml. Hearn.

Dortch, James - Amanda M. Parker, 15 Dec. 1837, (w) Jo. Bell, C. C.

Dortch, Lewis J. - Nancy J. Adams, 10 Oct. 1844, John Wilkinson.

Dortridge (Daughtridge), John - Zela Cobb, 20 Sept. 1825, Dorson Cobb, (w) N. Mathewson.

Dowd, Henry A. - Laura Baker, 19 Jan. 1859, m. 20 Jan. 1859 by Thomas R. Owen, M. G., John Norfleet, (w) J. H. Dozier.

Dowd, Patrick W. - Martha A. Austin, 21 Oct. 1830, Reading S. Long, (w) L. H. Hearn.

Downing, Henry - Martha Z. Leggett, 24 Dec. 1855, James K. Harper, (w) W. S. Pitt, Clk.

Downing, James Jr. - Britania Savidge, 9 Jan. 1828, Thomas Gatlin, (w) Ml. Hearn.

Dozier, Frederick - Mary Ann Trevathan, 11 May 1848, William R. Hunter, (w) John Norfleet.

Dozier, James H. - Catherine E. Jones, 24 Jan. 1855, m. 24 Jan. 1855 by Thomas R. Owen, M. G., Thomas A. Macnair, (w) T. M. Arrington.

Dozier, Philip - Coatney Shurley, 24 Dec. 1865, m. 25 Dec. 1865 by Thomas R. Owen, M. G., Jesse B. Hyatt, (w) Irvin Thigpen.

Dozier, Thomas - Nancy Lewis, 14 Feb. 1825, Alanson Powell, Stephen Bradley, Jr., (w) Ml. Hearn.

Dozier, W. L. - William A. Knight, 6 Aug. 1850, A. H. Macnair, (w) John Norfleet, Clk.

Drake, Edmund - Mary Mann, 3 Dec. 1763, Nathaniel Drake, (w) Edward Hall.

Drake, George Gustus - Louisiana Brown, 14 Dec. 1853, m. 16 Dec. 1853 by J. C. Knight, J. P., (w) K. H. Lewis.

Drake, Henry - Mary Nettle, 6 July 1822, Levi Drake, (w) Ml. Hearn.

Drake, Levi - Frances Drew, 22 Nov. 1865, m. 22 Nov. 1865 by R. Norfleet, J. P., James J. Price, (w) Irvin Thigpen.

Drane, Robert B. - Catherine C. Hargrave, 3 Dec. 1850, Ben M. Jackson, (w) John Norfleet.

Draper, John - Francis Porter, 22 May 1855, J. J. Johnson, (w) W. S. Pitt, Clk.

Draughan, James H. - Arretta Braswell, 9 Mar. 1858, m. 11 Mar. 1858 by William F. Mercer, J. P., (w) W. A. Jones.

Draughan, William - Susan Lyon, 29 Oct. 1836, Burrell Dunn, (w) T. C. Hearn.

Draughon, John - Winnifred Williams, 24 Jan. 1827, Josiah Williams, (w) Ml. Hearn.

Draughon, John W. - Elizabeth Draughon, 29 Jan. 1832, Moses Robbins, (w) L. H. Hearn.

Draughon, Miles W. - William Ann Whitehead, 12 Apr. 1862, m. 13 Apr. 1862 by John I. Proctor, J. P., James H. Draughon, (w) W. A. Jones.

Drew, John - Priscilla Bryant, 28 Jan. 1828, Drew King, (w) Ml. Hearn.

Drew, Thomas - Mary Pippen, 30 Jan. 1843, William W. Batts, (w) John Norfleet.
Drew, William - Iley Bell, 2 Jan. 1836, Richard Bell, (w) T. C. Hearn.
Duggan, John S. - Mary Sasnett, 28 Dec. 1830, Thomas Gatlin, (w) Ml. Hearn.
Duggin, James B. - Mary Ann Alsobrook, 17 Jan. 1835, William S. Duggan, T. C. Hearn.
Dun, Alexander R. - Mary Barnes, 8 Aug. 1850, Edwin G. Clark, (w) L. D. Farmer.
Duncan, Richard - Martha A. Pitman, 26 Sept. 1852, m. 23 Oct. 1852 by A. Weaver, M. G., Oliver P. Pittman, (w) W. A. Jones.
Dunford, William - Henrietta Atkinson, 24 Feb. 1845, John Harrell, (w) John Norfleet.
Dunford, William P. - Winnafred Pitt, 29 Jan. 1855, m. 29 Jan. 1855 by James Carney, J. P., Nathan Everett, (w) T. M. Arrington.
Dunfred, William A. S. - Elizabeth Femings (Fleming?), 13 Aug. 1833, William Taylor, (w) T. C. Hearn.
Dunn, Ashly - Martha Whitehead, 24 Oct. 1849, Anson Dunn, (w) John Norfleet, Clk.
Dunn, Bennett - Kesiah Whitly, 25 Sept. 1858, m. 27 Sept. 1858 by Theo. Atkinson, J. P., Richard Dunn, (w) W. A. Jones, Clk.
Dunn, Burrell - Lucinda Draughon, 21 Jan. 1828 Lamon Dunn, (w) Ml. Hearn.
Dunn, Charles - Mary Knight, 18 Sept. 1866, m. 30 Sept. 1866 by E. D. Macnair, W. T. Macnair, (w) Irvin Thigpen.
Dunn, David W. - Henrietta Price, 26 Dec. 1855, m. 27 Dec. 1855 by Jordan Thigpen, J. P., L. S. Dunn, (w) W. S. Pitt, Clk.
Dunn, Jacob - Polly Pitt, 25 Apr. 1818, James R. Dupree, (w) Ml. Hearn.
Dunn, James - Mary Stallings, 3 Aug. 1836, Joseph B. Braddy, (w) T. C. Hearn.
Dunn, James B. - Nancy Howerton, 7 Oct. 1845, Larry Dunn, (w) John Norfleet, Clk.
Dunn, John - Julia Whitley, 26 July 1842, Jacob Whitley, (w) John Norfleet, Clk, (w) S. Cooper Benjamin, (w) Dinion Fergusson.
Dunn, Joseph - Maomi (Naomi?) Owens, 21 Dec. 1852, Richard Dunn, (w) John Norfleet.

Dunn, Lemon S. - Georgiana V. Gatlin, 10 May 1851, m. 13 May 1851 by Thomas R. Owen, M. G., Charles E. Neal, (w) John Norfleet.

Dunn, Nicholas - Jane Gardner, 14 Feb. 1859, m. 16 Feb. 1859 by Bennett P. Pitt, J. P., Richard Dunn, (w) W. A. Jones, Clk.

Dunn, Ralph - Frances Hogans, 2 Sept. 1858, m. 2 Sept. 1858 by John W. Johnson, J. P., Allen Mosely, (w) W. A. Jones, Clk.

Dunn, Stephen - Elizabeth Dew, 16 Jan. 1852, m. 18 Jan. 1852 by B. B. Barron, J. P., Jesse A. B. Thorn, (w) John Norfleet, Clk.

Dunn, Thomas - Easter Owens, 12 Nov. 1845, Joab Johnson, (w) E. D. Macnair.

Dunn, William - Nancy Stallings, 11 Feb. 1828, John Dunn, (w) Ml. Hearn.

Dupree, Allen F. - Margarett E. Cobb, 10 Nov. 1866, m. 13 Nov. 1866 by Wm. Harrell, J. P., C. H. Jenkins, (w) Irvin Thigpen.

Dupree, Allen R. - Mary Thigpen, 12 Aug. 1843, Kenneth Thigpen.

Dupree, James - Winniford Wells, 12 Feb. 1861, m. 12 Feb. 1861 by Bennett P. Pitt, J. P., T. W. Hussey, (w) W. A. Jones, Clk.

Dupree, Louis - Mary E. Shurley, 2 June 1846, Henry Belcher, (w) John Norfleet.

Dupree, Sharper - Jane Jenkins, 25 Dec. 1866, m. 25 Dec. 1866 by John S. Dancy, Nelson Dupree, (w) Irvin Thigpen.

Dupree, William R. - James (?) C. Boone, 26 Dec. 1827, Geraldus Shurley, (w) Ml. Hearn.

Durden, Mackinley - Sally Brantley, 20 Dec. 1823, Levi Daniel, Peter Knight, (w) Ml. Hearn.

E

Eaeson, Ithiel - Penelope Eason, 21 Nov. 1831, Whitmell K. Bulluck, (w) Ml. Hearn.

Eagles, Richard T. - Penelope Eason, 20 Dec. 1831, William W. Edwards, (w) Ml. Hearn.

Earle, John W. - Martha C. Pope, 11 Aug. 1846, William J. Drake, (w) John Norfleet.

Eason, Abner - Elizabeth Pettaway, 24 May 1825, Johnathan Thomas, (w) Ml. Hearn.

Eason, Asa R. - Amanda Dilder, 12 Dec. 1854, m. 13 Dec. 1854 by Jesse Baker, Bennett Burrus, (w) W. S. Pitt, Clk.

Eason, James - Lydia Hotlett, 11 Sept. 1844, Joseph Forbes, (w) John Norfleet.
Eason, John S. - Winnefred W. Carr, 1 Nov. 1822, John Williams, (w) Ml. Hearn.
Eason, Nathan - Penelope Haddock, 1 June 1818, Elijah Owens, (w) Ml. Hearn, Spencer L. Hart.
Eason, Obed - Frances Lester, 17 Feb. 1800, Jesse Barnes.
Eason, Thomas - Nancy Anderson, 21 June 1823, Joseph R. Lloyd, (w) N. Mathewson.
Eason, Thomas E. - Caroline Eason, 22 Nov. 1848, Theophilus F. Eason, (w) John Norfleet.
Eatmon, Haman - Chasy Bath, 25 June 1853, m. 26 June 1853 by D. W. Barnes, David Batts, (w) John Norfleet.
Eatmon, Edwin - Francis Wilkinson, 3 Oct. 1850, John W. Farmer, (w) Jos. C. Taylor, J. P.
Eborn, Benjamin F. - Delia A. Little, 13 July 1858, m. 13 July 1858 by William Closs, Louis G. Little, (w) W. A. Jones, Clk.
Edge, James - Mary Ann Griffith, 31 Oct. 1840, G. W. Killebrew, (w) John Norfleet, Clk.
Edge, James - Mary Griffin, 9 Dec. 1841, G. W. Killebrew.
Edmonds, William - Dolly Hopkins, 19 Sept. 1856, m. 21 Sept. 1856 by William S. Long, J. P., Henry Griffin, (w) J. H. Dozier.
Edmondson, Alfred - Lucinda Hawkins, 14 Mar. 1832, Thomas Howard, (w) Ml. Hearn, C. C.
Edmondson, Andrew Mc. - Felitha Ann Barfield, 25 Jan. 1859, N. Mathewson.
Edmondson, Asa - Louisa Bradley, 10 Oct. 1826, Pollard Edmondson, (w) T. C. Hearn.
Edmondson, Asa - Nancy Porter, 30 Oct. 1832, Thomas Howard, (w) Ml. Hearn, C. C.
Edmondson, Elias - Hannah Cutchen, 8 Dec. 1825, John Edmondson, (w) Ml. Hearn.
Edmondson James - Cinderilla Crisp, 14 Aug. 1846, John Mooring, (w) John Norfleet.
Edmondson, John - Elizabeth Wilkinson, 19 Aug. 1845, B. A. Thigpen, (w) John Norfleet.
Edmondson, John - Nancy Parker, 3 Dec. 1828, C. C. Knight, (w) M. Hearn.
Edmondson, Josiah - Margarett E. Stallings, 21 Aug. 1860, m. 22 Aug. 1860 by Henry T. Clark, J. P., James W. J. House, (w) W. A. Jones.

Edmondson, Mansel - Mary Smith, 31 Dec. 1855, m. 1 Jan. 1856 by David Cobb, J. P., Joseph Edmondson, (w) W. S. Pitt, Clk.

Edmondson, McG. - Mary Parker, 19 Dec. 1855, m. 20 Dec. 1855 by Wm. S. Long, J. P., Horris E. Barfield, (w) W. S. Pitt, Clk.

Edmondson, Pollard - Susan Howard, 2 Oct. 1839, Thomas Edmondson, (w) Jo. Bell, C. C.

Edmondson, Pollard Patsy Manning, 7 Jan. 1845, James S. Long, (w) John Norfleet.

Edmondson, Pollard - Peggy Harrell, 22 Nov. 1848, R. H. Pender, (w) John Norfleet.

Edmondson, Willie - Ann Smith, 24 Dec. 1853, Mansel Edmondson, (w) W. S. Pitt, Clk.

Edmonson, Willie - Ann Smith, 20 Dec. 1853, m. 20 Dec. 1853 by Jesse Harrell, J. P., (w) W. S. Pitt, Clk.

Edmund, John B. (of Halifax) - Martha Dillard, 14 Jan. 1841, Jethro Edmund, (w) John Norfleet, Clk.

Edmunds, William - Amelia Bell, 5 Oct. 1848, Thomas Karr, (w) John Norfleet.

Edmundson, Anderson Mc. - Tabitha Ann Barfield, 24 Jan. 1859, m. 25 Jan. 1859 by Wm. K. Cherry, J. P., (w) W. A. Jones, Clk.

Edwards, Benjamin - Sally Eagles, 13 Apr. 1826, Grandy Etheridge, Frederick Etheridge, (w) Ml. Hearn.

Edwards, Brittain - Winnefred Byrum, 24 Mar. 1846, Levi Edwards, (w) John Norfleet, Clk.

Edwards, Edmund - Rachel Causey, 21 Dec. 1822, Cullen Causey, Henry Austin, (w) Ml. Hearn.

Edwards, Edward - Zilphy Batts, 16 Jan. 1838, William Batts, (w) Jo. Bell, C. C.

Edwards, Edwin - Elizabeth Batts, 10 Apr. 1841, John J. Winstead.

Edwards, Elbert - Celia Crisp, 27 Nov. 1857, m. 27 Nov. 1857 by W. Y. Moore, J. P., David Langley, (w) W. A. Jones, Clk.

Edwards, Elsberry - Jane Mosely, 29 Aug. 1855, m. 29 Aug. 1855 by James Carney, J. P., Benjamin Hathaway, (w) W. S. Pitt, Clk.

Edwards, Ely - Presay Wooten, 15 Mar. 1841, Job Deal, (w) John Norfleet, Clk.

Edwards, Ephrain W. - Cyrenia Edwards, 15 Oct. 1860, m. 16 Oct. 1860 by Bennett P. Pitt, J. P., William W. Edwards, (w) J. H. Dozier.

Edwards, Frederick - Elizabeth Howard, 4 Aug. 1849, William D. Petway, (w) John Norfleet.

Edwards, James G. - Prudence· H. Philips, 24 Nov. 1835, William W. Edwards, (w) T. C. Hearn.

Edwards, Joel - Mary Ann Lewis, 3 Apr. 1833, Gray Edwards, (w) Ml. Hearn.

Edwards, John B. - Person Edwards, 22 Sept. 1824, Turner Whitehead, (w) Ml. Hearn.

Edwards, John H. - Acena Parker, 26 Dec. 1865, m. 28 Dec. 1865 by John A. Stamper, M. P. Edwards, (w) Irvin Thigpen.

Edwards, Jonas - Mary Gay, 14 Jan. 1845, Levi W. Edwards, (w) John Norfleet, Clk.

Edwards, Joseph - Sarah Mangum, 4 Mar. 1843, John B. Edwards, (w) John Norfleet, Clk.

Edwards, Kinchen - Elizabeth Flowers (?), 17 Sept. 1849, Benjamin Edwards, (w) John Norfleet, Clk.

Edwards, Levi N. - Gatsy Ann Cobb, 11 Mar. 1844, Stephen W. Wooten, (w) John Norfleet, Clk.

Edwards, Littleberry - Tab P. Glover, 6 July 1815, (w) Ml. Hearn.

Edwards, Littleberry - Susan A. Hyman, 26 Dec. 1865, m. 28 Dec. 1865 by John A. Stamper, M. P. Edwards, (w) Irvin Thigpen.

Edwards, Micajah - Tabitha Weeks, 20 Apr. 1843, B. B. Bradley.

Edwards, Randall - Delphia A. Cobb, 21 Sept. 1841, Hines Cobb, Moses Edwards, (w) John Norfleet.

Edwards, Redding - Polly Langley, 7 Nov. 1829, William Edwards, (w) L. H. Hearn.

Edwards, Rial - Sally Reasons, 25 May 1840, Benjamin Moore, (w) John Norfleet.

Edwards, Stephen - Charity Wooten, 22 Jan. 1836, (w) Ml. Hearn.

Edwards, Thomas W. - Treasy Felton, 18 Dec. 1854, m. 21 Dec. 1854 by J. R. Pitt, J. P., Elias Summerlin, (w) W. S. Pitt, Clk.

Edwards, Titus - Rebecca Dyott, 19 Dec. 1822, John S. Edwards, Francis M. Wood, (w) Ml. Hearn.

Edwards, Weldon - Amanda Daughtery, 12 May 1851, m. 12 May 1851 by J. C. Knight, J. P., (w) John Norfleet, Clk.

Edwards, William B. - Alice Moore, 2 Jan. 1856, m. 4 Sept. 1856 by W. Y. Moore, James R. Moore, (w) W. S. Pitt.

Edwards, William H. - Delphia Ann Howard, 2 Feb. 1847, Everaitt Edwards.

Edwards, William J. - Jane E. Howell, 10 Jan. 1857, m. 10 Jan. 1857 by David Cobb, J. P., E. G. Worsley, (w) W. A. Jones, Clk.

Edwards, William J. - Mary F. Lawrence, 8 July 1861, m. 9 July 1861 by Wm. R. Cherry, J. P., M. P. Edwards, (w) W. A. Jones, Clk.

Edwards, William W. - Malvina Philips, 20 Dec. 1831, Richard T. Eagles, (w) Ml. Hearn.

Elinor, Lawrence - Louisa J. Cutchen, 20 Dec. 1859, m. 20 Dec. 1859 by W. P. Lewis, J. P., W. F. Lewis, (w) J. H. Dozier, D. C.

Ellinor, James - Martha Cromwell, 18 June, 1844, John Norfleet.

Ellinor, James Jr. - Zilpha Braswell, 18 Dec. 1823, Joseph Bell, (w) Ml. Hearn.

Ellinor, Josiah - Nancy Pender, 8 Mar. 1831, William Alsobrook, (w) Ml. Hearn.

Ellis, Alfred - Martha A. N. Edwards, 28 May 1850, Washington M. Stanton.

Ellis, Benjamin - Elizabeth Howard, 3 Jan. 1849, Cofield Ellis, (w) John Norfleet.

Ellis, Benjamin - Sally Howard, 15 Aug. 1849, William Ellis, (w) John Norfleet.

Ellis, Benjamin - Alvana Jones, 15 Oct. 1859, m. 27 Oct. 1859 by Theo. Atkinson, J. P., Robert S. Pitt, (w) W. A. Jones.

Ellis, Charles - Betsey Summerlin, 20 Dec. 1852, m. 23 Dec. 1852 by Lewis Ellis, J. P., Redmond Ellis, (w) John Norfleet.

Ellis, Charles - Fanny Lewis, 30 July 1822, John Carter, Robert Simms, (w) Ml. Hearn.

Ellis, Edwin - Eldy Farmer, 20 Mar. 1827, James D. Farmer, Henry Shirley, (w) Ml. Hearn.

Ellis, Edwin - Elizabeth Mattocks, 18 June 1845, Hyrum Forbes, (w) John Norfleet.

Ellis, Enas - Lovey Proctor, 23 Aug. 1821, Ision Gardner, (w) Ml. Hearn.

Ellis, Gray (alias Gray Flora) - Mary Gay, 5 Aug. 1856, m. Aug. 1856 by W. Y. Moore, J. P., Gray Webb, (w) J. H. Dozier.

Ellis, Hickman - Queen Esther Ellis, 1 Jan. 1838, Willie Robbins, (w) Jo. Bell, C. C. C.

Ellis, Ira G. - Harriet S. Ranton, 25 Jan. 1848, John Norfleet.
Ellis, James - Penelope Baker, 26 Aug. 1834, Blake Baker, (w) T. C. Hearn.
Ellis, James - Christana Winstead, 23 Oct. 1851, Redmond Ellis, (w) Benjamin Norfleet.
Ellis, John - Sally Gay, 25 May 1824, James Bradley, (w) Ml. Hearn.
Ellis, John, Sr. - Nancy Gay, 13 Sept 1831, Elisha Felton, (w) Ml. Hearn.
Ellis, John - Tempy Scott, 3 Apr. 1866, m. 7 Apr. 1866 by Allen Warren, J. P., J. A. Vines, (w) Irvin Thigpen, Clk.
Ellis, Joseph - Celia Mattocks, 11 Nov. 1851, m. 13 Nov. 1851 by William H. Hines, J. P., Henry Robbins, (w) John Norfleet.
Ellis, Josiah R. P. - Elizabeth Hollan, 14 July 1845, Bryant Little, (w) Willie Holon.
Ellis, Lewis - Zelia Simms, 30 April 1825, Charles Ellis, (w) Ml. Hearn.
Ellis, Redmon - Elislina Barnes, 31 Dec. 1847, Charles Ellis, (w) John Norfleet.
Ellis, Reuben - Lucy Johnston, 20 Jan. 1804, Jordan Forehand, (w) E. Hall.
Ellis, William - Nancy Baker, 25 Oct. 1830, Blake Baker, (w) L. H. Hearn.
Ellis, William - Sally Peacock, 27 Dec. 1853, m. 29 Dec. 1853 by Nathan Anderson, James Barnes, (w) W. S. Pitt, Clk.
Ellis, Willie - Quean Easter Sharpe, 16 Dec. 1833, Patrick Felton, (w) T. C. Hearn.
Ellis, Willie - Ellender Cobb, 14 July 1834, Elbert Amason, (w) Ml. Hearn.
Ellis, Willie - Rissa Webb, 2 Sept. 1856, m. 4 Sept. 1856 by W. Y. Moore, J. P., Gray Ellis, (w) J. H. Dozier, D. C.
Elvington, Thomas - Nancy Farmer, 25 Aug. 1840, Edwin Barnes, (w) John Norfleet, Clk.
Emory, Aaron - Ruth Cain, 28 Dec. 1816, Elijah Cain, (w) Michl. Hearn.
Ennis, James T. - Clary Andrews, 3 Dec. 1790, Rich. S. Wills, (w) S. Wren.
Ennis, Joshua - Amanda Philips, 3 Feb. 1834, Joel J. Bullock, James Grace, (w) Martha Sutton.
Etherage, Holliday - Parma Edwards, 18 Dec. 1823, Levi Edwards, (w) N. Mathewson.
Etherage, James - Avilla Dozier, 18 Jan. 1825, Solomon Pender, (w) Ml. Hearn.

Etheridge. Cobel - Ann Greene, 27 Oct. 1860, m. 28 Oct. 1860 by W. B. Jordan, J. P., Jesse H. Jones, Elijah Williams, (w) W. A. Jones.

Etheridge, David - Patsy Pittman, 11 Nov. 1830, Richard Bradley, (w) L. H. Hearn.

Ethridge, Frederick - Mary Flora, 10 May 1823, James Sherrod, (w) Ml. Hearn.

Ethridge, Frederick - Elizabeth Pitman, 24 Aug. 1829, Reddick Etheridge, (w) Ml. Hearn.

Etheridge, Holloway - Mary Todd, 17 Jan. 1827, Grandy Etheridge, (w) Ml. Hearn.

Etheridge, Holloway - Mary Barrow, 29 Dec. 1846, James R. Daniel, (w) W. L. Dozier.

Etheridge, Indan (?) - Lucy Moseley, 23 Sept. 1842, Perry Farrow, (w) John Norfleet, Clk.

Etheridge, Jesse B. - Mary Mourning, 18 Sept. 1830, Ransom Etheridge, (w) L. H. Hearn.

Etheridge, Kader - Keddy Sherrod, 24 Apr. 1824, Granday Etheridge, (w) Nn. Mathewson.

Etheridge, Lewis - Eliza Patterson, 23 Dec. 1834, Nathaniel M. Terrell, (w) T. C. Hearn.

Etheridge, Ransom - Penelope A. M. Shelton, 23 Oct. 1828, James Etheridge, (w) Ml. Hearn.

Etheridge, W. J. - Lucy Bellamy, 28 Oct. 1858, H. A. Taylor, W. H. Ruffin.

Etheridge, Willoughby - Nancy Robbins, 3 Feb. 1840, Willie Robbins, (w) Jo. Bell, C. C. C.

Ethridge, James - Anny Manning, 26 Mar. 1854, m. 27 Mar. 1854 by Joshua Barnes, J. P., Isaac B. Farmer, (w) Josh Barnes.

Ethridge, James T. - S. F. Fountain, 11 July 1846(?), m. 12 July 1866 by L. R. Cherry, J. P., John B. Savage, (w) Irvin Thigpen.

Ethindge (?), Ranson - Elizabeth Moore, 15 Dec. 1846, Joseph J. Marks, (w) John Norfleet.

Eure, Mills - Elizabeth Flood, 24 Dec. 1850, Wilber Robbins, (w) John Norfleet.

Euere, Stephen B. - Zilpha Thomas, 27 July 1822, Eason Thomas, (w) Ml. Hearn.

Evans, Elias - Susan Vasser, 1 July 1822, John Horn, (w) Ml. Hearn.

Evans, George W. - Sarah Owens, 4 May 1825, Jonathan Roberson.

Evans, Ruffin - Nancy Farmer, 18 Nov. 1833, William Barnet, (w) T. C. Hearn.

Evans, Sparkman - Milly Carter, 21 Apr. 1831, Geraldus Shurley, Zachariah Carter, (w) Ml. Hearn.

Evans, Winbon - Eveline Dixon, 15 Feb. 1839, Edmund Bleaset.

Everett, James - Elizabeth Johnston, 7 Dec. 1842, Joshua Everett, (w) John Norfleet, Clk.

Everett, John - Mary Ann Meranda Smith, 2 June 1842, Joshua Everett, James Everett, (w) John Norfleet, Clk.

Everett, John T. - Creacy Green, 17 Mar. 1842, Enos Green.

Everett, Joseph - Caroline Owens, 15 Feb. 1858, m. 16 Feb. 1858 by W. Y. Moore, J. P., James Everett, (w) W. A. Jones, Clk.

Everett, Nathan B. - Bytha Dunfood, 19 Jan. 1849, Exum Everett, (w) Benjamin Norfleet.

Exum, Edwin - Mollie Oneal, 19 Sept. 1826, Ely Porter.

Exum, Etheldred - Nancy Ing, 25 Feb. 1823, Willie Price, (w) Ml. Hearn.

Exum, James H. - Mary J. Belcher, 20 Mar. 1862, m. 25 Mar. 1862 by James T. Simpson, M. G., J. B. Belcher, (w) W. A. Jones.

Exum, John - Susanna Benton, 18 July 1766, Etheldred Exum.

Exum, Joseph W. - F. A. H. Johnston, 21 Sept. 1851, William T. Braswell, (w) John Norfleet.

Exum, Micajah - Martha Van, 29 Dec. 1800, Richard Pitt, (w) Samuel Wrenn.

Exum, Thomas - Elizabeth King, 31 July 1800, Jacob Coker, (w) J. H. Hall.

Ezzell, John W. - Susan E. McMahan, 13 Sept. 1849, Jesse M. Hursey, (w) John Norfleet.

F

Faircloth, Bright - Elizabeth Shingleton, 15 Apr. 1831, Jonas Cobb, (w) Ml. Hearn.

Faircloth, Turner F. - Mary C. Bryan, 3 Nov. 1846, William T. Braswell, (w) John Norfleet.

Faircloth, William - Susanna Edwards, 13 Feb. 1828, Newson Faircloth, (w) Ml. Hearn.

Faircloth, David - Elizabeth J. Haguns, 11 Feb. 1847, Joseph Pitman, (w) John Norfleet.

Faithful, Joseph J. - Sarah J. Pitt, 19 July 1851, m. 20 July 1851 by B. B. Baron, Jesse A. B. Thorn, (w) Benjamin Norfleet.

Faithful, Lewis - Sallie Higgs, 24 Sept. 1852, m. 24 Sept. 1852 by W. F. Lewis, J. P., Elias Bradley, (w) John Norfleet.

Faithful, Mike - Bedy Faithful, 8 Aug. 1851, R. H. Austin.

Faithful, Richard - Lizzy Bell, 3 Aug. 1847, Noah Leggett, (w) John Norfleet.

Faithful. William - Mary Parker, 28 Dec. 1854, m. 31 Jan. 1855 by Aaron Davis, H. L. Staton, (w) W. S. Pitt, Clk.

Farmer. Albert - Nancy Harrison, 20 Jan. 1847, Larry D. Farmer.

Farmer, Arthur - Catherine Farmer, 1 May 1847, David B. Bell, (w) W. L. Dozier, Clk.

Farmer, Arthur D. - Perry Eason, 31 Mar. 1822, Larry Dew, (w) Ml. Hearn.

Farmer, Augustine - Harriett Harris, 25 May 1827, John W Barnes, (w) Ml. Hearn.

Farmer, Augustine - Martha Robbins, 14 Aug. 1849, Josiah Farmer, (w) John Norfleet.

Farmer, Benjamin - Evelina Coleman, 21 Jan. 1851, Josiah Farmer, (w) John W. Farmer (w) Jas. J. Taylor, J. P.

Farmer, Ceaburn - Teresa Thomas, 9 Oct. 1849, A. D. Farmer, (w) L. D. Farmer.

Farmer, Gray - Mary Batts, 18 Jan. 1849, Willis W. Batts, (w) John Norfleet, Clk.

Farmer, Isaac - Polly Williams, 8 Jan. 1813, William White, Jr., (w) Ml. Hearn.

Farmer, Isaac - Treacy Barnes, 3 Feb. 1829, (w) Ml. Hearn.

Farmer, Isaac W. - Rebecca Gardner, 13 Aug. 1853, m. 14 Aug. 1853 by D. W. Barnes, J. P., James B. Gardner, (w) Benjamin Norfleet.

Farmer, James - Treacey Farmer, 15 Dec. 1845, William D. Thorn, (w) John Norfleet.

Farmer, Jesse - Mary Batts, 15 Oct. 1843, James B. Batts, (w) H. Austin.

Farmer, John L. - Anna Farmer, 11 Nov. 1822, Henry Shirly, William Farmer, James D. Farmer, (w) Ml. Hearn.

Farmer, John W. - Martha Rountree, 4 Dec. 1842, Ira G. Ellis, (w) John Norfleet, Clk.

Farmer, Josiah - Catherine Farmer, 17 Dec. 1842, Isaac Farmer, (w) John Norfleet.

Farmer, Larry D. - Sarah Dew, 18 Feb. 1839, James D. Barnes, (w) Larry Dew, J. P.

Farmer, Moses - Elizabeth Barnes, 13 Jan. 1835, Edwin Barnes, (w) Ml. Hearn.

Farmer, Moses - Patience Woodard, 23 Nov. 1853, m. 24 Nov. 1853 by Jesse Baker, M. G., William B. Myers, (w) J. W. Farmer.

Farmer, Pharoh - Makala (?) Daniel, 9 Mar. 1854, m. 9 Mar. 1854 by Elisha Barnes, J. P., Joseph F. Moore, (w) Elisha Barnes.

Felton, Elbert - Laura F. Felts, 6 Nov. 1863, m. 8 Nov. 1863 by Jesse Baker, M. G., Brittain Edwards, (w) T. N. Hussey.

Felton, Elisha - Basheba Varnell, 26 Aug. 1852, m. 26 Aug. 1852 by Mark Bennett, John Carter (w) .

Felton, Ely - Mary Harrell, 21 Feb. 1859, m. 22 Feb. 1859 by R. J. Johnson, J. P., Richard Felton, (w) W. A. Jones, Clk.

Felton, Job - Tresina Wooten, 30 Jan. 1866, m. 30 Jan. 1866 by J. H. Daniel, James G. Owen, (w) Irvin Thigpen, Clk.

Felton, John - Tamey Felton, 8 Jan. 1832, Thomas Felton, (w) T. C. Hearn.

Felton, Stephen - Jemimah Amason, 25 Nov. 1823, Thomas Amason, (w) N. Mathewson.

Felton, Thomas - Letha Sparkman, 9 Sept. 1828, David Holland, (w) Ml. Hearn.

Felton, William - Lydia Skinner, 3 Feb. 1836, Starky Howard, (w) T. C. Hearn.

Ferrell, J. D. T. - Fannie Langston, 22 Feb. 1866, m. 25 Feb. 1866 by H. S. Taylor, A. B. M. G., E. Ferrell, (w) N. M. Lawrence.

Fields, William B. - Mary F. King, 5 June 1855, m. 5 June 1855 by C. B. Hassell, David B. Knight, (w) W. S. Pitt, Clk.

Fitts, William - Annie Webb, 8 Aug. 1850, David Webb, (w) John Norfleet.

Flemings, Charles - Rhoda Sherrod, 22 Sept. 1848, James Stallings, (w) Benjamin Norfleet.

Flemings, Charles - Gilliana Burras, 20 Dec. 1866, m. 23 Dec. 1866 by C. L. Bonner, J. P., J. R. Griffin, (w) Irvin Thigpen.

Flemings, James - Titia Bell, 13 Aug. 1861, m. 13 Aug. 1866 by Bennett P. Pitt, J. P., Josiah Edmondson, (w) W. A. Jones.

Flemings, James S. - Sarah C. Flemings, 2 Jan. 1858, m. 7 Jan. 1858 by Bennett P. Pitt, J. P., Robert Walston (w).

Flemings, Minion B. - Sarah C. Little, 27 Feb. 1855, m. 28 Feb. 1855 by Jordan Thigpen, J. P., Jordan Thigpen, (w) W. S. Pitt, Clk.

Flemings, William - Juliana Bradley, 21 Apr. 1854, m. 21 Apr. 1854 by Thomas Norfleet, J. P., Thomas Norfleet, (w) W. A. Jones.

Fleming, Benjamin - Chacy Tolson, 11 Jan. 1827, William Fleming, (w) Ml. Hearn.

Fleming, Benjamin - Talitha A. House, 17 Sept. 1860, m. 20 Sept. 1860 by J. H. Jenkins, J. P., Gray Andrews, (w) J. H. Dozier.

Fleming, Frederick D. L. - Mary Ann Miranda Webb, 2 Jan. 1849, Bennett Hagans, (w) John Norfleet, Clk.

Fleming, Jesse - Elizabeth Williams, 18 Dec. 1849, James Stallings, (w) John Norfleet, Clk.

Fleming, Peter - Mary Howenton, 22 Nov. 1830, Thomas Moore, Noah Leggett, (w) L. H. Hearn.

Flemmons, Adam - Harriett House, 1 Dec. 1835, Starling Hicks, (w) Ml. Hearn.

Fletcher, John - Polly Bradley, 25 Feb. 1823, Willie Price, Stephen Bradley Jr., (w) Ml. Hearn.

Fletcher, John R. - Nancy Ruffin, 23 Sept. 1828, Micajah Rose, (w) Ml. Hearn.

Flewelling, John - Sarah Hobby, 24 Dec. 1761, Joseph Howell, (w) James Hall.

Flood, Enoch - Fanny Cherry (sister of Obediah Cherry), 19 June 1801, Obediah Cherry, Lemuel Thigpen, (w) Thos. E. McNair.

Flood, John W. - Martha Ann Weaver, 20 Dec. 1856, m. 28 Dec. 1856 by C. W. Spiers, J. P., Isaac Robbins, (w) W. A. Jones.

Flood, John W. - Nancy Williams, 14 Sept. 1858, m. 16 Sept. 1858 by Hilliard S. Taylor, A. B. M. G., Isaac Robbins.

Flood, Obediah - Patsey Jackson, 22 Aug. 1825, Burrel Land, (w) N. Mathewson.

Flora, Enoch - Elizabeth Varnell, 11 July 1827, W. D. Petway, (w) Ml. Hearn.

Flora, Enoch - Polly Pittman, 18 Mar. 1849, Willis Robbins, (w) John Norfleet, Clk.

Flora, John - Elsey Todd, 19 Mar. 1851, m. 19 Mar. 1851 by John Norfleet, Clk., Thomas Johnson (w) John Norfleet.

Flora, John - Jane Felton, 28 Aug. 1854, Nathan Webb, (w) W. S. Pitt, Clk.

Flora, Larry - Martha Ann Baker, 28 Sept. 1846, Eason Sharp, (w) John Norfleet.

Flora, Lewis - Jane Guinn, 7 Mar. 1842, Amos Robbins, (w) John Norfleet, Clk.

Flora, Willie - Kiddy Etheridge, 27 Sept. 1826, Ephraim Flora, (w) N. Mathison.

Flora, Willis - Sally Bateman, 10 Dec. 1840, William Woodard, (w) John Norfleet, Clk.

Flowers, Andrew J. - Piatia (Piety) Proctor, 18 Jan. 1840, (w) Jo. Bell, C. C.

Flowers Duncan L - Elizabeth Gill, 31 Dec. 1827, Augustin Mann, (w) Ml. Hearn.

Flowers, Elbert H. - Mary Ann Williford, 9 Dec. 1859, m. 13 Dec. 1859 by Hillard L. Taylor, A. B. M. G., David Sharp, (w) J. H. Dozier.

Flowers, Hardy G. - Sally Batts, 8 Sept. 1832, Hardy Flowers, (w) Ml. Hearn.

Flowers, Jacob - Mary Johnson, 20 Nov. 1764, Reneson Tisdale, (w) J. Hall.

Flowers, Jacob, Jr. - Elizabeth Cane, 19 Apr. 1763, Jacob Flowers (sr.), (w) John Spendelow.

Fly, Elisha - Nancy Hill, 28 Nov. 1847, William H. Hines, (w) John Norfleet, Clk.

Fly, John - Winny Powell, 30 Dec. 1845, Bennett Gay, (w) John Norfleet.

Fly, John - Margaret Thomas, 14 June 1865, m. 15 June 1865 by L. C. Pender, J. P., (w) Irvin Thigpen.

Fly, Thomas - Eliza Thigpen, 14 July 1849, Bythal G. Brown, (w) John Norfleet, Clk.

Forbes, Benjamin - Mary Webb, 26 Aug. 1845, Calvin Forbes, (w) John Norfleet, Clk.

Forbes, Britton - Penny Ellis, 13 May 1844, Calvin Forbes, (w) John Norfleet, Clk.

Forbes, Calvin - Penina Pippen, 15 Dec. 1846, Benjamin Forbes, (w) John Norfleet, Clk.

Forbes, Calvin - Rachel Marlow, 26 May 1851, m. 29 May 1851 by W. Y. Moore, J. P., Joseph Forbes, (w) John Norfleet, Clk.

Forbes, Hyrum - Milly Harrell, 10 Jan. 1835, John Harrell, (w) T. C. Hearn.

Forbes, John - Ann Edwards, 17 Oct. 1855, m. 18 Oct. 1855 by James Carney, J. P., J. W. Pollard, (w) T. M. Arrington.

Forbes, Joseph - Elizabeth Eason, 26 Aug. 1839, Hyrum Forbes, David Webb, (w) Jo. Bell, C. C.

Forbes, Peter - Catherine B. Exum, 1 Mar. 1850, John Manning, (w) John Norfleet, Clk.

Forbes, Randolph - Delphia Harrell, 9 Aug. 1864, m. 10 Aug. 1864 by J. R. Pitt, J. P., Ashley Page, (w) Irvin Thigpen.

Ford, Redin - Elizabeth Harris, 17 Apr. 1854, John H. Leigh.

Forehand, David - Letha Holland, 4 Dec. 1830, Moore Carter, (w) L. H. Hearn.

Forehand, Solomon - Rachel Hale, 24 Sept. 1763, Jacob Dunn, (w) John Spendelow.

Foreman, Agisalaus - Delha Dancy, 10 Nov. 1836, James Weddell, (w) T. C. Hearn.

Foreman, George - Lecey Devry, 24 Dec. 1866, John Ws. Johnson, (w) Irvin Thigpen.

Foreman, Peter P. - Marina Moore. 22 Feb. 1866, m. 22 Feb. 1866 by Jos. Blount Cheshire, Epis. Min., James E. Simonson, (w) Irvin Thigpen.

Foreman, William J. - Annie B. Sparrow, 31 Jan. 1865, m. 1 Feb. 1865 by Jos. Blount Cheshire, M. G., R. W. Singletary, (w) T. W. Hussey, D. C.

Fort, Edwin - Patsy Bell, 15 Jan. 1823, Thomas Dickerson, Duncan Hargrove, (w) Ml. Hearn.

Fort, Elias - Lucy Adkinson, 7 Mar. 1764, Joshua Johnson.

Fort, Jacob G. - Priscilla Horn, 3 Oct. 1822, James S. Battle, (w) Ml. Hearn.

Fort, John - Martha Batts, 2 Aug. 1837, William A. Pope, (w) T. C. Hearn.

Fort, Lewis - Nancy Battle, 28 May 1800, Adam L. Haywood.

Fort, Nelson - Peggy Patterson, 20 July 1826, Jos. Lackey, (w) N. Matheson.

Fort, Ricks - Priscilla Coffield, 24 Sept. 1823, John Coffield, (w) Ml. Hearn.

Fort, Ricks - Mary E. A. Bradley, 28 July 1827, Robert Joyner, Sol. T. Braddy, (w) Ml. Hearn, C. C.

Fountain, Edward - Eliza Pittman, 13 June 1848, Willis Pittman, (w) John Norfleet, Clk.

Fountain, Henry - Lizzie A. Etheridge, 4 July 1866, m. 5 July 1866 by L. R. Cherry, J. P., John Anderson, (w) Irvin Thigpen.

Fountain, James - Elizabeth Pitman, 10 Mar. 1825, James Coker, Jr., (w) Ml. Hearn.

Fountain, Joseph J. (son of O. Fountain) - Charlotte E. Pitt (dau. of James Pitt), 6 Feb. 1868, m. 13 Feb. 1868 by Lunsford R. Cherry, (w) Irvin Thigpen, Clk.

Fountain, Lawrence - Mary, E. Cottin, 29 June 1857, m. 30 June 1857 by Lunsford R. Cherry, John Coker.

Fountain, Lewis - Margaret Ann Smith, 9 Dec. 1856, m. 10 Dec. 1856 by W. F. Lewis, J. P., Spear Coker, (w) W. A. Jones.

Fountain, Loderick - Priscilla Dixon, 15 Feb. 1832, Matthew H. Dicken, (w) Ml. Hearn.

Fountain, Timothy - Prissy Exum, 21 Jan. 1817, James Coker Jr., David Lane, (w) Ml. Hearn.

Fountain, William - Martha Cutchin, 11 Dec. 1849, John J. R. Parker, (w) John Norfleet.

Fountain, Joseph - Susan Mary Pittman, 7 Sept. 1855, m. 10 Sept. 1855 by Lunsford R. Cherry, William Pittman, (w) W. S. Pitt, Clk.

Foxhall, Frank D. - Annie E. Barlow, 17 Dec. 1860, m. 18 Dec. 1860 by Thos. R. Owens, M. G., Willie Walston, (w) W. A. Jones.

Foxhall, William - Sarah Wilkins, 13 Nov. 1823, Ben Boykin (w) Ml. Hearn.

Freeman, Arthur - Eliza Bryan, 26 Mar. 1832, John Freeman, (w) Ml. Hearn.

Freeman, Berry - Mary E. Taylor, 4 June 1861, m. 6 June 1861 by Hylard S. Taylor, A. B. M. G., James Freeman, (w) T. W. Hussey.

Freeman, Berry - Viney Watson, 8 Mar. 1866, m. 10 Mar. 1866 by John A. Stamper, Isaac W. Bass, (w) Irvin Thigpen, Clk.

Freeman, George W. - Theresa Tart, 8 Dec. 1825, Jesse Battle, Joseph Bell, (w) Ml. Hearn.

Freeman, James - Mary Brake, 24 Oct. 1854, m. 26 Oct. 1854 by C. C. Bonner, J. P., R. S. Petway, (w) W. S. Pitt Clk.

Freeman, John - Emily Williams, 4 Sept. 1865, m. 9 Sept. 1865 by H. S. Taylor, M. G., R. H. Taylor, (w) Irvin Thigpen.

Freeman, John H. - Margaret Bradley, 21 Aug. 1858, m. 15 Apr. 1860 by Thos. L. Maner, J. P., (w) H. Banks.

Freeman, Joseph J. - Eliza Jones, 4 Feb. 1839, Henry Austin, (w) Jo. Bell, C. C.

Freeman, Miles - Amy Bryan, 23 June, 1866, m. 8 July 1866 by J. F. Batts, J. P., Thos. R. Owens, Jr., (w) I. Thigpen.

Fryer, James - Rebecca Haynes, 17 Jan. 1840, Stephen Bradley, (w) Jo. Bell, C. C.

Fryer, Richard K. - Mary Pender, 10 Apr. 1830, Nathanael G. Womble, (w) Ml. Hearn.

G

Gaiter, Kenneth - Lydia Ann Edmondson, 21 Dec. 1859, m. 15 Jan. 1860 by J. W. Howard, J. P., Harris E. Barfield, (w) W. A. Jones, Clk.

Gaitor, Nathan - Nancy Whitley, 6 Jan. 1862, m. 7 Jan. 1862 by J. H. Daniel, (w) W. A. Jones.

Gallaway, Jesse - Chacy Barter, 10 Dec. 1823, Stephen Felton, (w) Ml. Hearn.

Gallaway, Jesse - Lucinda Ritter, 27 Aug. 1850, William Ellis, (w) John Norfleet.

Gardner, Bailey - Peninah Batts, 12 Sept. 1853, m. 13 Sept. 1853 by John G. Williams, Calvin Moore, (w) William M. Pippin.

Gardner, (or Brown) Brittain B. - Edney Drawhorn, William Gardner, (w) Ml. Hearn. (No dates.)

Gardner, Calvin - Pennina Moseley, 24 May 1851, m. 26 May 1851 by W. J. Armstrong, James Wiggins, (w) John Norfleet, Clk.

Gardner, Charles - Francis Johnson, 23 Jan. 1861, m. 23 Jan. 1861 by J. R. Pitt, J. P., Martin Gardner, (w) T. W. Hussey.

Gardner, David - Patience Booth, 18 Sept. 1822, Lewis Booth, (w) Ml. Hearn.

Gardner, David - Elizabeth Robbins, 11 Mar. 1823, Elijah Robbins, Sion Gardner, (w) Ml. Hearn.

Gardner, Edwin - Matilda Darden, 15 Dec. 1828, Simeon Gardner, (w) Ml. Hearn.

Gardner, Edwin - Clarenda Edmunds, 14 Apr. 1837, (w) Ml. Hearn.

Gardner, Edwin T. - Winifred Wiggins, 25 Dec. 1849, William W. Batts, (w) John Norfleet.

Gardner, Edwin T. - Eliza Vick, 30 Apr. 1856, m. 1 May 1856 by Thomas L. Maner, J. P., George Gardner, (w) D. Pender.

Gardner, Eli - Temperance Whitley, 22 Dec. 1835, Henry Dunford, (w) Ml. Hearn, C. C.

Gardner, George - Elizabeth Cahoon, 1 Jan. 1811, Thomas Wells, (w) Ml. Hearn.

Gardner, George - Elizabeth Whithead, 11 Mar. 1828, William Gardner, (w) Ml. Hearn.

Gardner, George - Frances A. G. Vick, 26 Mar. 1855, m. 3 Apr. 1855 by Thomas L. Maner, J. P., Zadock R. Braswell, (w) W. A. Jones.

Gardner, James W. - Ellen Savage, 28 Jan. 1856, m. 31 Jan. 1856 by S. W. Pender, J. P., Edwin S. Gardner, (w) W. S. Pitt, Clk.

Gardner, James W. - Susan A. Luper, 27 Nov. 1863, (?) m. 29 Jan. 1863 by John I. Proctor, J. P., David Lane, (w) Irvin Thigpen.

Gardner, Jesse - Elizabeth Fleming, 27 June 1857, m. 28 June 1857 by L. C. Pender, J. P., Willie Jones, (w) J. H. Dozier.

Gardner, Joel - Sally Cherry, 18 Nov. 1852, m. 18 Nov. 1852 by John Norfleet, J. P., Joseph Dunn, (w) Benjamin Norfleet, Clk.

Gardner, John - Hariet Sikes, 20 Nov. 1834, James Griffin, (w) Theo. C. Hearn.

Gardner, Martin - Martha A. Foxhall, 21 Sept. 1844, A. H. Macnair.

Gardner, Martin - Jane Davis, 10 Mar. 1846, Leaster S. Cobb, (w) John Norfleet, Clk.

Gardner, Martin - Eveline Barnes, 8 May 1849, W. G. Dunn, (w) John Norfleet.

Gardner, Nathan - Martha Davis, 12 Mar. 1832, Lemon P. Stanton, (w) Ml. Hearn.

Gardner, Sion - Mary Scarborough, 12 Feb. 1823, David Gardner, Eliphas Lewis, (w) Ml. Hearn.

Gardner, Solomon - Lucinda Moore, 9 Oct. 1865, m. 26 Dec. 1865 by John Norfleet, J. P., D. W. Batts, (w) Irvin Thigpen, Clk.

Gardner, Taylor - Elizabeth Ruffin, 9 Feb. 1832, Cannon Windham, (w) Ml. Hearn.

Gardner, Taylor - Ann Allsbrook, 20 Nov. 1855, m. 20 Nov. 1855 by R. Norfleet, J. P., Joseph Stallings, (w) W. S. Pitt, Clk.

Gardner, Theophilus - Ohdina Ethridge, 15 Mar. 1850, Jordan Ethrich, (w) John Norfleet.

Gardner, William - Scyntha Batts, 3 Jan. 1828, Edwin Gardner, (w) Ml. Hearn.

Garner, Starlin - Betsey Parmenter, 31 Oct. 1831, Jno. Morgan, (w) L. H. Hearn.

Garner, Taylor - Margaret Sherrod, 6 Oct. 1862, m. 6 Oct. 1862 by L. C. Pender, Jacob Whitly, (w) T. W. Hussey.

Garrett, Charles W. - Mary Sugg, 10 June 1851, m. 12 June 1851 by Jos. Blount Cheshire, M. G., Bolin B. Barrow, (w) John Norfleet, Clk.

Garrett, Francis M. - Dellah Williams, 26 Nov. 1855, m. 27
    Nov. 1855 by Robert J. Carson, M. G., Joseph J. Gar-
    rett, (w) W. A. Jones.
Garrett, Geraldus - Charlotte Barfield, 20 Mar. 1823, John
    Gaitor, (w) Ml. Hearn.
Garrett, Henry W. - Sally Sasnett, 24 Oct. 1826, John Garrett.
Garrett, James J. - Susan Knight, 6 Feb. 1830, Henry W.
    Garrett, (w) Ml. Hearn.
Garrett, John - Elizabeth Nettle, 14 Apr. 1836, James Wilkins,
    (w) T. C. Hearn.
Garrett, J. W. - Lucy Suggs, 10 Nov. 1862, m. Nov. 1862 by
    James P. Simpson, Meth. Min., James P. Simpson, (w)
    Irvin Thigpen.
Garrett, John J. - Henrietta S. Williams, 30 Apr. 1861, m. 1
    May 1861 by L. S. Burkhead, R. H. Pender, (w) W. A.
    Jones, Clk.
Garrett, John Q. - Nancy Lawrence, 9 Jan. 1854, m. 12 Jan.
    1854 by Elisha Cromwell, J. P., William L. Hyman,
    (w) W. S. Pitt.
Garrett, Joseph J. - Nancy Miner, 12 May 1846, William H.
    Hines, (w) John Norfleet, Clk.
Garrett, Joseph J. - Henrietta Mercer, 12 Sept. 1851, m. 18
    Sept. 1851 by Mark Bennett, V. D. M., William George
    Thomas, (w) John Norfleet.
Garrett, R. H. - Sally Ann Mercer, 11 June 1861, m. 12 July
    1861 by William H. Barnes, (w) W. A. Jones, Clk.
Garrett, Richard H. - Louisa Jenkins, 4 Oct. 1852, m. 5 Oct.
    1852 by Wright Barnes, J. P. James H. Dozier, (w)
    John Norfleet.
Garrett, William - Nicey Edmondson, 29 Aug. 1825, John Ed-
    mondson, (w) Ml. Hearn.
Garris, Thomas - Betsy Ann Gay, 22 Oct. 1851, m. 26 Oct.
    1851 by W. Y. Moore, J. P., Elisha Bergeron, (w) Ben-
    jamin Norfleet.
Garvey, James - Peggy Boon, 1 Dec. 1855, Simon Gay, (w)
    W. S. Pitt, Clk.
Gaskins, Henry J. - Elizabeth Manning, 14 Feb. 1843, Andrew
    Gunter, (w) John Norfleet.
Gaston, Calvin - William Ann Thomas, 2 Jan. 1856, m. 3 Jan.
    1856 by L. C. Pender, J. P., William Shurly, (w) W. S.
    Pitt, Clk.
Gater, James - Sabra Ellinor, 12 Dec. 1832, William Alsobrook,
    (w) Ml. Hearn.

Gatlin, Bryan - Emily Sessums, 24 Nov. 1825, Henry Austin, (w) Ml. Hearn.

Gatlin, James R. - Mary Amanda Morgan, 24 Apr. 1857, m. 27 Apr. 1857 by L. C. Pender, J. P., Bryant B. Gatlin, (w) J. H. Dozier.

Gatlin, Patrick H. - Louisa Stallings, 25 July 1865, m. 31 July 1865 by L. C. Pender, Bryant Gatlin (w).

Gatlin, Thomas - Julia Pender, 18 June 1829, Levi Wilkinson, (w) Ml. Hearn, C. C.

Gay, Asa - Salley Allen, 14 Jan. 1830, Lewis Gay, (w) L. H. Hearn.

Gay, Benjamin - Leucretia Harrison, 13 May 1854, m. 14 May 1854 by Theo. Thomas, J. P., Simon Gay, (w) W. S. Pitt.

Gay, Bryant - Matilda Webb, 22 Jan. 1845, Willie Owens, (w) John Norfleet, Clk.

Gay, C. B. - Mary Ann Williford, 14 Mar. 1854, m. 17 Mar. 1854 by John W. Farmer, B. E. Farmer, (w) W. S. Pitt, Clk.

Gay, Dempsey - Mary Ward, 26 Feb. 1835, Henry Owens, (w) Ml. Hearn.

Gay, Dempsey - Sally Ann Harrell, 7 Mar. 1854, m. 9 Mar. 1854 by W. Y. Moore, Gray Elles, (w) W. S. Pitt.

Gay, Dempsey - Polly Andre, 6 Feb. 1800, Zarababel Gay, Hezekiah Langley, (w) E. Hale.

Gay, Henry - Delphia Owens, 24 Dec. 1832, Elnathan T. Eason, (w) Ml. Hearn.

Gay, Isham - Sarah Owens, 19 Dec. 1838, William Felton, (w) Jo. Bell, Clk.

Gay, Jonathan - Sally May, 1 Feb. 1831, Littleton Walston, (w) L. H. Hearn.

Gay, Levin - Orpy Boozman, 9 Dec. 1824, Jo. P. Pitt, Henry Skinner, (w) Ml. Hearn.

Gay, Levin - Ginnetta Sumlin, 13 Nov. 1863, m. 15 Nov. 1863 by Bennett P. Pitt, J. P., J. A. Williamson, (w) T. W. Hussey.

Gay, Lewis - Nancy Wood, 23 Dec. 1831, Thomas Amason, (w) Ml. Hearn.

Gay, Perry W. - Obedience A. Owens, 1 Apr. 1845, Henry Gay, Benjamin Owens, (w) John Norfleet.

Gay, Richard - Levina Robertson, 30 Dec. 1811, Benjamin Gay, (w) Ml. Hearn.

Gay, Richard - Penninah Sumertin, 29 Sept. 1838, Henry Gay, (w) Jo. Bell, Clk.

Gay, Simon - Polly Gay, 16 Dec. 1834, Henry Gay, (w) T. C. Hearn.

Gay, Theophilus - Sarah Amason, 23 Jan. 1832, Edmon Gay, (w) T. C. Hearn.

Gay, Thomas - Evelina Ellis, 21 Jan. 1836, Benjamin Gay, (w) T. C. Hearn.

Gay, William - Sally Eason, 19 Nov. 1817, Absalom Wooten, (w) Ml. Hearn.

Gay, William - Piety Ricks, 9 Mar. 1826, Rich'd Jordan, Josiah Cutchen, Ml. Hearn.

Gay, William G. - Harriett Beeman, 17 Mar. 1866, m. 18 Mar. 1866 by H. S. Taylor, M. G., John Davis, (w) Irvin Thigpen, Clk.

Gilbert, Jesse - Sarah Green, 28 Feb. 1764, Thomas Hall.

Gill, Thomas G. - Rhoda Proctor, 15 Feb. 1836.

Gill, Zachariah - Sally Stakes, 12 Dec. 1844, James Bridgers.

Glasgow, Issac - Penny Ann Reid, 31 July, 1860, m. 5 Aug. 1860 by J. R. Pitt, J. P., Thomas Johnson, (w) James H. Dozier, (w) W. A. Jones.

Glisson, Samuel T. - Abscilla Lawrence, 8 Dec. 1840, Hansel Moore, (w) John Norfleet.

Godwin, William T. - Jane Flora, 22 Mar. 1865, m. 23 Mar. 1865 by W. H. Knight, J. P., R. S. Williams, (w) Irvin Thigpen.

Goff, George W. - Susan Langly, 13 May 1856, m. 18 May 1856 by Peter E. Hines, J. P., Richard B. Buck, (w) W. A. Jones, Clk.

Good, John J. - Mary Sorey, 7 Apr. 1832, Thomas D. Price, (w) Ml. Hearn.

Gooden, Druey - Teresay Knight, 15 July, 1763, Dempsey Speir, (w) Thomas Cavenah.

Goodwin, William - Tabitha Merrit, 8 Mar. 1768, James Hill, (w) Edward Hall.

Gorham, Henry W. - Josephine Cherry, 24 Jan. 1866, m. 25 Jan. 1866 by Jesse H. Page, M. G., W. T. Gorham, (w) Irvin Thigpen.

Gorham, John C. - Delah F. Mabrey, 30 Jan. 1866, m. 6 Feb. 1866 by C. B. Hassell, Erastus Cherry, (w) Irvin Thigpen, Clk.

Gorham, Richard H. - Mary Cherry, 22 Jan. 1851, William Hyman, (w) John Norfleet, Clk.

Gray, William F. - Lucy Johnson, 5 Oct. 1858, John F. Speight.

Gray, William T. - William Ann Pender, 7 Apr. 1857, m. 8 Apr. 1857 by Thomas R. Owen, M. G., Spencer L. Hart, (w) W. A. Jones.
Green, Enos - Mary Peel, 31 Mar. 1827, Jesse Friar, (w) Ml. Hearn.
Green, Enos - Patsey H. Peel, 22 Feb. 1830, Elisha Peel, (w) Ml. Hearn.
Green, James J. - Margarett P. Anderson, 13 Aug. 1865, m. 14 Aug. 1865 by Thomas R. Owens, M. G., Thomas H. Matthews, (w) Irvin Thigpen, Clk.
Green, John R. - Elizabeth Flemming, 11 Jan. 1853, m. 11 Jan. 1853 by J. C. Knight, J. P., Thomas W. Green, (w) John Norfleet.
Green, Thomas W. - Nancy Bullock, 22 Dec. 1831, Enos Green, (w) Ml. Hearn.
Green, Washington - Betsey Reid, 30 May, 1825, Allen Rayner, John Carter, (w) Ml. Hearn.
Green, William E. - Winifard Moore, 8 Apr. 1856, m. Apr. 1856 by William F. Mercer, J. P., Thomas W. Green, (w) W. A. Jones.
Grice, John - Mary Simms, 28 Sept. 1826, Isaac F. Wood, (w) N. Mathewson,
Griffin, Benjamin - Sally Williams, 22 Apr. 1858, Jo. D. Jenkins.
Griffin, Benjamin W. - Mary Bozeman, 21 Mar. 1863, Theophilys Thomas, (w) T. W. Hussey.
Griffin, David - Elizabeth Proctor, 25 Aug. 1856, Arthur D. Taylor.
Griffin, Dempsy - Gatsey Gardner, 13 May, 1862, m. 13 May 1862 by John W. Johnson, J. P., Staton Cummings, (w) W. A. Jones.
Griffin, George Henry - Elizabeth P. Seabrook, 18 Jan. 1854, m. 19 Jan. 1854 by James Stratton, M. G., Pomeroy Clark, (w) John W. Farmer.
Griffin, James - Elizabeth Whitley, 21 Jan. 1824, Joab P. Pitt, (w) Ml. Hearn.
Griffin, James - Rachael Anderson, 29 Aug. 1825, Burrell Hill, (w) N. Mathewson.
Griffin, James H. - Mary E. Lane, 9 Dec. 1857 by C. B. Killebrew, J. P., James W. Waller, (w) J. H. Dozier.
Griffin, James Henry - Mary Baker, 21 Sept. 1848, William Barnes, (w) Benjamin Norfleet.
Griffin, John - Martha Jones, 27 Apr. 1761, Isaac Hillard, (w) Thomas Hall.

Griffin, John - Sally Bell, 13 Aug. 1856, m. 14 Aug. 1856 by Theo. Thomas, J. P., Amos Brake, (w) W. A. Jones.

Griffin, John - Lucy Clark, 12 May 1868, m. 12 May 1868 by W. F. Lewis, J. P., (w) Irvin Thigpen.

Griffin, Simeon - Martha Curl, 1 Aug. 1822, Jetty Griffin, (w) N. Mathewson.

Griffin, Robert - Rachel Gay, 1 Dec. 1835, Henry Gay, (w) Theo. C. Hearn.

Griffin, Simmons - Meniza Medford. 13 May 1856, m. 21 May 1856 by Wm. S. Long, J. P., Ricard Holland, (w) W. A. Jones.

Griffin, Thomas - Jenny Waller, 11 Feb. 1823, Jesse Ruffin, Willie Summerlin, (w) Ml. Hearn.

Griffin, Thomas - Amanda Page, 30 Sept. 1857, m. Oct. 1857 by J. R. Pitt, J. P., Irvin Thigpen, (w) W. A. Jones.

Griffin, Thomas H. - Joanna Trevathan, 13 Dec. 1852, m. 14 Dec. 1852 by C. B. Killebrew, J. P., William M. Qualls, (w) John Norfleet.

Griffin, Thomas H. - Mary E. Daughtry, 29 Dec. 1865, m. 2 Jan. 1866 by Thos. R. Owen, V. D. M., Robert A. Watson, (w) Irvin Thigpen.

Griffin, Theophilus - Esther Hicks, 9 May 1859, m. 10 May 1859 by J. P. Pitt, J. P., Benjamin Griffin, (w) W. A. Jones.

Griffin, William - Catherine Jones, 26 Mar. 1835, William W. Armstrong, (w) T. C. Hearn.

Griffin, Willie - Elizabeth Williams, 7 Feb. 1827, Gray Armstrong, (w) Ml. Hearn.

Griffin, Willie - Leas Jackson, 29 Oct. 1831, John Parker, (w) L. H. Hearn.

Griffin, Wille C. - Mary Eliza Bradley, 25 Jan. 1860, m. 29 Jan. 1860 by W. B. Jordan, J. P., W. B. Jordan, (w) W. A. Jones, Clk.

Griffin, Zacariah - Margaret Brake, 30 Jan. 1831, Thomas D. Dickerson, (w) L. H. Hearn.

Griffis, Edmund - Sarah Hales, 4 Mar. 1839, John W. Bishop, (w) Jo. Bell.

Griffis (Griffin), Lewis - Mary Braswell, 28 June 1764, Francis Griffis, (w) Thomas Cavenah.

Griffith, Roger - Faithy Wall, 14 Feb. 1765, Thomas Merritt.

Grimes, Thomas - Nancy Best, 3 Aug. 1835, Samuel Hyman, (w) T. C. Hearn.

Grimmer, Drewry - Silphia Sparkman, 30 Dec. 1854, m. 9 Jan. 1855 by R. J. Johnson. J. P., Staton Cummings, (w) W. S. Pitt, Clk., Jonas Walston.

Grimmer, Drury - Julia Pittman, 9 Mar. 1852, m. 14 Mar. 1852 by R. Bynum, J. P., Joel Gardner, (w) John Norfleet, Clk.

Grisson, Fryley - Eliza Crisp, 19 Nov. 1839, Mayo Worsley, (w) Jo. Bell, C. C.

Groves, James D. - Amanda W. Ward, 19 Aug. 1855, m. 19 Aug. 1855 by Henry T. Clark, J. P., Alonzo W. Ballance, (w) W. S. Pitt, Clk.

Guion, Isaac D. - Susan Waller, 21 May 1822, Zachariah Sasnett, Warren Waller, (w) N. Mathewson.

H

Hackney, Thomas - Martha Edwards, 26 May 1856, m. 29 May 1856 by W. Y. Moore, J. P., Micajah P. Edwards, (w) W. A. Jones.

Hackney, Thomas - Celestia Westry, 17 Feb. 1866, m. 18 Feb. 1866 by W. F. Lewis, J. P., William H. Hackney, (w) Irvin Thigpen.

Hackney, William - Martha Weeks, 17 Aug. 1765, Joseph Stevenson, (w) J. Hall.

Hackney, William - Joan Parker, 28 Oct. 1850, Micajah P. Edwards, (w) John Norfleet.

Haell, William H. - Absala Blackburn, 10 Dec. 1827, John Fort, (w) Ml. Hearn.

Hagan, William - Nancy Page, 4 Jan. 1860, m. 5 Jan. 1860 by J. R. Pitt, Gray Dunn, (w) J. H. Dozier.

Hagans, Amos - Polly Walker, 1 Apr. 1846, John S. Duggan, (w) John Norfleet.

Hagans, Dempsey - Cilvana Sumner, 12 Oct. 1835, Samuel Corbet, (w) T. C. Hearn.

Hagans, Hampton - Mary Ann Price, 2 Jan. 1832, (w) Ml. Hearn.

Hagans, Lamon - Catherine Whitley, 13 Nov. 1833, Thomas B. Cherry, (w) Ml. Hearn.

Hagans, Richard - Ann Faithful, 1 May 1849, Lamon S. Dunn, (w) John Norfleet.

Hagans, Robert - Sally Ann Evans, 11 June 1852, m. 16 June 1852 by William Ellis, J. P., Littleton Walston, Jr., (w) John Norfleet.

Hagins, Bennett - Evelina Stokes, 21 July 1844, David Harrell.

Hains, William - Betsy Savidge, 31 May 1834, Henry Savidge, (w) T. C. Hearn.
Hail, William - Martha Lodge, 12 Mar. 1840, William Peel, (w) Jo. Bell, C. C.
Hale, Hardy - Frances Mullen, 5 June 1865, m. 6 June 1865 by Hilyard S. Taylor, A. B. M. G., (w) Irvin Thigpen, Clk.
Hales, George - Frances Barnes, 22 Aug. 1864, m. 23 Aug. 1864 by Hiliard Taylor, A. B. M. G., John Young, (w) Irvin Thigpen.
Hales, Henry - Martha Anderson, 1 Mar. 1843, Redding B. Sasnett.
Hales, John - Betsy Weeks, 20 May 1848, Corsby Lane, (w) John Norfleet, Clk.
Hales, William - Eliza Walker, 7 Sept. 1848, Joseph J. Faithful, (w) John Norfleet, Clk.
Hales, William - Nancy Lane, 14 Jan. 1854, m. 15 Jan. 1854 by Henry T. Clark, J. P., (w) W. S. Pitt, Clk.
Hall, Isaac - Eliza Evans, 15 May 1834, Robert A. Smith, (w) Ml. Hearn.
Hall, James - Mason Hall, 17 Dec. 1764, John Hall, (w) Aquila Sugg.
Hall, Joseph J. - Celia Burgess, 20 Mar. 1851, m. 20 Mar. 1851 by Theo. Thomas, J. P., Hilliard L. Williford, (w) John Norfleet, Clk.
Hamlet, John G. - Sally Read - 5 Dec. 1826, Aaron Johnson, Jesse Ruffin, (w) Ml. Hearn.
Hamlet, John W. - Zylpha Farmer, 14 Dec. 1848, Augustin Farmer, (w) Benjamin Norfleet.
Hammons, Cain - Mary Butler, 14 Nov. 1836, Henry Austin, (w) T. C. Hearn.
Hammonds, Edwards - Lucy Knight, 10 July 1828, Bythel Stone, (w) Ml. Hearn.
Hammons, Burrell - Betsy Jenkins, 11 Sept. 1811, James Coker, Jr., (w) M. L. Hearn.
Hammons, James - Nancy Jackson, 6 July 1822, Eaton L. Philips, (w) Ml. Hearn.
Hancock, John - Mary Teak, 11 Dec. 1850, Joseph Pitman, (w) J. Norfleet.
Hardy, Haywood - Winnefred Cholington, 26 Mar. 1831, Thomas D. Gatling, (w) Ml. Hearn.
Hardy, James - Amelizer Shelton, 3 Jan. 1865, James J. Lawrence, (w) Irvin Thigpen.
Hardy, John - Judy Edwards, 26 Nov. 1825, (w) Ml. Hearn.

Hardy, Ruffin - Polly Edmondson, 14 Feb. 1842, John Hathaway.

Hardy, Thomas - Elizabeth Lawrence, 1 Jan. 1832, Benjamin Boykin, (w) Ml. Hearn.

Harell, Christopher Jr. - Lazina Mayo, 16 Dec. 1822, Christopher Harell Sr., (w) Ml. Hearn.

Hargrave, F. G. - M. W. Parker, 24 Feb. 1841, William G. Thomas.

Hargrove, Duncan - Sally Land, 15 Jan. 1823, Thomas Dickerson, (w) ·Ml. Hearn.

Hargrove, Gray L. - Martha A. Gardner, 31 Mar. 1853, m. 31 Mar. 1853 by Jordan Thigpen, J. P., D. Williams, (w) John Norfleet, Clk., David McDaniel.

Hargrove, Gay L. - Felitia Little, 25 Jan. 1859, m. 25 Jan. 1859 by David Cobb, Jordan Thigpen, (w) W. A. Jones, Clk.

Hargrove, James B. - Ama Warren, 9 Nov. 1858, m. 11 Nov. 1858 by John W. Johnson, J. P., Joseph Cobb, (w) W. A. Jones.

Hargrave, John - Caroline Parker, 22 Feb. 1837, Danford Richards, (w) T. C. Hearn.

Hargrove, Samuel H. - Lucinda Killebrew, 22 Feb. 1851, m. 27 Feb. 1851 by William H. Hines, J. P., Gray L. Hargrove, (w) John Norfleet, Clk.

Harper, Abner - Massey Howell, 10 Dec. 1763, Samuel Skinner.

Harper, Bennett - Charlotte Lewis, 26 Apr. 1822, Amos A. Atkinson, (w) Ml. Hearn.

Harper, James K. - Sarah A. Lawrence, 8 Oct. 1849, R. A. Savage, (w) John Norfleet.

Harper, Joseph - Lurana Adams, 18 June 1829, Micajah Alsobrook, (w) Ml. Hearn.

Harper, James K. - Nancy Staton, 7 Dec. 1854, m. 7 Dec. 1854 by Elisha Cromwell, J. P., James H. Dozier, (w) W. S. Pitt, Clk.

Harper, John - Mary Barnes, 10 Nov. 1827, Edwin Barnes, (w) Ml. Hearn.

Harper, Joseph John - Gracy Staton, 31 Dec. 1855, m. 1 Jan. 1856 by Elisha Cromwell, J. P., Elisha Cromwell, (w) John S. Baker.

Harper, Kindred - Mary Eliza Stallings, 6 May 1852, m. 6 May 1852 by Wright Barnes, J. P., David Neal, (w) John Norfleet.

Harper, R. M. - Netty E. Bradley, 16 Jan. 1866, m. 17 Jan. 1866 by Jesse Bulluck, J. P., A. L. Joyner, (w) Irvin Thigpen.

Harper, Spencer H. - Sarah S. Williard, 3 Feb. 1864, m. 9 Feb. 1864 by W. B. Jordan, J. P., Thomas P. Braswell, (w) Irvin Thigpen, Clk.

Harper, Stephen - Nancy Hainey, 7 July 1846, Henry T. Clark, (w) W. L. Dozier.

Harper, William B. - Mary A. S. Barnes, 5 Aug. 1857, m. 6 Aug. 1857 by Bennet P. Pitt, J. F., Silas Warren, (w) J. H. Dozier, D. C.

Harper, William B. - Elizabeth Purvis, 30 Mar. 1861, m. 2 Apr. 1861 by David Cobb, J. P., William T. Whitehurst, (w) W. A. Jones.

Harper, William B. - Mary E. Bynum, 25 Oct. 1866, m. 1 Nov. 1866 by J. H. Daniel, M. G., Joseph Cobb, (w) Irvin Thigpen.

Harrell, Amos - Cythia Felton, 4 Dec. 1858, m. 7 Dec. 1858 by R. J. Johnson, J. P., John Harrel.

Harrel, Asa - Martha Eason, 15 Feb. 1840, David Webb, (w) Jo. Bell, C. C. C.

Harrell, Asa - Nancy Wells, 23 Nov. 1847, David Webb, (w) John Norfleet, Clk.

Harrell, Asa - Mary Jenkins, 29 Apr. 1851, m. 1 May 1851 by W. Y. Moore, J. P., David Webb, (w) John Norfleet.

Harrell, David - Litha Webb, 1 Dec. 1842, Lewis Harrell, David Harrell, (w) John Norfleet.

Harrell, David - Tilitha Marras, 18 June 1866, James Warren, (w) Irvin Thigpen.

Harrell, E. T. - Lussetta Pitt, 23 May, 1860, m. 31 May 1860 by R. J. Johnson, J. P., Joseph H. Payne, (w) J. H. Dozier, D. C.

Harrell, Elisha - Ann Eliza Raynor, 1 Aug. 1854, m. 1 Aug. 1854 by R. H. Pender, J. P., (w) W. S. Pitt, Clk.

Harrell, Elisha - Jacky Ann Webb, 18 Nov. 1854, m. 21 Nov. 1854 by W. Y. Moore, J. P., John Harrell, (w) W. S. Pitt, Clk.

Harrell, Greenberry - Sarah C. Alsobrook, 8 Feb. 1847, Nathan Mathewson.

Harrell, Jesse - Sally Thigpen, 8 Mar. 1834, Eaton Cobb, (w) Ml. Hearn.

Harrell, Jesse - Betsy Webb, 22 Feb. 1836, John Harrell, (w) T. C. Hearn.

Harrell, John - Susan Dunford, 28 Feb. 1839, Elisha Harrell, (w) Ml. Hearn.

Harrell, John - Catharine Owens, 20 Mar. 1852, m. 25 Mar. 1852 by W. Y. Moore, J. P., James R. Harper, (w) John Norfleet.

Harrell, John - Martha A. Harrell, 18 Dec. 1866, James Warren, (w) Irvin Thigpen.

Harrell, Joseph C. - Amanda A. Worsly, 18 Jan. 1860, m. 1 Feb. 1860 by William Harrell, J. P., Jesse Hanson, (w) John Norfleet.

Harrell, Kinchen - Elizabeth Ann Lawrence, 7 Jan. 1852, Franklin G. Pitt, (w) John Norfleet.

Harrell, Lewelling - Sally Ann Mayo, 11 Nov. 1847, William Harrell, John Norfleet, Clk.

Harrell, Lewis - Tamsey Thigpen, 5 Jan. 1824, Theophilus Brown, (w) Ml. Hearn, Pitman Worsley.

Harrell, Peter - Celia Webb, 19 Sept. 1844, Elisha Harrell, (w) John Norfleet.

Harrell, Peter - Vicey Webb, 3 Apr. 1866, m. 5 Apr. 1866 by Allen Warren, J. P., William Webb, (w) Irvin Thigpen.

Harrell, Warren C. - Lucy Brown, 2 Jan. 1866, m. 4 Jan. 1866 by William Harrell, J. P., John H. Leigh, (w) Irvin Thigpen.

Harrell, Watson - Elizabeth Webb, 10 Jan. 1835, Hyrum Forbes, John Harrell, (w) T. C. Hearn.

Harrell, Watson - Amanda Webb, 11 Mar. 1851, m. 11 Mar. 1851 by William Y. Moore, J. P., Hyrum Forbes, (w) John Norfleet.

Harrell, Watson - Lucinda Carr, 14 Dec. 1852, m. 16 Dec. 1852 by William Y. Moore, J. P., John Norfleet, (w) John Norfleet.

Harrell, William - Temperance Lee, 15 July 1845, James Reddick, (w) John Norfleet, Clk.

Harrell, William - Emily Webb, 25 Oct. 1847, John Norfleet, (w) John Norfleet.

Harrell, Willie - Wealthy Felton, 18 Nov. 1850, Jesse Harrell, (w) John Norfleet.

Harrell, Wilson, (s. of Asa Harrel) - Manda Jones, (dau. of James Jones), 25 Feb. 1868, m. 28 Feb. 1868 by R. J. Johnson, J. P., (w) Irvin Thigpen, Clk.

Harrell, William - Mary Ann Skinner, 30 Mar. 1854.

Harrell, Zachariah - Martha Everit, 10 Sept. 1764, Sarah Neal, (w) Thomas Cavenah.

Harrington, Joshua - Mary Francis Elixon, 1 Dec. 1859, m. 1 Dec. 1859 by E. D. Macnair, J. P., J. L. Duggan, (w) W. A. Jones.

Harrington, Thomas - Henrietta Bradly, 19 Dec. 1844, William D. Bryan, (w) John Norfleet.

Harris, Benjamin - Elizabeth Bynum, 13 Dec. 1832, Benjamin W. Sharpe, (w) Ml. Hearn.

Harris, Burwell - Sally A. Shingleton, 28 Dec. 1838, Spencer Stokes, (w) Jo. Bell.

Harris, David - Nancy Wilkins, 21 Mar. 1866, James E. Simanson, (w) Irvin Thigpen.

Harris, Eli - Nelly Ford, 16 Dec. 1856, m. 23 Dec. 1856 by Jesse Harrell, J. P., Henry Ford, (w) W. A. Jones, Clk.

Harris, Eli - Polly Moore, 29 Sept. 1863, William F. Lewis.

Harris, George W. - Parmetta Smith, 13 Feb. 1849, Robert H. Austin, (w) John Norfleet.

Harris, Irvin J. - Elizabeth Everett. 9 Jan. 1866, m. 9 Jan. 1866 by R. J. Johnson, J. P., Timothy Harris, (w) Irvin Thigpen, Clk.

Harris, James - Sally Howell, 20 Jan. 1825, Pitman Worsley, (w) Ml. Hearn.

Harris, James - Polly Harris, 7 Jan. 1851, Geo. Harris, John Norfleet, Clk.

Harris, James Henry - Sarah Smith, 3 Jan. 1859, John R. Cobb.

Harris, John - Grace Lawrence, 11 Mar. 1841, Henry Foxhall, (w) John Norfleet, Clk.

Harris, John - Laura Owens, 27 Feb. 1866, m. 1 Mar. 1866 by R. J. Johnson, J. P., Hymon Norville, (w) Irvin Thigpen, Clk.

Harris, Joseph - Lucy Lane, 31 Aug. 1857, m. 2 Sept, 1857 by J. W. Johnson, J. P., Micajah Anderson, (w) W. A. Jones, Clk.

Harris, Kenith - Sarah Price, 17 June 1841, John Hathaway.

Harris, Reuben - Nancy Reasons, 9 Dec. 1829, Samuel Reasons, Kenan Sumrell, (w) Ml. Hearn.

Harris, Thomas - Mary Ricks, 25 Nov. 1829, Bennett H. Bunn, (w) Ml. Hearn.

Harris, Thomas - Mary Barfield (of Halifax Co.), 10 Mar. 1838, Alexander Barfield, (w) Joseph Bell, C. C. C.

Harris, Timmey - Ann Everett, 19 Nov. 1864, m. 20 Nov. 1864 by R. J. Johnson, J. P., John T. Harrell, (w) T. W. Hussey, D. C.

Harriss, Allen - Elizabeth Ford, 13 Jan. 1849, John Knight, (w) John Norfleet, Clk.

Harriss. Bias - Rebecca Crisp, 21 Apr. 1834, Laurence Buntyn, (w) T. C. Hearn.

Harriss, John H. - Sarah Bell, 13 May 1856, m. 29 May 1856 by John Stamper, Joseph Anderson, (w) W. A. Jones.

Harriss. Spencer S. - Margaret Taylor, 14 May 1830, Caswell Horn, (w) L. H. Hearn.

Harriss. Tobias - Tabitha Bradley, 22 Feb. 1825, Christopher Harrell, (w) Ml. Hearn.

Harriss. William - Nancy Jones, 28 Nov. 1836, Bennett Oneal, (w) T. C. Hearn.

Harrison. Charles - Eliza Bell, 29 June 1832, Josiah Lawrence, (w) T. C. Hearn.

Harrison, N. C. - Elizabeth R. Linch, 29 June 1834, B. D. Mann, (w) John Norfleet, Clk.

Hart, Benjamin T. - Emma P. Lyon, 22 Oct. 1866, m. 23 Oct. 1866 by Thomas R. Owen, V. D. M., W. P. Lloyd, (w) Irvin Thigpen, Clk.

Hart, Franklin - Sarah R. E. Bryan, 4 Nov. 1845, David Barlow, (w) John Norfleet, Clk.

Hart, Walter - Pattie Wimberly, 6 Feb. 1866, m. 11 Feb. 1866 by S. L. Hart, J. P., William Bryan, (w) N. M. Lawrence, D. C.

Hartmus, James H. - Frances Outlaw, 19 Jan. 1830, Henry Austin, (w) L. H. Hearn.

Hatcher, Hancock - Margaret Watkins, 16 Aug. 1763, John Hatcher, (w) John Spendelow.

Hatcher, William - Martha Vickers, 21 Feb. 1765, John Coleman, George Vickers, (w) T. Cavenah.

Hathaway, Augustus - Esther Robinson, 27 Feb. 1850, Jacob Byrum, (w) John Norfleet, Clk.

Hathaway, Benjamin - Eliza Moseley, 1 Nov. 1849, Allen Moseley, David Cummings, (w) John Norfleet.

Hathaway, Franklin - Sarah James, 15 May 1848, Thomas Smith, (w) John Norfleet.

Hathaway, Gaston - Sarah Little, 17 Nov. 1851, m. 18 Nov. 1851 by Elisha Cromwell, J. P., Samuel E. Moore, (w) John Norfleet.

Hathaway, Irvy (?) - Fanny Corbit, 31 Jan. 1842, Meridy Corbitt, (w) John Norfleet, Clk.

Hathaway, Jack - Lucy Mayo, 13 Jan. 1824, Reuben Hearn, (w) N. Mathewson.

Hathaway, Richard - Lucy Everett, 24 Nov. 1865, m. 25 Nov. 1865 by C. L. Vines, J. P., James B. W. Norville, (w) Irvin Thigpen.

Hawkins, David - Henrietta Ward, 17 Jan. 1854, m. 19 Jan. 1854 by Wright Barnes, J. P., John W. Davis, (w) W. S. Pitt, Clk.

Hawkins, Elzy - Lavina Taylor, 7 Jan. 1836, Wm. Hyman, (w) T. C. Hearn.

Hawkins, Frederick - Martha Griffin, 27 May 1834, Bennett Oneal, (w) Ml. Hearn.

Hawkins, John - Spicey Hawkins, 17 Sept. 1840, Bennet O'Neal, (w) John Norfleet, Clk.

Hawkins, John G. - Amanda Lane, 7 Jan. 1858, m. 12 Jan. 1858 by Joel W. Tucker, M. G., John Manning, (w) J. H. Dozier.

Hawkins, Thomas H. - Martha Read, 9 May 1831, Thomas D. Gatlin, (w) Ml. Hearn.

Hayes, James B. - Eliza Wasdon, 15 May 1845, Thomas Williams.

Hayles, Cader - Polly Ellis, 3 Feb., Burrell Stallings, Henry Austin, (w) Ml. Hearn.

Hayles, William - Mary Ann Stallings, 17 Feb. 1857, m. 19 Feb. 1857 by J. R. Pitt, J. P., James F. Jenkins, (w) W. A. Jones.

Hayles, William - Rhoda Braswell, 12 May 1836, Jacob Braswell, (w) T. C. Hearn.

Hayles, William - James Tedder, 28 Jan. 1858, m. 31 Jan. 1858 by L. C. Pender, J. P., Jesse Gorden, (w) W. A. Jones.

Haynes, Eaton - Mary Haynes, 23 Jan. 1804, Allen Savage, (w) E. Hall.

Haynes, Herbert - Anne Thompson, 6 Mar. 1771, Robert Thompson.

Haynes, William Jr. - Nancy Knight, 2 Oct. (1818), Fredrick Bell, (w) Ml. Hearn.

Hayns, Jesse - Polly Barnes, 17 Feb. 1848, James D. Barnes.

Hays, Levi M. (or Len) - Martha Batts, 27 Aug. 1850, Willie J. Batts.

Head, John - Patsey Woollard, 26 Aug. 1811, George Gardner, (w) Ml. Hearn.

Hearn, Absalom - Amelia Carter, 20 Aug. 1828, J. G. Williams, Ml. Hearn.

Hearn, Amos - Nancy Mayo, 24 Jan. 1831, Elisha Hearn, (w) John H. Matheson.

Hearn, Amos - Rody Ann Robinson, 18 Dec. 1858, m. 23 Dec. 1858 by R. J. Johnson, J. P., Staton Cummings, (w) W. A. Jones, Clk.

Hearn, John - Mary M. Philips, 29 Nov. 1859, m. 4 Dec. 1859 by Bennett P. Pitt, J. P., John Hearn, (w) W. A. Jones.

Hearn, L. H. - Margaret Ann Bell, 12 May 1836, Henry King, (w) T. C. Hearn.

Hearn, William - Martha Gay, 16 March 1854. (No wit.)

Heath, A. I. - Maria Sims, 14 Feb. 1854, m. 14 Feb. 1854 by J. B. Jackson, J. D. Edmondson, A. G. Brooks, J. H. Barnes, (w) W. S. Pitt, Clk.

Hedgepeth, Jesse - Penny Lawrence of Nash Co., 1810.

Hedgepeth, Jesse - Mary Eliza Parker, 3 Jan. 1849, Thomas Macnair, (w) W. L. Dozier.

Hedgepeth, Josiah - Sylvester Harris, 11 Dec. 1866, m. 3 Jan. 1867 by L. R. Cherry, J. P., Robert Adkins, (w) Irvin Thigpen.

Hedgepeth, R. R. - Elizabeth Bradley, 25 Jan. 1841, Elias Bradley.

Hegan, Watson - Jackie A. Wilkins, 2 Feb. 1864, m. 2 Feb. 1864 by Jos. Blount Cheshire, Epis. Min., William Mitchel (w) Irvin Thigpen.

Hegans, Jesse B. - William Ann Gaiter, 14 Dec. 1865, m. 14 Dec. 1865 by E. D. Macnair, J. P., J. H. Mears, (w) Irvin Thigpen.

Heggans, Jesse - Mary D. Landing, 29 Nov. 1866, m. 2 Dec. 1866 by J. I. Proctor, J. P., Lafayette Landing, (w) Irvin Thigpen.

Henderson, Walter - Elizabeth Bradley, 25 Feb. 1853, m. 25 Feb. 1853 by A. J. Battle, M. G., William Raynor, (w) John Norfleet.

Hendley, John - Elsa Laurence, 5 June 1819, George Laurence, (w) Michl. Hearn.

Hendley, Ransom - Edney Chilton, 25 Nov. 1818, Elisha Cromwell, (w) Ml. Hearn.

Hendley, Ransom - Martha Waters, 12 Jan. 1826, Burrel Shelton, (w) N. Matheson.

Hester, James - Martha Proctor, 27 Nov. 1848, William H. Hines.

Hickman, William - Luerelia Stricklin, 19 Dec. 1762, Nathaniel Hickman, (w) John Spendelow.

Hicks, Joseph C. - Margaret A. Shelton, 31 July 1865(?), m. 30 July 1865 by William Harrell, Jesse Harrell, (w) Irvin Thigpen.

Hicks, Joshua - Lady Ann Mayo, 23 Jan. 1837, Robert H. Austin, (w) Jo. Bell, C. C.

Hicks, Lemon - Nancy Laurence, 8 Oct. 1827, Reading Thigpen, (w) Ml. Hearn.
Hicks, Phesenton S. - Cittury Proctor, 24 Dec. 1856, m. 25 Dec. 1856 by Theo. Thomas, J. P., J. H. Dozier, (w) J. H. Dozier.
Hicks, Seth S. - Margaret Harrell, 22 Dec. 1857, m. 24 Dec. 1857 by David Cobb, J. P., W. W. Gay, (w) W. A. Jones, Clk.
Hicks, Spencer - Mary Mayo, 4 Jan. 1830, Cullen Adams, (w) Ml. Hearn.
Hicks, Starling - Elizabeth Boothe, 18 May 1829, James Hicks, (w) Ml. Hearn.
Hicks, Stephen - Sally Vasser, 27 Aug. 1832, Larry Dew, (w) Ml. Hearn.
Higgs, Joseph - Finella Staton, 16 Mar. 1835, Samuel Whitehead, (w) T. C. Hearn.
Hill, Asa - Rebbecca Hill, 29 Oct. 1840, Blake Williford.
Hill, Asbury - Emeliza Sessoms, 2 Aug. 1860, m. 2 Aug. 1860 by E. D. Macnair, J. P., J. B. Peel, (w) J. H. Dozier, I. B. Peal.
Hill, Burrell - Della Lodge, 28 Aug. 1862, m. 11 Sept. 1862 by J. I. Proctor, J. P., Taylor Garner, (w) Allen Warren.
Hill, Burwell - Nancy Long, 8 July 1834, Whitmil Williams, (w) L. H. Hearn.
Hill, Duffy - Polly Jackson, 19 May 1862, m. 20 May 1862 by Hilyard S. Taylor, A. B. M. G., Micajah Jackson, (w) W. A. Jones.
Hill, Fielding - Harriet Bond, 18 Dec. 1849, William Worsley, (w) John Norfleet.
Hill, Fielding - Zana A. Proctor, 12 Oct. 1859, m. 13 Oct. 1859 by R. H. Gatlin, R. H. Gatlin.
Hill, Green - Harriett Jackson, 12 Mar. 1855, m. 15 Mar. 1855 by Theo. Thomas, J. P., John Proctor, (w) W. S. Pitt.
Hill, Isaac - Julia Hagan, 8 July 1862, m. 10 July 1862 by Hilyard S. Taylor, A. B. M. G., Asa Hill, (w) Irvin Thigpen, Clk.
Hill, James - Bashuba Jones, 14 Sept. 1858, m. 17 Oct. 1858 by Lunsford R. Cherry, J. P., Lunsford R. Cherry (w).
Hill, Marcus - Martha A. Jackson, 4 Apr. 1859, m. 4 Apr. 1859 by Hilyard S. Taylor, A. B. M. G., John Proctor, (w) W. A. Jones, Clk.
Hill, Nathaniel - Melvina Weaver, 17 Apr. 1860, m. 17 Apr. 1860 by Hilyard S. Taylor, A. B. M. G., Hilliard Davis, (w) W. A. Jones.

Hill, Theophilus - Tresa Thomas, 3 Sept. 1762, Benjamin Emerson.

Hill, Thomas G. - Rhoda Proctor, 15 Feb. 1836, Micajah E. Armstrong, Benjamin Wilkinson, Newson Long, (w) Ml. Hearn.

Hilliard, James C. - Mary Ann Ruffin, 9 Feb. 1835, Turner Rogers, (w) Theo. C. Hearn.

Hines, John E. - Mary House, 19 Aug. 1835, Michael Watson, (w) T. C. Hearn.

Hines, Kinchen - Charity A. Ross, 16 May 1823, Henry Bryan, (w) Ml. Hearn.

Hines, Peter R. - Sarah McNair, 18 Feb. 1834, Simon J. Baker, (w) Theo. Hearn, D. C.

Hinton, Malachi - Sarah Wimberely, 6 June 1764, George Wimberely, (w) James Hall.

Hobbs, Isaac - Elizabeth Whitley, 7 Jan. 1825, Garret Knight, (w) Ml. Hearn.

Hobby, Joseph W. - Georgiana Marks, 27 Sept. 1859, m. 29 Sept. 1859 by Thomas F. Cherry, J. P., George B. Lipscomb, (w) W. A. Jones, Clk.

Hocott, James - Delphia Morgan, 1 Sept. 1845, Richard Hocott, (w) John Norfleet.

Hocott, Lewis - Betsy Brinkley, 9 Jan. 1836, David Lloyd, (w) Theo. C. Hearn.

Hocott, Richard - Nancy Turnage, 25 July 1844, Evan Howard, (w) John Norfleet, Clk.

Hodge, Allen - Mary Braddy, 4 Nov. 1826, Benjamin Boykin, (w) Ml. Hearn.

Hodge, James - Nancy Best, 20 Jan. 1857, m. 20 Jan. 1857 by E. W. Cox, B. W. Mabry, (w) J. H. Dozier.

Hodge, Mac - Martha Ann Staton, 1 Sept. 1860, m. 2 Sept 1860 by Kenneth Thigpen, J. P., Joseph Henry Drew, (w) W. A. Jones.

Hodge, Pollard - Catherine Bryan, 10 Apr. 1839, Charles Mabry, (w) D. C. Bell.

Holden, Jerry - Elizabeth Wingate, 27 Feb. 1866, m. 8 Mar. 1866 by A. M. Lowe, M. G., Jo. J. Garrett, (w) Irvin Thigpen, Clk.

Holland, Abraham - Rebecca Lane, 11 Mar. 1839, John Lane, (w) Jo. Bell.

Holland, Abram - Martha Wells (Widow), 28 Apr. 1846, James J. Vick, (w) John Norfleet.

Holland, B. - Martha Shelton, 1 Mar. 1866, John Harriss, (w) Irvin Thigpen.

Holland, Elias - Louiza Summerlin, 13 Mar. 1845, William Sessoms, (w) John Norfleet.
Holland, Elisha - Patsey Gardner, 16 Apr. 1830, Dempsey Webb, (w) L. H. Hearn.
Holland, James - Barbary Blackburn, 4 Jan. 1854, m. 5 Jan. 1854 by Kenneth Thigpen, J. P. (No wit.)
Holland. Kenneth - Mary Jane House, 29 Dec. 1858, William H. Holland.
Holland, Thomas - Mary Ross, 7 May 1764, John Whitehouse, (w) Thomas Cavenah.
Holloman, Isham - Sarah Wiggins, 29 Oct. 1799, David Forehand, (w) J. H. Hall.
Holloway, John - Mary Ship, 21 Oct. 1765, Jacob Sessoms.
Holtzcheister, Julius - Lucy E. Newsom, 11 Dec. 1861, m. 11 Dec. 1861 by Thomas R. Owen, Thomas W. Hussey, (w) T. W. Hussey.
Hopkins, Daniel - Mary Jenkins, 29 Dec. 1827, Joshua Pender, (w) Ml. Hearn.
Hopkins, Ezekiah (Hezekiah?) - Susan Hammons, 17 Oct. 1861, m. 17 Oct. 1861 by J. B. Bobbitt, Blount Barfield, (w) T. W. Hussey.
Hopkins, John - Talitha Cutchins, 16 Mar. 1827, James Downing, (w) Ml. Hearn.
Hopkins, Joseph John - David Lavinia Hopkins, 21 June 1853, m. 21 June 1853 by W. F. Lewis, J. P., Johnson Tyler, (w) John Norfleet.
Hopkins (or Worsley), Littleberry - Renny Cherry, 5 Mar. 1832, Staton Hopkins, (w) Ml. Hearn.
Hopkins, Staton - Susan Crisp, 20 Dec. 1831, Silas Wilkinson, (w) Ml. Hearn.
Hopkins, William - Sally Stancil, 22 Oct. 1799, William Cherry, (w) S. Wrenn.
Hopkins, William D. - Julia Best, 27 May 1830, William C. Leigh, (w) Ml. Hearn.
Horn, Caswell - Mary Taylor, 23 Sept. 1829, George W. Killebrew, (w) Ml. Hearn.
Horn, Dick - Linda Locust, 21 May 1853, m. 2 June 1853 by L. C. Pender, J. P., William Bryan, (w) John Norfleet.
Horn, Duke William - Mary E. A. Laurence, 28 Sept. 1829, Clemmons Darden, (w) Ml. Hearn.
Horn, Elias - Sarah Gay, 26 Jan. 1763, Elijah Horn, (w) Duncan Lamon.
Horn, Elijah - Susannah Killebrew, 18 Aug. 1799, Simeon Horn (w) S. Wren.

Horn, Henry H. - Peninah Philips, 24 Nov. 1831, Jno. A. Cotton, (w) Michl. Hearn.
Horn, Isaac - Mary B. Horn, 24 Dec. 1827, James G. Barnes, Joab Horne, (w) Ml. Hearn.
Horn, James - Elizabeth Price, 18 May 1799, Cullen Jones, (w) E. Hall.
Horn, James - Patsy Gill, 19 Dec. 1840, Guilford Horn, (w) John Norfleet, Clk.
Horn, James J. - Celia Ruffin, 19 Jan. 1828, Ely Gay, (w) Ml. Hearn.
Horn, Jordan - James Flowers, 18 Jan. 1845, James Horn, (w) John Norfleet.
Horn, Josiah - Delitha D. Berry, 23 Feb. 1818, Blake Little, (w) Michl. Hearn.
Horn, Joshua L. - Mary E. Mercer, 2 Nov. 1832, Joseph S. Battle, (w) T. C. Hearn.
Horn, William - Mary Thomas, 20 July, 1761, Edward Moore, (w) David Mann.
Horn, William - Nancy Holland, 26 Feb. 1800, William Sims, (w) J. H. Hale.
Horne, David - Martha Ann Elizabeth Morris, 13 Apr. 1854, m. 16 Apr. 1854 by D. W. Barnes, J. P., Augustin Farmer, (w) W. S. Pitt, Clk.
Hoskins, Richard T. - Elizabeth A. Lawrence, 5 Oct. 1846, Nathan Matheson, (w) John Norfleet.
House, Benjamin - Sally Young, 11 Oct. 1847, Jeremiah Odom, (w) John Norfleet, Clk.
House, Berry A. - Nancy Andrews, 7 Oct. 1845, John Whitehurst, (w) John Norfleet, Clk.
House, Joseph - Winny Bedford, 22 July 1845, Archelous Braswell, (w) John Norfleet, Clk.
House, William T. - Sallie Bryant, 26 Feb. 1861, m. 27 Feb. 1861 by John Ws. Johnson, J. P., (w) W. A. Jones, Clk.
Howard, David H. - Harriet Chilton, 16 Mar. 1818, Willie A. Howard, (w) Michl. Hearn.
Howard, Don Edgar - Sarah E. Mills, 25 Feb. 1853, m. 25 Feb. 1853 by John S. Dancy, J. P., James Walsh, William M. Pippen, John Norfleet, Isaac Palamountain, (w) John S. Dancy.
Howard, Evan - Amy Barns, 16 Feb. 1836, Lewis Hocott, (w) T. C. Hearn.
Howard, Irvy (?) - Bethane Ruffin, 7 Mar. 1849, Calvin Forbes, (w) John Norfleet, Clk.

Howard, James - Gracy Gater, 5 Apr. 1826, John Gaiter, (w) Ml. Hearn.

Howard, Joseph - Elizabeth Best, 2 Dec. 1839, Peter E. Knight, (w) Jo. Bell, C. C.

Howard, Micajah - Elizabeth Pitt, 26 Sept. 1826, Willie R. Howard, (w) N. Matheson.

Howard, Robert - Sarah Moore, 30 Oct. 1857, m. 3 Nov. 1857 by William S. Long, J. P., Thomas Howard, (w) W. A. Long.

Howard, Starky - Casia Felton, 14 Jan. 1833, William Felton, (w) T. C. Hearn.

Howard, Starky - Emeliza Pippen, 29 Oct. 1852, m. 30 Nov. 1852 by M. W. Moore, J. P., William Y. Moore, J. P., (w) John Norfleet.

Howard, Stephen - Elizabeth Mercer, 28 Mar. 1844, Jos. R. Broom, (w) John Norfleet.

Howard, Wilson - Betsy Best, 1 Sept. 1825, Peter E. Knight, (w) N. Matheson.

Howell, B. D. - Mary L. MacDowell, 18 Dec. 1860, m. 18 Dec. 1866(?) by J. H. Daniel, B. G. Howell (w) Thomas W. Hussey.

Howell, Bythal - Henretta Long, 7 Jan. 1833, Brittain Howell, (w) T. C. Hearn.

Howell, Ervin - Martha Pippin, 12 Jan. 1847, Joshua L. Laurence.

Howell, James D. - Martha A. Gray, 29 July 1847, Matthew Weddell, (w) John Norfleet, Clk.

Howell, Jonathan - Mary Fort (Widow), 20 May 1766, Elias Fort.

Howell, Willis - Ginnie Savage, 22 Jan. 1866, m. 30 Jan. 1866 by William F. Bell, John H. L. Best, (w) Irvin Thigpen, Clk.

Howerton, Baker - Sarah Benson, 7 Dec. 1853, m. 15 Dec. 1853 by John F. Speight, S. Boliver Bradley (w).

Howett, Benjamin - Margaret A. H. Tyson, 21 Jan. 1850, James Eason (w) John Norfleet.

Howington, Alexander - Martha J. Pitman, 3 Jan. 1857, m. 8 Jan. 1857 by L. R. Cherry, J. P., Joel Savage, (w) J. H. Dozier.

Howland, John - Clarky Bozeman, 25 Oct. 1848, Guilford Horn, (w) John Norfleet, Clk.

Hudnall, Robert - Lucresia Kitchen, 2 Dec. 1765, John Hudnell.

Hudnell, William - Elizabeth Bridges, 21 Feb. 1766, Nathan Bridges, (w) James Hall.

Hughes, John F. - Martha P. Randolph, 8 Oct. 1822, Nathan Matheson.

Hughes, John F. - (illegible,———, 18——, ——, 18——,), John Williams, (w) N. Matheson.

Humphrey, Ezekiel - Sarah Bishop, 15 Jan. 1825, James Liggs, (w) Ml. Hearn.

Hunt, David - Susan Wood, 1 May 1834, Richard Pond, (w) Ml. Hearn.

Hunter, Richard D. - Charity J. Poland, 21 Feb. 1859, m. 24 Feb. 1859 by C. B. Killebrew, J. P., W. Gray Billips, (w) W. A. Jones.

Hunter, Thomas - Mary Ann Lewis, 23 Nov. 1824, Exum Lewis, (w) Ml. Hearn.

Hunter, Wildon S. - Nancy Griffiths, 12 Feb. 1844, George A. Grimes, John Norfleet.

Hussey, Thomas C. - Emily Rountree, 7 July 1849, J. M. Hussey, (w) Benjamin Norfleet.

Hyatt, Jesse B. - Margaret A. Shurly, 15 Apr. 1847, David Neal, (w) John Norfleet, Clk.

Hyatt, Jesse B. - Martha C. Horne, 11 Feb. 1851, m. 11 Apr. 1851 by Jesse Harrell, J. P., David Neal, (w) John Norfleet.

Hyatt, William - Temperance Braswell, 9 Dec. 1857, m. 10 Dec. 1857 by Hilliard S. Taylor, A. B. M. G., Thomas J. Braswell, (w) J. H. Dozier.

Hyde, James T. - Martha Ann Pittman, 18 Jan. 1859, m. 20 Jan. 1859 by John A. Stamper, Edmon Alford, (w) J. H. Dozier.

Hyde, Stephen - Milissa Alsbrook, 8 Jan. 1844, Bythel Howell, John Hyde, (w) John Norfleet, Clk.

Hyman, Arthur B. - Sally Howard, 26 Feb. 1831, Kenneth Hyman, (w) L. H. Hearn.

Hyman, Benjamin F. - Mehala Garrett, 21 Apr. 1857, m. 23 Apr. 1857 by J. W. Howard, J. P., Robert Howard, (w) W. A. Jones.

Hyman, Henry - Martha E. Porter, 27 Feb. 1834, Robert H. Austin, (w) T. C. Hearn.

Hyman, Hunter, - Anacha Hyman, 15 Sept. 1865, m. 16 Sept. 1865 by E. D. Macnair, J. P., William Lloyd, (w) T. W. Hussey.

Hyman, John - Mary J. Best, 3 July 1848, William Hyman Sr., (w) John Norfleet, Clk.

Hyman, Nedam - Emily F. Jones, 27 Oct. 1853, m. 27 Oct. 1853 by William Hyman, William G. Moore.

Hyman, Turner - Louisa Battle, 8 Sept. 1866, Eli Norfleet, (w) Irvin Thigpen.

I

Ing, Allen - Lydia Wells, 13 Jan. 1831, Micajah Rose, (w) Ml. Hearn.

Irwin, Jeremiah - Elizabeth George, 11 Dec. 1766, Thomas Harris.

Israel, Jailand - Mary Jane Peoples, 18 Dec. 1855, m. 19 Dec. 1855 by C. B. Killebrew, J. P., William Summerlin, (w) W. S. Pitt, Clk.

Ivey, James - Nancy O'Neal, 20 Dec. 1843, James Coker, (w) John Norfleet, Clk.

Ivy, John R. - Sallie E. Turner, 24 Apr. 1866, m. 1 May 1866 by T. G. Lowe, William G. Lewis, (w) Irvin Thigpen, Clk.

J

Jackson, Alfred - Elizabeth Fareless, 18 Mar. 1833, Robert Jackson, Bird Land, (w) T. C. Hearn, C. C.

Jackson, Amos W. - Nancy W. Jackson, 23 Aug. 1858, m. 24 Aug. 1858 by Hilliard S. Taylor, A. B. M. G., William Proctor, (w) W. A. Jones, Clk.

Jackson, Antney (Anthony) - Lucinda Staton, 27 Feb. 1866. m. 3 Mar. 1866 by J. F. Batts, J. P., H. C. Dixon, (w) Irvin Thigpen.

Jackson, Edward P. - Viletta Dunn, 7 Apr. 1866, m. 12 Apr. 1866 by W. H. Knight, J. P., James H. Dixon, (w) Irvin Thigpen.

Jackson, Elisha W. - Atsey Masingale, 22 May 1824, Abraham Price, (w) Ml. Hearn.

Jackson, Elisha Willis - Nancy Mares, 6 Jan. 1831, Abraham Price, (w) Ml. Hearn.

Jackson, Henry - Polly Barnhill, 6 July 1822, James Hammond, (w) Ml. Hearn.

Jackson, James - Mary Leigh, 2 May 1859, m. 5 May 1859 by Hilliard S. Taylor, A. B. M. G., James Mullin, (w) W. A. Jones.

Jackson, James H. - Crissy Williams, 28 Oct. 1851, m. 28 Oct. 1851 by W. J. Armstrong, J. P., Elza Taylor, (w) John Norfleet, Clk.

Jackson, Jeremiah - Mary Boon, 12 Nov. 1825, Thomas Boon, (w) Ml. Hearn.
Jackson, Jeremiah - Priscilla Barrett, 19 Oct. 1827, James Jackson, Whitmel Williams, (w) Ml. Hearn.
Jackson, Jeremiah - Harriet Trevaithan, 7 Apr. 1841, David Williams.
Jackson, Jeremiah - Elizabeth Braswell, 17 May 1843, Joel D. Braswell, (w) John Norfleet, Clk.
Jackson, Jeremiah - Margaret M. Lancaster, 6 July 1844, Reddin Worsley, (w) John Norfleet.
Jackson, John Irving - Mary Ann Dancy, 7 Jan. 1791, David Pender, (w) E. Hall.
Jackson, John W. - Frances Proctor, 5 Mar. 1850, Elisha Thomas, (w) John Norfleet, Clk.
Jackson, Micajah - Temperance Ricks, 22 Jan. 1828, Simeon Griffin, (w) Ml. Hearn.
Jackson, Micajah - Sally Williams, 9 Dec. 1844, Hardy G. L. Calhoon, (w) John Norfleet.
Jackson, Micajah - Frances Gay, 28 Feb. 1852, m. 29 Feb. 1852 by Theo. Thomas, J. P., James Henry Jackson, (w) John Norfleet.
Jackson, Orren - Catherine Boon, 28 Jan. 1858, m. 28 Jan. 1858 by Hilliard S. Taylor, A. B. M. G., Saml. Ruffin, (w) W. A. Jones, Clk.
Jackson, William - Frances Ford, 6 Feb. 1841, William Smith, (w) John Norfleet, Clk.
Jackson, William - Sallie Ann Jackson, 1 Jan. 1855, m. 2 Jan. 1855 by Theo. Thomas, J. P., Orren L. Jackson, (w) W. S. Pitt, Clk.
Jakway, Stephen E. - Elizabeth Williford, 22 July 1847, William L. Hart, (w) John Norfleet.
James, Cliffin - Marina Taylor, 25 Feb. 1843, Josiah Counsel, (w) John Norfleet, Clk.
James, Elijah - Rachel Pew, 16 Feb. 1827, Charles Worrell, (w) Ml. Hearn.
Jeffreys, Henry - Penny Lloyd, 19 May 1866, m. 20 May, 1866 by Jos. Blount Cheshire, Epis. Min., William Howard, (w) Irvin Thigpen.
Jeffreys, James R. - Annie E. Laurence, 22 Jan. 1850, Leonidas A. Jeffreys, (w) John Norfleet.
Jeffreys, William - Mary Gray, (3)0 July 1773, Simon Gray, (w) James Gray, (w) John Hall.

Jenkins, Charles H. - Mary Jane Dupree, 19 Oct. 1857, m. 20 Oct. 1857 by Elisha Cromwell, J. P., W. H. Knight, (w) W. A. Jones, Clk.

Jenkins, F. H. - Hannah G. Staton, 12 Sept. 1855, m. 13 Sept. 1855 by Elisha Cromwell, J. P., Elisha Cromwell, (w) W. S. Pitt, Clk.

Jenkins, Henry - Sarah Pitman, 16 Aug. 1854 (?), m. 17 Aug. 1855 by John G. Williams, James Jenkins, (w) W. A. Jones, D. C.

Jenkins, James D. - Frances Killebrew, 11 June 1866, m. 12 June 1866 by Thomas R. Owen, V. D. M., A. J. Cotton, (w) Irvin Thigpen.

Jenkins, James F. - Marina Hopkins, 15 Nov. 1831, Silas Wilkinson, (w) L. H. Hearn.

Jenkins, Joab - Mary E. Carney, 28 July 1851, m. 31 July 1851 by Elisha Cromwell, J. P., Elisha Cromwell, (w) Benjamin Norfleet.

Jenkins, John - Susan Clark, 6 May 1837, Nicholas Warren, (w) Ml. Hearn.

Jenkins, Josiah D. - Rilla Hopkins, Jan. 10, 1832, Silas Wilkinson, (w) Ml. Hearn.

Jenkins, Josiah D. - Barsheba A. Daughtry, 6 July 1852, m. 8 July 1852 by William H. Hines, J. P., John Norfleet, (w).

Jenkins, Samuel H. - Temperance Bynum, 9 Oct. 1832, Benjamin Sharp.

Jenkins, Thomas - Eliza Etherage, 8 Oct. 1835, Thomas Smith, (w) T. C. Hearn.

Jenkins, William - Winnifred Corbitt, 22 Dec. 1825, Elisha Harrell, (w) Ml. Hearn.

Jenkins, William D. - Celia J. Philips, 10 Dec. 1822, Benjamin Boykins, (w) Ml. Hearn.

Johnson, Benjamin - Rebecca Norris, 5 May 1845, Henry Anderson, (w) John Norfleet, Clk.

Johnson, Benjamin - Martha Pernton, 7 Apr. 1866, m. 8 Apr. 1866 by W. F. Lewis, J. P., George Foreman, (w) Irvin Thigpen.

Johnson, David - Sally Vettel, 25 Jan. 1800, William Hines, (w) S. Wren.

Johnson, Edward - Mary Langly (Widow), 25 May 1761, Simon Johnson, (w) James Hall.

Johnson, Henry - Mary A. Griffin, 25 Aug. 1846, Dempsy Trevathan.

Johnson, James - Catherine Dunn, 23 Nov. 1839, Jacob Whitley, (w) Jo. Bell, C. C.

Johnson, James J. - Mary Edwards, 1 Jan. 1857, m. 11 Jan. 1857 by W. Y. Moore, J. P., Silas E. Crisp, (w) W. A. Jones, Clk.

Johnson, John - Susan Crisp, 26 Sept. 1859, m. 27 Sept. 1859 by Erastus Cherry, J. P., Theos. C. Hyman, (w) J. H. Dozier.

Johnson, Joseph J. - Nancy Barfield, 27 Dec. 1847, James R. King, (w) W. L. Dozier.

Johnson. Joseph J. - Elizabeth Pope, 21 Jan. 1860, m. 26 Jan. 1860 by Thomas F. Cherry, J. P., S. B. Bradley, (w) W. A. Jones.

Johnson, Lemuel T. - Sevesta Teel, 28 Mar. 1859, m. 30 Mar. 1859 by Bennett P. Pitt, J. P., F. D. Foxhall.

Johnson, Meredith - Molly Matthews, 1 Jan. 1763, Nathan Jones.

Johnson, Purviss - Mary Little, 2 Nov. 1825, William Little, (w) Ml. Hearn.

Johnson, Robert A. - Prudence Bullock, 28 March 1861, m. 4 Apr. 1861 by C. B. Killebrew, J. P., John W. Johnson, (w) T. W. Hussey.

Johnson, Robert A. - Lucinda Bullock, 19 June 1862, m. 19 June 1862 by W. F. Lewis, J. P., William F. Lewis, (w) Irvin Thigpen.

Johnson, Stephen - Clemmy Cook, 2 Jan. 1841, James M. Redmond, (w) John Norfleet, Clk.

Johnson, Will - Dilla Braswell, 10 Nov. 1840, (w) John Ward, John Norfleet, Clk.

Johnson, William C. - Sarah E. Johnson, 23 Dec. 1856, m. 23 Dec. 1856 by L. R. Cherry, J. P., Robert A. Johnson, (w) W. A. Jones.

Johnson, William C. - Martha A. Britt, 6 Apr. 1858, m. 9 Apr. 1858 by W. F. Lewis, J. P., William F. Lewis, (w) W. A. Jones, Clk.

Johnson, Willie - Eliza Dunn, 12 Apr. 1849, James Barrow, (w) John Norfleet, Clk.

Johnston, Aaron - Sally Williams, 10 Jan. 1823, Henry Bryan, (w) Ml. Hearn.

Johnston, Alexander S. - Nancy Norfleet, 29 March 1812, John Hogun, (w) Ml. Hearn.

Johnston, Amos - Dolly Vassar, 22 Dec. 1827, Thomas Johnston, (w) Ml. Hearn.

Johnston, Greenberry Laurence - Caroline Legett, 26 Aug. 1859, Robert H. King.

Johnston, Henry - Harriett B. Pittman, 20 Feb. 1826, David Barnes, (w) Ml. Hearn.

Johnston, Henry - Emily Norfleet, 11 Jan. 1830, Henry Austin, (w) Ml. Hearn.

Johnston, James M. - Sarah Cutchen, 12 May 1866, m. 15 May 1866 by A. M. Lowe, M. G., W. D. Pittman, (w) Irving Thigpen, Clk.

Johnston, John - Susan Edwards, 25 Nov. 1835, Thomas Johnston, (w) T. C. Hearn.

Johnston, John W. - Sarah Dicken, 6 Apr. 1846, John F. Speight.

Johnston, Joshua - Charity Bartee, 8 Aug. 1828, Levi Amason, (w) Ml. Hearn.

Johnston, Moses - Elizabeth R. Trevathan, 17 Dec. 1832, Thomas H. Hawkins, (w) Ml. Hearn.

Johnston, Nathan - Martha Pettaway, 17 Dec. 1831, John Morriss, (w) Ml. Hearn.

Johnston, Richard - Sophia Vines, 7 Jan. 1824, James Johnson.

Johnston, Robert - Nelley Griffin, 15 March 1838, Reubin Johnson, Kindred C. Taylor, (w) Jo. Bell, C. C.

Johnston, Stuart L. - Claudia Davenport, 19 May 1862, Cadar Abrams, (w) W. A. Jones.

Johnston, Thomas - Nancy Stokes, 30 Aug. 1837, Thomas Johnston, Jr., (w) Jo. Bell.

Johnston, William - Mary Ruffin, 15 May 1834, James Griffin, (w) Ml. Hearn.

Johnston, William G. - Sarah Ann Etheridge, 20 Jan. 1838, Michael Watson.

Johnston, William H. (s. of Henry Johnston) - Caroline Anthony, 15 Apr. 1868, m. 15 Apr. 1868 by Jos. Blount Cheshire, Epis. Min., (w) Irvin Thigpen, Clk.

Johnston, Zadock - Ailsey Amason, 1 Feb. 1828, Enos Amason, Joshua Johnston, (w) Ml. Hearn.

Joiner, Drewery Jr. - Piety Calhoun, 1 Aug. 1836, Andrew A. Calhoun, (w) Ml. Hearn.

Joiner, Guilford D. - Evelina Robbins, 19 Oct. 1866, m. 21 Oct. 1866 by Hilyard S. Taylor, A. B. M. G., Orren E. Joyner, (w) Irvin Thigpen.

Joiner, Jordan Jr. - Lucretia Adams, 23 Dec. 1856, m. 24 Dec. 1856 by C. W. Spiers, J. P., Jordan Joiner, Sr., (w) W. A. Jones, Clk.

Joiner, Redden - Ann Calhoun, 29 Dec. 1865, m. 30 Dec. 1865 by John E. Baker, J. P., B. Lancaster, (w) Irvin Thigpen, Clk.

Jolly, James - Priscilla Fort, 15 Oct. 1764, William Sharrod, (w) J. Hall.

Jolly, Lavin - Nancy Ann Penelope Dunn, 17 Apr. 1848, Theophilus Moore.

Jones, Aaron, Jr. - Martha O. Lawrence, 18 Dec. 1850, Thomas R. Owen, (w) Benjamin Norfleet.

Jones, Abram - Patsy Farrow, 18 Sept. 1811, Dennis Ellis, (w) N. Mathewson.

Jones, Adin - Sally Crisp, 20 Aug. 1811, John Rainer, (w) Ml. Hearn.

Jones, Allen - Elizabeth Pitman, 11 May 1826, Benjamin Whitfield, (w) Ml. Hearn.

Jones, Allen - Catherine Williams, 17 Apr. 1828, Benjamin Wilkinson, (w) Ml. Hearn.

Jones, Benjamin - Susan Killebrew, 17 Aug. 1842, Willie Pitman, (w) John Norfleet, Clk.

Jones, Berry - Mary Harrell, 26 May 1866, m. 27 May 1866 by Erastus Cherry, J. P., G. W. Bell, (w) Irvin Thigpen, Clk.

Jones, Burrell P. - Mary Ricks, 12 Mar. 1834, Robert Ricks, (w) Theo. C. Hearn.

Jones (Green), Berry - Elizabeth Pitt, 10 Sept. 1835, m. 12 Sept. 1853 by Thomas Norfleet, J. P., Jonas Walston, Kinchen Worrell.

Jones, Blount - Rebecca Boon, 21 Mar. 1860, m. 21 Mar. 1860 by Theo. Atkinson, J. P., Levi L. Lancaster, (w) W. A. Jones, Clk.

Jones, Calvin - Mary E. Staton, 11 Oct. 1842, Mc. Jones, (w) R. Norfleet.

Jones, Calvin - Emily Bilbury, 28 Jan. 1848, Willis Bradley, (w) John Norfleet.

Jones, Calvin - Mary Dillard, 25 Feb. 1856, m. 28 Feb. 1856 by Wm. F. Mercer, J. P., Martin Gordon, (w) W. A. Jones, D. C.

Jones, David - Cindarilla Savage, 10 Sept. 1863, m. 10 Sept. 1863 by Henry T. Clark, J. P., J. B. Hyatt, (w) T. W. Hussey.

Jones, Dempsey - Scynthia Webb, 3 May 1828, Ely Jones, (w) Ml. Hearn.

Jones, Edward - Sarah Porter, 21 Dec. 1838, David Biggs, William Biggs.

Jones, Edwin - Eliza Price, 30 Jan. 1834, George Anderson, Jr., (w) Ml. Hearn.

Jones, Edwin - Philicia Morgan, 17 Jan. 1853, m. 18 Jan. 1853 by Wright Barnes, J. P., Seth Hicks, (w) Benjamin Norfleet.

Jones, Eli - Elizabeth Wood, 7 Oct. 1829, John Ritter, (w) Ml. Hearn.

Jones, Elisha - Luvenia Sessoms, 16 Jan. 1855, m. 16 Jan. 1855 by Thomas Norfleet, J. P., Jesse Gardner, (w) W. S. Pitt, Clk.

Jones, Granville - Jane Chesson, 6 Jan. 1866, m. 20 Mar. 1866 by Erastus Cherry, J. P., Joseph B. Coffield, (w) Irvin Thigpen, Clk.

Jones, Guilford J. - Pheraby Sherrod, 18 Dec. 1861, m. 19 Dec. 1861 by Hilyard S. Taylor, A. B. M. G., Elisha Jones, (w) W. A. Jones.

Jones, Heziciah - Sally Dillard, 31 Jan. 1854, m. 7 Feb. 1854 by Theo. Thomas, J. P., Joshua L. Horn, (w) W. S. Pitt, Clk.

Jones, James - Dolly Spell, 4 Oct. 1809, James Booth, John Booth, (w) Ml. Hearn.

Jones, James - Nancy Corbitt, 17 Nov. 1828, Allen Rayner, (w) Ml. Hearn.

Jones, James - Eliza Dorman, 4 Jan. 1843, William E. Howell.

Jones, James - Auzy (Anzy?) Corbitt, 7 July 1852, m. 21 July 1852 by L. C. Pender, J. P., W. S. Hunter, (w) John Norfleet, Clk.

Jones, Jesse - Peggy Hagans, 25 Mar. 1834, Charles Ellis, (w) Theo. C. Hearn.

Jones, Jesse - Rhody Etheridge, 6 May 1843, John Carter, (w) John Norfleet, Clk.

Jones, John - Ann Spaw (or Ann S. Pace), 6 Nov. 1762, John Pace.

Jones, John - Ann Coffield, 20 Dec. 1766, James Jones, George Bryant, (w) Jas. Hall.

Jones, John - Ann Smith, 16 June 1788, Larance Smith, (w) John H. Hall.

Jones, John T. - Pennie O'Neal, 28 Aug. 1866, m. 30 Aug. 1866 by John T. Bellamy, J. P., B. T. Pittman, (w) Irvin Thigpen.

Jones, Joseph (John) T. - Mary Pittman, 19 May 1843, (w) John Norfleet, Clk.

Jones, Justice - Gimima H. J. Gay, 30 Mar. 1854, m. 30 Mar. 1854 by J. S. Barnes, J. P., Grey Wasdon, James R. Harper, (w) John Boyce.
Jones, Levi - Mahala Carter, 2 Jan. 1866, m. 2 Jan. 1866 by John Norfleet, J. P., Isaac Carter, (w) Irvin Thigpen.
Jones, Lewis - Merica Barnes, 28 ―― 1764, Edward Tucker, (w) Edward Hall.
Jones, Matthew - Nancy Tucker, 10 Mar. 1830, Lunsford R. Cherry, (w) Ml. Hearn.
Jones, Moses - Sallie Ann Mitchell, 21 Nov. 1844, William Norfleet, (w) John Norfleet.
Jones, Moses - Emily Horn. 17 Feb. 1857, m. 17 Feb. 1857 by W. F. Lewis, J. P., Elias Bradley, (w) W. A. Jones, Clk.
Jones, Nathan - Chordy Bell, 1 Jan. 1762, Meredith Johnson.
Jones, Orange - Mary S. Page, 29 Mar. 1849, John W. Davis, (w) John Norfleet, Clk.
Jones, Richard - Elizabeth S. L. Johnson, 2 Dec. 1854, m. 2 Dec. 1854 by J. H. Daniel, J. P., John W. Purvis, (w) W. S. Pitt, Clk.
Jones, Robert - Cherry Garrett, 27 Feb. 1866, Jo. J. Garrett, (w) Irvin Thigpen.
Jones, Rodric - Emilza Ellis, 28 Jan. 1854, m. 1 Feb. 1854 by Jacob S. Barnes, J. P., Thomas Allen, (w) W. S. Pitt, Clk.
Jones, Simmons - Jack Eliza Savage, 13 Apr. 1834, Bartholomew Bryan, (w) T. C. Hearn.
Jones, Spencer - Mourning Anderson, 4 Oct. 1830, George W. Killebrew, (w) L. H. Hearn.
Jones, William - Peggy Howard, 19 Oct. 1840, Rial Edwards, (w) John Norfleet, Clk.
Jones, William - Sarah Savage, 15 Feb. 1854, m. 16 Feb. 1854 by Thomas Norfleet, J. P., William Gaitor, (w) W. S. Pitt, Clk.
Jones, William - Nancy Robbins, 23 Mar. 1863, m. 23 Mar. 1863 by Wm. Pippen, J. P., Abram Stallings, (w) Irvin Thigpen.
Jones, William - Margaret Titus, 11 Dec. 1866, Henry F. Sessoms, (w) Irvin Thigpen.
Jones, William Albert - Virginia Staton, 31 May 1855, m. 31 May 1855 by Thomas R. Owen, M. G., (w) W. S. Pitt, Clk.
Jones, Willie - Sarah Tetter, 20 May 1856, m. 22 May 1866 by S. C. Pender, J. P., Joshua Killebrew, (w) ――――.

Jones, Wilson - Polly Ann Heggans, 2 Feb. 1865, Brittian Edwards, (w) Irvin Thigpen.

Jones, Wilson - Reana Glasco, 24 Feb. 1866, m. 25 Feb. 1866 by Erastus Cherry, J. P., H. R. Cherry, (w) Irvin Thigpen, Clk.

Jordan, Andrew - Mary Mares (Mears), 31 May 1858. m. 3 June 1858 by Hyllard S. Taylor, A. B. M. G., William D. Long, (w) J. H. Dozier.

Jordan, Cornelius - Nancy A. Smith, 19 Dec. 1859, m. 19 Dec. 1859 by Hilliard S. Taylor, A. B. M. G., William Long, (w) W. A. Jones.

Jordan, Etheldred - Lidia Beland, 24 Sept. 1840, Randall Dixon, (w) John Norfleet.

Jordan, Etheldred - Mary Land, 4 Jan. 1853, m. 5 Jan. 1853 by W. J. Armstrong, J. P., Charles Land, (w) Benjamin Norfleet.

Jordan, Gray - Sally Baley (Bailey), 20 Jan. 1831, William Worsley, (w) Ml. Hearn.

Jordan, Henry - Milbry Williams, 21 June 1828, Wright W. Joyner, (w) Ml. Hearn.

Jordan, James - Tempy Daniel, 29 Dec. 1834, William Morris, (w) Ml. Hearn.

Jordan, Josiah - Elizabeth Jordan, 15 Sept. 1840, Edwin Barnes.

Jordan, Josiah D. - Mary Barnes, 29 Nov. 1836, Edwin Barnes, (w) T. C. Hearn.

Jordan, Richard - Elizabeth Gay, 9 Mar. 1826, Josiah Cutchen, (w) Ml. Hearn.

Jordan, Thomas - Mary Rountree, 6 Feb. 1836, Blake Williford, (w) Jo. Bell, Clk.

(See Joiner)

Joyner, Alexander - Elizabeth Laurence, 29 Apr. 1768, David Carter, (w) Edward Hall.

Joyner, Asbury - Drucilla Nolly, 14 Nov. 1836, Jordan Gardner, (w) T. C. Hearn.

Joyner, Blount - Martha Pope, 6 Mar. 1833, J. B. Joyner, (w) T. C. Hearn.

Joyner, Emison H. - Nancy J. Weaver, 5 May 1859, m. 5 May 1859 by Hiliard S. Taylor, A. B. M. G., William L. Hart, (w) W. A. Jones.

Joyner, Howell - Susan Philips, 31 July 1852, m. 3 Aug. 1852 by Peter E. Hines, M. G., (w) John Norfleet, Clk.

Joyner, John H. (s. of Drew Joyner) - Christanie Robins, (dau. of William Robbins), 7 Mar. 1868, m. 12 Mar. 1868 by H. S. Taylor, A. B. M. G., (w) Irvin Thigpen.
Joyner, Owen - Mary Ann Parker, 30 Jan. 1839, William A. Joyner, (w) Jo. Bell, C. C.
Joyner, Thomas - Amy Land, 10 Sept. 1827, Joseph Lancaster, (w) Ml. Hearn.
Joyner, Thomas - Polly Barrett, 9 Jan. 1829, Jeremiah Jackson, (w) Ml. Hearn.
Joyner, Wilkinson - Temperance Batts, Wilkinson Mabry, (w) Ml. Hearn.
Joyner, Wright W. - Emily Batts, 23 May 1836, Drewry Joyner, (w) Ml. Hearn.

K

Kail, Elisha - Sally Forbes, 14 Mar. 1836, Hyrum Forbes, (w) T. C. Hearn.
Kail, Elisha - Mourning Webb, 25 Aug. 1846, Calvin Forbes.
Keal, James - Polly Cobb, 22 Feb. 1851, Quincy Lawrence, (w) John Norfleet.
Keal, Reubin - Delphia Harriss, 11 Feb. 1852, m. 12 Feb. 1852 by Bennett P. Pitt, J. P., Jordan Knight, (w) John Norfleet.
Keal, Richard - Talitha Brown, 5 July 1841, Robert Belcher.
Keal, William - Jane Gordon, 2 April 1845, Quincy Lawrence, (w) John Norfleet, Clk.
Keel, Henry - Mary Hicks, 29 Jan. 1837, James Little.
Keel, William - Sarah Moseley, 24 Sept. 1852, m. 23 Sept. 1852(?) by Wright Barnes, J. P., Joseph J. Faithful, (w) John Norfleet.
Keele, Willie - Delpha Kelly, 30 June 1830, William C. R. Summerell, (w) L. H. Hearn.
Kelly, James E. - Elsa Barron, 12 Apr. 1845, Kenneth Pippin, (w) John Norfleet, Clk.
Kelly, William - Delphia Moore, 14 July 1766, Thomas Hall.
Kenedy, William - Gracy Windham, 10 Apr. 1837, Benjamin Sharpe, (w) T. C. Hearn.
Kerson, Thomas - Lydia Crisp, 11 Oct. 1838, Laurence Buntyn, (w) Jo. Bell.
Kertland, Hezekiah C. - Eliza H. Macnair, 3 July 1823, N. Matthewson.
Killebrew, Churchwell - Maryann Jinkins, 9 Jan. 1840, Henry Hyman, (w) Jo. Bell, C. C.

Killebrew Isam - Olive Mitchell, 21 May 1866, m. 24 May 1866 by L. C. Pender, M. F. Grilly, (w) Irvin Thigpen.

Killebrew, John J. - Mary Ann Thorne, 19 Oct. 1853, m. 21 Oct. 1852(?) by Wright Barnes, J. P., Henry R. Johnson, (w) John Norfleet.

Killebrew, Joshua - Sally Gay, 31 Oct. 1835, Gideon Walston, (w) Ml. Hearn.

Killebrew. Samuel - Mary Bullock, 10 Aug. 1866, m. 11 Aug. 1866 by James F. Jenkins, J. P., William R. Ricks, (w) Irvin Thigpen.

King, Coffield - Louisa Bradley, 19 Apr. 1823, William W. Watson, (w) Ml. Hearn.

King, Drury - Elizabeth Cotten, 9 Oct. 1828, Marmaduke D. Braddy, (w) Ml. Hearn.

King, John - Sarah Pinnell, 13 Oct. 1763, John Flewelling, (w) J. Hall.

King, John - Elizabeth Cobb, 17 Dec. 1860, m. 18 Dec. 1860 by Kenneth Thigpen, J. P., Willie Walston, (w) W. A. Jones.

King, Kenneth - Eliza A. H. Thomas, 5 Aug. 1834, David Hagadon, (w) T. C. Hearn.

King, Micajah - Pamelia Joyner, 5 Apr. 1826, Coffield King, (w) Ml. Hearn.

King, Robert - Martha J. Wills, 30 Aug. 1859, m. 31 Aug. 1859 by W. F. Lewis, J. P., James P. Cross, (w) W. A. Jones.

King, Robert H. - Eliza Ann Weeks, 26 Dec. 1854, m. 27 Dec. 1854 by W. F. Lewis, J. P., W. F. Lewis, (w) W. S. Pitt, Clk.

King, Robert H. - Elizabeth Prigen, 19 Nov. 1866, m. 22 Nov. 1866 by Robert J. Powell, J. P., David Daniel, (w) Irvin Thigpen.

King, Thomas - Martha Porter, 16 Sept. 1819, David Bradley, (w) Michl. Hearn.

Kitchin, Boaz - Arabella Smith, 4 Mar. 1819, John Knight, (w) Ml. Hearn.

Knight, Alfred - Nerva Staton, 29 Dec. 1865, m. 30 Dec. 1865 by J. H. Daniel, Sandy Knight, (w) Irvin Thigpen.

Knight, Arthur - Lavina Booth, 13 Feb. 1834, William Little, (w) Theo. C. Hearn.

Knight, Arthur B. - Charlotte A. Knight, 17 Aug. 1865, m. 17 Aug. 1865 by Thomas R. Owen, M. G., William H. Weathersby, (w) Irvin Thigpen.

Knight, Charles C. - Louisiana Lawrence, 22 Dec. 1828, Thomas Gatlin, (w) Ml. Hearn.

Knight, Daniel - Mary Davis, 17 Jan. 1843, Thomas A. Macnair, (w) John Norfleet, Clk.

Knight, Francis H. - Sarah Knight, 4 Sept. 1834, James Ellinor, (w) T. C. Hearn.

Knight, George W. - Jane E. Howell, 9 Sept. 1853, John L. Knight, (w) W. S. Pitt.

Knight, James C. - Sally Bryan, 20 Aug. 1823, Henry Bryan.

Knight, James W. Jr. - Mary A. Dancy, 30 Nov. 1853 by Thomas R. Owens, M. G., (w) W. S. Pitt, Clk.

Knight, John - Martha A. Cromwell, 26 Nov. 1835, Edwin C. Dancy, (w) Theo. C. Hearn.

Knight, John H. - Elizabeth A. Harrison, 28 Feb. 1854, m. 29 Feb. 1854 by K. Thigpen, David B. Knight, (w) W. S. Pitt, Clk.

Knight, John L. - Martha E. Knight, 15 Nov. 1852, m. 18 Nov. 1852 by Blount Cooper, Kinchen H. Dicken, (w) John Norfleet.

Knight, John W. - Elizabeth O. McDowell, 10 Dec. 1847, John H. Knight, (w) John Norfleet.

Knight, Jordan - Frances Little, 8 Dec. 1829, Benjamin Boykin, (w) Ml. Hearn.

Knight, Moses - Charity Benton (wid.), 22 Sept. 1761, (w) J. Hall.

Knight, Peter E. - Martha Pippen, 4 Jan. 1853, m. 5 Jan. 1853 by R. Norfleet, J. P., William Norfleet, (w) Benjamin Norfleet.

Knight, Robert A. - Ann Pitt, 14 Dec. 1861, Jos. C. Hicks, (w) T. W. Hussey.

Knight, Samuel - Lydia Whitaker, 6 Feb. 1866, J. B. Coffield, (w) Irvin Thigpen.

Knight, William - Emelina Freeman, 3 Jan. 1828, Henry Austin, (w) Ml. Hearn.

Knight, William F. - Nancy Laurence, 28 Aug. 1846, James Harris, (w) John Norfleet.

Knight, William H. - Carolina V. Bellamy, 5 Jan. 1847, W. D. Bryan, (w) John Norfleet, Clk.

Knight, William H. - Amelia A. Dupree, 11 Mar. 1858, m. 11 Mar. 1858 by Elisha Cromwell, J. P., C. H. Jenkins, (w) William A. Jones.

L

Lacky, John - Penninah Fountain, 15 Jan. 1833, Henry T. Clark, (w) L. H. Hearn.

Lamm, Jones - Abashaby Barnes, 16 Oct. 1853, m. 20 Oct. 1853 by Joshua Barnes, J. P., William Barnes, (w) J. W. Farmer.

Lancaster, Benjamin H. - Susan Farmer, 14 Jan. 1854, m. 15 Jan. 1854 by Elisha Barnes, J. P., Sander L. Spicer, (w) W. S. Pitt, Clk.

Lancaster, Berry J. - Delha Armstrong, 3 Jan. 1855, m. 9 Jan. 1855 by John G. Williams, J. P., Colby S. Braswell, (w) W. S. Pitt, Clk.

Lancaster, David - Sally Edwards, 8 Apr. 1846, Matthew Whitehead, Sr., (w) John Norfleet.

Lancaster, David - Martha Braswell, 3 Mar. 1847, Matthew Whitehead, Sr., (w) John Norfleet.

Lancaster, David - Louisa Landing, 29 Jan. 1856, m. 31 Jan. 1856 by Theo. Thomas, J. P., Elisha Landing, (w) W. L. Pitt, Clk.

Lancaster, George - Sarah Williams, 9 Sept. 1841 Joseph Moore, David Williams, (w) John Norfleet, Clk.

Lancaster, Henry - Persey Houghton, 14 Mar. 1822, Philip Lupo, (w) Ml. Hearn.

Lancaster, James L. - Cherry Lancaster, 16 Apr. 1827, Jesse Brake, (w) Ml. Hearn.

Lancaster, Robert - Cynthanetta Braswell, 6 Feb. 1847, Daniel Land, (w) John Norfleet, Clk.

Lancaster, Thomas (s. of L. Lancaster) - Kittrena Roberson (dau. of Joshua Roberson), 23 Mar. 1868, m. 24 Mar. 1868 by Hilyard S. Taylor, A. B. M. G., (w) Irvin Thigpen, Clk.

Lancaster, William D. - Nancy Williams, 9 Feb. 1847, Willie A. Lancaster, (w) John Norfleet, Clk.

Lancaster, Willie - Martha Moore, 26 Sept. 1843, Moses Moore, (w) John Norfleet, Clk.

Land, Charles - Patsy Daws, 6 Nov. 1822, Ephraim Daws, (w) Ml. Hearn.

Land, Charles - Joana Flood, 18 Aug. 1863, m. 19 Aug. 1863 by Hilyard S. Taylor, A. B. M. G., Nathaniel Gay, (w) Irvin Thigpen.

Land, John - Rebecca Taylor, 15 June 1825, Isaac Braswell, Jr., Henry Austin, (w) Ml. Hearn.

Landen, Elisha - Catharine Ellinor, 9 Sept. 1829, John B. Edwards, (w) Ml. Hearn.

Landen, John - Nancy Odom, 30 Nov. 1812, John Wiggins, (w) Ml. Hearn.

Landin, John - Mary A. Moore, 17 Jan. 1866, m. 18 Jan. 1866 by John I. Proctor, J. P., Jesse Mercer, (w) Irvin Thigpen.

Landing, Elisha - Temprance Price, 21 Mar. 1848, William H. Odom, (w) John Norfleet, Clk.

Landing, Joseph John - Adeline Rose, 22 Oct. 1842, Micajah Rose, (w) John Norfleet.

Landing, Lafayette - Martha Thomas, 8 May 1866, m. 10 May 1866 by James F. Jenkins, J. P., Jesse Mercer, (w) Irvin Thigpen.

Landing, Lemuel N. - Martha Ann Bell, 12 Sept. 1851, m. 18 Sept. 1851 by Blount Cooper, William H. Powell, (w) John Norfleet.

Landing, Lewis A. - Martha Proctor, 27 Feb. 1865, m. 28 Feb. 1865 by Theo. Thomas, J. P., Mills Landing, (w) Irvin Thigpen, Clk.

Landing, Mills - Mary Friar, 28 Nov. 1839, Washington Friar, (w) Hy. Bryan.

Landing, William - Patsey Pearce, 22 Mar. 1847, Marmaduke Bell, (w) John Norfleet, Clk.

Lane, Cordy - Mary Faithful, 26 Oct. 1830, William Dancy (w) Ml. Hearn.

Lane, David - Rebecca Fountain, 21 Jan. 1817, James Coker, Jr., (w) Michl. Hearn.

Lane, David - Lucretia Land, 23 Nov. 1844, David Neale, (w) John Norfleet, C.

Lane, Henry - Patsey Weeks, 13 May 1833, John Weeks, (w) T. C. Hearn.

Lane, John A. - Sarah Applewhite, 23 Nov. 1852, m. 7 Dec. 1852 by Nathan Anderson, Robert S. Yelverton, (w) John Norfleet.

Lane, Joseph - Elizabeth Freeman, 31 Jan. 1866, m. 5 Feb. 1866 by William F. Bell, Dr. Jo. Lawrence, (w) Irvin Thigpen.

Lane, Joshua - Lugenia Hawkins, 22 May 1866, m. 24 May 1866 by W. F. Lewis, J. P., W. F. Lewis, (w) Irvin Thigpen.

Lane, Levi - Peggy Freeman, 14 Apr. 1835, Nathan Freeman, (w) Theo. C. Hearn.

Lane, Patrick - Zilphy Bradley, 7 July 1856, m. 13 July 1856 by W. F. Lewis, J. P., Dickerson Ruffin, (w) J. H. Dozier.

Lane, Robert J. - Elizabeth Marks, 15 May 1866, m. 17 May 1866 by John T. Bellamy, J. P., Robert A. Johnson, (w) Irvin Thigpen.

Lane, Theophilus - Susan Armstrong, 23 Dec. 1846, Henry Foxhall, (w) John Norfleet, Clk.

Lang, John - Elizabeth Rogers, 11 Nov. 1826, William Gay, (w) Ml. Hearn.

Langley, David - Elizabeth Ann Cobb, 29 Sept. 1854, m. 7 Jan. 1855 by W. Y. Moore, J. P., John Hearn, (w) T. M. Arrington.

Langley. Enos - Winniford Edwards, 20 Jan. 1864, m. 24 Jan. 1864 by R. J. Johnson, J. P., Henry Brinkley, (w) Irvin Thigpen, Clk., (w) T. W. Hussey.

Langley, Franklin - Emily Edwards, 25 Jan. 1864, m. 26 Jan. 1864 by Theo. Atkinson, J. P., W. J. Langley, (w) Irvin Thigpen.

Langley, Hezekiah - Celia Owens, 23 May 1825, Goodman Owens, (w) Ml. Hearn.

Langley, James - Susan Pettway, 30 July 1830, Thomas Amason, (w) L. H. Hearn.

Langley, John - Sally Owens, 13 Mar. 1848, Brittain Edwards.

Langley. Willis - Nancy Peal, 13 Mar. 1823, Benjamin Moore, W. D. Petway.

Langly, James - Emily Killebrew, 6 Dec. 1855, m. 9 Dec. 1855 by W. Y. Moore, J. P., John Whitley, (w) W. S. Pitt, Clk.

Langley, Thomas - Betsey Edmondson, 18 May 1830, Ezekiel Staton, Silas Wilkinson, (w) L. H. Hearn.

Lansdell, Thomas - Harriett J. Lawrence, 20 Nov. 1855, m. 21 Nov. 1855 by Thomas R. Owen, M. G., James L. Battle, (w) W. S. Pitt, Clk.

Laurence, Bennett B. - Frances Knight, 19 May 1835, Lemuel W. Lawrence, (w) Ml. Hearn.

Laurence, Henry - Rhoda Price, 14 July 1829, Solomon Laurence, (w) Ml. Hearn.

Laurence, James - Sarah Lawrence, 17 Aug. 1799, Vincent Smith, (w) S. Wren.

Laurence, James - Maria Lawrence, 20 Dec. 1849, Elisha Cromwell, Joseph J. Lawrence, (w) John Norfleet, Clk.

Laurence, John G. - Emily Billups, 18 Nov. 1829, Thomas Cromwell, (w) Ml. Hearn.

Laurence, Joseph J. - Mary Everett, 14 Jan. 1850, Perry Pitt, (w) John Norfleet.

Laurence, Joseph J. - Francis Cobb, 23 May 1850, Elisha Cromwell, (w) John Norfleet, C.

Laurence, Joshua - Tallitha Pippen, 9 Dec. 1844, James Laurence, (w) John Norfleet.

Laurence, Joshua L. - Harriet Mayo, 28 Sept. 1836, Joseph John B. Pender.

Laurence, Lemuel - Margarett Bryan, 8 Mar. 1825, Bartholomew Bryan, (w) Ml. Hearn.

Laurence, Lemuel - Gracey Staton, 2 Oct. 1826, Charles Mabrey.

Laurence, Peter P. - Mary B. Dancy, 11 Apr. 1833, Henry Johnston, (w) T. C. Hearn.

Laurence, William - Emma L. King, 5 Apr. 1859 by Thomas R. Owen, M. G., Robert Brown, (w) W. A. Jones.

Laurence, William J. - Laura F. Harrison, 4 May 1863, m. 5 May 1863 by Thomas R. Owen, M. G., J. F. Batts, (w) T. R. Hussey.

Lawrence, Arthur - Martha Baker, 17 Apr. 1828, Henry Austin, (w) Ml. Hearn.

Lawrence, Gray - Brittania Lawrence, 28 Dec. 1829, John Lawrence, Sr., (w) Ml. Hearn.

Lawrence, Handy - George Anna Tillery, 4 Oct. 1866, m. 10 Oct. 1866 by J. I. Proctor, J. P., W. E. Robbins, (w) Irvin Thigpen.

Lawrence, James - Sidney Howard, 22 May 1843, William Little, (w) L. T. Braddy.

Lawrence, James J. - Adeline Mason, 27 Feb. 1845, Elisha Cromwell.

Lawrence, Joshua - Lucinda Lawrence, 17 Nov. 1832, Kinchen Pippen, Thomas Hawkins, (w) Ml. Hearn.

Lawrence, Patrick McD. (s. of John) - Martha A. Bradley (dau. of Jonathan), 23 June 1868, m. 25 June 1868 by W. F. Lewis, J. P., (w) Irvin Thigpen.

Lawrence, Whitmel - Catherine Lawrernce, 15 Feb. 1866, m. 17 Feb. 1866 by J. F. Batts, J. P., James Denton, (w) Irvin Thigpen, Clk.

Lawrence, Zack - Ann Sessoms, 9 Dec. 1865, m. 12 Dec. 1865 by Henry E. Odom, J. P., Charles Pender, (w) Irvin Thigpen, Clk.

Lee, Edwin - Marina Worsley, 28 Dec. 1865, m. 28 Dec. 1865 by J. H. Daniel, John Worsley, (w) Irvin Thigpen.

Lee, Henderson - Celista Joyner, 15 July 1844, Willie Weaver, (w) John Norfleet.

Lee, James - Agnis Cade, 3 Nov. 1760, Edward Moore, (w) John Whiteous (Whitehurst).

Lee, John - Nancy Harris, 5 Nov. 1799, John Harris, (w) S. Wren.

Lee, John - Nanny Harris, 5 Nov. 1799, John Harris, (w) S. Wren.

Lee, William - Amey Best, 26 Oct. 1824, William Hopkins.

Lee, Willie - Finetta Womble, 27 Dec. 1826, Eli Harris, (w) Ml. Hearn.

Lee, Willie - Mary Anderson, 18 Mar. 1829, Doctor W. Womble, (w) Ml. Hearn.

Lee, Zachariah - Lucy Farmer, 11 Oct. 1763, Thomas Farmer, (w) Edward Hall.

Leggett, Lafayette - Laura Johnson, 16 Mar. 1859, m. 17 Mar. 1859 by W. F. Lewis, J. P., David A. Leggett, (w) W. A Jones, Clk.

Leggett, Noah - Martha Bradley, 25 Feb. 1828, John White, Levin Leggett, (w) Ml. Hearn.

Leggett, Noah - Mary Walker, 1 Mar. 1850, William T. Braswell.

Leggett, Stanly - Maryan E. Griffin, 3 Mar. 1853, m. 3 Mar. 1853 by William Hyman, John A. Purvis, (w) John Norfleet.

Leggett, William R. - Cindarilla Nelson, 6 Jan. 1844, Jordan Jenkins, (w) John Norfleet, Clk.

Leigh, Bryant - Pearcy Lancaster, 27 Apr. 1836, Abraham Price, (w) T. C. Hearn.

Leigh, Dorsey - Jane Faithful, 23 Mar. 1852, m. 24 Mar. 1852 by Thomas Norfleet, J. P., John J. Killebrew, (w) John Norfleet.

Leigh, Jesse W. - Winney C. L. Wilkinson, 19 Feb. 1850, Jesse B. Hyatt, (w) John Norfleet, Clk.

Leigh, John H. - Ruth House, 16 Sept. 1857, m. 17 Sept. 1857 by Elisha Cromwell, J. P., Chas. H. Jenkins, (w) William A. Jones, Clk.

Leigh, Jonathan - Elizabeth Pope, 25 Nov. 1841, James George.

Leigh, Norfleet - Mary Harrell, 28 Dec. 1837, Jesse Harrell, (w) Jo. Bell.

Leigh, Theophilus - Cresey Williams, 30 Oct. 1866, m. 31 Oct. 1866 by W. H. Knight, J. P., C. B. Killebrew, (w) Irvin Thigpen, Clk.

Leonard, Caleb - Martha Ruffin, 27 Apr. 1829, Thomas Gatlin, (w) Ml. Hearn.

Lewis, Allen - Nancy Ruffin, 29 Feb. 1832, (w) Ml. Hearn.

Lewis, Caswell - Arsena Mayo, 15 Dec. 1849, John H. Jenkins, (w) John Norfleet.

Lewis, Christoper Columbus - Emeline Sarah Elizabeth Eason, 10 Dec. 1855, m. 11 Dec. 1855 by David Cobb, J. P., John Warren, (w) W. S. Pitt, Clk.

Lewis, Exum - Jane Cotten, 26 Sept. 1835, Benjamin D. Battle, (w) Ml. Hearn.

Lewis, George - Cassandra Jones, 11 Jan. 1851, L. S. Jones, (w) John Norfleet, Clk.

Lewis, Guilford - Harriet W. Bryan, 23 April 1863, m. 23 Apr. 1863 by J. G. Barkley, M. G., A. C. Taylor, (w) Irvin Thigpen, Clk.

Lewis, Howell - Mary Wood, 22 July 1834, William Felton, (w) Ml. Hearn.

Lewis, James T. - Sarah Walston. 30 Sept. 1865, m. 1 Oct. 1865 by R. J. Johnson, J. P., B. B. Lewis, (w) Irvin Thigpen.

Lewis, Jason - Eliza Ward, 26 Feb. 1866(?), m. 28 Feb. 1861 by Thomas L. Maner, J. P., J. R. Bryan, (w) Irvin Thigpen, Clk.

Lewis, Joel - Elizabeth Griffin 2 Apr. 1829, James Lewis, (w) Ml. Hearn.

Lewis, John D. - Catherine Waller, 6 July 1855, m. 6 July 1855 by L. C. Pender, Joshua Killebrew, (w) W. S. Pitt, Clk.

Lewis, Kinchen - Millesent Eason, 2 Nov. 1839, Reddin S. Lewis, Levi Harrell, (w) Jo. Bell.

Lewis, Nicholas - Delilah Revel, 21 Sept. 1832, William Revel, (w) Ml. Hearn.

Lewis, Robert H. - Sarah Howard, 1 Nov. 1854, m. 1 Nov. 1854 by Jos. Blount Cheshire, Epis. Min., David Hinton, (w) T. M. Arrington.

Lewis, Thomas - Lydia Thigpen, 13 Sept. 1842, Jesse Harrell.

Lewis, Thomas - Marina Meeks, 28 Nov. 1843, Jesse Harrell, (w) John Norfleet, Clk.

Lewis, William E. - Emily Dew, 9 Oct. 1866, m. 11 Oct. 1866 by R. S. Sugg, J. P., Gray Cobb, Irvin Thigpen.

Lewis, William G. - Martha L. Pender, 14 Mar. 1864, m. 15 Mar. 1864 by Thomas R. Owen, M. G., W. P. Lloyd, (w) Irvin Thigpen.

Lilley, George L. - Amanda Strickland, 5 Feb. 1866, m, 8 Feb. 1866 by J. F. Batts, J. P., H. D. Lilley, (w) Irvin Thigpen.

Lilley, Henry D. - Cathrine Strickland, 9 Oct. 1866, m. 19 Oct. 1866 by J. H. Batts, J. P., G. L. Lilley, (w) Irvin Thigpen.

Lilly, Stanly - Martha Andrews, 12 Mar. 1834, Gray Andrews, (w) Ml. Hearn.

Linch, David - Susanah Newsom, no Date, (during the term of Gov. Benj. Williams, 1800-1803), Abraham Jones, (w) J. H. Hall.

Linch, John - Milly Stallings, 1 Jan. 1801, Abraham Jones.

Linch, Redding - Nancy Dixon, 17 May 1824, Henry Bryan.

Lipscomb, John W. - Elizabeth A. Peebles, 13 Mar. 1858, m. 14 Mar. 1858 by Thomas R. Owens, M. G., R. J. W. Carson, (w) William A. Jones, Clk.

Lipscomb, John W. - Elizabeth A. Wilson, 12 Sept. 1865, m. 12 Sept. 1865 by Thomas R. Owens, M. G., T. W. Hussey, (w) Irvin Thigpen.

Lipscomb, George B. - J. E. Dixon, 20 Jan. 1864, m. 20 Jan. 1864 by Thomas R. Owen, M. G., Robert A. Watson, (w) Irvin Thigpen, Clk.

Lipscomb, Oswel - Penelope Rountree, 26 Dec. 1854, m. 2 Jan. 1855 by Nathan Anderson, L. J. Sauls, (w) W. S. Pitt, Clk.

Little, Allen - Penelope Stallings, 25 Jan. 1825, Philip Dunford, (w) Ml. Hearn.

Little, Cullen - Lucy Alford, 4 Jan. 1830, Burrel Shelton, (w) Ml. Hearn.

Little, Frederick D. - Harriet Knight, 17 May 1830, Little Berry Thigpen, (w) Ml. Hearn.

Little, Henry D. - Lydia E. Cobb, 16 Feb. 1847, Jordan Knight, (w) John Norfleet.

Little, James - Fanny Edmondson, 5 Sept. 1825, James Thigpen, (w) N. Mathewson, C. C.

Little, Jesse C. - Lydia Ann May, 26 Sept. 1859, Henry C. Shelton, (w) James H. Dozier.

Little, William - Polly Hardy, 22 Apr. 1846, Joshua Lawrence, (w) John Norfleet, Clk.

Little, William G. - Margaret Drake, 20 Nov. 1829, Henry Miller, (w) Ml. Hearn.

Little, William - Elizabeth Toulson, 7 Dec. 1851, William R. Toulson, (w) John Norfleet, Clk.

Little, Willis - Sarah Hardy, 19 Oct. 1858, m. 21 Oct. 1858 by David Cobb, Leonidas Little, (w) Wm. H. Jones.

Lloyd, David - Sarah Brinkley, 21 Jan. 1830, William Norvill, (w) L. H. Hearn.

Lloyd, Henry A. - Polly A. Edwards, 23 Jan. 1843, William D. Petway, Shff.

Lloyd, John - Elizabeth Braswell, 8 Jan. 1825, Henry Cotten, (w) Ml. Hearn.

Lloyd, John - Polly Gay, 11 Feb. 1859, m. 20 Jan. 1859 by W. B. Killebrew, J. P., (w) W. A. Jones.

Lloyd, Joseph W. - Sarah E. Barlow, 8 Apr. 1856. m. 9 Apr. 1856 by Thomas R. Owen, M. G., John Leo. Williams.

Lloyd, Whitmel P. - Harriet E. Howard, 13 Jan. 1858, m. 13 Jan. 1858 by Jos. Blount Cheshire, Epis. Min., Joel B. Lewis. (w) W. A. Jones.

Lloyd, Whit P. - Laura F. Pender, 20 Dec. 1866. m. 20 Dec. 1866 by Thomas R. Owen, V. D. M., E. D. Foxhall, (w) Irvin Thigpen.

Locus, Augustus - Piety Hagons. 20 Sept. 1855, m. 20 Sept. 1855 by Jordan Thigpen, J. P., Right Locus, (w) W. S. Pitt, Clk.

Locust, Josiah - Lively Thomas, 5 July 1841, Robert Belcher.

Locust, Richard - Elizabeth Evans, 27 Aug. 1851, m. 30 Aug. 1851 by James W. Barnes, J. P., Henry Dixon, (w) John Norfleet, Clk.

Lodge, Amos - Celia A. Stallings, 15 Jan. 1844, William W. Sessums, (w) John Norfleet, Clk.

Lodge, John - Harriot Bosman, 17 Aug. 1829, Zacheriah Sasmutt, (Sasnett?), (w) L. H. Hearn.

Lodge, Joshua - Nancy Sorey, 9 Jan. 1829, Josiah Freeman, (w) Ml. Hearn.

Lodge, Redmond - Temperance Braswell, 4 Jan. 1830, Christopher Harrell, Jr., James Lewis, (w) Ml. Hearn.

Lodge, Richard - Eliza Alsobrook, 5 Apr. 1842, A. P. Sessums, (w) John Norfieet, Clk.

Lodge, Richard - William Delah Sessums, 17 Mar. 1857, m. 17 Mar. 1857 by R. H. Pender, J. P., R. Worsley, (w) W. A. Jones.

Lodge, Robert - Winefred Marlow, 16 May 1799, Joseph Morgan, (w) S. Wren.

Lodge, William - Fanny Sasnett, 23 Dec. 1834, James F. Jenkins, (w) T. C. Hearn.

Long, Calvin (s. of H. Long) - Elizabeth Baker, 7 Apr. 1868, m. 9 Apr. 1868 by B. P. Pitt, J. P., (w) Irvin Thigpen, Clk.

Long, David - Nancy Wood, 25 June 1834, Robert Long, (w) T. C. Hearn.

Long, Hartwell - Nancy Ricks, 26 Feb. 1833, Robert Braswell, (w) Ml. Hearn.

Long, Hartwell - Polly Gay, 29 Jan. 1851, m. 30 Jan. 1851 by Theo. Thomas, J. P., Newsom Long, (w) John Norfleet.

Long, James R. - Dolly Jones, 18 Feb. 1864, m. 18 Feb. 1864 by Theo. Thomas, J. P., (w) Irvin Thigpen.

Long, James S. - Louisa Laurence, 20 Jan. 1836, Peter E. Knight, (w) Theo. C. Hearn.

Long, John - Penelope Wilson, 9 Feb. 1829, William W. Armstrong, (w) Ml. Hearn.

Long, John - Mary Ann Mayo, 22 Mar. 1836, Arthur S. Cotten, (w) Theo. C. Hearn.

Long, Joseph - Margaret E. Anderson, 10 May 1856, John Long, (w) W. A. Jones, Clk.

Long, Joseph - Ony Williams, 10 July 1860, m. 11 July 1860 by L. C. Pender, J. P., Josh Killebrew, (w) W. A. Jones.

Long, Lovet - Betsy Proctor, 16 Dec. 1833, Robert R. Braswell, (w) T. C. Hearn.

Long, Matthew - Tabitha Taylor, 10 Jan. 1826, Whitmil Wiliams, (w) Ml. Hearn.

Long, Newsom - Oney Williams, 5 Feb. 1823, Peoples Hill, (w) Ml. Hearn.

Long, Newsom - Martha Proctor, 22 May 1829, Peoples Hill, (w) Ml. Hearn.

Long, Paskin - Mahaly Looper, 1 May 1866, m. 3 May 1866 by H. S. Taylor, A. B. M. G., J. R. Wells, (w) Irvin Thigpen.

Long, R. W. - Nancy Curls, 25 Feb. 1862, m. 26 Feb. 1862 by Hilyard S. Taylor, A. B. M. G., John Long, (w) W. A. Jones.

Long, Robert - Nancy J. Mares, 26 Feb. 1855, m. 1 Mar. 1855 by Theo. Thomas, J. P., Theo. Thomas, (w)

Long, Rubin - Prissilla Hunt, 19 Jan. 1763, William Williams, (w) Thomas Cavenah.

Long, Thomas - Elizabeth Judkins, 12 Oct. 1849, Thomas H. Cutchin, (w) John Norfleet, C.

Long, William D. - Kishy Ann E. Jordan, 1 June 1848, Gray Jordan, (w) John Norfleet, C.

Long, William S. - Mary Batts, 30 Dec. 1862, m. 25 Dec. 1862 by William H. Knight, J. P., Harry Long, (w) T. W. Hussey.

Long, Wilson - Winiford Peel, 25 Dec. 1862, m. 25 Dec. 1862 by William H. Knight, J. P., Harry Long, (w) T. W. Hussey.

Looper, Bennett C. - Sally A. Weaver, 18 Jan. 1853, m. 18 Jan. 1853 by Henry T. Clark, J. P., Jacob D. Robbins, (w) John Norfleet.

Looper, James -' Mourning Weaver, 22 Sept. 1846, Theophilus Moore, (w) John Norfleet.

Looper, Philip - Priscilla Ruffin, 1 June 1846, Theophilus Moore, (w) John Norfleet.

Lowry, John - Winney Beacham, 20 Dec. 1772, Richard Bell, (w) Edward Hall.

Lupo, Micajah - Elizabeth Atkinson, 12 Jan. 1855, m. 16 Jan. 1855 by J. R. Pitt, J. P., James Stallings, (w) W. A. Jones.

Lupo, Molen - Elizabeth Williams, 18 Aug. 1857, m. 18 Aug. 1857 by Hilyard S. Taylor, A. B. M. G., Miles Davis, (w) W. A. Jones.

Lupo, Philip - Sarah Braswell, 22 Jan. 1856, m. 24 Jan. 1856 by Hillard S. Taylor, M. G., Eliza Taylor, (w) W. S. Pitt, Clk.

Lupo, Phiilip - Susanna Moore, 1 June 1863, m. 2 June 1863 by Hilyard S. Taylor, A. B. M. G., J. P. Dixon, (w) Irvin Thigpen.

Luster, George W. - Mary Stokes, 12 Nov. 1835, Willie Robbins, (w) T. C. Hearn.

Lynch, James - Drucilla Kite, 25 Jan. 1845, Joseph Kane, (w) John Norfleet.

Lynch, Mark - Priscilla Winborne, 21 Feb. 1849, L. B. Manning, (w) John Norfleet, Clk.

Lynch, Noah - Piety Rose, 2 Mar. 1853, m. 4 Mar. 1853 by John W. Farmer, J. P., Barron C. Watson, (w) John Norfleet.

Lyon, Bennet - Penelope Pitman(?), 10 May 1836, William Draughon, (w) T. C. Hearn.

Lyon, Harrison P. - Mary D. Mayo, 2 Feb. 1864, m. 3 Feb. 1864 by Thomas R. Owen, M. G., B. T. Lyon, (w) Irvin Thigpen.

Lyon, Henry Lewis - Mary J. Hart, 3 Nov. 1826, Ephraim Dickens, (w) Ml. Hearn.

Lyon, Joshua L. - Martha Cherry, 15 May 1841, William Draughan, (w) John Norfleet, Clk.

Mc

McCabe, Alexander - Mary Ann Moore, 1 Dec. 1866, m. 4 Dec. 1866 by Joseph Blount Cheshire, Epis. Min., John Owen, (w) Irvin Thigpen.

McDaniel, Daniel, Jr. - Meriam Horn, 27 Feb. 1766, Sion Horn, (w) J. Hall.

McDaniel, W. J. - Frances Barfield, 30 Jan. 1861, m. 31 Jan. 1861 by W. F. Lewis. J. P., J. M. Cutchin, (w) W. A. Jones, Clk., (w) T. W. Hussey.

Mc. Dowell, Patrick - Mary S. Cromwell, 27 Jan. 1825, Ephraim Dickens, Henry Bryan, (w) Ml. Hearn.

McKenzie, James G. - Mary Bishop (Bishup), 17 Aug. 1826 William Crocket, (w) N. Mathewson.

McNair, Hugh - Margaret A. Baker, 15 Mar. 1859. m. 16 Mar. 1859 by Thomas R. Owen, M. G., W. T. McNair, (w) W. A. Jones, Clk.

McNair, William T. - Hattie E. Dunn. 19 Jan. 1865, m. 19 Jan. 1865 by Thomas R. Owen, M. G., Benjamin Norfleet, (w) Irvin Thigpen.

McPherson, Edward - Margaret Sugg, 19 Jan. 1859, m. 19 Jan. 1859 by Thomas R. Owen, M. G., H. McNair, (w)· J. H. Dozier.

M

Mabrey, Baker W. - Lucy B. Laurence, 7 Oct. 1856, m. 7 Oct. 1856 by Thomas R. Owen, M. G., J. F. Batts, (w) W. A. Jones.

Mabrey, Baker W. - Mary E. Freeman, 19 Dec. 1859, m. 20 Dec. 1859 by Thomas R. Owen, M. G., J. W. Jones, (w) W. A. Jones, Clk.

Mabrey, Bythel - M. L. Barlow, 24 Dec. 1861, m. 24 Dec. 1861 by Thomas R. Owen, M. G., B. W. Mabrey, (w) T. W. Hussey.

Mabrey, Charles - Frances Staton, 31 Oct. 1826, Henry Johnston, (w) N. Matheson.

Mabrey, Fenton - Rhoda Phelps, 1 Dec. 1866, m. 2 Dec. 1866 by J. F. Batts, J. P., John H. Edwards, (w) Irvin Thigpen.

Mabrey, John - Luvenia Key, 25 Dec. 1865, m. 15 Apr. 1866 by J. F. Batts, J. P., Joseph H. Pippin, (w) Irvin Thigpen.

Mabrey, Wilkinson - Rebecca Braddy, 8 Apr. 1801, Spencer D. Cotton, (w) Samuel Wren.

Mabrey, William A. S. - Louisa Knight, 19 Oct. 1847, Blount Bryant, (w) John Norfleet, Clk.

Madra (Madry), Thomas - Laney Downing, 10 Feb. 1840, (w) Jo. Bell, C. C. C.

Madrid, Micajah - Nancy Edmundson, 17 Feb. 1836, William Garrett, (w) T. C. Hearn.

(See Mares)

Mairs, (Mears) William - Elizabeth Hart, 13 Jan. 1824, Thomas Dickinson, (w) N. Matheson.

Maner, Jethro -. Milly Mainer, 6 Nov. 1801, William Price.

Maner, Joseph W. - Martha Wells, 26 Apr. 1839, Allen W. Ing, (w) D. C. Bell, D. C.

Maner, Robert - Mary Odom, 1 Apr. 1822, Elijah Price, (w) Ml. Hearn.

Mann, Augustine - Peninah Flowers, 18 Feb. 1823, Edwin Bullock, (w) Ml. Hearn, Ormon Cobb, William Gardner.

Mann, Thomas L. - Catharine Pitt, 28 July 1832, James George, (w) Ml. Hearn.

Mannen (Manning), John - Clarender Rountree, 9 Feb. 1854, m. 9 Feb. 1854 by John W. Farmer, J. P., Benjamin Morris, (w) W. S. Pitt, Clk.

Manning, John W. - Sallie Ann Parker, 9 Dec. 1850 by William S. Long, J. P., Thomas S. Manning, (w) John Norfleet.

Manning, L. B. - Mary E. Johnston, 27 June 1854, Matthew Exum, (w) W. S. Pitt, Clk.

Manning, Littleberry - Penina Exum, 21 Oct. 1842, Andrew Gunter.

Manning, Nathan - Margaret Laurence, 28 July 1832, John H. Wells, (w) Ml. Hearn.

Manning, Richard - Clary Avery, 22 Feb. 1800, Thomas Carson, (w) J. H. Hall.

Manning, Thomas S. - Emily Pitt, 25 Apr. 1851, m. 1 May 1851 by Henry T. Clark, J. P., William J. Edwards, (w) John Norfleet.

Mansfield, J. C. - A. M. Knight, 21 Jan. 1861, m. 22 Jan. 1861 by F. H. Jenkins, J. P., S. B. Staton, (w) J. H. Dozier.

Mares, Gilbert - Sally Hart, 18 Dec. 1828, Thomas Dickinson, (w) Ml. Hearn.

Mares, Hiram - Polly Jordan, 12 Nov. 1823, James Ricks, Nathan H. Rountree, (w) Ml. Hearn.

Mares, Hyram - Nancy Gay, 6 Nov. 1832, Gilbert Mares, (w) Ml. Hearn.

Mares, John - Sally Curl, 4 Mar. 1834, Gilbert Mares, (w) Ml. Hearn.

Mares, John - Sarah Ann Tanner, 17 May 1860, m. 17 May 1860 by E. D. MacNair, J. P., James Tanner, (w) J. H. Dozier.

Mares, Willie - Chaney Edwards, 28 Sept. 1827, Thomas Dickinson, (w) Ml. Hearn.

Mares, Willie - Elizabeth Peel, 27 Aug. 1833, Moses Spicer, (w) Ml. Hearn.

Mariner Thomas - Sabra Ann Savage, 12 Jan. 1859, m. 13 Jan. 1859 by Orren Williams, Orren Williams, (w) J. H. Dozier.

Marks, James - Rosena McWilliams, 5 Sept. 1835, Nathaniel M. Terrell, (w) Theo. C. Hearn, D. C.

Marks, Joseph J. N. - Amanda Weeks, 28 Mar. 1842, Littleberry B. Manning.

Marley, Benjamin - Patsey Lodge, 19 Mar. 1825, Nathan Marley, (w) Ml. Hearn.

Marley, Dempsey - Martha Page, 29 Dec. 1827, Nathan Marley, Benjamin Marley, (w) Ml. Hearn.

Marley, Nathan, Jr. - Elizabeth Mills, 23 Dec. 1828, James Burris, Ithial Eason, (w) Ml. Hearn.

Marley, William - Elizabeth Page, 23 Dec. 1828, Nathan Marley, (w) Ml. Hearn.

Marlow, Samuel - Martha Ann Morgan, 5 Feb. 1846, Nathaniel M. Ferrell, (w) John Norfleet.

Marriner, William - Sarah Bozeman, 14 Aug. 1863 (?), m. 13 Aug. 1863 by W. M. Pippin, J. P., John Norfleet, (w) Irvin Thigpen.

Marrinor, William - Louisa Varb, 18 Sept. 1833, John Wilson, (w) Ml. Hearn.

Marshall, John H. - Evelina Gardner, 1 May 1837, Edwin Gardner, (w) T. C. Hearn.

Mason, James - Murphy Proctor, 27 May 1844, Robert R. Braswell.

Mason, James - Susan O'Neal, 26 Feb. 1855, m. 1 Mar. 1855 by W. F. Lewis, J. P., Stephen Bradley, (w) W. S. Pitt, Clk.

Mathes, Jacob - Meady Johnston, 12 Sept. 1763, Hardy Griffin, (w) Thomas Cavenah.

Mathewson, Nathan - Mary Jane Austin, 10 May 1847, Robert Norfleet.

Mathis, Willie - Dolly Eavens, 21 Oct. 1851, m. 23 Oct. 1851 by John W. Farmer, J. P., William Tomlinson, (w) John Norfleet, Clk.

Mattocks, Nicholas - Celia Brently, 12 Mar. 1839, Philip Pitman, (w) Jo. Bell, C. C.

Mattocks, Riley - Cherry Baker, 11 Jan. 1847, James S. Barnes, (w) John Norfleet, Clk.

Mattocks, William W. - Gatsy Stokes, 22 Jan. 1850, Dempsey Baker, (w) John Norfleet, Clk.

May, Benjamin - Elizabeth Edwards, 14 Oct. 1824, Benjamin Joiner, (w) N. Matheson.

May, James W. - Tabitha Bynum, 20 June 1844, Allen Bynum.

May, John - Anny Kelly, 27 Nov. 1828, Gray Little, (w) Ml. Hearn.

May, Kinchen - Sarah Saunders, 22 Feb. 1836, James B. Woodard, (w) T. C. Hearn.

May, William - Maple (Mable?) Alsbrook, 11 Jan. 176(4), James Alsbrook (w) Edward Hall.

Mayer, Willie W. - Virginia Proctor, 11 Apr. 1855, m. 12 Apr. 1855 by J. C. Knight, J. P., Charles E. Neal, (w) W. S. Pitt, Clk.

Mayo, Allen - Eliza Wilkinson, 9 Mar. 1841, William C. Leigh, (w) John Norfleet, Clk.

Mayo, Amos - Patsy Kelly, 18 Dec. 1833, John Shelton, (w) T. C. Hearn.

Mayo, Benjamin C. - Evelina S. Jones, 17 Jan. 1844, Benjamin Staton, (w) John Norfleet.

Mayo, Benjamin F. - Laura E. Bellamy, 17 Dec. 1866, m. 19 Dec. 1866 by Orren Williams, J. P., Orren Williams, (w) Irvin Thigpen.

Mayo, Berry - Martha A. Thomas, 2 Jan. 1866, m. 4 Jan. 1866 by L. C. Pender, J. P., Henry A. Shurley, (w) Irvin Thigpen.

Mayo, Ezekiel P. - Berthana Nolly, 16 Sept. 1854, m. 17 Sept. 1854 by Theo. Thomas, J. P., H. R. Davis, (w) Theo. Thomas.

Mayo, James - Spicey Pippin, 10 Dec. 1842, (w) John Norfleet.

Mayo, John - Maria Shelton, 2 Aug. 1834, John Shelton, (w) L. H. Hearn.

Mayo, Kinchen - Nancy Knight, 23 Aug. 1826, Cullen Mayo, (w) Michl. Hearn.

Mayo, Ralph (s. of J. Mayo) - Treacy Lewis, 29 May 1868, m. 2 June 1868 by William Harrell, J. P., (w) Irvin Thigpen.

Mayo, Rebuen - Lucinda Best, 19 Dec. 1832, William C. Leigh, (w) Ml. Hearn.

Mayo, Thomas - Mary Bryan, 16 Feb. 1833, Isaac B. Brady, (w) T. C. Hearn.

Mayo, William - Faithy Taylor, 26 Dec. 1828, Jonathan Gay, (w) Ml. Hearn.

Mayo, William - Sarah M. A. Harrell, 19 Dec. 1865, m. 20 Dec. 1865 by William Harrell, J. P., Luellen Harrell, (w) Irvin Thigpen, Clk.

Meares, Redmond - Elizabeth Brinkley, 23 Dec. 1841. (No wit.)

Mears, Henry (s. of Willie Mears) - Drusilla Pitt, 22 Jan. 1868 m. 23 Jan. 1868 by S. L. Hart, J. P., (w) Irvin Thigpen, Clk.

Mears, Jesse - Sarah Griffin, 11 Dec. 1865, m. 12 Dec. 1865 by Jesse Bulluck, J. P., Thomas Norfleet, (w) Irvin Thigpen.

Mears, William - Louiseanna Brake, 23 Dec. 1865, m. 23 Dec. 1865 by Jesse Bulluck, J. P., Kinchen Gay, (w) Irvin Thigpen.

Measells (Mizell?), Silas - Wealthea Savage, 15 Oct. 1859, m. 20 Oct. 1859 by William R. Cherry, J. P., Adolphus Measells, (w) W. A. Jones.

Meeks, Henry - Peggy Norris, 15 Mar. 1833, John Hathaway, (w) Ml. Hearn.

Meeks, Joshua - Elizabeth Pittman, 1 Mar. 1851, m. 1 Mar. 1851 by Henry T. Clark, J. P., Everett Mills, (w) John Norfleet, Clk.

Meeks, Taylor - Elizabeth Thigpen, 10 Feb. 1834, Thomas Howard, (w) T. C. Hearn.

Meeks, William J. - Garsey Ann Mayo, 26 May 1868, m. 28 May 1868 by William Harrell, J. P., (w) Irvin Thigpen, Clk.

Mehagan, James - Emily G. Bond, 20 Jan. 1853, m. 20 Jan. 1853 by Thomas R. Owen, M. G., John W. Saunders, (w) John Norfleet.

Melone, Willie - Rosy Hammonds, 12 Nov. 1825, Henry Morgan, (w) Ml. Hearn.

Melton, Bennett - Susan Sumerlin, 11 Jan. 1836, George Anderson (w) T. C. Hearn.

Melton, Cullen - Melbry Gay, 3 Oct. 1835, George Melton, (w) Ml. Hearn.

Melton, George - Frances Nolly, 8 Dec. 1840, Cullen Melton, (w) John Norfleet, Clk.

Melton, John - Elizabeth Jones, 1 Oct. 1763, Zacariah Melton, (w) John Spendelow.

Melton, John W. T. - Jane Mares, 17 Jan. 1860, m. 19 Jan. 1860 by C. B. Killebrew, J. P., R. A. Savage, (w) W. A. Jones, Clk.

Mercer, David V. - Martha A. E. Dupree, 20 Nov. 1854, m. 22 Nov. 1854 by Bennett P. Pitt, Robert H. Pender, (w) W. S. Pitt, Clk.

Mercer, Dennis - Eliza Ann M. Jane Owens, 14 Oct. 1856, m. 21 1856 by W. Y. Moore, J. P., (w) W. A. Jones, Clk.

Mercer, Eli - Peggy Gardner, 3 Mar. 1823, Thomas Barren, Robert Joyner, (w) Ml. Hearn.

Mercer, Jesse - Margaret Norfleet, 16 June 1844, Robert R. Bridgers, (w) John Norfleet.

Mercer, John D. - Rebecca Lewis, 14 Oct. 1835, Jacob Mercer, Jr., William D. Petway, (w) Martha E. Sutton.

Mercer, John Nl. - Esther Pitt, 23 Dec. 1826, David Williams, (w) Ml. Hearn.

Mercer, Levi - Eliza Wooten, 2 Feb. 1846, Jacob Mercer, (w) John Norfleet.

Mercer, Riley - Harriet Joyner, 11 Jan. 1866, m. 12 Jan, 1866 by J. I. Proctor, J. P., John J. Proctor, (w) Irvin Thigpen.

Mercer William D. - Lucinda Bradley, 18 Aug. 1836, Joshua L. Horn, (w) T. C. Hearn.

Mercer, William F. - Emily A. Parker, 12 Oct. 1852, m. 12 Oct. 1852 by Mark Bennett, John O. Oates, (w) John Norfleet.

Meritt, Ethington J. - Margaret M. Gunter, 29 Dec. 1828, Henry Gunter, (w) Ml. Hearn.

Merriott (Marriott?), Dr. Robert H. - Tempy A. Battle, 7 Nov. 1853, m. 8 Nov. 1853 by James L. Cotton, M. G., J. G. Fort, (w) W. S. Pitt, Clk.

Merritt, James - Mary Scutchins (Cutchins?), 30 Jan. 1768, James Hill, (w) Edward Hall.

Mial, John - Elizabeth Gully, 20 Jan. 1764, Hancock Hacher, (w) Thomas Cavanah.

Miller, Frederic - Piety Robbins, 23 May 1825, Stephen Robbins, (w) Ml. Hearn.

Mills, Abner B. - Martha Garner, 10 July 1828, David Barnes, (w) Ml. Hearn.

Mills, Churchwell - Elizabeth Little, 28 Apr. 1858(?), m. 29 Mar. 1858 by Bennett P. Pitt, J. P., William Lodge, (w) J. H. Dozier.

Mills, Everitt - Sally Weeks, 8 Nov. 1828, Willis Bradley, (w) Ml. Hearn.

Mills, Everitt - Eliza Sory, 14 Nov. 1851, m. 15 Nov. 1851 by W. F. Lewis, J. P., Henry Hales, (w) John Norfleet.

Minnis, John A. - Penninah Horne, 21 June 1831, Amos J. Battle, (w) T. C. Hearn.

Minor, John - Lavina Lee, 26 Dec. 1836, Eli Boon, (w) Ml. Hearn.

Mitchell, John - Sarah Locus, 22 Nov. 1863, m. 22 Nov. 1863 by W. M. Pippin, J. P., Pierce Jones, (w) Irvin Thigpen.

Mitchel, Peter - Christian Miller, 22 Dec. 1769, James Hall, (w) William Hall.

Mitchel, Henry C. B. - Rebecca Barnes, 27 Mar. 1850, Robert R. Bridgers, (w) John Norfleet.

Mitchell, Mordecai - Dilly McDade, 28 Oct. 1828, Abraham Price, (w) Ml. Hearn.

Mitchell, Thomas - Martha Jane Reed, 3 Jan. 1859, m. 4 Jan. 1859 by J. R. Pitt, J. P., Jesse B. Hyatt, (w) W. A. Jones.

Mitchell, William - Mary Wilkins, 9 Oct. 1856, m. 9 Oct. 1856 by Thomas Norfleet, J. P., George B. Lipscomb, (w) J. H. Dozier.

Mizell, Frank - Maggie House, 30 June 1864, m. 3 July 1864 by Kenneth Thigpen, J. P., Silas Mizell, (w) T. W. Hussey.

Mizzeles, Timothy - Elizabeth Baker, 27 Mar. 1849, Henry Griffin, (w) John Norfleet.

Montague, John D. - Jullier A. Farmer, 11 Jan. 1855, m. 11 Jan. 1855 by E. Barnes, J. P., Peter Brinkley, Jackson Lasiter, (w) E. Barnes.

Montgomery, William - Elizabeth Pitman, 21 Aug. 1851, m. 21 Aug. 1851 by Elisha Barnes, J. P., William D. Thorn, (w) John W. Farmer.

Mooneyham, Duke - Martha Hill, 12 Dec. 1833, Thomas Dickinson.

Moore, Abraham - Rebecca Moore, 24 Nov. 1835, Philip Luper, (w) Ml. Hearn.

Moore, Alfred - Nancy Pelt, 26 May 1824, John Horn, (w) Ml. Hearn.

Moore, Alfred - Nancy Sorey, 19 Dec. 1835, (w) Ml. Hearn.

Moore, Andrew J. - Dellah Cotten, 31 Jan. 1859, m. 3 Feb. 1859 by John W. Johnson, J. P., B. T. Pittman, (w) W. A. Jones.

Moore, Brittain - Martha Harrell, 28 Feb. 1837, Jesse Harrell, (w) T. C. Hearn.

Moore, Burrell - Rhoda Hedgepeth, 11 Mar. 1826, Thomas Taylor, (w) Ml. Hearn.

Moore, Burrell - Penelope Dixon, 30 July 1831, William Taylor.

Moore, Calvin - Emeliza Gardner. 31 Dec. 1853, m. 3 Jan. 1854 by D. W. Barnes, J. P., Willie J. Batts, (w) William M. Pippin.

Moore, David - Mary Gardner, 19 Feb. 1829, Joab Moore, Whitnel Williams, (w) Ml. Hearn.

Moore, Edwin J. - Maomi A. E. Armstrong, 26 Dec. 1865, m. 28 Dec. 1865 by H. S. Taylor, A. B. M. G., Lawrence Lancaster, (w) Irvin Thigpen.

Moore, Guilford - Mary Ann Ward, 8 Jan. 1850, Spencer Ward, (w) John Norfleet, Clk.

Moore, Henry - Polly Proctor, 13 Dec. 1849, Joshua L. Boon, (w) John Norfleet. Clk.

Moore, Isaac - Blanchy Daughtridge, 4 May 1837, Abraham Moore, (w) Ml. Hearn.

Moore, James - Letha Mercer, 2 Jan. 1835, Hezekiah Langley, (w) Ml. Hearn.

Moore, James E. - Rebecca Coker, (No dates), Stephen Coker, (w) W. L. Dozier, D. C.

Moore, Joab - Martha Price, 16 Oct. 1827, Abraham Price, (w) Ml. Hearn.

Moore, John - Rutha Carney, 28 Nov. 1840, Winfield D. Staton.

Moore, John O. - Ann S. C. Carlisle, 11 Sept. 1855, m. 11 Sept. 1855 by Thomas Norfleet, J. P., (w) W. S. Pitt, Clk.

Moore, John W. - Jane Taylor, 20 Dec. 1848, Jesse Price, (w) John Norfleet, Clk.

Moore, Joseph - Ann Toole, 4 July 1765, Henry Irvin.

Moore, Joseph - Louisiana Hargrove, 5 Mar. 1848, Elijah Moore, (w) John Norfleet, Clk.

Moore, Joseph F. - Sarah A. S. Fryer, 10 Aug. 1853, m. 11 Aug. 1853 by E. Barnes, J. P., Robert H. Pender.

Moore, Joshua L. - Axcy Williams, 27 Sept. 1848, Bary Bailey, (w) James H. Dozier.

Moore, Joshua L. - Mary D. Wells, 5 Nov. 1860, m. 6 Nov. 1860 by Hilyard S. Taylor, A. B. M. G., William Long, (w) J. H. Dozier.

Moore, Lemuel - Mary Beeman, 7 May 1832, Henry Shurly, (w) Ml. Hearn.

Moore, Moses - Rebecca Griffin, 16 Jan. 1830, Robert Foxhall, (w) Ml. Hearn.

Moore, Moses - Elizabeth Hearn, 28 Jan. 1859, m. 1 Feb. 1859 by R. J. Johnson, J. P., Eli W. Sumerlin, (w) W. A. Jones.

Moore, Dr. R. A. - Margaret Griffin, 11 Oct. 1853, m. 12 Oct. 1853 by W. J. Armstrong, J. P., Powell Bullard, (w) W. S. Pitt.

Moore, Redding A. - Lucinda Sory, 22 Jan. 1848, Thomas A. Macnair, (w) John Norfleet, Clk.

Moore, Roderick - Mary Grimes, 2 Mar. 1829, Theop. Cherry, (w) Ml. Hearn.

Moore, Rufus S. - Sally Ann Dunford, 6 Jan. 1866, m. 9 Jan. 1866 by R. J. Johnson, J. P., J. C. Forbes, (w) Irvin Thigpen.

Moore, Samuel - ————, 9 May ————, William Hall, (w).

Moore, Samuel - Susanna Alsbrook, 27 Oct. 1823, Patrick McDowell, (w) N. Mathewson.

Moore, Samuel - Melly Leigh, 1 Nov. 1832, James Ellinor, (w) T. C. Hearn.

Moore, Samuel - Mary Ann Williford, 27 Feb. 1831, James Tropolet.

Moore, Samuel E. - Alice Ann Elliott, 7 Jan. 1845, Nathan Mathewson, (w) John Norfleet, Clk.

Moore, Spencer - Piety Hicks, 16 Apr. 1844, Enos Womble, (w) John Norfleet.

Moore, Theophilus - Catherine Proctor, 12 May 1847, William D. Lancaster, (w) John Norfleet, Clk.

Moore, Theophilus - Delha Mears, 28 Feb. 1853, m. 1 Mar. 1853, James J. Taylor, J. P., David Sharp, (w) John Norfleet.

Moore, William - Molly Swinney, 10 Jan. 1762, Thomas Spell, (w) Thomas Cavenough.

Moore, William - Sally Powell, 24 Dec. 1824, Wells Draughon, (w) Ml. Hearn.

Moore, William - Sally Little, 4 Jan. 1831, John R. Scarbrough, (w) L. H. Hearn.

Moore, William - Pamelia Baxter, 31 Dec. 1832, Thomas D. Price, (w) T. C. Hearn.

Moore, William A. - Mary Ann O'berry, 11 Nov. 1858, m. 11 Nov. 1858 by Thomas R. Owens, M. G., John L. Littlepage, (w) W. A. Jones.

Morgan, Canady - Sally Daniel, 11 Nov. 1830, Thomas Barron, (w) Ml. Hearn.

Morgan, David - Sally Linch, 6 Feb. 1827, William Pitman, (w) Ml. Hearn.
Morgan, Francis M. - Mary J. Lodge, 18 Apr. 1854, m. 20 Apr. 1854 by Wright Barnes, J. P., L. F. Morgan, (w) W. S. Pitt.
Morgan, Henry - Elizabeth Hammonds, 15 Jan. 1826, Joseph Pitman, (w) Ml. Hearn.
Morgan, Henry T. - Louisa Wammack, 8 Apr. 1865, m. 13 Apr. 1865 by W. F. Lewis, J. P., John J. Meeks, (w) Irvin Thigpen.
Morgan, James - Lydia Lodge, 7 Mar. 1860, m. 7 Mar. 1860 by Lunsford R. Cherry, J. P., J. T. Jones, W. A. Jones, Clk.
Morgan, Joseph - Emily Sessoms, 4 Apr. 1825, Isaac D. Guion, (w) Ml. Hearn.
Morgan, Joseph - Mourning Jones, 8 Oct. 1833, Willis Bradley, (w) T. C. Hearn.
Morgan, Joseph - Creasy Little, 24 Nov. 1826, Isaac D. Guion, Warren Waller, (w) Ml. Hearn.
Morgan, Stephen - Mariah Due (Dew), 7 Apr. 1858, m. 8 Apr. 1858 by L. C. Pender, J. P., Jesse Gardner, (w) W. A. Jones, Clk.
Morgan, Willie - Jacky A. Norris, 21 Jan. 1854, m. 22 Jan. 1854 by James Carney, J. P., F. G. Pitt, (w) W. S. Pitt, Clk.
Morriss, Bythal - Lurany Stokes, 4 Feb. 1832, Joab P. Pitt, (w) Ml. Hearn.
Morris, Garry - Arrinna Harrison, 22 Sept. 1863, m. 24 Sept. 1863 by Hilyard S. Taylor, A. B. M. G., Joseph Cobb, (w) Thomas Hussey.
Morris, John A. - Elizabeth Wilkinson, 13 May 1851, m. 13 June 1851 by J. C. Knight, J. P., Charles G. Wilkinson, (w) John Norfleet.
Morris, Joseph - Julia Hales, 6 Dec. 1843, John Williams, John Hales, (w) John Norfleet.
Morris, Joseph - Mary Eliza Summerlin, 4 July 1846, Joseph Moore, (w) W. L. Dozier.
Morris, Nathan - Catherine Medford, 26 Jan. 1810, Dolphin Drew, (w) Michl. Hearn.
Morriss, Nathan - Keziah Batts, 14 Mar. 1835, William Morris, (w) Ml. Hearn.
Morriss, Thomas - Virginia Ann Parker, 2 Aug. 1855, m. 2 Aug. 1855 by R. H. Pender, J. P., John H. Freeman, (w) W. A. Jones, D. C.

Morse, Joseph - Selecta (Celesta?) Woollard, 27 Aug. 1822, Lewis Bond, (w) Ml. Hearn.

Morton, George - Nanny Oneil, 26 June 1763, John Skinner, (w) John Spendelow.

Moseley, Allen - Patsy Dunn, 6 Feb. 1845, Thomas Dunn, (w) John Norfleet.

Moseley, Amos - Acenith Rodgers, 21 Mar. 1842, Elias Summerlin, (w) John Norfleet, Clk.

Mosely, David - Zilpha Durden, 9 Jan. 1828, Isaac Farmer Jr., (w) Ml. Hearn.

Mosley, David - Polly Eason, 5 June 1830, Cophel (Coffield?) Dixon, (w) L. H. Hearn.

Mosely, Elisha - Elizabeth Cobb, 5 Mar. 1836, Samuel D. Proctor, (w) T. C. Hearn.

Mosely, Henry - Mary Looper, 11 Aug. 1851, m. 12 Aug. 1851 by W. J. Armstrong, J. P., Ethelred Jordan, (w) John Norfleet.

Moseley, James - Nancy Dunn, 6 Aug. 1859, m. 7 Aug. 1859 by Theo. Atkinson, J. P., Joseph H. Payne, (w) James H. Dozier.

Moseley, John - Polly Brann, 15 Apr. 183—, Cophel Dixon, (w) Ml. Hearn.

Moseley, John - Leecy or Lucy Lunengham, 14 Aug. 1835, James Dixon, (w) T. C. Hearn.

Moseley, Thomas - Celia Barnes, 8 May, 1829, Augustin Farmer, (w) Ml. Hearn.

Moseley, William - Elizabeth Beland, 15 Oct. 1823, Henry Taylor, Edwin Bullock, (w) Ml. Hearn.

Mourning, Lewelling - Sally Wilkinson, 18 Dec. 1833, William Little, (w) T. C. Hearn.

Mullens, James - Drewcilla Joyner, 5 May 1852, m. 5 May 1852 by Jacob S. Barnes, J. P., M. Bennett Nolly, Emeriah Nolly, (w) Zadoc Johnson.

Mumford, James H. - Clemmy Eason, 11 Sept. 1836, Edwin Barnes, (w) Ml. Hearn.

Mumfred, William - Rebecca Johnston, 16 Mar. 1836, Larry Dew, (w) T. C Hearn.

Mumfred, George - Edith Ellis, 23 May 1835, Jacob S. Barnes, (w) T. C. Hearn.

Murphee, Josiah - Pherebe Wimberly, 7 June 1764, John Murphee, (w) James Hall.

Murphree, James - Sarah Strawther (Strother?), 25 Feb. 1770, John Strother, (w) William Hall.

Murray, John - Tempey Bland, 9 May 1810, Mark Murray, (w) M. Hearn.
Murray, William, Jr. - Margaret Rountree. 18 Oct. 1854, m. 18 Oct. 1854 by H. H. Gibbons, M. G., Thomas J. Stewart, (w) W. S. Pitt, Clk.

N

Nadal, Anthony - Sarah M. Nadal, 3 Feb. 1855, F.L. Bond, (w) W. S. Pitt, Clk.
Neal, Charles E. - Penetta Jenkins. 8 May 1852, m. 11 May 1852 by William H. Hines, J. P., Lennard S. Dunn, (w) John Norfleet.
Neal, David - Delha Horn, 2 July 1855, m. 3 July 1855 by Thomas R. Owen, M. G., David B. Knight, (w) W. S. Pitt, Clk.
Nelson, James R. - Mary M. Taylor, 24 Nov. 1857, m. 27 Nov. 1857 by James W. Howard, J. P., John W. Nelson, (w) W. A. Jones, Clk.
Nelson, John W. - Elizabeth Ann Grimes, 21 Dec. 1857, m. 22 Dec. 1857 by James W. Howard, J. P., William A. Mayo, (w) W. A. Jones, Clk.
Nelson, Kinchen - Martha Crisp, 21 Dec. 1825, Aldredg Andrews, Robert Jenkins, (w) Ml. Hearn.
Nelson, William - Albena Whitfield, 24 Nov. 1822, Benjamin Whitfield, Frederick Taylor, (w) Ml. Hearn, C. C.
Newton, John - Latetia Vines, 24 Sept. 1834, Edward Cobb, (w) T. C. Hearn.
Neville, Elijah - Emily Bradley, 4 Jan. 1851, John J. Battle, (w) John Norfleet, Clk.
Newsom, David A. - Sarah Strickland, 11 July 1866, m. 11 July 1866 by J. F. Batts, J. P., W. L. Petway, (w) Irvin Thigpen, Clk.
Newsom, Henry - Nancy B. Cotten, 24 Dec. 1849, Josiah Anderson, (w) John Norfleet.
Newsom, Simon - Chloe Williamson, 26 June, 1764, James Williamson, (w) Thomas Cavenah.
Newsom, William T. - Mary L. Strickland, 12 Mar. 1866, m. 13 Mar. 1866 by J. F. Batts, J. P., W. L. Petway, (w) Irvin Thigpen.
Nicholson, David - Rhoda Whitehead, 15 Aug. 1761, Edward Moore, (w) Benjamin Whitehead.
Nicholson, John - Penelope Mann, 2 Nov. 1770, Lemuel Nicholson.

Noble, Allen B. - Susan E. Garrett, 19 May 1855, m. 20 May 1855 by Wright Barnes, J. P., P. G. Foster, (w) W. A. Jones, D. C.

Nobles, Daniel - Cecelia Macnair, 27 Mar. 1866, m. 7 Apr. 1866 by W. H. Knight, J. P., W. T. Macnair, (w) Irvin Thigpen.

Nolley, Marke B. - Ellen A. Knight, 14 Nov. 1852, m. 14 Nov. 1852 by Theo. Thomas, J. P., A. J. Armstrong, (w) John Norfleet.

Nolly, Ananiah - Matilda Boon, 2 Feb. 1850, Francis W. Taylor, (w) John Norfleet.

Noly, William - Charlotte Proctor, 4 July 1838, William A. Joyner, (w) Jo. Bell.

Norfleet, Robert - Margaret Williams, 19 Dec. 1849, Henry T. Clark, (w) John Norfleet.

Norfleet, Thomas - Azula Mahegan, 1 Sept. 1858, m. 1 Sept. 1858 by Thomas R. Owen, (w) W. A. Jones, Clk. Joseph S. Staton.

Norvell, Enos - Sally Bolton, 6 Apr. 1824, Asa Bolton, (w) N. Mathewson.

Norvill, William - Sally Waller, 3 Sept. 1829, Isaac D. Guion, (w) Ml. Hearn.

Norville, Hardy - William Ann Wilkins, 22 Mar. 1851, m. 25 Mar. 1851 by Theo. Atkinson, J. P., Bury Norvill, (w) John Norfleet.

Norville, Ivey - Eliza Edwards, 25 Jan. 1845, William Dunford, John Norfleet.

Norville, James - Margaret Griffin, 8 Feb. 1855, m. 11 Feb. 1855 by James Carney, J. P., William S. Crisp, (w) W. S. Pitt, Clk.

Norville, L. B. - Vina Edwards, 17 Jan. 1857, m. 20 Jan. 1857 by W. Y. Moore, J. P., John Dail, (w) W. A. Jones, Clk.

Nowells, Luke - Sally Billups, 29 Jan. 1817, Francis M. Wood, Josiah Wood, Elisha Cromwell, Joshua Pender, (w) Michl. Hearn.

Nunnery, William - Adeline Fountain, 24 Feb. 1853, m. 27 Feb. 1853 by L. R. Cherry, J. P., William M. Pippen, (w) John Norfleet, Clk.

O

Oats, John O. - Martha M. Mercer, 20 July 1852. m. 20 July 1852 by John H. Daniel, M. G., William M. Gay, (w) John Norfleet.

O'berry, Green - Elizabeth Day, 22 July 1847, A. H. Macnair, (w) W. L. Dozier, D. Clk.

O'berry, Green - Elvira Parker, 3 Mar. 1852. m. 4 Mar. 1852 by Blount L. Cooper, George L. Winborn, (w) John Norfleet.

O'berry, Joseph - Harriet E. Edwards, 24 Jan. 1848, David Neal, (w) W. L. Dozier.

O'Berry, Joseph - Elizabeth Bridges, 11 July 1854, m. 11 July 1854 by J. H. Daniel, John H. Daniel, (w) W. S. Pitt, Clk.

Odenheimer, Falk - Margaret Spath (Speight?), 13 Nov. 1847, Josiah H. Brooks, (w) John Norfleet, Clk.

Odom, Allen - Ann Odom, 23 June 1866, m. 7 July 1866 by Thomas L. Maner, J. P., William H. Odom, (w) Irvin Thigpen.

Odom, James R. - Martha A. Pope, 10 Jan. 1859, m. 11 Jan. 1859 by Thomas L. Maner, J. P., Henry E. Odom, (w) J. H. Dozier.

Odom, Jeremiah - Catherine Pitt, 17 Feb. 1823, Blake H. Wiggins, Malichi Odom, (w) Ml. Hearn.

Odom, Lewis - Cornelia Drake, 22 Mar. 1866, m. 24 Mar. 1866 by Thomas L. Maner, J. P., Shade Hilliard, (w) Irvin Thigpen.

Odom, Malachi - Mary Griffin, 26 June 1822, Jeremiah Odom, (w) N. Mathewson.

Odom, William H. - Fredrica A. Braswell, 22 May 1855, m. 23 May 1855 by Thomas L. Maner, Coffield Mason, (w) W. S. Pitt.

Olford, Edmunds - Sarah Jones, 6 Aug. 1831, Benjamin Boykin, (w) Ml. Hearn.

Oliver, Richard - Prissa Ann Talbert, (dau. of Torq. Talbert), 4 Mar. 1868, m. 5 Mar. 1868 by John T. Bellamy, J. P., (w) Irvin Thigpen.

Ollidge, Mathew - Cathalina Bozeman, 25 Oct. 1848, Guilford Horn, (w) John Norfleet.

Onail, Benjamin - Elizabeth Ross, 12 Jan. 1764, John Onail, (w) Thomas Cavenah.

O'Nail, Isham - Mary Stallions, 6 Apr. 1764, William O'Nail.

Oneal, Arthur - Frances Bedford, 4 June 1833, John Coggins, Weeks Parker, (w) Ml. Hearn.

O'Neal, Arthur - Lydia Bishop, 24 Jan. 1848, Robert H. Pender, (w) John Norfleet.

O'Neal, Elisha - Susan Meeks, 20 Jan. 1845, Bennett O'Neal, (w) William Norfleet.

O'Neal, James - Elizabeth Faithful, 17 Oct. 1832, William Dancy, (w) Ml. Hearn.

Oneal, Wyatt - Elizabeth Exum, 1 Mar. 1825, Richard Bradley, (w) Ml. Hearn.

Oneal, Wyatt - Elizabeth Sory, 15 Oct. 1828, Richard Bradley, (w) Ml. Hearn.

O'Neale, Whitmill - Mary Price, 14 Apr. 1838, William Dancy.

Oneals, John - Louisa Bradley, 14 July 1851, m. 14 July 1851 by Jordan Thigpen, J. P., Joshua Meeks, (w) Benjamin Norfleet.

Oneil, Bennet - Bethia Hawkins, 4 May 1830, John Hawkins, Jr., (w) Ml. Hearn.

Oneil, David - Nancy Vick, 6 Sept. 1855, John W. Johnson.

Overstreet, James H. - Elizabeth J. Ellinor, 14 Jan. 1862, m. 22 Jan. 1862 by W. F. Lewis, J. P., Joel Savage, (w) Thomas W. Hussey.

Owen, John W. - Anna Owen, 8 May, 1866, m. 10 May 1866 by R. J. Johnson, J. P., Henry Owen, (w) Irvin Thigpen.

Owen, Thomas R. - Mary B. McCotter, 8 Oct. 1839, Benjamin M. Jackson.

Owens, Amos - Sally Felton, 1 Feb. 1837, Henry Owens, (w) Ml. Hearn.

Owens, Bennett - Elizabeth Page, 16 Dec. 1845, Henry Gay, (w) John Norfleet.

Owens, David - Elizabeth Kea, 5 Oct. 1817, Smith Hogan, (w) Ml. Hearn.

Owens, Dempsey - Mary A. Pippen, 17 Sept. 1853, m. 20 Sept. 1853 by ———? William Owens, (w) W. S. Pitt, Clk.

Owens, Dempsey - Celia A. E. Howard, 20 Mar. 1855, m. 21 Mar. 1855 by W. Y. Young, J. P., William Owen, (w) W. S. Pitt, Clk.

Owens, Eli - Penny Owens, 24 Feb. 1841, Henry Gay, Dempsey Gay, (w) John Norfleet, Clk.

Owens, Elisha - Mary Peoples, 18 Jan. 1827, Lemon Wheeler, (w) Ml. Hearn.

Owens, Elisha - Delphia A. Thigpen, 16 Jan. 1849, Ely Owens, (w) John Norfleet, Clk.

Owens, Henry - Sally Page, 7 Apr. 1826, Benjamin Moore, (w) Ml. Hearn.

Owens, Henry - Nisey Ellis, 18 May 1853, m. 22 May 1853 by William Y. Moore, J. P., Eli Owens, (w) John Norfleet, Clk.

Owens, Hilliard - Betsey Owens, 15 Dec. 1840, Rial Edwards, (w) John Norfleet, Clk.

Owens, James - Barbara Killebrew, 28 Dec. 1858, m. 4 Jan. 1859 by R. J. Johnson, J. P., James Wooten, (w) J. H. Dozier, D. C.

Owens, Jesse - Patsey Joyner, 10 Sept. 1811, Benjamin Gay, (w) Ml. Hearn.

Owens, John - Polly Wootten, 11 Jan. 1853, m. 12 Jan. 1853 by William Y. Moore, J. P., Ephraim Wooten, (w) John Norfleet, Clk.

Owens, Lasarus - Sally Burass, 2 Jan. 1835, Willie Burass, (w) T. C. Hearn.

Owens, Lin - Sally Dunn, 6 Dec. 1848, Dennis Mercer, (w) John Norfleet.

Owens, Lott - Letty Lester, 29 Jan. 1800, Patrick O'Keefe, (w) S. Wren.

Owens, Nasworthy - Sarah Buras, 13 Jan. 1835, Geraldus Shurly, (w) Ml. Hearn.

Owens, Nathan - Martha Ann Owens, 7 Oct. 1846, Hilyard Owens, (w) John Norfleet, Clk.

Owens, Newit D. - Mary Ann Thigpen, 6 Jan. 1841, James R. Broom, John Norfleet, Clk.

Owens, Reuben - Phenetta Miner, 13 Mar. 1848, Hardy Burnit, Jr.

Owens, Robert M. - Elizabeth L. Thorne, 5 May 1825, Levi Wooten, Bolene J. Boone, (w) Ml. Hearn.

Owens, William - Elizabeth Deverson, 1 July 1835, Benjamin Gay, (w) Ml. Hearn.

P

Page, Ashly - Elizabeth Lancaster, 10 Mar. 1845, Martin Gardner, (w) T. T. Braddy.

Page, Eason - Polly Flemming, 1 Sept. 1824, Joshua B. Eason, (w) N. Mathewson.

Page, Isaac - Lucinda Whitley, 3 Jan. 1856, m. 6 Jan. 1856 by J. R. Pitt, J. P., (w) W. S. Pitt, Clk.

Page, James - Elizabeth Lewis, 16 Mar. 1826, John Thigpen, (w) Ml. Hearn.

Page, Johnston - Lydia Gardner, 21 Dec. 1835, Theophilus Atkinson, (w) T. C. Hearn.

Page, Theophilus - Mary Ruffin, 26 Jan. 1847, Jonas Brown, (w) W. L. Dozier, D. P.

Page, William - Susan Hicks, 10 Mar. 1845, Martin Gardner, (w) T. T. Braddy.

Page, William - Rachel Hicks, 31 May 1848, Bennet P. Pitt, (w) John Norfleet.

Parker, Arthur - Letha Cutchens, 15 Dec. 1823, Weeks Parker, (w) Ml. Hearn.

Parker, Arthur T. - Fayettie ———, 26 Dec. 1865, m. 28 Dec. 1865 by John A. Stamper, M. P. Edwards, (w) Irvin Thigpen.

Parker, Edwin - Elizabeth Rountree, 29 Sept. 1848, Jordan Horn, (w) Benjamin Norfleet.

Parker, Eli - Martha Adams, 11 Nov. 1839, (w) Jo. Bell, C. C.

Parker, Ellic - Kiddy Taylor, 28 Feb. 1854, James G. Williford.

Parker, Francis M. - Sarah T. Philips, 17 Dec. 1851, m. 17 Dec. 1851 by Jos. Blount Cheshire, Epis. Min., William H. Powell, (w) John Norfleet, Clk.

Parker, Frederick - Mary B. Ellis, 11 Sept. 1826, William Parker, (w) Ml. Hearn.

Parker, Guilford - Priscilla Farmer, 27 Feb. 1833, Frederick F. Robbins, (w) Ml. Hearn.

Parker, Henry - Mary Rainer, 28 Feb. 1854, m. 2 Mar. 1854 by William S. Long, J. P., Thomas Dunn, (w) W. S. Pitt.

Parker, Irwin - Elizabeth Proctor, 20 Dec. 1823, John Hayes, Benjamin Braswell, (w) Ml. Hearn.

Parker, James - Mary Owens, 4 Jan. 1829, William Owens, (w) Ml. Hearn.

Parker, Jesse W. - Nancy Bryant, 15 Dec. 1858, Laurence Lancaster, (w) J. H. Dozier.

Parker, John - Mary Weeks, 27 Sept. 176—, William Hudnall, (w) Edward Hall.

Parker, John - Margaret Jones, 22 May 1770, John Jones, (w) J. Hall.

Parker, John - Dolly Washington, 21 Aug. 1800, William A. White.

Parker, John - Lucy Bell, 12 Apr. 1825, Stephen Harper, Ml. Hearn.

Parker, John - Martha Tart, 22 Sept 1829, (w) Ml. Hearn.

Parker, John - Eliza Jane Philips, 14 Oct. 1851, m. 15 Oct. 1851 by Jos. Blount Cheshire, Epis. Min., Frank M. Parker, (w) John Norfleet.

Parker, Joseph J. R. - Jane Aberthnot Howell (or James?), 2 Dec. 1851, m. 4 Dec. 1851 by Blount Cooper, David Neale, Andrew M. Parker, (w) John Norfleet.

Parker, Kenneth - Malissa D. Bradley, 24 Feb. 1858, m. 2 Mar. 1858 by Thomas L. Maner, J. P., W. K. Parker, (w) W. A. Jones, Clk.

Parker, Mark - Mary Ann Whitehead, 12 Mar. 1857, m. 12 Mar. 1857 by Henry T. Clark, J. P., J. M. Edwards, (w) J. H. Dozier.

Parker, Martin - Tempy Brady, 2 Sept. 1848, Jeremiah Odom, (w) John Norfleet, Clk.

Parker, Seth - Peggy Skinner, 5 Jan. 1811, John Ellis, (w) N. Mathewson.

Parker, Weeks Jr. - Winnifred Cockburn, 11 June 1814, Hardy Proctor, (w) Michl. Hearn.

Parker, Weeks B. - Anna Pitt, 14 June 1866, m. 19 June 1866 by J. H. Daniel, John Owen, (w) Irvin Thigpen.

Parker, William - Celia Williams, 15 Mar. 1828, Augustin Farmer, (w) Ml. Hearn.

Parker, William Weeks - Sarah P. Edwards, 11 Feb. 1857, m. 12 Feb. 1857 by Henry T. Clark, J. P., (w) W. A. Jones.

Parris, John - Sally Ann A. Bellamy, 10 Dec. 1845, William D. Bryan.

Peal, John Jr. - Mary Johnston, 1 Oct. 1834, William W. Armstrong, (w) Ml. Hearn.

Peal, Miles - Fruny Farless, 9 Dec. 1828, James Waller, (w) Ml. Hearn.

Peebles, John - Carolina Worsley, 13 Feb. 1851, m. 18 Feb. 1851 by Elisha Cromwell, J. P., Walter Newton, (w) Norfleet, Clk.

Peebles, Ralph - Naomi Hill, 12 Feb. 1863, m. 12 Feb. 1863 by R. M. Pippen, J. P., Thomas Norfleet, (w) Irvin Thigpen.

Peel, David - Sally Evans, 7 Aug. 1848, Cornelius Jordan.

Peel, Henry - Matilda Brake, 24 Dec. 1834, Zachariah Ponds, (w) T. C. Hearn.

Peel, Henry W. - Zilly Ann Flemming, 20 Jan. 1845, Amos Walston, (w) John Norfleet.

Peel, John L. - Jacky Dew Braswell, 8 Aug. 1835, William Taylor, (w) T. C. Hearn.

Peel, Joshua - Lucinda Brake, 15 Feb. 1857 (?), m. 18 Feb. 1856 by Thomas Norfleet, J. P., (w) W. A. Jones, Clk.

Peel, Josiah - Elizabeth Britt, 5 Jan. 1860, m. 5 Jan. 1860 by L. C. Pender, J. P., William Peel, Jr., (w) W. L. Dozier.

Peel, Stephen - Maryan Dew, 29 Apr. 1851, m. 29 Apr. 1851 by Joshua Barnes, J. P., Daniel Hocott, (w) Joshua Barnes.

Peele, Richard - Viney Bottom, 21 Apr. 1811, Joseph Pitman, (w) Ml. Hearn.

Pender, Allen - Elizabeth Porter, 12 May 1866, m. 13 May 1866 by Jos. Blount Cheshire, Epis. Min., Warren Jones, (w) Irvin Thigpen.

Pender, Andrew J. - Any Elizabeth Joyner, 4 Mar. 1841, Wright W. Joyner, (w) John Norfleet, Clk.

Pender, Cullin - Lucy Bradley, 5 Jan. 1836, James Fryer, (w) T. C. Hearn.

Pender, Cullen W. - Peninah Gardner, 2 Apr. 1851, m. 6 Apr. 1851 by W. E. Spiers, J. P., W. S. Hunter, (w) John Norfleet, Clk.

Pender, David - Mary C. Johnston, 25 July 1859, Thomas H. Peters, (w) W. A. Jones, Clk.

Pender, James - Patsey Pitman, 27 Dec. 1825, Bernard Cowell, Charles Wilkinson, (w) Ml. Hearn.

Pender, John - Silvia Harrell, 12 Jan. 1828, Solo. Pender, David Holland, (w) Ml. Hearn.

Pender, Joseph J. - Elizabeth Bridgers, 4 Mar. 1829, Stephen Robbins, (w) Ml. Hearn.

Pender, Joseph J. - Luckins L. Wilkins, 13 Feb. 1855, m. 15 Feb. 1855 by Theo. Atkinson, J. P., W. S. Pitt, (w) W. S. Pitt.

Pender, Joshua (son of L. C. Pender) - Kate D. Pender (dau. of Josiah Pender), 11 July 1868, m. 14 July 1868 by Thos. R. Owen, V. D. M., (w) Irvin Thigpen.

Pender, Josiah S. - Laura M. Pender, 22 Sept. 1862, m. 23 Sept. 1862 by Thomas R. Owen, M. G., (w)———.

Pender, Littleton - Martha Harper, 9 Mar. 1852, m. 11 Mar. 1852 by L. C. Pender, J. P., John W. Davis, (w) John Norfleet.

Pender, Lorenzo D. - Martha Louisa Howard, 20 Oct. 1852, m. 20 Oct. 1852 by R. J. Carson, William M. Pippen, (w) John Norfleet.

Pender, Reddick B. - Elizabeth Pender, 8 July 1799, Benjamin Jourdan, (w) S. Wren.

Pender, Robert - Polly Gardner, 1 Apr. 1856, m. 3 Apr. 1856 by L. C. Pender, J. P., Lewis C. Pender.

Pender, Robert H. - James(?) Pender, 24 Oct. 1843, Robert R. Bridgers, (w) John Norfleet, Clk.

Pender, Solomon - Elizabeth Hines, 20 Dec. 1827, Exum L. Lowe, (w) Ml. Hearn.

Pender, Solomon M. - Mary J. Ward, 27 Jan. 1864, m. 28 Jan. 1864 by Thomas R. Owen, M. G., William Howard, (w) Irvin Thigpen.

Pender, Thomas E. - Sarah R. Carstarphen, 10 Dec. 1835, Stephen W. C. Lewellen, (w) Thos. C. Hearn.

Pender, William, Jr. - Elizabeth Bilbry, 22 Jan. 1851, Braswell Britt, (w) John Norfleet.

Pender, Wright - Druscilla Cowell, 17 Dec. 1829, (w) L. H. Hearn.

Peoples, Anderson - Elizabeth Ann Cherry, 27 Feb. 1856, m. 27 Feb. 1856 by Elisha Cromwell, J. P., James M. Harper, (w) W. S. Pitt.

Peoples, Ashly A. - Polly Ann Rayner, 14 Jan. 1843, (w) John Norfleet, Clk.

Peoples, David - Rebecca Jenkins, 10 Nov. 1824, Benjamin Hearn, (w) Ml. Hearn.

Peoples, Martin - Lewesa Anderson, 15 Jan. 1857, m. 23 Jan. 1857 by J. R. Pitt, J. P., Joel D. Gardner, (w) W. A. Jones.

Peoples, W. L. - Bettie A. Battle, 9 Jan. 1866, m. 10 Jan. 1866 by Thomas R. Owen, V. D. M., James L. Battle, (w) Irvin Thigpen.

Pepper, Robert - Eliza Lewis, 5 Apr. 1830, Peter E. Knight, (w) L. H. Hearn.

Perkins, William S. - Susan E. Leggett, 21 Sept. 1841, Levin Leggitt, (w) John Norfleet, Clk.

Permenter, John - Sarah Evans, 16 Mar. 1763, Charles Jones, (w) John Spendelow.

Perry, John M. (s. of B. L. Perry) - Delah Barlow, (dau. of David Barlow), 14 Apr. 1868, m. 15 Apr. 1868 by Thomas R. Owen, V. D. M., (w) Irvin Thigpen, Clk.

Perry, Thomas - Temperance Dawson, 31 Jan. 1834, Benjamin White, (w) T. C. Hearn.

Perry, William - Mary Lenoir, 26 Apr. 1762, Thomas Lenoir, (w) James Hall.

Peters, Samuel - Ann George, 7 Apr. 1764, John Irvin, John Morris, (w) Thomas Cavenah.

Peton, George - Rhoda Walke, 20 Mar. 1799, James Turner, (w) S. Wren.

Petway, Joseph L. - Melvina Williams, 30 Jan. 1849, William H. Skinner, (w) John Norfleet.

Petway, Dr. P. S. - Fannie T. Mercer, 7 Nov. 1862, m. 11 Nov. 1862 by James P. Simpson, M. G., (w) Irvin Thigpen.

Petway, Redding S. - Elizabeth J. Edmondson, 6 Nov. 1843, Jesse Mercer, (w) John Norfleet, Clk.

Petway, William L. - Lucy Knight, 22 May 1849, Henry Hyman, (w) John Norfleet, Clk.

Petway, William L. - Ann E. Brown, 9 July 1861, David Cobb, (w) W. A. Jones.

Petway, Willie J. - Elizabeth Ward, 10 Jan. 1842, James W. Barnes.

Pew, Benjamin - Polly Worrell, 28 Feb. 1831, Zachariah Samet, Henry W. Garrett, (w) Ml. Hearn.

Peyton, John W. - Nancy Booth, 4 Sept. 1799, John Booth, (w) S. Wren.

Philips, Andrew - Elizabeth Parker, 30 Dec. 1803, Ezekiel Phillips, (w) E. Hall.

Philips, Eaton L. - Mary Causey, 28 Sept. 1829, Charles Wilkinson, (w) Ml. Hearn.

Philips, Fred - Martha S. Hyman, 26 Jan. 1864, m. 26 Jan. 1864 by Thomas R. Owen, M. G., James S. Staton.

Philips, John - Sally Anderson, 14 Nov. 1826, James Ellinor, Jr., (w) Ml. Hearn.

Philips, Jordan - Lazina Coker, 3 Dec. 1851, m. 4 Dec. 1851 by R. Pittman, J. P., Lewis Faithful, (w) John Norfleet.

Philips, Joseph - Maria Cobb, 20 Aug. 1818, Joshua Bell, Henry Adams, (w) Ml. Hearn.

Philips, Joseph - Mary Booth, 10 Jan. 1824, Joshua Pender, (w) Ml. Hearn.

Philips, Peter - Mary Wilkins, 15 Dec. 1866, m. 23 Dec. 1866 by Hilyard S. Taylor, A. B. M. G., Joseph Page, (w) Irvin Thigpen.

Philips, Peter P. - Raney Norville, 5 Dec. 1839, Benjamin Gay.

Philips, William B. - Susan Edwards, 3 Jan. 1839, William W. Edwards, (w) Jo. Bell, C. C.

Phillips, Richard T. - Elizabeth Warren, 2 Mar. 1857, m. 3 Mar. 1857 by Bennett P. Pitt, J. P., Allen Warren, (w) J. H. Dozier.

Phillips, William H. - Mary Causey, 17 Dec. 1855, m. 18 Dec. 1855 by W. F. Lewis, J. P., Eaton L. Philips, (w) W. S. Pitt, Clk.

Philpot, Eason - Spicy Andrews, 17 Dec. 1841, Gray Andrews.

Pippen, Arthur - Polly Hudnall, 6 Feb. 1800, John Lawrence.

Pippen, E. G. - Sally Bardin, 11 Jan. 1854, m. 15 Jan. 1854 by W. Y. Moore, J. P., William Owen, (w) W. S. Pitt, Clk.

Pippen, Elisha - Letha Tolson, 11 Mar. 1822, John Booth, (w) Ml. Hearn.

Pippen, Frank - Jane Stancell, 24 Dec. 1866, m. 1 Jan. 1867 by James R. Thigpen, J. P., (w) William Biggs, Clk.

Pippen, Jeffrey - Judia Cobb, 14 Aug. 1866, m. 17 Aug. 1866 by James R. Thigpen, J. P., James R. Thigpen, (w) Irvin Thigpen.

Pippen, Joseph - Temperance Lee, 9 Feb. 1827, Henry Austin, (w) Ml. Hearn.

Pippen, Joseph John Jr. - Mary Harper, 20 July 1852, m. 20 July 1852 by Henry T. Clark, J. P., William J. Edwards, (w) John Norfleet, Clk.

Pippen, Luke - Cella (Celia?) Knight, 27 Nov. 1865, m. 27 Nov. 1865 by Jos. Blount Cheshire, Epis. Min., Jesse B. Hyatt, (w) Irvin Thigpen, Clk.

Pippen, Roderick - Lear Gardner, 27 Feb. 1845, Dawson Gardner, (w) William D. Petway.

Pippen, William M. - Mary H. Powell, 20 Mar. 1855, m. 21 Mar. 1855 by Jos. Blount Cheshire, M. G., Joseph H. Baker, (w) W. S. Pitt, Clk.

Pippin, Elisha - Nancy Stallings, 23 Dec. 1819, Ely Deal, (w) Ml. Hearn.

Pippin, James S. - Susan F. Mabray, 23 Feb. 1861, m. 27 Feb. 1861 by Thos. R. Owen, M. G., F. B. Staton, (w) W. A. Jones, Clk.

Pippin, Silas - Mamie Lewis, 15 June 1849, John Norfleet, (w) William W. Batts.

Pippen, Silas - Elizabeth Little, 28 Dec. 1835, Josiah Lawrence, (w) Ml. Hearn.

Pippin, Silas M. - Sally Ann Madrey, 9 July 1860, m. 12 July 1860 by John W. Johnson, J. P., Campbell Denton, (w) W. S. Jones, Clk.

Pitman, David - Elizabeth Anderson, 18 Mar. 1826, Jalon Ezell, Spencer L. Hart, (w) Ml. Hearn.

Pitman, Delmanutha - Margaret Forbes, 4 Jan. 1837, Willie Atkinson, (w) Ml. Hearn.

Pitman, Gresham Coffield - Polly Linch, 18 Dec. 1801, James Knight.

Pitman, Harrison - Tirzah Linch, 11 Apr. 1799, Exum Lewis.

Pitman, Jacob - Hannah Best, 19 Mar. 1764, Isaac Wilson, (w) Thos. Cavenah.

Pitman, Jesse - Rachel Horn, 26 Sept. 1765, James Jolly, (w) T. Cavenah.
Pitman, Jesse - Christian Hickmen, 19 Oct. 1765, William Hickmen, (w) Thomas Cavenah.
Pitman, John - Penelope Pitman, 23 Feb. 1827, Fredrick Etheridge, (w) Ml. Hearn.
Pitman, John - Julia Ellis, 30 Dec. 1833, (w) Ml. Hearn.
Pitman, John - Litha Tolson, 28 Oct. 1835, Dempsey Etheridge, (w) Ml. Hearn.
Pitman, Philip - Sopha Farrow, 1 Feb. 1837, John Sparkman, (w) Ml. Hearn.
Pitman, William - Nelly Hayes, 23 Dec. 1826, David Williams, (w) Ml. Hearn.
Pitman, William - Mary Ann Rose, 13 Apr. 1833, James Coker, (w) Ml. Hearn.
Pitman, Willie - Catherine Cobb, 22 June 1833, David Pender, (w) Ml. Hearn.
Pitman, Willie - Elizabeth Parker, 3 Dec. 1838, Joseph Pitman, Jo. Bell, C. C. C.
Pitt, Bennet - Nancy Fountain, 14 Jan. 1830, John P. Stewart, (w) L. H. Hearn.
Pitt, Bennett - Katura Mercer, 11 Feb. 1840, David G. Baker, (w) Jo. Bell, C. C. C.
Pitt, Bryant - Mary Ann Shurley, 25 Dec. 1862, m. 25 Dec. 1862 by William H. Knight, J. P., G. B. Jones, (w) T. W. Hussey.
Pitt, Franklin G. - Sarah A. F. Knight, 8 Oct. 1849, Irvin Thigpen, (w) John Norfleet.
Pitt, Franklin G. - Susan E. Knight, 3 Oct. 1855, m. 4 Nov. 1855 by James Carney, J. P., William T. Macnair, (w) T. M. Arrington.
Pitt, Henry B. S. - Susan A. Bennett, 18 Dec. 1847, Bolin B. Barron, (w) John Norfleet, Clk.
Pitt, James - Rebecca Atkinson, 11 Sept. 1822, Jacob Dunn, (w) Ml. Hearn.
Pitt, James - Charlotte Maner, 10 May 1828, (w) Ml. Hearn.
Pitt, James A. - Harietta Turner, 9 Sept. 1856, m. 15 Sept. 1856 by Thomas L. Maner, J. P., C. H. Jenkins, (w)——
Pitt, John - Mary Baker, 22 Jan. 1825, Robert Joyner, (w) Ml. Hearn.
Pitt, John R. - Mary Moon, 28 Jan. 1832, Guilford Stringer, (w) Ml. Hearn.
Pitt, Nathan - Emily Weaver, 14 Oct. 1841, Jeremiah Odom.

Pitt, Nathan - Mary E. Spivy, 7 Dec. 1845, Joab Price, (w) John Norfleet.

Pitt, Perry - Sarah E. Harper, 4 Sept. 1855, m. 4 Sept. 1855 by Henry T. Clark, J. P., David Knight, (w) W. S. Pitt, Clk.

Pitt, Ralph - Lucy Atkinson, 9 Feb. 1831, Theophilus Atkinson, (w) Ml. Hearn.

Pitt, Theophilus - Martha J. Blount, 18 Sept. 1866, m. 25 Sept. 1866 by J. H. Daniel, M. G., F. G. Pitt, (w) Irvin Thigpen.

Pitt, Thomas - Sarah Whitley, 11 Nov. 1865, m. 14 Nov. 1865 by Battle Bryan, J. P., Joseph Elmondson, (w) Irvin Thigpen.

Pitt, Warren - Elizabeth S. Wiggins, 2 Oct. 1847, Amos Walston, (w) Wm. Norfleet.

Pitt, William C. - Drucilla Melton, 27 Nov. 1855, m. 28 Nov. 1855 by W. E. Spicer, J. P., Cullen Melton, (w) W. S. Pitt, Clk.

Pittman, Arthur - Elizabeth Little, 12 Feb. 1831, Benjamin Little, (w) L. H. Hearn.

Pittman, Arthur - Nelly Strickland, 8 July 1851, m. 17 July 1851 by William Ellis, J. P., William Felton, (w) Benjamin Norfleet.

Pittman, Ben - Elmouth Gardner, 23 May 1854, m. 30 May 1854 by Robert Bynum, J. P., John Carter, (w) W. S. Pitt, Clk.

Pittman, Beverly T. - Elizabeth Johnson, 24 Jan. 1859, Andrew J. Moore.

Pittman, George - Penny Gardner, 23 Nov. 1847, Starlin Gardner, (w) John Norfleet, Clk.

Pittman, George - Sally A. Carr, 10 Mar. 1850, William Jenkins, (w) John Norfleet.

Pittman, Henry - Lucy Anderson, 28 Jan. 1850, Joseph Pitman, (w) John Norfleet.

Pittman, James - Nancy Price, 10 Nov. 1831, William Ellis. (w) L. H. Hearn.

Pittman, James - Elizabeth Tolbert, 26 Aug. 1856, m. 28 Aug. 1856 by L. R. Cherry, J. P., Lewis Fountain, (w) W. A. Jones, Clk.

Pittman, Joseph - Mary Edwards, 9 Oct. 1845, John Norfleet.

Pittman, Joseph W. - Nancy E. Pitt, 27 Nov. 1866, m. 5 Dec. 1866 by William F. Bell, R. E. Pittman, (w) Irvin Thigpen.

Pittman, Josiah - Sally Waller, 8 Nov. 1856, m. 11 Nov. 1856 by R. J. Johnson, J. P., James Pittman, (w) J. H. Dozier.

Pittman, Newsom - Mary Pittman, 28 Apr. 1858, m. 29 Apr. 1858 by Jos. Blount Cheshire, Epis. Min., R. Chapman, (w) W. A. Jones.

Pittman, Reden E. - Sarah E. Pitt, 27 Nov. 1866, m. 5 Dec. 1866 by William F. Bell, Joseph W. Pittman, (w) Irvin Thigpen.

Pittman, Reddin - Martha Bryan, 8 Mar. 1831, Lunsford R. Cherry, (w) Ml. Hearn.

Pittman, Theophilus - Repsy Dildy, 3 Jan. 1848, Benjamin Dildy, (w) John Norfleet, Clk.

Pittman, Thomas - Lucy Winborne, 11 June 1846, Green O'Berry, (w) John Norfleet.

Pittman, Warren - Gatsy Proctor, 9 Mar. 1853, m. 9 Mar. 1853 by R. H. Pender, J. P., Robert Petway, (w) John Norfleet.

Pittman, Wesley - Charlotte Edwards, 11 Oct. 1837, Joseph Pitman, (w) Theo. C. Hearn.

Pittman, William - Olivia Womack, 12 Sept. 1844, John Jones, (w) John Norfleet, Clk.

Pittman, William H. - Martha Knight, 16 Aug. 1841, Andrew Gunter, (w) John Norfleet, Clk.

Pittman, Willie - Charlotte Killebrew, 27 Oct. 1833, Jesse Stallings, (w) T. C. Hearn.

Ponds, Edwin - Lydia Ward, 3 Jan. 1850, William Griffin, (w) John Norfleet.

Ponds, John - Sally Dilliard, 3 June 1826, Benjamin Wilkinson, Thomas Dickinson, (w) Ml. Hearn.

Ponds, Robert - Arrena Harris, 1 Aug. 1866, m. 2 Aug. 1866 by S. L. Hart, J. P., Elias Grimmer, (w) Irvin Thigpen.

Ponds, Zachariah - Sally Lodge, 18 Nov. 1829, Jackson Griffin, (w) Ml. Hearn.

Pope, Carter - Martha A. Worsley, 5 Jan. 1864, m. 14 Jan. 1864 by Thomas L. Maner, J. P., (w) Irvin Thigpen.

Pope, Harris - Catharine Anderson, 24 Nov. 1846, Thomas O'Berry, (w) John Norfleet, Clk.

Pope, Jacob R. - Martha F. Parker, 6 Aug. 1844, Willie Bradley, (w) John Norfleet, Clk.

Pope, John W. - Eliza Taylor, 31 Jan. 1840, John H. Wells, Bryant C. Pope.

Pope, Martin - Sidney Hopkins, 28 Feb. 1854, m. 1 Mar. 1854 by Thomas L. Maner, Coffield Mason, (w) W. S. Pitt, Clk.

Pope, Pilgrim - Ollive Surgrner, 26 Jan. 1762, Edward Moore.

Pope, Woodard - Elizabeth Ellis, 25 May 1834, Roderick Amason, (w) T. C. Hearn.

Porter, Benjamin F. - Eliza King, 16 Jan. 1833, Elias Bryan, (w) T. C. Hearn.

Porter, John - Susan R. Blount, 28 Sept. 1858, m. 30 Sept. 1858 by David Cobb, J. P., John McJenkins, (w) W. A. Jones, Clk.

Porter, Joseph J. - Susan Wilkins, 15 Feb. 1837, Theophilus Bryan, (w) T. C. Hearn.

Portis, James - Caroline Horn, 25 Jan. 1855, m. 25 Jan 1855 by R. H. Pender, J. P., William B. Bell, (w) W. S. Pitt, Clk.

Portis, William - Lazina Downing, 10 Oct. 1850, George Davenport, (w) John Norfleet.

Powel, William - Sally Johnston, 17 Jan. 1829, William More, (w) Ml. Hearn.

Powell, Allen - Cinta Powell, 14 Apr. 1868, m. 18 Apr. 1868 by Thomas L. Maner, J. P., (w) Irvin Thigpen.

Powell, James - Martha Bell, 8 Nov. 1836, William Biggs, (w) Ml. Hearn.

Powell, James - Chaney Wimberly, 14 Oct. 1865, m. 14 Oct. 1865 by E. D. Macnair, J. P., Fred Philips, (w) Irvin Thigpen.

Powell, Jesse - Nancy Philips, 1 Sept. 1823, (w) Ml. Hearn, C. C.

Powell, Jesse H. - Mary Ann Battle, 12 Dec. 1857, m. 15 Dec. 1857 by W. F. Lewis, J. P., W. F. Lewis, (w) W. A. Jones, Clk.

Powell, John - Isabella Powell, 21 Dec. 1866, m. 30 Dec. 1866 by E. D. Macnair, J. P., Smith Loshad, (w) Irvin Thigpen.

Powell, Joseph - Frances Braswell, 3 Feb. 1859, m. 3 Feb. 1859 by C. B. Killebrew, J. P., John Fly, (w) W. A. Jones.

Powell, William - Rosa Boon, 12 Oct. 1865, m. 12 Oct. 1865 by L. C. Pender, J. P., Robert H. Austin, (w) Irvin Thigpen.

Powell, William H. - Anne B. Lawrence, 24 Nov. 1852, m. 24 Nov. 1852 by Thomas R. Owen, M. G., William M. Pippin, (w) John Norfleet.

Power, Edward - Abigal Coker, 26 Feb. 1800, D. Coffield, (w) J. H. Hall.

Powers, Marryman - Eliza Walston, 24 Dec. 1857, m. 27 Dec. 1858(?) by R. J. Johnson, J. P., Thomas Harriss, (w) J. H. Dozier.

Presson, James - Sarah Taylor, 15 Aug. 1799, Walker Knight, (w) S. Wren.

Price, Abraham - Martha Parker, 29 Dec. 1846, (w) W. L. Dozier.

Price, Abram - Patsey Jackson, 7 July 1823, William H. Horn, (w) Ml. Hearn.

Price, Asa - Nancy Thorn, 3 Nov. 1835, John H. Wells, (w) Ml. Hearn.

Price, Daniel - Mary Portis, 20 Mar. 1843, Joseph Stallings, (w) John Norfleet, Clk.

Price, Elijah - Elizabeth Little, 22 Dec. 1810, John Laurence, (w) Ml. Hearn.

Price, Hardy W. B. - Jacky Eliza Howell, 9 Sept. 1839, John P. Turner.

Price, Jackson - Frances Melton, 18 Aug. 1846, Epenetos G. Armstrong, (w) John Norfleet.

Price, James - Mary Ann Jackson, 29 Jan. 1828, Bythal Braswell, (w) Ml. Hearn.

Price, James J. - Ellen Bradley, 16 Apr. 1866, m. 17 Apr. 1866 by John Stamper, Henry F. Sessums, (w) Irvin Thigpen.

Price, Jesse - Elizabeth Lawrence, 16 Oct. 1823, Solomon Lawrence, (w) N. Mathewson.

Price, Joab - Milbry Landin, 18 Dec. 1824, Henry Austin, (w) Ml. Hearn.

Price, Joel - Penelope Pitt, 10 Jan. 1864, m. 19 Jan. 1864 by W. F. Lewis, J. P., Jesse Price.

Price, John - Mary Folsom, 9 Mar. 1827, Jesse Price, (w) Ml. Hearn.

Price, John H. - Martha Weeks, 9 Nov. 1859, m. 10 Nov. 1859 by W. F. Lewis, J. P., William R. Pitt, (w) W. A. Jones.

Price, John Henry - Martha Ann Sessums, 25 Apr. 1854, m. 27 Apr. 1854 by W. F. Lewis, J. P., Louis D. Johnson, (w) W. A. Jones.

Price, John W. - Elizabeth Bradley, 11 Jan. 1831, Alexander D. Bradley, (w) Ml. Hearn.

Price, Jo. John - Lewesa Price, 8 Jan. 1861, m. 10 Jan. 1861 by Thomas F. Cherry, J. P., Etheldred Pitt, (w) W. A. Jones.

Price, Joseph J. - Phoebe Ricks, 23 Nov. 1831, Henry Austin, (w) L. H. Hearn.

Price, Joseph J. - Elizabeth Ann Warren, 22 May 1852, m. 23 May, 1852 by Jordan Thigpen, J. P., David Barton, (w) John Norfleet.
Price, Moses - Sally McDade, ——— 1799, James Horn, (w) S. Wren.
Price, Purvis - Margaret Shelton, 20 Dec. 1855, m. 20 Dec. 1855 by Elisha Cromwell, J. P., H. G. Shelton, (w) W. S. Pitt, Clk.
Price, Redmond - Catherine Odom, 7 Jan. 1831, Malacha Odom, (w) L. H. Hearn.
Price, Thomas Jr. - Susan Shurly, 10 July 1848, William H. Hirn, (w) W. L. Dozier, D. C.
Price, William - Lavina Maner, 20 Dec. 1799, Joseph Price, (w) S. Wren.
Price, William - Celia Weeks, 23 Nov. 1830, Silas Wilkinson, (w) L. H. Hearn.
Price, William - Nancy Braswell, 30 Dec. 1857, m. 31 Dec. 1857 by Hilyard Taylor, A. B. M. G., Jesse Price, (w) W. A. Jones.
Price, William - Rachel Bynum, 24 Dec. 1859, m. 25 Dec. 1859 by J. I. Proctor, J. P., Jo. John Price, (w) W. A. Jones.
Price, William H. - Mary E. M. Wells, 9 June 1854, m. 13 June 1854 by Thomas L. Maner, J. P., Joseph John Price, (w) W. S. Pitt, Clk.
Pridgen, David - Amey Evans, 26 June 1763, John Evins, (w) Thomas Cavenah.
Pridgen, David - Nancy Teat, 13 Sept. 1843, James C. Marks.
Pridgen, Henry T. - Mary E. Warmick, 28 Aug. 1866, m. 29 Aug. 1866 by W. H. Powell, J. P., John Coker, (w) Irvin Thigpen.
Pridgen, Thomas - Martha Ruffin, 15 June 1763, Benjamin Bunn.
Pridgen, William - Elizabeth Land, 22 May 1854, m. 18 July 1854 by Theo. Thomas, J. P., Henry Crumply, W. S. Pitt, Clk.
Pridgeon, William - Mourning Thomas, 13 Nov. 1761, George Brown, (w) Dun. Lamon.
Pridgin, William - Harriet Hubbard, 24 Jan. 1837, Henry Austin, (w) Ml. Hearn.
Prince, Thomas M. - Lucilla Carr, 20 Aug. 1829, Richard Henry Lewis, (w) L. H. Hearn.
Prince, Turner - Sarah Foremon, 5 May 1866, m. 6 May 1866 by William H. Pitts, Elder A. M. E. Zion Church, Buckner Rogers, (w) Irvin Thigpen.

Procter, Absalom - Letha Gay, 9 Dec. 1814, John Gay, (w) Ml. Hearn.

Procter, Fredrick - Celia Taylor, 28 Dec. 1824, Newton Taylor, (w) Ml. Hearn.

Proctor, Isaac - Nancy Mosely, 4 Mar. 1857, m. 4 Mar. 1857 by Hylard S. Taylor, A. B. M. G., J. Lawrence Proctor, (w) W. A. Jones.

Procter, James - Zany Williford, 4 Aug. 1850, Coffield Dixon, (w) John Norfleet, C.

Procter, Joab - Lucy Bullock, 21 Jan. 1823, Henry Whitehead, (w) Ml. Hearn.

Procter, John - Louisa Hinton, 1 Nov. 1853, m. 1 Nov. 1853 by R. H. Pender, J. P., Alfred White, (w)———.

Procter, John J. - Leah Armstrong, 28 Feb. 1856, John H. Leigh, (w) W. A. Jones.

Procter, Jonathan - Sally Cuthen, 8 Mar. 1808, Jonas Dunn, (w) E. Hall.

Proctor, Absalom - Anzelina Moore, 4 Jan. 1841, R. R. Braswell.

Proctor, Alsy Wright Evans - Mary Frances Powell, 18 Mar. 1851, m. 20 Mar. 1851 by W. E. Spicer, J. P., (Willie) W. S. Proctor, (w) John Norfleet, Clk.

Proctor, Charles W. - Phenetta Braswell, 12 Dec. 1866, m. 13 Dec. 1866 by Hilyard S. Taylor, A. B. M. G., John Proctor, (w) Irvin Thigpen.

Proctor, Dennis - Sally Daws, 19 Mar. 1823, Ephraim Daws, (w) Ml. Hearn, C. C.

Proctor, Elisha - Eliza Lewis, 15 Jan. 1834, Geraldus Shurly, (w) T. C. Hearn.

Proctor, Hardy - Elizabeth Parker, 13 Apr. 1825, William G. Bulluck, (w) Ml. Hearn.

Proctor, Henry - Sally Boon, 15 July 1831, Daniel Land, (w) L. H. Hearn.

Proctor, Hines B. - Frances C. Ricks, 21 June 1847, Robert H. Pender, (w) John Norfleet, Clk.

Proctor, James S. - Visa Williams, 24 July 1841, Bryant Williams, (w) John Norfleet, Clk.

Proctor, John - Mourning Gardner, 9 Aug. 1799, Richard Holland, (w) S. Wren.

Proctor, John - Celia Flora, 13 May 1828, John G. Williams, James Pender, (w) Ml. Hearn.

Proctor, John - Lucinda Williford, 17 Jan. 1839, Josiah B. Williford, (w) Jo. Bell, C. C.

Proctor, Josiah - Mary Moore, 5 Nov. 1860, m. 6 Nov. 1860 by Hylard S. Taylor, A. B. M. G., William Long, (w) J. H. Dozier.

Proctor, Lawrence - Mary Moore, 18 Apr. 1848, Absalom Proctor, (w) John Norfleet.

Proctor, Orren J. - Sarah Thorn. 28 Feb. 1853, m. 28 Feb. 1853 by Wright Barnes, J. P., Wright Barnes, (w) John Norfleet.

Proctor, Orren J. - Nelly Barnes, 28 May 1855, m. 7 June 1855 by Theo. Thomas, J. P.

Proctor, Samuel D. - Elizabeth Bell, 27 May 1834, Cader Cherry, (w) T. C. Hearn.

Proctor, Thomas - Harriet Thomas, 20 Feb. 1850, William H. Thomas, (w) John Norfleet, Clk.

Proctor, Whitmel - Betsy Elizabeth Williams, 6 June 1853, m. 8 June 1853 by William F. Mercer, J. P., Baker S. Brown, (w) John Norfleet, Clk.

Proctor, William - Mourning Gay, 25 June 1827, Richard Gay, Joseph R. Lloyd, Michl. Hearn.

Proctor, William - Elizabeth Lancaster, 14 Oct. 1846, John Norfleet.

Proctor, William - Talitha Hill, 27 Apr. 1847, William H. Hines, (w) John Norfleet.

Proctor, William - Fanny P. Daws, 27 Mar. 1854, m. 28 Mar. 1854 by Theo. Thomas, J. P., David B. Knight, (w) W. A. Jones.

Proctor, William - Tamperance Faithful, 22 July 1858, m. 22 July 1858 by L. C. Pender, J. P., Jonas Walston, (w) W. A. Jones.

Proctor, William E. - Susan Wells, 29 Nov. 1849, B. G. Braswell, (w) R. H. Pender.

Proctor, Willie G. W. - Murphy Ann Proctor, 25 May 1859, m. 26 May 1859 by Hilyard S. Taylor, A. B. M. G., Jesse Bulluck, (w) W. A. Jones.

Proctor, Young - Martha Horton, 21 Jan. 1832, Abraham Price, (w) Ml. Hearn.

Purvis, John A. - Julina Howell, 5 Mar. 1849, Gray Andrews, (w) John Norfleet, Clk.

Purvis, Reuben T. - Margilly Best, 22 Feb 1848, John A. Purvis, (w) John Norfleet.

Purvis, William W. - Martha Howell, 27 Nov. 1854, m. 29 Nov. 1854 by William Hyman, J. P., Joseph Wethesbe, (w) W. S. Pitt, Clk.

Q

Qualls, William S. - Sarah W. Edmundson, 29 July 1853, Malachi Weston, (w) Benjamin Norfleet.

R

Raley, John Michael - Hannah Dawson, 26 Jan. 1767, Thomas Norman.

Randolph, Robert - Jaque A. Ruffin, 22 Dec. 1831, William Wootten, (w) Ml. Hearn.

Rascoe, Thomas W. - Penina Hyman, 27 Nov. 1832, Cannon Windham, (w) T. C. Hearn.

Rawlings, Mark - Judith Nelson, 25 July 1800, James Bracewell, (w) J. H. Hall.

Rawlings, William - Sally A. Savidge, 2 Oct. 1832, James Savidge, (w) L. H. Hearn.

Rawls, Thomas - Martha Ellis, 3 Mar. 1831, Reddic Barnes, Jr., Ml. Hearn.

Ray, Houston - Mariah Wiggin, 30 Oct. 1866, m. 9 Dec. 1866 by A. M. Lowe, M. G., John K. Cherry, (w) Irvin Thigpen.

Ray, John - Sally Corbitt, 25 Apr. 1848, William Varnall, (w) John Norfleet.

Rayner, Allen H. - Elizabeth Proctor, 11 Aug. 1832, (w) Ml. Hearn.

Rayner, John - Thaney Corbitt, 13 Jan. 1848, Charles Ellis, (w) John Norfleet.

Rayner, John - Creasy Kelly, 5 Feb. 1823, Allen Rayner, Joshua Pender, (w) Ml. Hearn.

Rayner, Lewelling - Elizabeth Worsley, 26 Dec. 1834, Josiah Lawrence, (w) Ml. Hearn.

Rayner, Willie - Susan Lewis, 7 Mar. 1837, Clemons Darden, (w) Ml. Hearn.

Read, William - Eliza Thomas, 23 May 1831, William Brown, (w) Ml. Hearn.

Read, William, Nancy Rose, 13 Oct. 1838, William Dancy, (w) William Norfleet.

Read, William - Sally Mitchell, 25 May 1849, Robert S. Pitt, (w) John Norfleet, Clk.

Reasons, Randall, Dicy Robinson, 25 Nov. 1850, John Robinson, (w) John Norfleet.

Reasons, Richard - Millicent Allen, 1 June 1846, George Thigpen, (w) John Norfleet, Clk.

Ricks, Elisha - Susannah L. Mayo, 29 Jan. 1819, Weeks P. Hadley, (w) Michl. Hearn.

Redmond, James M. - Catherine Stillman, 6 Feb. 1839, David C. Bell.

Redmund, William - Martha E. Gaiter, 13 May 1862, m. 13 May 1862 by L. C. Pender, J. P., Calvin Gaither, (w) W. A. Jones.

Reed, Arthur - Phereby Thomas, 22 Dec. 1829, Miles Reed, Joseph Kelly, (w) Ml. Hearn.

Reed, Bryant - Elizabeth Ann Brown, 24 Dec. 1859, m. 25 Dec. 1859 by J. R. Pitt, J. P., Edwin Jones, (w) W. A. Jones.

Reed, David - Penelope Brown, 22 Dec. 1835, John Carter, (w) Ml. Hearn.

Reed, Hardy - Emeliza Simpson, 18 Feb. 1830, John Ellis, (w) Ml. Hearn.

Reed, Joel - Louisa Reed, 8 May 1857, m. 10 May 1857 by Theo. Atkinson, J. P., David Pender, (w) W. A. Jones.

Reed, Miles - Patsy Thomas, 10 Jan. 1844, John Carter, (w) John Norfleet, Clk.

Reid, David C. (s. of Willis Reid) - Vester Garvey (dau. of James T. Garvey), m. 30 Jan. 1868 by D. T. Towles, M. G.

Reid, James - Catherine Howell, 15 Feb. 1855, m. 15 Feb. 1855 by Aaron Davis, Thomas O'berry, (w) W. S. Pitt, Clk.

Reid, Miles - Mary Hagons, 22 Dec. 1853, m. 17 Jan. 1854 by J. R. Pitt, J. P., William H. Harrell, (w) W. S. Pitt.

Revel, Humphrey - Dilly Hammonds, 28 Dec. 1811, Barnabus Revel, (w) Ml. Hearn.

Revel, William N. - Phebe Brake, 19 Sept. 1832, Henry Johnston, (w) Ml. Hearn.

Revell, Elijah H. - Susannah Hamons, 5 Apr. 1833, Willie Malone, (w) T. C. Hearn.

Rhodes, Archebold - Louisa Battle, 13 Nov. 1854, m. 14 Nov. 1854 by Thomas J. Lathain, M. G., Thomas C. Davis, (w) Joshua Barnes.

Rhodes, Edmund H. - Catherine T. Pettaway, 27 Nov. 1826, Micajah Petway, (w) Ml. Hearn.

Richard, William - Ann Maria Redmond, 9 Nov. 1846, Greenberry Causey.

Richardson, Dick - Nancy Caroline Landing, 23 Dec. 1858, m. 24 Dec. 1858 by James H. Hyman, J. P., Elisha Landing, (w) J. H. Dozier.

Richardson, Thomas - Sarah Eason, 27 Mar. 1763, Mathias Manning, (w) Thomas Cavenah.

Ricks, Isaac W. - Mary Jane Pender, 25 Dec. 1849, William F. Mercer, (w) John Norfleet, Clk.

Ricks, James - Mary Crudup, 23 July 1762, James Oliver.

Ricks, James - Pheebe Horn, 29 Sept. 1770, James Ricks, William McClellan, (w) J. Hall.

Ricks, John - Esther Ross (widow), 13 July 176 (3?), George Wimberly, (w) J. Hall.

Ricks, John C. - Mary Ann Warren, 26 Feb. 1857, m. 1 Mar. 1857 by L. S. Burkhead, M. G., Thomas D. Gay, (w) W. A. Jones, Clk.

Ricks, John W. - Nancy Jackson, 22 June 1833, Abraham Price, (w) Ml. Hearn.

Ricks, Robert - Frances A. Fort, 4 Oct. 1844, Reddin Daughtry.

Ricks, William - Mahala Williford, 4 Apr. 1856, m. 7 Apr. 1857 by L. S. Burkhead, M. G., William Ricks, (w) J. H. Dozier.

Ricks, William - Mary Ann Johnson, 3 Jan. 1861, m. 3 Jan. 1861 by E. D. Macnair, J. P., Thomas W. Hussey, (w) W. A. Jones, Clk.

Ricks, William B. - Elenora Barnes, 12 June 1846, John W. Ricks, (w) John Norfleet.

Ricks, William B. - Elenora Barnes, 8 Mar. 1847, Isaac Robbins.

Ricks, Willie - Polly Brake, 7 Oct. 1824, Dorris Brake, (w) N. Matthewson.

Riley, William - Martha Gardner, 7 Apr. 1854, Cullen Pender.

Ritter, Bennett H. - Sally Ricks, 27 Feb. 1840, Dempsey Trevathan, (w) Jo. Bell, C. C.

Ritter, Elisha - Celia Brown, 23 Feb. 1836, William Jenkins, (w) T. C. Hearn.

Ritter, Lewis - Elizabeth Coletrain, 20 Apr. 1836, Joab P. Pitt, (w) T. C. Hearn.

Ritter, Lewis - Martha Carr, 18 Nov. 1850, Willie Harrell, (w) John Norfleet, Jesse Harrell.

Rives, John G. - Lucy D. Foxhall, 20 Sept. 1848, David Barlow, (w) John Norfleet, Clk.

Robards, William H. - Ann Elisa Toole, 11 Dec. 1827, Nathan Mathewson, (w) Ml. Hearn.

Robards, William P. - Clary Ann Adams, 4 Dec. 1832, Thomas D. Gatlin, (w) Theodore C. Hearn.

Robberson, Joshua - Elizabeth Forbs, 27 July 1839, (w) Jo. Bell, C. C.

Robbins, Arthur - Treacy Barnes, 26 May 1824, Fredrick F. Robbins, (w) Ml. Hearn.
Robbins, Benjamin - Charity Amason, 17 Oct. 1831, Theophilus Gay, (w) Ml. Hearn.
Robbins, Birt - Amanda Land, 4 May 1854, O'berry Cromply, (w) W. S. Pitt, Clk.
Robbins, Cornelius - Polly Williams, 21 Jan. 1853, m. 30 Jan. 1853 by Theo. Thomas, J. P., Elza Taylor, (w) John Norfleet.
Robbins, Duncan - Peninah Barnes, 18 Feb. 1831, Bird Land, (w) Ml. Hearn.
Robbins, Edwin - Nancy Moore, 17 Dec. 1845, William Armstrong, (w) John Norfleet.
Robbins, Isaac - Catherine Daws, 3 Jan. 1828, John Daws, (w) Ml. Hearn.
Robbins, Isaac - Mary Catherine Jackson, 7 Feb. 1859, m. 16 Feb. 1859 by Hillard S. Taylor, A. B. M. G., Isaac Robbins, (w) W. A. Jones.
Robbins, Jacob D. - Frances Ann Skinner, 10 Nov. 1837, Jacob Robbins, (w) Jo. Bell.
Robbins, James W. - Nancy Draughon, 20 Dec. 1830, Stephen Robbins, (w) Ml. Hearn.
Robbins, John W. - Rebecca Jackson, 7 July 1831, Isaac Robbins, (w) L. H. Hearn.
Robbins, John W. - Louisa H. Braswell, 17 Feb. 1846, Isaac Robbins, (w) John Norfleet, Clk.
Robbins, John - Temperance Tomlinson, 21 Dec. 1827, Robert Whitehead, (w) Ml. Hearn.
Robbins, John D. - Evilina Weaver, 7 Feb. 1859, m. 8 Feb. 1859 by Hylard S. Taylor, A. B. M. G., Isaac Robbins, (w) W. A. Jones.
Robbins, Jordan - Eliza Barnes, 22 Dec. 1834, Duncan Robbins, (w) Ml. Hearn.
Robbins, Starky - Elizabeth Flood, 25 Jan. 1860, m. 26 Jan. 1860 by R. H. Gatlin, J. P., Duffy Hill, (w) W. A. Jones.
Robbins, Simon - Patsy Morriss, 28 Nov. 1836, Nathan Morriss, (w) T. C. Hearn.
Robbins, Stephen Jr. - Lovey Taylor, 29 Dec. 1827, Stephen Robbins, Sr., (w) Ml. Hearn.
Robbins, Warren B. - Thaney Whitehead, 12 Sept. 1865, m. 14 Sept. 1865 by H. S. Taylor, A. B. M. G., D. L. Williams, (w) Irvin Thigpen.
Robbins, William - Milly Woody, 26 Oct. 1830, Elijah Robbins, (w) Ml. Hearn.

Robbins, William Jr. - Martha Farmer, 29 Aug. 1799, William Robbins Sr., (w) S. Wren.

Robbins, William, Jr. - Talitha White, 13 Sept. 1823, Stephen Robbins, (w) Ml. Hearn.

Robbins, Willie - Elizabeth Proctor, 4 Aug. 1849, Henry Robbins, John Norfleet, Clk.

Robbins, Willie H. R. S. - Sally L. Farmer, 13 Jan. 1852, m. 25 Jan. 1852 by John W. Farmer, J. P., Augustin Farmer, (w) Benjamin Norfleet.

Roberson, Jonathan - Nancy Peoples, 13 Nov. 1826, Elijah Roberson, (w) Ml. Hearn.

Robertson, John J. - Martha E. Bradley, 29 Apr. 1865, Joseph J. Alston, (w) T. W. Hussey.

Robertson, Robert F. - Mary E. Wilson, 17 June 1868, m. 18 June 1868 by J. H. Daniel, John H. Daniel, (w) Irvin Thigpen.

Robins, Arthur - Penelope Sellers, 14 Apr. 1764, Thomas Dixon, (w) J. Hall.

Robins, Elisha - Rachael R. C. Robins, 6 Jan. 1857, m. 6 Jan. 1857 by Hilard Taylor, M. G., Isaac Robins, (w) J. H. Dozier.

Robins, Willie - Sallie Ann Williams, 6 Feb. 1856, m. 7 Feb. 1856 by William F. Mercer, J. P., John C. Robbins, (w) W. S. Pitt, Clk.

Robinson, Andrew J. - Caroline Philips, 9 Dec. 1847, Henry T. Clark, (w) John Norfleet.

Robinson, David - Amelia Dunn, 1 May 1843, Elijah Robinson, (w) R. Norfleet.

Robinson, John - Delphia Reasons, 26 Aug. 1851, m. 30 Aug. 1851 by Bennett Pitt, J. P., Joshua Roberson, (w) John Norfleet.

Rochester, John (alias Rogester) - Martha Ann Freeman, 25 Apr. 1851, m. 27 Apr. 1851 by Blount Cooper, M. G., Theophilus Blann, (w) John Norfleet, Clk.

Rodgers, John - Polly O'day, 23 July 1843, Wester Rodgers, (w) John Norfleet, Clk.

Rodgers, John A. - Deliza Eason, 12 Jan. 1847, Alfred J. Ellis, (w) John Norfleet, Clk.

Rodgers, Pelich - Elizabeth Allen, 5 Jan. 1764, John Hoxie, (w) John Spendelow.

Rogers, Buck - Betsey Ann Hussey, 29 May, 1849, J. C. Holt.

Rogers, Calvin - Jane Ellis, 29 Apr. 1844, Jonathan Page, (w) John Norfleet.

Rogers, Pegleg - Mary Ann Exum, 24 Sept. 1852, m. 26 Oct. 1852 by Lunsford R. Cherry, J. P., Peter Forbes, (w) John Norfleet, Clk.

Rogers, Redmund - Mary E. Philips, 3 Mar. 1855, A. J. Cotton.

Rogers, Robert - Ann Woods, 26 May 1764, Thomas Holland, (w) Edward Hall.

Rogers, William - Thruby Harris, 25 ——, 1835, James E. Lewis, (w) Ml. Hearn.

Rogers, Willie - Olive Wasdon, 27 May 1819, James B. Woodard, (w) Ml. Hearn.

Rogester, James - Patsey Drew, 29 Aug. 1822, John Drew, Thomas Watson, Jr., (w) Ml. Hearn.

Rogister, John - Sarah Roberts, 16 June 1866, m. 17 June 1866 by Joseph Blount Cheshire, Epis. Min., Willie Hammond, (w) Irvin Thigpen.

Rogister, William - Catherine Lawrence, 4 Sept. 1866, John H. Best, (w) Irvin Thigpen.

Rose, Bennett - Rosa Trevathan, 19 May 1829, Jonas Trevathan, (w) Ml. Hearn.

Rose, Duke - Mary Exum, 13 Mar. 1855, m. 15 Mar. 1855 by W. F. Lewis, J. P., James H. Dozier, (w) W. A. Jones.

Rose, John - Elizabeth Landing, 19 Dec. 1842, William H. Wells.

Rose, Micajah - Celia Trevathan, 28 Dec. 1836, John H. Wells, (w) T. C. Hearn.

Rose, Micajah - Penelope Landing, 21 Oct. 1843, John Rose, Joseph Landing, (w) John Norfleet.

Rose, Timothy G. - Amanda M. Philips, 9 Sept. 1852, m. 9 Sept. 1852 by W. F. Lewis, J. P., Weldon S. Hunter, (w) Benjamin Norfleet.

Rose, William C. - Malvina J. Vick, 30 Apr. 1866, m. 3 May 1866 by Thomas L. Maner, J. P., Edwin T. Gardner, (w) Irvin Thigpen.

Ross, Ezekiel - Elizabeth Cross, 11 Sept. 1799, Jacob Green, (w) S. Wren.

Rountree, Benajah - Mary Johnston, 22 Dec. 1827, Thomas Johnston, Amos Johnston, (w) Ml. Hearn.

Rountree, Calvin - Rebecca Robbins, 7 Apr. 1852, m. 20 Apr. 1852 by Joshua Barnes, J. P., Augustin Farmer, (w) John Norfleet.

Rountree, Jonathan D. - Malvina E. Gill, 9 Mar. 1847, Robert S. Adams, (w) John Norfleet, Clk.

Rountree, Lewis D. - Martha E. Braswell, 9 Aug. 1858, Lewis D. Rountree.

Rountree, Nathan H. - Emeliza Bell, 10 Dec. 1832, Daniel Knight, (w) Ml. Hearn.

Rouse, Joshua - Anna E. T. Thigpen (wid.), 18 Dec. 1855, m. 18 Dec. 1855 by Elisha Cromwell, J. P., William I. Staton, (w) W. S. Pitt, Clk.

Rowe, Robert H. - Mary S. C. Bond, 23 Dec. 1852, m. 23 Dec. 1852 by Thomas R. Owen, M. G., James Mehegan, (w) Benjamin Norfleet.

Ruffin, A. J. - Mary Ann E. Pittman, 21 Apr. 1868, m. 21 April 1868 by S. L. Hart, J. P., (w) Irvin Thigpen, C. C. C.

Ruffin, Benjamin - Pressy Bealand, 10 Feb. 1835, Duncan Flowers, (w) T. C. Hearn.

Ruffin, David - Louisiana Daughtry, 29 Mar. 1851, m. 30 Mar. 1851 by Theo. Thomas, J. P., Elisha Thomas, (w) John Norfleet, Clk.

Ruffin, Dickerson - Martha Ann Billups, 27 Sept. 1847, David Allsbrook, (w) E. D. Macnair.

Ruffin, Frederick - Sukey Clark, 19 Feb. 1823, Reading Sugg, (w) Ml. Hearn.

Ruffin, Gray L. - Mourning Winstead, 8 Jan. 1849, Zadock R. Braswell, (w) John Norfleet, Clk.

Ruffin, James - Lucinda Cobb, 26 Feb. 1830, James Stallings (or Staley), (w) Ml. Hearn.

Ruffin, Jesse - Sarah Stephenson, 1 Jan. 1800, John Ruffin, (w) S. Wren.

Ruffin, John D. - Mary Ann Edna Mercer, 26 Feb. 1856, m. 4 Mar. 1856 by W. Y. Moore, J. P., Dennis Mercer, (w) W. A. Jones, D. C.

Ruffin, Lamon - Eliza Powell, 12 Mar. 1832, Benjamin Wilkinson, (w) Ml. Hearn.

Ruffin, Lemon (Lamon?) - Elizabeth Jones, 11 Feb. 1829, Benjamin Wilkinson, (w) Ml. Hearn.

Ruffin, Lamon Jr. - Treacy White, 9 Jan. 1813, James Thomas, (w) Ml. Hearn.

Ruffin, Samuel H. - Charity Boon, 20 May 1858, m. 20 May 1858 by Hilliard S. Taylor, A. B. M. G., (w) W. A. Jones.

Ruffin, Samuel - Martha Ann Jordan, 22 Jan. 1861, m. 24 Jan. 1861 by Hillard S. Taylor, A. B. M. G., C. H. Jordan, (w) W. A. Jones, Clk.

Ruffin, Thomas - Lisandy Wilson, 7 Jan. 1841, S. D. Proctor, (w) John Proctor, Clk.

Ruffin, William H. - Martha J. Ruffin, 18 Dec. 1856, m. 18 Dec. 1856 by Thomas Norfleet, J. P., Lemon Atkinson, (w) J. H. Dozier.

Ruffin, William J. - Felicia Little, 12 Jan. 1824, Samuel Ruffin.

Ruffin, William J. - Martha Fleetwood, 20 Feb. 1826, William Tyson, (w) Ml. Hearn.

Rutter (Ritter?), John - Susan Reasons, 15 Jan. 1859, m. 16 Jan. 1859 by R. J. Johnson, Martin Gardner, (w) J. H. Dozier.

S

Samson, James - Rebecca J. Cadett, 13 Feb. 1864, m. 18 Feb. 1864 by Joseph Blount Cheshire, Epis. Min., Thomas W. Hussey.

Sanders, W. H. - Jane Sutton, 26 Feb. 1865, m. by W. B. Jordan, J. P., Charles C. Fleming, (w) Irvin Thigpen.

Sasnett, Zachariah - Peninah Sessums, 27 Jan. 1830, (w) L. H. Hearn.

Sasnett, Zachariah - Lucy Morgan, 27 Dec. 1830, Joseph Morgan, Warren Waller, (w) L. H. Hearn.

Sassnett, R. B. - Martha Grimes, Oct. 1843, ——— (No wit.).

Sassnett, Henry - Caroline Pitt, 17 Nov. 1847, William Lodge, (w) John Norfleet.

Sassnett, Reddin B. (of Pitt Co.) - Jane Mayo, 31 July 1852, m. 1 Aug. 1852 by Jesse Harrell, Jr., Allen Mayo (of Pitt Co.), (w) Benj. Norfleet.

Saul, Abraham - Anna Screw, 1 Dec. 1762, John Evans, (w) John Spendelow.

Saunders, John F. - Martha Edmundson, 25 Sept. 1847, James P. Edmundson, (w) William Norfleet.

Savadge, Britton - Angelina Savadge, 13 June 1832, Charles Mabry, (w) T. C. Hearn.

Savage, Allen - Sally Haynes, 23 Jan. 1804, Eaton Haynes, (w) E. Hall.

Savage, Burrell - Elizabeth Pender, 18 July 1865, m. 20 July 1865 by Battle Bryan, J. P., H. A. Shurley, (w) Irvin Thigpen.

Savage, Bythal - Mahala A. Alford, 4 July 1860, m. 5 July 1860 by William F. Bell, John T. Worrell, (w) W. A. Jones, Clk.

Savage, Frederick - Martha Downing, 12 May 1857, m. 13 May 1857 by Kenneth Thigpen, J. P., Kenneth Thigpen, (w) J. H. Dozier.

Savage, Harry - Luvenia Downing, 1 Jan. 1866, m. 2 Jan. 1866 by W. F. Bell, Jasper Savage, (w) Irvin Thigpen.

Savage, Henry - Sally Ann Savage, 17 Jan. 1838, Jacob Laurence, (w) Jo. Bell.

Savage, Isaac - Polly Pender, 13 Dec. 1823, Micajah Anderson, (w) Ml. Hearn.

Savage, James - Pherabe Laurence, 16 July 1844, Blount Bryan, (w) John Norfleet.

Savage, James D. - Jane F. Johnston, 3 Oct. 1853, m. 6 Oct. 1853 by Jordan Thigpen, J. P., Augustus Dun, (w) W. S. Pitt.

Savage, Jessy T. - Eliza Downing, 19 Dec. 1865, m. 20 Dec. 1865 by Eld. W. F. Bell, W. R. Savage, (w) Irvin Thigpen.

Savage, John - Hettie Staton, 23 June 1866, John Owen, (w) Irvin Thigpen.

Savage, John B. - Rebecca J. Bryan, 12 Apr. 1850, James L. Battle, (w) Benjamin Norfleet.

Savage, John H. - Pennina Savage, 21 Jan. 1861, m. 22 Jan. 1861 by William F. Bell, James H. Staton, (w) T. W. Hussey.

Savage, Joseph - Jane Stallings, 29 Dec. 1858, m. 30 Dec. 1858 by W. F. Lewis, J. P., Eliga K. Nevill, (w) W. A. Jones, Clk.

Savage, Raymond - Harriett Sevanner, 3 Mar. 1866, W. R. Savage, (w) Irvin Thigpen.

Savage, Richard A. - Sarah Louise Mabrey (Widow), 6 Mar. 1860, m. by Henry T. Clark, J. P., F. D. Foxhall, (w) J. H. Dozier.

Savage, Richard H. - Janie (James?) M. Killebrew, 16 May 1848, William H. Hines, (w) John Norfleet, Clk.

Savage, Sherrod - Mary Sessums, 31 Jan. 1800, Allen Davis, (w) S. Wren.

Savage, Solomon - Martha Brady, 13 Sept. 1763, Solomon Braswell, (w) J. Hall.

Savage, Wesley - Catherine Stallings, 23 Feb. 1857, m. 25 Mar. 1857 by John L. Michaux, James H. Griffin, (w) W. A. Jones, Clk.

Savedge, James H. - Catherine Barfield, 12 Aug. 1834, John Barfield, Jr., (w) T. C. Hearn.

Savidge, Absalom - Martha Laurence, 26 Sept. 1764, John Laurence, (w) Tho. Cavenah.

Savidge, Brittain - Lucinda Crisp, 26 Apr. 1830, Charles Mabrey, (w) Ml. Hearn.

Savidge, Sherwood - Nancy Atkins, 13 Mar. 1826, Drewry Pender, (w) Ml. Hearn.
Savidge, Thomas - Elizabeth Harrell, 9 Oct. 1828, Britain Howell, (w) Ml. Hearn.
Savidge, Warren - Wealthy Boyt, 23 Sept. 1823, Fred Bell, (w) Ml. Hearn.
Savidge, Warren - Routh Cutchin, 26 Nov. 1825, Kenneth Bembry, (w) Ml. Hearn.
Sawyer, Hardy - Delilah Hawkins, 20 Oct. 1834, Elza Hawkins, (w) Michl. Hearn.
Sawyer, Isaac - Winnifred Griffin, 12 May 1830, David Matthews, (w) L. H. Hearn.
Scarborough, James - Martha Eason, 26 Nov. 1823, Samuel Ruffin.
Scarbrio, Isaac - Nancy Tyson, 13 Sept. 1848, Lewis Dildy, (w) John Norfleet, C.
Schutte, Henry - Amelia Zoeller, 19 Aug. 1863, m. 20 Aug. 1863 by J. H. Daniel, Sr., Edward Zoeller, (w) Irvin Thigpen.
Screws, Henry - Lydia Sauls, 11 June 1766, Thomas Denton, (w) James Hall.
Sears, Charles E. - Delphia D. Draughn, 20 Feb. 1856, m. 20 Feb. 1856 by Jeremiah Johnson, M. G., N. W. Arrington, Jr., (w) William S. Pitt, Clk.
Seay, George - Julia Wilkerson, 16 Nov. 1859, m. 17 Nov. 1859 by Thomas R. Owen, M. G., Orren Williams, (w) J. H. Dozier.
Sessoms, Richard - Julian Ruffin, 26 Jan. 1856, W. A. Jones.
Sessums, Richard - Laura Lane, 27 Feb. 1861, m. 28 Feb. 1861 by R. H. Cotton, J. P., Ashly Vick, (w) W. A. Jones.
Sessoms, Wilson - Mary Foxhall, 25 Aug. 1834, Drew Bryan, (w) T. C. Hearn.
Sessums, Alunson P. - Talitha Canady, 17 July 1837, (w) M. L. Hearn.
Sessums, Jacob - Elizabeth Harper, 19 Dec. 1836, William Dancy, (w) M. L. Hearn.
Sessums, Nathan H. - Eliza Killebrew, 12 Feb. 1835, Alonson P. Sessums, (w) Ml. Hearn.
Sessums, Nathan H. - Martha Harris, 10 June 1857, m. 11 June 1857 by Thomas Norfleet, J. P., Irvin Howell, (w) W. A. Jones, Clk.
Sessums, William W. - Priscilla Alsobrook, 9 Jan. 1852, m. 11 Jan. 1852 by L. C. Pender, J. P., Joseph Stallings, (w) John Norfleet, Clk.

Shallington, David P. - Penne Barnes, 22 Oct. 1838, Willie Bridgers.

Sharp, Abraham T. - Elizabeth Taylor, 24 June, 1835, Benjamin Sharpe, (w) Ml. Hearn.

Sharp, Benjamin - Mary Ann Edwards, 22 Nov. 1838, John Morgan, (w) Jo. Bell, C. C.

Sharp, Benjamin W. - Martha R. Pender, 19 Aug. 1828, Thomas Sharp, Jr., (w) Ml. Hearn.

Sharp, Benjamin W. - Martha Barnes, 31 Dec. 1833, Benj. Sharp, (w) M. L. Hearn.

Sharp, David - Emily Sharp, 6 Mar. 1855, m. 8 Mar. 1855 by Alexander Gattis, E. H. Flowers, (w) W. S. Pitt, Clk.

Sharp, John - Margaret Taylor, 2 Jan. 1829, Stephen Robbins, (w) Ml. Hearn.

Sharp, John - Nancy Todd, 7 May 1837, Thomas Sharp, (w) T. C. Hearn.

Sharp, John - Mazy Wells, 16 Nov. 1854, John B. Wells, (w) W. S. Pitt, Clk.

Sharp, Thomas - Annis Taylor, 14 Aug. 1827, Isaac Robbins, Henry Austin, (w) M. L. Hearn.

Sharpe, Eason - Barsheba Flora, 18 May 1846, Willie G. Barnes, (w) John Norfleet.

Sharpe, Edward P. - Martha A. Belcher, 17 Oct. 1864, m. 18 Oct. 1864 by E. A. Yates, M. G., W. B. Harper, (w) Irvin Thigpen, Clk.

Sharpe, Gray B. - Nancy Farmer, 6 Dec. 1852, m. 7 Dec. 1852 by Joshua Barnes, J. P., Jonathan T. Dew, (w) John W. Farmer.

Sharpe, James B. - Elizabeth Howell, 1 Nov. 1857, m. 1 Nov. 1859(?) by Jos. H. Hyman, J. P. John H. Edwards, (w) W. A. Jones.

Sharpe, John P. - Nancy Bynum, 3 June 1844, Louis D. Wilson.

Sharpe, Moses B. - Mary Ann Gill, 13 June 1843, Samuel F. Sharpe.

Sharpe, Van Buren - Emily Cobb, 16 Dec. 1857, m. 17 Dec. 1857 by William A. Ross, Joseph H. Payne, (w) J. H. Dozier.

Shaw, Curtis - Clarecey Bonner, 6 June 1866, m. 9 June 1866 by C. C. Bonner, J. P., R. A. Watson, (w) Irvin Thigpen.

Shields, Robert - Sidney Parker, 29 Dec. 1865, J. B. Coffield, (w) Irvin Thigpen.

Shelton, Burrell - Sarah Booth, 10 July 1829, (w) L. H. Hearn.

Shelton, Henry G. - Margarett Little, 11 Dec. 1855, m. 13 Dec. 1855 by Elisha Cromwell, J. P., William Shelton, (w) T. M. Arrington.

Shelton, John - Elizabeth Connor, 17 Mar. 1825, William Shelton, (w) M. L. Hearn.

Shelton, Pheasanton - Polly Mayo, 4 Oct. 1848, John Mayo, Jr., William Shelton, (w) John Norfleet.

Shelton, Pheasanton - Martha Ann Deal, 27 Aug. 1861, William Shelton, (w) W. A. Jones.

Shelton, William - Caroline Shelton, 25 Feb. 1845, John Shelton.

Sherrod, Albert - Harriet Sherrod, 13 Jan. 1866, m. 15 Jan. 1866 by W. F. Bell, G. L. Lilley, (w) Irvin Thigpen.

Sherrod, Geraldus - Lucindy Taylor, 19 Feb. 1840, William Taylor, (w) Jo. Bell, C. C.

Sherrod, John - Elizabeth Savidge, 15 Dec. 1829, Nathan H. Rountree, (w) L. H. Hearn.

Sherrod, Reddin - Martha Pender, 13 Nov. 1855, m. 14 Nov. 1855 by L. C. Pender, J. P., Isaac Brinn, (w) W. A. Jones.

Sherrod, Redmond - Temperence Barnes, 22 Apr. 1825, Simon Robbins, (w) M. L. Hearn.

Sherrod, William W. - Margarett E. Hyman, 9 Nov. 1858, m. 11 Nov. 1858 by H. H. Gibbons, M. G., James M. Earl, (w) W. A. Jones, Clk.

Sherrod, John H. - Sarah E. Tart, 2 Aug. 1824, John A. Irvin, Jr.

Sherwood, James - Lucinda Pender, 24 Jan. 1861, m. 24 Jan. 1861 by L. C. Pender, J. P., William H. Tolston, (w) J. H. Dozier.

Shirley, Henry A. - Lewisa Horn, 3 June 1858, m. 3 June 1858 by Henry T. Clark, J. P., W. W. Gay, (w) W. A. Jones, Clk.

Shirley, Nathan - Martha Fort, 21 Aug. 1839, Henry Morgan, (w) Jo. Bell, C. C.

Shirley, Nathan - Penny Bilberry, 8 Jan. 1859, m. 9 Jan. 1859 by L. C. Pender, J. P., William Shirley, (w) W. A. Jones, Clk.

Shollington, William E. J. - Jilly Barnes, 29 Nov. 1843, James J. Taylor, (w) John Norfleet, Clk.

Shollington, William H. - Rhoda Pender, 23 Feb. 1811, David Forhand, (w) Ml. Hearn.

Shurley, Bird - Louisiana Edwards, 11 Mar. 1826, Benjamin Marley, (w) M. L. Hearn.

Shurley, Geraldus - Temperance Amason, 14 Feb. 1827, Solomon Pender, (w) M. L. Hearn.

Shurley, Geraldus - Susan Bridgers, 13 Jan. 1841. (No wit.)

Shurley, Nathan - Mary Ann Brake, 31 Jan. 1825, Joshua K. Bulluck, Joseph Morgan, (w) M. L. Hearn.

Shurley, Nathan - Lucy Johnson, 20 June 1828, Samuel Ruffin, (w) Ml. Hearn.

Shurley, Nathan - Polly Johnson, 6 May 1846, Cullen Pender, (w) John Norfleet.

Shurley, William - Delha Thomas, 24 Dec. 1855, m. 26 Dec. 1855 by L. C. Pender, J. P., Calvin Gaitor, (w) W. S. Pitt, Clk.

Sikes, Bassett - Mary Ann Edwards, 24 Sept. 1830, Riley Stokes, (w) L. H. Hearn.

Simmons, Willoughby - Maria Braddy, 18 Mar. 1826, Coffield King, John Sprivey, (w) M. L. Hearn.

Simms, Robert - Sally Horn, 26 Nov. 1823, Elnathan Tart, N. Mathewson.

Simpson, James P. - Nancy Williams, 25 Nov. 1862, m. 25 Nov. 1862 by Charles F. Deems, R. H. Garrett, (w) T. W. Hussey.

Singletary, Richard W. - Mary Pitt, 12 Oct. 1865, Robert C. Brown, (w) Irvin Thigpen.

Singleton, Adam - Winny Faircloth, 25 Feb. 1831, Brittain Edwards, (w) L. H. Hearn.

Sinyear, William - Tillitha Grimes, 21 Jan. 1839, Benjamin C. Mayo, (w) Jo. Bell, C. C.

Sizer, Robert A. - Caroline M. Bell, 22 Sept. 1857, m. 23 Sept. 1857 by L. S. Burkhead, Meth. Min., Thomas U. Gatlin, (w) Wm. A. Jones, Clk.

Skinner, Andrew J. - Arsenia Fleming, 29 Mar. 1841, Jesse L. Fleming, (w) John Norfleet, Clk.

Skinner, H. C. - Elizabeth Cotton, 28 Oct. 1865, m. 2 Nov. 1865 by John Ws. Johnson, J. P., Jordan W. Johnson, (w) Irvin Thigpen.

Skinner, Henry - Charlotte Webb, 1 Jan. 1849,.Starky Howard, (w) John Norfleet, Clk.

Skinner, Hiram - Elizabeth Hicks, 24 Jan. 1827, Gardner Skinner, (w) M. L. Hearn.

Skinner, Immanuel - Milly Jenkins, 20 Jan. 1830, James Dunford, John Skinner, (w) L. H. Hearn.

Skinner, James C. - Obedience Weaver, 1 Jan. 1844, Willie G. Barnes, (w) R. Norfleet.

Skinner, John - Penninah Sessums, 14 Mar. 1831, William Webb, (w) L. H. Hearn.

Skinner, John - Emily Weaver, 22 Aug. 1860, m. 23 Aug. 1860 by E. D. Macnair, J. P., Lemuel N. Landin, (w) W. A. Jones.

Skinner, William - Rebecca Gill, 17 Feb. 1829, Silas Ward, (w) Ml. Hearn.

Skinner, William - Junnetta Webb, 3 Oct. 1845, David Walston, (w) John Norfleet.

Smith, Abel - Fannie Parker, 29 Mar. 1844, Amraphel Beeman, (w) John Norfleet, C. C.

Smith, Alexander - Susan R. Edwards, 14 Jan. 1860 (?) m. 9 Jan. 1860 by Bennett P. Pitt, J. P., R. T. Eagles, (w) W. A. Jones, Clk.

Smith, Arthur C - Frances Sugg, 4 Dec. 1854, m. 5 Dec. 1854 by James H. Brent, James H. Brent, (w) W. S. Pitt, Clk.

Smith, Eugene D. - Elizabeth Hanks, 27 Nov. 1866, m. 28 Nov. 1866 by Joseph Blount Cheshire, Epis. Min., Robert Whitehurst, (w) Irvin Thigpen.

Smith, George W. - Sarah Mears, 2 Nov. 1862, m. 7 Dec. 1862 by Theo. Thomas, J. P., Joshua Killebrew, (w) Irvin Thigpen.

Smith, Lemuel - Ann Little, 19 June 1844, David Neale, (w) John Norfleet.

Smith, Moses - Nancy Hodges, 14 May 1800, Smith Bryan, (w) J. H. Hall.

Smith, Moses - Annetta Wilkinson, 27 Aug. 1850, Nathan G. Pitt, (w) John Norfleet. C.

Smith, Sipha - Susan Webb, 19 Dec. 1842, Lewis Howell, (w) John Norfleet, Clk.

Smith, Thomas - Nancy Gardner, 23 Apr. 1823, John Parker, Exum L. Lowe, John Williams, Weeks P. Hadley, William Harrell, (w) Ml. Hearn.

Smith, Thomas - Elizabeth Brown, 26 May 1857, m. 26 May 1857 by W. Y. Moore, J. P., H. Belcher, (w) W. A. Jones, Clk.

Smith, William - Finetta Thigpen, 24 Jan. 1835, Littleberry Brown, (w) Ml. Hearn.

Smith, William - Sally Riddick, 8 Jan. 1861 by Wm. Harrell, J. P., Willie Edmondson, (w) W. A. Jones.

Smith, William R. - Susan Evans, 17 Dec. 1827, Jonas J. Carr, (w) Ml. Hearn.

Snakenburg, William - Delpha J. Gardner, 17 Nov. 1862. m. 18 Nov. 1862 by Thomas R. Owen, V. D. M., George Gardner, (w) John H. Mathewson.

Sorey, Josiah - Sally Vann, 23 Dec. 1822, Bernard Cowell, (w) Ml. Hearn.

Sorey, Josiah - Celia Womble, 17 Aug. 1830, (w) Ml. Hearn.

Sorey, Robert - Ann Wiggins, 16 June 1849, Dempsey Trevathan, (w) John Norfleet, Clk.

Sorey, Solomon - Celia Hubbard, 22 Dec. 1831, Enos Green, (w) Ml. Hearn.

Sorg, Andrew - Lucinda R. Leigh, 12 Nov. 1861, m. 12 Nov. 1861 by J. B. Bobbitt, N. M. Terrell, (w) Thomas W. Hussey.

Sory, Solomon - Lotty Alsobrook, 25 Oct. 1847, Richard Purdy, (w) John Norfleet, Clk.

Sothall, Stephen W. - Martha F. Mallory, 8 Jan. 1861, m. 9 Jan. 1861 by Joseph Blount Cheshire, Epis. Min., William Foreman, (w) Thomas W. Hussey.

Southerland, Samuel - Mary A. Evans, 9 Jan. 1830, Jonas J. Carr, (w) L. H. Hearn.

Spain, Ruffin - Jamima Brake, 18 Feb. 1800, Richard Powell.

Sparkman, John - Nancy Wootten, 12 Dec. 1825, Reuben Sparkman, (w) Ml. Hearn.

Sparkman, Reuben - Letha Wootten, 12 Mar. 1822, John Sparkman, Charles Ellis, (w) Ml. Hearn.

Sparks, Andrew J. - Martha Ann Mayo, 21 Nov. 1860, m. 21 Nov. 1860 by L. C. Pender, J. P., Laurence Bradley, (w) W. A. Jones.

Sparks, Jackson - Martha Dickson, 23 Dec. 1848, Henry H. Bryan.

Sparks, James T. - Susan Tanner, 11 Aug. 1864, m. 17 Sept. 1864 by W. M. Pippin, J. P., C. B. Couch, (w) Irvin Thigpen.

Speight, Henry - Lydia E. Moore, 17 Jan. 1850, William H. Speight, (w) John Norfleet.

Speight, John F. - Emma Lewis, 28 Sept. 1840, Jesse H. Powell.

Speight, John F. - Clio C. Lewis, 27 Feb. 1866, m. 28 Feb. 1866 by Jesse H. Page, M. G., R. H. Speight, (w) Irvin Thigpen.

Speight, Samuel - Nancy Amason, 5 Jan. 1831, Henry Johnston, (w) L. H. Hearn.

Speight, Thomas - Sabry Gaiter, 27 Feb. 1838, William E. Billips, (w) Jo. Bell.

Spellings, Gideon C. - Nancy Crisp, 23 Oct. 1827, Joel Whitfield, Benjamin Whitfield Jr., (w) Ml. Hearn.
Spicer, Bryant - Betsy Griffin, 13 May 1834, Henry Gay, (w) T. C. Hearn.
Spicer, Bryant W. - Leonora Wabbleton, 22 Sept. 1845, Whitmel Williams, (w) John Norfleet.
Spicer, James - Sally Ruffin, 26 Nov. 1823, Burnett Hill, Spencer L. Hart, (w) Ml. Hearn.
Spicer, Jason -.Sarah Tillery, ———, m. 5 Jan. 1868 by L. C. Pender, J. P., (w) Irvin Thigpen.
Spicer, Joseph - Mary Fitzpatrick, 31 July 1764, Josiah Horn, (w) J. Hall.
Spicer, Joseph Wells - Charlotte Tunnell, 11 Oct. 1831, Garry Daughtry, (w) Ml. Hearn.
Spicer, Joseph W. - Martha Mears, 10 Oct. 1838, William D. Petway.
Spicer, Warren E. - Sally Ann Worsley, 19 Apr. 1843, Gray Armstrong, (w) John Norfleet, Clk.
Spiers, Kindred - Sylvester Bradley, 25 Jan. 1831, Little B. Bryan, (w) Ml. Hearn.
Spikes, James - Jinny Whittonton, 23 Mar. 1763, William Spikes, (w) John Spendelow.
Spivey, John - Lucinda Mills, 24 Mar. 1825, John Parker, Henry Austin, (w) Ml. Hearn.
Spivey, John T. - Annaliza Wilkinson, 1 Apr. 1854, m. 1 Apr. 1854 by K. Thigpen, William T. Gray, (w) W. S. Pitt, Clk.
Spragins, James M. - Martha A. Williams, 31 Jan. 1856, m. 31 Jan. 1856 by Thomas R. Owen, M. G., John W. White, (w) W. S. Pitt, Clk.
Spruill, Benjamin J. - Margaret S. Ross, 14 Dec. 1830, Richard Hines, (w) L. H. Hearn.
Stallings, Baker - Elizabeth Moseley, 18 May 1853, m. 19 May 1853 by W. S. Armstrong, J. P., Elbert H. Flowers, (w) Benjamin Norfleet.
Stallings, Burrell - Rebecca Peal, 27 Jan. 1825, Nathan Sessums, (w) Ml. Hearn.
Stallings, Eason - Priscilla Dupree, 22 Dec. 1851, m. 23 Dec. 1851 by Wright Barnes, J. P., Willaba Davis, (w) John Norfleet.
Stallings, Eason - Penelope Warren, 19 Feb. 1861, m. 20 Feb. 1861 by L. C. Pender, J. P., (w) J. H. Dozier, D. C.
Stallings, Etheldred - Franky Sherrod, 28 Sept. 1846, Robert D. Wimberley, (w) John Norfleet, Clk.

Stallings, Etheldred - Patsy Jackson, 4 July 1850, James Stallings, (w) Benjamin Norfleet.

Stallings, Franklin - Patsy Green, 4 Aug. 1853, m. 11 Aug. 1853 by Wright Barnes, J. P., Richard H. Garrett, (w) Benjamin Norfleet.

Stallings, Harmon - Mary Bullock, 23 Dec. 1826, John Garrett, (w) Ml. Hearn.

Stallings, James - Mary Peele, 5 Jan. 1829, John Garrett, (w) Ml. Hearn.

Stallings, James - Martha Holland, 13 Aug. 1846, Etheldred Stallings, (w) John Norfleet, Clk.

Stallings, James - Elizabeth S. Pitt, 22 Oct. 1856, m. 22 Oct. 1856 by Bennet P. Pitt, William L. Wiggins, (w) J. H. Dozier.

Stallings, Jesse - Elizabeth Pitman, 14 May 1827, John Garrett, (w) Ml. Hearn.

Stallings, John - Elizabeth Dunning, 26 Feb. 1824, Nathan Sessums, (w) Ml. Hearn.

Stallings, Joseph - Celia Windham, 15 Dec. 1838, Jesse Stallings, (w) Jo. Bell, C. C.

Stallings, Langden C. - Mary A. Wright, 10 Jan. 1859, m. 12 Jan. 1859 by Thomas F. Cherry, J. P., Thomas D. Wright, (w) J. H. Dozier.

Stallings, Phillip - Amanda Long, 31 Mar. 1855, m. 3 Apr. 1855 by C. W. Spicer, J. P., Joseph Rophan, (w) W. S. Pitt, Clk.

Stallings, S. P. - Cornelia Belcher, 23 Nov. 1866, m. 27 Nov. 1866 by Thomas R. Owen, B. D. M., W. B. Harper, (w) Irvin Thigpen.

Stallings, Thomas - Mary Hail (Hale?), 26 April 1800, Mills Stallings.

Stallions, John - Elizabeth Staton, 8 Mar. 1824, Joseph Winstead, (w) Ml. Hearn.

Stancil, Jesse - Harriett Hopkins, 8 Jan. 1834, Caswell Stansel, (w) Ml. Hearn.

Stancil, Thomas - Elizabeth Woodard, 8 Jan. 1846, Joshua Barnes.

Standard, William - Dorothy Jones, 7 Jan. 1763, Daniel Standard, (w) Thomas Cavenah.

Stanton, Archibald - Elizabeth Staton, 26 Oct. 1832, Baker Staton, (w) T. C. Hearn.

Staton, Arthur - Emily Howard, 28 Sept. 1846, Nathan Mathewson, (w) John Norfleet, Clk.

Staton, Baker - Genet Young, 19 Dec. 1827, William Hyman, (w) Ml. Hearn.

Staton, Berry - Malvina Dunn, 7 Mar. 1868, m. 7 May (?) 1868 by W. S. Long, J. P., (w) Irvin Thigpen, Clk.

Staton, Bythal Jr. - Elizabeth Cloman, 28 Feb. 1827, Solomon Pender, (w) Ml. Hearn.

Staton, Edmund - Armitta Cobb, 22 Sept. 1866, Hinter Jeffreys, (w) Irvin Thigpen.

Staton, Ezekiel - Nancy Strautige, 2 Jan. 1838, Mayo Worsley.

Staton, Henry L. - Margaret Batts, 10 Jan. 1848, John Norfleet.

Staton, James - Elizabeth Bell, 19 May 1858, m. 20 May 1858 by Orren Williams, J. P., James Hodge, (w) W. A. Jones, Clk.

Staton, James B. - Nancy J. Pippen, 13 Feb. 1854, m. 15 Feb. 1854 by J. H. Daniel, J. P., Baker W. Mabrey, (w) W. S. Pitt, Clk.

Staton, James H. - Emmalizar L. Savage, 10 Dec. 1861, m. 12 Dec. 1861 by John A. Stamper, Elder, James H. Griffin, (w) W. A. Jones.

Staton, Lewelling - Susan M. Hopkins, 6 Nov. 1837, Bythal Richard Bell.

Staton, Robert - Barbara A. Hadley, 12 Oct. 1847, Robert Norfleet.

Staton, Simmons B. - Drucilla Knight, 30 June 1835, Joshua Pender, (w) T. C. Hearn.

Staton, Thomas - Jane Jones, 10 Feb. 1866, m. 3 Mar. 1866 by Erastus Cherry, J. P., S. B. Staton, (w) Irvin Thigpen.

Staton, Willey - Mary Ann Bell, 7 May 1835, Simmons B. Staton, (w) Theo. C. Hearn.

Staton, William - Elizabeth Cockburn, 25 Jan. 1800, John Howell, (w) S. Wrenn.

Staton, William - Betsey Jordan, 26 Nov. 1833, William Proctor, (w) T. C. Hearn.

Staton, William - Amandy Bell, 1 Apr. 1837, John Watson, (w) T. C. Hearn.

Staton, William A. - Louisa Jones, 16 Feb. 1847, Robert Staton, (w) John Norfleet.

Staton, William J. - Gatsey A. Daniel, 13 Feb. 1851, m. 13 Feb. 1851 by Elisha Cromwell, J. P., Baker W. Mabrey, (w) John Norfleet.

Steptoe, William N. - Eugenia Daniel, 19 Nov. 1857, m. 1 Dec. 1857 by Joseph Blount Cheshire, Epis. Min., J. H. Laurence, (w) W. A. Jones, Clk.

Stewart, John P. - Mary P. Warren, 15 Nov. 1830, Bennett Pitt, (w) L. H. Hearn.

Stewart, Joseph C. - Jennett Hussey, 16 Jan. 1850, Jesse B. Hyatt, (w) John Norfleet, Clk.

Stewart, William - Mary Ann Tart, 13 Oct. 1831, John Parker, (w) Ml. Hearn.

Stokes, Bryant - Elizabeth Wells, 9 Aug. 1841, Ira G. Ellis.

Stokes, Drury - Martha Permenter, 17 Jan. 1804, Malachi Permenter, (w) E. Hall.

Stokes, George W. - Loura A. Ricks, 7 Feb. 1865, m. 8 Feb. 1865 by W. F. Lewis, J. P., Marcus J. Battle, (w) T. W. Hussey.

Stokes, John - Treacy Woodard, 4 May 1825, Randolph Johnson, Reading White, (w) Jo. Bell, C. C.

Stokes, Spencer - Tillitha Louis, 5 Mar. 1839, I. G. Ellis, (w) Jo. Bell, C. C.

Stokes, William - Sarah Gwinn, 7 Nov. 1767, Thomas Norman, (w) Edward Hall.

Strickland, Davis - Nancy Howell, 10 Jan. 1829, Dunkin C. Howell, (w) Ml. Hearn.

Strickland, Isaac - Elizabeth Jordan, 6 Nov. 1828, Hiram Chamblee, (w) Ml. Hearn.

Strickland, Soloman - Amey Pace, 19 Sept. 1764, Jacob Strick (?), (w) Tho. Cavenah.

Strickland, Stephen - Nellie Jones, 5 May 1837, Wright Edmundson, (w) T. C. Hearn.

Strictly, Robert - Catherine Sessums, 28 Dec. 1824, Micajah Alsobrook.

Stringer, Guilford - Mary Pitt, 11 Apr. 1827, Moses Baker, (w) Ml. Hearn.

Stringer, William - Kiziah Davis, 27 July 1799, John Stringer, (w) J. H. Hall.

Stuart, John P. - Nancy Warren, 24 Dec. 1824, James W. Wilson.

Stubbs, John - Elizabeth I. Leggett, 16 Mar. 1856, m. 19 Mar. 1856 by E. W. Cox, M. G., James R. Leggett, (w) W. A. Jones, D. C.

Sugg, Geo. C. - Nancy B. Sharpe, 10 June 1851, m. 10 June 1851 by Blount Cooper, Bolin B. Barron, (w) John Norfleet, Clk.

Sugg, Noah - Murphree Howell, 16 Jan. 1763, Lemuel Sugg, Peter Mitchell, (w) Thomas Cavenah.

Sugg, Pheasanton - Lucinda Pender, 9 Jan. 1827, Duke W. Horne, (w) Ml. Hearn.

Sugg, Redding S. - Mary S. Vines. 28 Feb. 1865, m. 1 Mar. 1865 by Thomas R. Owen, M. G., William F. Mercer, (w) Irvin Thigpen.

Sugg, Warren - Martha Walters, 27 Feb. 1866, m. 14 Apr. 1866 by A. M. Lowe, M. G., Jo. J. Garrett, (w) Irvin Thigpen.

Sugg, William - Elizabeth Lovett, 31 Oct. 1765, Arthur Richardson, (w) Mason Hall, (w) James Hall.

Sumerlin, Eaphram - Bitha Mosely, 30 Aug. 1854, m. 25 Sept. 1854 by J. Weaver Moore, M. G., John Hearn, (w) W. S. Pitt, Clk.

Sumerlin, J. M. - Lucrecy Moonyham, 18 Nov. 1854, m. 21 Nov. 1854 by Thomas Thomas, J. P., B. G. Braswell, (w) W. S. Pitt, Cik.

Summerlin, Jesse - Cornelia Parker, 25 Sept. 1858, m. 14 Oct. 1858 by Henry T. Clark, J. P., William Hearn, (w) W. A. Jones, Clk.

Sumerlin, William - Lydia Tolson, 30 Dec. 1857, m. 31 Dec. 1857 by W. Y. Moore, J. P., Jarrett Webb, (w) W. A. Jones.

Sumlin, Charles - Betsy Sumlin, 3 Oct. 1833, Green Berry Causey, (w) Theo. C. Hearn.

Sumlin, John - Martha Harris, 6 Nov. 1864, m. 6 Nov. 1864 by R. J. Johnson, J. P., William Keel, (w) T. W. Hussey.

Sumlin, William F. L. - Margaret Ann Melton, 7 Mar. 1866, m. 8 Mar. 1866 by S. L. Hart, J. P., Richard Watkins, (w) Irvin Thigpen.

Summerlin, Elias - Susan Edwards, 27 Sept. 1842, Amos Mosely.

Summerlin, George - Gatsy Webb, 21 Apr. 1852, m. 22 Apr. 1852 by W. Y. Moore, J. P., William H. Harrell, (w) John Norfleet.

Summerlin, Howell - Lurana Cox, 26 Apr. 1826, Joseph Morgan, Josiah Freeman, (w) Ml. Hearn.

Summerlin, James - Elizabeth Gardner, 25 Aug. 1828, Elijah Price, (w) Ml. Hearn.

Summerlin, Jonas - Peggy Little, 3 May 1813, Jacob Summerlin, (w) Ml. Hearn.

Summerlin, Theophilus - Elizabeth Pittman, 23 Aug. 1852, m. 29 Aug. 1852, by Robt. Bynum, J. P., John Proctor, (w) John Norfleet.

Summerlin, William - Pennina Anderson, 29 Mar. 1842, Weldon S. Hunter, (w) William Norfleet.

Summerling - Elizabeth Hearn, 25 May 1824, Stephen Milbern, (w) Ml. Hearn.

Sures, Richard - Judy Hambleton, 3 Sept. 1763, Richard Thomas.

Sutton, William - Martha E. Hearn, 1 Dec. 1829, Michael Hearn.

Swain, Elias - Mary Eliza Etheridge, 28 Aug. 1857, m. 3 Sept. 1857 by Mark Bennett, Ransom Etheridge, (w) J. H. Dozier.

Swift, Westley - Anna S. Petway, 23 Feb. 1854, m. 23 Mar. 1854 by Mark Bennett, Joshua Barnes, (w) W. S. Pitt, Clk.

T

Tannahill, William - Susan McNair, 4 Jan. 1832, Danford Richards, (w) L. H. Hearn.

Tanner, Hezekiah B. - Eliza Vick, 3 Nov. 1863, m. 3 Nov. 1863 by W. J. Lewis, J. P., (w) Irvin Thigpen, Clk.

Tanner, James - Penelope Tolbert, 14 Jan. 1851, John Coker, (w) John Norfleet.

Tanner, James - Susan Bilberry, 7 June 1860, m. 7 June 1860 by E. D. Macnair, J. P., John Mears, (w) W. A. Jones, Clk.

Tanner, Joseph - Elizabeth Boykin, 24 Dec. 1823, Henry Markes.

Tanner, William - Ony Griffin, 29 Jan. 1840, (w) Jo. Bell, C. C.

Tarniage, Carnell - Eliza Causey, 15 June 1831, Cullen Causey, (w) Ml. Hearn.

Tartt, Elnathan - Martha M. Andrews, 31 May 1824, Louis D. Wilson, (w) Ml. Hearn.

Taylor, Abraham - Charity Robbins, 23 Dec. 1799, William Taylor, (w) S. Wren.

Taylor, Allen - Gracy Garrett, 8 Jan. 1866, m. 14 Jan. 1866 by W. H. Knight, J. P., I. W. Garrett, (w) Irvin Thigpen.

Taylor, Alpha - Mary Bell, 9 Feb. 1830, Merrit Taylor, (w) L. H. Hearn.

Taylor, Arthur - Nancy Lancaster, 15 June 1846, Willie Lancaster, (w) John Norfleet.

Taylor, B. H. (Bukron Henry) - Martha Mayo, 3 Dec. 1866, m. 6 Dec. 1866 by James T. Howard, J. P., J. B. Coffield, (w) Irvin Thigpen.

Taylor, Burkett - Martha Griffin, 23 Dec. 1854, James C. Griffin, (w) W. S. Pitt, Clk.
Taylor, Bythel - Sally Haines, 3 Aug. 1831, Calvin Jones, (w) T. C. Hearn.
Taylor, Daniel R. - Barshaba Robbins, 11 Sept. 1830, Elza Taylor, (w) L. H. Hearn.
Taylor, Daniel R. - Harriet Proctor, 18 Apr. 1848, Absalom Proctor, (w) John Norfleet.
Taylor, David - Lucy Holland, 3 Feb. 1831, David Forehand, (w) L. H. Hearn.
Taylor, Dawson - Gilly Ann Best, 8 Dec. 1836, Jos. Jno. B. Pender, (w) T. C. Hearn.
Taylor, Demsey - Annis Jenkins, 26 Aug. 1865, m. 28 Aug. 1865 by William Harrell, J. P., Thomas W. Crisp, (w) Irvin Thigpen.
Taylor, Dempsey C. - Mary Daffin, 13 Jan. 1847, John H. Wells, (w) John Norfleet, Clk.
Taylor, Egbert H. - Evelina Pender, 13 Dec. 1845, James W. Barnes.
Taylor, Elza - Laura A. Worsley, 12 Sept. 1844, Redding Worsley, (w) John Norfleet, Clk.
Taylor, Elza - Mahala Daws, 4 Jan. 1849, Patrick Taylor, (w) Benjamin Norfleet.
Taylor, Elza - Angelina Ethridge, 16 Sept. 1853, m. 17 Sept. 1853 by Jesse Baker, M. G., W. W. Barnes, (w) W. S. Pitt, Clk.
Taylor, Francis W. - Rebecca A. Braswell, 5 Feb. 1850, Amariah Nolly, (w) John Norfleet.
Taylor, Gray - Spicy Felton, 26 Sept. 1844, John Walston, (w) John Norfleet.
Taylor, Henry - Casanda Parker, 7 Jan. 1837, Henry Savage, (w) T. C. Hearn.
Taylor, Hilliard S. - Mary M. Daws, 30 April 1842, Daniel R. Taylor, (w) John Norfleet, Clk.
Taylor, Isaiah - Sarah L. Taylor, 3 Jan. 1850, John Taylor, (w) John Norfleet, C.
Taylor, James - Nancy Andrews, 27 Oct. 1816 Lewis Purvis, (w) Michl. Hearn.
Taylor, James J. - Sarah Barnes (wid.) 31 Oct. 1842, Caswell Horne, (w) John Norfleet, Clk.
Taylor, Jesse - Sarah Ellis, 29 Aug. 1825, John Ellis, Jr., (w) John H. Mathewson.
Taylor, Jesse - Elizabeth Hairgrove, 19 Feb. 1829, David Williams, (w) Ml. Hearn.

Taylor, Jesse - Penninah Hedgepeth, 4 Jan. 1831, Stephen Taylor, (w) L. H. Hearn.

Taylor, Jesse I. - Isabella Purvis, 15 Dec. 1855, m. 18 Dec. 1855 by David Cobb, J. P., Mc. G. Taylor, (w) W. S. Pitt, Clk.

Taylor, Joel - Charlotte Weeks, 10 Sept. 1829, Baker Staton, (w) Ml. Hearn.

Taylor, John - Phereby Owens, 18 Mar. 1825, Willis Knight, (w) Ml. Hearn.

Taylor, John - Rachel Edwards, 18 Oct. 1831, Thomas Taylor, (w) L. H. Hearn.

Taylor, John B. - Polly Bozeman, 1 Feb. 1847, Daniel R. Taylor, (w) John Norfleet, Clk.

Taylor, John F. - Penelope Caroline Maner, 11 Apr. 1855, m. 12 Apr. 1855 by C. C. Bonner, A. C. Taylor, (w) W. S. Pitt, Clk.

Taylor, John N. - Burthania Proctor, 16 Jan. 1861, m. 17 Jan. 1861 by Hilyard S. Taylor, A. B. M. G., John B. Taylor, (w) J. H. Dozier.

Taylor, Johnston - Lucy Medford, 22 Sept. 1831, John Knight, (w) Michl. Hearn.

Taylor, Kindred C. - Lucy Clark, 11 Dec. 1833, Wilson Sessums, (w) T. C. Hearn.

Taylor, Lemuel - Gilly Jones, 29 Oct. 1822, Laurence Buntyn, (w) Ml. Hearn.

Taylor, Mac. G. - Sally E. Best, 21 May 1860, m. 22 May 1860 by T. H. Jenkins, J. P., Louis K. Purvis, (w) W. A. Jones.

Taylor, Newsom - Ellen Brown, 17 Dec. 1866, m. 20 Dec. 1866 by Hilyard S. Taylor, A. B. M. G., A. Proctor, (w) Irvin Thigpen.

Taylor, Newton - Christianna Robbins, 24 July, 1822, William Robbins, (w) Ml. Hearn.

Taylor, Noah - Caroline Howard, 27 Feb. 1866, m. 18 Mar. 1866 by J. W. Howard, J. P., H. E. Barfield, (w) Irvin Thigpen.

Taylor, Patrick - Mary Proctor, 17 May 1848, Daniel R. Taylor, (w) John Norfleet.

Taylor, Perry - Sally Winstead, 3 Nov. 1834, Thomas Taylor, (w) Ml. Hearn.

Taylor, Rascoe - Sally Anderson, 23 Jan. 1833, George Anderson, (w) T. C. Hearn.

Taylor, Redmond Hesekiah - Mary Frances Freeman, 23 Oct. 1860, m. 24 Oct. 1860 by Hilyard S. Taylor, A. B. M. G., Patrick C. Taylor, (w) W. A. Jones.

Taylor, Samuel - Drucilla Wooten, 17 Apr. 1844, Levi Mercer, (w) John Norfleet, Clk.

Taylor, Teagle - Selia Little, 14 June, 1763, William Wombell, (w) John Spendelow.

Taylor, Thomas - Maria Cockburn, 19 Apr. 1817, William Staton, (w) Ml. Hearn.

Taylor, Thomas - Elizabeth Edwards, 14 Dec. 1826, William Taylor, Isaac Farmer, (w) Ml. Hearn.

Taylor, Thomas - Jane Mooring, 14 Nov. 1844, Dawson Taylor, (w) John Norfleet, Clk.

Taylor, Thomas - Marina Taylor, 31 Jan. 1866, m. 4 Jan. 1866 by William Harrell, J. P., Mayo Worsley, (w) Irvin Thigpen.

Taylor, William - Mary Hart, 13 Oct. 1821, Willie Howard, (w) Ml. Hearn.

Taylor, William Jr. - Talitha Hedgepeth, 5 Dec. 1823, William Taylor, Sr., (w) Ml. Hearn.

Taylor, William - Elizabeth Taylor, 3 Oct. 1836, Dawson Taylor, (w) T. C. Hearn.

Taylor, William A. - Elizabeth Kelly, 11 Jan. 1842, Kinchen Taylor, (w) John Norfleet, Clk.

Taylor, William I. - Fannie Dunn, 18 Jan. 1856, m. 22 Jan. 1856 by Bennet P. Pitt, J. P., B. S. Taylor, (w) B. S. Pitt, Clk.

Taylor, William R. - Fanny Nelson, 31 Dec. 1845, Joseph Howard, (w) John Norfleet, Clk.

Taylor, Wilson G. - Lucy Ann Drake, 28 Feb. 1860, m. 1 Mar. 1860 by Thomas F. Cherry, J. P., Cofield Mason, (w) W. A. Jones.

Teal, Green - Sally Ann Moore, 5 May 1846, Little Berry Manning.

Tedder, Blount - Viney Bottoms, 2 Jan. 1862, m. 5 Jan. 1862 by L. C. Pender, J. P., (w) T. W. Hussey, D. C.

Tedder, Haywood - Amanda Hagens, 6 Apr. 1858, m. 11 Apr. 1858 by L. C. Pender, J. P., Jonas Walston, (w) W. C. Jones.

Tedder, Mathew - Mary E. Morgan, 21 Apr. 1859, m. 21 Apr. 1859 by L. C. Pender, J. P., Jesse Gardner, (w) J. H. Dozier.

Teel, Kinny M. - Elizabeth Edwards, 19 Oct. 1830, Bassett Sikes, (w) L. H. Hearn.

Telfair, Octavus W. - Pauline D. Macnair, 22 Mar. 1853, m. 23 Mar. 1853 by Jos. Blount Cheshire, Epis. Min., David T. Tayloe, Ed. C. Yellowley, (w) John Norfleet, Clk.

Terrell, Nathaniel - Alice Redmond, 26 Dec. 1832, Isaac B. Brady, (w) T. C. Hearn.

Thigpen, Dennis - Lewey Edwards, 27 Apr. 1827, James Thigpen, (w) Ml. Hearn.

Thigpen, D. LaFayette - Jane Allen, 4 Nov. 1850, George Thigpen, (w) John Norfleet, Clk.

Thigpen, Ellick - Edney Thigpen, 12 May 1866, m. 12 May 1866 by Jas. R. Thigpen, J. P., W. B. Whitley, (w) Irvin Thigpen.

Thigpen, Gray - Penelope Stallings, 28 Jan. 1815, Lemuel Thigpen, (w) Ml. Hearn.

Thigpen, Gray - Louisa Stancil, 27 Dec. 1865, m. 30 Dec. 1865 by William Harrell, J. P., William Thigpen, (w) Irvin Thigpen.

Thigpen, Ivy - Sally Edwards, 11 Apr. 1827, Dennis Thigpen, Lemuel Thigpen, (w) Ml. Hearn.

Thigpen, James - Lydia Mayo, 18 Oct. 1765, John Thigpen, (w) Thomas H. Hall, (w) Thomas Cavenah.

Thigpen, James - Patsey Brown, 24 July 1834, Lemuel Thigpen, (w) T. C. Hearn.

Thigpen, James - Martha Cobb, 24 Dec. 1850, Irvin Thigpen, (w) John Norfleet, Clk.

Thigpen, James R. - Gatsey Pitt, 11 Aug. 1851, m. 12 Aug. 1851 by Elisha Cromwell, J. P., Irvin Thigpen, (w) John Norfleet.

Thigpen, Job - Larina Cromwell, 7 Sept. 1829, Little Berry Little, Gray Little, (w) Ml. Hearn.

Thigpen, John - Penny Price, 9 June 1830, Lemon Hicks, (w) L. H. Hearn.

Thigpen, Jordan - Avith Atkinson, 10 Jan. 1843, Eaton Cobb.

Thigpen, Jordan - Mary F. Little, 18 Apr. 1849, Amariah Cobb, (w) John Norfleet.

Thigpen, Kenneth - Ann Lane, 10 July 1849, James Little, (w) John Norfleet.

Thigpen, Lemuel - Anne O'Berry, 5 Dec. 1815, John Hogun, (w) Ml. Hearn.

Thigpen, Little Berry - Ann Little, 1 Aug. 1827, Ollen Cobb, (w) Ml. Hearn.

Thigpen, Rufus C. - Ann E. T. Daniel, 19 Mar. 1851, m. 20 Mar. 1851 by William Hyman, M. G., Irvin Thigpen, (w) John Norfleet.

Thomas, Aaron - Anne Boothe, 6 Feb. 1840, (w) Jo. Bell, C. C. C.
Thomas, Archelaus B. - Lydia Price, 27 Dec. 1825, Benjamin Miller, Charles Wilkinson, (w) Ml. Hearn.
Thomas, Curtis - Elizabeth Jones, 17 Apr. 1849, William S. Duggan.
Thomas, Eason - Polly Eure, 28 Aug. 1823, Stephen B. Eure, (w) Ml. Hearn, Clk.
Thomas, Elisha' - Martha A. S. Ruffin, 7 Sept. 1847, James B. Thomas, (w) John Norfleet.
Thomas, Hilliard - Nancy Sharpe, 19 Dec. 1843, William Thomas, (w) John Norfleet, Clk.
Thomas, Ichabob - Susanna Barnes, ———, 1799, Benjamin Amason, (w) S. Wren.
Thomas, Jacob - Amanda R. Bridgers, 10 July 1830, William S. Baker, (w) L. H. Hearn.
Thomas, James A. - Fanny Little, 29 Dec. 1858, Colin Macnair, (w) W. A. Jones, Clk.
Thomas, James B. - Margaret F. Whitehead, 28 Sept. 1847, James H. Dozier, (w) E. D. Macnair.
Thomas, Jonathan - Tabitha Little, 23 May 1815, John Little, Dempsey Eure, (w) Ml. Hearn.
Thomas, Jordan - Charity Locus, 9 Feb. 1837, Ephraim Vaun, (w) Ml. Hearn.
Thomas, Josiah - Mary A. F. Proctor, 26 Mar. 1866. m. 27 Mar. 1866 by H. S. Taylor, A. B. M. G., Elisha Thomas, (w) Irvin Thigpen.
Thomas, Josiah R. - Nancy Williams, 8 Sept. 1841, Drewry Williams, (w) John Norfleet, Clk.
Thomas, Josiah R. - Sarah Walker, 2 Feb. 1845, James W. Thomas, (w) John Norfleet.
Thomas, Lorenzo D. - Margaret Jackson, 22 Dec. 1847, Exum F. Vick, (w) James H. Dozier.
Thomas, Morrisson, Sarah Turner, 16 Sept. 1826, Nathan H. Rountree, (w) Ml. Hearn.
Thomas, Morrison - Patience B. Horn, 12 Feb. 1828, (w) Ml. Hearn.
Thomas, Theophilus - Thaney Whitehead, 7 Dec. 1841, Aaron Thomas.
Thomas, Theophilus - Nancy C. Whitehead, 7 Mar. 1854, m. 7 Mar. 1854 by C. W. Spicer, J. P., Elisha Thomas, (w) W. S. Pitt, Clk.
Thomas, Theophilus - Nancy A. Horn, 24 Jan. 1856, m. 24 Jan. 1856 by C. C. Bonner, W. G. Proctor, (w) W. S. Pitt, Clk.

Thomas, Wade R. - Millicent Horn, 6 Jan. 1827, Nathan H. Rountree, (w) Ml. Hearn.

Thomas, William - Sarah Braswell, 1 Mar. 1825, Thomas Southerland, (w) Ml. Hearn.

Thomas, William - Elizabeth Stallings, 6 Jan. 1837, Coffield King, (w) Ml. Hearn.

Thomas, William G. - Mary S. Clark, 1 Nov. 1843, Nathan Mathewson.

Thomas, William H. - Mary Thomas, 18 Jan. 1839, Elisha Woodard, (w) Jo. Bell, C. C.

Thomas, William H. - Araanna F. Horne, 4 Dec. 1857, m. 10 Dec. 1857 by R. D. Hart, V. D. M., W. G. Billips, (w) James H. Dozier.

Thompson, Andrew W. - Mary Goff, 2 Oct. 1823, Daniel Hopkins, (w) N. Mathewson.

Thompson, Noah - Martha Eliza W. Collin, 15 Feb. 1832, Richard H. Lewis, (w) Ml. Hearn.

Thompson, Noah - Harriet Eliza Wright, 18 Oct. 1838, Charles G. Hunter.

Thompson, Zadock L. - Annie S. Barnes, 8 Feb. 1850, Wyatt Moye, (w) John Norfleet.

Thorn, George - Laura Vaughn, 22 June 1866, R. A. Watson, (w) Irvin Thigpen.

Thorn, James R. - Martha Batts, 14 Nov. 1840, Andrew J. Pender, (w) John Norfleet, Clk.

Thorne, Jesse A. B. - Elizabeth J. Sassnett, 3 Nov. 1852, m. 4 Nov. 1852 by Wright Barnes, J. P., John H. Leigh, (w) John Norfleet, Clk.

Thorne, Jesse A. B. - Elizabeth A. Norval, 10 Dec. 1857, m. 15 Dec. 1857 by Bennett P. Pitt, J. P., Thomas Norfleet, (w) J. H. Dozier.

Thorne, Punch (s. of Mary) - Rose Pender (dau. of Rose), 23 May 1868, m. 23 May 1868 by W. H. Powell, J. P., (w) Irvin Thigpen, Clk.

Thorne, Samuel H. - Frances Stallings, 30 Aug. 1849, Richard A. Savage, (w) John Norfleet, Clk.

Thorne, Theophilus T. - Mary D. Cutchin, 28 Dec. 1849, J. J. Barnes, (w) John Norfleet, Clk.

Thorne, William D. - Sarah Robbins, 7 Oct. 1846, Solo. Pender, Jr., (w) John Norfleet.

Thorne, William D. - Felicia Skinner, 27 Aug. 1849, William Tomlinson, (w) John Norfleet.

Thornell, Benjamin F. - Prescilla Williams, ———, 1844 Benjamin Thornell, (w) R. Norfleet.

Thornell, Henry - Nancy Land. 24 July 1823, E. T. Bullock, Lemuel Lancaster, (w) Ml. Hearn.

Thornell, Henry G. - Martha A. Thomas (or Robbins), 4 Dec. 1866, m. 6. Dec. 1866 by J. I. Proctor, J. P., J. M. Neal, (w) Irvin Thigpen.

Thornell, Thomas - Serena Braswell, 18 Dec. 1835, Benjamin Thornell, (w) Ml. Hearn.

Tillery, William H. - Mary A. Battle, 13 Feb. 1849, Redin Daughtry, (w) William L. Dozier, Clk.

Tison, Abner - Nancy Barnes, 12 Oct. 1833, Canady Morgan, (w) T. C. Hearn.

Tison, Benjamin - Lucy Hines, 31 Mar. 1823, William D. Jenkins, Jacob Powell, (w) Ml. Hearn.

Tison, George W. - Sally Cherry, 25 Nov. 1834, Whitmell K. Bulluck, (w) Ml. Hearn.

Tison, William - Esther Ruffin, 4 Nov. 1824, Peter Evans, (w) Ml. Hearn.

Titus, Lunsford - Eliza Portis, 19 June 1843, William Little.

Todd, Henry A. - Martha Marshburn, 11 Feb. 1854, m. 14 Feb. 1854 by Thomas L. Maner, Thomas F. Cherry, (w) W. S. Pitt, Clk.

Todd, James - Susan Gill, 14 July 1840, William Skinner, (w) John Norfleet, C. C. C.

Tolbert, William T. - Prescilla Pittman, 20 May 1846, Stephen Cocker, (w) John Norfleet.

Tolbert, Isaac - Martha Banks, 10 Feb. 1830, James Tolbert, (w) L. H. Hearn.

Tolson, Moses - Saveny Draughan, 4 Apr. 1825, Harry Sykes, (w) Ml. Hearn.

Tolson, Moses - Mary Webb, 19 Dec. 1832, John Hays, (w) Ml. Hearn.

Tomblinson, William - Martha Barnes, 9 May 1854, m. 9 May 1854 by Joshua Barnes, J. P., Arthur B. Dew, (w) Josh Barnes.

Tomlinson, Thomas - Nancy Eavens, 8 Dec. 1851, m. 11 Dec. 1851 by John W. Farmer, J. P., Edwin Barnes, William Tomlinson, (w) John W. Farmer.

Tompkins, John S. - Rosanna Hines, 23 Apr. 1823, David Barnes, William J. Andrews, (w) Ml. Hearn, C. C.

Toulson, Henry - Louisa Worrell, 21 Feb. 1849, Kinchen Worrell, (w) John Norfleet, Clk.

Treevathan, Mathew G. - Elvina Batts, 13 Mar. 1854, m. 16 Mar. 1854 by D. W. Barnes, J. P., John O'Callaghan, (w) W. S. Pitt, Clk.

Trevathan, Aaron - Lavina Odom, 3 Aug. 1818, Elijah Price, (w) Michl. Hearn.

Trevathan, Benjamin - Sally Williams, 20 May 1846, William J. Armstrong, (w) John Norfleet.

Trevathan, Dempsey - Elizabeth Sorey, 15 Dec. 1827, Dennis Sorey, (w) Ml. Hearn.

Trevathan, Dempsey - Polly Jones, 15 Mar. 1850, Henry R. Anderson, (w) John Norfleet.

Trevathan, Eli - Polly Robertson, 29 July 1826, Henry Bryan, (w) Ml. Hearn.

Trevathan, Henry - Mary Ing, 18 Dec. 1826, Willie Price, (w) Ml. Hearn.

Trevathan, Jonas - Keddy Rose, 15 Apr. 1824, Burrel Rose, (w) Ml. Hearn.

Trevathan, Meedy - Obedience Bulard, 22 June 1847, James Bulard, (w) John Norfleet, Clk.

Trevathan, Meedy - Harriet Taylor (widow), 21 Dec. 1853, m. 22 Dec. 1853 by Theo. Thomas, J. P., Miles Daws, (w) W. S. Pitt, Clk.

Trevathan, Saunders - Mahala Beland, 19 Dec. 1851, Eason Sharpe, (w) R. H. Pender.

Trevathan, Saunders - Esther Batts, 26 Mar. 1853, m. 29 ——— 1853 by D. W. Barnes, J. P., David W. Batts, (w) John Norfleet, Clk.

Trevathan, William - Emily Bedford, 14 Sept. 1844, Jeremiah Odom, (w) William D. Petway.

Trevathan, William C. - Sarah Jane Price, 27 Apr. 1854, m. 11 May 1854 by C. C. Bonner, J. P., Charles H. Jenkins, (w) W. S. Pitt, Clk.

Tucker, Haverson - Emily Jones, 19 Dec. 1863, m. 21 Dec. 1863 by W. F. Lewis, J. P., Lawrence Fountain, (w) Irvin Thigpen.

Tumbrow, A. D. - Elizabeth S. Knight, 31 Aug. 1859, m. 1 Sept. 1859 by J. H. Daniel, Sr., J. S. Barnes, (w) W. A. Jones, Clk.

Tunnell, Bird B. - Drucilla Baker, 19 June 1854, m. 22 June 1854 by C. C. Bonner, William Rose, (w) W. A. Jones.

Turner, Alford - Tazzy Ann Sena Joyner, 23 Mar. 1843, Josiah Turner, (w) John Norfleet, Clk.

Turner, Benjamin D. - Margaret M. Andrews, 7 Sept. 1829, Thomas Gatlin, (w) Ml. Hearn.

Turner, Caswell - Bitha Flood, 14 Feb. 1854, m. 16 Feb. 1854 by Theo. Thomas, J. P., James W. Jackson, (w) W. S. Pitt, Clk.

Turner, E. M. - Virginia L. Staton, 29 Dec. 1858, David Neal.
Turner, John P. - Penelope King, 30 Nov. 1852, John Whitaker, (w) John Norfleet.
Turner, Josiah - Nancy Jackson, 6 Apr. 1833, Abraham Price, (w) T. C. Hearn.
Tyler, Johnson - Louisa King, 10 Jan. 1853, m. 11 Jan. 1853 by W. F. Lewis, J. P., A. H. Macnair, (w) John Norfleet.
Tyler, Lorenzo D. - Emily L. Pittman, 29 Dec. 1843, Stephen Coker, (w) John Norfleet.
Tyler, Robert - Elizabeth Fountain, 20 Nov. 1866, m. 23 Nov. 1866 by L. R. Cherry, J. P., Beverly T. Pittman.
Tyler, Thomas K. - Mary Lewesa Dorman, 24 May 1859, m. 28 May 1859 by John A. Stamper, Joshua L. Lawrence, (w) W. A. Jones, Clk.

U

Underwood, Samuel - Elizabeth Burgess, 2 Sept. 1863, R. A. Watson.

V

Vainright, James - Edy Webb, 18 Nov. 1857, m. 24 Nov. 1857 by W. Y. Moore, J. P., James S. Eason, (w) W. A. Jones.
Vann, Dempsey - Julia Barnes, 24 May 1853, m. 7 June 1853 by Joshua Barnes, J. P., A. D. Farmer, (w) J. W. Farmer.
Vannaford, Noah - Elizabeth Edwards, 23 Sept. 1819, Riddick Etheridge, (w) Michl. Hearn.
Van Pelt, James - Barsheba Brake, 31 Jan. 1829, Wright Wiggins, (w) Ml. Hearn.
Vanpelt, John - Polly Taylor, 8 May 1822, John Williams Sr., Michl. Hearn.
Varnell, Kinchen - Martha Carter, 14 Apr. 1851, m. 16 Apr. 1851 by Theo. Atkinson, J. P., Patrick Byrum, (w) Benjamin Norfleet.
Varnell, Levi - Bersheby Brinkley, 26 Dec. 1822, Isaiah Varnell, (w) Ml. Hearn.
Varnold, William - Sally Barnes, 2 June 1846, William W. Barnes, (w) John Norfleet.
Vaughan, Maurice H. - Camilla H. Cook, 12 May 1862, T. M. Cook, (w) T. W. Hussey.
Vaughn, Benjamin - Lisby Wilkins, 4 Oct. 1844, John Jones, (w) John Norfleet.
Vaughn, Claiborne - Sally Ann Morgan, 19 Aug. 1845, Stephen Coker, (w) John Norfleet.

Vaughn, Thomas - Cinda Mosely, 20 Nov. 1858(?), m. 21 Nov. 1853(?) by R. J. Johnson, J. P., Thomas O'berry, (w) J. H. Dozier.

Vester, Nathan A. - Mary Ann Jane Webb, 20 Apr. 1854, m. 30 Apr. 1854 by W. Y. Moore, J. P., Abner Eason, (w) W. A. Jones, D. C.

Vick, Ashley - Penny Lane, 15 Mar. 1860, m. 22 Mar. 1860 by John W. Johnson, J. P., John W. Johnson, (w) W. A. Jones.

Vick, Burton C. - Martha Ann Lee, 14 Sept. 1847, Roderick C. Vick, Exum F. Vick, (w) John Norfleet.

Vick, David - Emaliza Harris, 24 Apr. 1851, m. 29 Apr. 1851 by L. S. Dunn, J. P., John W. Johnson, (w) John Norfleet, Clk.

Vick, Elisha - Letha Page, 6 Aug. 1832, John Walston, (w) T. C. Hearn.

Vick, Exum F. - Martha Harris, 21 Aug. 1847, David W. Bulluck.

Vick, James - Polly Sorey, 14 Apr. 1842, Frederick Vick, (w) John Norfleet, Clk.

Vick, James J. - Mary Landing, 22 Oct. 1845, Abram Holland, (w) John Norfleet, Clk.

Vick, John - Polly Lane, 19 Dec. 1842, Exum F. Vick, Frederick Vick, (w) John Norfleet.

Vick, Roderick C. - Tabitha Hopkins, 16 June 1848, Exum F. Vick, (w) John Norfleet, Clk.

Vick, William B. - Martha Philips, 29 May 1860, m. 31 May 1860 by Thomas F. Cherry, J. P., Exum F. Vick, (w) W. A. Jones.

Vick, William H. - Della F. Denton, 6 Feb. 1865, m. 9 Feb. 1865 by John W. Johnson, J. P., James B. Keith, (w) T. W. Hussey.

Vines, John - Prudence Ruffin, 22 Dec. 1837, Wiley Belcher.

Vines, Jordan - Ann Clark, 2 Feb. 1866, m. 3 Feb. 1866 by Allen Warren, J. P., John A. Vines, (w) Irvin Thigpen.

Viverette, Micajah - Ann Eliza Armstrong, 30 Jan. 1833, James Viverette.

W

Waddell, Abel - Rachel Standard, 15 Mar. 1762, Joseph Cotton, (w) James Hall.

Wadkins, George W. - Margarett E. Pittman, 27 Feb. 1866, m. 28 Feb. 1866 by S. L. Hart, J. P., Joseph J. Hales, (w) Irvin Thigpen.

Wadkins, Robert - Jane Iseral, 28 Dec. 1866. m. 28 Dec. 1866 by S. L. Hart, J. P., James R. Williams, (w) Irvin Thigpen.

Wadsworth. John - Elizabeth Whitley. 8 Oct. 1866, m. 11 Oct. 1866 by A. M. Lowe, M. G., John H. Carlisle, (w) Irvin Thigpen.

Walker, Hartwell - Martha S. A. Bulluck, 31 Mar. 1855, m. 3 Apr. 1855 by Lunsford R. Cherry, J. P., Thomas Bulluck, (w) W. S. Pitt, Clk.

Walker Hartwell - Catherine Bell, 25 Jan. 1859, m. 27 Jan. 1859 by W. F. Lewis, J. P., Lawrence Billups, (w) W. A. Jones.

Walker, James - Caroline Farmer, 27 Feb. 1855, m. 2 Mar. 1855 by C. C. Bonner, J. P., E. T. Mayo, (w) W. S. Pitt, Clk.

Walker. James R. - Martha A. Hart, 27 Nov. 1851, K. H. Dicken, (w) John Norfleet, Clk.

Walker, Lawrence H. - Martha Baker, 24 Dec. 1840, (w) John Norfleet, Clk.

Walker. William - Elsey Walls. 19 Sept. 1855, m. 20 Sept. 1855 by J. R. Pitt, J. P., Joel Gardner, (w) W. S. Pitt, Clk.

Wall, Dorsey - Ailsey Nainey (Nairney?), 18 June 1830, James Pender, (w) L. H. Hearn.

Wall, Jesse - Susanna Ship, 4 Jan. 1765, Jeremiah Irvin, (w) J. Hall.

Wallace, George S. - Jane Drake, 28 June 1826, Thomas Taylor, Meedy Williford.

Waller, James W. - Margaret L. Lawrence, 24 May 1859. m. 27 May 1859 by Henry T. Clark, J. P., Joseph Stallins, (w) W. A. Jones, Clk.

Waller, Warren - Caty Morgan, 13 Feb. 1823, Edward Waller, Henry Austin, (w) Ml. Hearn.

Walston, Bennett - Sally Ann Pitt, 2 Jan. 1850, Littleton Walston, (w) W. L. Dozier.

Walston, Drewry - Lavina Langley, 31 Jan. 1834, Robert Owens, (w) T. C. Hearn.

Walston, James - Weltha Webb, 11 Jan. 1858, m. 12 Jan. 1858 by W. Y. Moore, J. P., Hyram Webb, (w) W. A. Jones, Clk.

Walston, Jonas - Martha Peel, 7 Dec. 1845, Amos Walston, (w) John Norfleet, Clk.

Walston, John - Treacy Felton, 27 May 1834, James Barron, (w) T. C. Hearn.

Walston, Joshua - Anna Felton, 22 Dec. 1840, Amos Owens, (w) John Norfleet.

Walston, Josiah - Sally Green 8 Feb. 1836, Littleton Walston, Enos Green, (w) Ml. Hearn.

Walston, Kinchen - Viney Webb, 24 Jan. 1840, Hyrum Forbes, (w) Jo. Bell, C. C.

Walston, Levi - Pennina Pittman, 26 Nov. 1845, Kinchen Walston, (w) John Norfleet, Clk.

Walston, Levi - Martha E. Lewis, 30 Sept. 1865, m. 1 Oct. 1865 by R. J. Johnson, J. P., B. B. Lewis, (w) Irvin Thigpen, Clk.

Walston, Littleton - Delpha Cherry, 28 Jan. 1841, John Walston, (w) John Norfleet, Clk.

Walston, Littleton - Zilpha Smith, 14 Nov. 1843, John Walston, (w) John Norfleet, Clk.

Walston, Littleton - Eliza Cobb, 17 June 1845, Josiah Walston, (w) John Norfleet.

Walston, Phesenton - Jackey Ann E. Carr, 26 Sept. 1863, m. 1 Oct. 1863 by Bennet P. Pitt, J. P., J. T. Weaver, (w) Irvin Thigpen, Clk.

Walston, Robert - Mary Ann Fleming, 15 Nov. 1858, m. 18 Nov. 1858 by Bennet P. Pitt, J. P., William Walston, (w) J. H. Dozier.

Walston, William - Elizabeth Dilday, 26 Sept. 1843, David Walston, (w) John Norfleet, Clk.

Walston, William - Penetta Peel, 26 Dec. 1846, Amos Walston, (w) W. L. Dozier.

Walston, William - Sally Ann Barron, 14 Dec. 1858, m. 16 Dec. 1858 by R. J. Johnson, J. P., Brittain Edwards, (w) W. A. Jones.

Walston, Willie - May Cobb, 24 Oct. 1854, m. 26 Oct. 1854 by Jesse Harrel, J. P., (w) W. A. Jones, D. C.

Walton, Aron - Zany Braswell, 10 May 1866, m. 13 May 1866 by C. C. Bonner, J. P., (w) Irvin Thigpen, Clk.

Walton, Hardy - Luvinia Mosely, 2 May 1863, m. 3 May 1863 by Bennet P. Pitt, J. P., Reuben Harris, (w) Irvin Thigpen.

Wammack, William - Lucinda Pittman, 23 Sept. 1840, David W. Bulluck, (w) John Norfleet.

Warbleton, James - Mary E. Anderson, 19 Dec. 1855, m. 19 Dec. 1855 by C. B. Killebrew, J. P., Willie Long, (w) John L. Baker.

Warbritton, Simeon - Elizabeth Wilson, 3 Oct. 1822, Joseph R. Lloyd, James S. Battle, (w) Ml. Hearn.

Ward, A. M. - Mary P. Pender. 26 May 1857, m. 26 May 1857 by Thomas R. Owen, M. G., J. H. Dozier, (w) W. A. Jones, Clk.

Ward, Benjamin - Martha Worrell, 27 Feb. 1850, John Norfleet.

Ward, George Washington - Cathrine Cobb, 16 Jan. 1849, Thomas W. Ward, (w) Benjamin Norfleet.

Ward, Harmon - Catharine E. Pippen, 1 Jan. 1834, Lunsford R. Brown, (w) Ml. Hearn.

Ward, Henry - Polly Barkley, 2 Aug. 1824, William Barfield, (w) N. Mathewson.

Ward, John - Lydia Peal, 11 Feb. 1832, James Stallings, (w) Ml. Hearn.

Ward, John F. - Lucy Tyler, 23 Aug. 1858, m. 26 Aug. 1858 by Thomas R. Owens, M. G., G. B. Lipscomb, (w) W. A. Jones.

Ward, Luke - Nancy Mayo, 10 May 1824, Joseph John Pippen, (w) Ml. Hearn.

Ward, Luke - Mahala Legget, 16 June 1834, Lanier Ward, (w) T. C. Hearn.

Ward, Needham - Susan Woodard, 25 Aug. 1850, Willie J. Pettway, (w) Benjamin S. Ward.

Ward, Robert L. - Phebe H. Williams, 15 Apr. 1851, m. 24 Apr. 1851 by William H. Hines, J. P., William H. Hines, (w) Benjamin Norfleet.

Ward, Solomon - Zilpha Barnes, 16 May 1831, (w) L. H. Hearn.

Ward, T. W. - Mary Pender, 21 Mar. 1859, James B. Coffield, (w) W. A. Jones, Clk.

Ward, Willie - Lucea Leggett, 27 Feb. 1837, James P. Tropolet.

Ward, Willie - Telitha Leggett, 29 June 1845, Thomas Parker, (w) John Norfleet, Clk.

Warren, Alfred - Nancy Jane Edmondson, 6 Jan. 1857, m. 6 June 1857 by L. S. Dunn, J. P., Richard H. Gatlin, (w) J. H. Dozier.

Warren, Alfred - Susan I. Bryant, 2 Apr. 1861, m. 5 Apr. 1861 by John W. Johnson, J. P., William Warren, (w) T. W. Hussey.

Warren, Allen - Mary L. Edwards, 15 Oct. 1855, m. 18 Oct. 1855 by Bennet P. Pitt, J. P., R. T. Phillips, (w) W. S. Pitt, Clk.

Warren, Eli - Margaret A. Little, 26 Jan. 1858, m. 27 Jan. 1858 by David Cobb, J. P., Benjamin J. Thigpen, (w) J. H. Dozier.

Warren, Henry O. - Winnefred Dunn. 24 Oct. 1857, m. 25 Oct. 1857 by L. S. Dunn, J. P., William Warren, (w) W. A. Jones, Clk.

Warren, Ivey - Polly Windham, 10 June 1845, Ollen Warren, (w) John Norfleet, Clk.

Warren, James Sr. - Patsey Harrell, 3 Dec. 1861, m. 3 Dec. 1861 by William Harrell, J. P., Henry S. Warren, (w) T. W. Hussey.

Warren, James R. - Tabitha Harrell, 8 Dec. 1857, m. 9 Dec. 1857 by David Cobb, J. P., John M. Bunting, (w) W. A. Jones, Clk.

Warren, John - Jennette Hopkins, 2 July 1847, Reed A. Norvill, (w) John Norfleet.

Warren, Joshua - Rebecca Etheridge, 25 Sept. 1833, Joseph Stallings, (w) Ml. Hearn.

Warren, Lemuel - Lovey Warren, 19 Aug. 1865, m. 20 Aug. 1865 by William Harrell, J. P., Mayo Worsley, (w) Irvin Thigpen.

Warren, Richard - Elizabeth Thigpen, 6 Oct. 1835, Ollen Warren, (w) Ml. Hearn.

Warren, William - Sarah Atkinson, 28 Jan. 1845, Amos Walston, (w) John Norfleet, Clk.

Wasdon, Grey - Martha Ann D. Rogers, 1 June 1854, m. 1 June 1854 by Jacob S. Barnes, Justice Jones, Kintchen Corbit, (w) Willie Rogers.

Washington, George - Caroline Gorham, 17 July 1866, m. 29 July 1866 by W. H. Powell, J. P., P. H. Gorham, (w) Irvin Thigpen.

Watkins, James T. - Lowis Cutchen, 27 Aug. 1832, Norfleet Cutchen, (w) Ml. Hearn.

Watkins, Laborn - Elizabeth Barnes, 23 Jan. 1823, (Geraldus) Geerry Anderson, George W. Killebrew, (w) Ml. Hearn.

Watkins, Leavin - Edith Hinnant, 9 Oct. 1770, John Permenter.

Watkins, Orren - Sarah A. Lancaster, 23 Mar. 1852, m. 25 Nov. 1852 by Theo. Thomas, J. P., Amos J. Armstrong, (w) John Norfleet, Clk.

Watkins, Richard - Elizabeth Anderson, 21 Feb. 1862, m. 23 Feb. 1862 by C. B. Killebrew, J. P., William Davison, (w) W. A. Jones.

Watkins, Sion - Pennina Gay, 4 Dec. 1848, Joseph J. Price, (w) John Norfleet, Clk.

Watson, Charles - Sarah Beckworth, 17 Apr. 1764, William Hunt, (w) J. Hall.

Watson, Henry - Sally A. Watson, 5 Dec. 1849, William F. Bell, (w) John Norfleet, Clk.

Watson, John - Catharine Long 21 Dec. 1850, Daniel R. Taylor, (w) John Norfleet, Clk.

Watson, R. A. - Georgianna Smith. 21 June 1864. m. 21 June 1864 by Thomas R. Owen, M. G., R. W. Thomas, (w) T. W. Hussey.

Weathersbee, William H. - Sarah F. Knight, 28 Nov. 1865, m. 29 Nov. 1865 by Thomas R. Owen, V. D. M., Brinkley G. Howell, (w) Irvin Thigpen.

Weathersby, William H. - Sarah Knight. 21 Dec. 1863. m. 22 Dec. 1863 by William F. Bell, William R. Howell, (w) Irvin Thigpen, Clk.

Weaver, Benjamin F. - Rebecca A. Taylor, 4 June 1851. m. 5 June 1851 by W. F. Lewis, J. P., Henry E. Odom, (w) John Norfleet, Clk.

Weaver Benjamin Hines - Peninah Braswell, 17 Nov. 1835, Daniel R. Taylor, (w) Ml. Hearn.

Weaver. David W. - Sarah Wiggins, 14 May 1838, Drewry Williams, (w) Jo. Bell, C. C.

Weaver, William D. - Mourning Curle, 12 Jan. 1859(?), m. 14 Jan. 1857 by Theo. Thomas, J. P., John T. Weaver, (w) W. A. Jones.

Weaver. William S. - Martha A. Eason, 22 Dec. 1855, m. 23 Dec. 1855 by Bennett P. Pitt, J. P., J. T. Weaver, (w) W. S. Pitt, Clk.

Weaver, Willie - Emliza Joyner, 11 Dec. 1839, Willie J. Weaver, (w) Jo. Bell, C. C.

Weaver. Zachariah - Finetta Griffin, 4 Feb. 1828, Benjamin Weaver, (w) Ml. Hearn.

Webb, Bennett - Elizabeth Forbes, 12 Nov. 1849, James Eason, (w) John Norfleet.

Webb, Cullen - Nanny Brinkley. 27 Nov. 1849, Kinchen Walston, (w) John Norfleet, Clk.

Webb, David - Wealthy Felton, 1 Mar. 1825, Dempsey Webb, Jr., (w) Ml. Hearn.

Webb, David - Elizabeth Felton, 26 Aug. 1850, James S. Eason, (w) John Norfleet.

Webb, Dempsey, Sr. - Polly Ritter, 20 Nov. 1830, Thomas Felton, David Holland, (w) Ml. Hearn.

Webb, Dempsey - Sealy Ann Webb, 7 Nov. 1864, m. 8 Nov. 1864 by R. J. Johnson, J. P., Kinchen Walston, (w) T. W. Hussey.

Webb, Elbert - Louisana Webb, 10 Dec. 1861, m. 12 Dec. 1861 by R. J. Johnson, J. P., Joseph Edwards, (w) W. A. Jones, Clk.

Webb, Elisha - Edith Forbes, 26 Aug. 1835, William Webb, (w) Ml. Hearn.

Webb, Garrett - Jane Barron, 31 Dec. 1850, Hyrum Forbes, (w) John Norfleet, Clk.

Webb, Gray - Sally Gay, 30 Dec. 1857, m. 31 Dec. 1857 by Bennet P. Pitt, J. P., Elbert Webb, (w) I. H. Dozier.

Webb, Hardy - Vicy Orrins, 25 Nov. 1845, Kinchen Walston, (w) John Norfleet.

Webb, Henry - Hester J. Bridgers, 4 May 1863, m. 5 May 1863 by J. R. Pitt, J. P., Bennett Hagens, (w) Irvin Thigpen, Clk.

Webb, Hyram - Catharine Barron, 23 Feb. 1852, m. 26 Feb. 1852 by W. Y. Moore, J. P., James S. Eason, (w) John Norfleet, Clk.

Webb, Jesse R. - Mary A. Robinson, 8 Jan. 1848, William Harrell, (w) John Norfleet, Clk.

Webb, John - Mary A. J. Burriss, 21 Feb. 1848, Bassett Sikes.

Webb, Joseph - Christiana Webb, 12 Feb. 1851, James S. Eason, (w) John Norfleet, Clk.

Webb, Morison - Gatsey Felton, 23 Jan. 1860, m. 24 Jan 1860 by R. J. Johnson, J. P., William Walston, (w) W. A. Jones.

Webb, Nathan - Elizabeth Barnes, 4 July 1842, Watson Harris.

Webb, Redding - Nancy Brinkly, 27 Mar. 1848, Jeptha Webb, (w) John Norfleet, Clk.

Webb, Riley - Milly Owens, 20 Dec. 1834, Hyrum Forbes, (w) Ml. Hearn.

Webb, Wilie - Sally Cobb, 12 Aug. 1850, John Norfleet.

Webb, William - Sarah Amerson, 3 Jan. 1840, David Webb, (w) Jo. Bell, C. C.

Webb, Willie - Betsey Barnes, 31 July 1824, Jobe Felton, (w) N. Mathewson.

Weddell, James - Margaret Ward, 24 Feb. 1835, Danford Richards, (w) Theo. C. Hearn.

Weddell, Mathew - Maria T. Clark, 20 Oct. 1852, m. 20 Oct. 1852 by Joseph Blount Cheshire, Epis. Min., Almon Hart, (w) John Norfleet.

Weddell, Mathew - Mary M. Norcom, 6 Oct. 1862, m. 7 Oct. 1862 by Joseph Blount Cheshire, Epis. Min., R. T. Haskins, (w) Irvin Thigpen, Clk., (w) T. W. Hussey.

Weeks, Archelaus - Louisana Exum, 5 Mar. 1845, James C. Marks, (w) William Norfleet.

Weeks, Benjamin - Mary Anderson Harris, 28 Nov. 1766, Moses Feild.

Weeks, Henry - Peggy Ann Pittman, 24 Dec. 1853 (?), m. 25 Dec. 1852 by L. R. Cherry, J. P., Micajah Anderson, (w) W. S. Pitt, Clk.

Weeks, Silas - Celestia A. P. Leggett, 9 Mar. 1852, m. 11 Mar. 1852 by R. Pittman, J. P., Elias Bradley, (w) John Norfleet, Clk.

Weeks, William - Mary Edmondson, 30 Jan. 1841, Littleberry Bradley, John Norfleet, Clk.

Wells, James R. - Drucella Long, 14 Jan. 1861, James R. Long, (w) J. H. Dozier.

Wells, John B. - Jane Williams, 17 Feb. 1852, m. 17 Feb. 1852 by W. J. Armstrong, J. P., Willie S. Wells, (w) John Norfleet.

Wells, John H. - Nancy W. Pope, 2 Jan. 1827, Burrell Rose, (w) Ml. Hearn.

Wells, Redmond - Amanda Ritter, 18 Feb. 1848, Willie Atkinson, (w) Jo. Bell, C. C. C.

Wells, William H. - Martha A. Cutchens, 10 Dec. 1839, Joseph W. Maner, (w) Jo. Bell, Clk.

Wells, Willis - Lidia Hudnall, 1 Apr. 1766, John Hudnall.

West, Henry - Rebecca Robertson, 22 Jan. 1830, Malachi Odom, Henry Trevathan, Jr., (w) Ml. Hearn.

Wethersby, Lewis - Elizabeth Howard, 11 Jan. 1825, Sovereign Purvis, (w) Ml. Hearn.

Wethersby, Willis - Delha Bellamy, 10 Nov. 1856, m. 11 Nov. 1856 by R. Thigpen, J. P., E. M. C. Bryan, (w) J. H. Dozier.

Wheeler, Isham - Milly Summerlin, 21 Sept. 1826, Lemon Wheeler.

Wheeler, Isom - Melbry Pitman, 23 Feb. 1835, Jacob Byrum, (w) T. C. Hearn.

Wheeler, Noah - Martha Baily, 2 Jan. 1851, Richard Baily, (w) John Norfleet.

Whitaker, Ferdinand H. - Louisa Ed. Deberry, 18 Nov. 1850, Cary Whitaker, (w) John Norfleet.

Whitaker, James C. - Delphia Lyon, 5 Oct. 1827, William Stewart, (w) Ml. Hearn.

Whitaker, John - Christian Benton, 6 Aug. 1770, Gough Whitaker, (w) William Hall.

Whitaker, John - Mary P. Marshall, 27 Nov. 1826, L. H. B. Whitaker, James C. Whitaker, (w) Ml. Hearn.

White, Albert - Pamelia Leggett, 23 Jan. 1845, Levin Leggett, (w) John Norfleet, Clk.

White, Blount - Casanda Taylor, 26 Jan. 1863, m. 3 Feb. 1863 by John A. Stamper, Elder, John W. Manning, (w) Irvin Thigpen.

White, Burton - Isabella Leggett, 6 Jan. 1849, Levin Leggett, Mayo Worsley, (w) John Norfleet.

White, James A. - Charlotte Leggett, 2 Aug. 1865, m. 3 Aug. 1865 by John W. Johnson, J. P., Edwin G. Worsley, (w) Irvin Thigpen, Clk.

White, Jarrett - Mary A. Pitt, 25 Dec. 1854, m. 27 Dec. 1854 by W. F. Lewis, Thomas F. Cherry, (w) W. S. Pitt, Clk.

White, John P. - Charlotte Savage, 25 Feb. 1851, m. 27 Feb. 1851 by William S. Long, J. P., James S. Long, (w) John Norfleet, Clk.

White, John W. - Martha L. Hunter, 29 Feb. 1860, m. 1 Mar. 1860 by Thomas R. Owen, M. G., John F. Ward, (w) W. A. Jones.

White, Robert - Treacy Leggit, 18 Dec. 1826, John Curry, (w) Ml. Hearn.

White, William - Elizabeth Lawrence, 28 Aug. 1854, m. 31 Aug. 1854 by W. F. Lewis, J. P., Thomas F. Cherry, (w) W. S. Pitt, Clk.

Whitehead, Augustin - Mary Vaughn, 24 Nov. 1831, Richard Harrison, (w) L. H. Hearn.

Whitehead, Augustin J. M. - Caroline Petway, 14 Jan. 1850, Benjamin Norfleet, (w) John Norfleet, Clk.

Whitehead, Benjamin - Mary Arrington, 24 July 1764, Hardy Griffin, (w) J. Hall.

Whitehead, Henry A. - Lucy Joyner, 29 Nov. 1836, Alexander P. Alsobrook, (w) T. C. Hearn.

Whitehead, Henry A. - Martha Proctor, 28 Aug. 1837, Elijah Williams, William Proctor, (w) Jo. Bell.

Whitehead, James - Harriet Braswell, 22 Sept. 1827, Matthew Whitehead, (w) Ml. Hearn.

Whitehead, James H. - Mahala Beeland, 3 Feb. 1853, m. 11 Feb. 1853 by W. J. Armstrong, John Whitehead, (w) John Lawrence, Clk.

Whitehead, John - Sarah Batts, 22 Oct. 1828, Josiah Williams, (w) Ml. Hearn.

Whitehead, John - Elizabeth Harrell, 15 Apr: 1835, Joseph S. Cherry, (w) Theo. C. Hearn.

Whitehead, John - Piety Whitehead, 29 Dec. 1857, m. 31 Dec. 1857 by Hilyard Taylor, A. B. M. G., James W. Williams, (w) W. A. Jones, Clk.
Whitehead, Jordan - Elizabeth Batts, 9 Jan. 1826, David Williams, (w) N. Mathewson.
Whitehead, Leonidas L. - Emiliza Elliot, 18 Apr. 1843, Wester Rodgers, (w) John Norfleet, Clk.
Whitehead, M. L. - Mary A. Cutchen, 2 Jan. 1866, m. 2 Jan. 1866 by J. W. Johnston, J. P., Lawrence Billips, (w) Irvin Thigpen.
Whitehead, Mathew, Sr. - Phoeby Langley, 21 Dec. 1842, Mathew Whitehead, Jr., (w) John Norfleet, Clk.
Whitehead, Ralph - Mariah Battle, 24 Feb. 1866, m. 2 Mar. 1866 by Thomas L. Maner, J. P., P. J. Williams, (w) Irvin Thigpen.
Whitehead, Robert - Treacy Tomberlinson, 8 Jan. 1825, Thomas Tomberlinson, (w) Ml. Hearn.
Whitehead, Robert - Mary Freeman, 17 May 1826, Henry Austin, (w) Ml. Hearn.
Whitehead, Thaddeus - Nicey Leggett, 19 Dec. 1865, m. 21 Dec. 1865 by John Ws. Johnson, J. P., Willie Cherry, (w) Irvin Thigpen, Clk.
Whitehead, Thomas - Elizabeth Culpepper, 4 June 1768, Erasmus Culpepper, (w) James Hall.
Whitehead, Thomas - Mary Mangum, 30 July 1831, William Biggs, (w) Ml. Hearn.
Whitehead, Turner - Harriet Folk, 16 Feb. 1825, John B. Edwards, (w) Ml. Hearn.
Whitehouse, John - Lucy Holland, 14 June 1763, Edward Moore.
Whitehurst, Delany - Maria Taylor, 31 Mar. 1824, Frederick Taylor, John Mooring, Jr., (w) Ml. Hearn.
Whitehurst, James - Tabitha Taylor, 7 Feb. 1828, John Mooring, (w) Ml. Hearn.
Whitehurst, James - Nancy Staton, 17 Feb. 1842, James A. Staton, (w) John Norfleet, Clk.
Whitehurst, Marshal D. - Mary A. E. Taylor, 27 Jan. 1855, m. 1 Feb. 1855 by William R. Cherry, J. P., William A. Whitehurst, (w) W. S. Pitt, Clk.
Whitehurst, Newton - Sarah A. Howard, 18 Oct. 1852, m. 20 Oct. 1852 by William Hyman, McG. Whitehurst, (w) John Norfleet.
Whitfield, Benjamin - Temperance Manning, 8 June 1825, Daniel Hopkins, (w) Ml. Hearn, C. C.

Whitfield. Benjamin, Jr. - Nancy Council, 5 Jan. 1826, Joel Whitfield, James Knight, (w) Ml. Hearn.

Whitfield, George W. - Mary L. Wimberly. 13 Dec. 1849, Robert H. Winborne, (w) John Norfleet, Clk.

Whitfield, John G. (of Virginia) - Martha C. Coffield, 28 Jan. 1856, m. 29 Jan. 1856 by G. A. Whitaker, M. G., Cary Whitaker, (w) W. S. Pitt, Clk.

Whitley. Edwin - Charity Galloway, 24 Feb. 1852, m. 8 Apr. 1852 by William Ellis, J. P., Calvin Rogers, (w) John Norfleet, Clk.

Whitley, Edwin G. - Elizabeth Garman(?), 17 Feb. 1837, Andrew E. Gill.

Whitley, Jacob - Mary Johnston, 15 Jan. 1836, Joab Johnston, (w) Ml. Hearn.

Whitley, Jacob - Lucy Dunn, 2 May 1848, Joseph Dunn, (w) John Norfleet, Clk.

Whitley, James W. H. - Harriet W. Ethridge, 3 Jan. 1860, m. 5 Jan. 1860 by Thomas F. Cherry, J. P., Thomas F. Cherry, (w) W. A. Jones, Clk.

Whitley, John - Harriet L. Thigpen. 1 June 1848, Kenneth Thigpen, (w) John Norfleet, Clk.

Whitley. John B. - Nancy A. Daniel, 3 Nov. 1851, m. 11 Nov. 1851 by Elisha Cromwell, J. P., Rufus C. Thigpen, (w) John Norfleet, Clk.

Wichard, Alfred - Caroline Whitehurst, 12 Dec. 1850, Staton Whitchard, (w) Benjamin Norfleet.

Wiggins, Blake - Nancy Wilkinson, 1 Feb. 1823, John Wilkinson, Spencer L. Hart, (w) Ml. Hearn.

Wiggins, Garratt - Temperance Boone, 29 Dec. 1823, George W. Woodman, (w) N. Mathewson.

Wiggins, Isaac - E. Wiggins, 23 Jan. 1866, R. H. Garrett, (w) Irvin Thigpen.

Wiggins, James - Milley Taylor, 6 Dec. 1838, David W. Weaver.

Wiggins, Jesse - Frances Williams, 23 Jan. 1855, m. 25 Jan. 1855 by John G. Williams, J. P., David W. Weaver, (w) W. A. Jones, D. C.

Wiggins, Lawrence - Esther Sasnett, 27 Jan. 1827, John Garrett, (w) Ml. Hearn.

Wiggins, Mordecai - Martha J. Lawrence, 8 Apr. 1866 (?), m. 7 Apr. 1866 by W. H. Knight, J. P., Edward Zoeller, (w) Irvin Thigpen.

Wiggins, Noah - Julia F. Braswell, 23 Apr. 1845, John Webb, (w) John Norfleet, Clk.

Wiggins, Thomas - Mary Porter, 9 June 1824, Augustus W. King, Solomon T. Braddy, (w) Ml. Hearn.
Wiggins, William L. - Sally Ann Bridgers, 1 Jan. 1855, m. 2 Jan. 1855 by Bennett P. Pitt, J. P., R. H. Pender, (w) W. A. Jones, D. C.
Wiggins, Wright - Elizabeth Gardner, 26 May 1836, John Garrett, (w) Ml. Hearn.
Wilkins, Benjamin - Patsey Faithful, 24 Feb. 1831, Isaac Tolbot, (w) Ml. Hearn.
Wilkins, David - Martha Vaughn, 10 Jan. 1845, Jesse Rawlings, (w) John Norfleet.
Wilkins, James - Ann Eliza Armstrong, 29 Dec. 1832, Clemmons Darden, (w) T. C. Hearn.
Wilkins, West - Priscilla Rawls, 23 July 1770, Philip Perry, (w) William Hall.
Wilkinson, Abner - Nancy Bynum, 1 A g. 1835, Silas Wilkinson, (w) L. H. Hearn.
Wilkinson, Benonie M. - Sarah Caroline Jones, 17 Feb. 1840, Mayo Worsley, (w) Jo. Bell, C. C.
Wilkinson, Charles G. - Delphia Wiggins, 26 Dec. 1850, James Harrison, (w) Benjamin Norfleet.
Wilkinson, John E. - Amanda Anderson, 28 Aug. 1861, m. 28 Aug. 1861 by James B. Bobbitt, Charles E. Bennett, (w) T. W. Hussey, D. C.
Wilkinson, Joshua - Mary Bridgers, 13 Jan. 1835, Willie Atkinson, (w) Ml. Hearn.
Wilkinson, Silas - Sally Jenkins, 23 Sept. 1822, John Wilkinson, (w) Ml. Hearn.
Wilkinson, William - Belenda Wilkinson, 12 Jan. 1837, Llewelling R. Mooring, (w) T. C. Hearn.
Williams, Abram - Emily Mayo, 5 May 1866, m. 20 May 1866 by Erastus Cherry, J. P., Gus Williams, (w) Irvin Thigpen.
Williams, Bartley - Louisiana Proctor, 12 Jan. 1847, William W. Batts.
Williams, Bartley R. - Delilah Bailey, 28 Dec. 1838, Willie J. Weaver, (w) Jo. Bell, C. C.
Williams, Bennett - Lucinda Staton, 4 Dec. 1850, Hilyard Taylor, (w) John Norfleet.
Williams, Bennett - Polly Lancaster, 29 Nov. 1854, m. 1 Dec. 1854 by Theo. Thomas, J. P., Elza Taylor, (w) W. S. Pitt, Clk.
Williams, Bisha (Abisha)- Amanda Moore, 19 Jan. 1847, Bary (Berry) Bailey, (w) John Norfleet.
Williams, David - Frances Ruth, 31 Jan. 1831, John Mercer, (w) Ml. Hearn.

Williams, Dempsey - Amanda Fryer, 13 Apr. 1852, m. 13 Apr. 1852 by E. Barnes, Charles B. Gay, (w) John W. Farmer, J. P.

Williams, Drewry - Rebecca Baily, 23 Jan. 1843, Willie J. Weaver.

Williams, Eason - Polly Robbins, 5 Sept. 1840, Martin Daws, (w) John Norfleet.

Williams, Edmund - Martha Winstead, 22 June 1827, Jeremiah Winstead, (w) Ml. Hearn.

Williams, Elijah - Nancy Williams, 1 Feb. 1830, Willie Williams, (w) L. H. Hearn.

Williams, Gray L. - Surity (Purity) Moore, 29 Oct. 1840, John Williams, (w) John Norfleet, C. C.

Williams, Henry - Patsey Williams, 1 Feb. 1830, Benjamin Braswell, (w) L. H. Hearn.

Williams, James - Polly Moody, 5 Sept. 1835, James Adams, (w) T. C. Hearn, C. C.

Williams, James - Elizabeth May, 19 Feb. 1859, George B. Lipscombe, (w) W. A. Jones, Clk.

Williams, James H. - Mary A. Sessums, 13 May 1861, m. 14 May 1861 by Thomas L. Maner, J. P., Benjamin T. Hart, (w) W. A. Jones, Clk.

Williams, James W. - Mary Ann Margaret Whitehead, 7 Sept. 1855, Robert Braswell, (w) W. S. Pitt, Clk.

Williams, Jesse - Nancy Perry, 26 June 1833, Bird Land, (w) T. C. Hearn.

Williams, Jesse - Susanna Beland, 20 Feb. 1863, m. 20 Feb. 1863 by Hilvard S. Taylor, A. B. M. G., Jesse P. Dixon, (w) Irvin Thigpen, Clk.

Williams, Joel - Joice Proctor, 6 Feb. 1832, Benjamin Braswell, (w) L. H. Hearn.

Williams, John - Priscilla Barnes, 31 Jan. 1763, Jacob Barnes.

Williams, John - Carolina Matthewson, 26 May 1829, (w) M. L. Hearn.

Williams, John - Sarah Braswell, 21 Feb. 1833, Thomas B. Cherry, (w) Ml. Hearn.

Williams, John - Elizabeth Morris, 6 Dec. 1843, John Hales, (w) John Norfleet.

Williams, John G. - Nancy Barnes, 8 Jan. 1828, William Hall, (w) Ml. Hearn.

Williams, John R. - Martha E. Landing, 11 Nov. 1851, m. 11 Nov. 1851 by William H. Hines, J. P., Jonathan H. Bulluck, (w) John Norfleet.

Williams, Joseph - Anne Wall, 24 Aug. 1848, Charles Land, (w) John Norfleet.

Williams, Josiah - Elizabeth Whitehead, 13 Jan. 1823, Matthew Whitehead, (w) Ml. Hearn.

Williams, Michael - Mary E. Brinkley, 22 June 1852, Duncan Ferguson, (w) John Norfleet.

Williams, Nathan - Temperance Howell, 28 Feb. 1826, Ezekiel Staton, (w) Ml. Hearn.

Williams, Orren - Alice Howard, 7 Mar. 1859, m. 8 Mar. 1859 by Joseph Blount Cheshire, Epis. Min., Thomas H. Peters, (w) J. H. Dozier.

Williams, Redmond - Martha Griffin, 17 Jan. 1833, Bird Land, (w) T. C. Hearn.

Williams, Richard - Susan Right, 16 Aug. 1834, Daniel Land, (w) T. C. Hearn.

Williams, Robert - Roana Gay, 11 Nov. 1856, m. 13 Nov. 1856 by J. C. Knight, J. P., William J. Bulluck, (w) W. A. Jones.

Williams, Roderick - Nancy Garrett, 23 Dec. 1826, Christopher Harrell, (w) Ml. Hearn.

Williams, Robert - Holly Coggins, 29 July 1846, Arthur M. Barlow, (w) W. L. Dozier, D. C.

Williams, Stephen - Mary Williams, 20 Sept. 1830, Bird Land, (w) Ml. Hearn.

Williams, Thomas - Sally Ann Ward, 21 Jan. 1852, m. 22 Jan. 1852 by William F. Mercer, J. P., Guilford Moore, (w) John Norfleet.

Williams, Thomas - Susan Williams, 30 June 1857, m. 30 June 1857 by William F. Mercer, J. P., Baker S. Brown, (w) W. A. Jones, Clk.

Williams, W. B. - Margaret Ruffin, 29 July 1857, m. 30 July 1857 by Hylyard S. Taylor, A. B. M. G., Elza Taylor, (w) J. H. Dozier.

Williams, W. H. - Mary Ann J. Lancaster, 17 Dec. 1853, m. 20 Dec. 1853 by D. W. Barnes, J. P., Willie G. Barnes, (w) W. S. Pitt, Clk.

Williams, Whitmel - Betzada Taylor, 21 Jan. 1824, John Long, (w) Ml. Hearn.

Williams, William A. - Elmyra E. Wynn, 27 Feb. 1850, Hilyard Taylor, (w) John Norfleet, Clk.

Williams, William D. - Margaret E. Jones, 12 Sept. 1854, m. 12 Oct. 1854 by C. C. Bonner, J. P., W. W. Parker, (w) W. S. Pitt, Clk.

Williams, Willie - Susan Pitt, 14 Aug. 1827, Isaac Robbins, (w) Ml. Hearn.

Williams, Willie - Elizabeth Ruffin, 28 Oct. 1829, Peoples Hill, (w) Ml. Hearn.

Williams, Worsley - Letha Taylor, 11 Oct. 1866, m. 11 Oct. 1866 by Hilyard Taylor, A. B. M. G., Richard Flood, (w) Irvin Thigpen.

Williams, Wright I. - Margaret L. Anderson, 27 May 1856, m. 27 May 1856 by C. W. Spicer, J. P., James B. Thomas, (w) W. A. Jones, Clk.

Williford, Andrew J. - Lucy Lancaster, 2 Jan. 1860, m. 3 Jan. 1860 by Hilliard S. Taylor, A. B. M. G., S. L. Spicer, (w) W. A. Jones.

Williford, Bennett L. - Mary A. Meares, 26 Aug. 1850, William W. Batts, (w) John Norfleet, Clk.

Williford, Blake - Martha Ann Jordan, 17 Mar. 1837, William D. Petway, (w) Ml. Hearn.

Williford, Elijah - Julia A. Batchelor, 14 Nov. 1852, m. 14 Nov. 1852 by W. F. Lewis, J. P., Irvin Thigpen, (w) John Norfleet, Clk.

Williford, Hartwell - Elizabeth Sharpe, 4 Nov. 1848, James G. Williford, (w) John Norfleet.

Williford, Hilliard - Bashaby Batts, 23 Dec. 1835, Benjamin D. Battle, (w) T. C. Hearn.

Williford, Hilliard L. - Peninah Batts, 26 Nov. 1834, Benjamin D. Battle, (w) Ml. Hearn.

Williford, James G. - Polly Curl, 26 Nov. 1834, Hartwell Williford, (w) T. C. Hearn.

Williford, James G. - Nancy Mears, 11 June 1853, m. 16 June 1853 by James J. Taylor, J. P., David W. Weaver, (w) John Norfleet, Clk.

Williford, John - Catalina Long, 22 Apr. 1839, Robert R. Braswell.

Williford, John D. - Sally Jones, 31 Dec. 1856, m. 1 Jan. 1857, by Hilliard S. Taylor, M. G., Jesse Dixon, (w) W. A. Jones, Clk.

Williford, John G. - Mary Williford, 17 Mar. 1845, Meedy E. Williford, (w) John Norfleet.

Williford, Joseph (s. of Harmon Williford) - Margaret F. Cutchin (dau. of T. H. Cutchin), 9 Mar. 1868, m. 12 Mar. 1868 by M. C. Hepinstall, Meth. Min., (w) Irvin Thigpen.

Williford, Meady - Elizabeth Moore, 11 Nov. 1845, William Y. Moore, (w) E. D. McNair.

Williford, Meedy B. - Jaruthy A. Whitley, 25 Jan. 1866, m. 1 Feb. 1866 by Hilyard S. Taylor, A. B. M. G., Joseph B. Coffield, (w) Irvin Thigpen.

Williford, Thomas - Mary Calhoon, 14 Feb. 1832, Meedy Williford, (w) Ml. Hearn.

Williford, William - Matilda Robbins, 10 Feb. 1850, Henry Marshburn, (w) John Norfleet.

Wilson, Asa - Emily A. Edwards, 23 Jan. 1836, Edwin Bulluck, (w) T. C. Hearn.

Wilson, John - Susan Dunn, 8 May 1834, (w) Ml. Hearn.

Wimberly, George - Charity Thomas, 1 Sept. 1764, Malachi Hinton, (w) Edward Hall.

Wimberly, George - Catherine Hart, 28 May 1827, Henry Bryan, Edwin L. Moore, (w) Ml. Hearn.

Wimberly, Joseph W. - Martha Lawrence, 1 Dec. 1859, m. 1 Dec. 1859 by Thomas R. Owen, M. G., William T. Macnair, (w) W. A. Jones, Clk.

Winborne, Augustus (s. of Joseph Winborne) - Susan Tyler, (dau. of Lorenza D. Tyler), 12 Feb. 1868, m. 13 Feb. 1868 by Lunsford R. Cherry, J. P., (w) Irvin Thigpen, Clk.

Winborne, George Lawrence - Martha A. Parker, 15 Jan. 1852, m. 15 Jan. 1852 by Henry T. Clark, J. P., John H. Leigh, (w) John Norfleet.

Winborne, Henry - Nancy Luper, 9 Jan. 1866, m. 9 Jan. 1866 by John Norfleet, J. P., D. Griffin, (w) Irvin Thigpen.

Winbourne, Joseph J. - Lavina Dixon, 15 Nov. 1832, Harrod Pitman, (w) Ml. Hearn.

Windham, Cannon - Susan Taylor, 16 Aug. 1830, Caswell Horn, (w) L. H. Hearn.

Windham, Willie - Sally Rogers, 26 Aug. 1823, Henry T. Stonton (Staton?), (w) Ml. Hearn.

Wingate, Elias - Delpha Mercer, 23 Jan. 1866, m. 28 Feb. 1866 by A. W. Lowe, M. G., R. H. Garrett, (w) Irvin Thigpen.

Winstead, Edwin - Elizabeth Ellis, 22 Dec. 1851, m. 23 Dec. 1851 by Lewis Ellis, J. P., G. M. Winstead, (w) John Norfleet, Clk.

Winstead, Elijah G. - Elizabeth Pitt, 23 Dec. 1847, Flowers Winstead, (w) James H. Dozier.

Winstead, Flowers - Mary Ann Catherine Joiner, 26 Aug. 1841, Wright W. Joyner.

Winstead, George - Mary Ellis, 18 Jan. 1850, Joseph Dunn, John Norfleet, Clk.

Winstead, John G. - Nancy Land, 16 Sept. 1841, Andrew A. Calhoon.

Winstead, Redmond - Polly Loe, 12 Dec. 1851, m. 14 Dec. 1851 by Jos. J. Taylor, Willie S. Wells, (w) John Norfleet, Clk.

Winstead, Willie - Betsy Horn, 24 Nov. 1840, James Thorn, (w) John Norfleet, Clk.

Womble, Edward - Betsy Crisp, 26 Aug. 1826, Samuel Stillman, (w) John H. Mathewson.

Womble, Enos - Lucinda Ford. 30 May 1854, m. 31 May 1854 by John S. Dancy, J. P., Enos Womble, (w) W. A. Jones.

Womble, Jacob Y. - Nancy Fryar, 2 Feb. 1830, Nathaniel G. Womble, (w) L. H. Hearn.

Womble, Nathaniel G. - Martha Taylor, 3 July 1857, m. 12 July 1857 by Hilyard S. Taylor, A. B. M. G., Lucian B. Battle, (w) W. A. Jones.

Womble. Nathaniel G. - Elizabeth Ethridge, 2 May 1864. m. 2 May 1864 by Theo. Thomas, J. P., (w) Irvin Thigpen.

Womble. Nathaniel Green - Celia Sorrell. 9 Jan. 1823, Doctor Warren Womble, Weeks Parker, Jr., (w) Ml. Hearn.

Womble. Nathaniel Green - Martha Frier, 3 Dec. 1823, Doctor Warren Womble, (w) Ml. Hearn.

Wood, John - Judith Brooks (widow), 23 July 1761, (w) James Hall.

Wood, Joseph - Elizabeth Corbitt, 17 Feb. 1866, m. 28 Feb. 1866 by J. F. Batts, J. P., William L. Dixon, (w) Irvin Thigpen, Clk.

Wood, Joshua - Nancy Savage, 27 Dec. 1866, m. 27 Dec. 1866 by E. D. Macnair, J. P., Burrell Savage, (w) Irvin Thigpen, Clk.

Woodard, Daniel - Sarah Pitt, 12 Dec. 1767, Kadar Coleman, (w) Edward Hall.

Woodard, Elisha - Betsy Boyt, 21 Nov. 1823, (w) N. Mathewson.

Woodard, Gaston - Martha Ann Hays, 13 July 1855 (?), m. 13 Feb. 1855 by J. L. Barnes, Jr., William Barnes, Jr., (w) W. S. Pitt, Clk.

Woodard, Gray W. - Mary Barnes, 28 Aug. 1854, W. W. Batts.

Woodard, James - Susannah Menshaw, 24 May 1823, Henry T. Stanton, (w) Ml. Hearn.

Woodard, James B. - Nancy Daniel, 8 Oct. 1822, Josiah Daniel, (w) N. Mathewson.

Woodard, James B. - Sally Peel, 27 Feb. 1827, Willie Ellis.

Woodard, James B. - Sarah B. King, 7 Apr. 1841, William L. Dozier, (w) John Norfleet, Clk.

Woodard, Lamuel - Beedy Barnes, 22 May 1799, Elisha Woodard, (w) S. Wrenn, (w) Archelaus Barnes.

Woodard, Phelix - Patience Simms, 27 Dec. 1828, Nathan H. Rountree, (w) Ml. Hearn.

Wooten, Amos, Jr. - Sally A. E. Norvill, 25 Jan. 1837, Stephen Edwards, (w) Ml. Hearn.

Wooten, Amos - Fanny Wootten, 28 Jan. 1845, Spencer W. Wootten, John Norfleet, Clk.

Wooten, Benajah - Parmelia Edwards, 23 Feb. 1846, Stephen Edwards, (w) John Norfleet.

Wootten, Henry - Elizabeth Cobb, 31 July 1832, John R. Scarborough, (w) L. H. Hearn.

Wooten, James - Litha Mercer, 14 Feb. 1831, William D. Jenkins, (w) Ml. Hearn, C. C.

Wootten, James - Nancy Page, 10 Dec. 1833, John Walston, Jacob Mercer, (w) Ml. Hearn.

Wooten, Mansel - Sally Cobb, 8 Jan. 1850, William P. Dunford, (w) John Norfleet.

Wooten, Spencer W. - Jenetta Edwards, 30 Dec. 1843, William P. Dunford, (w) John Norfleet, Clk.

Wooten, Stephen C. - Susan E. Wilkinson, 18 Dec. 1860, m. 20 Dec. 1860 by Bennett P. Pitt, Hardy Norville, (w) Thomas W. Hussey.

Wooten, Stephen W. - Delpha Ann Wooten, 23 Jan. 1845, Benejah Wooten, (w) John Norfleet, Clk.

Wooten, Worrell W. - Tamsey Corbett, 28 Dec. 1858, m. 30 Dec. 1858 by R. J. Johnson, J. P., Mansel Wooten, (w) J. H. Dozier.

Wootten, George W. - Julia A. Gay, 3 Apr. 1849, Jos. John Williams, (w) Benjamin Norfleet.

Wormick, William D. - Mary E. Jones, 29 Apr. 1863, m. 31 Apr. 1863 by W. F. Lewis, Silas Weeks, (w) Irvin Thigpen, Clk.

Worrell, John - Rebecca Webb, 27 Mar. 1847, Cullen W. Pender, (w) John Norfleet.

Worrell, John T. - Sally Ann Harper, 31 Mar. 1852, m. 1 Apr. 1852 by W. F. Lewis, J. P., John W. Johnson, (w) John Norfleet, Clk.

Worrell, William - Elizabeth Manning, 18 Mar. 1764, Joshua Johnson, (w) Thomas Cavanah.

Worsely, Henry Guilford - Elizabeth Proctor, 12 Dec. 1859, m. 14 Dec. 1859 by Hilliard S. Taylor, A. B. M. G., William Worsley, Jr., (w) W. A. Jones, Clk.

Worseley, Nathan G. - Evelina Anderson, 1 Jan. 1845, Robert Johnson, (w) William Norfleet.

Worsely, Etheldred - Brittania Spelling, 15 Oct. 1828, Frederick Mayo, (w) Ml. Hearn.

Worsley, John - Emeliza Spicer, 2 Nov. 1831, Thomas Dickinson, (w) Michl. Hearn.

Worsley, (or Hopkins) Littleberry - Renny Cherry, 5 Mar. 1832, (w) Ml. Hearn.

Worsley, Mayo - Nancy Wiggins, 8 Dec. 1828, Cullin Adams, (w) Ml. Hearn.

Worsley, Mayo - Mary L. Staton, 22 Feb. 1842, Joseph John Pippin.

Wright, John - Obedience Brownrigg, 12 Sept. 1828, Willie Brownrigg, (w) Ml. Hearn.

Wright, Jordan - Hariot E. Pugh, 17 July 1832, Joseph B. G. Roulhac, (w) T. C. Hearn.

Wright, Thomas - Susan Moore, 16 Oct. 1827, Job Felton, (w) Ml. Hearn.

Wright, Thomas D. - Mary R. Pope, 17 Dec. 1860, m. 18 Dec. 1860 by Thomas L. Maner, J. P., Richard Odom, (w) J. H. Dozier.

Wyatt, James - Sarah Foreman, 14 May 1766, Samuel Foreman, (w) James Hall.

Wynn, John P. - Catharine Daws, 26 Feb. 1857, m. 26 Feb. 1857 by Hylard S. Taylor, A. B. M. G., Kinchen Edwards, (w) W. A. Jones, Clk.

Y

Yellowby, Charlton W. - Carolina Toole, 10 Feb. 1858, m. 11 Feb. 1858 by Joseph Blount Cheshire, Epis. Min., Wm. Macnair, (w) ———.

Yelverton, George T. - Edith Farmer, 31 Jan. 1848, John Farmer, (w) John Norfleet, Clk.

York, John - Mary Gray, 18 Mar. 1823, Louis D. Wilson, (w) Ml. Hearn.

Young, John - Mary Whitehouse, 26 Jan. 1763, Robert Young, (w) J. Hall.

Young, William - Sarah Sellers, 19 Aug. 1763, Arthur Sellers, (w) John Spendelow.

MARRIAGE RECORDS FROM THE REGISTER EDGECOMBE COUNTY COURT HOUSE

Tarboro, N. C.
1867 - 1868

A

Abanathy (Abernathy), William to Louisa Andrews, Dec. 19, 1867, William Harrell, J. P.

Andres, (Andrews) to Fanny Mayo. (Dates illegible.)

Atkins, Bartlett E. to Vickie Armstrong, Nov. 21, 1867, Rocky Mount, D. T. Tawles (Toles?).

Atkinson, Laurin (Lamon?) to Angelina Summerlin, Mar. 8, 1868, H. T. Clark, J. P.

B

Beland, William B. to Louisanna Williams, Dec. 19, 1867, H. S. Taylor, A. B. M. G.

Bennett, George to Ellen Webb, Feb. 14, 1868, James F. Jenkins, J. P.

Bradley, Cornelius to Martha Bradley, May 21, 1868, F. L. Ward, J. P.

Braswell, Asberry (Asbury) to Sally Walls, Nov. 25, 1868, Hilyard (Hilliard) Taylor, A. B. M. G.

Braswell, Duncan B. R. to Cathrine Hinton, Dec. 24, 1867, H. S. Taylor, A. B. M. G.

Braswell, John H. to Sallie Hinton, Oct. 13, 1868, William V. Taylor, A. B. M. G.

Braswell, William to Martha A. Bailey, Aug. 20, 1867.

Brown, George A. to Mary A. Hooker, Oct. 3, 1867, E. Cherry.

Brown, Gray L. to Harriet M. Stancil, Nov. 14, 1867, R. K. Hearn, Minister.

Bullock, T. E. to Lucinda Williams, Jan. 30, 1868, Jas. F. Jenkins, J. P.

Burras, Thomas L. to Louisa Tyler, Apr. 2, 1868, Thos. R. Owens, V. D. M.

Burrop, (Burros) Willie to Mary D. House, May 30, 1867, Thos. D. Maner, J. P.

Butterworth, Joseph W. to Mattie Southall, Oct. 28, 1867, M. Jenkins, M. G.

Bynum, Thomas W. to Harriett Little, Sept. 8, 1868, Joseph Cobb, J. P.

C

Chesson, James A. to Sarah R. Pender, Jan. 16, 1868, Jos. Blount Cheshire, Epis. Rector.

Clark, William to Cinda Armstrong, Jan. 16, 1868, Orren Williams, J. P.

Cobb, Joseph to Catherine A. Bynum, May 24, 1867, Thomas R. Owens, V. D. M.

Cobb, William R. to John Ella Pitt, Sept. 29, 1868, C. S. Nius, J. P.

Corbett, Henry to Elizabeth Eason, Dec. 11, 1868, Joseph Cobb, J. P.

Cutchin, Green J. S. to Anna C. Manina, Dec. 29, 1868, John Purvis, M. G.

D

Dillard, Levi to Mary Tailor (Taylor), July 15, 1867, J. J. Proctor, J. P.

Dixon, James W. to Elizabeth Canady, Jan. 30, 1868, W. H. Knight, J. P.

Dunn, Joseph to Anna Griffin, Jan. 16, 1868.

E

Edwards, Adam to Pennina Shelton, Oct. 28, 1867, B. P. Pitt, J. P.

Edwards, Willie to Elizabeth Braswell, June 18, 1867, Hilliard S. Taylor, A. B. M. G.

Edmondson, Joseph E. to Meduvia (?) Ruffin, Feb. 27, 1867, S. L. Hart, J. P.

Everett, John D. to Sallie Ann Everett, Dec. 29, 1868, Joseph Cobb, J. P.

F

Farley, John M. to Sarah A. Worrell, July 4, 1867, I. F. Batts, J. P.

Felton, Elisha to Selequa (?) Edwards, Dec. 30, 1867, R. I. Johnson.

Fountain, Joseph I. to Charlotte Pitt, Feb. 13, 1868, Lunsford R. Cherry, J. P.

Friar, Jepe (Jesse) to Catherine Gardner, May 29, 1867, J. H. Daniel, M. G.

G

Gay, James to Elizabeth Dunsford, June 4, 1867, R. I. Johnson, J. P.

Gay Silas W. to Mary Atkinson, Dec. 17, 1868, H. S. Taylor, M. G.

Gorham, Samuel to Nancy Williams, Oct. 7, 1867, J. J. Proctor, J. P.

Gorham, William F. to Mary A. Cherry, Mar. 4, 1868, Kenneth Thigpen.

Griffin, Simon H. to Nannie Trevathan, May 8, 1867, Thomas R. Owen, V. D. M.

Green, William F. to Louisa F. Williams, June 25, 1867, T. M. Jones.

Griffin, Henderson to Martha A. Proctor, Dec. 3, 1867, H. S. Taylor, A. B. M. G.

Griffin, John to Lucy Clark, May 12, 1868, W. F. Lewis.

H

Harrell, Edward E. to Mary Bland, Dec. 17, 1867, W. F. Bell.

Harrell, Jepe (Jesse) to Edu (Edie) Vainwright, July 30, 1867, R. I. Johnson, J. P.

Harrell, Wilson to Maudia Jones, Feb. 28, 1868, R. I. Jones, (Johnson?), J. P.

Hardy, John to Emily L. Shelton, Jan. 8, 1868, William Harrell, J. P.

Harris, James to Evelina Shelton, Nov. 26, 1868, A. M. McCabe, J. P.

Holden, Timpronous to Mahala Jane Batts, Nov. 12, 1868, J. W. Jenkins, M. G.

J

Joyner, John H. to Christina Robbins, Mar. 12, 1868, H. S. Taylor, A. B. M. G.

L

Lawrence, John J. to Laura Knight, Dec. 13, 1867, John H. Daniel, M. G.

Landing, Mills to Lucinda Braswell, Dec. 5, 1867, Jas. F. Jenkins, J. P.

Lanier, James B. to Cornelia V. Ricks, Oct. 8, 1867, Thomas R. Owens, V. D. M.

Lancaster, Thomas to Kittuna (Kitturah) Roberson, Mar. 24, 1868, H. S. Taylor, A. B. M. G.

Lawrence, Patrick McD. to Martha A. Bradley, June 25, 1868, William F. Lewis, J. P.

Lane, Lawrence to Lucy Ann Ruffin, Nov. 19, 1868, L. Fountain, J. P.

Leigh, Francis M. to Perlina Reddick, July 11, 1867, Wm. Harrell, J. P.

M

Mallory, Wm. L. to Pamela Sheppard, Aug. 6, 1867, Jos. Blount Cheshire, Epis.
Mayo, Augustus to Louisa Deal, July 13, 1867, Wm. Harrell, J. P.
Mayo, Ralph to Trecy Lewis, June 2, 1868, Wm. Harrell, J. P.
Mayo, James M. to Florence A. Lyon, Oct. 9, 1868, G. S. G. Whitaker, M. G.
Meeks, William J. to Gatsey Mayo, May 28, 1868, Wm. Harrell, J. P.
Mears, Henry to Drusilla Pitt, Jan. 23, 1868, L. L. Hart, J. P.
Mills, L. R. to Anna H. Lewis. (No further data.)

Mc

McClarron, Benj. to Mary Stephenson, Aug. 29, 1867, J. H. Howard, J. P.
McDowell, William to Mary F. Farmer, Nov. 10, 1868, J. W. Jackson, M. G.

N

Nelson, R. James to Jennett Whichard, Dec. 10, 1867, Jas. F. Howard, J. P.
Newton, Joseph to Sarah Etheridge, Sept. 17, 1868, John H. Carlisle, J. P.
Neal, William D. to Jenny Ann Hanson, Jan. 12, 1868, Jas. R. Thigpen, J. P.
Norville, William to Mary Eagles, June 18, 1868, Jesse Baker, Elder.

O

Oliver, Richard to Pripa Talbot, Mar. 5, 1868, John T. Bellamy, J. P.
Owen, George to Nancy Griffin, Oct. 3, 1867, R. I. Johnson, J. P.
Owens, Thomas W. to Treacy (Tremmy) Edwards, Nov. 5, 1867, R. I. Johnson, J. P.

P

Pender, Joshua to Kate D. Pender, July 14, 1868, Thos. R. Owens, V. D. M.
Pender, Robert H. to M. E. Hanks, Aug. 2, 1867, P. H. Dalton, M. G.
Perkins, David B. to Lucy A. Vick, Feb. 6, 1868, E. Cherry, J. P.
Perry, John M. to Delah Barlow, Apr. 15, 1868, Thos. R. Owens, V. D. M.

Phillips, William E. to ——(?), Nov. 21, 1867, B. P. Pitt, J. P.

Pitt, Campbell B. to Mary E. Ricks, Oct. 8, 1867, Thomas R. Owens, V. D. M.

Pittman, N. J. to M. E. Dancy, Apr. 21, 1867, Thos. Atkinson, Bishop.

Pitt, M. B. to Fannie P. Cobb, Dec. 8, 1868, John H. Daniel, M. G.

Pitt, James A. to Sarah L. Crisp, Dec. 10, 1868, John H. Daniel, M. G.

Powell, Allen to Cuita Powell, Apr. 18, 1868, Thos. L. Maner, J. P.

R

Reed, David C. to Vester Garvy, Jan. 30, 1868, D. F. Towl, M. G.

Rodgers, Augustus to Della Lewis, Oct. 25, 1868, L. Fountain, J. P.

Roberts, Ashwell to Sarah A. Mears, Sept. 3, 1868, Henry T. Clark, J. P.

Roberson, David R. to Julia Gay, Jan. 7, 1868, H. S. Taylor, A. B. M. G.

Ruffin, John R. to Amanda Gardner, Aug. 29, 1867, H. S. Taylor, A. B. M. G.

Ruffin, A. J. to Mary Ann E. Pittman, Apr. 21, 1869, F. L. Hart, J. P.

S

Skinner, Seth to Manda ———, Aug. 4, 1867, D. T. Tomley, M. G.

Sparks, Henry to Jane Fountain, Nov. 7, 1867, L. R. Cherry, J. P.

Stancil, George W. to Alsey Gavaltney (Gwaltney?), Dec. 12, 1867, R. K. Hearns, M. G.

Starke, Lucien D. to Telitha L. M. Pippen, Jan. 8, 1868, Joseph Blount Cheshire, Rector.

Sparks, Henry to Jane Fountain, Nov. 7, 1867, L. R. Cherry, J. P.

Staton, Berry to Melvina Dunn, May 7, 1868, W. L. Long, J. P.

T

Thomas, George W. to Mary E. Fly, Sept. 10, 1868, N. S. Taylor, A. B. M. G.

Thorn, Punch to Rose Pender, May 23, 1868, W. H. Powell, J. P.

Trevathan, James D. to Elizabeth Brown, Dec. 22, 1868, H. S. Taylor, A. B. M. G.

V

Vick, John B. to Elisa S. Drake, May 8, 1867, H. L. Leggett, J. P.

W

Walston, John to Susan R. Porter, Sept. 10, 1868, Joshua Harrell, M. G.

Waller, Henry to Mrs. Margaret Waller, Oct. 29, 1868, W. T. Godwin, J. P.

Walker, George to Leona Worsley, Dec. 24, 1868, J. H. Daniel, M. G.

Webb, John to Bedy Webb, July 30, 1867, R. I. Johnson, J. P.

West, John to Sallie Ann Mason, Dec. 23, 1867, Thos. L. Maner, J. P.

Wells, John to Fannie Circey, Dec. 26, 1868, L. Fountain, J. P.

White, Thomas to Nancy Bradley, May 30, 1867, H. L. Leggett, J. P.

Whitehead, Frederick to Mary E. Anderson, Dec. 6, 1867, H. L. Leggett, J. P.

Williams, John to Susan Proctor, Dec. 12, 1867, Jas. F. Jenkins, J. P.

Williams, Franklin to Louisa Peeples, Dec. 5, 1867, H. S. Taylor, A. B. M. G.

Williams, James D. to Joanna Flood, Nov. 5, 1867, Hilliard S. Taylor, A. B. M. G.

Williams, David L. to Elizabeth L. Austin, Sept. 10, 1867, Thomas R. Owen, V. D. M.

Williams, James H. to Charity Weaver, May 14, 1867, Hilliard S. Taylor, A. B. M. G.

Williams, William A. to Harriett P. Latham, Jan. 15, 1868, Thos. R. Owens, V. D. M.

Williams, Joseph to Anna McDaniel, Nov. 10, 1868, T. R. Owens, V. D. M.

Williford, Joseph to Margaret F. Cutchin, Mar. 12, 1868, M. C. Hepinstall, M. G.

Winborn, Augustus to Susan F. Tyler, Feb. 13, 1868, Lunsford R. Cherry, J. P.

Worsley, William to Mary M. Long, Nov. 1, 1868, R. P. Petway, J. P.

PART II

Marriages Proved by Edgecombe County Wills

Marriages from The Raleigh Register and North Carolina Gazette, 1799-1868

Marriages from The Tarboro Free Press, 1826-1845

Marriages from The Battle Book

Marriages from the Files of Hugh B. Johnston, Jr.

Marriages Proved by Records in Halifax County

Miscellaneous

MARRIAGES PROVED BY EDGECOMBE COUNTY WILLS
By Margarette Glenn Griffin

Unless otherwise noted, testator of will was usually a parent.

Where two dates appear, the first signifies date of will, the second represents date of probation.

A

Abrams, Elijah m. Mary F. Dupree, (dau. of William R. Dupree), W. Bk. G, p. 84, Will of Temperance Pippen, 1852-1854.

Adams, ? m. Unity House, W. Bk. C, p. 167, Will of John House, 1791-1791,

Adams, Henry? m. Martha Ann Fountain, W. Bk. F, p. 19, Will of James Fountain, 1824-1824.

Addams, ? m. Martha Lloyd, Will of Nicholas Lloyd, 1781-1781,

Adkins, John m. Lucy Phillips, Will of Arthur Phillips, 1789-1790.

Alexander, ? m. Crystal Jones, Will of Hardy Jones, 1796-1796.

Alford, ? m. Mary E. Barnes, W. Bk. F, p. 252, Will of Charlie Barnes, 1840-1841.

Allen, ? m. Mary Savage, Will of Loveliss (Lovelace) Savage, 1802-1807.

Allen, ? m. Rachel Price, Will of Thomas Price, 1779-1781.

Allen, ? m. Susannah Taylor, Will of James Taylor, 1782-1783.

Alsobrook, ? m. Dolly Dillard, W. Bk. E, p. 172, Will of Elizabeth Dillard, 1817-1817.

Alsobrook, ? m. Mary Braddy, Will of Joseph Braddy, 1802-1804.

Alsobrook, ? m. Penelope Hyett, Will of Thomas Hyett, 1781-1783.

Alsobrook, David m. Thenah (Pheby) Wall, W. Bk. B, p. 50, Will of John Wall, Halifax Co., 1778-1779.

Amason, ? m. Elizabeth Farmer, W. Bk. F, p. 65, Will of Benjamin Farmer, 1825-1827.

Amason, ? m. Martha Bailey, W. Bk. F, p. 470, Will of Jonathan Bailey, 1852.

Amason, ? m. Sarah Barnes, Will of Edward Barnes, 1760-1762.

Amason, Benjamin m. ? Lewelling, Will of Alexander Lewelling, 1791-1792.

Amason, Thomas? m. Martha Bailey, W. Bk. F, p. 470, Will of Jonathan Bailey, 1852.

Amason, Thomas m. Nancy Robbins, W. Bk. E, p. 217, Will of John Robbins, 1819-1819.

Amerson, Benjamin m. Martha Woodard, W. Bk. D, p. 50, Will of Elisha Woodard, 1798-1798.

Amerson, Isaac m. Delanah Woodard, W. Bk. D, p. 50, Will of Elisha Woodard, 1798-1798.

Amerson, William? m. Jerusha Moore, Will of Samuel Moore, 1793-1794.

Anderson, ? m. Ann McDaniel, Will of Daniel McDaniel, 1768-1769.

Anderson, ? m. Delilah Horn, Will of Michael Horn, 1785.

Anderson, ? m. Jacque Thompson, W. Bk. F, p. 495, Will of Mary Thompson, 1849-1853.

Anderson, James m. Patience O'Neel, W. Bk. E, p. 7, Will of Isham O'Neel, 1811-1811.

Andrews, ? m. Lovey Staton, W. Bk. E, p. 58, Will of Jesse Staton, 1812-1813.

Andrews, John m. Elizabeth Maund, W. Bk. D, p. 352, Will of John Andrews, 1809.

Andrews, ? m. Clarey Bentley, Will of Joshua Bentley, 1799-1799.

Andrews, ? m. Mourning Price, Will of Thomas Price, 1779-1781.

Andrew, Joseph m. Cloah Forehand, W. Bk. D, p. 146, Will of Solomon Forehand, 1798-1802.

Andry, ? (Andre'?) m. Venah Barfield, W. Bk. D, p. 349, Will of Charles Barfield, 1809.

Applewhite, ? m. Elizabeth Barnes, Will of Dempsey Barnes, 1807.

Applewhite, Council m. Sally Bynum, W. Bk. F, p. 259, Will of Joseph Bynum, 1841-1841; W. Bk. F, p. 408, Will of brother, Samuel V. Bynum, 1848-1848.

Arrington, ? m. Mourning Ricks, Will of James Ricks, 1792-1792.

Arrington, Thomas James m. Ann Willis, W. Bk. A, p. 245, Will of William Willis, 1776-1776.

Artice, ? m. Sally Laseter, W. Bk. F, p. 502, Will of Hardy Laseter, 1851-1853.

Ashburn, ? m. Susanah Daughtis, Will of brother, Dempsey Daughtis (Daughty), 1761-1778.

Austin, Henry? m. Lydia Pippen, W. Bk. F, p. 146, Will of Joseph Pippen, 1827-1833; W. Bk. F, p. 330, Will of Martha Porter, 1845-1845; Will of Henry Austin, 1843-1845.

B

Baggett, ? m. Dicy Davis, W. Bk. F, p. 15, Will of John Davis, 1822-1824.

Baggett, ? m. Elizabeth Jones, Will of Hardy Jones, 1796-1796.

Baggett, ? m. Martha Amason, Will of William Amason, 1793.

Baggett, ? m. Obedience Amason, Will of William Amason, 1793.

Bailey, ? m. Kesiah Spicer, W. Bk. E, p. 308, Will of William Spicer, 1820-1822.

Baker, Aaron or Moses m. Mary Vickers, W. Bk. A, p. 110, Will of Ralph Vickers, 1761.

Baldwin. ? m. Sarah Carlile or Bell, Will of Sarah Carlile, 1772-1776.

Ballard, ? m. Sarah Cromwell, W. Bk. C, p. 66, Will of Alexander Cromwell, 1788-1789.

Ballard, ? m. Leady Evens, W. Bk. A, p. 155, Will of Elizabeth Evens, 1766-1766.

Ball, ? m. Mourning Kinchen, Will of William Kinchen, 1779.

Banks, Thomas? m. West Pitt, W. Bk. E, p. 264, Will of Ann Pitt, 1809-1821; Will of Ethelred Pitt, 1798-1799, s. of James and Ann Pitt.

Barefoot, ? m. Zilpha Barnes, W. Bk. F, p. 324, Will of James W. Barnes, 1844-1845.

Barfield, ? m. Elizabeth Staton, W. Bk. E, p. 297, Will of Nehemiah Staton, 1820-1822.

Barfield, John m. ? Savage, W. Bk. F, p. 164, Will of James Savage, 1834-1834.

Barfoot, ? m. Sarah Sanders, Will of Thomas Sanders, 1801-1802.

Bargam, ? m. Sally Simms, W. Bk. E, p. 79, Will of Benjamin Simms, 1814-1815.

Barlow, David m. Nanney Proctor, W. Bk. C, p. 21, Will of Joshua Proctor, 1785-1785.

Barnes, ? m. Elizabeth Simms, W. Bk. F, p. 459, Will of Zilla Simms, 1851-1851.

Barnes, ? m. Elizabeth Skinner, Will of Elizabeth Barnes, 1789-1794.

Barnes, ? m. Elizabeth Thomas, Will of Mary Thomas, 1802-1802.
Barnes, ? m. Jane Robbins, W. Bk. F, p. 339, Will of Simon Robbins, 1848-1850.
Barnes, ? m. Martha Foort, Will of George Foort, 1761-1761.
Barnes, ? m. Oney Tisdal, W. Bk. E, p. 2, Will of Renison Tisdal, 1808-1811.
Barnes, ? m. Orfee Foort, Will of George Foort (Fort), 1761-1761.
Barnes, ? m. Patience Amason, Will of William Amason, 1793.
Barnes, ? m. Patsey Simms, W. Bk. E, p. 79, Will of Benjamin Simms, 1814-1815.
Barnes, ? m. Polly Horn, W. Bk. E, p. 74, Will of brother, Michael Horn, 1814-1814.
Barnes, ? m. Selah Deloach, Will of Mary Deloach, 1773-1774.
Barnes, ? m. Tempy Parker, W. Bk. E, p. 151, Will of Mary Parker, wid. of William Parker, 1817-1817.
Barnes, Edwin m. Elizabeth Simms, W. Bk. F, p. 459, Will of James Simms, 1846-1847; W. Bk. F, p. 459, Will of Zillah Simms, 1851-1851.
Barnes, Elias? m. Mahaly Sharpe, W. Bk. F, p. 336, Will of John P. Sharpe, 1845.
Barnes, James m. Louisa Ellis, W. Bk. G, p. 51, Will of Coffield Ellis, 1854-1854.
Barnes, James m. Martha Daniel, W. Bk. E, p. 61, Will of Asa Daniel, 1813-1813.
Barnes, James A. m. Sarah Daniel, Will of Judieth Daniel, 1837-1837.
Barnes, Joseph m. Sarah Whitehead, W. Bk. D, p. 286, Will of William Bond Whitehead, 1805-1807; Will of Sarah Whitehead, 1808-1810.
Barnes, Nathan? m. Patience Amason, Will of William Amason, 1793.
Barnes, William m. Sally Ellis, W. Bk. G, p. 51, Will of Coffield Ellis, 1854-1854.
Bartley, ? m. Catherine Barfield, Will of James Barfield, 1770.
Basel, ? m. Nancy or Jemima Cox, Will of Joseph Cox, 1821-1825.
Basel, Jonathan m. Jemima Cox, W. Bk. F, p. 31, Will of Joseph Cox, 1821-1825.
Bass, ? m. Judieth Daniel, Will of Judieth Daniel, 1837-1837.
Bass, John m. Melisha Mabry, W. Bk. F, p. 231, Will of Wilkinson Mabry, 1833.

Bass, Turner m. Rebecca Mabry, W. Bk. F, p. 231, Will of Wilkinson Mabry, 1833.

Baton, ? m. Edah Averitt, W. Bk. F, p. 4, Will of James Averitt, Sr., 1822-1823.

Battle, ? m. Rhoda Ricks, Will of James Ricks, 1792-1792.

Battle, Rev. Amos J. m. Margaret H. Parker, W. Bk. F, p. 303, Will of Weeks Parker, Sr., 1843-1844.

Battle, Col. Benjamin m. Henrietta S. H. Parker, W. Bk. F, p. 303, Will of Weeks Parker, Sr., 1843-1844.

Battle, Joel m. Mary Johnston, W. Bk. E, p. 133, Will of Amos Johnston, 1814-1816.

Battle, William S. m. Elizabeth M. Dancy, W. Bk. F, p. 404, Will of Francis L. Dancy, 1845-1848.

Batts, ? m. Elizabeth Knight, W. Bk. E, p. 122, Will of Jesse Knight, 1815-1816.

Batts, ? m. Lucy Knight, W. Bk. E, p. 25, Will of Peter Knight.

Batts, ? m. Sarah Booth, W. Bk. D, p. 303, Will of James Booth, 1806-1808.

Batts, Benjamin m. Lucy Bryan, W. Bk. F, p. 352, Will of Dempsey Bryan, 1847.

Beckingham, ? m. Sarah Hendrick, Will of William Hendrick, 1766-1767.

Beckwith, Amos m. Rhoda Willis, W. Bk. A, p. 245, Will of William Willis, 1776-1776.

Belcher, ? m. Elizabeth Barnes, W. Bk. F, p. 20, Will of Julan Barnes, 1823-1824.

Belcher, ? m. Mary Lane, W. Bk. 3, p. 103, Will of James Lane, 1789.

Belcher, ? m. Sarah Little, W. Bk. C, p. 85, Will of Abraham Little, 1785-1789.

Belcher, Beverly? m. Mary Hines, W. Bk. B, p. 67, Will of Richard Hines, 1781-1781.

Belcher, Henry m. Martha Shearley, Will of Henry Shearley, 1849-1849.

Bell, ? m. Amy Battle, Will of John Battle, 1774.

Bell, ? m. Sally Goldsmith Lloyd, Will of Nicholas Lloyd, 1781-1781,

Bell, ? m. Sophia Ansley, W. Bk. F, p. 57, Will of Joseph Ansley, 1826.

Bell, Benjamin? m. Taby Jelks, W. Bk. B, p. 96, Will of brother, William Jelks, 1781-1782.

Bell, Frederick m. Sally Goldsmith Loyd, Will of Frederick Bell, 1803; Will of Nicholas Loyd, 1781-1781.

Bell, John m. Lucy Williams, W. Bk. C, p. 254, Will of John Williams 1792-1793.
Bell, Joshua m. Peggy Adams, W. Bk. B, p. 233, Will of James Adams, 1818-1820.
Bell, Marmaduke m. ? Boddie (dau. of Geo. Boddie), W. Bk. F, p. 111, Will of Marmaduke Bell, 1830-1830.
Bell, William m. Elizabeth Bell, W. Bk. F, p. 337, Will of Frederick Bell, 1844-1846.
Bell, William? m. Nancy Kea, W. Bk. E, p. 242, Will of Henry Kea, 1842.
Bellamy, ? m. Nancy Nicholson, W. Bk. E, p. 238, Will of Penelope Nicholson, 1820-1820.
Bellamy, John m. Sarah Exum, W. Bk. C, p. 316, Will of William Exum, 1790-1795.
Bellflower, ? m. Polly Carlile, W. Bk. E, p. 81, Will of Robert Carlile, 1808-1815.
Bembrey, ? m. Merina Mayo, W. Bk. F, p. 28, Will of John W. Mayo, 1824-1825.
Bennett, ? m. Eleanor Crisp, W. Bk. F, p. 129, Will of Jesse Crisp, Sr., 1829-1831.
Bennett, ? m. Ellen Taylor, Will of John Taylor, 1823-1825.
Bennett, ? m. Nancy Crisp, W. Bk. F, p. 129, Will of Jesse Crisp, Sr., 1829-1831.
Bentley, ? m. Alice Amason, Will of William Amason, 1811-1811.
Bentley, Joshua m. Martha Jarrel, Will of Joshua Bentley, 1799-1799; W. Bk. D, p. 238, Will of Martha Bentley, 1804-1808.
Bergman, John m. Nancy M. Felts, W. Bk. G, p. 92, Will of William Felts, 1853-1854.
Bettis, ? m. Mary Evans, Will of Charles Evans, 1759-1759.
Biggs, ? m. Eliza Parker, W. Bk. G, p. 78, Will of Hardy Parker.
Biggs, ? m. Elizabeth Hart, Will of Priscilla Hart, 1798-1798.
Billups, ? m. Charlotte Hicks, W. Bk. F, p. 254, Will of James Hicks, 1840-1841.
Blackburn, ? m. Sarah Barnes, Will of Dempsey Barnes, 1807.
Blacklidge, Richard m. Louisa Blount, Will of Louisa Blacklidge, 1786-1789.
Bloodworth, Thomas m. Sarah Griffis (Griffin?), W. Bk. D, p. 100, Will of John Griffin, 1796-1799.
Bloodworth, William? m. Milly Deloach, Will of Mary Deloach, 1773-1774.

Blount, ? m. Esther J. Carr, W. Bk. F, p. 246, Will of Celia Carr, 1839-1840.

Blount, (Bunting?), m. Elizabeth Council, W. Bk. D, p. 236, Will of Charles Council, 1805-1806.

Boddie, ? m. Jean Toole, Will of sister, Sabra Garner, 1800-1801.

Bolten, ? m. Jemmimay Amason, Will of William Amason, 1811-1811.

Bond, ? m. Sabra Harrell, Will of Thomas Harrell, 1763-1763.

Bonner, ? m. Caroline Gray, W. Bk. G, p. 111, Will of Charlotte Ward.

Bonner, Redding (Warren Co., Tenn.) m. Mary Bilberry, W. Bk. F, p. 191, Will of Nathaniel Bilberry, 1830-1836.

Boon, ? m. Elizabeth Barfield, Will of James Barfield, 1770.

Booth, Robert m. Venetia Cromwell, W. Bk. C, p. 66, Will of Alex Cromwell, 1788-1789.

Booth, Robert? m. Pattey Newsome, W. Bk. B, p. 12, Will of Thomas Newsome, 1778-1779.

Boswell, ? m. Delana Daniel, Will of Judieth Daniel, 1837-1837.

Bottom, ? m. Mary Pitman, Will of Benjamin Pitman, 1755-1756.

Bowen, ? m. Polly Everitt, Will of brother, Silas Everitt, 1835.

Boykin, ? m. Sarah Knight, Will of John Knight, 1769-1770.

Braddy, Patrick m. Mary Thorp, Will of Solomon Thorp, 1788-1793.

Bradford, John m. (1) Polly Eelbeck, W. Bk. F, p. 179, Will of Daniel Barksdale, 1835.

Bradford, John m. (2) Elizabeth Barksdale, W. Bk. F, p. 179, Will of brother, Daniel Barksdale, 1835.

Bradford, Thomas m. Elizabeth Eelbeck, W. Bk. F, p. 179, Will of Daniel Barksdale, 1835.

Bradley, ? m. Anney Hyett, Will of Thomas Hyett, 1781-1783.

Bradley, ? m. Elizabeth Carlile or Bell, Will of Sarah Carlile, 1772-1776.

Bradley, ? m. Rachel Lee, Will of Richard Lee, 1756-1756.

Bradley, Agy m. Honour Dilliard, W. Bk. E, p. 248, Will of Agy Bradley, 1820-1820.

Bradley, Job or Willis m. Elizabeth Kitchen, W. Bk. F, p. 44, Will of Elizabeth Kitchen, 1825-1825.

Brake, ? m. Sarah Lane, W. Bk. 3, p. 103, Will of James Lane, 1789.

Brake, Jacob? m. Absle (Absala?) Stallions (Stallings?), Will of Greggre (Gregory?) Stallions (Stallings?),1788-1790.

Brake, Jesse m. Patience Price, W. Bk. F, p. 55, Will of Charity Price, 1824-1826; W. Bk. E, p. 47, Will of Jesse Price, 1812.

Brake, Nathan m. Barsheba Holland, Will of Jacob Holland, 1798-1799.

Brand, ? m. Sarah Bryant, Will of Gayle Bryant, 1788-1793.

Brantley. ? m. Elizabeth Amason, Will of William Amason, 1793.

Brantley, ? m. Molly Thomas, Will of Mary Thomas, 1802-1802.

Brantley, ? m. Polly Thomas, Will of Mary Thomas, 1802-1802.

Braswell, ? m. Molley Deloach, Will of Samuel Deloach, 1764-1764.

Braswell, ? m. Mary Permenter, W. Bk. 3, p. 106, Will of James Permenter, 1789-1789.

Braswell, Isaac m. Charity Robbins, W. Bk. B, p. 90, Will of William Robbins, 1826-1831.

Braswell, Zadock? m. Polly Soary, W. Bk. E, p. 185, Will of Andrew Soary, 1818-1818; W. Bk. F, p. 265, Will of Lucy Soary, 1836-1842.

Brazwell, ? m. Lucy Bailey, W. Bk. F, p. 470, Will of Jonathan Bailey, 1852.

Brett, ? m. Charity Parker, Will of Francis Parker, 1746-1747.

Bridges (Bridgers?), James m. Millison Freeman, W. Bk. F, p. 229, Will of Josiah Freeman, 1838-1838

Bridgers, ? m. Mary Barnes, W. Bk. F, p. 20, Will of Julan Barnes, 1823-1824.

Bridgers, ? m. Mary Barnes, W. Bk. D, p. 223, Will of James Barnes, 1805.

Bridgers, ? m. Pernitee (?) Pitt, Will of James Pitt, Sr., 1830-1831.

Bridgers, William? m. Mary Barnes, W. Bk. D, p. 221, Will of James Barnes, 1805-1805.

Brinkley, ? m. Polly Harrell, W. Bk. F, p. 32, Will of Samuel Harrell, 1825-1825.

Britt, ? m. Eliza Weaver, W. Bk. F, p. 389, Will of Jonathan W. Weaver, 1847-1848.

Brown, ? m. Bethinae M. Pippen, W. Bk. F, p. 519, Will of Joseph L. Pippen, 1851-1853.

Brown, ? m. Charity Holmes, Will of John Holmes, 1835-1836.

Brown, ? m. Dolly Thornell, W. Bk. D, p. 365, Will of Benjamin Thornell, 1810-1810.

Brown, Asa? m. Polley Pippen, W. Bk. D, p. 235, Will of Mary Pippen, 1805-1805.

Brown, Solomon m. Lucie Gaddey, W. Bk. 3, p. 73, Will of Thomas Gaddey, 1787-1788.

Brown, Theophilus? m. Sally Harrell. W. Bk. F, p. 30, Will of Christopher Harrell, 1843-1844.

Browne, ? m. Cressy Fort, W. Bk. E, p. 314, Will of Jane Fort, 1818-1822.

Brownrigg, ? m. Obedience Thomas, W. Bk. D, p. 363, Will of Mary Thomas, 1810-1810.

Bruce, ? m. Nannie Barnes, Will of Nathan Barnes, 1777.

Brun, ? m. Ann Coker, Will of Caleb Coker, 1748-1748.

Bryan, ? m. Martha Knight, W. Bk. F, p. 143, Will of Walker Knight, 1830.

Bryan, ? m. Martha Weeks, W. Bk. E, p. 93, Will of James Weeks, 1809-1815; W. Bk. F, p. 77, Will of Cely Weeks, 1827-1827.

Bryan, Brittain? m. Elizabeth Harriss, W. Bk. C, p. 40, Will of Thomas Harris, 1786-1787.

Bryant, ? m. Drucilla Lane, Will of brother, Joseph Lane, 1757-1758.

Bryant, William? m. Elizabeth Harrell, W. Bk. A, p. 119, Will of Thomas Harrell, 1763-1763.

Bulluck, Bennett m. Martha Barnes, W. Bk. D, p. 298, Will of Sarah Barnes, 1833-1834.

Bulluck, Edwin m. Elizabeth Lee, W. Bk. E, p. 42, Will of Henry Lee, 1812-1812.

Bulluck, Whitmel m. Lucy Bell, W. Bk. F, p. 337, Will of Frederick Bell, 1844-1846.

Bulluck, William G. m. Polly Bell, W. Bk. F, p. 337, Will of Frederick Bell, 1844-1846.

Bumpass, John m. Martha Etheridge, W. Bk. F, p. 63, Will of Caleb Etheridge, 1826-1826.

Bunn, ? m. Charity Fort, Will of Sarah Horn, 1799.

Bunn, ? m. Mary H. Bryan, Will of Rosa H. Bryan, 1850.

Bunn, Benjamin m. Mary Foort, W. Bk. A, p. 84, Will of George Foort (Fort), 1761-1761.

Bunn, John m. ? Ricks, Will of John Bunn, 1760-1760.

Buntyn (Bunting?), m. Elsey Averitt, W. Bk. F, p. 4, Will of James Averitt, Sr., 1822-1823.

Burk, ? m. Louisa Lawrence, W. Bk. F, p. 282, Will of Joshua Lawrence, 1841-1843.

Burn, Michael m. Ann Swinson (wid.), Will of Michael Burn, 1780.

Burrous, ? m. Jane Connell, Will of Thomas Connell, 1769.

Bynum, ? m. Faith Lane, Will of brother, Joseph Lane, 1757-1758.

Bynum, Benjamin m. Catherine W. Hines, W. Bk. G, p. 106, Will of Prudence Hines, 1850-1855.

C

Cain, ? m. Sarah Braswell, Will of James Braswell, 1760-1765.

Cain, Jonathan? m. Barbery Harrell, Will of Thomas Harrell, 1763-1763.

Calhoon, ? m. Elizabeth Flowers, W. Bk. A, p. 161, Will of Jacob Flowers, 1766-1766.

Calhoon, ? m. Priscilla Flowers, Will of Jacob Flowers, 1766-1766.

Calhoon, John m. Elizabeth or Priscilla Flowers, W. Bk. A, p. 161, Will of Jacob Flowers, 1766.

Calhoun, ? m. Polly Braswell, W. Bk. F, p. 498, Will of Crissey Braswell, 1848-1853.

Canady, ? m. Sarah Rose, W. Bk. E, p. 245, Will of Robert Rose, 1816-1820.

Cane, Jonathan m. Barberry Harrell, W. Bk. A, p. 119, Will of Thomas Harrell, 1763.

Cannon, ? m. Mary Hines, Will of Peter Hines, Sr., 1783-1783.

Carpenter, ? m. Mary Lee, Will of James Lee, 1771-1777.

Carr, ? m. Mary Williams, Will of Elisha Williams, 1751-1755, (brother).

Carr, ? m. Milly Dunn, Will of John Dunn, 1793-1793.

Casway (Causey?), Leven m. Nancy McDowell, W. Bk. F, p. 98, Will of John McDowell, 1825-1829.

Caswell, ? m. Sary Brown, Will of James Brown, 1795-1797.

Caulwell, ? m. Mary Cartwright, Will of John Cartwrightt, 1780-1780.

Causey, Ezekiel? m. Anne Morgan, Will of Joseph Morgan, 1791-1792.

Causway, Philip? m. Rachel Davis, Will of Emory Davis, 1795; Will of Rachel Davis, 1800-1800.

Cherry, ? m. Charlotte Council, W. Bk. D, p. 236, Will of Charles Council, 1805-1806.

Cherry, ? m. Elizabeth Harrell, W. Bk. F, p. 307, Will of Christopher Harrell, 1843-1844.

Cherry, William R. m. Julia Grimes, W. Bk. F, p. 450, Will of William Grimes, 1850-1850.

Cherry, Thomas B. m. Emily Bell, W. Bk. F, p. 337, Will of Frederick Bell, 1844-1846.

Cherry, Willie m. Polly Hardie, W. Bk. E, p. 239, Will of Robert Hardy, 1820-1820.

Clark, ? m. Pennina Brake, W. Bk. G, p. 94, Will of Patience Brake, 1854-1854.

Clark, Jesse? m. Polly Bryant, W. Bk. D, p. 208, Will of Faithful Bryant, 1803-1804.

Claud, ? m. Sarah Hodges, W. Bk. E, p. 17, Will of Anthony Hodges, 1811-1811.

Coleman, John? m. Sally Jordan, Will of Henry Jordan, 1836-1837.

Coleman, John? m. Sally Jordan, W. Bk. F, p. 210, Will of Henry Jordan, 1836-1837.

Collins, ? m. Mary Lowry, Will of Robert Lowry, 1768-1774.

Cone, ? m. Elizabeth Duggan, Will of Thomas Hyman, 1796-1796.

Cook, Woodard m. Judea Barnes, W. Bk. G, p. 57, Will of Sarah Barnes, 1849-1854.

Cooper, ? m. Drusilah Jolley, W. Bk. 3, p. 73, Will of Thomas Gaddey, 1787-1788.

Corbin, ? m. Polly Knight or Benton? W. Bk. E, p. 22, Will of Charity Benton, 1818-1818.

Corbett, Dempsey m. Milley Wooten, W. Bk. F, p. 193, Will of Absalam Wooten, 1836.

Cotten, John m. Kezziah Savage, W. Bk. D, p. 274, Will of Loveliss, (Lovelace) Savage, 1802-1807.

Cotten, ? m. Elizabeth Horn, Will of Priscilla Horn, 1837-1850.

Cotton, ? m. Laura P. Clark, W. Bk. F, p. 303, Will of James W. Clark.

Cotton, ? m. Mary Nobleland, Will of John Nobleland, 1755-1755.

Cotton, ? m. Zylpha Wimberley, Will of George Wimberley, Sr., 1764-1768.

Counsell, ? m. Julia Purvis, W. Bk. F, p. 454, Will of Lewis Purvis, 1851-1851.

Cravey, Owen m. Seley Johnston, W. Bk. B, p. 101, Will of Jacob Johnston, 1780-1782.

Crenshaw, ? m. Catherine E. Austin, Will of Henry Austin, 1843-1845.

Crisp, ? m. Louisa Cobb, W. Bk. F, p. 198, Will of John Cobb, 1837-1837.

Cromwell, ? m. Peninah Little, W. Bk. F, p. 124, Will of Sylvia Little, 1827-1831.

Cromwell, Newsome? m. Martha McDowell, W. Bk. F, p. 177, Will of Elizabeth McDowell, 1831-1835.

Crowell, Edward m. Nancy Wiggins, W. Bk. D, p. 168, Will of Robert Wiggins, 1803-1803.

Crowell, Samuel m. Latitia Nicholson, W. Bk. D, p. 81, Will of John Nicholson, 1779-1779.

Clybun, ? m. Jean Clark, Will of Robert Clark, 1752-1753.

Cobb, ? m. Elizabeth A. Pippen, W. Bk. F, p. 519, Will of Joseph L. Pippen, 1851-1853.

Cobb, ? m. Elsey Bolton, W. Bk. E, p. 241, Will of Richard Bolton, 1818-1820.

Cobb, ? m. Elizabeth Thomas, W. Bk. D, p. 363, Will of Mary Thomas, 1810-1810.

Cobb, ? m. Lydia Thigpen, W. Bk. F, p. 420, Will of James Thigpen, 1840-1849.

Cobb, ? m. Mourning Horn, W. Bk. F, p. 68, Will of Jacob Horn, 1826-1827.

Cobb, Edward m. Mary Barnes, Will of Bryan Barnes, 1839.

Cobb, John m. Winnie Wooten, W. Bk. F, p. 193, Will of Absalam Wooten, 1836; W. Bk. F, p. 198, Will of John Cobb, 1837-1837.

Cobb, Joseph m. Sarah Carney (Moore?), W. Bk. F, p. 449, Will of Rutha Moore, 1850-1850.

Coffield, ? m. Patience Sessums, W. Bk. E, p. 173, Will of Richard Sessums, 1769-1769.

Coffield, Benjamin? m. Elizabeth Knight, W. Bk. C, p. 268, Will of James Knight, 1786-1794.

Coffield, David m. Elizabeth Whitaker, W. Bk. E, p. 180, Will of David Coffield, 1817-1818; W. Bk. F, p. 170, Will of Elizabeth Coffield, 1835-1835.

Coffield, Thomas? m. Elizabeth Bryan, Will of Thomas Bryan, 1785-1785; Will of Evin Bryant, 1808-1810.

Cohoon, ? m. Charity Horn, Will of Michael Horn, 1785.

Cook, ? m. Courtney Downing, Will of James Downing, Sr., 1808-1808.

Cohoon, ? m. Jemimah Dixon, Will of Thomas Dixon, 1790-1790.

Coker, ? m. Elizabeth Porter, Will of Charles Porter, 1794-1794.

Coker, ? m. Olive McDaniel, W. Bk. D, p. 302, Will of Campbell McDaniel, 1807-1808.

Coker, ? m. Rebecca George, Will of Selah George, 1808-1808.

Coleman, ? m. Kiziah Price, Will of Thomas Price, 1779-1781.

Coleman, ? m. Sarah Powell, Will of William Powell, 1792-1793.
Coleman, Charles m. Elizabeth Whitehead, W. Bk. D, p. 286, Will of William Bond Whitehead, 1807; Will of Sarah Whitehead, 1808-1810.
Crudup, ? m. Elizabeth Battle, Will of Elisha Battle, 1799.
Cullers, John m. Mary Jones, Will of Francis Jones, 1750-1755.
Cutchin, ? m. Hester M. F. Lynch, Will of Eaton Lynch, 1851-1851.

D

Dancy, ? m. Charlotte Sessums, W. Bk. F, p. 173, Will of Elizabeth Sessums, 1834-1835; Will of Solomon Sessums, 1817-1818.
Dancy, ? m. Sally Bell, W. Bk. E, p. 293, Will of Nancy Bell, 1822-1822.
Dancy, Francis L. m. Charlotte Sessums, W. Bk. F. p. 173, Will of Elizabeth Sessums, 1834-1835; W. Bk. F, p. 404, Will of Francis L. Dancy, 1845-1848; W. Bk. E, p. 173, Will of Solomon Sessums, 1817-1818.
Dandridge, ? m. Elizabeth Bulluck, W. Bk. F, p. 337, Will of Frederick Bell, 1844-1846.
Daniel, ? m. Hannah E. Purvis, W. Bk. F, p. 454, Will of Lewis Purvis, 1851-1851.
Daniel, ? m. Manize Long, W. Bk. F, p. 432, Will of William R. Long, 1848-1849.
Daniel, ? m. Sally Barnes, W. Bk. F, p. 324, Will of James W. Barnes, 1844-1845.
Daniel, ? m. Sarah Barnes, Will of Nathan Barnes, 1777.
Daniel, ? m. Sarah Wells, Will of Thomas Wells, 1800-1801.
Daniel, ? m. Susannah Barnes, Will of Dempsey Barnes, 1807.
Daniel, Elias m. Mary Woodard, W. Bk. D, p. 50, Will of Elisha Woodard, 1798-1798.
Daniel, Willie m. Eliza Roundtree, W. Bk. F, p. 445, Will of Lewis Roundtree, 1849-1850.
Darnold (Donald), ? m. Barsheba Brinkley, Will of Abraham Brinkley, 1835-1838.
Daughtry, ? m. Elizabeth Williams, Will of Elisha Williams, 1751-1755, (brother).
Davenport, ? m. Zilpha Winstead, Will of Sally Winstead, 1837-1838.
Davis, ? m. Aday Amason, Will of William Amason, 1811-1811.
Davis, ? m. Elizabeth Foort, Will of George Foort (Fort), 1761-1761.

Davis, ? m. Elizabeth Moore, Will of Samuel Moore, 1793-1794.

Davis, John m. Elizabeth Peel, W. Bk. F, p. 500, Will of Hillary Peel, 1849-1853.

Davis, Richard m. Mary Peel, W. Bk. D, p. 332, Will of Robert Peel, 1807-1808.

Dawson, ? m. Nelly Edwards, Will of Kinchen Edwards, 1847-1851.

Dawson, ? m. Edith White, Will of John White, 1800.

Deal, James m. Emily Billeps, W. Bk. F, p. 437, Will of Isobel Billeps, 1847-1850.

Deans, James m. Penny Barnes, W. Bk. F, p. 178, Will of Nancy Barnes, 1835-1835.

Deloach, Samuel m. Mary Boykin, dau. of Francis Boykin of Northampton Co., W. Bk. A, p. 134, Will of Samuel Deloach, 1764-1764.

Denning, ? of Washington Co., m. Mary Cotten, dau. of Alexander Cotten, W. Bk. F, p. 482, Will of Randolph Cotten, 1852.

Denton, ? m. Agnes McDaniel, W. Bk. D, p. 302, Will of Campbell McDaniel, 1807-1808.

Deshields, Noah of Arkansas, m. Martha Dupree, dau. of William R. Dupree of Edgecombe Co., W. Bk. G, p. 84, Will of Temperance Pippen, 1852-1854.

Dew, ? m. Nancy Farmer, W. Bk. F, p. 65, Will of Benjamin Farmer, 1825-1827.

Dew, ? m. Martha Simms, W. Bk. F, p. 459, Will of Zilla Simms, 1851-1851.

Dew, ? m. Martha Taylor, Will of Arthur Taylor, 1765-1765.

Dew, John m. Elizabeth Barnes, W. Bk. F, p. 21, Will of Joseph Barnes, 1824-1824; W. Bk. F, p. 178, Will of sister, Nancy Barnes, 1835-1835.

Dew, John m. Sally Thomas, Will of Mary Thomas, 1802-1802.

Dew, John m. Martha Simms, W. Bk. F, p. 377, Will of James Simms, 1846-1847; W. Bk. F, p. 459, Will of Zilla Simms, 1851-1851.

Dew, Samuel m. Selah Horn, W. Bk. E, p. 83, Will of Elijah Horn, 1804-1815.

Dewall (Duval?) ? m. Martha Dew, Will of Millicent Dew, 1786-1786.

Dicken, Richard m. Polly Harris, W. Bk. D, p. 360, Will of Nathan Harris, 1809-1810.

Dickens, ? m. Ann Lowry, Will of Robert Lowry, 1768-1774.

Digges, Starling m. Elizabeth Hodges, W. Bk. E, p. 17, Will of Anthony Hodges, 1811-1811; Will of Thomas Hodges, 1800-1806.

Dilda, Benjamin m. Absilla Howard, W. Bk. F, p. 381, Will of Evan Howard, 1847-1847.

Dillard, ? m. Fanny Dickinson, Will of John Dickinson, 1779-1780.

Dillard, ? m. Mary Dickinson, Will of Ava Dickinson, 1837-1838.

Dilliard, ? m. Elizabeth Davis, Will of Emory Davis, 1795.

Dilliard, Luke m. Winefred Ruffin, W. Bk. C, p. 320, Will of Benjamin Ruffin, 1795-1795.

Dixon, ? m. Martha Irwin, Will of Andrew Irwin, 1772.

Dixon, ? m. Sarah Hickman, Will of Nathaniel Hickman, 1790-1795.

Donaldson, William m. Sarah Phillips, W. Bk. E, p. 214, Will of William Donaldson, 1817-1819.

Douglis, ? m. Mary Clark, Will of Robert Clark, 1752-1753.

Dowden, ? m. Mary Everitt, W. Bk. E, p. 326, Will of Keton Everitt, 1823-1823.

Dowdna, ? m. Senah Simms, Will of Joseph Simms, 1795-1795.

Downing, ? m. Mary Hudnall, Will of Robert Hudnall, 1762-1763.

Drake, ? m. Polly Nettle, W. Bk. F, p. 115, Will of John Nettle, 1830-1830.

Drake, William m. Nancy Maund or Killebrew? Will of Mary Maund, 1795-1795.

Draughon, John m. Martha Stallings, wid. of William Robertson, W. Bk. F, p. 157, Will of Jas. Stallings, 1830-1834.

Drew, (Dew?), John m. Phereby Bell, Will of Joshua Bell, 1793-1793.

Drew, ? m. Talitha Staton, W. Bk. E, p. 297, Will of Nehemiah Staton, 1820-1822.

Dunford, Thomas m. Salley W. Edwards, W. Bk. E, p. 165, Will of Brittain Edwards, 1813-1817.

Duffield, ? m. Elizabeth Sessums, Will of Nicholas Sessums, 1764-1764.

Duggan, ? m. Cloanna Hyman, Will of brother, Thomas Hyman, 1796-1796.

Duggin, ? m. Mary Sasnett, Will of Joshua Sasnett, 1833-1834.

Dunford, ? m. Susanna Hobbs, W. Bk. E, p. 222, Will of Mary Hobbs, 1819-1819.

Dunford. Thomas m. Salley W. Edwards, W. Bk. E, p. 165, Will of Britain Edwards, 1813-1817; W. Bk. G, p. 99, Will of Nancy Edwards, 1853-1855.

Dunn, ? m. Ann Sessums, Will of Nicholas Sessums, 1764-1764.

Dunn, ? m. Lurana Sessums, Will of Nicholas Sessums, 1764-1764.

Dunn, ? m. Mary Wilkinson, W. Bk. E, p. 194, Will of Joshua Wilkinson, 1817-1819.

Dunn, John ? m. Ann Sessums, Will of Nicholas Sessums, 1764-1764; W. Bk. E, p. 508, Will of John Dunn. 1793-1793; W. Bk. D, 351, Will of Ann Dunn, 1809-1809.

Dunn, Larry m. Polly Williams, W. Bk. F, p. 416, Will of Winifred Williams, 1848-1849.

Dupree, Lewis B. m. Eliza Shearley, Will of Henry Shearley, 1849.

Durden, ? m. Maria Brownrigg, W. Bk. F, p. 242, Will of Obedience Brownrigg, 1839-1840.

E

Eagles, ? m. Bytha Edwards, W. Bk. E, p. 165, Will of Britain Edwards, 1813-1817; W. Bk. G, p. 99, Will of sister, Nancy Edwards, 1853-1855.

Eagles, Richard T. m. Penelope Eason, W. Bk. F, p. 189, Will of James Scarborough, 1835-1836.

Eason, ? m. Frances Lester, W. Bk. F, p. 38, Will of Moses Lester, 1825-1826.

Eason, ? m. Vicey Thigpen, Will of Gilliard Thigpen, 1831-1838.

Eason, ? m. Martha Peele, W. Bk. E, p. 71, Will of Catherine Peele, 1812-1814.

Eason, Coburn m. Elizabeth Barnes, dau. of Joshua Barnes, W. Bk. D, p. 183, Will of Coburn Eason, 1801-1803.

Eason, Joshua m. Polly P. Scarborough, W. Bk. F, p. 189, Will of James Scarborough, 1835-1836.

Edmondson, ? m. Lydia Downing; Will of James Downing, Sr., 1808-1808.

Edmundson, ? m. Nancy B. Parker, W. Bk. G, p. 78, Will of Hardy Parker.

Edmondson, Richard m. Mary A. Felts, W. Bk. G, p. 92, Will of William Felts, 1853-1854.

Edwards, ? m. Mary Lewis, W. Bk. F, p. 350, Will of James Lewis, 1844-1846.

Edwards, ? m. Mary Kitchen, W. Bk. F, p. 44, Will of Elizabeth Kitchen, 1825-1825.

Edwards, Briant m. Elizabeth Wooten, W. Bk. F, p. 193, Will of Absalam Wooten, 1836.
Edwards, Edmund? m. Nancy Shearley, W. Bk. F, p. 13, Will of Richard Shearley, 1816-1823.
Edwards, Samuel m. Elizabeth Brown, Will of John Brown, 1758-1759.
Edwards, Siley m. Nanny Wooten, W. Bk. F, p. 193, Will of Absalom Wooten, 1836; W. Bk. F, p. 298, Will of Siley Edwards, 1841-1843.
Edwards, William m. Delpha Howard, W. Bk. F, p. 381, Will of Evan Howard, 1847-1847.
Ellis, ? m. Elizabeth Hines, Will of Peter Hines, Sr., 1783-1783.
Ellis, ? m. Fanny Lewis, W. Bk. F, p. 350, Will of James Lewis, 1844-1846.
Ellis, Gray m. Nancy Wilkins, W. Bk. E, p. 144, Will of William Wilkins, 1810-1816.
Ellis, J. G. m. Harriet Roundtree, W. Bk. F, p. 445, Will of Lewis Roundtree, 1849-1850.
Ellis, John m. Nancy Gay, W. Bk. F, p. 251, Will of Dempsey Gay, 1840-1841.
Ellener, ? m. Sarah Davis, Will of Emory Davis, 1795.
Elliner, James m. Martha Cromwell, wid. W. Bk. F, p. 318, Will of James Elliner, 1845-1845.
Ellinor, ? m. Jane Fort, W. Bk. E, p. 314, Will of Jane Fort, 1818-1822.
Emeson (Amason?) m. Hannah Stallings, Will of Griggre Stallions, (Gregory Stallings), 1788-1790.
Etheridge, ? m. Agnes Clark, Will of Robert Clark, 1752-1753.
Etheridge, ? m. Mourning Whitaker, W. Bk. F, p. 170, Will of sister, Elizabeth Coffield, 1835-1835.
Etheridge, ? m. Rachel Clark, Will of Robert Clark, 1752-1753.
Etheridge, Lott? m. Rachel Clark, Will of Robert Clark, 1752-1753.
Evans, ? m. Ann Hines, Will of Peter Hines, 1783-1783.
Evans, ? m. Elizabeth Howard, Will of Stephen Howard, 1834-1838.
Evans, John m. Kezziah (Savage) Cotten, wid. of John Cotten, W. Bk. D, p. 274, Will of Loveliss (Lovelace) Savage, 1802-1807.
Evans, Peter m. Nancy Johnston, W. Bk. E, p. 133, Will of Amos Johnston, 1814-1816.
Evins, ? m. Elizabeth Mitchell, Will of Peter Mitchell, 1770.

Evins, Isham m. ? Jordan, Will of Cornelius Jordan, Sr., 1792-1794.

Exum, ? m. Molly O'Neal, W. Bk. F, p. 309, Will of Edmund O'Neal, 1843-1844.

F

Fail, ? m. Fereby Tart, W. Bk. 3, p. 87, Will of Jonathan Tart, 1789.

Faircloth, ? m. Elizabeth Lane, W. Bk. 3, p. 103, Will of James Lane, 1789.

Faircloth, Newsome m. Sally Everett, W. Bk. E, p. 326, Will of Keton Everitt, 1823-1823.

Faircloth, William m. Susan Edwards, W. Bk. F, p. 298, Will of Siley Edwards, 1841-1843.

Faithful, ? m. Elizabeth Price, Will of William Price, 1793.

Farmer, ? m. Elizabeth Barnes, W. Bk. F, p. 397, Will of Polly Barnes, 1845-1848.

Farmer, ? m. Elizabeth Dew, W. Bk. E, p. 149, Will of Arthur Dew, 1816-1816.

Farmer, ? m. Elizabeth Peele, W. Bk. E, p. 71, Will of Catherine Peele, 1812-1814.

Farmer, ? m. Milicent Horn, W. Bk. F, p. 68, Will of Jacob Horn, 1826-1827.

Farmer, ? m. Nancy Barnes, W. Bk. F,.p. 296, Will of Jesse Barnes, 1841-1843.

Farmer, Benjamin m. Elizabeth Dew, dau. of William Dew, W. Bk. F, p. 65, Will of Benjamin Farmer, 1825-1827; W. Bk. F, p. 490, Will of Elizabeth Farmer, 1844-1852.

Farmer, Isaac m. Tresee Barnes, W. Bk. D, p. 298, Will of Sarah Barnes, 1833-1834.

Farmer, Jesse? m. Elizabeth Dew, Will of Mary Dew, 1801-1801; W. Bk. E, p. 149, Will of brother, Arthur Dew, 1816-1816.

Faulk, ? m. Patience Pitman, Will of Benjamin Pitman, 1755-1756.

Fiveash, ? m. Mourning Barnes, Will of Edward Barnes, 1760-1762.

Fleming, ? m. Sarah Little, W. Bk. F, p. 42, Will of Jesse Little, 1824-1825.

Floyd, Francis? m. Elizabeth Bell, Will of George Bell, 1751-1752.

Foreman, ? m. Delha M. Dancy, W. Bk. F, p. 404, Will of Francis L. Dancy, 1845-1848.

Foreman, ? m. Elizabeth Parker, Will of Francis Parker, 1746-1747.
Foreman, ? m. Judah Knight, Will of John Knight, 1769-1770.
Foreman, ? m. Mary Knight, Will of John Knight, 1769-1770.
Forman, ? m. Elizabeth Gainer, Will of sister, Mary Gainer, 1751-1751; Will of William Gainer, 1746-1750.
Forehand, ? m. Oliff Nettle, W. Bk. F, p. 115, Will of John Nettle, 1830-1830.
Fort, ? m. Anna Barrow, Will of William Barrow, 1758.
Fort, ? m. Elizabeth Dickinson, Will of John Dickinson, 1779-1780.
Fort, ? m. Jane Dickinson, W. Bk. E, p. 314, Will of Jane Fort, 1818-1822.
Fort, ? m. Nancy Hart, Will of Priscilla Hart, 1798-1798.
Fort, ? m. Mary Barnes, Will of Mary Fort, 1782-1782.
Fort, ? m. Piety Horn, Will of Sarah Horn, 1799.
Fort, ? m. Priscilla Horn, Will of Priscilla Horn, 1837-1850.
Fort, ? m. Sarah Harriss, Will of Thomas Harris, 1786-1787.
Fort, Joseph m. Nancy Kea, W. Bk. E, p. 88, Will of Faithy Kea, 1814-1815.
Foort, ? m. Nancy Powell, W. Bk. D, p. 348, Will of Nancy Powell, 1809-1809.
Foort, ? m. Elizabeth Powell, W. Bk. D, p. 348, Will of Nancy Powell, 1809-1809.
Fossett, ? m. Priscilla Price, Will of William Price, 1793.
Fossett, ? m. Nanny Price, Will of William Price, 1793.
Fountain, ? m. Patsey Kea, W. Bk. E, p. 88, Will of Faithy Kea, 1814-1815.
Furnivall, ? m. Sarah Forehand, Will of Solomon Forehand, 1798-1802.

G

Gandy, Edward m. Elizabeth Allen, W. Bk. A, p. 102, Will of Roger Allen, 1762-1762.
Gardner, ? m. Ann Little, W. Bk. C, p. 85, Will of Abraham Little, 1785-1789.
Gardner, ? m. Elizabeth Little, W. Bk. C, p. 85, Will of Abraham Little, 1785-1789.
Gary ? m. Sally Eason, W. Bk. E, p. 223, Will of Abner Eason, 1819-1819.
Gater, ? m. Leviny Davis, Will of John Davis, 1794-1799.
Gay, ? m. Mary Daughtery, Will of Samuel Daughtery, Sr., 1787-1787.

Gay, Burrel? m. Sally Thigpen, W. Bk. F, p. 215, Will of Gilliad Thigpen, 1831-1838.
Gilbert, Nathan m. Charity Ricks, W. Bk. E, p. 36, Will of Phebe Ricks, 1806-1812; Will of James Ricks, 1792-1792.
Gilchrist, Thomas m. Martha Jones? W. Bk. C, p. 109, Will of Thomas Gilchrist, 1789-1789.
Glanden, Mazah? m. Jemima Horn, W. Bk. C, p. 323, Will of William Horn, 1795-1795; Will of Ruth Horn, 1803-1803.
Godard, ? m. Sally Averitt, W. Bk. F, p. 4, Will of James Averitt, Sr., 1822-1823.
Gray, Etheldred m. Patsy D. Lyon, W. Bk. F, p. 186, Will of Thomas Lyon, 1834-1836.
Grice, ? m. Patty Simms, Will of Joseph Simms, 1795-1795.
Griffith, ? m. Faithey Wall, Will of John Wall of Halifax Co., N. C., 1778-1779.
Griffin, James m. Margaret Whitehead, Will of Matthew Whitehead, Sr., 1848.
Griffin, Thomas m. ? Waller, W. Bk. F, p. 109, Will of Margaret Waller.
Griffis (Griffin), John? m. Delilah Davis, W. Bk. D, p. 1, Will of Emory Davis, 1795-1796; Will of Rachel Davis, 1800-1800.
Griffes (Griffin) William m. Oney Gosney, W. Bk. A, p. 18, Will of John Gosney, 1779-1779.
Grimes, ? m. Phereby Robertson, Will of Hardy Robertson, 1795-1795.
Grimes, ? m. Mary Ann Jones, Will of sister, Nancy Jones, 1794-1794.
Grimes, ? m. Tabitha Mayo, W. Bk. E, p. 11, Will of Nathan Mayo, 1808-1811.
Gwin, ? m. Ann Price, Will of Thomas Price, 1779-1781.
Goin (Gwin?), ? m. Polly Simms, Will of William Simms, 1827-1827.
Gunter, John? m. Sarah Goodson, W. Bk. A, p. 101, Will of Thomas Goodson, 1761-1762.

H

Hackney, ? m. Rachel Knight, Will of John Knight, 1769-1770.
Hackney, William m. Martha Weeks, Will of Sarah Weeks, 1792-1792.
Hall, ? m. Sarah Amason, Will of Thomas Amason, 1792-1792.
Hall, ? m. Ann Lane, W. Bk. 3, p. 103, Will of James Lane, 1789.

Hallsey, Benjamin F. m. Cleopatra Barksdale, W. Bk. F, p. 179, Will of Daniel Barksdale, 1835.

Hamby, ? m. Mary Bullock, Will of David Bullock, 1774.

Hammond, ? m. Sarah White, Will of John White, 1800.

Hammond, Edward G.? m. Lucy L. Knight, W. Bk. F, p. 143, Will of Walker Knight, 1830.

Hanby, William m. Amee Merritt, Will of John Merritt, 1757.

Hardy, ? m. Martha Mitchell, Will of Peter Mitchell, 1770.

Hardy, ? m. Polly Lawrence, W. Bk. F, p. 310, Will of John Lawrence, 1841-1844.

Hargrove, ? m. Caroline C. Parker, W. Bk. F, p. 414, Will of Theophilus Parker, 1848-1849.

Hargrove, ? m. Mary W. Parker, W. Bk. F, p. 414, Will of Theophilus Parker, 1848-1849.

Hargrove, ? m. Sally Land, W. Bk. F, p. 102, Will of Littleberry Land, 1827-1829.

Harper, ? m. Charlotty Lewis, W. Bk. F, p. 350, Will of James Lewis, 1844-1846.

Harper, ? m. Polly Barnes, W. Bk. F, p. 397, Will of Polly Barnes, 1845-1848.

Harper, Stephen m. Susannah Kitchen, W. Bk. F, p. 44, Will of Elizabeth Kitchen, 1825-1825.

Harper, ? m. Sarah Weeks, W. Bk. E, p. 93, Will of James Weeks, 1809-1815; W. Bk. F, p. 77, Will of Cely Weeks, 1827-1827.

Harrell, ? m. Mary Gewin (Gwin), Will of Christopher Gewin (Gwin), 1748-1749.

Harrell, ? m. Mary Proctor, Will of William Proctor, 1779-1780.

Harrell, ? m. Sally Mayo, W. Bk. G, p. 54, Will of William Mayo, 1853-1854.

Harrell, ? m. Susannah Dunford, W. Bk. F, 264, Will of Thomas Dunford, 1841-1842.

Harrell, ? m. Winny Bell, W. Bk. F, p. 26, Will of Whitmel Bell, 1824-1824.

Harrell, ? m. Molly Moore, Will of Samuel Moore, 1793-1794.

Harrell, Elisha? m. Charlotte Webb, W. Bk. F, p. 271, Will of John Webb, Sr., 1841-1842.

Harrell, William m. Temperance Leigh, W. Bk. G, p. 103, Will of William C. Leigh, 1854-1855.

Harris, ? m. Mary Phillips, Will of Arthur Phillips, 1789-1790.

Harris, ? m. Brittania Hicks, W. Bk. F, p. 254, Will of James Hicks, 1840-1841.

Harriss, ? m. Mizy Hawkins, Will of Elza Hawkins, 1828-1837.

Harrison, ? m. Charity Williams, W. Bk. 3, p. 91, Will of James Williams, 1789-1789.

Harvey, ? m. Ann Blount, Will of Louisa Blacklidge, 1786-1789.

Hatcher, ? m. Martha Vickers, Will of John Vickers, 1784-1784.

Hatton, Francis m. Frances Grimes, Will of Thomas Grimes, 1795-1797.

Hawkins, Elza m. Gracy Taylor, dau. of Tabbitha Taylor, W. Bk. F, p. 206, Will of Elza Hawkins, 1828-1837.

Hawkins, Frederick m. Martha Griffin, W. Bk. F, p. 233, Will of Zacheriah Griffin, 1837.

Hay, ? m. Martha Draughan, W. Bk. F, p. 170, Will of William Draughan, 1835-1835.

Haywood, ? m. Hannah Gray, Will of Robert Gray, 1781-1781.

Haywood, ? m. Sally Ruffin, W. Bk. E, p. 203, Will of Mary Ruffin, 1817-1818.

Hearn, ? m. Margaret Ann Bell, Will of Winnefred Bell, 1837-1837.

Hearn, Michael m. Martha Hall, W. Bk. F, p. 11, Will of Edward Hall, 1821-1823.

Hedgepeth, ? m. Winny Turner, Will of Henry Turner, 1819-1819.

Henley, ? m. Eleny Lawrence, W. Bk. F, p. 310, Will of John Lawrence, 1841-1844.

Hill, ? m. Treasy Thomas, W. Bk. 3, p. 80, Will of John Thomas, 1788-1789.

Hill, ? m. Ony Griffin, Will of Zachariah Griffin, 1837.

Hill, Abraham? m. Christian Lane, Will of Christian Lane, 1747-1748.

Hill, Henry m. Susannah Swales, Will of Mary Swales, 1796-1800.

Hines, Peter m. Prudence Johnston, W. Bk. F, p. 249, Will of Esther Johnston, 1840-1841.

Hinson, Richard m. Salley Rogers, W. Bk. F, p. 316, Will of Josiah Rogers, 1844-1844.

Hinton, ? m. Martha Moore, Will of Joseph Moore, 1753-1757.

Hinton, William m. ? Johnson, W. Bk. 3, p. 101, Will of Simon Johnson, 1789.

Hocott, ? of Tenn. m. Delphia Morgan, W. Bk. F, p. 419, Will of James S. Morgan, 1848-1849.

Hodges, ? m. Catherine Parker, Will of Francis Parker, 1746-1747.

Hodges, ? m. Mary Cromwell, W. Bk. C, p. 66, Will of Alexander Cromwell, 1788-1789.

Hogg, Thomas m. Elizabeth Gilchrist, W. Bk. C, p. 109, Will of Thomas Gilchrist, 1789-1789.

Holland, James m. Sarah Woodard, Will of John Woodard, 1765-1765.

Holley, ? m. Elizabeth Simmons, Will of Edward Simmons, 1735-1746.

Holley, ? m. Jane Simmons, Will of Edward Simmons, 1735-1746.

Holloway, ? m. Mary Ship, Will of Richard Ship, 1778-1778.

Hollowell, ? m. Sally Farmer, W. Bk. F, p. 65, Will of grandfather, Benjamin Farmer, 1825-1827.

Hood, ? m. Mary Daughtery, W. Bk. E, p. 170, Will of Elizabeth Daughtery, 1817-1817.

Hood, ? m. Mary Hendrick, Will of William Hendrick, 1766-1767.

Hooper, ? m. Sarah Syms, Will of William Syms, 1755.

Hopkins, ? m. Elizabeth Pender, W. Bk. E, p. 186, Will of John Pender, 1818-1818.

Hopkins, ? m. Sabry Staton, W. Bk. E, p. 113, Will of Ezekiel Staton, 1821-1821.

Horne, ? m. Mary E. A. Lawrence, W. Bk. G, p. 101, Will of Peter P. Lawrence, 1852-1855.

Horne, ? m. Betsy Bloodworth, Will of William Bloodworth, 1793-1795.

Horn, ? m. Fereby Peele, W. Bk. D, p. 332, Will of Robert Peele, 1807-1808.

Horn, ? m. Luraney Robbins, Will of William Robbins, 1779-1781.

Horn, ? m. Sarah Lee, Will of Richard Lee, 1756-1756.

Horn, ? m. Tabitha Barnes, W. Bk. E, p. 66, Will of Williamson Barnes, 1814.

Horn, Abisha m. Ann Ricks, Will of James Ricks, 1792-1792.

Horn, Elisha m. ? Tisdal, W. Bk. E, p. 2, Will of Renison Tisdal, 1808-1811.

Horn, Guilford m. Mary Dixon, Will of Coffield Dixon, 1833-1838.

Horn, Jacob? m. Millison (Millicent?) Thomas, W. Bk. 3, p. 80, Will of John Thomas, 1788-1789.

Horn, James m. Betsy Price, W. Bk. E, p. 78, Will of Joseph Price, 1811-1815.
Horn, Thomas, m. Sally Barnes, W. Bk. F, p. 21, Will of Joseph Barnes, 1824-1824; W. Bk. F, p. 178, Will of Nancy Barnes, 1835-1835.
Horn, William m. Elizabeth Dancy, W. Bk. D, p. 299, Will of William Dancy, 1805-1807.
Hoskins, ? m. E. A. Lawrence, W. Bk. G, p. 101, Will of Peter P. Lawrence, 1852-1855.
House, ? m. Nicey Staton, W. Bk. E, p. 300, Will of Arthur Staton, 1821-1822.
Howard, ? m. Gracey Gator, W. Bk. F, p. 457, Will of brother, John Gator, 1849-1851.
Howard, ? m. Harriet Shelton, W. Bk. E, p. 107, Will of William Shelton, 1827-1829.
Howard, ? m. Polly Howell, W. Bk. F, p. 364, Will of John Howell, 1845.
Howard, ? m. Susannah Joyner, W. Bk. E, p. 274, Will of Drewry Joyner, 1820-1821.
Howard, Hardy? m. Dianner Davis, W. Bk. F, p. 69, Will of John Davis, 1794-1799.
Howell, ? m. Gracie Staton, W. Bk. E, p. 113, Will of Ezekiel Staton, 1815-1815.
Howell, ? m. Nancy Waller, W. Bk. D, p. 315, Will of James Waller, 1808-1808.
Howell, ? m. Polly Cox, Will of Joseph Cox, 1821-1825.
Howell, ? m. Martha Ann Gray, W. Bk. G, p. 111, Will of Charlotte Ward, 1855-1855.
Howell, Brittain m. Dice Kitchen, W. Bk. F, p. 44, Will of Elizabeth Kitchen, 1825-1825.
Hudnall, Amos m. Lucresia (Lurena?) Kitching, Will of Boaz Kitching, 1767-1776.
Hudnall, ? m. Prissy Alsobrook, W. Bk. E, p. 40, Will of Parthinia Alsobrook, 1808-1812.
Hudnall, ? m. Sereny Braswell, W. Bk. F, p. 266, Will of Bythal Braswell, 1841-1842.
Huise, (Hughes) ? m. Anne Taylor, Will of Robert Taylor, 1758.
Hunter, Thomas m. Mary Ann Lewis, Will of Ann Lewis, 1843-1844; W. Bk. F, p. 226, Will of Exum Lewis, 1831-1839.
Hyatt, Jesse m. ? Shearley, Will of Henry Shearley, 1849-1849.
Hyman, Henry m. Martha E. Porter, W. Bk. F, p. 279, Will of Ely Porter, 1842-1843; W. Bk. F, p. 330, Will of Martha Porter, 1845.

I

Ingram, ? m. Mary Merrett, Will of Thomas Merrett, 1757.

Irwin, John Alexander m. Sally Sessums, W. Bk. E, p. 173, Will of Solomon Sessums, 1817-1818.

Irvin, James m. ? Savage, Will of Charles Savage, 1789-1794.

J

Jackson, ? m. Molley Coker, Will of James Coker, 1796-1796.

Jackson, ? m. Rebecca Carlile, W. Bk. E, p. 81, Will of Robert Carlile, 1808-1815.

Jackson, Elisha m. Winnefred Brake, W. Bk. F, p. 118, Will of Jacob Brake, 1827-1830.

Jackson, J. J. m. Mary Ann Dancy, W. Bk. D, p. 299, Will of William Dancy, 1805-1807.

Jackson, John J. m. Charlotte Philips, W. Bk. D, p. 79, Will of John J. Jackson, 1779-1799.

Jannett, ? m. Mary C. Williams, W. Bk. F, p. 515, Will of Ann D. Williams of Petersburg, Va., 1852-1853.

Jeffreys, William m. Mary Gray, W. Bk. B, p. 64, Will of Robert Gray, 1781-1781.

Jelks, ? m. Polly Nicholson, W. Bk. E, p. 238, Will of Penelope Nicholson, 1820-1820.

Jenkins, ? m. Martha Dickinson, Will of John Dickinson, 1779-1780.

Jenkins, ? m. Polly Ellis, W. Bk. F, p. 25, Will of Elisha Ellis, Sr., 1824-1824.

Jenkins, ? m. Martha Nicholson, W. Bk. E, p. 238, Will of Penelope Nicholson, 1820-1820.

Jenkins, ? m. Keddy Morgan, Will of William Morgan, 1794-1795.

Jerkins, Charles m. Sarah Jones, Will of John Jones, 1757-1758.

Jinkens, ? m. Rebecca Pitt, Will of James Pitt, Sr., 1830-1831.

Johnson, ? m. Elizabeth Downing, Will of James Downing, Sr., 1808-1808.

Johnson, Jesse m. ? Lewis, Will of Exum Lewis, 1790-1790.

Johnson, ? m. Martha Exum, Will of John Exum, 1775-1775.

Johnson, ? m. Christian Amason, Will of Thomas Amason, 1792.

Johnson, ? m. Mary Roberson, Will of Archelaus Roberson, 1803-1804.

Johnston, ? m. Elizabeth Bruce, W. Bk. D, p. 278, Will of George Bruce, 1806-1807.
Johnston, ? m. Emily Norfleet, W. Bk. F, p. 264, Will of Emily Johnston, 1841-1841.
Johnston, ? m. Rachel Wells, Will of Thomas Wells, 1800-1801.
Johnston, Amos m. Catherine Hines, wid., W. Bk. E, p. 205, Will of William Hines, 1816-1818.
Jolley, ? m. Elizabeth Gaddey, W. Bk. 3, p. 73, Will of Thomas Gaddey, 1787-1788.
Jones, ? m. Ann Coffield, Will of Benjamin Coffield, 1770-1770.
Jones, ? m. Bytha Staton, W. Bk. E, p. 113, Will of Ezekiel Staton, 1821-1821.
Jones, ? m. Elizabeth Bullock, Will of David Bullock, 1774.
Jones, ? m. Margaret Spicer, W. Bk. E, p. 308, Will of William Spicer, 1820-1822.
Jones, ? m. Mary Powell, Will of William Powell, 1792-1793.
Jones, ? m. Mary Spicer, W. Bk. E, p. 308, Will of William Spicer, 1820-1822.
Jones, ? m. Mary Webb, Will of John Webb, 1785-1785.
Jones, ? m. M. O. Lawrence, W. Bk. G, p. 101, Will of Peter P. Lawrence, 1852-1855.
Jones, ? m. Patience Proctor, Will of John Proctor, 1761-1772.
Jones, ? m. Patty Quinn, Will of William Quinn, 1790-1790.
Jones, ? m. Rachel Horn, Will of Ruth Horn, 1803-1803.
Jones, ? m. Rachel Stallings, Will of Griggre Stallions, (Gregory Stallings), 1788-1790.
Jones, ? m. Sarah R. Cherry, W. Bk. F, p. 182, Will of Aaron Cherry, 1835-1835.
Jones, Asa m. Lydia Grimes, W. Bk. F, p. 450, Will of William Grimes, 1850-1850.
Jones, Jesse m. Nancy Bryant, W. Bk. E, p. 1, Will of brother, Evin Bryant, 1808-1810; W. Bk. D, p. 208, Will of Faithful Bryant, 1803-1804.
Jones, Willie, m. Ellen Gilchrist, Will of Thomas Gilchrist, 1789-1789.
Jordan, ? m. Elizabeth Taylor, Will of James Taylor, 1782-1783.
Jordan, ? m. Mary Daniel, W. Bk. E, p. 286, Will of Lemuel Daniel, 1821-1822.
Jordan, ? m. Polly Barnes, W. Bk. F, p. 324, Will of James W. Barnes, 1844-1845.
Jordan, James m. Tempa Barnes, W. Bk. G, p. 57, Will of Sarah Barnes, 1849-1854.

Jordan, ? m. Temperance Daniel, Will of Judieth Daniel, 1837-1837.

Jordan, Joseph? m. Edah Bryant, W. Bk. D, p. 240, Will of Gayle Bryant, 1793.

Jordan, Randolph ? m. Sally Thornell, W. Bk. D, p. 365, Will of Benjamin Thornell, 1810-1810.

Jordan, Thomas m. Sarah Rountree, W. Bk. F, p. 445, Will of Lewis Rountree, 1849-1850.

Joyner, ? m. Amy Land, W. Bk. F, p. 102, Will of Littleberry Land, 1827-1829.

Joiner, ? m. Piety Calhoun, W. Bk. F, p. 326, Will of Pherabe Calhoun, 1839-1845.

Joyner, ? m. Sarah White, Will of Ann White, 1805-1810.

Joyner, Guilford m. Nancy Dixon, W. Bk. F, p. 223, Will of Coffield Dixon, 1833-1838.

Joyner, Merit m. Sarah Dixon, W. Bk. F, p. 223, Will of Coffield Dixon, 1833-1838.

Joyner, Wrightson m. Tabitha Tisdale, W. Bk. E, p. 234, Will of grandmother, Mary Tisdale, 1820; W. Bk. E, p. 2, Will of grandfather, Renison Tisdale, 1818-1811.

K

Kelley, Giles m. Selah Wall, W. Bk. B, p. 15, Will of John Wall of Halifax Co., 1778-1779.

Key, ? m. Mary Dicken, Will of Christopher Dicken, 1779-1779.

Killebrew, ? m. Rebecca Maund, Will of Mary Maund, 1795-1795.

Killibrew, George m. Frances Bilberry, W. Bk. F, p. 191, Will of Nathaniel Bilberry, 1830-1836.

Kinchen, ? m. Elizabeth Bellamy, Will of William Bellamy, 1779-1780.

Kitchen, ? m. Elizabeth Weeks, W. Bk. E, p. 93, Will of James Weeks, 1809-1815; W. Bk. F, p. 77, Will of Cely Weeks, 1827-1827.

Kitchen, ? m. Sally Savidge, W. Bk. E, p. 119, Will of Absalom Savidge, 1815-1816.

Knight, ? m. Edith Wilkinson, W. Bk. E, p. 194, Will of Joshua Wilkinson, 1817-1819.

Knight, ? m. Louisa Barlow, W. Bk. F, p. 127, Will of Lewis Barlow, 1831-1831.

Knight, ? m. Marthyan Cromwell, Will of Elizabeth Cromwell, 1838-1840.

Knight, ? m. Patty Linch, W. Bk. D, p. 354, Will of George Linch, 1808-1810.

Knight, ? m. Sukey Braddy, Will of Joseph Braddy, 1802-1804.

Knight, Charles m. Sally Adams, W. Bk. E, p. 223, Will of James Adams, 1818-1820.

Knight, James m. Priscilla Carter, W. Bk. A, p. 260, Will of Kindred Carter, 1777.

Knight, James m. Sarah Bandy, W. Bk. F, p. 270, Will of Susan Bandy, 1840-1842.

Knight, Moses m. Charity Carter, W. Bk. A, p. 260, Will of Kindred Carter, 1777.

Knight, Peter m. Phereby Bell, W. Bk. F, p. 337, Will of Frederick Bell, 1844-1846.

Knight, Robert, m. ? Spier, Will of James Spier, 1761-1761.

Knight, William m. Emerlina Freeman, W. Bk. F, p. 229, Will of Josiah Freeman, 1838-1838.

Knight, Willis m. Polly Knight, wid. of Jesse Knight, W. Bk. F, p. 343, Will of Willis Knight, 1845-1846.

L

Lancaster, ? m. Anne Lupo, W. Bk. E, p. 20, Will of James Lupo, 1811-1811.

Lancaster, ? m. Polly Land, W. Bk. F, p. 102, Will of Littleberry Land, 1827-1829.

Lancaster, Jesse m. Prudence Whitehead, W. Bk. F, p. 357, Will of Augustine Whitehead, 1846-1847.

Lancaster, Robert m. Mary Williams, W. Bk. C, p. 254, Will of John Williams, 1792-1793.

Land, Charles? m. Piety Weaver, W. Bk. E, p. 107, Will of Benjamin Weaver, 1812-1815.

Lang, John? m. Elizabeth Rogers, W. Bk. F, p. 500, Will of mother, Priscilla Warren of Pitt Co., N. C., 1811-1820.

Langdon, ? m. Elizabeth George, Will of Elizabeth George, 1833-1833.

Langford, ? m. Frankey Lowry, Will of Robert Lowry, 1768-1774.

Langley, ? m. Charity Mial, Will of John Mial, 1775-1785.

Langley, Isaac m. ? Lodge, Will of Luis Lodge, 1794-1794.

Langston, Leonard m. Ann Woodard, W. Bk. A, p. 146, Will of John Woodard, 1765-1765.

Lanier, ? m. Tabitha Grimes, W. Bk. F, p. 450, Will of William Grimes, 1850-1850.

Lattimore, ? m. Betty Lenoir, Will of Thomas Lenoir, 1765-1765.

Lawrence, ? m. Absilla Bell, Will of Joshua Bell, 1793-1793.

Lawrence, ? m. Comfort Cromwell, W. Bk. C, p. 66, Will of Alexander Cromwell, 1788-1789.

Lawrence, ? m. Elizabeth Norris, W. Bk. D, p. 310, Will of Charity Norris, 1807-1808.

Lawrence, ? m. Lucy Mayo, W. Bk. F, p. 154, Will of David Mayo, 1824-1834.

Lawrence, John m. Mildred Batts, Will of Lucy Batts, 1847-1847.

Lawrence, Joshua m. Harriet P. Ward, W. Bk. G, p. 57, Will of Nancy Ward, 1853-1854.

Laws, George m. ? Mulkey, Will of Philip Mulkey, 1736-1737.

Lee, ? m. Mary Woodard, Will of John Woodard, 1765-1765.

Leigh, ? m. Elizabeth Barnes, Will of Edward Barnes, 1760-1762.

Leigh, ? m. Lucy Harrell, W. Bk. F, p. 307, Will of Christopher Harrell, 1843-1844.

Leigh, ? m. Polly Harrell, W. Bk. F, p. 307, Will of Christopher Harrell, 1843-1844.

Little, ? m. Chrischaney Downing, Will of James Downing, Sr., 1808-1808.

Little, ? m. Fannie Thigpen, W. Bk. F, p. 420, Will of James Thigpen, 1840-1849.

Little, ? m. Harriett Knight, W. Bk. F, p. 343, Will of Willis Knight, 1845-1846.

Llewelling, ? m. Sarah Bruce, W. Bk. D, p. 278, Will of George Bruce, 1806-1807.

Lloyd, ? m. Sally Brinkley, Will of Abraham Brinkley, 1835-1838.

Lodge, Joshua m. ? Soary, W. Bk. G, p. 113, Will of Solomon Soary, 1850-1855.

Lodge, Lewis m. Martha Sarsnett, W. Bk. E, p. 251, Will of Henrietta Sarsnett, 1820-1820.

Long, ? m. Annie Staton, W. Bk. E, p. 113, Will of Ezekiel Staton, 1815-1815.

Long, Bennett? m. Catherine Hill, W. Bk. F, p. 59, Will of Penelope Hill, 1826-1826.

M

Mabry, ? m. Hepsebah Braddy, Will of Joseph Braddy, 1802-1804.

Mabry, Charles? m. Penelope Bryan, W. Bk. B, p. 277, Will of Drewry Bryan, 1843-1843.

Mace, ? m. Polly Griffis, Will of John Griffis (Griffin), 1796-1799.

Manning, ? m. Claracy Averitt, W. Bk. F, p. 4, Will of James Averitt, Sr., 1822-1823.

Manning, ? m. Elizabeth Cherry, W. Bk. D, p. 340, Will of Solomon Cherry, 1808.

Manning, ? m. Martha Culpepper, Will of Benjamin Culpepper, 1767-1772.

Manning, ? m. Sarah Staton, W. Bk. E, p. 58, Will of Jesse Staton, 1812-1813.

Manning, ? m. Patience Phillips, Will of Arthur Phillips, 1789-1790.

Manning, John? m. Martha Kitchen, W. Bk. F, p. 44, Will of Elizabeth Kitchen, 1825-1825.

Marks, ? m. Annis Coker, W. Bk. F, p. 118, Will of James Coker, 1830-1830.

Marley, ? m. Elsey Shearley, Will of Richard Shearley, 1816-1823.

Marley, ? m. Sarah Sessums, Will of Nicholas Sessums, 1764-1764.

Marley, Benjamin m. Ann Drake, Will of Lazarus Drake, 1774-1785.

Marley, Nathan m. Sarah Sessums, Will of Nicholas Sessums, 1764-1764; W. Bk. F, p. 124, Will of Nathan Marley, 1824-1831.

Marlow, Bolling m. Providence Cromwell, W. Bk. C, p. 66, Will of Alexander Cromwell, 1788-1789.

Mason, ? m. Polly Everitt, Will of brother, Silas Everitt, 1835.

Mathewson, ? m. Mary I. Austin, Will of Lydia Austin, 1852-1853.

Matthews, ? m. Elener Averitt, W. Bk. F, p. 4, Will of James Averitt, Sr., 1822-1823.

May, ? m. Rebecca Bailey, W. Bk. F, p. 470, Will of Jonathan Bailey, 1852.

May, ? m. Sarah Lowry, Will of Robert Lowry, 1768-1774.

May, ? m. Harriett Pippen, W. Bk. F, p. 146, Will of Joseph Pippen, 1827-1833.

Mayo, ? m. Fanny Cobb, W. Bk. E, p. 167, Will of Edward Cobb, 1812-1817.

Mayo, ? of Miss. m. Nancy Knight, W. Bk. F, p. 343, Will of Willis Knight, 1845-1846.

Mayo, Nathan m. Elizabeth Hyman, wid., W. Bk. E, p. 11, Will of Nathan Mayo, 1808-1811.

Mayo, Thomas m. Mary Bryan, W. Bk. F, p. 352, Will of Dempsey Bryan, 1847.

Mc

McDowell, ? m. Mary Cromwell, Will of Elizabeth Cromwell, 1838-1840.

McDowell, John m. Elizabeth Savidge, W. Bk. E, p. 119, Will of Abasalom Savidge, 1815-1816.

McGee, ? m. Ann Moore, Will of Joseph Moore, 1753-1757.

McGee, William m. Eugenia Bell, Will of Frederick Bell, 1844-1846.

McMullen, Robert? m. Pheriby Bryan, W. Bk. D, p. 166, Will of John Bryan, 1801-1803.

M

Melton, ? m. Sarah Thomas, Will of John Thomas, 1774-1777.

Mercer, ? m. Rebecca Lewis, W. Bk. F, p. 350, Will of James Lewis, 1844-1846.

Mercer, Jesse m. Margaret Norfleet, dau. of Isam Norfleet, W. Bk. F, p. 491, Will of Margaret Mercer, 1852-1852; W. Bk. F, p. 509, Will of Christian Norfleet, 1852-1853.

Merrit, William? m. Elizabeth Goodson, W. Bk. A, p. 101, Will of Thomas Goodson, 1762.

Meritt, ? m. Margaret Gunter, W. Bk. F, p. 339, Will of Priscilla Gunter, 1844-1846.

Merrit, ? m. Mary Goodson, Will of Thomas Goodson, 1761-1762.

Mials, Thomas m. Sarah Exum, W. Bk. A, p. 236, Will of John Exum, 1775-1775.

Miller, ? m. Mary Louisa Blount, dau. of William Blount, Will of Anna Harvey, 1802-1805.

Miller, ? m. Martha Knight, W. Bk. E, p. 122, Will of Jesse Knight, 1815-1816.

Minshew (Michaux?), m. Polly Simms, W. Bk. E, p. 79, Will of Benjamin Simms, 1814-1815.

Mitchell, ? m. Delilah McDade, Will of sister, Mary McDade, 1832.

Mitchell, Peter m. ? Jones, Will of John Jones, 1757-1758.
Montgomary, ? m. Elizabeth Dixon, Will of Thomas Dixon, 1790-1790.
Moore, ? m. Elizabeth Dillard, W. Bk. E, p. 172, Will of Elizabeth Dillard, 1817-1817.
Moore, ? m. Judith Ricks, Will of James Ricks, 1792-1792.
Moore, ? m. Martha Harrell, W. Bk. F, p. 307, Will of Christopher Harrell, 1843-1844.
Moore, ? m. Mary Grimes, W. Bk. F, p. 450, Will of William Grimes, 1850-1850.
Moore, ? m. Newton Dillard, W. Bk. E, p. 172, Will of Elizabeth Dillard, 1817-1817.
Moore, ? m. Rebecca Coker, W. Bk. F, p. 409, Will of James Coker, 1846-1848.
Moore, ? m. Rebecca Griffin, Will of Zachariah Griffin, 1837.
Moore, ? m. Rebecca Harrell, W. Bk. F, p. 307, Will of Christopher Harrell, 1843-1844.
Moore, ? m. Sally Lewis, Will of Exum Lewis, 1790-1790.
More (Moore), Benjamin m. Honor Wells, W. Bk. F, p. 194, Will of Mathew Wells, 1834-1836.
Moore, Burwell m. Penny Dixon, W. Bk. F, p. 223, Will of Coffield Dixon, 1833-1838.
Moore, Moses m. Easter Peel, W. Bk. F, p. 500, Will of Hillary Peel, 1849-1853.
Mooring, John Jr.? m. Susannah Staton, W. Bk. E, p. 300, Will of Arthur Staton, 1821-1822.
Morgan, ? m. Jenny Waller, W. Bk. D, p. 315, Will of James Waller, 1808-1808.
Morgan, ? m. Lucy Soary, W. Bk. G, p. 113, Will of Solomon Soary, 1850-1855.
Morgan, ? m. Mary Jelks, Will of brother, William Jelks, 1781-1782.
Morgan, Joseph m. Mary Atkinson, Will of Joseph Morgan, 1791-1792.
Morris, ? m. Dilly Knight, Will of James Knight, 1786-1794.
Morris, ? m. Sarah Wilkinson, W. Bk. E, p. 194, Will of Joshua Wilkinson, 1817-1819.
Morris, John m. Mary Vickers, W. Bk. B, p. 152, Will of John Vickers, 1784-1784.
Morris, Nathan m. Feby Hunt, dau. of Elizabeth Hunt, W. Bk. F, p. 106, Will of Nathan Morris, 1820-1829.
Murphy, ? m. Catey Bryan, W. Bk. E, p. 14, Will of Smith Bryan, 1809-1811.

N

Narron, ? m. Mary Coker, Will of Caleb Coker, 1748-1748.

Nelson, Kinchen m. Fanny or Patsy Crisp, W. Bk. F, p. 103, Will of Samuel Crisp, 1829-1829.

Nelson, Jonas m. Fanny or Patsy Crisp, W. Bk. F, p. 103, Will of Samuel Crisp, 1829-1829.

Newsome, Joseph m. Julian Pope, Will of William Pope, 1749-1749.

Nicholson, ? m. Elizabeth Knight, W. Bk. E, p. 22, Will of Charity Benton, 1818-1818.

Norsworthy, ? m. Delilah (Delia?) Clark, Will of Henry Clark, 1784-1785.

Norsworthy, Ogburn m. ? Lodge, Will of Luis Lodge, 1794-1794.

Norville, Chapman m. Lucinda Edwards, W. Bk. E, p. 165, Will of Brittain Edwards, 1813-1817; W. Bk. G, p. 99, Will of sister, Nancy Edwards, 1853-1855.

Nowell, ? m. Henryetta Long, W. Bk. F, p. 432, Will of William R. Long, 1848-1849.

Nunnery, ? m. Sarah Coker, Will of James Coker, 1796-1796.

Nunry, Grifen (Griffin) m. Penstope (Penelope) Horn, W. Bk. A, p. 52, Will of Henry Horn, 1761-1761.

O

O'Berry, ? m. Amy Pitman, W. Bk. F, p. 156, Will of Sally Pitman, 1833-1834.

Odom, ? of Tenn. m. Mary Crisp, Will of Samuel Crisp, Sr., 1829-1829.

Odom, ? m. Milbry Davis, W. Bk. F, p. 15, Will of John Davis, 1822-1824.

O'Neal, ? m. Lucy Vines, wid., W. Bk. E, p. 334, Will of son, Charles Vines, 1823-1823.

O'Neal, ? m. Sarah or Mary Stallings, Will of Griggre Stallions (Gregory Stallings), 1788-1790.

O'Neal, Isham m. Sarah or Mary Stallions (Stallings), Will of Greggre (Gregory?) Stallions (Stallings), 1788-1790.

Owen, ? m. Elizabeth Kea, W. Bk. F, p. 242, Will of Henry Kea, 1842.

Owen, ? m. Mary Ellis, W. Bk. E, p. 118, Will of Jean Ellis, 1815-1815.

Owens, ? m. Nancy Lester, W. Bk. F, p. 38, Will of Moses Lester, 1825-1826.

Owens, ? m. Martha Joyner, W. Bk. E, p. 274, Will of Drewry Joyner, 1820-1821.

Outland, ? m. Margaret Peele, W. Bk. D, p. 332, Will of Robert Peele, 1807-1808.

P

Pace, James? m. Sarah Knight, W. Bk. B, p. 88, Will of Moses Knight, 1781.

Page, ? m. Elizabeth Lewis, W. Bk. F, p. 350, Will of James Lewis, 1844-1846.

Parish, ? m. Patsey Robertson, Will of Hardy Robertson, 1795-1795.

Parish, ? m. Sarah Moore, Will of Samuel Moore, 1793-1794.

Parit, ? m. Sarah Bradley, Will of John Bradley, 1772-1772.

Parker, ? m. Jerusha Benton, W. Bk. B, p. 229, Will of brother, Jethro Benton, 1774-1775.

Parker, ? m. Mary Weeks, Will of Sarah Weeks, 1792-1792.

Parker, ? m. Rachel Sessums, Will of Nicholas Sessums, 1764-1764.

Parker, Kadah m. Ann Weeks, Will of Sarah Weeks, 1792-1792.

Parrot, Joseph m. Martha Belcher, W. Bk. E, p. 283, Will of Beverley Belcher, 1820-1821.

Paton, ? m. Nancy Booth, W. Bk. D, p. 303, Will of James Booth, 1806-1808.

Peal, ? m. Jackey D. Braswell, W. Bk. F, p. 266, Will of Bythal Braswell, 1841-1842.

Peal, ? m. Rebekah Gray, W. Bk. E, p. 168, Will of Benjamin Gray, 1817-1817.

Pearce, ? m. Elizabeth Tisdal, W. Bk. E, p. 2, Will of Renison Tisdal, 1808-1811.

Pearman, ? m. Selah Coker, Will of James Coker, 1796-1796.

Peel, Henry W. m. Zilla Fleming, W. Bk. G, p. 96, Will of Willis Fleming, 1850-1855.

Peck, ? m. Abby Matthewson, W. Bk. F, p. 133, Will of Nathan Matthewson, 1826-1832.

Pender, ? m. Elizabeth Daughtis, Will of brother, Dempsey Daughtis (Daughty), 1761-1778.

Pender, ? m. Elizabeth Robbins, W. Bk. E, p. 217, Will of John Robbins, 1819-1819.

Pender, ? m. Maria Louisa Williams, W. Bk. F, p. 515, Will of Ann D. Williams of Petersburg, Va., 1852-1853.

Pender, Robert H. m. Janis? Pender, W. Bk. F, p. 480, Will of William Pender, 1850-1852.

Perry, ? m. Milley Crocker, Will of Drewry Crocker, (Halifax Co.), 1779-1779.

Perry, ? m. Mary Lenoir, Will of Thomas Lenoir, 1765-1765.

Perry, Benjamin m. Elizabeth Middleton, Will of John Middleton, 1750-1750.

Perkins, ? m. Susan Leggett, W. Bk. G, p. 102, Will of Levin Leggett, 1854-1855.

Pettaway, Micajah m. ? Sugg, W. Bk. D, p. 207, Will of Noah Sugg, 1804-1804.

Petway, William D. m. Cinderella Cromwell, Will of Elizabeth Cromwell, 1838-1840, W. Bk. F, p. 239.

Philips, ? m. Arrena Norvel, W. Bk. F, p. 441, Will of Chapman Norvel, 1850-1850.

Philips, ? m. Elizabeth Nicholson, W. Bk. E, p. 238, Will of Penelope Nicholson, 1820-1820.

Philips, ? m. Sarah Exum, Will of John Exum, 1775-1775.

Philips, Frederick m. dau. of Catherine Peele, W. Bk. E, p. 71, Will of Catherine Peele, 1812-1814.

Philips, Joseph m. Nancy Taylor, dau. of John Taylor of Martin Co., Will of Joseph Philips, 1819-1822.

Philips, Matthew m. Elizabeth Nicholson, W. Bk. E, p. 238, Will of Penelope Nicholson, 1820-1820.

Pippen, ? m. Mary Weeks, W. Bk. E, p. 93, Will of James Weeks, 1809-1815; W. Bk. F, p. 77, Will of Cely Weeks, 1827-1827.

Pippen, ? m. Selah Weeks, W. Bk. E, p. 93, Will of James Weeks, 1809-1815.

Pippen, ? m. Tellitha Tolson, Will of Winder Tolson, 1837-1837.

Pitman, ? m. Absala Spier, Will of John Spier, 1783-1790.

Pitman, ? m. Ann Gardner, W. Bk. 3, p. 97, Will of George Gardner, 1786-1789.

Pitman, ? m. Elizabeth Bryan, W. Bk. E, p. 276, Will of Elias Bryan, 1821-1821.

Pitman, ? m. Phereby Gardner, W. Bk. 3, p. 97, Will of George Gardner, 1786-1789.

Pitman, ? m. Sary Pitt, W. Bk. E, p. 264, Will of Ann Pitt, 1809-1821; Will of James Pitt, 1797-1797.

Pitman, ? m. Tazzy Linch, W. Bk. D, p. 354, Will of George Linch, 1808-1810.

Pitman, Edward m. Elizabeth Barnes, W. Bk. E, p. 191, Will of Briton Barnes, 1818-1818.

Pitman, Jesse m. Lucy Barnes, W. Bk. E, p. 191, Will of Briton Barnes, 1818-1818.

Pitman, Reddin m. Martha Bryan, W. Bk. F, p. 352, Will of Dempsey Bryan, 1847.

Pitt, Archibald m. Polly Coffield, W. Bk. E, p. 45, Will of Thomas Coffiield, 1812-1812.

Pittman, ? m. Elizabeth Cotten, W. Bk. F, p. 482, Will of Randolph Cotten, 1847-1852.

Pittman, ? m. Mary Linch, W. Bk. F, p. 36, Will of Olive Linch, Sr., 1824-1825.

Pittman, ? m. Polly Summerlin, W. Bk. E, p. 162, Will of Barnes Summerlin, 1815-1817.

Pittman, ? m. Sally Spicer, W. Bk. E, p. 308, Will of William Spicer, 1820-1822.

Pittman, Robert J. m. Elizabeth Cotten, sister of Frederick Cotten, W. Bk. E, p. 102, Will of Frederick Cotten, 1814-1815.

Pittman, William m. ? Ross, Will of Andrew Ross, 1761-1761.

Pond, Stephenson m. Mourning Griffin, Will of Benjamin Griffin, 1808-1808.

Poovy, ? m. Winnie Wells, Will of Stephen Wells, 1773-1775.

Pope, ? m. Olive Surginer, Will of Robert Surginer, 1773-1778.

Pope, ? m. Mary Ricks, Will of Isaac Ricks, 1748-1748.

Pope, ? m. Priscilla Wells, Will of Stephen Wells, 1773-1775.

Pope, Barnaby m. Angelina McKinne Parish, wid., Will of Mary McKinne, 1754-1754; Will of John McKinne, 1753-1753.

Pope, John m. Rhoda Robertson, W. Bk. F, p. 27, Will of Peter Robertson, 1823-1824.

Pope, John ? m. Patience Brown, Will of John Brown of Halifax Co., N. C., 1758-1759.

Pope, Thomas m. Mary Lee, W. Bk. A, p. 215, Will of Joshua Lee, 1767-1774.

Pope, William of Tenn. m. ? Stallings, W. Bk. F, p. 157, Will of James Stallings, 1830-1834.

Porter, Ely m. Martha Pippen, dau. of Joseph and Temperance Pippen, W. Bk. F, p. 279, Will of Ely Porter, 1842-1843; W. Bk. F, p. 330, Will of Martha Porter, 1845-1845.

Porter, Moodie m. Elizabeth Phillips, W. Bk. E, p. 214, Will of William Donaldson, 1817-1819.

Powell, ? m. Seale Harrell, Will of Thomas Harrell, 1763-1763.

Price, ? m. Jack Elizer Howell, W. Bk. F, p. 364, Will of John Howell, 1845.

Price, ? m. Mary Tolson, Will of Winder Tolson, 1837-1837.

Price, ? m. Martha Morgan, Will of William Morgan, 1794-1795.

Price, ? m. Sarah McDade, Will of sister, Mary McDade, 1832.

Price, John m. ? Perritt, Will of Ann Perritt, 1788; Will of John Perritt, 1785-1786.

Price, Jonathan? m. Polly O'Neel, W. Bk. E, p. 7, Will of Isham O'Neel, 1811-1811.

Price, John m. Maria Adams, W. Bk. E, p. 233, Will of James Adams, 1818-1820.

Price, Jonathan m. Polley O'Neel, W. Bk. E, p. 7, Will of Isham O'Neel, 1811-1811.

Pridgen, David m. ? Evins, Will of Elizabeth Evins, wid. of Abraham Evins, 1766.

Pridgen, Hardy m. ? Tisdal, W. Bk. E, p. 2, Will of Renison Tisdal, 1808-1811.

Proctor, ? m. Charity Williams, W. Bk. F, p. 72, Will of Thomas Williams, 1825-1827.

Proctor, ? m. Phebe (Phoebe) Gardner, W. Bk. 3, p. 97, Will of George Gardner, 1786-1789.

Proctor, ? m. Susanna Gwin, Will of Daniel Gwin, 1795-1796.

Proctor, Aaron? m. Anna Williams, W. Bk. E, p. 63, Will of Absalom Williams, 1802-1814.

Proctor, John? m. Frances Clark, W. Bk. C, p. 8, Will of Henry Clark, 1784-1785.

Pyrent, ? m. Mary Bell, Will of William Bell, 1752-1754.

R

Radock, ? m. Mary Daughtis, Will of brother, Dempsey Daughtis, (Daughty), 1761-1778.

Rawling, William G. m. ? Savage, W. Bk. F, p. 164, Will of James Savage, 1834-1834.

Read, ? m. Rhoda Williams, W. Bk. E, p. 228, Will of John Williams, 1819-1819.

Reaves, ? m. Mary Ann Long, W. Bk. F, p. 432, Will of William R. Long, 1848-1849.

Reddick, ? m. Drucilla Mayo, W. Bk. F, p. 369, Will of Rebecca Mayo, 1846-1847.

Richardson, ? m. Hannah Mitchell, Will of Peter Mitchell, 1770.

Richardson, Benjamin m. Ann Spell, dau. of Thomas Spell and gr. dau. of John Jones, Will of John Jones, 1757-1758.

Ricks, ? m. Ann Ross, Will of Kallum Ross, 1760-1760.

Ricks, ? m. Jude Ross, Will of Kallum Ross, 1760-1760.

Ridley, ? m. Amelia Toole, Will of Geraldus Toole, 1834-1834.

Riley, ? m. Nancy Carlile, W. Bk. E, p. 81, Will of Robert Carlile, 1808-1815.

Ritter, John? m. Elizabeth Ellis, W. Bk. F, p. 25, Will of Elisha Ellis, 1824-1824.

Roads, ? m. Nancy Gator, W. Bk. E, p. 236, Will of Samuel Gater, Sr., 1820-1820.

Roane, ? m. Christian Powell, Will of William Powell, 1792-

Robards, ? m. Eliza Toole, Will of Geraldus Toole, 1834-1834. 1793.

Robbins, ? m. Mary Wells, Will of Stephen Wells, 1773-1775.

Robbins, Frederick m. Polly Barnes, W. Bk. F, p. 21, Will of Joseph Barnes, 1824-1824.

Robertson, Henry m. Clary Bentley, W. Bk. D, p. 328, Will of Martha Bentley, 1804-1808.

Robertson, ? m. Elizabeth Powell, Will of William Powell, 1792-1793.

Robertson, William m. Martha Stallings, W. Bk. F, p. 157, Will of James Stallings, 1830-1834.

Rodgers, ? m. Sally Dew, Will of Milicent Dew, 1786-1786.

Rogers, ? m. Ledy Robbins, W. Bk. D, p. 346, Will of Sarah Robbins, 1809-1809.

Rogers, ? m. Milley Robbins, W. Bk. D, p. 346, Will of Sarah Robbins, 1809-1809.

Rollings, ? m. Martha Davis, Will of Emory Davis, 1795.

Ross, ? m. Martha Cherry, W. Bk. D, p. 340, Will of Solomon Cherry, 1808.

Ross, James? m. Sarah Ricks, Will of Isaac Ricks, 1760-1760.

Rountree, ? m. Susannah Whitehead, Will of William Bond Whitehead, 1805-1807; Will of Sarah Whitehead, 1808-1810.

Routh, William m. ? Wilkins, W. Bk. E, p. 144, Will of William Wilkins, 1810-1816.

Ruffin, ? m. Averilla Deloach, Will of Samuel Deloach, 1764-1764; Will of Mary Deloach, 1773-1774.

Ruffin, ? m. Lucy Fort, W. Bk. E, p. 314, Will of Jane Fort, 1818-1822.

Ruffin, ? m. Mary Brownrigg, W. Bk. F, p. 242, Will of Obedience Brownrigg, 1839-1840.

Ruffin, ? m. Mary Haywood, Will of William Haywood, 1779-1780.

Ruffin, ? m. Mary Johnston, W. Bk. F, p. 249, Will of Esther Johnston, 1840-1841.

Ruffin, ? m. Millie Braswell, Will of Benjamin Braswell, 1789-1792.

Ruffin, ? m. Milly Davis, Will of Emory Davis, 1795.

Ruffin, ? m. Sarah Bullock, Will of David Bullock, 1774.

Ruffin, Jesse m. Sarah Lee, W. Bk. E, p. 42, Will of Henry Lee, 1812-1812.

Ruffin, John m. Maria Griffin, W. Bk. F, p. 233, Will of Zacheriah Griffin, 1837-1839.

Ruffin, Richard m. Averilla Deloach, W. Bk. A, p. 205, Will of Mary Deloach, 1773-1774.

Ruffin, Samuel m. Selah Braswell, W. Bk. C, p. 194, Will of Benjamin Braswell, 1789-1792.

S

Samon, Sammon (Salmon?) James? m. Elizabeth Passmore, Will of John Passmore, 1754.

Sanders, ? m. Ann Holmes, Will of John Holmes, 1735-1736.

Sanders, ? m. Mary Hedgepeth, Will of brother, John Hedgepeth, 1816-1823.

Sanders, Thomas m. ? Jordan, Will of Cornelius Jordan, Sr., 1792-1794.

Sanders, Willie m. ? Dickinson, W. Bk. F, p. 183, Will of Turner Dickinson, 1835-1836.

Sandifor, ? m. Olif Harris, Will of Thomas Harris, 1786-1787.

Sandiser, ? m. Nancy Quinn, Will of William Quinn, 1790-1790.

Sasnett, ? m. Charity Dillard, W. Bk. E, p. 172, Will of Elizabeth Dillard, 1817-1817.

Savage, ? m. Silvah Norriss, Will of John Norriss, 1801-1801.

Savage, ? m. Susan Dickens, W. Bk. F, p. 488, Will of William Dickens, 1852-1852.

Savage, Lemuel? m. Tabitha Long, W. Bk. F, p. 432, Will of William R. Long 1848-1849.

Sawyer, ? m. Winnefred Griffin, Will of Zachariah Griffin, 1837.

Sasnet, Richard m. Henrietta Maria Gosney, W. Bk. A, p. 181, Will of John Gosney, 1779-1779.

Sauls, Frederick m. Frances Spier, W. Bk. A, p. 38, Will of James Spier, 1761-1761.

Scarborough, ? m. Grace Clark, Will of Henry Clark, 1784-1785.

Scarborough, ? m. Jemimah Drake, Will of Jesse Drake, 1796-1796.

Scarborough, ? m. Rachel Vickers, Will of Ralph Vickers, 1761-1762.

Scrues (Screws), Henry m. Mary Saul, W. Bk. A, p. 186, Will of Abraham Saul, 1769-1771.

Sealf, ? m. Edea Carlile, W. Bk. E, p. 81, Will of Robert Carlile, 1808-1815.

Sears, Davis m. Charity Robbins, W. Bk. B, p. 90, Will of William Robbins, 1779-1781.

Seebery, ? m. Mary Gardner, W. Bk. 3, p. 97, Will of George Gardner, 1786-1789.

Sessoms, Isaac? m. Elizabeth Lloyd, Will of Nicholas Lloyd, 1781-1781.

Sharpe, ? m. Elizabeth Taylor, W. Bk. F, p. 391, Will of Stephen Taylor, 1848-1848.

Shelton, ? m. Mary Mayo, W. Bk. G, p. 54, Will of William Mayo, 1853-1854.

Shelton, ? m. Pheriba Nicholson, W. Bk. E, p. 238, Will of Penelope Nicholson, 1820-1820.

Sherley, ? m. Delia Edwards, W. Bk. E, p. 75, Will of Nathan Edwards, 1812-1814.

Sherrod, ? m. Elizabeth Savage, W. Bk. F, p. 328, Will of Frances Savage, 1843-1845.

Sikes, ? m. Hannah Suringer, Will of Robert Suringer, 1773-1778.

Sikes, Bassett m. Mary Ann Edwards, W. Bk. F, p. 298, Will of Siley Edwards, 1841-1843.

Sketre ? m. Nancy Davis, W. Bk. F, p. 15, Will of John Davis,

Skinner, ? m. Elizabeth Little, W. Bk. F, p. 42, Will of Jesse Little, 1824-1825.

Skinner, ? m. Obedience Weaver, W. Bk. F, p. 389, Will of Jonathan W. Weaver, 1847-1848.

Skinner, Andrew m. Arcena L. Fleming, W. Bk. G, p. 96, Will of Willie Fleming, 1850-1855.

Skinner, Henry m. Elizabeth Vines? W. Bk. F, p. 49, Will of Henry Skinner, 1825.

Sims, ? m. Charity Barnes, Will of Edward Barnes, 1760-1762.

Sims, ? m. Mary Barnes, Will of Edward Barnes, 1760-1762.

Simms, ? m. Christian Thomas, Will of Mary Thomas, 1802-1802.

Simms, ? m. Edie Horn, W. Bk. F, p. 68, Will of Jacob Horn, 1826-1827.

Simms, ? m. Martha Dew, W. Bk. E, p. 149, Will of brother, Arthur Dew, 1816-1816; Will of Mary Dew, 1801-1801.

Simms, ? m. Milicent (Thomas) Eason, wid., W. Bk. D, p. 363, Will of Mary Thomas, 1810-1810; W. Bk. D, p. 172, Will of Theophilus Thomas, 1803-1803.

Simms, ? m. Tabitha Thomas, W. Bk. D, p. 363, Will of Mary Thomas, 1810-1810; W. Bk. D, p. 172, Will of Theophilus Thomas, 1803-1803.

Simms, ? m. Tresey Daniel, W. Bk. E, p. 286, Will of Lemuel Daniel, 1821-1822.

Simon, Benjamin? m. Mrs. Dinah Gerrad, wid. of Forbes Gerrad (Gerhard), Will of Charles Gerhard, 1797-1798.

Singleton, ? m. Ann Amason, Will of Thomas Amason, 1792.

Singleton, ? m. Peggy Lawrence, W. Bk. F, p. 310, Will of John Lawrence, 1841-1844.

Smiley, ? m. Elizabeth Daughtery, W. Bk. E, p. 170, Will of Elizabeth Daughtery.

Smith, ? m. Ann Coker, Will of James Coker, 1796-1796.

Smith, ? m. Cypy Webb, W. Bk. F, p. 271, Will of John Webb, Sr., 1841-1842.

Smith, ? m. Nancy Hodges, W. Bk. E, p. 17, Will of Anthony Hodges, 1811-1811; Will of Thomas Hodges, 1800-1806.

Smith, ? m. Levinia Averitt, W. Bk. F, p. 4, Will of James Averitt, Sr., 1822-1823.

Smith, ? m. Luvyce Averitt, W. Bk. F, p. 4, Will of James Averitt, Sr., 1822-1823.

Smith, ? m. Mary Thomas, Will of John Thomas, 1774-1777.

Smith, Reubin m. Ann Swales, Will of Mary Swales, 1796-1800.

Smith, Sypa? m. Elizabeth M. Felts, W. Bk. G, p. 92, Will of William Felts, 1853-1854.

Smith, William m. Penetta Thigpen, W. Bk. F, p. 258, Will of Lemuel Thigpen, 1839-1841.

Southerland, John L.? m. Nancy Mayo, W. Bk. F, p. 28, Will of John W. Mayo, 1824-1825.

Spaight, ? m. Sary Barnes, W. Bk. D, p. 230, Will of Aziel Barnes, 1804-1805.

Spear, ? m. Elizabeth Fountain, Will of Henry Fountain, 1797-1797.

Spear, ? m. Faithy Hyett, Will of Thomas Hyett, 1781-1783.

Speed, Joseph m. Ann Bignall, Will of Robert Bignall, 1786-1787.

Speight, ? m. Catherine Eason, W. Bk. E, p. 223, Will of Abner Eason, 1819-1819.
Speight, ? m. Emma Lewis, Will of Ann Lewis, 1843-1844.
Spell, Thomas m. ? Jones, Will of John Jones, 1757-1758.
Spelling, Britain? m. Luvina (Luvinia?) Pippen, W. Bk. F, p. 146, Will of Joseph Pippen, 1827-1833.
Spicer, ? m. Elizabeth Griffin, Will of Zachariah Griffin, 1837.
Spier, ? m. Christian Benton, W. Bk. B, p. 229, Will of brother, Jethro Benton, 1774-1775.
Spier, ? m. Dorothy Holmes, Will of John Holmes, 1835-1836.
Spier, ? m. Beatrix Holmes, Will of John Holmes, 1835-1836.
Spier, James m. Elizabeth Coker, Will of Caleb Coker, 1748-1748.
Spruill, Benjamin m. Elizabeth Hines, W. Bk. D, p. 215, Will of Peter Hines, Sr., 1804-1805.
Stallings, ? m. Martha Ann Holland, W. Bk. F, p. 394, Will of David Holland, 1847-1848.
Stallings, James? m. Sealy Odum, W. Bk. F, p. 66, Will of Abraham Odum, 1826-1827.
Stallings, James m. ? Ross, Will of Andrew Ross, 1761-1761.
Stallings, James m. Mary Peel, W. Bk. F, p. 500, Will of Hillary Peel, 1849-1853.
Stallings, John m. Martha Anderson, W. Bk. 3, p. 145, Will of William Anderson, 1789-1790.
Stalins (Stallings), James? m. Sealy Odum, W. Bk. F, p. 66, Will Abraham Odum, 1826-1827.
Stancil, ? m. Liddy Cherry, W. Bk. D, p. 340, Will of Solomon Cherry, 1808.
Stanfield, ? m. Betty Lowry, Will of Robert Lowry, 1768-1774.
Stansell (Stancil) Jessey? m. Harriet Hopkins, W. Bk. F, p. 345, Will of Daniel Hopkins, 1845-1846.
Staton, ? m. Absal Lawrence, wid. of John Lawrence, Sr., W. Bk. D, p. 218, Will of John Lawrence (Jr.), 1799-1805; Will of John Lawrence, (Sr.), 1795-1797.
Staton, ? m. Cecelia Knight, W. Bk. F, p. 143, Will of Walker Knight, 1830.
Sterling, ? m. Betty Wells, Will of Stephen Wells, 1773-1775.
Stewart, William? m. Mollie (Mary) Pitt, W. Bk. E, p. 264, Will of Ann Pitt, 1809-1821; Will of Etheldred Pitt, 1798-1799, s. of James and Ann Pitt; Will of James Pitt, 1797-1797.
Stinson, ? m. Olive Braswell, Will of James Braswell, 1760-1765.

Stinson, Micajah m. Mary Baker, W. Bk. C, p. 28, Will of Moses Baker, 1781-1786.

Stockdale, Matthew? m. Eauphania (Euphemia?) Sugg, W. Bk. 3, p. 57, Will of William Sugg, 1787-1788.

Stockdale, ? m. Martha Hines, Will of Richard Hines, 1781-1781.

Stokes, ? m. Patience Vickers, Will of John Vickers, 1784-1784.

Stone, John m. Pegee (Peggy?) Merritt, Will of John Merritt, 1757-1757.

Strickland, ? m. Mary Dunn, Will of John Dunn, 1793-1793.

Stricklen, ? m. Mary Hickman, Will of Nathaniel Hickman, 1790-1795.

Stricklin, Isaac? m. Elizabeth Jordan, W. Bk. F, p. 210, Will of Henry Jordan, 1836-1837.

Stringer, John? m. Selah Davis, W. Bk. D, p. 1, Will of Emory Davis, 1795.

Stubbs, ? m. Debrough Everitt, Will of brother, Silas Everitt, 1835.

Sturdivant, ? m. Sarah Hines, Will of Richard Hines, 1781-1781.

Sugg, ? m. Seely Fort, Will of Sarah Horn, 1799.

Sumerell, ? m. Nancy Everitt, W. Bk. E, p. 326, Will of Keton Everitt, 1823-1823.

Sumrell, ? m. Mary Dunford, Will of Philip Dunford, 1821-1829.

Summerlin, Willie m. Elizabeth Freeman, W. Bk. F, p. 229, Will of Josiah Freeman, 1838-1838.

Sumner, John m. Catherine Sherrod, W. Bk. A, p. 264, Will of J. William Sherrod, 1778.

Surgenor, ? m. Joana Foxhall, Will of Thomas Foxhall, 1791-1792.

Surginer, John m. Mary Pope, Will of Jacob Pope, 1770-1772.

Swearingan, ? m. Lidia Permenter, W. Bk. 3, p. 106, Will of James Permenter, 1789-1789.

Swearingan, ? m. Martha Permenter, W. Bk. 3, p. 106, Will of James Permenter, 1789-1789.

Sykes, ? m. Rebecca Pope, Will of Jacob Pope, 1770-1772.

T

Tannabile, William m. Susan M. Macnair, W. Bk. F, p. 274, Will of Edmund D. Macnair, 1842-1843.

Tatum, Thomas? m. Ann Clark, Will of Robert Clark, 1752-1753.

Tart, ? m. Treacy Thomas, W. Bk. D, p. 363. Will of Mary Thomas, 1810-1810; W. Bk. D, p. 172, Will of Theophilus Thomas, 1803-1803.

Tart, Enos m. ? Peele, W. Bk. E, p. 71, Will of Catherine Peele, 1812-1814.

Tartt, ? m. Sally Barnes, W. Bk. E, p. 143, Will of Peggy Barnes, 1816.

Taylor, ? m. Martha Lawrence, Will of Solomon Lawrence, 1801-1804.

Taylor, ? m. Mary Waller, W. Bk. D, p. 315, Will of James Waller, 1808-1808.

Taylor, ? m. Mourning Weaver, W. Bk. E, p. 107, Will of Benjamin Weaver, 1812-1815.

Taylor, ? m. Polly Ruffin, W. Bk. F, p. 458, Will of Elizabeth Ruffin, 1850-1851.

Taylor, ? m. Rhoda Jordan, Will of Henry Jordan, 1836-1837.

Taylor, ? m. Sarah Lawrence, Will of Solomon Lawrence, 1801-1804.

Taylor, ? m. Selah Little, W. Bk. C, p. 85, Will of Abraham Little, 1785-1789.

Taylor, ? m. Winnaford Carter, W. Bk. A, p. 260, Will of Kindred Carter, 1777-1777.

Taylor, Joseph m. Sally Wooten, W. Bk. E, p. 265, Will of James Wooten, 1821-1821.

Teale, ? m. Sally Ann Moore, Will of Elizabeth Moore, 1851-1852.

Teat, ? m. Mary Pitman, W. Bk. F, p. 271, Will of Nancy Pitman, 1842-1842.

Tennison, Abraham m. Jane Adams, W. Bk. D, p. 86 Will of Hopewell Adams, 1794-1799.

Thigpen, ? m. Lavinia Cromwell, Will of Elizabeth Cromwell, 1838-1840.

Thigpen, ? m. Sally Cobb, W. Bk. E, p. 167, Will of Edward Cobb, 1812-1817.

Thomas, ? m. Sally Soary, W. Bk. E, p. 185, Will of Andrew Soary, 1818-1818; W. Bk. F, p. 265, Will of Lucy Soary, 1836-1842.

Thomas, ? m. Susanna Barnes, W. Bk. E, p. 143, Will of Peggy Barnes, 1816.

Thomas, Ichabob m. Suckey Barnes, W. Bk. D, p. 264, Will of Archilaus Barnes, 1807-1807.

Thomas, Law m. ? Jones, Will of John Jones, 1757-1758.

Thomas, ? m. Betty Proctor, Will of William Proctor, 1779-1780.

Thomas, ? m. Elizabeth Ann Ruffin, W. Bk. F, p. 458, Will of Elizabeth Ruffin, 1850-1851.

Thomas, Theophilus m. ? Gibbs, Will of Frederick Gibbs, 1780-1781.

Thomas, Theophilus m. Thaney Whitehead, Will of Matthew Whitehead, 1846-1848.

Thompkins, ? m. Ann Hines, Will of Richard Hines, 1781-1781.

Thornton, ? m. Lucinda Braswell, W. Bk. F, p. 473, Will of Zadock Braswell, 1851-1852.

Thornton, ? m. Mary Foxhall, Will of Thomas Foxhall, 1791-1792.

Tisdal, ? m. Mary Flowers, Will of Edward Flowers, 1775-1778.

Tice, Washington m. Sarah Taylor, W. Bk. F, p. 391, Will of Stephen Taylor, 1848-1848.

Toler, ? m. Betty Stokes, Will of John Stokes, 1783-1784.

Toole, ? m. Elizabeth Haywood, Will of William Haywood, 1779-1780.

Trevathan, ? m. Martha Pope, W. Bk. F, p. 315, Will of Mary Pope, 1837-1844.

Trevathan, ? m. Sarah Pender, W. Bk. E, p. 329, Will of bro., Josiah Pender, 1823-1823; Will of Solomon Pender, 1783.

Trevathan, Henry m. Elizabeth Rose, W. Bk. E, p. 245, Will of Robert Rose, 1816-1820.

Trevathan, Lewis m. Sarah Weeks, W. Bk. E, p. 329, Will of brother, Josiah Pender, 1823-1823.

Tucker, ? m. Goodwin Marshall, Will of John Marshall, 1757-1758.

Tucker, Willaby m. ? Ross, Will of Andrew Ross, 1761-1761.

Tucker, ? m. Mary Barnes, Will of Thomas Barnes, 1761.

Tunnell, John m. Martha Bentley, W. Bk. D, p. 328, Will of Martha Bentley, 1804-1808.

Turlington, ? m. Priscilla Warren or Priscilla Rogers, W. Bk. E, p. 256, Will of Priscilla Warren of Pitt Co., N. C.

Turnal (Purnal?), ? m. Martha Bentley, Will of Joshua Bently, 1799-1799.

Tye, ? m. Mary Dickinson, Will of John Dickinson, 1779-1780.

Tyson, William m. Esther J. Ruffin, W. Bk. F, p. 82, Will of William Tyson, 1826-1828; W. Bk. F, p. 60, Will of Samuel Ruffin, 1826-1826.

U

Underwood, ? m. Hannah Clark, Will of Robert Clark, 1752-1753.

V

Vaughn, ? m. Absala Anderson, W. Bk. 3, p. 145, Will of William Anderson, 1789-1790.
Vickers, Ralph m. Ann Baker, W. Bk. C, p. 28, Will of Moses Baker, 1781-1786.
Vivret, ? Nancy Taylor, W. Bk. F, p. 391, Will of Stephen Taylor, 1848-1848.
Vivret, ? m. Patsey Taylor, W. Bk. F, p. 391, Will of Stephen Taylor, 1848-1848.
Vivrett, ? m. Elizabeth Hickman, Will of Nathaniel Hickman, 1790-1795.

W

Wall, ? m. Frances Coker, Will of Caleb Coker, 1748-1748.
Wall, ? m. Sukey Ship, Will of Richard Ship, 1778-1778.
Waller, Willis m. Nancy Weston, W. Bk. E, p. 28, Will of Amos Weston, 1811-1811.
Ward, ? m. Alley Gaddey, W. Bk. 3, p. 73, Will of Thomas Gaddey, 1787-1788.
Ward, ? m. Catherine E. Pippen, W. Bk. F, p. 519, Will of Joseph L. Pippen, 1851-1853.
Ward, ? m. Elizabeth Bolton, Will of Richard Bolton, 1787-1789.
Ward, ? m. Mahala Leggett, W. Bk. G, p. 102, Will of Levin Leggett, 1854-1855.
Ward, ? m. Nancy Pippen, W. Bk. F, p. 146, Will of Joseph Pippen, 1827-1833; W. Bk. F, p. 330, Will of sister, Martha Porter, 1845-1845.
Ward, ? m. Tabitha Leggett, W. Bk. G, p. 102, Will of Levin Leggett, 1854-1855.
Ward, Elijah m. Ada Daughtery, W. Bk. E, p. 170, Will of Elizabeth Daughtery, 1817-1817.
Ward, ? m. Sally Amason, W. Bk. F, p. 131, Will of Ellendor Amason, 1829-1832.
Ward, John m. Lydia Peel, W. Bk. F, p. 500, Will of Hilliary Peel, 1849-1853.
Ward, Mercer m. Rhoda Horn, W. Bk. E, p. 83, Will of Elijah Horn, 1804-1815.
Warren, Richard m. Elizabeth Thigpen, W. Bk. F, p. 258, Will of Lemuel Thigpen, 1839-1841.

Walton, (Walston?) ? m. Elizabeth Tart, W. Bk. 3, p. 87, Will of Jonathan Tart, 1789.
Walston, ? m. Nancy Atkinson, W. Bk. F, p. 392, Will of Aaron Atkinson, 1842-1848.
Walston, ? m. Polly Webb, W. Bk. F, p. 271, Will of John Webb, Sr., 1841-1842.
Waters, ? m. Milly Everitt, Will of brother, Silas Everitt, 1835.
Watkins, ? m. Betsey Robertson, W. Bk. F, p. 27, Will of Peter Robertson, 1823-1824.
Watkins, ? m. Betsey Robertson, Will of Hardy Robertson, 1795-1795.
Watkins, ? m. Charity Thomas, Will of Mary Thomas, 1802-1802.
Watkins, ? m. Dicey Horn, Will of Michael Horn, 1785.
Watson, ? m. Peninah Brownrigg, W. Bk. F, p. 242, Will of Obedience Brownrigg, 1839-1840.
Watson, ? m. Temperance Wells, Will of Thomas Wells, 1800-1801.
Watson, Silas m. ? Summerlin, W. Bk. E, p. 162, Will of Barnes Summerlin, 1815-1817.
Watts, ? m. Jemima Lowry, Will of Robert Lowry, 1768-1774.
Weatherby, ? m. Lyda (Lydia) Crisp, Will of Samuel Crisp, Sr., 1829-1829.
Weaver, ? m. Polly Land, Will of Charles Land, 1838-1838.
Weaver, Benjamin? m. Murphey Shearley, W. Bk. F, p. 70, Will of Delilah Shearley, 1827-1827.
Webb, ? m. Sally Lewis, W. Bk. F, p. 350, Will of James Lewis, 1844-1846.
Webb, ? m. Ann Wester, W. Bk. F, p. 38, Will of Moses Lester, 1825-1826.
Weeks, ? m. Rhoda Alsobrook, W. Bk. E, p. 40, Will of Parthenia Alsobrook, 1808-1812.
Weeks, ? m. Selah Pender, W. Bk. E, p. 329, Will of brother, Josiah Pender; Will of Solomon Pender, 1783.
West, ? m. Temperance Robertson, Will of Henry Robertson, 1749-1752.
West, Israel m. Priscilla West Coffield, Will of West Coffield, 1778.
Westmorland, ? m. Ann Lenoir, Will of Thomas Lenoir, 1765-1765.
Whibley (Whitley?) ? m. Mary Pridgen, Will of William Pridgen, 1762.

Whitaker, ? m. Catherine Wiggins, Will of Robert Wiggins, (brother), 1803-1803.
Whitaker, ? m. Elizabeth F. Lewis, Will of Ann Lewis, 1843-1844.
Whitaker, ? m. Leah Lenoir, Will of Thomas Lenoir, 1765-1765.
Whitaker, Carey m. Penelope Carter, W. Bk. A, p. 260, Will of Kindred Carter, 1777.
Whitaker, John m. Christian Benton, W. Bk. B, p. 241, Will of Absalom Benton, 1795-1806.
Whitaker, Speir m. Elizabeth F. Lewis, W. Bk. F, p. 226, Will of Ann Lewis, 1844; Will of Exum Lewis, 1839.
Whitaker, William B.? m. Delphia Lyon, W. Bk. F, p. 186, Will of Thomas Lyon, 1836.
White, ? m. Temperance Leggett, W. Bk. F, p. 33, Will of Noah Leggett, 1823-1825.
White, ? m. Charlotte Bradley, W. Bk. F, p. 477, Will of David Bradley.
White, ? m. Elizabeth Vickers, Will of John Vickers, 1784-1784.
White, ? m. Isabella Leggett, W. Bk. G, p. 102, Will of Levin Leggett, 1854-1855.
White, ? m. Nancy Whitehead, W. Bk. D, p. 286, Will of William Bond Whitehead, 1805-1807.
White, ? m. Pamelia Leggett, W. Bk. G, p. 102, Will of Levin Leggett, 1854-1855.
White, Henry m. Polly Rhoades, W. Bk. E, p. 269, Will of Abraham Rhoades, 1819-1821.
White, Jacob m. Mary Williams, W. Bk. B, p. 28, Will of Arthur Williams, 1779-1779.
White, John? m. Nicey Legget, W. Bk. F. p. 33, Will of Noah Legget, 1823-1825.
White, William m. Beedy Farmer, W. Bk. F, p. 65, Will of Benjamin Farmer, 1825-1827; Will of brother, Braswell Farmer, 1827-1827.
Whitehead, ? m. Fanny Land, Will of Charles Land, 1838-1838.
Whitehead, ? m. Oleof Goodson, Will of Thomas Goodson, 1761-1762.
Whitehead, ? m. Rahab Culpepper, Will of Benjamin Culpepper, 1767-1772.
Whitehead, ? m. Sally Higgs, W. Bk. F, p. 396, Will of Mary McWilliams, 1847-1848.
Whiteherst, ? m. Elizabeth Crisp, Will of Samuel Crisp, Sr., 1829-1829.

Whitfield, Hardy? m. Penelope Nicholson. W. Bk. E, p. 238, Will of Penelope Nicholson, 1820-1820.
Whitley, ? m. Nancy Staton, W. Bk. E, p. 113, Will of Ezekiel Staton, 1815-1815.
Whitley, ? m. Rachel Taylor, Will of William Whitley, 1783-1786.
Whitley, ? of Tenn. m. Sarah Crisp, Will of Samuel Crisp, Sr., 1829-1829.
Whitley, ? m. Winnaford Rodgers, Will of Tristram Rodgers, 1799-1799.
Whitley, ? m. Priscilla Amason, Will of Thomas Amason, 1792-1792.
Whitley, David m. Nancy Johnson, W. Bk. F, p. 100, Will of Nathan Johnson, 1829-1829.
Whitley, ? m. Millicent Amason, Will of Thomas Amason, 1792-1792.
Whitty, Jesse m. Nancy Hobbs, W. Bk. E, p. 222, Will of Mary Hobbs, 1819-1819.
Wiatt, ? m. Sally Fountain, Will of Henry Fountain, 1797-1797.
Wiggins, James m. Milbery Taylor, W. Bk. F, p. 391, Will of Stephen Taylor, 1848.
Wiggins, Laurence m. Esther Sasnett, W. Bk. F, p. 162, Will of Joshua Sasnett, 1833-1834.
Wilder, ? m. Winny Lee, Will of James Lee, 1771-1777.
Wilkins, ? m. Sarah Dancy, W. Bk. E, p. 249, Will of Lucy Dancy, 1820-1820.
Wilkins, James m. Esther Johnston, W. Bk. E, p. 133, Will of Amos Johnston, 1814-1816.
Wilkinson, ? m. Nancy Bynum, W. Bk. F, p. 259, Will of Joseph Bynum, 1841-1841.
Wilkinson, William m. Mourning Thomas, Will of Mary Thomas, 1802-1802.
Williams, ? m. Ann Davis, Will of John Davis, 1794-1799.
Williams, ? m. Brissulla Barnes, Will of Jacob Barnes, 1764.
Williams, ? m. Caty Curl, W. Bk. E, p. 231, Will of Sarah Curl, 1820-1820.
Williams, ? m. Frances Sugg, W. Bk. F, p. 257, Will of Redding Sugg, 1840-1841.
Williams, ? m. Mary West, Will of William West, 1748-1749.
Williams, Henry m. Martha Williams, W. Bk. F, p. 416, Will of Winifred Williams, 1848-1849.
Williams, James m. Elizabeth Exum, W. Bk. A, p. 236, Will of John Exum, 1775-1775.

Williams, Josiah m. Zada Moore, W. Bk. F, p. 140, Will of Elijah Moore, 1820-1833.

Williams, Thomas m. Elizabeth Robbins, W. Bk. B, p. 90, Will of William Robbins, 1781.

Williford, ? m. Chaney Winstead, Will of Sally Winstead, 1837-1838.

Williford, ? m. Charity Winstead, Will of Sally Winstead, 1837-1838.

Williford, ? m. Charity Curl, W. Bk. E, p. 231, Will of Sarah Curl, 1820-1820.

Williford, ? m. Polly Calhoun, W. Bk. F, p. 326, Will of Pherabe Calhoun, 1839-1845.

Williford, ? m. Zylphy Gardner, W. Bk. 3, p. 97, Will of George Gardner, 1786-1789.

Wilson, ? m. Judith Jones, Will of Francis Jones, 1750-1755.

Willis, ? m. Rhody McDade, Will of sister, Mary McDade, 1832.

Wills, Richard? m. Elizabeth Hyett, W. Bk. B, p. 111, Will of Thomas Hyett, 1781-1783.

Wimberly, ? m. Mourning Pope, Will of Jacob Pope, 1770-1772.

Wimberly, ? m. Sarah Fort, Will of George Fort, 1761-1761.

Wimberly, George? m. Sarah Diggs, W. Bk. C, p. 119, Will of Robert Diggs, 1786-1789.

Winstead, Thomas m. Elizabeth Dixon, W. Bk. F, p. 223, Will of Coffield Dixon, 1838-1838.

Wood, ? of Vicksburg, Miss. m. Dolly Hall, Will of brother, Thomas H. Hall, 1850-1853.

Wood, ? m. Charity Ann Ruffin, W. Bk. F, p. 458, Will of Elizabeth Ruffin, 1850-1851.

Wood, ? m. Patience Horn, Will of Ruth Horn, 1803-1803.

Woodard, ? m. Delilah Moore, Will of Samuel Moore, 1793-1794.

Woodard, Noah m. Delilah Bryant, W. Bk. E, p. 1, Will of brother, Evin Bryant, 1808-1810.

Wooten, ? m. Elizabeth Bolton, W. Bk. E, p. 241, Will of Richard Bolton, 1818-1820.

Wooten, ? m. Fanny Bolton, W. Bk. E, p. 241, Will of Richard Bolton, 1818-1820.

Wooten, ? m. Silar Edwards, W. Bk. G, p. 99, Will of Nancy Edwards, 1853-1855.

Wooten, ? m. Talitha Bolton, W. Bk. E, p. 241, Will of Richard Bolton, 1818-1820.

Wooten, Amos, m. ? Norvel, W. Bk. F, p. 441, Will of Chapman Norvel, 1850-1850.

Wooten, Josiah? m. Sarah Rogers, W. Bk. E, p. 256, Will of mother, Priscilla Warren of Pitt Co., N. C., 1811-1820.

Wright, William? m. Sarah Garner, W. Bk. A, p. 13, Will of John Garner, 1760-1760.

Wright, ? m. Obedience Brownrigg, W. Bk. F, p. 242, Will of Obedience Brownrigg, 1839-1840.

Y

York, John m. Catherine MacDade, W. Bk. F, p. 8, Will of Willis MacDade, 1823.

EDGECOMBE COUNTY MARRIAGE RECORDS

Copied From
MARRIAGE AND DEATH NOTICES
Which Appeared in the
RALEIGH REGISTER AND NORTH CAROLINA GAZETTE
1799 - 1868

Compiled by the late Miss Carrie Broughton, State Librarian, and published in the Biennial Reports of the State Librarian.

1799 — None
1800 — None
1801 — None
1802

Clarke, James to Arabella Toole, Jan. 4, Tarborough, R. R., Jan. 12, 1802.

1803 — None
1804

Lewis, Green, of Edgecombe County, to Martha Wiggins, Martin County, R. R., Mar. 12, 1804.

1805

Lamon, Olen, to Polly Battle, June 27, Edgecombe County, R. R., July 8, 1805.
Hunter, Harry, of Williamston, to Mrs. Gerard, Tarborough, June 24, Tarborough, R. R., July 8, 1805.
Sessoms, Roderic, to Polly Lloyd, June 27, Tarborough, R. R., July 8, 1805.

1806

Cotton, Henry to Sophia Mumford, Sept. 23, Tarborough, R. R., Oct. 6, 1806.

1807

Parker, Weeks, to Mrs. Cook, Nov., Tarborough, R. R. Nov. 26, 1807.
Redmond, Daniel, to Eliza M. Porie, June 30, Tarborough, R. R., July 23, 1807.

1808

McNair, Edmund, of Tarborough, to Eliza Harvey of Washington, Beaufort County, Dec. 21, Washington, R. R., Dec. 29, 1808.

Parker, Theophilus, to Mary Toole, Nov. 23, Tarborough, R. R., Jan. 14, 1808.

1809

Stuart, Robert, to Mary R. Thompson. of Fayetteville, Jan. 4, Tarborough, R. R., Jan. 19, 1809.

1810

Foxhall, William, to Nancy Jackson, Apr. 3, Edgecombe County, R. R., Apr. 12, 1810.

Lewis, Dr. Mills, of Virginia, to Polly Wiggins, of Edgecombe County, July 10, R. R., Aug. 22, 1810.

1811

O'Brien, Lawrence, to Nancy Ferguson, Dec. 29, Tarborough, R. R., Jan. 17, 1811.

Vines, Samuel, of Greene County, to Polly Brownrigg, of Edgecombe County, July 21, Edgecombe County, R. R. Aug. 16, 1811.

1812

Simons, Thomas, of Tarborough, to Ann Sheals, of Plymouth, Dec. 18, R. R., Jan. 24, 1812.

1813 — None

1814 — None

1815

Leigh, John Roscoe, of Tarborough, to Elizabeth Nixon, Dec. 26, New Hanover County, R. R., Jan. 27, 1815.

1816 — None

1817 — None

1818

Exum, John, to Olza Johnson, of Granville County, Dec., Edgecombe County, R. R., Jan. 2, 1818.

Spruill, George, of Edgecombe County, to Louise Hill, Dec., Halifax County, R. R., Dec. 18, 1818.

1819

Hines, Richard, of Washington to Susan Wilkins, of Edgecombe County, Dec. 10, Edgecombe County, R. R. Jan. 1, 1819.

1820 — None

1821

Lloyd, James R., of Tarborough, to Ann Slade, Oct., Martin County, R. R., Oct. 26, 1821.

Lowe, Exum H., to Elizabeth Sessums, Nov., Tarborough, R. R., Nov. 23, 1821.

1822

Battle, James S., of Edgecombe County, to Sallie Westray, Dec. 3, Nash County, R. R., Dec. 27, 1822.

Price, Elijah, of Statonsburg, to Temperance Thomas, Dec. 11, Edgecombe County, R. R., Jan. 18, 1822.

1823 — None

1824 — None

1825

Battle, William H., of Edgecombe County, to Lucy M. Plummer, June 1, Warrenton, R. R., June 7, 1825.

Freeman, Geo. W., of Franklin County, to Theresa T. Tart, of Edgecombe County, Dec. 13, Edgecombe County R. R., Dec. 27, 1825.

1826

Garrett, Henry W. to Sarah Sasnett, Oct. 26, Edgecombe County, R. R., Nov. 17, 1826.

Hodge, Allen, of Kentucky, to Mary Brady, Nov., Edgecombe County, R. R., Nov. 24, 1826.

Lyon, Thomas to Mary Heartt, Nov., Edgecombe County, R. R., Nov. 24, 1826.

M'Kenzie, J. G. of Scotland Neck to Mary Bishop, Aug. 17, Edgecombe County, R. R., Sept. 8, 1826.

Mabrey, Chas. to Frances Staton, Nov., Edgecombe County, R. R., Nov. 24, 1826.

Mayo, Kinchen to Nancy Knight, Aug. 24, Edgecombe County, R. R., Sept. 8, 1826.

Powell, Jesse H. of Edgecombe County, to Hester Ann Moore, Nov. 28, Halifax County, R. R., Dec. 15, 1826.

1827

Bass, Turner to Mrs. Susan Dickens, Jan., Tarborough, R. R., Feb. 2, 1827.

Dixon, Capt. William to Wilmouth Boxwell, Jan., Tarborough, R. R., Feb. 2, 1827.

Sugg, Dr. Pheasanton S. to Lucinda Pender, Jan., Tarborough, R. R. Feb. 2, 1827.

Thomas, Wade R. to Milliscent Horn, Jan., Tarborough, R. R., Feb. 2, 1827.

Lloyd, Joseph R., of Tarborough, to Maria A. Pugh, of Bertie County, July 19, Oxford, R. R., Aug. 3, 1827.

Whitaker, James C. to Delphia Lyon, Oct. 16, Edgecombe County, R. R., Oct. 19, 1827.

1828

Banks, T. to Patsey Cone, Jan. 22, Edgecombe County, R. R., Feb. 8, 1828.

Blakely, Thomas J., of Petersburg, Va., to Ann Stafford, of Halifax, Oct. 13, Tarborough, R. R., Oct. 31, 1828.

Bradley, Willie to Mrs. Lynch, Jan. 22, Edgecombe County, R. R., Feb. 8, 1828.

Cherry, Cado to Mary Bell, Nov. 16, Edgecombe County, R. R., Nov. 28, 1828.

Dunn, Burrill to Drusilla Draughon, Jan. 22, Edgecombe County, R. R., Feb. 8, 1828.

Gardner, Wm. to Eliza Batts, Jan. 22, Edgecombe County, R. R., Feb. 8, 1828.

Jackson, Micajah to Miss Temperance Ricks, Jan 22, Edgecombe County, R. R., Feb. 8, 1828.

Hopkins, Daniel to Mrs. Jenkins, Dec. 28, Edgecombe County, R. R. Jan. 22, 1828.

Mayo, Frederick to Manisia Ganer Menetta Anders Sylvester Maivia Lewellen Sherrod, Mar. 27, Edgecombe County, R. R., Apr. 11, 1828.

Pender, John to Sylvia Harrell, Jan. 22, Edgecombe County, R. R., Feb. 8, 1828.

Petway, Micajah to Elizabeth Skinner, Jan. 22, Edgecombe County, R. R., Feb. 8, 1828.

Smith, William R., of Halifax County, to Susan Evans, Jan. 22, Edgecombe County, R. R., Jan. 29, 1828.

Staton, Baker to Jeanette Young, Dec. 20, Edgecombe County, R. R., Jan. 22, 1828.

1829

Anderson, Joshua L. to Catharine Bradley, Dec. 25, Edgecombe County, R. R., Jan. 9, 1829.

Knight, Charles C. to Louisiana Lawrence, Dec. 22, Edgecombe County, R. R. Jan. 9, 1829.

Lawrence, David, of Tarboro, to Emily G. Bond, Oct., Greenville, Pitt County, R. R. Oct. 22, 1829.

Lewis, Dr. John W. to Catharine Battle, Feb. 5, Edgecombe County, R. R., Feb. 20, 1829.

Parker, Jno. to Martha Tartt, Sept., Edgecombe County, R. R., Oct. 1, 1829.

Prince, Thomas M. C., of Chatham County, to Lucille Carr, Sept., Edgecombe County, R. R., Sept. 4, 1829.

Toole, Henry, of Tarborough, to Margaret Telfair, of Pitt County, Oct. 20, Washington, R. R., Nov. 12, 1829.

Williams, Benjamin to Mary Kewell, June, Tarborough, R. R., June 5, 1829.

Williams, John to Caroline Mathewson, June, Tarborough, R. R., June 5, 1829.

Williams, Joshua to Cherry Langley, May 23, Edgecombe County, R. R., July 2, 1829.

1830

Battle, Amos J. to Margaret H. Parker, Jan. 7, Edgecombe County, R. R., Jan. 28, 1830.

Cherry, Thomas to Emily Bell, Mar. 4, Tarborough, R. R., Mar. 25, 1830.

Dowd, Rev. P. W., of Raleigh, to Martha Austin of Tarborough, R.R., Nov. 4, 1830.

Hinton, James J., of Johnston County, to Frances A. Hart, of Edgecombe County, June 17, R. R., June 31, 1830.

Johnston, Henry to Emily Norfleet, Jan. 7, Edgecombe County, R. R., Jan. 28, 1830.

Southerland, Dr. Samuel L., of Warrenton, to Mary Ann Evans, Jan. 7, Edgecombe County, R. R., Jan. 28, 1830.

1831

Arrington, Arthur, of Nash County, to Elizabeth Irwin, Dec., Edgecombe County, R. R., Jan. 13, 1831.

Bilbry, James to Anne Walker (Waller?), Jan., Edgecombe County, R. R., Jan. 13, 1831.

Hawkins, Thomas H. to Martha Reed, May, Edgecombe County, R. R., May 25, 1831.

Spruill, Benj. to Margaret Ross, Dec., Edgecombe County, R. R., Jan. 13, 1831.

1832

Dicken, Ephraim, of Edgecombe County, to Charlotte Whitehead, Nov. 6, Edgecombe County, R. R., Nov. 23, 1832.

Horne, Lawrence to Elizabeth Mercer, Nov. 6, Edgecombe County, R. R., Nov. 23, 1832.

1833

Andrews, William J., of Edgecombe County, to Virginia Hawkins, May 8, Franklin County, R. R., May 28, 1833.

Cotten, John W. to Laura P. Clark, Dec., Tarborough, R. R., Jan. 4, 1833.

Horne, John R., of Edgecombe County, to Eliza Jane Burt, Oct. 24, Nash County, R. R., Nov. 12, 1833.

Lawrence, Dr. Josiah, of Tarboro, to Mary Eliza Toole, Feb. 20, Greenville, R. R., Mar. 12, 1833.

Mayo, Thomas to Mary Bryan, Feb. 19, Edgecombe County, R. R., Mar. 12, 1833.

Richards, Danford to Mary R. Hearn, Feb. 3, Tarborough, R. R., Feb. 26, 1833.

1834

Dillard, Joseph J., of Raleigh, to Arabella Battle, of Rocky Mount, May 27, Chatham County, R. R., June 3, 1834.

Hines, Peter to Sarah P. Macnair, Feb., Tarboro, R. R., Feb. 25, 1834.

Hines, Richard H., of Edgecombe County, to Caroline Snead, Nov. 11, Newbern. R. R., Dec. 30, 1834.

Philips, Dr. James, of Edgecombe County, to Harriet Amanda Burt. Apr. 23, Hilliardston, Nash County, R. R., May 13, 1834.

Potts, Dr. John W., of Tarboro, to Lucy Nelson Boyd, Edgecombe County, Nov. 4, Boydton, Va., R. R., Nov. 18, 1834.

Sessums, Wilson to Mary Foxhall, Sept., Edgecombe County, R. R., Sept. 16, 1834.

Ward, Harmon to Catharine E. Pippen, Jan. 9, Edgecombe County, R. R., Jan. 28, 1834.

1835

Bryan, Wm. D. to Peggy Beaton, Aug. 13, Edgecombe County, R. R., Sept. 8, 1835.

Hill, Daniel to Susan Irwin Toole, of Edgecombe County, Dec. 5, Franklin County, R. R., Dec. 29, 1835.

Lewis, Exum Jr. to Jane Cotton, Sept. 29, Edgecombe County, R. R., Oct. 13, 1835.

Warren. Richard, of Pitt County, to Elizabeth Thigpen, Oct. 8, Edgecombe County, R. R., Nov. 3, 1835.

Wilkinson, Abner to Nancy Bynum, Aug. 16, Edgecombe County, R. R., Sept. 8, 1835.

1836

Brown, Wm. R. of Martin County, to Ellen Hyman of Edgecombe County, Dec. 7, R. R., Feb. 2, 1836.

Foreman, Agesilaus S., of Virginia, to Delha Dancy, Nov., Tarboro, R. R., Nov. 22, 1836.

Hayles, William to Rhoda Bracewell, May, Edgecombe County, R. R., May 31, 1836.

Hearn, Lawrence H. to Margaret Bell, May, Tarboro, R. R., May 31, 1836.

Hines, Peter E., of Edgecombe County, to Mary May, Feb. 18, Pitt County, R. R., Mar. 8, 1836.

Lawrence, Joshua L. to Harriet Mayo, Oct., Edgecombe County, R. R., Oct. 11, 1836.

Lyon, Benton T. to Penelope C. Pittman, May, Edgecombe County, R. R., May 31, 1826.

Pender, Thomas, of Plymouth, to Sarah Carstaphen, Dec. 10, Edgecombe County, R. R., June 28, 1836.

Terrill, Nathaniel M., of Tarboro, to Mrs. Eliza A. Ellis, Sept., Washington, Beaufort County, R. R., Oct. 11, 1836.

1837

Hargrave, John L., of Davidson County, to Caroline C. S. Parker, Mar., Tarboro, R. R., Mar. 7, 1837.

Moore, Samuel, of Pitt County, to Mary Ann Williford, Mar., Edgecombe County, R. R., Mar. 21, 1837.

Parker, Edward C. to Mrs. Celia Price, Oct., Tarborough, R. R., Oct. 9, 1837.

1838 — None

1839 — None

1840

Blocker, John C., of Fayetteville, to Julia Ann Bradley, Jan., Tarboro, R. R., Jan. 24, 1840.

Speight, Rev. John F. to Emma Lewis, Sept. 29, Mount Prospect, Edgecombe County, R. R., Jan. 14, 1840.

1841

Burke, Harman H., of Chatham County, to Mrs. Louisiana Knight, May, Edgecombe County, R. R., May 28, 1841.

Davis, Robert to Russia Ann Nettle, Jan., Edgecombe County, R. R., Jan. 29, 1841.

Flemings, Jesse A., of Edgecombe County, to Ann Pittman, Nov., Halifax County, R. R., Nov. 9, 1841.

Hargrave, Franklin, of Lexington, to Mary W. Parker, Mar., Tarboro, R. R., Mar. 5, 1841.

Lyon, Joshua L. to Martha Cherry, May, Edgecombe County, R. R., May 28, 1841.

Shurley, Geraldus to Susan Bridgers, Jan., Edgecombe County, R. R., Jan. 29, 1841.

1842

Hines, Peter, of Edgecombe County, to Emma J. Snow, Mar. 22, Raleigh, R. R., Mar. 25, 1842.

1843

Cheshire, Rev. Joseph B. to Elizabeth Parker, Feb., Tarboro, R. R., Feb. 17, 1843.

Dancy, John S., of Tarboro, to Cornelia V. Battle, Dec., Edgecombe County, R. R., Dec. 22, 1843.

Pender, Robert H. to Amarilla James Pender, Nov., Edgecombe County, R. R., Nov. 10, 1843.

Shallington, Dr. Wm. E. J. to Sarah Barnes, Dec., Cool Springs, Edgecombe County, R. R., Dec. 22, 1843.

Thomas, Dr. Wm. Geo. to Mary Sumner Clark, Nov., Tarboro, R. R., Nov. 10, 1843.

1844

Barnes, Wright to Mrs. Mary A. S. Sharpe, Feb. 13, Edgecombe County, R. R., Feb. 27, 1844.

Dortch, Dr. Lewis J. to Nancy Jane Allen, Nov., Edgecombe County, R. R., Nov. 29, 1844.

Hunter, Weldon S. to Nancy Griffiths, Feb. 14, Tarboro, R. R., Feb. 27, 1844.

1845

Battle, William S. to Elizabeth M. Dancy, July, Tarboro, R. R., July 8, 1845.
Edmondson, Rufus W., of Stantonsburg, Edgecombe County, to Caroline Wilder, Oct. 16, Wake County, R. R., Oct. 21, 1845.
Hart, Dr. Franklin to Sarah Bryan, Nov., Edgecombe County, R. R., Nov. 25, 1845.
Long, William S. to Mary Batts, Jan., Edgecombe County, R. R., Jan. 14, 1845.
Moore, Samuel E. to Alice Ann Elliott, Jan., Tarboro, R. R., Jan. 17, 1845.

1846

Cotten, Frederick R., of Florida, to Elizabeth W. Coffield, Oct., Edgecombe County, R. R., Oct. 20, 1846.
Earle, John W. to Margaret Carter Pope, Aug., Edgecombe County, R. R., Aug. 25, 1846.
Hoskins, Rich'd T., of Alabama, to Elizabeth A. Lawrence, Oct., Tarboro, R. R., Oct. 13, 1846.
Vines, Chas. L., of Edgecombe County, to Martha Ann Williams, July 7, Falkland, Pitt County, R. R., July 17, 1846.

1847 — None

1848

Bryan, Hugh B., of Edgecombe County, to Mary P. Jenkins of Warrenton, Sept. 5, Warrenton, R. R. Sept. 13, 1848.
Porter, Joseph J., of Tarborough, to Cynthia Ann Patience, Dec., Franklin County, R. R., Jan. 2, 1848.

1849

Moye, Gen. Wyatt, of Edgecombe County, to Mrs. Jesse Speight, Oct., Lowndes County, Mississippi, R. R., Oct. 13, 1849.

1850 — None

1851

Parker, John, of Mobile, to Eliza J. Phillips, of Edgecombe County, Oct. 15, Edgecombe County, R. R., Oct. 29, 1851.

1852

Pender, L. D. to Martha L. Howard, Oct., Tarboro, R. R., Nov. 3, 1852.

1853

Telfair, O. W., of Washington, to Pauline D. Macnair, Mar. 30, Tarboro, R. R., Apr. 2, 1853.

1854

Lewis, Robert H., of Milton, to Sarah E. Howard, Nov. 3, Tarboro, R. R., Nov. 8, 1854.

1855

Burton, Conway W., of New Haven, Conn., to Lucinda R. Pender, Oct. 10, Tarboro, R. R., Oct. 17, 1855.

Battle, Kemp P., of Raleigh, to Martha S. Battle of Edgecombe County, Nov. 28, Cool Springs, R. R. Dec. 5, 1855.

1856

Carr, Wm. B., of Edgecombe County, to Bettie H. Irwin, of Warren County, June 10, Nash County, R. R., June 18, 1856.

King, Col. E., of Nash County, to Julia Harrison, formerly of Edgecombe County, May 20, Gonzales, Texas, R. R., June 18, 1856.

1857

Lewis, K. H., of Edgecombe County, to Battle Bryan, Apr. 15, Raleigh, R. R., Apr. 22, 1857.

Lewis, Dr. Richard H., of Edgecombe County, to Virginia A. Cull, of Washington, D. C., Dec. 8, R. R., Dec. 23, 1857.

Powell, Jesse H. to Mary Ann Battle, Dec. 15, Edgecombe County, R. R., Dec. 30, 1857.

1858

Battle, Dr. James to Kate Ruth Horne, Jan. 12, Edgecombe County, R. R., Feb. 17, 1858.

Dancy, John S. to Annie E. Hyman, Nov. 11, Tarboro, R. R., Nov. 24, 1858.

Dancy, Wm. F. to Mary Eliza Battle, Jan. 14, Cool Springs, Edgecombe County, R. R., Jan. 20, 1858.

Moore, William A. to Mary Ann O'Berry, Nov. 11, Tarboro, R. R., Nov. 24, 1858.

1859

Mishew (Michaux), John J. to Ann Cutchins, of Edgecombe County, Apr. 19, Nash County, R. R., Apr. 27, 1859.

1860 — None

1861 — None

1862 — None

1863 — None

1864 — None

1865 — None

1866

Bryan, Maj. J. C., of Ala., to Willie A. Staton, of Edgecombe County, Apr. 5, Edgecombe County, D. S., Apr. 24, 1866.

Charles, Francis M. to Augusta S. Jones, May 1, Tarboro, D. S., May 12. 1866.

Ivey, Capt. John R. to Sallie Turner, May 1, Rocky Mount, Edgecombe County, D. S., May 8, 1866.

1867

Mallory, Wm. S. to M. Pamela Sheppard, of Salem, Aug. 6, Tarboro, R. R., Aug. 16, 1867.

Hyman, Col. Joseph H., of Tarboro, to Sallie P. Rayner, of Coahoma County, Miss., Nov. 13, Columbia County, Miss., R. R., Nov. 22, 1867.

Pender, Robert H. to Martha E. Hanks, Aug. 7, Tarboro, R. R., Aug. 16, 1867.

Bridgers, Col. John L., of Tarboro, to Mary E. Battle, Apr. 4, D. S., Apr. 12, 1867.

Draughan, James W., of Edgecombe County, to Sue S. Hellen, (Ellen?), Feb. 12, Thomasville, D. S., Mar. 12, 1867.

Foxhall, Edwin D., of Edgecombe County, to Mary L. Hargrave, Jan. 13, Tarboro, D. S., Feb. 18, 1867.

Lloyd, Maj. W. P., of Tarboro, to Laura Pender, Dec. 20, Tarboro, D. S., Feb. 23, 1867.

1868

Battle, James S., of Edgecombe County, to Johanna John Somerville, of Warrenton, Oct. 28, Warrenton, D. S., Nov. 4, 1868.

EDGECOMBE COUNTY MARRIAGES

Abstracted From
TARBORO FREE PRESS, 1826 - 1845
On file in North Carolina Room.
University of North Carolina Library, Chapel Hill, N. C.

Contributed by
Dr. Claiborne T. Smith, Jr., Rocky Mount, N. C.

The first date is that of publication of Tarboro Free Press, and other refers to date of marriage.

1826

- 8-29 James G. McKenzie, of Halifax County, to Mary Bishop, Aug. 17.
- 8-29 Kenchen Mayo to Nony Knight, Aug. 24, by J. J. Pippen, Esq.
- 10- 3 Patrick S. Cromwell to Pennina Little, by Joshua Pender.
- 10- 3 Micajah Howard to Elizabeth Pitt, by Kinchen Hines, Esq.
- 10-10 James Downing, Esq. to Grace, dau. of William Staton, by Lemuel Lawrence.
- 11- 7 Henry W. Garrett to Sarah Sasnett, Oct. 26, by Jesse C. Knight, Esq.
- 11-14 Thomas Lyon to Mary Heartt, Tues. last.
- 11-14 Allen Hodge, of Kentucky, to Mary Brady, by William Bellamy, Esq.
- 11-14 Charles Mabry to Frances Staton, Nov. 2.
- 11-28 John Long, of Pitt County, to Elizabeth Rogers, relict of Stephen Rogers, Nov. 19, by Rev. Ichabod Moore.
- 12- 5 John Whitaker, of Halifax, to Penelope Marshall.
- 12-19 James Cobb to Elvy Bartee, Dec. 7.
- 12-26 Tom Taylor to Elizabeth(?) Edwards, by David Williams, Esq.

1827

- 1-16 Dr. Pheasanton Sugg to Lucinda, dau. of Solomon Pender, by Henry Bryan.
- 1-16 Wade R. Thomas to Millecent, dau. of Jacob Horn, by Elijah Price.

2-17   Joe Pippen, officer of Revolution, age 73, to Mrs. Temperance Lee, age 43.
3-10   Bytha Staton, Sr. to Elizabeth Cloman, Mar. 1, by Rev. Wm. Hyman.
3-24   Bennett Bradley to Sabra Griffin, by Ben Wilkinson.
5-19   Arthur Cotton to Louisa Mayo, May 10.
6- 2   George Wimberly, of Johnston County, to Mrs. Catherine Hart, by Rev. Joshua Lawrence.
8-11   Littleberry Thigpen to Ann, dau. of Jesse Little, Aug. 2.
8-11   Levi (Lem) Howell, of Martin County, to Dolly B., dau. of Thomas Watson, Sr., July 24.
8-18   William King, of Halifax County, to Prudence Howard, Aug. 9.
10-13 James C. Whitaker to Delphia, dau. of Thomas Lyon, by Rev. Eli Whitaker.
12-15 Henry Bryan to Mary P., dau. of Joseph Bell, Dec. 11, by Henry Austin, Esq.
12-15 William H. Robards, of Granville County, to Ann Eliza, dau. of Geraldus Toole, Dec. 11, by Rev. William Bellamy.
12-28 Solomon Pender, tavern keeper, to Elizabeth Hines, Dec. 20, by Exum Lowe, Esq.

1828

1-11   William J. Knight to Adelina, dau, of Josiah Freeman, Jan. 30, by H. Austin, Esq.
1-18   Daniel Hopkins to Mrs. Jenkins, Dec. 28, 1827.
1-18   Baker Staton to Jeanette Young, Dec. 20, 1827.
1-25   William R. Smith, Jr. of Scotland Neck, Halifax County, to Susan, dau. of Peter Evans, Jan. 22, by Rev. James Weatherly (Family record, Jan. 17.).
2- 1   Tom Banks, Revolutionary soldier, age 80, to Patsy Cone, age 25, Jan. 22.
2- 1   Burrell Dunn to Drucilla Draughon, Jan. 22.
2- 1   Willie Bradley to Mrs. Lynch, Jan. 22.
2- 1   Micajah Jackson to Temperance Ricks, Jan. 22.
2- 1   William Gardner to Eliza Batts, Jan. 22.
2- 8   Micajah Petway, Revolutionary soldier, to Mrs. Eliza Skinner, Jan. 22.
2- 8   John Pender to Sylvia Harrell, Jan. 22.
4- 4   Frederick Mayo to Manisia Ganer Menetta Anders Sylvester Malvia Lewellen Sherrard, 27 Mar.

5- 2 Arthur Laurence, of Hertford County, to Martha, dau. of Moses Baker, Apr. 17, by Wells Wilkinson, Esq.

5-30 Elisha Woodard, age 70, to Terece Deberry, age 18, May 27.

6- 6 Patrick Boyt to Elizabeth Benson(?) gr. dau. of Elisha Woodard, Sen.

7-18 Abner Mills, 70, to Mrs. Martha Carney, age 35, July 10, by R. Joyner, Esq.

11- 7 Gilbert Valentine, of Nash, to Sally Jenkins.

11-28 Drew King of Halifax County, to Eliza Cotten, Nov. 20, by James Biggs, Esq.

12-19 John Edmondson to Ann Parker, by J. Biggs, Esq., Dec. 4.

1829

1- 2 Joshua L. Anderson to Catherine Bradley, Dec. 25.

1- 2 Charles C. Knight to Louisiana, dau. of Rev. Joshua Lawrence, Dec. 22, 1828, by Rev. Wm. Hyman.

1- 9 Willie Atkinson to Sally Wilkinson, Jan. 5, by Dempsey Bryan, Esq.

1-16 John Sharpe to Margaret, dau. of Stephen Taylor, Jan. 6, by David Williams.

1-16 John G. Williams to Nancy, dau. of Burrill Barnes, Jan. 8.

1-23 Spencer Hart, Sheriff, to Louisiana Pender, Sunday last.

2- 6 David Strickland to Nancy Howell, Jan. 22.

2- 6 E. J. Merrit, of Halifax County, to Margaret Gunter.

2-13 Dr. John Lewis to Catherine, dau. of Joel Battle, Feb. 5.

2-27 William Skinner to Rebecca Guill, Feb. 19.

5-22 Caleb Leonard, Nash Connty, to Mrs. Martha Ruffin, May 3.

5-29 John Williams to Caroline, dau. of Nathan Mathewson, by Rev. John Armstrong.

6-26 Thomas Gatlin to Julia Pender, June 8.

7- 3 Joshua Williams, age 60, to Cherry Langley, age 25, June 23, by H. Austin.

7-24 Willie Braswell to Polly Bulluck, July 16, by Moses Baker, Esq.

7-31 Burwell Shelton to Sally Booth, July 12.

10-25 John Parker, Sheriff, to Martha Tartt, Oct. 23.

11- 2 Duke William Horn, of Marianna, Fla., to Mary Amelia Ann Laurence, dau. of Peter P. Laurence, Oct. 31, by Rev. P. W. Dowd.

11- 2 John E. Ridley, of Granville County, to Amelia M., dau. of Geraldus Toole, Oct. 15, by Rev. Thos. P. Hunt.

11-27 Stephen Bennett to Mrs. Eliza Bell, widow of Whitmel Bell, Nov. 19.

12- 4 William Sutton, of Martin County, to Martha, dau. of Michael Hearn, by Ben Boykin, Esq.

12-18 Alexander S. Bellamy to Sally Boykin, by Jones J. Philips.

1830

1- 8 Cullen Little to Lucy Alford by John F. Hughes, Esq.

1-15 A. J. Battle to Margaret H., dau. of Weeks Parker, Jan. 7, by P. W. Dowd.

1-15 Henry Johnson to Emily, dau. of J. Norfleet, Tues. last.

1-15 Dr. Samuel L. Southerland, of Warrenton, to Mary Ann, dau. of Peter Evans, Jan. 11, by Rev. T. Dupree.

2- 5 Henry West to Rebecca Robertson, Jan. 28, by N. Austin, Esq.

2-15 Hardiman Abington, of Halifax County, to Elizabeth, dau. of James Biggs, Esq., by James Downing.

2-19 James J. Garrett to Susan, dau. of J. C. Knight, Feb. 11, by John Mercer, Esq.

3-12 Tom Cherry to Emily, dau. of Frederick Bell, Mar. 4, by L. D. Wilson, Esq.

3-19 Elias Barnes to Mahala F., dau. of Col. Benjamin Sparp, by Willis Wilkinson, Esq.

5-28 Isaac Sawyer to Winfred Griffin, May 13, by Ben Wilkinson, Esq.

5-28 Spencer S. Hanes, of Pitt County, to Margaret Taylor, May 20, by Ben Wilkinson, Esq.

6- 2 Frederick Little to Harriet, dau. of Willis Knight, by Ben Boykin, Esq.

6- 2 John Knight to Sally Harper, by Joshua Pender, Esq.

6- 2 Capt. William D. Hopkins to Julia Best, by Louis D. Wilson.
"We are best pleased in giving publicity to the latter marriage in consequence of having received the best piece of wedding cake that has delighted our eyes and titillated our palate for sometime past. We tender our best wishes to the newly married pair for their delectable 'printer's fee.' "

7-23 Jacob Thomas to Amanda R. Bridges, July 17, by John Mercer, Esq.

9-21 John Coggin to Margaret Bedford, Sept. 19, by Dan Hopkins, Esq.

10- 5 Bazel Sikes to Mary Ann Edwards, Sept. 26, by Howell Hearn, Esq.

10-26 Rev. Patrick W. Dowd, of Raleigh, to Martha Ann, dau. of Henry Austin, by Rev. John Armstrong.

12- 7 James Bilbry to Ann Waller.

12-14 Arthur Arrington, of Nash County, to Elizabeth, dau. of J. A. Irvin, by Ben Boykin.

12-21 Benjamin S. Spruill, of Scotland Neck, Halifax County, to Margaret Ross, by Rev. Philip Wiley.

1831

1-18 William S. Baker to Julia, dau. of Henry Shurly, Tues. last, by James Biggs, Esq.

2- 8 Col. David Williams to Mrs. Catherine Ruth (Routh), dau. of Redding Sugg.

2-22 John R. Barnes to Margaret, dau. of Samuel Ruffin, Jan. 13.

3- 1 Arthur Hyman to Sally, dau. of Wilson Howard, Sr.

3-15 Redding Pittman to Martha, dau. of Dempsey Bryan.

5-17 Tom H. Hawkins to Martha Reed, Tues. last, by Rev. William Hyman.

10-11 Johnson Taylor to Lucy Medford, Sept. 23, by Theo. Cherry.

10-25 William Stewart to Mary Ann Tartt.

12-20 John Atkinson to Mrs. Esther Tyson.

1832

1-10 William Tannahill, of Washington, N. C., to Susan M., dau. of E. D. Macnair.

1-17 Joseph Jenkins to Rilla, dau. of Frederick Hopkins.

2-21 Noah Thompson, of Bertie County, to Eliza W., dau. of Spencer D. Cotten, by Rev. William Norwood.

2-21 John Day to Margaret Mitchell, by Benj. Boykin.

2-21 Edwin Doyle to Creecy Wimberley, by Charles Wilkinson, Esq.

3-13 Littleberry Worsley to Reanny Cherry, Mar. 5, by William C. Leigh.

3-27 Redmund Bunn, of Nash County, to Mary Bryan, by Rev. Mark Bennett.

3-27 Alfred Edmondson to Lucinda Hawkins, by J. J. Pippin, Esq.
5-29 Thomas Benson to Martha King, by L. R. Cherry, Esq.
7-10 Charles Harrison to Eliza, dau. of Col. Joseph Bell, by Rev. Joshua Lawrence.
7-17 Maj. Lunsford R. Cherry to Mary George, July 5, by C. W. Knight, Esq.
9- 4 James Watkins to Loes Cuthins, by Lunsford R. Cherry.
10-16 Dorsey Battle to Henrietta S. H. Parker, dau. of Weeks Parker, by Frederick F. Robbins.
10-23 Bennett B. Bell to Susan, dau. of Mathew Turner, desc.
11-13 Lawrence Horne to Elizabeth, dau. of John Mercer.
11-20 Asa Edmondson to Nancy, dau. of Moody Porter, desc.
12- 4 Joshua Lawrence to Lucinda Lawrence, Nov. 21, by William C. Leigh, Esq.
12-11 William P. Roberts to Clara Ann Adams, by L. R. Cherry, Esq.
12-11 Thomas W. Rascoe to Penina, dau. of Rev. William Hyman.
12-18 Nathan H. Rountree to Emiliza Bell, by Ben Boykin.
12-25 John W. Cotten to Laura P., dau. of Capt. James W. Clark, by Rev. William Norwood.

1833

1- 1 Nathaniel M. Terrell to Alicia M. Redmond, Dec. 1832, by Rev. J. A. Miller.
1- 1 Reuben Mayo to Lucinda Best, Dec. 19, by William C. Leigh, Esq.
1- 8 Danford Richards to Mary R., dau. of Michael Hearn, by Rev. William Norwood.
1-15 Bythal Howell to Henrietta, dau. of William R. Long, by J. J. Pippen, Esq.
1-15 Lemuel Savage to Talitha, dau. of William R. Long, by J. J. Pippen, Esq.
1-22 Benjamin Porter to Eliza, dau. of William C. King, by L. R. Cherry, Esq.
3- 5 Thomas Mayo to Mary, dau. of Dempsey Bryan, Feb. 19, by Rev. J. Lawrence.
4-13 Peter P. Lawrence to Mrs. Mary B. Dancy, by Rev. P. W. Dowd.
6-22 Lewis Bond to Polly Norman by Rev. P. W. Dowd.
6-29 William Billups to Elizabeth Ellinor, June 20.

12- 6   William Barnes to Jane, dau. of Wells Wilkins, Tues. last, by Ben Sharpe.

12-20   Kindred Taylor, of Nash County, to Lucy, dau. of William Clark, Dec. 12, by Richard Harrison.

1834

1-10   William T. Ellinor to Litha Hopkins, Jan. 2.

1-17   Harmon Ward to Catherine E., dau. of J. J. Pippen, Jan. 9, by Rev. William Hyman.

1-24   Jesse Stancell to Harriet, dau. of Col. Daniel Hopkins, Jan. 9, by William C. Leigh.

1-31   David G. Baker to Catherine R., dau. of Egbert H. Williams, by J. P. Pitt.

1-31   David Barlow to Peninah, dau. of Henry Shurley, Jan. 30, by Ben Boykin.

2- 7   Alexander Bradley, to ——, dau. of Thomas Edmondson, Jan. 28.

2- 7   Littleberry Bradley, to——, dau. of Thomas Edmondson, Jan. 30.

2-21   Peter E. Hines to Sarah, dau. of E. D. McNair, Feb. 16.

2-21   Arthur Knight to Lavina Booth, Feb. 13.

2-28   Henry Hyman to Martha, dau. of Eli Porter, Feb. 27, by Rev. Joshua Lawrence.

3- 7   Lunsford Brown to Bethia, dau. of J. J. Pippen, Mar. 6, by Rev. William Hyman.

3-14   Jesse Harrell to Sally, dau. of Howell Thigpen, desc., by William C. Leigh.

3-21   William H. Dicken to Lucy Thurston, Mar. 20, by Rev. J. Lawrence.

5-16   John Wilson to Susan Bunn, May 8.

5-23   Dr. Isaac Holt Jackson, of Northampton County, to Eliza Imogene Evans, dau. of Peter Evans, Esq., May 15, by Rev. William Norwood.

6-20   Luke Ward, of Pitt County, to Mahala, dau. of Levin Leggett, June 17, by Rev. William Hyman.

8- 8   James Thigpen, Sr. to Patsey Brown, July 24, by William C. Leigh, Esq.

8-15   John Mayo, Jr. to Maria Shelton, Aug. 3, by William C. Leigh, Jr.

9- 5   Wilson Sessums to Mary, dau. of Robert Foxhall, Aug. 26, by William Savage.

9- 5	James H. Savage to Catherine Barfield, Aug. 14, by William E. Bellamy, Esq.
9-12	Francis Henry Knight to Sally, dau. of Jesse C. Knight, Sept. 4, by Benj. Wilkinson, Esq.

1835

1-24	James Duggan, Halifax County, to Mary Ann, dau. of Michael Alsobrook.
2- 7	William Smith to Phenetta, dau. of Lemuel Thigpen, Jan. 27.
2-21	James Hilliard, of Nash County, to Mary Ruffin, Feb. 10.
2-28	James Weddell to Margaret, dau. of Dr. John F. Ward, desc., by Rev. J. Singletary.
3-14	Ezekiel Crisp to Louisa Cobb, Mar. 5, by William C. Leigh.
3-28	Joseph Higgs, of Halifax County, to Phenetta, dau. of Bythal Staton, desc., by Joshua Pender.
4- 4	William McGee, of Tenn., to Eugenia, dau. of Frederick Bell, by L. D. Wilson, Esq.
7-11	Simmons B. Staton to Drucilla L., dau. of James Knight, July 2.
8-15	Thomas Grimes to Nancy Best, by Rev. William Hyman, Aug. 4.
8-29	William D. Bryan to Peggy Benton, Aug. 13, by Rev. William C. Bellamy.
8-29	Abner Wilkinson to Nancy, dau. of Joe Bynum, Aug. 16, by Benj. Moore.
9-19	James Marks to Rosina, dau. of George McWilliams, desc., Sept. 6, by Henry Austin, Esq.
10- 3	Exum Lewis Jr. to June Cotten.
10-10	Thomas Jenkins to Eliza Etheridge, by Henry Austin.
10-10	Cullen Melton to Milbry, dau. of Richard Gay, by Henry Austin.
10-24	Richard Warren, of Pitt County, to Elizabeth, dau. of Lemuel Thigpen, Oct. 8, by William C. Leigh.
11-28	John Knight to Martha Cromwell, by Ben Boykin.
12-12	William R. Brown, of Martin County, to Ellen, dau. of Kenneth Hyman, desc., by Rev. William Hyman.

1836

1- 9	Thomas Pender, of Plymouth, m. Sarah Carstarphen, Dec. 10, 1835, by Rev. A. Battle.
1-16	Cullen Pender m. Lucy, dau. of Willis Bradley, Oct. 6, 1836, by Ben Batts.

1-30 James Long m. Mary Louisa, dau. of Joshua Lawrence, Oct. 21, 1836, by Rev. William Hyman.
3- 5 John L. Cotton to Emily, dau. of James Savage, Feb. 11.
4- 2 John Long, of Martin County, to Marion Mayo.
4-23 John Garrett to Elizabeth Nettles, Apr. 14, by Ben Sharpe.
5-21 Lawrence Henry Hearne to Margaret Ann, dau. of Henry Bell, desc., by L. D. Wilson.
5-21 William Hayles to Rhoda, dau. of Jacob Braswell, by Henry Austin.
5-21 Bennett T. Lyon to Penelope C., dau. of Harrison Pittman, May 12, by L. R. Cherry, Esq.
7- 2 Joseph John B. Pender to Elizabeth Mason, gr. dau. of Benjamin Coffield, by L. R. Cherry.
7- 2 Elias Bradley to Mary, dau. of Willis Bradley, June 23, by Benj. Batts, Esq.
8-27 Richard Bell to Sally Jones, Aug. 18, by S. B. Staton.
8-27 Thomas H. Cutchin to Hester Ann Lynch, Aug. 18, by L. R. Cherry, Esq.
10- 1 Joshua L. Lawrence to Harriet Mayo, by Rev. William Hyman.
10- 8 William Taylor to Elizabeth Taylor, by J. J. Pippen.
11-12 Agesilaus S. Foreman, of Va., to Delha, dau. of Francis L. Dancy, by Rev. Sam'l Harris.
12-17 Henry A. Whitehead to Lucy Joyner, Dec. 8, by Ben Batts.

1837

1- 7 Andrew A. Cohoun to Nancy Barnes, Dec. 27, 1936, by Robert Barnes, Esq.
1-31 William L. Wilkinson to Melinda Wilkinson by Daniel Hopkins.
2-11 Robert Belcher to Emily, dau. of Alex. S. Cotten, by Rev. Thomas Dupree.
2-25 Joseph John Porter to Susan, dau. of Welles Wilkins, Feb. 16, by Rev. Thomas Dupree.
2-25 John L. Hargrove, of Lexington, to Caroline C. S., dau. of Theo. Parker, by Rev. J. Singletary.
3-11 Sam Moore, Pitt County, to Mary Ann, dau. of Meedie Williford, by John Mercer.
3-18 Willie Ward, of Greene County, to Louisina (Louisiana?), dau. of Levin Leggett, Mar. 18, by Rev. William Hyman.

4-29	William Kennedy to Gracy Windham, Apr. 12, by Benj. Sharpe.
5- 6	Rev. Philemon Bennett to Lucretia Pope, by William S. Baker, Esq.
6-24	Dr. John A. Mennis to Mrs. Penina Horne, dau. of Frederic Philips, by Rev. A..J. Battle.
7- 1	William Coker to Charlotte Neal, June 22, by L. R. Cherry, Esq.
9- 9	Enos Womble to Elizabeth Skinner, Aug. 30, by Henry Austin.
9-23	William Burnett to Virginia Howerton, by L. D. Wilson.
9-30	Edward C. Parker to Mrs. Celia Price, Sept. 12, by Joseph George, Esq.
10- 7	Elijah Elliott to Margaret Ford, by Henry Austin, Esq.
11-25	Lewelling Staton to Mrs. Susan Hopkins, Nov. 7.

1838

1- 5	James Dortch, of Nash County, to Amanda, dau. of Weeks Parker, Dec. 21, 1837, by H. Austin.
1-12	Hickman Ellis to Mrs. Queen Esther Ellis, Jan. 4, by James Bridgers.
2-17	Lacy Alford to Sally Mayo, by W. C. Leigh, Esq.
2-17	Henry Keel to Mary Hicks, Feb. 1, by W. C. Leigh, Esq.
2-17	Joshua Hicks to Lydia Ann Mayo, Jan. 25.
3-17	Charles Baines, age 70, to Piety Gay, age 30, Feb. 20, by H. Austin.
3-17	Tom Hales to Mary Barfield, Mar. 10, by H. Austin.
3-17	John Walston to Margaret, dau. of Eason Cherry, Sunday last, by J. J. Pitt.
6-30	Simmons B. Parker to Emily, dau. of Nathan Mathewson, desc., by Rev. A. J. Battle.
10-20	Noah Thompson to Harriet Eliza Wright, by Rev. J. Singletary.
11-10	Josiah Council to Charlotte, dau. of Thomas Taylor, desc., Nov. 1.
12- 1	Col. Benjamin Sharp to Mary Ann Susan Edwards, Nov. 22, by Jesse C. Knight.
12- 8	Col. Joshua Pender to Mrs. Margaret H., wid. of Kenneth ? Nov. 29, by Rev. William Hyman.

1839

1- 5   Peter L. Lawrence to Abbe Mathewson, Dec. 23, 1838, by Rev. William Wills.

1- 5   Eli Sorey, Halifax County, to Nony, dau. of Eli Harris, Dec. 20, 1838, by S. L. Hart, Esq.

1-12   Hansel Cross to Mrs. Susan Braswell by H. Austin.

1-12   William Adams Sr. to Miss Robbins, dau. of Jacob Robbins.

2- 2   William Lanier, of Beaufort County, to Talitha, dau. of William Grimes, Jan. 24, by Rev. William Hyman.

2- 9   James M. Redmund to Catherine Stillman by Rev. William Wills.

2-16   William M. Crenshaw, M.D., of Wake Forest, to Catherine E., dau. of Henry Austin, by Rev. P. W. Dowd.

2-16   David C. Bell to Mary, dau. of Benjamin Williams, by L. D. Wilson.

2-16   Joseph J. Freeman to Eliza, dau. of Allen Jones, Feb. 5, by H. Austin.

2-16   Charles Mabry to Penny, dau. of Drury Bryan, Jan. 29, by B. Batts.

5-18   Levi Blount, of Plymouth, to Susan, dau. of John Brown, May 6, by W. C. Leigh.

8- 3   William F. Batly, of Nash County, to Mary E. Jenkins, July 17, by Rev. William Wills.

8-31   Peter Nixon to Mary Simmons, dau. of Mrs. Harrison Simmons, by H. Austin.

9- 7   William C. Leigh to Lucy, dau. of Chris. Harrell, Aug. 28, by W. D. Staton.

9- 7   Joseph Forbes to Elizabeth, dau. of Joe Eason, Aug. 29, by Ben Moore.

9-17   Daniel Batchelor, of Nash County, age 75, to Elizabeth Creekman, age 18.

10-12   Rev. Thomas R. Owen to Mary B. McCottor, by Rev. Mr. Shalton.

10-12   James S. Long to Wealthy Ann, dau. of Eli Howell, desc.

10-12   Lewis Pender to Mary, dau. of Kenneth Hyman, desc., Oct. 3, by J. J. Pippen.

10-12   Pollard Edmondson to Susan, dau. of James Howard, Oct. 3, by S. B. Staton.

10-12   William H. Hines to Malvina, dau. of John Mercer, Oct. 1, by D. Williams.

10-26 William D. Bell to Elizabeth, dau. of Frederick Bell, Oct. 17, by Demsey Bryan, Esq.
12-21 Elijah Robertson to Sally Britt, by Spencer L. Hart.

1840

1- 4 John C. Blocker, of Fayetteville, to Julia Ann Braddy.
1-18 Joseph Moore to Rebecca, dau. of Chris. Harrell, Dec. 24, by M. Williford.
1-18 Churchwell Killebrew to Mary, dau. of S. P. Jenkins, Jan. 7.
2- 8 John W. Pope to Eliza, dau. of Allen Taylor, Jan. 31, by D. W. Maner, Esq.
2- 8 William R. Dupree to Martha Tunnell, Jan. 29, by L. D. Wilson.
2-29 Benoni M. Wilkinson, Martin County, to Sarah Caroline, dau. of Frederick Jones, desc., by Joshua Pender, Feb. 18.
6- 6 Lorenzo Bell to Julia Bell by C. G. Hunter, Esq.
10-10 Rev. John F. Speight to Emma, dau. of Exum Lewis, desc., Sept. 29, by Rev. William Bellamy.
12- 5 John Moore to Mrs. Rutha Carney, Nov. 26, by W. D. Staton.

1841

1-23 Robert Davis to Russia Ann, dau. of Allen Nettle, Jan. 13.
1-23 Geraldus Shurley to Susan Bridgers, by John F. Hughes, Esq.
2-22 Dr. P. A. R. C. Cahoon to Mrs. Martha Sutton(?) dau. of Michael Hearn.
2-27 Franklin Hargrove, of Texas, to Mary W., dau. of Theo. Parker, by Rev. J. Singleton.
3-13 Andrew Jackson Pender to Anna Eliza, dau. of Wright W. Joiner, Mar. 4, by H. Austin.
3-20 Allen Mayo to Eliza, dau. of Abner C. Wilkinson, Mar. 10, by W. C. Leigh.
4- 3 Andrew Jackson Skinner, of Tenn., to Arcene, dau. of Willis L. Flemming.
4-10 James B. Woodard to Sarah B., dau. of William C. King, desc., by Rev. Joshua Lawrence.
5-22 Harmon H. Burke, of Chatham County, to Mrs. Louisiana Knight.
5-22 Joshua L. Lyon to Martha, dau. of Maj. Lunsford Cherry, by William S. Baker.

6- 5   Redding Lawrence to Elizabeth, dau. of John Lawrence, by H. Austin.
8-28   William H. Pittman, of Halifax, to Martha Ann, dau. of James C. Knight, by J. J. B. Pender.
10-23 Nathan Pitt to Emily, dau. of Richard Weaver, desc.
11-27 Dr. Samuel Carson to Mrs. Sarah Freeman, Nov. 26, by H. Austin.
12- 4 Jonathan Lee to Betsy Pope, by James George, Esq.
12-25 David Bullock to Margaret Ruth (Routh), Dec. 15 by William S. Baker.

1842

2-19   James Whitehurst to Nancy, dau. of Winfield Staton, by William S. Baker.
3- 6   Mayo Worsley to Mary L., dau. of Winfield Staton, Feb. 22, by J. J. Pippen.
3-26   Joseph Harvey to Nancy Eason by H. Austin.
4-23   James Vick to Polly Sorey, Apr. 14, by H. Austin, Esq.
4-30   Joseph J. N. Marks to Amanda, dau. of Silas Weeks, Apr. 30, by J. J. Pender.
9- 3   Redding Worsley, of Alabama to Anna Eliza, dau. of Gray Armstrong, by M. Price, Esq.
10-15 Calvin Jones to Mary, dau. of Bythal Staton, desc. by Rev. William Hyman.
10-29 Littleberry Manning to Pennina B. Exum, by Joseph J. Pender.
12-10 Elisha Cromwell to Sally Ann, dau. of Coffield King.

1843

1-21   Daniel Knight to Mary Davis by H. Austin.
2-11   Rev. J. B. Cheshire to Elizabeth, dau. of Theo. Parker, by Rev. Singletary.
3- 4   Col. Joab P. Pitt to Mrs. Winnfred G. Warren, by George Howard.
3- 4   Clinton James, of Pitt County, to Marina, dau. of Thomas Taylor, desc., Feb. 28.
5-27   James Lawrence to Sydney, dau. of Willie Howard, desc., by Wm. C. Leigh.
8-19   Allen Dupree to Mary, dau. of William Thigpen, by William C. Leigh.
9-16   Lewis Belcher to Rebecca S., dau. of Col. J. P. Pitt, by Rev. T. Dupree.

11- 4 Dr. William G. Thomas to Mary Sumner, dau. of Maj. James W. Clark, by J. B. Cheshire.

11- 4 Robert H. Pender to Amarilla James P., dau. of William Pender, by Rev. Mark Bennett.

12-16 John S. Dancy to Cornelia V., dau. of James S. Battle, Dec. 12, by Rev. Thomas Carter.

12-16 Dr. William E. J. Shallington to Sarah, dau. of Jesse Barnes, Jr., desc., Nov. 30, by John G. Williams, Esq:

1844

1-20 Benjamin C. Mayo to Evelina, dau. of Allen Jones, Jan. 11, by Rev. William Hyman.

1-20 William R. Leggett to Cinderella, dau. of Jonas Nelson, Jan. 11, by Harmon Ward.

2-17 Weldon S. Hunter to Nancy Griffiths by L. D. Wilson.

2-17 Wright Barnes to Mrs. A. S. Sharpe by J. C. Knight, Esq.

4-13 Jacob Turner to Patsy Lee.

4-13 Alfred Turner to Tassey Joiner.

4-13 Lawrence L. Boon to Esther Gay.

4-13 Commodore Stephen Decatur Daves, of Franklin County, to Rachel Gay.

4-20 Henry Belcher to Martha, dau. of Geraldus Shurley, desc., by Rev. T. Dupree.

6- 8 John P. Sharpe to Nancy, dau. of Turner Bynum, by L. D. Wilson.

6-22 Jesse Mercer to Margaret, dau. of Isaac Norfleet, by Rev. Mark Bennett.

6-29 James Ellinor to Mrs. Martha Cromwell by Rev. B. Cooper.

8- 3 James Savage to Pheribee, dau. of Rev. Joshua Lawrence, desc., July 18.

11- 2 Dr. Lewis J. Dortch to Nancy J. Adams, Oct. 10, by Rev. William Robertson.

11-16 Thomas Taylor, of Haywood County, Tenn., to Jane, dau. of John Mooring, Nov. 14.

MARRIAGE RECORDS
ABSTRACTED FROM THE BATTLE BOOK

By H. B. Battle, Lois Yelverton and W. J. Battle

Copied By Permission

Battle, John, (1684-1748) of Nansemond Co., Va., m. Sarah, (1684-1769), dau. of Dr. John Brown.

Battle, Sarah, dau. of John and Sarah Brown Battle, m. Richard Yates.

Battle, Mary, dau. of John and Sarah Brown Battle, m. James Norfleet.

Norfleet, Sally, dau. of James and Mary Battle Norfleet, m. (1) Elias Hilliard; (2) Col. William Horn.

Battle, Martha, dau. of John and Sarah Brown Battle, m. Isaac Dortch. (Moved to Tennessee.)

Battle, William m. Martha Drake.

Battle, John m. ———Moore. (Moved to Anson Co., N. C.)

Battle, Elizabeth m. Randolph Rutland, Hancock Co., Ga.

Battle, Priscilla m. Benjamin Forsett, Suffolk, Parish of Nansemond Co., Va.

Battle, Elisha (b. Nansemond Co., Va., Jan. 9, 1723; d. 1799), s. of John and Sarah Brown Battle, m. Elizabeth Sumner of Nansemond Co., Va. (History of Hepsibah Assn. pp. 135-136-137). Moved to Edgecombe Co. about 1743.

Battle, Jesse (1734———) m. Susan Forsett (1734———), (b. Nansemond Co. Va.), moved from Edgecombe Co. to Green (Hancock) Co., Ga., Feb. 20, 1787.

Battle, William Summer, s. of Jesse and Susan F. Battle, (b. 1761) m. May 24, 1783, Sally Whitehead (b. Sept. 24, 1784, d. Dec. 12, 1803), dau. of Lazarus Whitehead, Sr.

Battle, John Joseph, s. of William and Sally Whitehead Battle, m. Rhoda, dau. of William Whitehead.

Battle, Sarah, dau. of Elisha and Elizabeth Sumner Battle, m. (1) Jacob Hilliard, (2) Henry Horn.

Phillips, Joseph (b. 1763 in Edgecombe Co.), m. 1785, Milbry Horn (b. 1764); moved to Tennessee in 1791.

Battle, Elizabeth, dau. of Jethro Battle, m. Garry Fort, Jan. 2, 1794.

Battle, Capt. Turner Westry, of Cool Spring, Edgecombe Co., m. May 1, 1850, Lavinia Bassett Daniel, dau. of Joseph J. Daniel, Halifax Co.

Battle, Kemp Plummer (born Dec. 19, 1831, d. Feb. 4, 1919), s. of William Horn and Lucy Martin Plummer Batt'e, m. Nov. 28, 1885 (cousin), Martha Ann Battle (b. Feb. 14, 1833 at Cool Spring, Edgecombe Co., N. C.), dau. of James Smith Battle; (d. Chapel Hill, N. C., Mar. 16, 1913.)

Battle, Demcy (b. Dec. 4, 1758, d. Mar. 10, 1815), s. of Elisha Battle, m. 1784, Jane Andrews (who d. 1799).

Gilbert, Dr. John, s. of Elder Nathan and Charity Ricks Gilbert, m. Amelia Battle, dau. of Demcy and Jane Andrews Battle, (b. 1791, d. 1817.)

Gilbert, Elder Nathan (b. in Anson Co., N. C., Jan. 30, 1768.). Came to Edgecombe Co. in 1793. Married July 10, 1794, Charity Ricks, dau. of James Ricks, at Falls of the Tar River.

Phillips, Charles, of Chapel Hill, m. Dec. 8, 1847, Laura Caroline Battle (b. Nov. 5, 1824, Falls of the Tar River in Edgecombe Co., d. Oct. 4, 1919), dau. of Joel and Mary Johnston Battle.

Hilliard, Jacob, planter of Edgecombe Co., Falls of Tar River, m. Sarah Battle (b. Nansemond, Va., 1743, d. Mar. 19, 1802.).

Hilliard, Jeremiah (b. ca. 1760, d. Apr. 21, 1816), m. (1) Nancy Hilliard, dau. of Isaac Hilliard, (2) Mrs. John Hilliard (no children.).

Fort, William (b. June 23, 1759 in Edgecombe Co., d. Jan. 8, 1802), (See Will Chap. V, Battle Book), m. Mar. 6, 1782, Elizabeth Hilliard (b. in North Carolina, Sept. 6, 1763, d. Tennessee, Oct. 4, 1819.)

Fort, Jeremiah Hilliard (b. Edgecombe Co., Aug. 28, 1784, d. Cumberland, Tenn., Feb. 23, 1806, m. Temperence Battle, dau. of Jethro Battle and Martha Lane Battle; she m. (2) James Smith Battle, son of Jacob and Mrs. Penelope (Langley) Edwards Battle.

Fort, James, merchant (b. Edgecombe Co., Oct. 18, 1788, d. Tennessee, July 9, 1819), m. (1) Jan. 19, 1810, Jane Vernon Hampton (b. Mar. 1, 1791, d. Dec. 13, 1811), dau. of George and Mary Nugent Ballard Hampton; (2) Miss Ewing, who after death of James Fort, m. (2) William B. Ross.

Fort, Elias (b. Edgecombe Co., N. C., July 14, 1730, d. Robertson Co., Tenn., Jan. 14, 1819), Corpl. 1st. N. C. Reg., Rev. War, (removed with large number of relatives and neighbors in 1791 from Edgecombe Co. to Robertson, then Cumberland Co., Tenn.) m. 1758, Sarah Sugg (b. May, 1738, d. Mar. 19, 1802).

Phillips, Joseph (b. Oct. 31, 1763, d. May 22, 1822), m. in Edgecombe Co., 1785, Milberry Horn (b. Edgecombe Co., Dec. 4, 1764, d. Nashville, Tenn., Dec. 19, 1851).

Fort, Josiah (b. Edgecombe Co., N. C., Sept 8, 1762, d. Apr. 21, 1848), s. of Elias and Sarah Sugg Fort. Went to Tennessee in 1791 with father and brother William; m. in Edgecombe Co., Piety Horn, (b. Dec. 10, 1767, d. Nov. 27, 1815).

Sugg, Lemuel, II, s. of Acquilla Sugg, of Edgecombe Co., grandson Acquilla Sugg (Meth. minister), who came to North Carolina from Wales and removed to Tennessee about 1800.

Battle, John, Edgecombe Co., N. C., planter, (b. Nansemond Co., Va., 1745, d. 1796, s.s. Tar River below Little Falls), m. about 1770, Frances Davis (d. 1806).

Andrews, Cullen, near Little Falls of Tar River, m. Mary Battle (b. Edgecombe Co.) d. of John Battle, (b. in Nansemond Co., Va., 1745, d. Edgecombe Co., 1796), who m. about 1770, Frances Davis (d. 1806).

Andrews, Jesse (b. Edgecombe Co., Nov. 20, 1789), m. Sarah Battle, dau. of Elisha and Sarah Bunn Battle.

Andrews, John (b. Edgecombe Co., N. C.), m. Martha Pope, removed to Logan Co., Ky.

Cotton, John, Tar River Road, m. Elizabeth Andrews.

Battle, Davis (b. in Edgecombe Co., N. C., July 3, 1775, d. in Madison Co., Ala., Sept. 25, 1824), m. (1) May 20, 1802, Ann Applewhite, (d. Mar. 23, 1803), m. (2) May 8, 1805, Mrs. Margaret (Bunn) Lamon (b. Feb. 12, 1774, d. Aug. 22, 1838), wid. of John Duncan Lamon, who d. Oct. 1798.

Battle, Josiah Davis (b. Sept., 1811), m. Dec. 20, 1837, Mary Eliza McCrary, moved to Alabama or Mississippi.

Battle, Elisha, Shreveport, La., (b. in Edgecombe Co., N. C., Dec. 5, 1779, d. by accident in Shreveport, La., Aug. 26, 1844), moved about 1820 to Hancock Co., Ga., compiler of "A Collection of Hymns and Spiritual Songs for Public and Family Worship," pub. 1814; Baptist minister; m. Jan. 22, 1807, Olivia Ruffin Lamon (b. Dec. 10, 1789, d. Shreveport, La., Dec. 25, 1875), dau. of Archibald and Olivia Ruffin Lamon, granddaughter of John Duncan and Margaret Lamon of Edgecombe Co., N. C.

Crudup, Josiah m. Elizabeth Battle, Nov. 28, 1767.

Lee, James B. Falls of Tar River, m. Chloe Crudup, dau. of Joseph and Elizabeth Battle Crudup.

Perry, Solomon Ruffin m. Mary Louisa Crudup, dau. of Josiah and Elizabeth Battle Crudup.

Lee, James B. m. Chloe Crudup after 1767 and lived near Falls of Tar River.
Children: Susan Lee m. Lewis Fort and went to Tennessee; Eliza Lee, Temperance Lee, James Lee, Harry Lee, Mary Lee, Martha Lee, Dossy Lee.

Battle, Elisha II (b. 1749, d. 1830), lived s.s. Tar River, m. Sarah Bunn, dau. of Benjamin Bunn of Nash Co.

Andrews, Jesse (b. Edgecombe Co., Nov. 20, 1789, d. Jackson, Miss. about 1850), removed from North Carolina in 1811 to Logan, Ky., then to Mississippi; Bapt. minister; s. of Cullen and Mary Battle Andrews, m. Sarah Battle of Hinds Co., Miss., (b. in North Carolina, Aug. 14, 1792, d. in Hinds Co., Miss., Dec. 6, 1836).

Battle, William, Edgecombe Co., planter, (b. Nov. 8, 1751, d. Edgecombe Co., 1781), m. in Edgecombe Co., 1774, Charity Horn, dau. of Henry Horn, dismissed from her church because of m. to a non-Quaker; sister of Henry Horn, II, who m. Sarah Battle, dau. of Elisha Battle and Elizabeth Sumner.

Battle, Isaac (b. July 3, 1775, d. May, 1786), s. of William and Charity Horn Battle, m. Mar. 23, 1803, Lucinda Atkinson Mayo (b. Feb. 25, 1788), dau. of William Mayo and Elizabeth Atkinson. Moved to Tennessee in 1810.

Battle, Joel (b. May 16, 1779), s. of William and Charity Horn Battle, m. Mary Palmer Johnston.

Battle, Ann, dau. of William and Charity Horn Battle, (b. 1781), moved to Mississippi, m. Daniel Ross.

Battle, Charity Horn (b. Feb. 28, 1807, d. Feb. 10, 1880, in Nashville, Tenn.), m. Oct. 3, 1822, Rev. Martin Clark (b. Oct. 3, 1801, d. Feb. 25, 1859 in Edgecombe Co., N. C.), Meth. minister; s. of Samuel and Virginia Martin Clark.

Battle, Joel (b. in Edgecombe Co., N. C., May 16, 1779, d. in Rocky Mount, Aug. 25, 1829), m. May 9, 1801, Mary Palmer Johnston (b. Jan. 14, 1786, d. in Chapel Hill, Feb. 23, 1866), dau. of Amos and Dorcas Williams Johnston.

Johnston, Amos (b. Apr. 8, 1746, d. Edgecombe Co., 1816), s. of Jacob Johnston, from Va., (d. 1782), and Mary Waller, m. Jan. 2, 1777, Dorcas Williams (b. Feb. 19, 1760), dau. of John Williams of Pitt Co., granddaughter of Dr. Robert Williams of Pitt Co., s. of Richard Williams of Pitt Co., N. C.

Battle, Dossey (b. Rocky Mount. July 12, 1842, d. Mar. 28, 1900), m. Sept. 28, 1876, Mary Clark Bell, Washington, N. C., (b. Dec. 15, 1849, d. Rocky Mount, Jan. 24. 1929). Their dau., Helene, (b. June 21, 1885), m. Mar. 30, 1910, A. B. Willingham.

Battle, Richard (b. Rocky Mount, N. C., Dec. 22. 1845, d. Atlanta, Ga., Feb. 11, 1917), m. (1) Fayetteville, N. C., Oct. 10. 1882. Cornelia E. McDaniel (d. Mar. 7, 1887), dau. of Rev. James McDaniel, D.D.; m. (2) Wake Forest, N. C., Aug. 27, 1889, Isabella Wingate (b. Jan. 10, 1864).

Battle, Amos Johnston (b. Edgecombe Co., Jan. 11, 1805. d. Wilson, N. C., Sept. 24, 1870), m. Edgecombe Co., Jan. 7, 1830, Margaret Hearne Parker (b. Jan. 19, 1811. d. St. Louis, Mo., Jan. 6, 1889), dau. of Weeks Parker of Edgecombe Co., and Mrs. Sabra Irwin Hearne (Cooke) Parker.

Battle, Catherine Ann (b. Edgecombe Co., N. C., Aug. 1, 1809, d. Wake Forest, May 25, 1879), Baptist, m. Feb. 5, 1829, John Wesley Lewis, M,D., b. Mar. 2, 1804, d. Nov. 22, 1842), removed in 1837 to Warrenton and in 1839 to Raleigh, Methodist, s. of Exum Lewis and Ann Harrison.

Lewis, Richard Henry, physician and teacher (b. near Rocky Mt., Dec. 21, 1832, d. Kinston, N. C., May 15, 1917), m. (1) Dec. 8, 1857, Virginia Cull (b. Washington, D. C., 1833; d. Tarboro, N. C., Sept. 22, 1861), dau. of James Cull; m. (2) Dec. 23, 1863, Eleanor Mildred Betts (b. Halifax Co., July 9, 1844, d. Kinston, N. C., May 17, 1915), dau. of Capt. William Spencer Betts and Mary Faulkner.

Lewis, Exum (b. Edgecombe Co., N. C., Nov. 1837, d. Weldon, N. C., June 17, 1888), s. of John Wesley and Catherine Ann Battle Lewis. Methodist, m. (1) Rocky Mt., N. C., Nov. 20, 1867, Lou Hall (d. July 8, 1870), m. (2) Dec. 18, 1871, Fannie E. Walker (d. Dec. 4, 1873), m. (3) Jan. 22, 1883, Mrs. Pattie Moore.

Battle, Laura Caroline (b. Edgecombe Co., N. C., Nov. 5, 1824, d. Chapel Hill, Oct. 4, 1919), dau. of Joel and Mary Palmer Johnston Battle, Presbyterian; m. Chapel Hill, Dec. 8, 1847, Dr. Charles Phillips, (b. Harlem, N. Y., July 30, 1822, d. Columbia, S. C., May 10, 1889).

Battle, James Smith (b. Cool Spring Plantation, Edgecombe Co., N. C., June 25, 1786, d. Westryville, July 18, 1854), Baptist; m. (1) Jan. 1812, Mrs. Temperence (Battle) Fort (b. Edgecombe Co., d. Edgecombe Co., Sept. 9, 1814), dau. of Jethro and Martha Lane Battle; m. (2)

Nash Co., Dec. 3, 1822, Sally Harriett Westry (b. Nash Co., Feb. 7, 1803, d. Hicksford, Va., July 15, 1840), dau. of Samuel Westry (from Northampton Co. to Nash Co., N. C.), and Mrs. Sallie Bradford (Turner) Short.

Battle, William Smith, Lone Pine, Edgecombe Co. (b. Edgecombe Co., Oct. 4, 1823; d. near Tarboro, Nov. 10, 1915), m. Tarboro, June 25, 1845, Mary Elizabeth Dancy (b. Tarboro, Jan. 29, 1825, d. near Tarboro, July 21, 1907), dau. of Francis Little Dancy and wife Charlotte Dancy.

Dancy, William Francis (b. Tarboro, N. C., Oct. 11, 1818, d. Philadelphia, Pa., May 7, 1860), s. of Francis Little and Charlotte Sessums Dancy; m. (1) Cool Spring, Edgecombe Co., Jan. 14, 1858, Mary Eliza Battle (b. Nashville, N. C., Jan. 11, 1829, d. Tarboro, Aug. 13, 1905), Episcopalian.

Dancy, Francis Little (b. Aug. 2, 1776, d. June 18, 1848), was s. of William Dancy (b. Charles City Co., Va., d. ca. 1776), who m. in Edgecombe Co., 1765, Agnes Little. He was s. of John Dancy, Charles City Co., Va.

Battle, Mary Eliza (b. Nashville, N. C., Jan. 11, 1829, d. Tarboro, N. C., Aug. 13, 1905), Episcopalian; m. (1) Cool Spring, Edgecombe Co., Jan. 14, 1858, William Francis Dancy (b. Tarboro, N. C., Oct. 11, 1818, d. Philadelphia, Pa., May 7, 1860), s. of Francis Little and Charlotte Sessums Dancy; m. (2) Tarboro, N. C., Apr. 21, 1867, Dr. Newsom Jones Pitman (d. Tarboro, N. C., 1893).

Battle, Jethro (b. Edgecombe Co., 1756, d. Edgecombe Co., 1813), m. Martha (Patty) Lane of Halifax Co. (d. 1793).

Battle, Alford Lane (b. Jan. 8, 1784, d. Feb. 5, 1847), m. (1) Susanna Wilson (b. Dec. 26, 1781, d. May 14, 1807), dau. of William (b. Aug. 24, 1751, d. Apr. 4, 1807), and Elizabeth Wilson (b. Sept. 24, 1757, d. Mar. 4, 1811). William Wilson was s. of Isaac and Susanna Wilson. Alford Lane Battle m. (2) Oct. 8, 1809, Nancy Wilson (b. Jan. 24, 1778, d. Nov. 23, 1845).

Battle, James Lane (b. Edgecombe Co., Nov. 25, 1814, d. Falls of Tar River, Feb. 25, 1884), Baptist; m. (1) Mar. 28, 1843, Frances C. Powell (May 26, 1822-1854), dau. of Jesse and Charity Powell of Halifax Co., m. (2) Nov. 26, 1856, Mary Louise Peebles (b. Sept. 24, 1825- ——), dau. of Thomas E. and Susan Peebles.

Battle, James Alford (b. Tarboro, Mar. 7, 1844), Baptist; m. (1) Nov. 27, 1867, Annie R. Taylor of Greensville Co., Va.; m. (2) Murfreesboro, Aug. 1880, Sue Cotton.

Battle, Julia Elizabeth (b. Apr. 18, 1845, d. Tarboro, N. C., May 30, 1871), m. Jan. 10, 1866, William L. Peebles of Petersburg, Va.

Battle, Orren Datus (b. Edgecombe Co., Feb. 22, 1787, d. Texas, Jan. 21, 1869), m. Tennessee, Dec. 7, 1809, Sarah Coleman Fort (b. Edgecombe Co., Sept. 6, 1786, d. Bowie Co., Tex., Apr. 25, 1843), dau. of William Fort and Elizabeth Hilliard.

Battle, Temperence (d. Edgecombe Co., Sept. 9, 1814), Baptist; m. (1) Jeremiah Hilliard Fort, s. of William Fort and Elizabeth Hilliard; m. (2) Jan. 1812, James Smith Battle, s. of Jacob Battle and Mrs. Penelope (Langley) Edwards Battle.

Battle, Joseph Sumner (b. Edgecombe Co., July 18, 1791, killed by slave, Edgecombe Co., July 19, 1847), m. (1) Rebecca Dunn of Wake Co., N. C.; m. (2) Dec. 5, 1826, Mary Ann Horn, (b. Oct. 19, 1810), dau. of Josiah Horn. She m. (2) Jesse H. Powell.

Battle, Elizabeth (b. Edgecombe Co., Oct. 6, 1776), Bapt.; m. Jan. 2, 1793, Jacob Geraldus Fort, Tarboro. Descendants moved to Tennessee, Texas and Arkansas.

Battle, James Phillips, M.D. (b. Edgecombe Co., May 11, 1829, d. Rocky Mt., Oct. 3, 1865), Mason; Meth.; Class of 1856, Jefferson Med. Col. Phil.; m. Edgecombe Co., Jan. 12, 1858, Kate Routh Horne (b. Mar. 2, 1839, d. Dec. 23, 1910), dau. of Joshua Horne and Elizabeth Mercer.

Battle, Temperence Ann (b. Edgecombe Co., Nov. 18, 1835, d. Rocky Mt., Oct. 21, 1913), Meth.; m. Edgecombe Co., Nov. 8, 1853, Robert Henry Marriott (b. Wake Co., N. C., Sept. 10, 1819, d. Rocky Mt., Sept. 7, 1873), s. of Benjamin Marriott and Aley Terrell.

Battle, Demsey (b. Edgecombe Co., Dec. 4, 1758, d. Mar. 10, 1815), Bapt.; m. 1784, Jane Andrews (1767-1799), dau. of Cullen Andrews, Sr.; descendants moved to Georgia and Alabama.

Battle, William (b. Virginia, 1728, d. Nash Co., 1780), Virginia to Edgecombe Co., thence ca. 1740 to Northampton Co., 1748 Capt. Northampton Colonial Militia, thence to Nash at close of Revolutionary War; m. Mary Capell, dau. of John (Jack) Capell of Halifax Co., N. C.

EDGECOMBE COUNTY MARRIAGES
AS PROVED BY BIBLES, WILLS, AND DEEDS

From the files of
Hugh B. Johnston, Jr., Historian-Genealogist

A

Andrews, John and Elizabeth Johnston Bell, dau. of Jonas Johnston, 1795.

Armstrong, Gray and Martha Ann Williams, 1809.

Armstrong, Joseph and —— Bracewell, dau. of William Bracewell, Sr., before 1797.

RE Robert Armstrong will in 1798.

    d. Mary Armstrong married to John Long, Dec. 29, 1785, Sussex Co., Va.

    d. Elizabeth Armstrong m. October 23, 1792, William Land, Sussex Co., Va.

Armstrong, William W., and Edney Griffin, dau. of John and Sabra Griffin, 1821. (D. B. 22, p. 301.)

Atkinson, John A. and Esther Ruffin Tyson, dau. of Samuel Ruffin, Dec. 1. 1831. (Bible).

B

Bailey, Berry and Martha Williams, 1842.

Barbee, Joseph D. and Harriet Dew Barnes, dau. of Larry Dew, Sept. 22, 1839. (Bible).

Bardin, Benjamin H. and Nancy Rountree, dau. of Willie Rountree, June 15, 1854.

Barnes, Archelaus Jr. and Penelope Dickinson, dau. of Shadrach Dickinson of Wayne County, June 10, 1815. (Bible).

Barnes, Brittain Jr. and Patience Farmer, dau. of Isaac Farmer Jr., after 1811.

Barnes, Burrell and Elizabeth Flowers, dau. of Hardy Flowers, about 1803.

Barnes, Dempsey D. and Temperance Winstead, dau. of David Winstead of Nash County, 1821.

Barnes, Dempsey D. and Harriet Dew, dau. of Larry Dew, Aug. 4, 1836. (Bible).

Barnes, Edwin and Theresa Simms, dau. of Benjamin Simms, Sept. 25, 1828.

Barnes, Edwin W. and Elizabeth Simms, dau. of James Simms, June 20, 1839. (Bible).

Barnes, Jacob S. and Fannie Bynum, dau. of Gideon Bynum, Apr. 2, 1929. (Bible).

Barnes, James R. and Louisa O. Ellis, dau. of Coffield Ellis, Nov. 27, 1849.

Barnes, James Stephen and Obedience Johnson, 1823.

Barnes, Jesse and Mary Dew, dau. of Arthur Dew, 1790.

Barnes, Jesse and Edith Jordan, dau. of Joshua Jordan, 1797.

Barnes, Jethro and Nancy Pender, dau. of Joseph Pender, before 1814. Deed Book 15, page 83.

Barnes, John and Mary Dew, dau. of John Dew, 1803.

Barnes, John and Margaret Huett Ruffin, dau. of Samuel Ruffin, about 1828.

Barnes, Joshua and Matilda Bynum, dau. of Turner Bynum, May 16, 1843. (Bible).

Barnes, Wright and Mary A. S. Edwards, dau. of Edmund Edwards, 1845.

Barrett, Thomas and Ann Thomas, dau. of Philip Thomas, before 1789.

Battle, Joel and Mary Palmer Johnston, dau. of Amos Johnston, April 9, 1801. (Bible).

Battle, Joseph S. and Mary Ann Horn, dau. of Josiah Horn, Dec. 5, 1826. (Bible).

Battle, William and Charity Horne, dau. of Henry Horne in 1775.

Batts, Bailey and Esther Jordan, dau. of Jesse Jordan of Pitt County, 1800.

Batts, Isaac and Lucy Knight, dau. of Peter Knight, 1802.

Batts, Isaac B. F. and Fannie O. Little of Greene County, Jan. 10, 1864. (Bible).

Batts, Jeremiah and Elizabeth Williams, dau. of John Williams, 1793

Batts, John and Mary Taylor, dau. of William Taylor, 1807.

Batts, Redmond and Sally Batts, widow of David Batts, 1858.

Batts, Wiley J. and Elizabeth Williford, dau. of Hartwell Williford, 1839.

Batts, William Sr. and Martha Woodard, dau. of Elisha Woodard Jr., Nov. 12, 1822. D. Bk. 21, p. 408.

Batts, William W. and Margaret Peelle Woodard, dau. of James B. Woodard, Dec. 6, 1853. (Bible).

Beal, John, of Johnston County, and Barsheba Farmer, dau. of Isaac Farmer Jr., before 1810.

Bell, John and Elizabeth Maund Johnston, dau. of Jonas Johnston, 1789.

Borden, Arnold, of Wayne County, and Maria Ann Brownrigg, dau. of George Brownrigg, 1824.

Boswell, James R. and Harriet Eliza Farmer, dau. of Absalom Farmer, 1845.

Bradley, Reuben and Frances Horn, widow of Josiah Horn, 1816.

Braswell, Jacob and Nancy Cotton, July 9, 1789. (Bible).

Braswell, Robert R. and Anselana Wilkinson, widow of John Wilkinson Jr., Dec. 4, 1823. (Bible).

Brinkley, Jackson W. and Martha Farmer, dau. of Isaac Farmer, Jan. 21, 1853. (Bible).

Brownrigg, George and Obedience Tartt, widow of Elnathan Tartt, by 1797.

Bridgers, Britain and Mary Rice, before 1780.

Bridgers, Edwin B. and Mary Atkinson, dau. of Aaron Atkinson, March 15, 1851. (Bible).

Bridgers, John and Elizabeth Kettlewells Routh, dau. of William Routh, 1815.

Bridgers, John and Catherine Pender, dau. of James Pender, Dec. 23, 1831. (Bible).

Bridgers, John L. and Louisa Dicken, of Halifax County, Apr. 20, 1847.

Bridgers, Redden and Mary Ann Thomas, dau. of Eason Thomas, Feb. 20, 1855. (Bible).

Bridgers, William and Mary Barnes, dau. of James Barnes, 1797.

Bryant, George A. and Priscilla Farmer, dau. of James D. Farmer, 1851.

Bullock, David W. and Mary Margaret Routh, dau. of Robert William Routh, Dec. 15, 1841. (Bible.

Bullock, John and Sarah Ruffin, 1771.

Bullock, Joshua and Emily Vines, dau. of Samuel Vines, of Pitt County, Nov. 19, 1839. "Tarboro Press."

Bunn, Burrell and Charity Horn, dau. of Henry Horn, Jr. by 1794.

Bunn, David, of Nash County, and Elizabeth Thomas, dau. of Jacob Thomas, June 30, 1831. (Bible).

Bynum, Benjamin and Jedidah Pitt, dau. of James Pitt Sr., Sept. 24, 1837. (Bible).

C

Cahoon, William and Sarah Powell, dau. of John Powell, before 1744. (Halifax deed book 5, p. 265.)

Carr, Elias, of Pitt County, and Celia Johnston Hines, dau. of Jonas Johnston, 1797.

Clark, Edwin G. and Martha Ann Barnes, dau. of James J. Barnes, Nov. 2, 1847. (Bible).

Cobb, James and Mourning Horn, dau. of Jacob Horn, before 1826.

Cohoon, Joel and Naomy Futrell, Aug. 4, 1785. (Publishing of banns.)

Cohoon, Lamon and Winny Bracewell, dau. of Solomon Sr., before 1799.

Cohoon, Micajah and Jemina Dixon, dau. of Thomas Dixon, before 1790.

Cohoon, William and Elizabeth Flowers, widow, 1766, July Court, 1766.

Coleman, —— and Mary Cahoon, dau. of Simon Cahoon, before 1819. (D. B. 17, p. 114.)

Coleman, Moses and Treasey Cohoon, dau. of Wm. Cohoon, before 1795. (D. B. 8, p. 420.)

Cotten, John L. and Nancy B. P. T. Johnston, dau. of Aaron Johnston, 1837.

Cotton, Dr. A. S. and Sarah Vick, dau. of late Josiah Vick, of Nash County, Nov. 28, 1854.

Coward, Solomon and Charity Dillard, dau. of John Dillard, Jr., prior to 1807. (D. B. 12, p 304.)

Cravey, Owen and Seley Johnston, dau. of Jacob Johnston, Sr., by 1770.

D

Daniel, Lemuel and Anna Brown, before 1791.

Daniel, Nathan P. and Margaret M. Bynum, dau. of Gideon Bynum, Apr. 9, 1846. (Bible).

Daniel, Simon and Elizabeth Bentley, dau. of William Bentley, of Halifax Co., prior to 1747. (Halifax County D. B. 3, p. 182.)

Davis, David and Keziah Pitt, dau. of Robert Pitt, 1796.

Davis, Joseph and Keziah Howell, dau. of Joseph Howell Jr., 1788.

Deans, Willie and Martha Simms, dau. of Robert Simms, Nov. 10, 1840. (Bible).

Dempsey, Eure Jr. and Nancy Thomas, dau. of Jonathan Thomas Jr., before 1820.

Dew, Jonathan and Nancy Farmer, dau. of Benjamin Farmer, about 1810.

Dew, Arthur B. and Edith Barnes, dau. of Dempsey Barnes, 1844.

Dew, John and Sarah Thomas, dau. of Jonathan Thomas Sr., 1784.

Dew, John and Elizabeth Barnes, about 1810.

Dew, John and Martha Simms, dau. of James Simms, Feb. 26, 1844. (Bible).

Dew, Larry and Nancy Bardin, dau. of Arthur Bardin, Nov. 15, 1818. (Bible).

Dew, William and Delphia Rountree, about 1819.

Dickinson, Jacob and Mourning Thomas, dau. of Joseph Thomas, Nov. 19, 1770. (Bible).

Dillard, Edward and Wealthy Ann Williams, dau. of Pilgrim F. Williams, Jan. 19, 1869.

Dillard, James and Elizabeth Davis, widow of Amos Moore, 1791.

Dillard, John and Mary Dickinson, dau. of Thomas Dickinson, before 1810. (D. B. 24, p. 518.)

Dillard, Joseph and Mary Williams, widow, prior to 1776. (D. B. E, p. 78.)

Dillard, Mark and Milberry Ellinor, before 1807.

Dillard, Matthew and Nancy Marley, dau. of Benjamin Marley, before 1807. (D. B. 12, p. 202.)

Dillard, Thomas James R. and Mary Elizabeth Long, dau. of Edward Long, Dec. 19, 1831.

Dixon, Wrightson and Martha Irving, dau. of Andrew Irving, by 1772.

Dunn, John Jr. and Anne Sessums, dau. of Nicholas Sessums, 1753.

Dunn, Jonas and Patsey ———, Apr. 7, 1808. (Bible).

Dunn, Lamon and Mary Ann Wilkinson, dau. of Joshua Wilkinson, 1804.

Dunn, Lamon and Anna Rey, 1827.

Dunn, Lamon S. and Ann Eliza Gay, 1843.

E

Eagles, Richard T. and Penelope S. Eason, dau. of Joshua Barnes Eason, Jan. 12, 1832. (Bible).

Eason, Abner and Martha Tartt, dau. of Jonathan Tartt, Sr., before 1789, (W. B. C, p. 87).

Eason, Coburn and Elizabeth Barnes, dau. of Elder Joshua Barnes, about 1786.

Eason, Joshua B. and Polly Scarborough, dau. of James Scarborough, July 8, 1812. (Bible).

Edwards, Jonas and Cilicia Johnston, dau. of William Johnston, about 1808.

Edwards, William Henry and Mary Jane Woodard, dau. of James B. Woodard, Feb. 25, 1858. (Bible).

Edmundson, Wright and Susanna Dickinson, dau. of Shadrach Dickinson, of Wayne County, Apr. 6, 1817. (Bible).

Ellis, Lewis and Mary Peele, dau. of Robert Peele, Jr., Aug. 10, 1820. (Bible).

Ellis, Lewis and Zilla Morris, widow of Robert Simms, May 8, 1825. (Bible).

Ellis, William and Elizabeth Stanton, dau. of James Stanton, Jr., before 1790.

Ellis, William Sr. and Unity Dixon, dau. of Thomas Dixon, Jr., before 1802.

Ellis, William and Theresa Dew, dau. of John Dew, about 1812.

Evans, Peter and Nancy Johnston, dau. of Amos Johnston, by 1807.

F

Farmer, Absalom and Elizabeth Dickinson, 1801.

Farmer, Azeal and Charlotte Coppage, 1797.

Farmer, Benjamin and Elizabeth Dew, dau. of Arthur Dew, before 1775.

Farmer, Braswell and Nancy White, before 1827.

Farmer, Isaac Jr. and Christian Barnes, dau. of John Barnes, of Wayne County, before 1785.

Farmer, Isaac D. and Elizabeth Barefoot, 1840.

Farmer, Jacob and Penelope Rountree, dau. of John Rountree, 1812.

Farmer, Jacob and Amanda Marcilla Ellis, dau. of Lewis Ellis, about 1850.

Farmer, James D. and Sarah Holland, 1822.

Farmer, Jesse and Elizabeth Tartt, dau. of Jonathan Tartt, Sr., before 1808.

Farmer, Jesse and Mary Batts, dau. of William Batts, Sr., Oct. 15, 1843.
Farmer, John and Nancy Barnes, dau. of Jesse Barnes, 1813.
Farmer, John R. and Elizabeth Stallings, Dec. 31, 1833. (Bible).
Farmer, John W. and Obedience Rountree, dau. of Willie Rountree, before 1850.
Farmer, Joseph and Zilpha Barnes, dau. of John Barnes, of Wayne County, about 1781. (D. B. A, p. 224.)
Farmer, Joseph and Polly Barnes, 1815.
Farmer, Joseph and Millicent Horn, dau. of Jacob Horn, before 1826.
Farmer, Joseph and Elizabeth Daniel, about 1848.
Farmer, Larry D. and Sarah Dew, dau. of Jonathan Dew, Feb. 19, 1839. (Bible).
Farmer, Moses and Elizabeth Dew, dau. of John Dew, Sept. 4, 1817. (Bible).
Farmer, Moses and Elizabeth Barnes, dau. of John Barnes, Jan. 13, 1835. (Bible).
Farmer, Moses, Jr. and Patience Woodard, dau. of William Woodard, Jr., Nov. 24, 1853. (Bible).
Farmer, Pharaoh L. and Mehala Elizabeth Daniel, Mar. 9, 1854. (Bible).
Farmer, Samuel B. and Temperance Ann Cox, dau. of Saunders B. Cox, 1856.
Farmer, Samuel and Jerusha Tyson, dau. of Aaron Tyson, about 1778.
Farmer, Thomas and —— Lee, dau. of Joshua Lee, about 1765.
Farmer, William D. and Elizabeth Batts, widow of Edwin Edwards, 1849.
Farmer, William H. and Julia Ann Darden, Oct. 25, 1856. (Bible).
Fitzgerald, Gibson and Mary Simms, dau. of Benjamin Simms, Apr. 13, 1826. (Bible).
Fort, Josiah and Piety Horn, dau. of Henry Horn, Jr., Jan. 17, 1788.
Fort, Jacob G. and Priscilla Horn, dau. of Josiah Horn, Oct. 13, 1822. (Bible).

G

Gay, William and Piety Horn, dau. of Jacob Horn, of Nash County, before 1829.
Gilbert, Nathan and Charity Ricks, dau. of James Ricks, July 10, 1794.

Glanden, Major and Jemina Horn, dau. of William Horn, before 1803.

Green, John A. and Diana Simms, dau. of Benjamin Simms, May 31, 1836. (Bible).

Guin, Edward and Martha Permenter, dau of John Permenter, before 1802.

H

Harper, John and Mary Barnes, dau. of John Barnes, Nov. 15, 1827. (Bible).

Hedgepeth, John and Elizabeth Farmer, dau. of Isaac Farmer, Jr., before 1810.

Herring, Bryan W. and Penelope Simms, dau. of Benjamin Simms, June 21, 1834. (Bible).

Hickman, William and Keziah Dixon, dau. of Thomas Dixon, Jr., before 1802.

Hillard, Jacob and Sarah Battle, dau. of Elisha Battle Sr., 1760.

Hilliard, James C., of Nash County, and Mary Ann Ruffin, dau. of Samuel Ruffin, Feb. 10, 1835. (Bible).

Hillard, Jeremiah and Mourning Pope, dau. of Jacob Pope, Sr., 1732.

Hines, Jesse and Celia Johnston, dau. of Jonas Johnston, 1791.

Hines, Peter and Prudence Johnston, dau. of Jonas Johnston, about 1793.

Hines, Richard and Susan Wilkins, dau. of James Wilkins, 1810.

Hollowell, William and Sarah Simms, dau. of Barnes Simms, before 1832. (Deed book 20, p. 290.)

Hood, Edward and Patience Horn, dau. of William Horn, before 1803.

Horn, Abishai and Ann Ricks, dau. of James Ricks, about 1780.

Horn, Bythal and Tabitha Barnes, dau. of Williamson Barnes, about 1809.

Horn, Henry Jr. and Sarah Battle, dau. of Elisha Battle Sr., by 1775.

Horn, Henry and Mary Simms, dau. of Jacob Simms, 1810.

Horn, Henry III and Lydia Read, dau. of Elder Jesse Read, of Halifax County, before 1815.

Horn, Jacob and Millicent Thomas, dau. of Elder John Thomas, Jr., 1781.

Horn, Jeremiah and Betsey Grice, dau. of Alexander Grice, Sept. 6, 1815. (Bible).

Horn, Joab and Nancy Ricks, before 1777.

Horn, John and Asenath Simms, dau. of Simon Simms, 1803.

Horn, Jordan and Elizabeth Dixon, dau. of William Dixon, 1796.

Horn, Josiah and Frances Thorpe, dau. of Henry Thorpe, 1803.

Horn, Josiah R. and Delitha Deberry, dau. of Lemuel Deberry, Feb. 23, 1818.

Horn, Thomas and Ann Grice, before 1818.

Horne, Whitmell and Mary F. Telfair of Washington, N. C., 1835.

Howell, Joseph and Ester Sugg, dau. of Aquilla Sugg, prior to 1760.

Howell, William, of Wayne County, and Dorcas Daniel, dau. of Simon Daniel Sr., before 1760.

Howenton, Thomas and Zerviah Horn, dau. of Henry Horn, before 1815.

Hyatt, David and Ruth Horn, dau. of Henry Horn, before 1785.

Hyatt, Jesse B. and Margaret Shirley, dau. of Geraldus Shirley, April 15, 1847. (Bible).

J

Jackson, Isaac and Winifred Proctor, July 4, 1798.

Jenkins, S. Perry and Rebecca Pitt, dau. of James Pitt Sr., about 1821.

Johnson, David and Sally Nettle, dau. of John Nettle, Jan. 26, 1800. Bonded by William Hines.

Johnson, Jesse and Rebecca Lewis, dau. of Exum Lewis, before 1790.

Johnston, Aaron and Winifred Walker, dau. of Daniel Walker, of Nash County, 1832.

Johnston, Amos and Dorcas Williams, dau. of John Williams, of Pitt County, Jan. 2, 1777. (Bible).

Johnston, Amos and Catherine Williams Hines, widow of Henry Hines, 1798.

Johnston, Bolden S. and Nancy Jane Dillard, dau. of Thomas James Ransome Dillard, Sept. 28, 1868. (Bible).

Johnston, Elisha and Mary Roberson, dau. of Archelaus Roberson, 1801.

Johnston, Jacob Jr. and Mary Randall, dau. of Alexander Randall, by 1768.

Johnston, James and Elizabeth Catherine Dunn, dau. of Jonas Dunn, Nov. 23, 1839.

Johnston, Jesse, and Keziah Pitt, dau. of Robert Pitt, 1805.

Johnston, Joab and Mary Ann Griffin, 1844.

Johnston, Jonas and Esther Maund, dau. of Lott Maund, 1769.

Johnston, Joseph J. and Charlotte Mason, 1825.

Johnston, Nathan and Elizabeth Henry, by 1761.

Johnston, Richard and Nancy Jenkins, by 1813.

Jones, Reuben and Rachel Horn, dau. of William Horn, before 1803.

Jones, Roderick and Emma Eliza Ellis, dau. of Lewis Ellis, 1853.

Jordan, Cornelius Jr. and Martha Woodard, dau. of Elisha Woodard, Sr., 1777.

Jordan, Cornelius, III and Christian Walton, dau. of John Walton, 1800.

Jordan, Cornelius (son of Joshua) and Mary Daniel, dau. of Lemuel Daniel, 1811.

Jordan, Gray and Penelope Hargrove, dau. of Aaron Hargrove, before 1801. (Deed book 10, p. 235.)

Jordan, Joseph and Edith Bryant, dau. of Gayle Bryant, before 1788

Jordan, Joshua and Edith Flowers, dau. of Henry Flowers of Nash County, before 1788.

Jordan, Joshua and Agnes Farmer, dau. of Isaac Farmer, Jr., before 1810.

Joyner, Wrightson W. and Tabitha Horn, dau. of Elisha Horn, by 1815.

L

Lancaster, Benjamin H. and Susan Farmer, dau. of Joseph Farmer, Jan. 27, 1854. (Bible).

Lawrence, John and Mildred Batts, dau. of Isaac Batts, 1833.

Lawrence, Joshua and Mary Knight, dau. of John Knight, about 1806.

Lawrence, Joshua L. and Harriet Penelope Mayo, dau. of Nathan Mayo, Jr., 1837.

Lewis, Reddin S. and Sarah Page, dau. of John Page, 1841.

Long, Henry and Narcissa Bullock, 1843.

Long, Newsome and Patsey Proctor, dau. of Aaron Proctor, before 1832.

Lyon, Richard and Elizabeth Eason, dau. of Obed Eason by 1798.

M

Mallison, Thomas H. and Frances Bynum, dau. of Benjamin Bynum, 1857.

Maund, William and Mary Howell, dau. of Joseph Howell, before 1759. Court record.

Mercer, Eli and Christian Farmer, dau. of Isaac Farmer Jr., before 1810.

Mewborn, Thomas and Elizabeth Pitt, dau. of Ralph Pitt, about 1823.

Moore, Benjamin and Martha Eason, dau. of Coburn Eason, before 1809.

N

Newsome, Henry and Nancy B. P. T. Cotten, widow of John L. Cotten, 1850.

Norvill, Enos and Elizabeth Eason, widow of Coburn Eason, before 1809.

Norvell, Enos and Elizabeth Langley, Apr. 14, 1828, bonded by Hezekiah Langley.

P

Parker, Calvin J. and Evelina Batts, dau. of John Batts, before 1840.

Parker, Guilford and Aggy Farmer, dau. of Isaac Farmer, before 1846.

Peelle, John J. and Elizabeth Woodard, dau. of Elisha Woodard Jr., 1797.

Peelle, Robert Sr. and Catherine Tartt, widow of Jonathan Tartt Sr., about 1798.

Pender, David and Mary C. Johnston, dau. of Henry Johnston, July 25, 1859. (Bible).

Pender, James and Sally Routh, dau. of William Routh, by 1814.

Pender, Joseph and Patience Cobb, dau. of Stephen Cobb, of Wayne County, before 1785.

Pender, Joseph J. and Elizabeth Bridgers, dau. of William Bridgers, March 4, 1829. (Bible).

Pender, Solomon and Mary Batts, dau. of Joseph Batts, Dec. 17, 1807. (Bible).

Permenter, James and Selisha Edwards, widow of Jonas Edwards, before 1818. (Deed Book 17, p. 7.)

Pettway, Micajah and Sarah Walton, dau. of John Walton, before 1808.

Phillips, Frederick and Sarah Tartt, dau. of Jonathan Tartt, Jr., before 1798.

Philips, Joseph and Milberry Horn, dau. of William Horn, about 1782.

Phillips, William and Penelope Eason, dau. of Obed Eason, by 1798.

Pippen, Joseph and Temperance Lee, Feb. 10, 1827, by David Hopkins, J. P.

Pitt, Bennett and Nancy Fountain, before 1832.

Pitt, Davis and Winny Phillips, dau. of David Phillips, 1798. (D. B. 10, p. 182.)

Pitt, Henry B. S. and Susan Routh Bennett, dau. of Mark H. Bennett, Dec. 22, 1847. (Bible).

Pitt, James and Leah Phillips, dau. of David Phillips, 1797. (Deed Book 10, p. 182.)

Pitt, Joab P. and Elizabeth Hopkins, Dec. 10, 1819. (Bible).

Pitt, Robert S. and Pennina Porter, dau. of Elisha Porter of Martin County, Jan. 15, 1849. (Bible).

Pittman, Jesse and Zilpha Eure, widow of Stephen B. Eure, 1839.

Pope, Sampson and Susannah Thomas, dau. of John Thomas, of Nansemond County, Va., 1741.

Price, Elijah and Temperance Thomas, dau. of Ichabod Thomas, Dec. 11, 1821. (Bible).

Proctor, Aaron and Anna Williams, dau. of Arthur Williams, before 1802.

Proctor, Aaron and Charity Williams, dau. of Thomas Williams, before 1820.

Proctor, John and Charlotte Pitt, dau. of Joseph Pitt, before 1819.

Q

Quinn, Amos and Susanna Permenter, before 1802.

R

Randolph, John and Jacky Ann Ruffin, dau. of Samuel Ruffin, 1831.

Ritter, William and Elizabeth Ellis, dau. of Elisha Ellis, before 1805.

Rountree, Lewis and Elizabeth Daniel, 1818.

Rountree, Moses, and Theresa Thomas, dau. of Jonathan Thomas, Sr., 1780.

Rountree, Nathan T. and Diana Barnes, dau. of Edwin Barnes, about 1855.
Rountree, Willie and Martha Dew, dau. of John Dew, 1817.
Rountree, Willie D. and Martha A. Hadley, 1851.
Ruffin, Etheldred and Mary Haywood, before 1778.
Ruffin, Henry J. G. and Mary Tartt, dau. of Elnathan Tartt, before 1820.
Ruffin, Samuel and Mary Ann Johnston, dau. of Jonas Johnston, Sept. 18, 1794. (Bible).
Ruffin, William J. and Martha Fleetwood, Nov. 23, 1826. (Bible).

S

Scarborough, Enos and Lucy Forehand, dau. of David Forehand, before 1809. (D. B. 13, p. 90.)
Scarborough, James and Penelope Eason, widow of Obed Eason, by 1793.
Scarborough, John R. and Martha Elizabeth Watkins, of Nash County, 1813.
Scarborough, Miles and Racheal Vickers, dau. of Ralph Vickers, by 1761.
Scarborough, Miles, and Jemina Drake, dau. of Jesse Drake, before 1796.
Scarborough, Samuel and Rachel Rogers, before 1783.
Sessums, Nicholas and Ann Benbow, dau. of John Benbow, 1754.
Sharpe, Benjamin and Mary Ann Susan Edwards, dau. of Edmond Edwards, before 1838.
Sherrod, John and Pherabah Braswell, dau. of James Braswell, before 1784.
Shirley, Geraldus and Temperance Amason, dau. of Benjamin Amason, Jr., about 1828.
Shirley, Henry and Elizabeth Davis, dau. of Joseph Davis, about 1809.
Simms, Barnes and Martha Dew, dau. of Arthur Dew Sr., 1785.
Simms, Benjamin and Tabitha Thomas, dau. of Theophilus Thomas, Feb. 15, 1799. (Bible).
Simms, Robert and Sarah Horn, dau. of John Horn, Dec. 30, 1823. (Bible).
Simms, Theophilus T. and Abigail Holland, Aug. 30, 1832. (Bible).
Simms, William and Edith Horn, dau. of Jacob Horn, before 1826.

Simmons, Jesse and Elizabeth Dixon, dau. of Thomas Dixon Jr., before 1802.

Skinner, Emanuel and Elizabeth Moore, dau. of John Moore, Sr., before 1780.

Smith, Ezekial and —— Simms, dau. of Barnes Simms, before 1832. (Deed Book 20, p. 290.)

Smith, Samuel G. and Catherine Tartt, dau. of Enos Tartt, by 1819.

Spicer, Moses and Delilah Calhoun, dau. of Etheldred Calhoun, before 1833. (D. B. 20, pp. 516-518.)

Stallings, Philip and Amanda Long, dau. of Newsome Long, April 3, 1855.

Stanton, James and Sallie May, 1797.

Stanton, Willie J. and Elizabeth Dickinson, dau. of Shadrach Dickinson, of Wayne County, 1794.

Stringer, Lawrence and Sally Pitt, dau. of Robert Pitt, before 1809.

Sugg, Lemuel and Celia Horn, dau. of Henry Horn, Jr. before 1800.

Sugg, Phesington S. and Lucinda Pender, dau. of Solomon Pender, Jan. 9, 1827. (Bible).

T

Tartt, Elnathan and Obedience Thomas, dau. of Theophilus Thomas, 1788.

Tartt, Enos and Theresa Thomas, dau. of Theophilus Thomas, by 1803.

Tartt, James and Sarah Barnes, dau. of Archelaus Barnes, 1815.

Taylor, Arthur D. and Nancy Lancaster, June 16, 1846. (Bible).

Taylor, Jack B. and Elizabeth Dillard, dau. of Thomas James Ransom Dillard, Jan. 24, 1867.

Taylor, James J. and Sarah Rountree, dau. of Willie Rountree, before 1850.

Taylor, William and Keziah Farmer, dau. of Isaac Farmer Jr., before 1810.

Thigpen, James R. and Gatsey Ann Pitt, dau. of Joab P. Pitt, Aug. 12, 1851. (Bible).

Thomas, Benjamin and Mary Ann Dickinson, dau. of Shadrach Dickinson, of Wayne County, 1797.

Thomas, Hillard and Zilpha Woodward, dau. of Elisha Woodward Jr., 1813.

Thomas, Hilliard and Nancy Sharpe, widow, about 1843.
Thomas, Jonathan and Mary Hillard, dau. of Jeremiah Hillard Sr., 1755.
Thomas, Jonathan Jr. and Elizabeth Eason, dau. of Isaac Eason Sr., of Pitt County, 1790.
Thomas, John Jr. and Patience Williams, about 1754.
Thomas, John R. and Mary Hooker, dau. of Hymerick Hooker, of Greene County, 1814.
Thomas, Joseph and Mourning Hilliard, widow of Jeremiah Hilliard, 1742.
Thomas, Micajah Sr. and Elizabeth Veal, April 11, 1751. (Bible).
Thomas, Micajah Sr. and Mourning Crudup, widow of John Crudup, Oct. 9, 1753. (Bible).
Thomas, Morrison and Sarah Turner, Sept. 16, 1826. (Bible).
Thomas, Morrison and Patience B. Horn, dau. of John Horn, Feb. 12, 1828.
Thomas, Richard and Rebecca Lewis, by 1760.
Thomas, Theophilus and Mary Rogers, dau. of Thomas Rogers, 1770.
Thomas, Theophilus and Dorothy Boothe, 1835.
Thomas, Treadwell D. and Mary Jane Thompson, 1841.
Thomas, Wade R. and Millicent S. Horn, dau. of John Horn, Jan. 6, 1827. (Bible).
Thomas, Warren and Nancy Warren, dau. of John Warren, 1829.
Thomas, Wilson and Nancy Proctor, dau. of Aaron Proctor, 1808.
Tisdall, Renison and Mary Flowers, dau. of Edward Flowers, before 1775.
Tyson, William and Esther Johnston Ruffin, dau. of Samuel Ruffin, Nov. 9, 1824. (Bible).

V

Vines, Charles and Prudence Celina Ruffin, dau. of Samuel Ruffin, Dec. 24, 1837. (Bible).

W

Walker, James and Caroline Farmer, March 2, 1855. (Bible).
Walton, John and Elizabeth Tartt, dau. of Jonathan Tartt, Sr., by 1780.
Ward, Silas and Sally Pitt, dau. of Thomas Pitt, before 1825.

Washington, George and Dolly Goodwin, dau. of William Goodwin, 1788.

Weaver, John and Nancy Horn, dau. of Jacob Horn, of Nash County, before 1815.

White, William and Rachel Brown, before 1791.

Whitehead, Augustine and Mary Proctor, dau. of Aaron Proctor, before 1832.

Wiggins, James and Milbrey Taylor, dau. of Stephen Taylor, Dec. 8, 1838. (Bible).

Wiggins, Noah and Julia F. Braswell, by 1852.

Wilkins, James and Esther Johnston, dau. of Amos Johnston, by 1803.

Wilkins, John and Delpha Farmer, dau. of John Farmer, 1845.

Wilkinson, Benjamin and Obedience Dew, dau. of John Dew, 1818.

Wilkinson, John Jr. and Anselana Stringer, dau. of William Stringer, 1818.

Williams, Abisha and Amanda Moore, dau. of Samuel Moore, Jan. 19, 1847. (Bible).

Williams, John G. and Elizabeth Barnes, dau. of Burrell Barnes, before 1830.

Williams, Joshua and Esther Pitt, dau. of Robert Pitt, before 1798.

Williams, Wiley G. and Piety Moore, dau. of Samuel Moore, after 1837.

Williamson, Kinchen and Rhoda Barefoot, dau. of John Barefoot, before 1825.

Williford, Harmon and Charity Winstead, of Nash County, before 1821.

Williford, Hartwell and Zilpha Gardner, dau. of George Gardner, before 1786.

Williford, Hartwell and Elizabeth Taylor, widow of Abraham T. Sharpe, Nov. 4, 1848. (Bible).

Williford, Meedy and Charity Curle, dau. of Willis Curle, about 1808.

Winstead, Jordan and Mary Horn, dau. of Guilford Horn, before 1852.

Wood, Daniel and Priscilla Farmer, before 1780.

Woodard, Asa and Julian Daniel, dau. of Lemuel Daniel, 1803.

Woodard, Calvin and Winifred Exum, dau. of John Exum, of Wayne County, Aug. 31, 1848.

Woodard, David and Elizabeth Bullock, dau. of John Bullock, Feb. 1793. (Bible).

Woodard, Elisha Jr. and Sarah Howell, dau. of William Howell, of Wayne County, before 1777.

Woodard, Gray W. and Mary Barnes, dau. of James Stephen Barnes, Sept. 7, 1854. (Bible).

Woodard, James B. and Nancy Daniel, dau. of Lemuel Daniel, Nov. 7, 1822. (Bible).

Woodard, James B. and Sarah Peelle, dau. of John Peelle, Mar. 20, 1827. (Bible).

Woodard, James B. and Sarah B. King, dau. of William C. King, Apr. 7, 1841. (Bible).

Woodard, Stephen, of Wayne County, and Mary Simms, dau. of Barnes Simms, 1817. (D. Bk. 20, p. 290.)

Woodard, Warren and Jerusha Farmer, dau. of Moses Farmer, Sept. 28, 1856. (Bible).

Woodard, William and Elizabeth Simms, dau. of Barnes Simms, 1823.

Woodard, William Jr. and Delpha Rountree, dau. of Wiley Rountree, Jan. 30, 1849.

Y

Young, Ezekial and Sally Cahoon, widow of Simon Cahoon, before 1819. (D. B. 17, p. 114.)

MARRIAGES OF EDGECOMBE COUNTY

Proved by Records in
Halifax County, North Carolina

These Halifax records are contributed by Susie Brickell Anderson, (Mrs. Leon W.) of Halifax, North Carolina, genealogist and historian. Mrs. Anderson has published Abstracts of Wills, Deeds and Marriage Records of Halifax County, North Carolina.

Halifax was cut from Edgecombe in 1758, keeping all records. The date given is date of recording, the marriages may have occurred many years earlier. For instance, James Easley to Betty, dau. of Samuel Norwood is dated 1796. But at this time Betty was dead, leaving four sons, all 21 or over. James had married again and had two sons by a second wife. So James and Betty were probably married in 1760 or earlier. For this reason dates include 1760s.

W 1 - 49/230 indicates Will Book 1, pp. 49 and 230.

W 1 - 354: 3-143 indicates Will Book 1, p. 354 and Will Book 3 p. 143.

Where two references are given as DB 8-39 and DB 9-301, we prove names, dates, and relationships better.

DB 1-341/354 indicates records on both pages, make proof clearer.

MARRIAGE RECORDS

Amis, John, of Northampton Co., N. C., to Mary, sister of Thos. Dillard, DB 7-268, 1761.

Amis, Thomas, of Northampton Co., N. C., to Rebecca, sister of Thos. Dillard, DB 7-268, 1761.

Andrews, Jesse to Milicent, dau. of Robert Warren.

Borden, Joseph to Jane, dau. of Robert Warren.

Raburn, Matthew to Sarah, dau. of Robert Warren.
> There is no definite proof of these three marriages; inferred from DB 10-360 and DB 18-151/164, 1769.

Arrington, —— to Agnes, dau. of Robert Bell,. W 1-139, 1767.

Baggot, Nicholas to Martha, dau. of Benjamin Wood, DB 7-101, 1759.

Bailes, Jesse to ——, dau. of Thos. Biell, W 1-103, 1762.

Bailey, John to Amy, dau. of William Andrews, W 1-49/230, 1761.

Bell, Joshua to Pheribe, dau. of Marmaduke Norfleet, Jr. (son of Thomas), DB 9-325, 1765.
Benbo, John to Elizabeth, widow of Jos. Watts, DB 4-487, 1753.
Bird, Barnabe to Ann Milton of Bertie Co., DB 4-115, 1751.
Blake, —— to Elizabeth, sister of Micajah Hobgood, W 1-106, 1763.
Blunt, —— to Sarah, dau. of Ann Bell, W 1-325, 1764.
Borden, Joseph —— see Andrews.
Braswell, —— to Sarah, dau. Peter Bruce, Sr., W 1-69, 1762.
Bryant, Arthur to Mary, sister Drew Smith, W 1-57, 1762.
Bryant, —— to Mary, dau. Robert Hill, W 1-159, 1762.
Bryant, Needham to Jemima (parents of Artnur) DB 18-162.
Bryant, William to Jane, dau. William Andrews, W 1-49/79, 1761.
Burt, Richard to Elizabeth, widow Daniel Williams, DB 10-123, 1767, Grimes 412, DB 9-
Chapman, —— to Tabitha, dau. Robert Hill, W 1-159, 1765.
Conner, James to Charity Carnal (Mar. Art.) DB 3-44, 1746.
Coupland, Joseph to ——, sister of Barnabe McKinne, W 1-49, 1761.
Cox, George to Mary, dau. Jesse Hammond, DB 8-39, 1763, DB 9-301.
Cox, John to Elizabeth, dau. Ignatius Hall, W 3-50/73, DB 17-820, 1779.
Crawford, Thomas to Elizabeth, dau. William Alston, DB 9-558, 1757.
Cureton, James to Elizabeth, dau. John Heath, W 1-169, 1765.
Daniel, James to Elizabeth, dau. Israel West, W 3-166/175, 1769.
Dill, Philip to Mony, dau. Jesse Rhymes, W 1-98, 1763.
Easley, James to Betty, dau. Samuel Norwood, DB 18-147, 17——. (They had 4 sons, all 21 in 1796.)
Easley, Rhoderick to Elizabeth, W 1-221, 1766.
Edwards, Samuel to Lidia, dau. Nathan Brown, W 1-151, 1764.
Eelbeck, Montfort to Mary, dau. Emanuel Rogers, DB 2-450, 1743. (Probably between 1727 and 1743, DB 5-247, Grimes 318.)
Emory, Edward to Rebecca, dau. Peter Hays, W 1-24, W 3-207, 1760.
Foort, Elias to Ann, dau. John Ricks, W 1-354, W 3-143, 1759.
Foort, Elias, Sr. to Priscilla Barrow, widow, DB 8-326, 1759.

Fountain, John (or Robert) to Ann, dau. Peter Bruce, Sr., W 1-69, 1762.

Geddy, John to Patience, dau. John McKinne, DB 9-460, 1757.

Goodloe, John to Susanna, dau. James Martin, W 1-121, 1763. (Susanna's 1st marriage. Second to Len H. Bullock.)

Green, Moses to Anne, dau. Michael Connell, W 1-100, 1760.

Green, William of Warren Co., N. C., to Ann Hunt, widow of John Alston, W 3-87/281, 1761. (Ann Hunt, dau. Gideon and Priscilla Jones Macon, DB 17-305.)

Griggs, —— to Mary, dau. John Corlew, W 1-54, 1761.

Grubbs, Benjamin to Jane, sister John Hardy, DB 6-165, 1754.

Gudge, John to Christian, dau. of Margret Hilliard, W 3-124, 1756, W 4-178.

Hardy, Benjamin to Mary, dau. William Alston, dec'd, late of Edgecombe Co., DB 7-332, 1767.

Harris, Richard to Margaret, sister Marmaduke Kembrough, DB 1-341/354, 1739.

Hayes, Peter, to Martha, W 1-24, 1760.

Hilliard, —— to Winny, dau. Peter Hays, W 1-24, 1760. 34, 1865.

Holderness, James to Patience, dau. Barnabe McKinne, DB 9-1769.

Huett, —— to Alice, dau. Peter Bruce, Sr., W 1-89, 1762.

Hurst, Spencer to Seilah, dau. William Cos (Cox?) W 1-300,

Jackson, —— to Elizabeth, dau. John Corlew, W 1-34, 1761.

Jones, Benjamin to Katherine, sister Susanna Reed, DB 9-431, 1766.

Joyner, Jesse to Priscilla, dau. William Whitehead, DB 15-246 and W 1-162, 1765.

Lane, —— to Martha, dau. Elias Fort, W 1-209, 1765.

Mayo, Nathan to Jileen(?), dau. John and Mary Williams, W 1-299, 1768; Martin Co., DB A-117.

Miliken, Col. Jas.(?) to Elizabeth, dau. Jos. Joyner, DB 1-229, 1737.

Montgomery, John, of Craven Co., N. C., to Ann, widow Wm. Hardy Jones, DB 1-255, 1739.

Norfleet, Reuben of Bertie Co., N. C., to Lucy, relative Thos. Langley, DB 9-418, 1766.

Norsford, —— to Susanna, sister Israel Campbell, W 1-107, 1762.

Norwood, Samuel of Halifax Co., N. C., to Mary, dau. Robert Smith, Surry Co., Va. Robert Smith moved from Surry Co., Va., to Bertie Co., N. C., 1727, DB 3-125, 1739.

Patrick, Paul to Agnes, dau. Col. Jas. Miliken, DB 6-190, 1754, DB 9-423.
Phillips, ――― to Edy, dau. Peter Hays, W 1-24, 1765.
Pope, ――― to Ann, dau. Elias Foort, W 1-208, 1765.
Pope, ――― to Mary, dau. Elias Foort, W 1-208.
Pope, Henry to Mourning, dau. Barnabe McKinne, DB 6-189, 1757.
Pope, Robert to Sarah, dau. Foust, DB 8-154, 1762.
Powell, William to Lucy, dau. Wm. Smith, W 3-197/450, 1764.
Powell, Zachariah to Mary, dau. Wm. Smith, W 3-197/450, 1764.
Raburn, Matthew to Sarah, dau. Robert Warren. (See Andrews.)
Ragland, Evin to Amy, dau. Mary Merritt, W 1-177, 1761.
Read, ―――to Susanna, widow Henry West, W 1-293, 1764.
Richmond, William to Ann, dau. Col. Jas. Miliken, DB 12-17, DB 9-423, 1751.
Ricks, Robert to Mary, dau. Nath'l Bradford, DB 9-339, DB 12-360, 1765.
Saxon, Benjamin to Sarah, dau. Wm. Green, W 1-22, 1760.
Sledge, Capt. Daniel, of Warren Co., N C., to Winifred, dau. Wm. House, W 1-96, 1763.
Smith, Joseph to Ann, dau. Mourning Payne, DB 10-122, 1759.
Smith, William to Patty, dau. Richard Powell, W 1-214, 1761, W 3-206.
Spann, John to Sarah, dau. James Smith, W 1-70, 1762.
Stewart, Thos. to Catherine, dau. Col. Jas. Miliken, DB 8-354, 1763.
Story, ――― to Elizabeth, dau. Green Emry, W 1-126, 1763.
Strickland, Moses to Rebecca, dau. John Grice, W 1-149, 1764.
Thomas, William to Mary, sister William Duglis, W 1-33/193, 1764.
Troughton, Andrew to Mary, widow, James Martin, W 1-121/202, 1764.
Vasser, Joel to Martha Dawson.
Ward, John to Elizabeth, sister Jas. Duglis, W 1-33/193, 1761.
Whitehead, Jacob (son of William, Jr., W 1-162.) to Hannah, dau. Dr. David Hopper, DB 6-262, 1757.
Williams, John to Mary, dau. William West, DB 3-284, 1748.
Young, John to Sarah, dau. Marmaduke Norfleet, Jr., DB 9-325, 1765.
Young, Thomas to Rutha, dau. Thos. Young, DB 18-574/804.

MISCELLANEOUS

Abstracted by Hugh B. Johnston, Jr., Historian for Wilson Co., N. C., from the original manuscripts now on file in The Library of N. S. D. A. R. in Washington, D. C., 31st day Oct. 1942.

Moore, Newton and Bathsheba Burnet: Nov. 29, 1809; Willie Causey.
Pierson, Berona and Tabitha ———: Aug. 24, 1800; Solomon Ward.
Whitehead, Jacob and Mary Bailey: Dec. 1, 1763: John Spendelow.
Williams, Burwell and Winney Braswell: July 19, 1799; Samuel Ruffin.
Williams, Joel and Phebe Atkins: Dec. 31, 1799; Augustine Whitehead.
Winstead, Jeremiah and Phereby Batts: Oct. 21, 1799; Drury D. Williams.

Marriages taken from the "Old Reporter's Column," Evening Telegram, Rocky Mount, N. C.

Price, Robert m. Cealy Johnston (b. Aug. 1, 1815).
Johnston, James m. Harriet Crews (He was killed in the Battle of Atlanta).
Watson, Mullion m. Patience Johnston (b. Aug. 18, 1825).
Johnston, John W. (b. 1832) m. Ann Williams (He was killed in the battle of Seven Pines).
Johnston, George Washington (b. Feb. 25, 1835) m. 1856, Margaret Leonora Kennedy. Moved to Jackson, Miss. after War between the States.
Braswell, Isaac m. Betsey Hyatt, Sept. 8, 1834.

Marriages taken from the files of Dr. Clairborne T. Smith, Jr., of Rocky Mount, North Carolina.

Bryán, Arthur m. Mary Smith, dau. of Nicholas Smith, (Will of her Bro. Drew Smith 1762. Halifax W. Bk. 1, p. 57.)
Bryan, William m. Sarah Smith, dau. of Nicholas Smith, who settled on s. side of Roanoke River 1732, then Bertie County, Edgecombe after 1740; Halifax after 1759. Bertie Deed Bk. A, p. 122.)

Arthur and William Bryan were sons of John Bryan, will dated 1734. Grimes "Abstracts of N. C. Wills" p. 54 and "Southside Va. Families" — Boddie.

Stewart, William m. Mary Ann Tartt of Edgecombe, Oct. 18, 1831 by Rev. Jos. R. Horn. Roanoke Advocate, Nov. 3, 1831.

Marriages taken from the files of Minnie Stone Dominick (Mrs. S. B.) of Rocky Mount, N. C.

Joyner, Baldy m. Leyan Crumply, Jan. 8, 1811.
Joyner, Jacob m. Mary Whitehead, Oct. 21, 1865.
Joyner, Peter m. Louisa Bonner, Aug. 2, 1861.
Cohoon, Lamon m. Nancy Joyner, (Edgecombe Deed, Feb. 25, 1815).
Morrison, Thomas m. Patience B. Horn, Feb. 12, 1828.
Godwin, William m. Tabitha Merritt, 1768.

RICKS MARRIAGE RECORDS

From the Ricks Family History

Contributed by Minnie Stone Dominick (Mrs. S. B.) of Rocky Mount, N. C.

Page 24: Joiner, Nathan m. Sarah Ricks, proved by will of Benamin Ricks, 1774 (Edgecombe Co.)
Page 24: Joiner, William m. Patience Ricks, proved by will of Benjamin Ricks, 1774.
Page 35: Ricks, Lewis m. Nancy Ann Joiner, 1768-9.
Page 36: Joiner, Jonathan m. Mourning Ricks (b. 1799).
Page 23: Ricks, Benjamin m. prior to 1735, Patience ———.

RECORDS EXTRACTED FROM OLD BIBLES

Arrington, Joseph s. of Arthur Arrington of Nash Co., m. Mourning Ricks of Edgecombe Co.

Atkinson, John A., b. Mar. 27, 1796; d. Jan. 1843; m. Dec. 1, 1831, Esther Johnston Ruffin Tyson, wid. of William Tyson.

Barnes, Jesse, s. of Dempsey and Sarah Barnes, b. Nov. 10, 1764; d. Oct. 11, 1843; m. (1) Mary "Polly" Dew, dau. of Arthur and Mary Dew; (2) m. Edith Jordan, (dau. of Joshua and Edith Jordan), b. May 27, 1775, d. May 28, 1849.

Barnes, Joseph James, s. of James F. and Mary Bowden Barnes, m. May 21, 1863, Frances Ann Bunting, b. ca. 1832, d. Feb. 10, 1869.

Boddie, Nathan, b. Isle of Wight Co., Va., Feb. 22, 1732; d. Nash Co., N. C., Dec. 7, 1797, s. of William and Mary Bennett Boddie, m. Chloe Crudup, b. 1745; d. Sept. 16, 1871, dau. of Mourning Dixon and John Crudup.

Bowers, James m. Sept. 19, 1839, Sally Ann Purvis.

Bradley, Benjamin F. b. Mar. 16, 1850; d. May 27, 1910; m. Martha Ann Brake, b. Feb. 18, 1851; d. Mar. 1, 1918.

Braswell, Jacob b. Mar. 7, 1763; d. July 25, 1837, s. of William and Anna Braswell, m. July 9, 1789, Nancy Cotten b. Dec. 3, 1772; d. after 1850.

Brown, Gray L. m. Nov. 14, 1867, Harriett M. Stancill.

Brown, Little Berry m. May 23, 1821, Lydia Cobb.

Bryan, David m. 17——, Lucy Barlow.

Bulluck, David William, s. of Jonathan and Elizabeth Bryan Bulluck, m. Dec. 15, 1841, Mary Margaret Routh, dau. of Robert William Routh and Mary Margaret Sutherland.

Bunting, James, s. of William and Penelope Carter Bunting of Nash Co., m. ca. 1829, Malany Ricks, b. ca. 1794.

Carr, Jonas Johnston b. Feb. 15, 1805; d. May 18, 1843, s. of Elias and Celia Johnston Carr, m. Sept. 20, 1832, Elizabeth Jane Hilliard b. Feb. 1. 1809, Nash Co.; d. Dec. 25, 1840.

Cherry, Theophilus m. Feb. 4, 1821, Julia Grimes, dau. of William and Talitha Grimes.

Chicken, Lewis of Halifax Co. m. Elizabeth Figures Moore, b. Jan. 7, 1803; d. Oct. 5, 1842.

Crudup, George, s. of John and Mourning Dixon Crudup of Halifax Co., N. C., m. May 3, 1761, Priscilla Thomas, dau. of Joseph and Mourning Thomas.

Crudup, Josiah, s. of John and Mourning Dixon Crudup of Halifax Co., N. C., m. Elizabeth, dau. of Elisha Battle of Edgecombe Co., progenitor of the Battle family in Edgecombe.

Eagles, Richard Tilghman m. Jan. 12, 1832, Penelope Scarborough Eason (1813-1869).

Eason, Joshua Barnes, s. of Coburn Eason and Elizabeth Barnes, dau. of Rev. Joshua Barnes of Pitt Co., m. Martha "Polly" Palmer Scarborough (1794-1812).

Fly, John b. Dec. 22, 1823; d. Mar. 8, 1874; m. Dec. 30, 1845, Winnaford Mary Powell, b. Jan. 30, 1830; d. Aug. 12, 1862.

Fountain, Cary b. 1797; d. Oct. 5, 1832, s. of Solomon and Auliff Fountain, m. Sarah McComb Power, b. Jan. 19, 1801; d. Nov. 2, 1838.

Fountain, Spencer b. Feb. 26, 1820; d. Mar. 26, 1878, s. of Cary and Sarah McComb Fountain, m. ca. 1845, Caroline Virginia Adams b. Halifax Co., N. C., July 18, 1826, dau. of George W. and Mary Jane Adams.

Gilbert, Elder Nathan b. Anson Co., N. C., Jan. 30, 1768; d. Aug. 1, 1809, Edgecombe Co.; m. July 10, 1794, Charity Ricks, dau. of James and Phebe Ricks of Edgecombe Co.

Graves, Stephen Arme Decatur, m. 1852, Sally Ann Figures Lowe, b. Aug. 25, 1825, wid. of Stephen Lowe and dau. of Sally Ann Lewis and Rev. William Lowe.

Griffin, James Haverson, s. of Thomas and Jane Griffin of Nash Co., m. Dec. 3, 1867 Martha Ann Proctor, dau. of Frederick and Celia Proctor.

Griffin, John b. ca. 1770; d. Nov. 1838; m. 1803, Susan Causey, b. 1780; d. Dec. 1, 1855.

Grimes, Thomas m. Chloe Llewelling, dau. of William and Frances Llewelling of Martin and Tyrrell Counties, N. C.

Grimes, William m. Mar. 19, 1795, Talitha Mayo, dau. of Nathan Mayo.

Hilliard, Isaac m. Apr. 20, 1765, Leah Crafford, dau. of Carter and Elizabeth Kearney Crafford, Jr. of Surry Co., Va.

Hines, Williams m. Sept. 23, 1828, Martha, dau, of John and Clara May Joyner of Pitt Co.

Horne, James J. of Pittsboro, N. C., m. Jan. 20, 1828, Cecilia Olivia Ruffin b. July 1, 1805; d. Oct. 20, 1880, dau. of Mary Johnston and Samuel Ruffin.

Hyman, Ebenezer m. Nov. 13, 1834, Temperance Jones, dau. of Asa and Lydia Grimes Jones.

Johnston, Amos, s. of Jacob (the elder) and Mary Johnston, m. Jan. 2, 1777, Darkis (Dorcas) Williams.

Johnston, Jesse m. Rebecca, dau. of Col. Exum Lewis (will prob. 1790) and moved to Tenn.

Jones, Asa m. Nov. 26, 1812, Liddia Grimes, dau. of William and Talitha Grimes.

Jordan, Gray, Sr. m. Dec. 29, 1801, Penelope Hargrove, dau. of Aaron and Unity Hargrove.

Langley, James m. July 30, 1830, Susan Petway.

Lawrence, Joshua L., s. of Rev. Joshua and Mary Knight Lawrence, m. Sept. 28, 1836, Harriett Penelope Mayo, dau. of Martha Nancy Pippen and Nathan Mayo, Jr.

Lawrence, Thomas David, s. of Rev. Joshua Lawrence, m. Mary Sherrod, dau. of John Sherrod of Martin Co.

Lee, Maj. Aaron of Maryland Heights m. 17—, Mary Williams.

Lewis, Bartholomew, s. of Col. Exum Lewis and wife Elizabeth Figures Lewis, m. Catherine Wiggins.

Lewis, Col. Exum (Revolutionary War) m. Elizabeth Figures of Southampton Co., Va.

Lewis, Exum, Jr. d. 1839, m. Ann Harrison, descendant of Benjamin Harrison of Virginia. No marriage date.

Lewis, Green d, 1814, m. Martha Patsy Wiggins, sister of Catherine Wiggins.

Lewis, Reddin Sugg b. Jan. 1, 1812, s. of James and Mary Lewis, m. Sarah Page b. Dec. 1, 1822, dau. of John and Patty Page.

Lewis, Richard Henry b. Edgecombe Co., m. (1) Mary Foreman, d. Sept. 24, 1840; (2) m. June 5, 1849, Mrs. Martha Elizabeth Haskins Foreman, wid. of John Foreman. She d. prior to 1857; (3) m. Mary Long Gordon, Apr. 16, 1890. Dr. Lewis was a resident of Raleigh, N. C.

Lowe, Exum Lewis, 1790-1834, s. of Sally Ann Lewis and Rev. William Lowe, m. 1821, Elizabeth Sessums.

Lowe, Figures b. Nov. 14, 1792; d. 1834, s. of Sally Ann Lewis and Rev. William Lowe, m. (1) Zelpha Powell, wid. of Cotten Powell, dau. of John Taylor of Martin Co. She d. 1834. (2) m. 1835, Ann Maria Crowell and moved to Mississippi.

Lowe, Stephen d. 1851, m. 1844, Sally Ann Figures Lowe b. Aug. 25, 1825, dau. of Sally Ann Lewis and Rev. William Lowe.

Mayo, James b. Edgecombe Co., Oct. 20, 1795; d. Aug. 30, 1848, Fayette Co., Tenn.; m. in Martin Co., N. C., Oct. 19, 1815, Sarah Elizabeth Melvina Dale Coakley, b. Dec. 9, 1795; d. Mar. 3, 1850, Fayette Co., Tenn.

Mayo, John Williams b. Apr. 13, 1772; d. Feb. 3, 1825. s. of Col. Nathan Mayo, m. (1) Catherine (Catey) Sherrod; (2) m. Nancy S. S. D.?, d. June 18, 1865. No date of marriage.

Mayo, Lawrence b. Sept. 30, 1793, Edgecombe Co.; d. Sept. 6, 1840, Fayette Co., Tenn.; m. Harriett Staton b. Feb. 8, 1794; d. Sept. 2, 1816, dau. of Arthur and Charlotte Staton of Edgecombe Co.

Mayo, Micajah m. (1) Bethia, dau. of John Sherrod; (2) m. Nancy, dau. of Ensign Joseph Pippen of the Revolutionary War. No dates.

Mayo, Micajah, Jr. m. Polly Watson, dau. of Jordan Watson. No dates.

Mayo, Col. Nathan m. (1) Julia Williams, dau. of John Williams of Halifax Co., N. C.; (2) m. Elizabeth Hyman, wid. of Thomas Hyman. Col. Mayo d. Mar. 14, 1811. Julia Williams Mayo d. Mar. 24, 1777.

Mercer, John b. Mar. 23, 1781; d. Mar. 27, 1864; m. Dec. 3, 1805, Nancy Routh b. Oct. 30, 1789; d. Feb. 16, 1850, dau. of William and Mary Routh.

Mills, Prof. Luther Rice of Halifax Co., Va., m. Ann Harrison Lewis, dau. of Dr. John Wesley Lewis and wife, Catherine A. Battle, 1868.

Moore, Bartholomew Figures b. Jan. 29, 1801, s. of James Moore, Jr. and Sally Ann Lewis (Lowe) Moore, m. Lucy Boddie of Nash Co.

Moore, Edwin b. Jan. 29, 1797, s. of James Moore, Jr. and Sally Ann Lewis (Lowe) Moore, m. Elizabeth Hart.

Moore, James, Jr. b. Jan. 7, 1765; d. Dec. 31, 1851, s. of James Moore, Revolutionary soldier and wife, Celah Williams of Southampton Co., Va., m. July 10, 1794, Sally Ann Lewis Lowe, wid. of Rev. William Lowe.

Moore, James b. Apr. 12, 1799; d. June 5, 1828, s. of James Moore, Jr. and Sally Ann Lewis (Lowe) Moore, m. Mahala Beckwith.

Moore, Roderick m. Mar. 5, 1829, Mary (Polly) Grimes.

Moore, Rev. Thomas of Virginia, m. Rebecca Moore b. June 17, 1795, dau. of James Moore, Jr. and Sally Ann (Lowe) Moore.

Myrick, Charles b. Apr. 18, 1767; s. of James and gr. s. of Moses Myrick, who moved to Granville Co. from Edgecombe; m. Dec. 2, 1792, Martha ———, b. Sept. 5, 1769.

Myrick, John C., 1824-1880, m. Nov. 19, 1852, Sarah R. Nicholson, d. Jan. 14, 1904.

Parker, Weeks m. Nov. 15, 1807, Sabra Hearn Cooke, wid. of James Maxwell Cooke.

Petway, (Pettaway) Micajah d. Apr. 12, 1849, age 92; m. (1) Mary Sugg, dau. of Lemuel Sugg (1749-1780) and wife, Mary Davis (1749-1824); (2) m. Elizabeth Skinner, wid. of William Skinner.

Petway, (Pettaway) William b. Oct. 1, 1799; d. Oct. 18, 1854; m. Cinderella Cromwell b. 1800, dau. of Elisha and Elizabeth Sutherland Cromwell.

Philips, James Jones m. Harriet Amanda Burt, dau. of William Burt of Nash Co., Apr. 23, 1834.

Pippen, Joseph John b. Sept. 1, 1796; d. Oct. 24, 1853, s. of Ensign Joseph Pippen of the Revolutionary War, m. Talitha Mayo b. July 11, 1790; d. Sept. 1, 1866, dau. of Micajah and Bithia Sherrod Mayo.

Pippen, Kinchen m. Nancy Knight and moved to Gibson Co., Tennessee.

Pippen, Nathan K. b. Apr. 9, 1842; d. Sept. 7, 1901, s. of Joseph John and Talitha Mayo Pippen, m. Feb. 14, 1867, Carrie E. Hyman, dau. of Ebenezer and Temperance Jones Hyman.

Powell, Jesse Harrison, s. of William H. and Mary Harrison Powell, m. Sally Hester Ann Moore b. Sept. 19, 1810, d. July 31, 1836.

Pullen, Blake Baker, s. of Lemuel and Phoebey Anderson Pullen, m. Nov. 7, 1865, Frances Sugg Bulluck, dau. of David William and Mary Margaret Routh Bulluck.

Ray, John m. Elizabeth, dau. of Col. Exum Lewis (will prob. 1790) and moved to Ft. Sterling, Ky.

Ricks, Isaac, 1702-1760, s. of Isaac and Sarah Ricks, m. Sarah Burke. No date.

Ricks, William b. 1750; d. June 10, 1832; m. Lydia Brantley b. 1760; d. July 18, 1835. He was a Revolutionary soldier, and was in Battle of Guilford Court House, Mar. 15, 1781, as was his brother, Lewis Ricks, (b. 1741).

Routh, Robert William, s. of William Routh and Mary Wilkins, m. Sept. 20, 1820, Frances Sutherland Sugg, dau. of Reddin Sugg and Mary Margaret Sutherland.

Routh, William d. 1808, m. Mary Wilkins, dau. of William Wilkins and Nancy Mercer, who was dau. of John Mercer, Jr. and wife, Mary Poyner.

Ruffin, Samuel b. Dec. 4, 1773, Northampton Co., N. C.; d. Edgecombe Co., May 17, 1826, s. of John Ruffin and Milisent, m. Sept. 18, 1794, Mary Johnston b. Dec. 30, 1777; d. Feb. 12, 1857, dau. of Col. Jonas and Esther Maund Johnston.

Ruffin, William Johnston b. May 19, 1797; d. Sept 21, 1826; m. Jan. 15, 1824, Felicia Little, d. Sept. 25, 1824; m. (2) Nov. 23, 1826, Martha Fleetwood.

Scarborough, David b. 1720; d. Edgecombe Co., 1744; m. in Virginia ca. 1745, Sarah Dunn b. ca. 1728, dau. of John Dunn, Sr., (b. ca. 1700-1771) and Esther (Easter) Kinsey (b. ca. 1713).

Scarborough, Maj. James (Revolutionary War) b. Nov. 28, 1748 in Southampton Co., Va.; m. (1) name unknown; m. (2) Grace Clark, dau. of Henry and Frances Clark;

m. (3) 1793, Penelope Palmer Eason, b. May 26, 1749; d. Oct. 16, 1832, wid. of Obed Eason; m. (4) Nov. 26, 1823, Martha Tart Eason, wid. of Abner Eason (d. 1819).

Speight, Dr. Richard H. m. (1) Jan. 25, 1871, Margaret (Maggie) A. Powell, m. (2) Margaret Whitfield.

Spicer, Moses b. Mar. 6, 1778; d. Jan. 28, 1838; m. June 18, 1813, Delilah Calhoun b. Feb. 17, 1797, dau. of Etheldred and Pharabe Calhoun.

Stallings, James Craig b. 1793, m. Jan. 5, 1829, Mary Peele, b. 1806, dau. of Hilary Peele; m. (2) Sarah Elizabeth Wiggins, b. Mar. 21, 1833; d. May 12, 1917, dau. of William Lawrence Wiggins.

Starke, Dr. Lucien Douglas m. Jan. 8, 1868, Talitha Lucretia Lavinia Pippen.

Sugg, Lemuel m. 17——, Elizabeth Cromwell.

Sugg, Reddin, s. of Lemuel and Elizabeth Cromwell Sugg, m. Jan. 9, 1803, Mary Margaret Sutherland, dau. of Daniel Sutherland and Mary McDowell.

Taylor, Kinchen, s. of Ford and Elizabeth Horne Taylor, m. Aug. 4, 1853, Sarah Lane, dau. of Lemmon and Nancy Cornell Lane.

Thomas, Micajah b. Feb. 13, 1725; d. Nov. or Dec. 14, 1769; m. (1) Apr. 11, 1751, Elizabeth Veal; m. (2) Oct. 9, 1753, Mourning Dixon Crudup b. Nov. 10, 1722; d. Jan. 29, 1781, wid. of John Crudup and dau. of Penelope and Thomas Dixon of Isle of Wight Co., Va.

Thomas, Micajah, Jr. m. Jan. 7, 1778, Anne Hawkins.

Thomas, William Howell, s. of Hilliard and Zilpha Woodard Thomas, m. Dec. 24, 1865, Mary Jane Woodard.

Tyson, William d. Dec. 12, 1827, m. Nov. 9, 1824, Esther Johnston Ruffin b. Feb. 16, 1803, d. Aug. 14, 1843, dau. of Mary Johnston and Samuel Ruffin.

Weathersbee, Joseph m. Apr. 25, 1849, Sally Purvis Bowers, wid. of James Bowers.

Williams, Dr. Robert T. of Pitt Co. m. 1804, Elizabeth Ellis, gr. dau. of Peter Hines.

Woodard, David b. May 10, 1771; d. Aug. 13, 1799, s. of Elisha and Mary Woodard, m. Feb. 1793, Elizabeth Bullock (1776-1805), dau. of John and Sarah Bullock.

Woodard, James Bullock, b. Sept. 4, 1793; d. July 2, 1863; m. (1) Nov. 7, 1822, Nancy Daniel, b. Dec. 4, 1792; d. Dec. 1, 1825; m. (2) Mar. 20, 1827, Sally Peele, b. May 23, 1800; d. Oct. 19, 1837; dau. of John and Elizabeth Peele.

ERRATA

- A -

Alsobrook, Parthenia 234, Rhoda 234
Amason, Milicent 236, Prisc. 236, Thos. 236 (2)
Amis, Jim 3
Atkinson, Aaron 234, Nancy 234
Avent, T. W. 6

- B -

Barlow, David 121
Barnes, Jacob 236, Jesse 9, Prisc. 236
Benton, Absalom 235, Christian 235
Bolton, Eliz. 237, Fannie 237, Rich. 237, Talitha 237
Bradley, Char. 235, David 235, Jonathan 95
Battle, Sarah 278
Batts, Meedy 8
Brownrigg, Obedience 234-238 (2), Peninah 234
Bryant, Delilah 237, Evin 237
Burras, Jas. 26
Bynum, Jos. 236, Nancy 236

- C -

Calhoun, Pharabe 237, Sally 237
Carter, Kindred 235, Penelope 235
Chapman, Norvell 237
Cherry, Obediah 54
Coffied, Prisc. 234, West 234
Crisp, Eliz. 235, Lyda 234, Sam. 234-235-236, Sarah 236
Culpepper, Benj. 235, Rahab 235
Curl, Caty 236, Charity 237, Sarah 236-237
Cutchin, T. H. 176

- D -

Dancy, Lucy 236, Sarah 236
Davis, Ann 236, John 236

Digges, Robt. 237, Sarah 237
Dixon, Coffield 237 Eliz. 237

- E -

Exum, Eliz. 236, John 236
Edwards, Nancy 237, Silar 237
Everitt, Milly 234, Silas 234

- F -

Farmer, Beedy 235, Benj. 235, Braswell 235
Flora, Gray 48
Fort, Geo. 237, Sarah 237
Fountain, Henry 236, Sally 236,

- G -

Gardner, Geo. 237 Zyphy 237
Garner, John 238, Sarah 238
Garvey, Jas. 133
Goodson, Oleof 235, Thos. 235
Grimes, Talitha 215

- H -

Hall, Dolly 237, Thos. 237
Harrell, Asa 69
Hart, Frank 6
Higgs, Sally 235,
Hobbs, Mary 236, Nancy 236
Horn, Dicey 234, Ml. 234, Patience 237, Ruth 237
Howard, Prudence 251
Hyett, Eliz. 237, Thos. 237,

- J -

Johnson, Nancy 236, Nathan 236
Johnston, Amos 236, Esther 236, Henry 234
Jones, Francis 237, Jas. 69, Judith 237
Joyner, Drew 89

- L -

Lancaster, L. 92

Land, Chas. 234-235, Fannie 235, Polly 234
Lawrence, John 95
Lee, Jas. 236, Winny 236,
Leggett, Isabella 235, Levin 235 (2), Nicey 235, Noah 235, Pamelia 235, Temp. 235
Lenoir, Ann 234, Leah 235, Thos 234-235
Lester, Moses 234
Lewis, Ann 235, Eliz. 235, Exum 235, Jas. 234, Sally 234
Linch, Olive, Sr. 233
Long, H. 99

- M -

Mayo, J. 105,
Mears, Willie 106

- P -

Pender, Josiah 120, L. C. 120
Perry, B. L. 121
Pitt, Jas. 56

- R -

Reid, Willis 133
Robbins, Wm. 89
Roberson, Joshua 92

- S -

Sugg, Dr. Pheasanton S. 242

- T -

Talbert, Tarq. 115,
Tyler, Lorenza 177

- W -

Weaver, Eliza 195
Williford, Harmon 176
Winborne, Jos. 177

INDEX

- A -

Abington, Hardiman 253
Abrams, Sally 33
Adams, Clara 255, Caroline 295, Clary 134, Geo. 295, Hopewell 231, Jas. 193-215-224, Jane 231, Lucretia 84, Lurana 67, Mariah 224, Martha 118, Mary 295, Nancy 38-41-263, Peggy 193, Sally 215-233, Wm. Sr. 260
Adkinson, Lucy 56
Alford, Lacy 259, Lucy 98-253, Mahala A. 139
Allen, Eliz. 27-136-206, Jane 156, Jean 16, Nancy 246, Roger 206, Sally 61
Alsbrook, Alsobrook, Ann 59, Eliza 99, Lotty 146, Maple 105, Mary 43-257, Milissa 79, Ml. 257, Parthenia 211, Priscilla 141, Prissy 211, Sarah C. 68, Susa. 110,

Alston, Eliz. 289, John 290, Mary 290, Wm. 289-290
Amason, Amerson, Aailsey (Elsie) 84, Aday 200, Alice 193, Ann 228, Benj. 283, Charity 135, Christian 212, Eliz. 32-195, Ellendor 233, Jemima 194, Martha 190, Nancy 146, Obediance 190, Patience 191, Sarah 14-53-62-168-207, Temp. 144-283, Thos. 207-212-228, Wm. 190-191-193-194-195-200,
Amey, Lewsey 14
Amis, Jim 3
Anderson, Absala 16-233, Amanda 173, Cath. 126, Eliz. 166, Evelina 180, Joshua 243-252, Lewesa 121, Lucy 125, Marg. 63-100-102-176, Martha 66-176-229, Mary 96-164-169-186, Mourning 87, Nancy 45, Pennina 152, Phoebey 298, Rachel 63, Sally 122-154, Susan 39, Susie B. 288, Tempy 14, Wm. 229-233
Andre, Polly 61

Andrews, Amy 288, C. C. 4, Clary 49, Cullen 266-267-270, Eliz. 18-266, Jane 265-270-289, Jesse 266-267, John 189-266, 271, Louisa 181, Marg. 160, Martha 98-152, Mary B. 267-Nancy 77-153, Sally 34, Spicy 122, Susan A. 16, Wm. 244-288-289
Ansley, Jos. 192, Sophia 192
Anthony, Caroline 84
Applewhite, Ann 266, Eliz. 7, Sarah 93
Armstrong, Ann 162-173, Cilla 17, Cinda 182, Delha 92, Eliz. 271, Gray 262-271, Jos. 271, Leah 130, Lucinda 30, Maomi 109, Marg. 28, Martha 41, Mary 11-271, Robt. 271, Susan 94. Vickie 181
Arrington, Arthur 243-254, 293, Jos. 293, Mary 170
Atkins, Lucy 18, Nancy 141, Phebe 292
Atkinson, Aaron 273, Avith 156, Eliz. 101-267, Henrietta 43, John 254-293, Lucy 125, Mary 21-182-219-273, Rebecca 124, Rhoda 21, Sarah 166, Willie 252
Austin, Cath. 34-198-260, Eliz. 186, Henry 190-198-254-260, Lydia 217, Martha 42-243-254, Mary 104-217
Avent, T. W. 6
Avery, Clary 103
Averitt, Claracy 217, Edah 192, Eleanor 217, Elsie 196, Jas. 192-196-207-217-228, Lavinia 228, Luvyce 228, Sally 207

- B -

Bailey, Delilah 173, Jonathan 189-195-217, Martha 2-169-181-188-189, Mary 292, Rebecca 174-217, Sally 88
Baines, Chas. 259
Baker, Ann 233, Cath. 5, Cherry 105, David 256, Drucella 160, Eliz. 99-108, Laura 41, Marg. 102, Martha 54-95-163-

252, Mary 10-63-124-230, Moses 230-233-252, Nancy 49, Neomi 4, Penelope 49, Wm. 254
Ballard, Mary 265
Bandy, Sarah 215, Susan 215
Banks, Martha 159, T. 242-251
Bardin, Arthur 275, Nancy 275, Sally 123
Barefoot, Eliz. 276, John 286, Rhoda 286
Barfield, Ann 46, Cath. 140-191-257, Chas. 189, Char. 60, Felitha 45, Jas. 191, Louiza 38, Martha H. 29, Mary 14-36-70-102-259, Nancy 83, Tabitha A. 46, Venah 189
Barkley, Polly 165
Barksdale, Cleo. 208, Dan. 194 (3)- 208, Eliz. 194
Barlow, Annie E. 57, David 121-256, Delah 121-184, Lewis 214, Louisa 214, Lucy 294, M. L. 102, Sarah 99
Barnes, Abashay 92, Amy 77, Annie 158, Arch. 231-284, Aziel 228, Beedy 179, Betsy 168, Britton (2) 223, Bryan 199, Burrill 252-286, Celia 112, Chas. 188, Charity 227, Christian 276, Demp. 189-193-200-275-283, Diana 283, Edie 25, Edith 275, Ed. 188-205-216-227 (2), Edwin 283, Elenora 134 (2), Elias 253, Elislina 49, Eliza 135, Eliz. 2-11-19-41-52-166-168-189-190-192-201-203-205-216-223-275-276-277-286-294, Eveline 59, Fran. 66, Harriett 38-271, Jas. 190-195 (2)-200-213-273-274-287-294, Jesse 9-205-263-277-293, Jilly 143, John 254-276-277 (2)-278, Jos. 201-211-225-294, Rev. Joshua 203-276-294, Judea 198, Julan 192-195, Julia 161, Lucy 223, M. 2, Martha 25-30-142-159-196-274, Mary 17-43-67-68-88-

178-188-195 (3)-199-206-227-232-273-278-287, Merica 87, Mourning 18-205, Nancy 7-27-159-174-201-205-211-252-277, Nannie 196, Nathan 196-200, Nelly 131, Obedience 38, Peggy 231, Peninah 41-135, Penny 39-142-201- Polly 72-205-208-213-225-277, Priscilla 174, Rebecca 108, Sally 2-9-36-37-161-200-211-231, Sarah 153-188-193-196-198-200-205-213-228-246-263-284-293, Sucky 231, Susanna 157-200-231, Tabitha 210-278, Temp. 33-143-213, Teresa 9-205, Thos. 232, Treacy 26-52-135, Wm. 256, Williamson 210-278, Wright 246-263, Zilpha 165-190-277

Barnhill, Liza 34, Polly 80
Barrett, Priscilla 81
Barron, Cath. 168, Elsa 89, Jane 168, Patsey 26, Sally 164
Barrow, Anna 206, Mary 50, Priscilla 289, Wm. 206
Bartee, Charity 84, Elvy 31-250
Barter, Chacy 58
Bass, Turner 242, Winney 11
Batchelor, Dan. 260, Julia 176
Bateman, Dorcas 2, Martha 36, Sally 55
Bath, Chasy 45
Batly, Wm. 260
Battle, A. J. 253, Alford 269, Amelia 265, Amos 243-268, Amy 192, Ann 267, Arabella 244, Bettie 121, Cath. 243- 252-268-297, Charity 267, Cornelia 36-246-263, Davis 266, Delah 31, Demp. 264-270, Dossey 268, Dorsey 255, Elisha 200-264-265-266-267-278-294, Elisha II 267, Eliz. 35-200-264-266-267-270-294, Helene 268, Isaac 267 Jacob 270, Jas. 263-269, Dr. Jas. 248-270, James S. 241-249-265-268-270, Jesse 264, Jethro 264-265-268-269, Joel 252-265-267-268, John 192-264 (3)-266, Jos. 270, Josiah D.

266, Julia 270, Kemp 248-265, Laura 265-268, Louisa 80-133, Mariah 171, Martha 12-248-264-265, Mary 11-36-127-159-248-249-264-266-269, Nancy 56, Orren 270, Peggy 12, Penelope 34-265-270, Phillis 32, Polly 239, Prisc. 264, Rich. 268, Sarah 264, 265, 266, 267-278, Temp. 107-265-270, Turner 264, Wm. 241-264-265-267-270, Wm. S. 247-264-269
Batts, Bashaby - 176, David 272, Eliza 242-251, Eliz. 46-171-277, Elvina 159-281, Emily 29-89, Esther 160, Hasty 25, John 281, Jos. 281, Isaac 280, Keziah 111, Lucy 216, Mahala 183, Marg. 149, Martha 56-158, Mary 52 (2)-100-247-277-281, Meedy 8, Mildred 216-280, Peninah 58-176, Phereby 292, Polly 89, Rebecca 31, S. A. 14, Sally 55-272, Sarah 170, Scyntha 59, Temp. 89, Wm. 277, Zilphy 46
Baxter, Pamelia 110
Beacham, Winney 101
Brake, Pennina 30
Beaton, Peggy 245
Beckwith, Mahala 297
Beckworth, Sarah 166
Bedford, Emily 160, Frances 115, Marg. 31-254, Winny 77
Beel, Laura 2
Beeman, Harriett 62, Mary 109
Beland, Beeland, Bealand, Eliz. 112, Lydia 88, Mahala 160-170, Pressy 138
Belcher, Beverly 221, Cornelia 148. Eliz. 33-149, Henry 263, Lewis 262, Martha 144-221, Mary 30-51, Robt. 258
Bell, Absala 216, Agnes 288, Amandy 149, Amelia 46, Ann 289, Bennett 255, Caroline 144, Chordy 87, David 260, Eliza 71-253-255, Eliz. 14- 15-131-193-194-205-271, Emeliza 137-255, Emily 29-243-253-197, Eugenia 218-257, Geo. 205, Fred. 192-193-196 (2)-197-

200-215-218-253-257-261, Henry 258, Iley 43, Jos. 251-255, Joshua 202-216, Julia 14-261, Lizzie 52, Lorenzo 261, Lucy 118- 196, Marg. 8- 19-73-209-245-258, Marmaduke 193, Martha 93- 127, Mary 18-23-28-149-224- 242-251-268, Nancy 200, Patsey 56, Phereby 202-215, Polly 196, Rich. 258, Robt. 288, Sally 64-200, Sarah 71- 190-289, Titia 53, Winnifred 209, Winny 208, Whilmel 208-253, Wm. 261-224.
Bellamy, Alex. 253, Caroline 91, Delha 169, Eliz. 214, Laura 105, Lucy 50, Rachel 14, Sally 119, Wm. 214
Benbow, Ann 283, John 283
Bennett, Mark 282, Mary 294, Rev. Phileman 259, Stephen 253, Susan 124-282
Benson, Eliz. 252, Sarah 78, Thos. 255
Bentley, Clary 189-225, Eliz. 274, Joshua 189-193-232, Martha 193, 225-232, Wm. 274
Benton, Charity 91-198-220, Christian 169-229, Evelina 15, Jerusha 221, Jethro 221-229, Marg. 24, Peggy 257, Polly 198, Susanna 51
Berry (Deberry?), Delitha D. 77
Best, Amey 96, Betsey 78, Eliz. 78, Gilly Ann 153, Hannah 123, Julia 76-253, Lucinda 106-255, Margilly 131, Mary 36-79, Nancy 64-75-257, Sally 35-154
Betts, Eleanor 268, Capt. Wm. 268
Biell, Thos. 288
Biggs, Bethelda P. 6, Eliz. 1- 253, Jas. 253 (3), Lovinah 18, Martha C. 34
Bignall, Ann 228, Robt. 228
Bilbry, Bilberry, Bellberry, Eliz. 121, Emily 85, Fran. 214, Jas. 243-254, Marg. 17, Mary 194 Nath. 194-214, Penny 143, Susan 152
Billups, Emily 94-201, Isabel 201, Martha A. 138, Sally 114, Wm. 255

302

Bird, Rachel 21
Bishop, Lydia 116, Mary, 102-241-250, Nancy 27, Sarah, 79
Blackburn, Absala 65, Barbarry 76
Blackledge, Louisa 193-209
Blakely, Thos. 242
Bland, Mary 183, Tempey 113
Blocker, John 246, 261
Bloodworth, Betsey 210, Wm. 210
Blount, Ann 209, Levi 16-260, Louisa 193, Martha 125, Mary 218, Susan 127, Wm. 218
Boddie, Geo. 193, Lucy 297, Nathan 294, Wm. 294
Bolton, Eliz. 233, Elsie 199, Rich. 233, Sally 114
Bond, Emily 106-243, Harriett 74, Julia 4, Lewis 255, Mary 138
Bonner, Clarecey 142, Louisa 293
Boone, Boon, Cath. 81, Charity 138, Jas. 44, Lawr. 263, Mary 4-81, Matilda 114, Peggy 60, Rebecca 85, Rosa 127, Sally 11-130, Temp. 172
Boothe, Booth, Anne 157, Dorothy 285, Eliz. 74, Jas. 192-221, Lavina 90, Lavinia 256, Mary 122, Nancy 122-221, Patience 58, Sally 252, Sarah, 142-192
Bottom, Viney 120-155
Bowdin, Mary 294
Bowers, James 294-299
Boxwell, Wilmouth 242
Boyd, Lucy 244
Boykin, Eliz. 152, Mary 201, Sally 253, Sarah 15, Viney 26
Boyt, Betsey 178, Patrick 252, Wealthy 141
Bozeman, Boazman, Boseman, Cathalina 115, Clarky 78, Harriot 99, Mary 63, Orpy 61, Polly 154, Sarah 104
Braddy, Hepsabah 217, Jos. 188-215-217, Julia 261, Louise 90, Maria 144, Mary 75-188, Rebecca 102, Sukey 215
Bradford, Mary 291, Nath. 291
Bradley, Bradly, Agy 194, Alex 256, Annie H. 15, Benj. 294, Bennett 251, Bethhelder 19, Cath. 3-243-252, Delphia 1, Dicey 20, Elias 258,
Eliz. 19-41-73 (2), Ellen 128, Henrietta 70, Honor 32, John 221, Jonathan 95, Julia 246, Juliana 54, Littleberry 256, Louisa 45-90- 116, Lucinda 107, Lucy 120-257, Malissa 119, Marg. 57, Martha 18-95-96-136-181-183, Mary 18-41-56-64, Nancy 186, Netty 68, Peggy 36, Polly 54, Sarah 221, Susan 19, Sylvester 147, Tabitha 71, Willie 242-251, Willis 258, Winifred 19, Zilphy 93
Brady, Martha 140, Mary 241-250, Tempy 119
Brake, Barsheba 161, Eliza 24, Emeliza 17, Jacob 212, Louisiana 106, Lucinda 119, Marg. 5-64, Martha 3-294, Mary 57-144, Matilda 119, Patience 198, Peninah 198, Phebe 133, Polly 134, Winnifred 212
Brand, Sally T. 19
Brann, Polly 112
Brantley, Celia 105, Lydia 298, Sally 44
Braswell, Anna 294, Arretta 42, Benj. 226, (2), Bythal 211-221, Crissy 197, Cynthanetta 92, Dellah 20, Dilla 83, Eliz. 5-81-99- 182, Fran. 127, Fredrica A. 115, Harriett 13-170, Isaac 292, Jacky 119-221, Jacob 258-294, Jas. 197-229- 283, Julia 172-286, Lavinia 1, Louisa 1- 135, Louisiana 13, Lucinda 183-232, Mahala 7, Marg. 31, Maria 40, Martha 92-138, Mary 27-36-64, Milly 35-226, Nancy 38-129, 168, Olive 229, Peninah 167, Phenetta 130, Phereby 283, Polly 197, Rebecca 153, Rhoda 72-245-258, Sarah 98-101-158-174-197, Selah 226, Serena 159, Sol. 274, Sophy 37, Susan 260, Temp. 79-99, Willie 252, Winney 20-274-292, Wm. 271-294, Zany 1-164, Zadock 232, Zilpha 48
Bridgers, Amanda 157-254, Eliz. 15-78-115-120-281, Hester 168, Col. John 249, Mary 9-173, Susan 144-246-261, Wm. 281
Brinkley, Abraham 200-216, Barsheba 161-200, Betsey 75, Eliz. 106, Gilly 22, Mary 175, Nanny 167, Sally 216, Sarah 98
Britt, Eliz. 119, Martha 83, Rachel 23, Sally 261
Brooks, Judith 178
Brown, Anna 274, Anne 122, Celia 134, Eliz. 133-145-185-204, Ellen 154, Gray 294, Jas. 197, John 204-223-260-264, Lidia 289, Little Berry 294, Louisa 17, Louisiana 142, Lucy 69, Lunsford 256, Nathan 289, Patience 223, Patsey 156-256, Penelope 133, Rebecca 25, Rachel 286, Sarah 197-264, Susan 260, Talitha 89, Wm. 245- 257
Brownrigg, George 273, Mary, 226, Obedience 180-203-226, Polly 240
Bruce, Alice 290, Ann 290, Eliz. 213, Geo. 213-216, Martha 17, Peter 289-290, Sarah 216-289
Bryan, Amy 57, Arthur 292-293, Battle 248, Catey 219, Cath. 75, David 294, Demp. 192-218-223-254-255, Drewry 217-260, Elias 222, Eliza 57, Eliz. 24-199-222-294, Emeliza 24, Harriet 97, Henry 251, Hugh 247, Maj. J. C. 249, John 218-293, Lucy 12-192, Marg. 95, Martha 126-223-254, Mary 25-51-106-196-244-254-255, Nancy 24, Penelope 217, Penny 260, Pheriby 218, Rebecca 140, Rosa 196, Sally 24-91, Sarah 71-247, Smith 219, Susan 165, Thos. 199, Wm. 245-257-292-293
Bryant, Edah 214, Edith 280, Evan 199-213, Faithful 198-213, Gayle 195-214-280, Nancy 118-213, Polly 198, Prisc. 42, Sally 77, Sarah 195

Bullard, Obedience 160
Bulluck, Bullock, David
 208-213-226-262- 294-
 298, Eliz. 200-213- 286-
 299, Fran. 298, John
 286-299, Jonathan 294,
 Len 290, Lucinda 83,
 Lucy 130, Martha 163,
 Mary 20-90-148-208-
 298, Nancy 63, Narcissa
 280, Polly 252, Pru-
 dence 83, Sarah 226-
 299
Bumpass, Nancy 7.
Bunn, Benj. 267, John
 196, Mary 26, Red-
 mund 254, Sarah 267,
 Susan 256
Bunting, Fran. 294, Jas.
 294, Polly 30, Wm. 294
Burgess, Eliz. 161, Celia
 66
Burke, Harmon 246-261,
 Sarah 298
Burn, Ml. 196
Burnet, Bathsheba 292,
 Wm. 259
Burras, Gilliana 53, Jas.
 26, Mary 168, Sally
 117, Sarah 117, Thos
 26, Winnifred 34
Burt, Eliza 244, Harriet
 244-298, Wm. 298
Burton, Conway 248
Butler, Jacky 4, Mary 66
Bynum, Benj. 281, Cath.
 182, Eliz. 70, Fannie
 272, Fran. 281, Gid.
 272-274, Joe 257, Jos.
 189, Julia A 37, Marg.
 274, Mary 68, Matilda
 10-34- 272, Nancy 142-
 173-245-257-263, Rachel
 129, Sally 189, Sam.
 189, Sarah 4, Tabitha
 105, Temp. 82, Turner
 272
Byrum, Charity 7, Matilda
 2, Winefred 46

- C -

Cade, Agnes 95
Cadett, Rebecca 139
Cain, Cane, Eliz. 55,
 Ruth 49
Calhoun, Cahoon,
 Cohoon, Andrew 258,
 Ann 85, Eliz. 58,
 Etheldred 284-299,
 Delilah 284-299,
 Lamon 293, Mary 177-
 274, Dr. P. A. R. C.
 261, Pherabe 214-299,
 Piety 84-214, Sally
 287, Simon 274-287,
 Treasey 274, Wm. 274
Campbell, Israel 290,
 Susa. 290

Canady, Eliz. 182,
 Talitha 141
Capell, "Jack" 270,
 Mary 270
Carnal, Charity 289
Carlisle, Ann 109,
 Edeah 227, Eliz. 194,
 Mary 2, Nancy 225,
 Polly 193, Rebecca
 212, Robt. 193-212-
 225-227, Sarah 190 (2)-
 194
Carney, Martha 252,
 Mary 82, Rutha 109-
 261, Sarah 199
Carr, Celia 194, Elias
 294, Esther 194,
 Jackey 164, Jonas
 294, Lucilla 129-243,
 Lucinda 69, Martha
 134, Sally 125, Wm.
 248, Winifred 45
Carson, Nancy 34,
 Dr. Sam. 262
Carstarphen, Sarah 121-
 245-257
Carter, Amelia 72, Ann
 11, Charity 215,
 Kindred 215 (2)-231,
 Mahala 87, Martha 161,
 Mary 15, Milly 51,
 Penelope 294, Peninah
 27, Prisc. 215, Winni-
 fred 231
Cartwright, John 197,
 Mary 197
Causey, Eliza 152,
 Marg. 5, Mary 122 (2),
 Rachel 46, Sallie 39,
 Susan 295
Charles, Francis 249
Cherry, Aaron 213, Cado
 242, Celia 11, Delia
 164, Fannie 54, Fran.
 27, Eason 259, Eliz.
 121-217, Henrietta 35,
 Josephine 62, Liddy
 229, Lunsford 255-
 261, Marg. 23-259,
 Martha 101-225-246-
 261, Mary 32-62-183,
 Obediah 54, Renny 76-
 180-254, Sabra 27,
 Sally 30-59-159, Sarah
 213, Sol 217-225-229,
 Theo. 294, Thos.
 243- 253
Cheshire, Rev. Jos.
 246-262
Chesson, Jane 86
Chicken, Lewis 294
Chilton, Edney 73,
 Harriet 77
Circey, Fannie 186
Clark, Agnes 204, Ann
 162-230, Delilah 220,
 Eliz. 22, Fran. 224-
 298, Grace 227-298,
 Henry 220-224-227-
 233-298, Jas. 198-239-
 263, Jean 199, Laura
 33-198-244-255, Lucy
 64-154-183-256, Rev.
 Martin 267, Mary 158-
 168-202-246-263, Re-
 becca 20, Robt. 199-
 202-204-230-233, Sam.
 267, Sukey 138, Susan
 82, Wm. 256
Clinton, Jas. 262
Cloman, Eliz. 149-251
Cobb, Armitta 149, Cath.
 124-165, Delphia A.
 47, Ed. 218-231, Eliza
 164, Eliz. 90-93-112-
 179, Ellender 49,
 Emily 142, Fannie 185-
 218, Fran. 93, Gatsey
 47, Jas. 250, John 198-
 199, Judia 123, Louisa
 198-257, Lucinda 34-
 138, Lydia 98-294,
 Marg. 44, Maria 122,
 Martha 156, Mary E.
 26, Matilda 40, May
 164, Milly 40, Patience
 281, Polly 89, Sally
 179-23-168-231,
 Stephen 281, Zella 41
Cockburn, Eliz. 149,
 Maria 155, Winnifred
 119
Coffield, Ann 86-213,
 Benj. 213-258, David
 199, Eliz. 33-199-204-
 247, Martha 172, Nancy
 15, Polly 223, Prisc.
 56, Sarah 15, Thos. 223
Coggin, John 254
Coggins, Holly 175
Coker, Abigail 127, Ann
 196-228, Annis 217,
 Caleb 196-220-229-
 233, Eliz. 229, Fran.
 233, Jas. 212-217-219-
 220-221-228, Lazina
 122, Mary 220, Mollie
 212, Rebecca 109-219-
 Sarah 220, Selah 221,
 Wm. 259
Coleman, Evelina 52,
 Prissy 10, Sarah 27
Coletrain, Eliz. 134
Collin, Martha 158
Colwell, Sarah 38,
Cone, Patsey 8-242-251
Connell, Anne 290, Jane
 196, Michael 290,
 Thos. 196
Conner, Eliz. 143
Cook, Cooke, Camilla
 161, Clemmy 83, Jas.
 297, Mrs. 239, Sabra
 268
Coppedge, Char. 276
Corbett, Auzy 86, Eliz.
 178, Fannie 71,
 Nancy 86, Sally 132,
 Tamsey 179, Thaney
 132, Winnifred 82

Corlew, Eliz. 290, Mary 290, John 290
Cotten, Cotton, Abba 27, Abselle 33, Alex. 201-258, Arthur 251, Dellah 108, Eliza 252-254, Eliza. 90-144-223, Emily 14-258, Fred. 223-247, Henry 239, Jane 97-245, John 204-244-255-258-266-281, June 257, Martha 14, Mary 57-201, Nancy 113-273-281-294, Randolph 201-223, Spencer 254, Sue 269
Council, Char. 197, Chas. 194-197, Eliz. 194, Nancy 172, Josiah 259
Cowell, Druscilla 121
Cox, Jemimah 191, Jos. 191-211, Lurana 151, Nancy 191, Polly 211, Saunders 277, Selah 290, Temp. 277, Wm. 290
Crafford, Carter 295, Leah 295
Creekman, Eliz. 260
Crenshaw, Wm. 260
Crews, Harriet 292
Crisp, Betsey 178, Celia 46, Cinderella 45,, Eleanor 193, Eliza 65, Eliz. 65, Ezekiel 257, Fanny 220, Jennett 34, Jesse, Sr. 193, Lucinda 140, Lydia 89, Martha 113, Mary 25-220, Nancy 34-147-193, Patsy 220, Rebecca 71, Sally 85, Sam., Sr. 220 (2), Sarah 185, Susan 76-83
Crocker, Drewry 222, Milly 222
Cromwell, Alex. 190-194-210-216-217, Cinderella 222-297, Comfort 216, Elisha 262-297, Eliz. 214-218-222-231-299, Laurina 156, Marg. 34, Martha 48-91-204-214-257, Mrs. Martha 263, Mary 102-210-218, Patrick 250, Providence 217, Sally 16, Sarah 190, Venetia 194
Crowell, Ann 296
Cross, Eliz. 137, Hansel 260
Crudup, Chloe 266-267-294, Eliz. 267, Geo. 294, Mary 134-267, Mourning 285, John 285-294-299, Jos. 266,

Josiah 266-267-294
Crumply (Crumpler), Leyan 293
Cull, Jas. 268, Virginia 248-268
Culpepper, Benj. 217, Eliz. 171, Martha 217
Cummings, Sishy 29
Curle, Curl, Charity 286, Martha 64, Mourning 167, Nancy 100, Polly 176, Sally 104, Willis 286
Cutchin, Cutchins, Cutchen, Ann 248, Eliz. 21, Hannah 45, Letha 118, Lois 166-255, Louisa 48, Marg. 19-176-186, Martha 57-169, Mary 107-158-171-Routh 141, Sally 130, Sarah 84, Talitha 76, T. H. 176, Thos. 258,

- D -

Daffin, Mary 153
Dancy, Delha 56-205-245-258, Eliz. 12-192-211-247, Francis 192-205-269, Indiana 36, John 246-248-260-263, Mary 81-91-95-212-255-269, Martha 16, M. E. 185, Rebecca 32, Wm. 211-212-248-269
Daniel, A, E. 23, Ann 156, Asa 191, Delana 17-194, Dorcas 279, Eliza 11, Eliz. 277-282, Eugenia 149, Gatsey 149, Hulda 41, Jos. 264, Judith 191-194-214, Julian 286, Lavinia 264, Lem. 213-228-280-286-287, Mahala 277, Makala·53, Mary 23-213-280, Nancy 172-178-287-299, Sally 9-110, Sarah 191, Simon 279, Temp. 88-214, Tresey 228
Darden, Julia 277, Matilda 58
Daughtridge, Blanchy 109
Daughtry, Daughtis, Daughtery, Ada 233, Amanda 47, Barsheba 82, Demp. 190-221-224, Eliz. 210-221-228- (2)-233, Louisiana 138, Mary 64-206-210-224, Prisc. 37, Sam. 206, Susa. 190
Davenport, Claudia 84
Daves, Stephen, 263
Davis, Delilah 207, Diana 211, Dicey 190, Eliz. 202-275-283,

Emory 197-202-204-207-225-226-230, Eveline 37, Fran. 266, Jane 59, John 190-206-211-220-227, Jos. 283, Keziah 150, Leviny 206, Martha 24-59-225, Mary 91-262-297, Milbry 220, Milly 226, Nancy 227, Peggy 37, Polly 27, Rachel 197 (2)-207, Robt. 246-261, Sarah 204, Selah 230
Daws, Cath. 135-180, Fan. 131, Mahala 153, Mary 153, Patsey 92, Sally 130, Susa. 9
Dawson, Hannah 132, Martha 291, Temp. 121
Day, Eliz. 115, John 254
Deal, Eliz. 1, Louisa 184, Martha A. 143, Sarah 1
Deberry, Delitha 279, Lem. 279, Louise 169, Terece 252
Deloach, Averilla 225, Mary 191-193-225, Milly 193, Mollie 195, Sam. 195-201-225-226, Selah 191
Denton, Asola 3, Delha 162, Peninah 32
Deverson, Eliz. 117
Devry, (Devereaux?) Lecey 56
Dew, Arthur 205-272-276-283-293, Cath. 41, Eliz. 44-205-276-277, Emily 97, Harriet 9-271, John 272-276-277-283-286, Larry 271, Maria 111, Martha 201-283-283, Mary 205-228-272-293, Mary (Polly) 293, Maryan 120, Milicent 201-225, Obedience 286, Sally 225, Sarah 52-277, Theresa 276, Wm. 205
Dicken, Chris. 214, Ephriam 244, Florence 17, Fran. 7, Louisa 273, Sarah 84, Susan 11, Wm. 256
Dickens, Susan 226, Mrs. Susan 242, Wm. 226
Dickinson, Ava 202, Eliz. 206-276-284, Fan. 202, Jane 206, John 202-206-212-232, Mary 202-214-232-275-284, Martha 212, Penelope 271, Shad. 271-276-284 (2), Susa. 276, Thos. 275, Turner 226
Dilday, Dilder, Dildy,

Amanda 44, Eliz. 164,
Repsey 126
Dillard, Charity 226-274,
Dolly 188, Eliz. 188-
219 (2)-226-284, Honor
194, John 274, Jos.
244, Martha 46, Mary
13-85-288, Nancy 279,
Newton 219, Rebecca
288, Sally 86-126,
Thos. 279-284-288 (2)
Dixon, Cath. 7,
Clarenda 40, Coffield
210-214-219, Eliz. 2-
219-279-284, Eveline
51, J. E. 98, Jemimah
199-274, Keziah 278,
Lavina 177, Martha
146, Mary 210, Mourn-
ing 294-299, Nancy
14-98-214, Penelope
109-299, Penny 219,
Prisc. 57, Thos. 199-
219-274-276-278-284
299, Wm. 279, Capt.
Wm. 242
Donaldson, Sally 36,
Wm. 202-224
Dorman, Eliza 86, Mary
161
Dortch, Isaac 264, Jas.
259, Dr. Lewis 246-
263
Dowd, Rev. Patrick 254,
Rev. P. W. 243
Downing, Chrischaney
216, Courtney 199,
Della 2, Eliza 140,
Eliz. 212, Laney 103,
Lasina 127, Liza Ann
8, Luvinia 140, Lydia
203, Jas. 216, Jas., Sr.
199-203-212-250,
Martha 139
Doyle, Edwin 254
Dozier, Avilla 49
Drake, Ann 217, Cornelia
115, Elisa 186, Jane
163, Jemima 227-283,
Jesse 227-283, Laz.
217, Lucy 155, Marg.
98, Martha 264, Tempy
9
Draughan, Drawhon,
Draughon, Delphia 141,
Drucilla 242-251, Edney
58, Eliz. 42, Lucinda
43, Jas. 249, Martha
209, Nancy 135, Sa-
vaney 159, Wm. 209
Drew, Fran. 42, Lydia 7,
Patsey 137, Sally 7
Duggan, Eliz. 198, Jas.
257
Duglis, Eliz. 291, Jas.
291, Mary 291, Wm. 291
Dunford, Bytha 51, Hen-
rietta 23, Mary 230,
Nancy 28, Prisc. 28,
Sally 110, Susan 69,
Wm. 230
Dunn, Amelia 136, Ann
203, Betty 1, Burrill
242-251, Cath. 83,
Eliza 83, Eliz. 35-
279, Fannie 155,
Hattie 102, John 197-
203-230-298, Jonas
279, Lucy 172, Mal-
vina 149, Mary 35-
230, Melvina 185,
Milly 197, Nancy 85-
112, Patsey 112, Re-
becca 270, Sally 117,
Susan 177, Sarah 298,
Violetta 80, Winnifred
166
Dunning, Eliz. 148
Dunsford, Eliz. 182,
Susa. 208, Thos. 208
Dupree, Allen 262,
Amelia 91, Martha
107-201, Mary 1-29-
82-188, Milly 16,
Prisc. 147, Rebecca
35, Wm. 188-201-261
Durden, Zilpha 112
Dyott, Rebecca 47

- E -

Eagles, Mary 184, Rich.
294
Earle, John 247
Eason, Abner 206-229-
299, Caroline 45, Cath.
229, Clemmy 112, Co-
burn 203-281 (2)-294,
Eliz. 55-182-228-260-
280-281-285, Emeline
97, Deliza 136, Isaac
285, Joe 260, Joshua
276-294, Martha 9-26-
68-141-167-281, Mili-
cent 97, Nancy 262,
Obed 280-282-283-
299, Penelope 44 (2)-
203-276-282-283-294;
Perry (Penny ?), 52,
Polly 112, Rosina 34,
Sally 46-62-206,
Sarah 133, Talitha 13
Eatman, Rilly 5
Edmondson, Edmundson,
Alfred 255, Asa 255,
Betsey 94, Eliz. 18-
122, Fannie 98, John
252, Lydia 18-58,
Martha 139, Mary 169,
Nancy 103-165, Nisey
29-60, Penelope 23,
Pollard 260, Polly 66,
Rufus 247, Sarah 132,
Thos. 256 (2), Winni-
fred 18
Edmunds, Clarenda 58
Edwards, Ann 55, Bar-
sha 24, Brittain 202-
203 (2)-220, Bytha 203,
Chaney 104, Char.
126, Cinderella 34,
Cyrenia 46, Delia 227,
Edmund 272-283, Ed-
win 277, Elisha 225,
Eliza 114, Eliz. 3-
105-155 (2)-161-225-
250, Emily 94-177,
Harriet 115, Jacky 33,
Jennetta 179, Jonas
281, Judy 66, Kinchen
201, Lewey 156,
Louisiana 143, Lu-
cinda 220, Martha 48-
65, Mary 83-125-165-
142-144-165-227-254-
259-272-283, Nancy
203 (2)-220, Nathan
227, Nelly 38-201,
Parma 49, Parmelia
179, Person 47, Polly
98, Rachel 154, Sally
38-92-156-202-203,
Sarah 119, Selequa
182, Selisha 281,
Siley 204-205-227,
Susan 84-122-145- 151-
205, Susa. 51, Tremmy
184, Venah 114, Winni-
fred 94, Zoa 34
Elbeck, Eliz. 194, Polly
194
Elixon, Mary 70
Ellinor, Cath. 92, Eliz.
15-116-225, Jas. 204-
263, Penelope 2, Mil-
berry 275, Sabra 60,
Wm. 256
Elliott, Alice 110-247,
Elijah 259
Ellis, Amanda 276, Cof-
field 191-272, Edith
112, Elisha 212-282,
Mrs. Eliza 245, Eliz.
127-177-225-282-299,
Emma 280, Emeliza
87, Evelina 62, Jane
136, Jean 220, Julia
124, Louisa 9-191-272,
Lewis 276-280, Martha
39-132, Mary 6-118-
177-220, Milicent 28,
Nicey 117, Peggy 8,
Penny 55, Polly 72-
212, Queen Esther 48,
Sally 191, Sarah 10-
153, Spicy 26, Susan 1,
Tempy 7, Unity 9
Emry, Eliz. 291, Green
291
Etheridge, Etherage,
Angelina 153, Caleb
196, Eliza 82-257,
Eliz. 178, Harriet 172,
Kiddy 55, Lizzie 56,
Martha 196, Mary 152,
Ohdina 59, Rebecca 166,
Rhoda 86, Sarah 84-184
Eure, Polly 10-157, Steph
en 282, Zypha 282
Evans, Evins, Abby 16,

Abraham 224, Amy 129,
Chas. 193, Dolly 105,
Edith 8, Eliza 66-256,
Eliz. 99-190-224,
Leady 190, Lucinda 14,
Mary 146-193-253, Nancy
159, Peter 251-253-256,
Polly 1, Sally 65-119,
Sarah 121, Susan 145-
242-251
Everitt, Ann 70, Debora
230, Eliz. 70, Keton
202-205-230, Lucy 71,
Martha 69, Mary 94-
202, Nancy 230, Polly
194-217, Sally 182-
205, Silas 194-217-230
Ewing, Miss 265
Exum, Cath. 55, Eliz. 10-
16, Louisiana 169,
Martha 212, Mary 137
(2), John 212-218-222-
240-286, Peninah 103-
262, Prissy 57, Sarah
193-218-222, Wm. 193,
Winnifred 286

- F -

Faircloth, Winny 144
Faithful, Ann 65, Bedy
52, Eliz. 116, Harriet
3, Jane 96, Mary 93,
Patsey 173, Temp. 131
Fareless, Eliz. 80,
Fruny 119
Farmer, Absalom 273,
Aggie 281, Agnes 280,
Anna 52, Barsheba 272,
Benj. 188-201-205-210-
275, Caroline 163-285,
Cath. 52 (2), Cinderella
10, Christian 281, Del-
phia 39-286, Eddy 48,
Edith 180, Eliz. 12-
188-205-278, Harriet
273, Isaac 271-272-273-
278-280-281-284, Jas.
273, Jerusha 287, John
286, Jos. 280, Julia
108, Keziah 284, Lucy
96, Martha 22-136-273,
Mary 22-38-184, Moses
287, Nancy 49-51-142-
201-275, Patience 271,
Prisc. 9-273-286, Sally
9-136-210, Susan 92-
280, Trecey 52, Zylpha
66

Farrar, Patsey 85, Sopha
124, Zilpha 66
Faulkner, Mary 268
Felton, Anna 164, Casia
78, Cynthia 68, Del-
phia 33, Eliz. 167,
Gatsey 168, Jas. 54,
Nancy 26, Spicey 153,
Sally 116, Tamey 53,
Treacy 47-163, Wealthy
167
Felts, Eliz. 228, Jane
26, Laura 53 Mary 203,
Nancy 193, Wm. 193-
203-228
Ferguson, Nancy 240
Figures, Eliz. 296,
Sally 295
Fleetwood, Martha 283-
298
Fleming, Flemings,
Flemin, Flemming,
Flemmings, Arsena 144-
227-261, Eliz. 43-59-
63, Jesse 246, Mary
164, Milly 27, Polly 117
Sally 18, Sarah 53,
Willie 227, Willis 72,
Zilla 119-221
Flood, Bytha 160, Eliz.
50-135, Joanna 92-186
Flora, Barsheba 142,
Celia 130, Gray 48,
Hester 21, Jane 62,
Martha 30, Mary 50
Flowers, Edith 280, Ed.
232-285, Eliz. 47-197-
271-274, Hardy 271,
Henry 280, Jacob 197,
(3), Jane 77, Mary
232-285, Nancy 30,
Obedience 11, Prisc.
197
Fly, Mary 185, John 295
Folk, Harriet 171
Folsom, Mary 128
Forbes, Edith 168, Eliz.
134-167, Jos. 260,
Marg. 123, Sally 89
Ford, Eliz. 70, Fran. 81,
Lucinda 178, Marg.
259, Nellie 70, Prisc.
37
Forehand, Cloah 189,
David 283, Lucy 283,
Sarah 206, Sol. 189-
206
Foreman, Agesilaus
245-258, Delha 6,
John 296, Mary 296,
Sarah 129-180
Forsett, Benj. 264,
Susan 264
Fort, Foort, Ann 291,
Charity 196, Cressy
196, Elias. 265-266-
290-291 (2), Eliz. 200,
Fran. 134, Geo. 191-
196-200-264, Jacob
270, Jas. 265, Jane
196-204-206-225, Jere-
miah 265-270, Josiah
266, Lewis 267, Lucy
225, Martha 143-191-
143-290, Mary 78-196-
206-291, Orpha 10,
Orfee 191, Prisc. 85,
Sarah 270, Sealy 230,
Temp. 268, Wm. 265-
266-270
Fountain, Adeline 114,
Auliff 295, Cary 295,
Delah 40, Eliza 3,
Eliz. 3-32-161-228,
Henry 228, Jas. 188,
Jane 185, Mahala 15,
Martha 188, Nancy 124-
282, O. 56, Peninah
92, Rebecca 93, S. F.
50, Spencer 295, Sol.
295
Foust, Sarah 291
Foxhall, Edwin 249,
Joanna 239, Lucy
134, Martha 59,
Mary 141-232-244-
256, Robt. 256,
Susan 7, Thos. 230-
232, Wm. 240
Freeman, Adelina 251,
Eliza 3, Eliz. 93-230,
Emelina 91-215, Geo.
241, Martha 136,
Mary 102-155-171,
Milicent 195, Milly
21, Jos. 260, Josiah
195-215-230-251,
Peggy 93, Sarah 28-
262
Friar, Fryar, Fryer,
Amanda 174, Martha
178, Mary 93, Nancy
178, Sarah 109
Futrell, Naomy 274

- G -

Gaddey, Alley 233,
Eliz. 213, Lucy 196,
Thos. 196-198-213-
233
Gainer, Eliz. 206, Mary
206, Sabra 194, Wm.
206
Galloway, Charity 172
Gardner, Amanda 185,
Ann 28-222, Cath.
182, Delpha 146,
Eliz. 21-151, Elmouth
125, Emeliza 109,
Evelina 19-104, Gat-
sey 63, Geo. 222,
224-227-286, Jane 44,
Leah 123, Lucretia
12, Lydia 117, Martha
67-134, Mary 109-
227, Matilda 12,
Mourning 130, Nancy
145, Patsey 76, Peggy
107, Peninah 120,
Penny 125, Phebe
224, Phereby 222,
Polly 120, Rebecca
52, Wm. 242-251,
Zylpha 286
Garman, Eliz. 172

Garrett, Cherry 87, Gracy 152, Henry 241-250, Jas. 253, John 258, Mahala 179, Nancy 175, Susan 114
Garvey, Jas. 133, Vesta 133-185
Gater, Gaitor, Gracy 78-211, John 211, Lavina 8, Martha 133, Nancy 225, Penelope 8, Sabra 146, Sally 8, Sam. 225, Wm. Ann 73
Gatlin, Caroline 4, Georgiana 44, Thos. 252
Gay, Ann 275, Betsey 60, Demp. 204, Easter 17, Edith 35, Eliza 20, Eliz. 88, Esther 263, Fran. 81, Jemima 87, Julia 179-185, Letha 130, Martha 73, Mary 47-48, Milbry 106-257, Mourning 131, Nancy 49-103-204, Peninah 166, Polly 62-99-100, Rachel 64-263, Roanna 175, Sally 49-90-168
George, Ann 121, Eliz. 80-215 (2), Mary 29-255, Rebecca 199, Selah 199
Gerard, Mrs. 239
Gerrard, Chas. 228, Mrs. Dinah 228, Forbes 228
Gibbs, Fred 232
Gilbert, Dr. John 265, Elder Nathan 265-295
Gilchrist, Eliz. 210, Ellen 213, Thos. 207-210-213
Gill, Eliz. 55, Malvina 137, Rebecca 145-252
Glover, Mary 36, Tab. 47
Godwin. Wm. 293
Goff, Mary 158
Goodson, Eliz. 218, Mary 28, Sarah 207, Thos. 218 (2)-207
Gordon, Jane 89
Gordan, Mary 296
Gorham, Caroline 166
Goodwin, Dolly 286, Wm. 286
Gosney, John 207-226, Henrietta 226, Oney 207
Graves, Stephen 295
Gray, Benj. 221, Carolina 16, Caroline 194, Hann. 209, Helen 28, Martha 78-211, Mary 81-180-212, Nancy 38, Rebecca 221, Robt. 209-212, Rosa 4
Green, Greene, Ann 50, Creasy 51, Patsey 148, Sally 164, Sarah 62-291, Wm. 291
Grice, Alex. 278, Ann 279, Betsey 278, John 291, Rebecca 291
Griffin, Anna 182, Benj. 223, Betsy 147, Cath. 19, Edney 271, Eliz. 19-97-229, Jas. 295, Jane 41-295, John 271-295, Marg. 19-110-114, Maria 226, Martha 72-153-175-209, Mary 13-45-82-96-115-280, Maryan 96, Mourning 223, Nancy 184, Nellie 84, Oney 152-209, Polly 37, Rebecca 110-219, Sabra 18-251-271, Sarah 106, Thos. 295, Winnefred 141-226-253, Zach. 209-219-226-229
Griffis, Griffith, Griffiths, John 193-217, Martha 16, Mary 45, Nancy 79-246-263, Polly 217, Sarah 193
Grimes, Eliz. 113, Fran. 209, Julia 197-294, Lydia 213-295 (2), Martha 139, Mary 29-110-219, Rhoda 41, Talitha 144-215-260-295 (2), Thos. 209-257-295, Wm. 197-213-215-219-260-294-295 (2),
Guinn, Jane 54
Guion, James C. 17
Gully, Eliz. 107
Gunter, Marg. 107-218-252, Prisc. 218
Guy, Eliz. 18
Gwaltney, Alsey 185
Gwin, Chris. 208, Dan. 224, Mary 208, Sara 150, Susa. 224

- H -

Haddock, Penelope 45
Hadley, Barbara 149, Martha 283
Hagan, Hagon, Hagans, Haguns, Haggans, Amanda 155, Eliz. 51, Fran. 44, Julia 74, Mary 133, Peggy 86, Piety 99, Polly Ann 88
Hainey, Nancy 68, Patsey 20
Hales, Hayles, Hails, Julia 111, Mary 148, Nancy 18, Rachel 56, Sarah 64, Tom 259, Wm. 245-258
Hall, Ed. 209, Eliz. 289, Ignatius 289, Lou 268, Martha 209, Mason 66
Hamilton, Judy 152
Hammond, Hammons, Dilly 133, Eliz. 111, Jesse 289, Mary 289, Rosy 106, Sally 17, Susan 76, Susa. 133
Hampton, Geo. 265, Jane 265
Hancy, Rosy 16-106
Hanes, Haynes, Haines, Char. 2, Martha 72, Mary 72, Nelly 124, Sally 139-153, Spencer 253
Hanks, Eliz. 145, Martha 249, M. E. 184
Hanson, Jenny 184
Hardy, Hardie, Polly 98-198, Robt. 198, Sarah 98, Temp. 22
Hargrave, Cath. 42, Frank. 246, John 245, Louisiana 109, Mary 249
Hardy, Jane 290, John 290
Hargrove, Hairgrove, Aaron 280-295, Amy 40, Anna 35, Eliz. 153, Frank. 261, John 258, Inda 24, Martha 20, Mary 20, Penelope 280-295, Unity 295
Harper, Elizabeth 19-141, Jane 1, Martha 24-120, Mary 123, Sally 179-253, Sarah 125, Susa. 19-22
Harrell, Asa 69, Barbara 197 (2), Chris. 196-197-216 (2)-219 (2), 260-261, Delphia 56, Eliz. 141-170-196-197-260, Emily 30, Jesse 256, Lucy 216, Marg. 74, Martha 69-109-219, Mary 53-85, Milly 55, Patsey 166, Peggy 46, Polly 195, 216, Rebecca 219, Sabra 194, Sally 61-196, Sam. 195, Sarah 23, Seale 224, Sylvia 120-242-251, Tabitha 166, Thos. 194-196-197 (2)-224, Wm. 208

Harris, Arena 126, Cath. 5, Delphia 89, Eli 260, Eliz. 56-196, Emeliza 162, Evelina 1, Louisa 40, Martha 141-151-162, Mary 31, Nancy 96, Nanny 96, Nathan 201, Nony 260, Olif 226, Polly 70-201 Sally 13, Sarah 206 Thos. 196-206-226, Thruby 137

Harrison, Ann 268-296, Benj. 296, Chas. 255, Julia 248, Mary 298
Hart, Heartt, Cath. 177-251, Eliz. 103-193-297, Ellen 35, Emily 6, Fran. 243, Frank. 6-247, Indiana 20, Marg. 32, Martha 163, Mary 101-155-241-250, Nancy 206, Olivia 28, Prisc. 193, 206, Sallie 103, Spencer 252
Harvey, Anna 218, Eliza 240, Jos. 262
Haskins, Mrs. Martha 296
Hathaway, Chloe 32
Hawkins, Anne 299, Bethia 116, Delilah 141, Elza. 209 (2), Lucinda 45-255, Lugenia 93, Mizy 209, Penny 33, Spicey 72, Thos. 244-254, Virginia 244,
Hayne, Rebecca 57
Hays, Edy 291, Eliza 17, Eliz. 2, Martha 178, Peter 289-290-291, Rebecca 289, Winney 290
Haywood, Eliz. 232, Mary 226-283, Wm. 226-232
Hearn, Eliz. 110-152, Lawr. 245-258, Martha 152-253, Mary 244-255, Ml. 253-255-261, Sabra 297,
Heath, Eliz. 289, John 289
Hedgepeth, Agatha 32, John 226, Mary 226, Penninah 154, Rhoda 109, Talitha 155
Hellen, Sue 249
Hendrick, Mary 210, Sarah 192, Wm. 192-210
Henry, Eliz. 280
Hickman, Chris. 124, Eliz. 39-144-233,

Ellis 259, Mary 230, Nat. 202-230-233, Sarah 202,
Hicks, Brittania 208, Char. 193, Esther 64, Jas. 193-208, Joshua 259, Mary 89-259, Piety 110, Rachel 118, Susan 118
Higgs, Jos. 257, Sally 52
Hill, Cath. 216, Dan. 245, Louise 240, Martha 108, Mary 289, Nancy 55, Naomi 119, Penelope 216, Polly 40, Rebecca 74, Robt. 289 (2), Tabitha 289, Talitha 131
Hilliard, Chris. 290, Elias 264, Eliz. 265-270-294, Isaac 265-295, Jacob 264-265, Jas. 257, Jeremiah 265-285, Mrs. John 265, Marg. 290, Mary 285, Mourning 285, Nancy 265
Hines, Ann 204-232, Celia 274, Cath. 197-213-279, Eliz. 121-204-229-251, Henry 279, Katey 26, Lucy 159, Martha 230, Mary 192-197, Peter 197-204-229-244-245-246-256-299, Prudence 197, Rich. 192-230-232-241-244, Rosana 159, Sarah 230, Wm. 213-260-295
Hinnant, Edith 166
Hinton, Betsy 23, Cath. 181, Jas. 243, Louisa 130, Sallie 22-181
Hobbs, Mary 202, Susa. 202
Hobgood, Eliz. 289, Micajah 289
Hobby, Rhoda 23, Sarah 24-54
Hodge, Allen 241-250
Hodges, Anthony 198-202-228, Eliz. 202, Nancy 145-228, Sarah 198, Thos. 202-228
Holland, Abigail 283, Abra 30, Barsheba 195, David 229, Eliz. 49, Jacob 195, Letha 56, Lucy 153-171, Martha 148-229, Nancy 77, Sarah 276,
Holmes, Ann·226, Beatrix 229, Charity 195, Dorothy 229, John 195-226-229 (2)
Hooker, Mary 181-285, Hymeric 285
Hopkins, Dan. 229-242-

251-256, David Lavinia 76, Dolly 45, Fred. 254, Eliz. 282, Harriett 148-229-256, Janette 166, Litha 256, Marina 82, Mary 27, Rilla 82-254, Sally 35, Sidney 126, Susan 149-259, Tabitha 162, Wm. 253
Hopper, Dr. David 291, Hannah 291
Horne, Areana 158, Betsy 178, Caroline 127, Cath. 11, Celia 284, Charity 199-272-267-273, Delha 113, Delilah 189, Duke Wm. 253, Edie 228, Edith 283, Elijah 201-233, Elisha 280, Eliz. 198-299, Emily 87, Guilford 286, Fran. 273, Harriett 35, Henry 220-264-267-272-273-277-279 (2)- 284, Jacob 199-205-228-250-274-277-283, Jas. 295, Jemima 207-278, John 244-283-285, Joshua 270, Josiah 270-272-273, Kate 248-270, Lawr. 244-255, Louisa 143, Martha 79, Mary 12-77-270-272-286-Ml. 189-191-199, Milbry 264-266-282, Milicent 158-205-242-250-277-285, Miriam 102, Mourning 199-274, Nancy 157-286, Patience 157-278-285-293, Penelope 220, Peninah 108-259, Phebe 134, Piety 206-266-277 (2), Prisc. 56- 198-206-277, Polly 191, Rachel 124-213- 280, Rhoda 233, Ruth 207-213-279, Sally 144-196-206- Sarah 230-283, Selah 201, Tabitha 280, Wm. 207-264-278-280-282, Zerviah 279
Horton, Houghton, Martha 131, Persey 92
Hoskins, Rich. 247
Hotlett, Lydia 45
House, Charlotte 34, Harriett 54, John 188, Maggie 108, Mary 75-76-181, Ruth 96, Talitha 54, Unity 188, Wm. 291, Winnifred 291
Howard, Absala 40-202, Alice 175, Caroline 154, Celia 116, Del-

phia 48-204, Eliz. 47-
48-169, Emily 148,
Evan 202-204, Har-
riett 33-99, Jas. 260,
Jannett 32, Martha
120-247, Mary 8,
Micajah 250, Peggy
87, Prud. 251, Sally
48-79-254, Sarah 97-
171-248, Sidney 95-
262, Willie 262,
Wilson 254
Howell, Bythal 255,
Cath. 133, Eli 260,
Eliz. 142, Henrietta
29, Jackie Eliza 128-
224, Jane 48-91-119,
John 211-244. Jos.
274-281, Juliana 131,
Keziah 274, Levi
(Lem) 51, Martha 131,
Mary 15-281, Massey
67, Murphree 150,
Nancy 150-252, Polly
211, Sallie 21-70,
Sarah 287, Susan 4,
Temp. 175, Wealthy
260, Wm. 287
Howenton, Mary 54,
Nancy 43, Virginia
259
Hubbard, Celia 145,
Harriet 129,
Hudnall, Lydia 169,
Mary 202, Polly 122,
Robt. 202
Hunt, Ann 290, Eliz.
219, Feby 219, Prisc.
100
Hunter, Harry 239,
Martha 170, Weldon
246-263
Hussey, Betsy 136,
Jennett 150
Hyett, Hyatt, Annie 194,
Betsey 292, Faithy
228, Penelope 188,
Thos. 188-194-228
Hyman, Anacha 79,
Ann 36, Annie 248,
Arthur 254, Carrie
298, Cloanna 202,
Ebenezer 295-298
Eliz. 218-297, Ellen
23-245-257, Henry
256, Col. Jos. 249,
Kenneth 257-260,
Marg. 143, Martha 122,
Mary 260, Penina 132,
255, Susan 47, Thos.
198-202-297, Wm. 255

- I -

Ing, Nancy 51, Mary 160
Irwin, Andrew 202,
Bettie 248, Eliz. 5-
243-254, J. A. 254,
Martha 202
Irving, Andrew 275,

Martha 275
Isaerel, Jane 163
Ivey, Capt. John 249

- J -

Jackson, Cath. 135,
Harriett 74, Dr.
Isaac 256, John 212,
Leas 64, Marg. 157,
Martha 74, Mary 16-
128, Micajah 242-
251, Nancy 66-80-
134-161-240, Patsey
54-128-148, Polly 74,
Rebecca 135, Sarah
81
James, Dicey 22, Sarah
22-71
Jameson, Eliz. 4
Jarrell, Martha 193
Jelks, Mary 219, Tabby
192, Wm. 192-219
Jenkins, Annis 153,
Betsey 66, Jane 44,
Jos. 254, Louisa 60,
Mrs. 242-251, Mary
13-33-68-76-89-247-
260-261, Milly 44,
Pennetta 113, Rebecca
121, Sally 173-252,
S. P. 261, Thos. 257
Jernigan, Penelope 3
Jones, Allen 260-263,
Alvana 48, Amanda 69,
Ann 290, Augusta 28-
249, Asa 295 (2),
Barsheba 74, Calvin
262, Casandra 97,
Cath. 42-64, Crystal
188, Delitha 40, Dolly
100, Dorothy 148,
Eliza 57-260, Eliz.
107-138-157-190,
Emily 80-160, Evelina
105-263, Francis 200,
Fred. 261, Gilly 154,
Hardy 188-190, Jas.
69, Jane 149, John
212-219-225-229-231,
Laura 15-29, Liley 21,
Louisa 149, Marg.
118-175, Martha 207,
Mary 29-179-200-207,
Maudia 183, Mourn-
ing 111, Nancy 71-
207, Nellie 150, Polly
160, Prisc. 290, Sally
14-22-176-258, Sarah
115-173-212-261,
Temp. 295-298, Wm.
Hardy 290
Johnson, Eliz. 87-125,
Fran. 58, Henry 253,
Laura 96, Lucy 62-
144, Martha 24, Mary
55-119-134, Obedience
272, Olza 240, Polly
144, Sarah 24-83,
Simon 209

Johnston, Aaron 274,
Aggy 14, Amos 192-
204-267-272-276-286-
295, Celia 198-278-
292-294, Cilicia 276,
Eliz. 51-273, Emily
213, Esther 209-226-
286, F. A. H. 51, Geo.
292, Henry 84-243-
281, Jacob 198-267-
274-295, Jas. 292,
Jane 140, Jesse 295,
John 294, Col. Jonas
271-273-274-278 (2)-
283-298, Joshua 280,
Lucy 49, Marg. 22,
Mary 103-120-137-172-
192-226-265-267-268-
272-281-283-295-298-
299, Meady 104, Nancy
17-204-274-276-280,
Patience 292, Prudence
209-278, Rebecca 112,
Sally 127, Seley 274,
Wm. 276
Jolly, Drucilla 198
Jordan, Edith 272-293,
Cornelius 205-226-
230-231, Eliz. 230,
Esther 272, Gray 295,
Jesse 272, Joshua
272-293, Rhoda 231,
Sally 198
Joyner, Annie 120,
Baldy 293, Drewry
89-221, Drucilla 112,
Elisa 27, Eliz. 290,
Emeliza 167, Harriett
12-107, Jacob 293,
Jonathan 293, John
295, Jos. 290, Lucy
170-258, Martha 221-
295, Mary 177, Nancy
293, Nathan 293,
Pamelia 90, Patsey
117, Peter 293,
Tassey 160-263, Wm.
293, Wright 261
Judkins, Eliz. 100

- K -

Kail (Keel), Nancy 2
Kea, Key, Eliz. 116-
220, Faithey 206 (2),
Henry 193-220, La-
vinia 102, Nancy 193-
206, Patsy 206
Kearney, Eliz. 295,
Sally 31
Kewell, Mary 243
Keel, Henry 259
Kelly, Delpha 89, Eliz.
155, Marg. 15, Patsy
105
Kennedy, Margaret 292,
Wm. 259
Kembrough, Marg. 290,
Marmaduke 290
Killebrew, Barbara 117,

Dolly 25, Char. 126,
Churchwell 261,
Eliza. 141, Emily 94,
Fran. 82, Janie
(James?) 140, Lu-
cinda 67, Marg. 29,
Nancy 202, Susan 85,
Susa. 76
Kinchen, Mourning 190,
Wm. 190
King, Anne 38, Coffield
262, Drew 252, Col. E.
248, Eliza 127-255,
Eliz. 51, Emma 95,
Louisa 161, Martha
15-255, Mary 53,
Penelope 161, Sally
262, Sarah 179-261-
287, Wm. 251-255-
261-287
Kinsey, Esther 298
Kitchen, Boaz 211,
Dicey 211, Eliz.
194 (2)-208-211-217,
Lucretia 78-211,
Martha 217, Mary 203,
Susa. 208
Kite, Drucilla 101,
Fannie 18
Knight, A. M. 103,
Arthur 256, Cecelia
229, Cella 123, Chas.
243-252, Char. 90,
Dan. 262, Dilly 219,
Drucilla 149-257,
Eliz. 160- 192-199-
220, Ellen 114, Eme-
liza 21, Fran. 94,
Francis 257, Harriett
98-216-253, Jas. 199-
219-257-262, J. C.
253, Jesse 192-215-
218-257, John 194-
206 (2)-207-253-257-
280, Judah 206, Laura
183, Louisa 103,
Louisiana 246-261,
Lucy 66-192-208-262,
Lydia 37, Martha 91-
126-177-196-218-262,
Mary 43-206- 296-280,
Moses 221, Nancy 72-
105-218-241-250-298,
Penny 4, Peter 192-
272, Polly 198-215,
Rachel 207, Sally 257,
Sarah 91-124-167-194,
221, Susan 60-122-124,
253, Walker 196-208-
229, Wm. 251, Wm. Ann
42, Willis 215-216-218-
253

- L -

Lamon, Arch. 266, Dun-
can 266, Marg. 266,
Olen 239, Olivia 266
Lancaster, Cherry 92,
Eliz. 117-131, L. 92,
Lucy 176, Marg. 81,
Martha 20-24, Mary
175, Nancy 152-284,
Pearcy 96, Polly 173,
Sarah 166
Land, Amanda 135, Amy
89-214, Eliz. 129,
Emily 5, Littleberry
208-214-215, Lucretia
12-93, Mary 88, Nancy
159-178, Polly 215,
Sally 67-208, Wm. 271
Landing, Eliz. 137,
Louisa 92, Martha
174, Mary 73-162,
Nancy 133, Penelope
137 Peninah 17
Landen, Mary 14, Mil-
brey 128
Lane, Amanda 72, Ann
156-207, Chris. 209,
Drucilla 196, Eliz.
205, Faith 197,
Henry 196, Jas. 192-
194-205-207, Jos. 196-
197, Laura 141, Lem-
mon 299, Lucy 70,
Martha 6-268-269,
Mary 63-192, Nancy
66-299, Penny 162,
Polly 162, Rebecca 75,
Sarah 194-299
Langley, Cherry 243-
252, Eliz. 281,
Hezekiah 281, Jas.
295, Lucy 290, Mary
82, Thos. 290
Langston, Sarah 16
Lanier, Wm. 260
Lassiter, Hardy 189,
Sally 189
Latham, Harriett P. 186
Lawrence, Absala 62-
229, Anne 127, Annie
81, Arthur 252, Brit-
tana 95, Cath. 95-
137, David 243, E. A.
211, Eleny 209, Eliz.
67-69-77-88-128-170-
247-262, Elsa 73,
Emily 38, Harriett 94,
Jas. 262, John 95-
208-209-228-229-262,
Joshua 196-245-255,
258-296, Rev. Joshua
252-263, Dr. Josiah
244, Louisa 100-196,
Louisiana 91-243-
252, Lucinda 95-255,
Lucy 102, Marg. 103-
163, Maria 94, Martha
85-140-172-177-231,
Mary 23-48-76-210-
253-258, M. O. 213m
Nancy 39-60-74-91,
Peggy 228, Peter
210-211-213-253-255-
260, Phereby 40-263,
Polly 208, Sarah 67-
94-231, Sol. 231,
Thos. 296
Lee, Maj. Aaron 296,
Dossy 267, Eliza 267,
Eliz. 196, Harry 267,
Henry 226, Jas. 197-
266-267, Jonathan
262, Joshua 223-277,
Lavinia 108, Martha
162-267, Mary 197-
223-267, Myra 28,
Patsy 263, Polly 178,
Rachel 194, Rich.
194-210, Col. Rich.
28, Sally 39, Sarah
210-226, Susan 267,
Temp. 69-123-251-
267-282, Temp. 282
Leggett, Caroline 84,
Celestia 169, Char.
170, Eliz. 150, Isa-
bella 170, Levin 222-
233 (2)-256-258,
Louisiana 258, Lucia
165, Mahala 165-233-
256, Martha 18-42,
Nicey 171, Pamelia
170, Sarah 32, Susan
121-222, Tabitha 233,
Talitha 165, Treacy
170, Wm. 263
Leigh, Lucinda 146,
Martha 23, Mary 80,
Melly 110, John 240,
Temp. 208, Wm.
208 (2)-260
Lenoir, Betty 216, Mary
121-122, Thos. 216-
222
Leonard, Caleb 252
Lester, Fran. 45-203,
Letty 117, Moses
203-221, Nancy 221
Lewis, Louis, Ann 211-
229-297, Anna H.
184, Barth. 296, Char.
67, Charlotty 208,
Clio 146, Della 185,
Eliza 121-130-146,
Eliz. 117-221-298,
Emma 146-229-246-
261, Exum 211-212-
219-245-257-261-
268-279-295-296-
298, Fannie 48-204,
Green 239-296, Jas.
203-204-218-221-
296, Dr. John 243-
252-268-297, K. H.
248, Malinda 33,
Mamie 123, Martha
164, Mary 47-79-203-
211-296, Dr. Mills
240, Nancy 42, Re-
becca 107-218-279-
285-295, Reddin 296,
Rich. 268-296, Dr.
Rich. H. 248, Robt.
248, Sally 219-295-
296, Susan 132,
Talitha 150, Treacy-

105-184,
Little, Abraham 192-206 (2)-231, Agnes 269, Ann 145-156-206-251, Celia 155, Creasy 111, Cullen 253, Delia 45, Eliz. 107-123-125-128-206-227, Fannie 157-272, Felicia 67-139, Fran. 91, Fred. 253, Harriett 181, Jesse 205-227-251, Julia 39, Marg. 143-165, Martha 30, Mary 83-156, Peggy 151, Peninah 35-198-250, Sally 110, Sarah 53-71-192-205, Selah 231, Sylvia 198, Tabitha 157
Llewellyn, Alex. 188, Chloe 295, Fran 295, Wm. 295
Lloyd, Eliz. 227, Jas. 241, Dr. Jos. 242, Lucinda 24, Martha 188, Nicholas 188, 192-227, Penny 81, Polly 239, Sally 26-192, Maj. W. P. 249
Locust, Locus, Charity 157, Linda 76, Sarah 108
Lodge, Della 74, Dolly 28, Luis 215-220, Lydia 111, Martha 66, Mary 111, Patsey 104, Vicey 28
Long, Amanda 148-284, Catalina 176, Cath. 167, Drucilla 169, Ed. 275, Eliz. 40, H. 99, Henrietta 78-220-255, Jas. 258-260, John 258-250-271, Maniza 36-200, Mary 186-224-275, Nancy 74, Newsome 284, Sally 22-126, Talitha 255, Tabitha 226, Wm. 200-220-224-226-247-255 (2), Winnefred 12
Lovett, Eliz. 151
Lowe, Exum 241-296, Figures 241-296, Polly 179, Mrs. Sally 297, Stephen 295-296, Rev. Wm. 295-296
Lowry, Ann 201, Betty 229, Frankey 215, Jemima 234, Mary 198, Robt. 198-201-215-217-229-234, Sarah 217
Luningham, Leecy 112
Luper, Looper, Anne 215, Jas. 215, Mahala 100, Mary 112, Nancy 177, Phebe 19, Susan

59
Lynch, Mrs. 242-251, Eaton 200, Eliz. 71, Geo. 215-223, Hattie 215, Hester 36-200-258, Mary 223, Nancy 18, Polly 123, Sally 111, Tazzy 223, Tirzah 123
Lyon, Bennett 258, Benton 245, Delphia 169-242-251-235, Emma 71, Florence A. 184, Joshua 246-261, Patsy 207, Susan 42, Thos. 207-241-250-251-235

Mabrey, Mabry, Arie 40, Chas. 241-250-260, Delah 62, Milisha 11-191, Rebecca 11-30-191, Sarah 140, Susan 40-123, Wilkinson 191,
MacNair, McNair, Cecelia 114, Eliza 89, E. D. 254-256, Edmund 230-239, Pauline 156-248, Sarah 75-244-256, Susan 152-230-254
Macon, Gideon 290
Madrey, Sally 123
Mahegan, Azula 114
Mallory, Martha 146, Wm. 249
Maner, Mainor, Mainer, Char. 124, Milly 103, Joanna 8, Levina 129, Penelope 154
Mangum, Mary 171, Sarah 47
Manina, Anna C. 182
Mann, Mary 42, Penelope 113, Polly 31
Manning, Annie 50, Eliz. 60-179, Harriett 39, Littleberry 262, Patsey 46, Temp. 171
Marks, Annis 16, Eliz. 94, Georgeanna 75, Jas. 257, Jos. 262
Marley, Benj. 275, Jenny 26, Nancy 275, Nathan 217
Marlow, Rachel 55, Winnifred 99
Marriott, Benj. 270, Robt. 270
Marshall, Goodwin 232, John 232, Penelope 250, Mary 170
Marshburn, Martha 159
Martin, Jas. 290-291, Mary 291, Susa. 290, Virginia 267
Mason, Adeline 95, Char. 280, Eliz. 258, Sally 186
Massingale, Atsey 80

Matthews, Mollie 83
Matthewson, Abby 221-260, Caroline 174-243-252, Nath. 221-252
Mattocks, Celia 49, Eliz. 48
Maund, Eliz. 189, Esther 298, Lott 280, Mary 202-214, Nancy 202, Rebecca 214
May, Eliz. 25-174, Lazina 67, Louisa 33, Lucinda 31, Lydia 98, Patsey 30, Sally 61
May, Clara 295
Mayo, Allen 261, Arsena 96, Benj. 263, David 216, Drucilla 27-224, Emily 173, Fanny 181, Fred. 242-251, Gatsey 106-184, Harriett 95-245-280-296, J. 105, Jas. 296, Jane 139, John 193-228-256-296, Kinchen 241-250, Lady 73, Lawrence 296, Louisa 251, Lucinda 267, Lucy 71-216, Lydia 25-156, Marina 193, Martha 17-100-146-152, Mary 14-15-74-101-227-245, Micajah 297 (2)-298, Nancy 72-165-228, Nathan 207-218-280-295-296, Polly 1-8-143, Rebecca 224, Reuben 255, Sally 69-133-208-259-284, Talitha 207-295-298, Thos. 244-255, Wm. 208-227-267

- Mc -

McCotter, Mary 116-260
McCrary, Mary 266
McDade, Cath. 238, Delilah 218, Dilly 108, Mary 218-224-237, Rhoda 237, Sally 129, Sarah 224, Willis 238
McDaniel, Agnes 201, Ann 189, Anna 186, Campbell 199-201, Cornelia 268, Dan. 189, Rev. Jas. 268, Olive 199
McDonald, Ann 4
McDowell, Eliz. 91-199, John 197, Martha 35-199, Mary 78-299, Nancy 197
McDuell, Nancy 28
McGee, Wm. 257
McKenzie, Jas. 250, J. G. 241

McKinne, Bar. 289,
  Barnaby 290-291, John
  290-233, Mary 223,
  Mourning 291, Patience
  290
McMahon, Susan 51
McWilliams, Geo. 257,
  Mary 235, Rosina 104-
  257

- M -

Mears, Mares, Delha 110,
  Faitha 25, Jane 107,
  Martha 147, Mary 88-
  176, Nancy 80-100-
  176, Sarah 145-185,
  Willie 106
Medford, Cath. 111,
  Lucy 154-254, Maniza
  64
Meeks, Lucy 25, Marina
  97, Susan 116
Melton, Cullen 257, Drucilla 125, Fran. 128,
  Marg. 151
Mennis, Dr. John 259
Mercer, Delpha 177,
  Eliz. 78-244-255-270,
  Fannie 122, Henrietta
  60, Jesse 263, John
  255-260-297-298,
  Ketura 124, Letha 109-
  179, Malvina 260,
  Marg. 218, Mariah 115,
  Mary 77-138, Nancy
  298, Sally 60
Merritt, Amy 208-291
  E. J. 252, John 208-
  230, Mary 212-291,
  Peggy 230, Tabitha
  62-293, Thos. 212
Mial, Charity 215, John
  215
Middleton, Eliz. 222,
  John 222
Milikin, Agnes 291, Ann
  291, Cath. 291, Col.
  Jas. 291 (2)
Miller, Christian 108
Mills, Abner 252, Eliz.
  104, Lucinda 147,
  Prof. Luther 297,
  Sarah 77
Milton, Ann 289
Minor, Harriett 37, Nancy
  60, Phenetta 117
Mishew (Michaux?) John
  248
Mitchell, Eliz. 204,
  Hannah 225, Marg. 38-
  354, Martha 208, Olive
  90, Peter, 204-208-
  225, Sally 87-132,
Moye, Gen. Wyatt 247
Moody, Charity 1, Polly
  174, Mary 124
Moonyham, Lucrecy 151,
  Mary 21
Moore, Alice 47, Amanda
  173-286, Amos 275,
Ann 218, Anzelina 130,
  Barth. 297, Cath. 22.
  Delilah 237, Delphia
  89, Edwin 297, Elijah
  237, Eliz. 20-26-50-
  176-201-231-284-294,
  Hester 241, Jas. 297
  (2), Jerusha 189, John
  261-284, Jos. 209-218-
  261, Lucinda 59, Lydia
  146, Marina 56, Martha
  92-209, Mary 40-102-
  131 (2), Mollie 208,
  Nancy 135, Newton
  292, Pattie 268, Penny
  20, Piety 286, Polly
  70, Rebecca 108-297,
  Roderick 297, Rutha
  199, Sally 155-231-
  298, Sam. 189-201-
  208-221-237-245-247-
  258-286 (2), Sarah 78-
  199-221, Surety 174,
  Susan 41-101-180,
  Susa. 101, Rev. Thos.
  297, Wm. 248, Winnefred 63, Zada 237
Mooring, John 263,
  Jane 155-263
Morgan, Ann 197, Cath.
  22, Caty 163, Delphia
  75-209, Elsie 11,
  Felicia 86, Jas. S.
  209, Jos. 197-219,
  Keddy 212, Lucy 139,
  Martha 104-224, Mary
  61-155, Sallie 161,
  Wm. 212-224
Morris, Eliz. 174,
  Martha 31-77, Milbry
  38, Nathan 219,
  Patsy 135, Talitha
  68, Thos. 293, Zilla
  276
Moseley, Bytha 151,
  Cinda 162, Eliza 71,
  Eliz. 147, Jane 46,
  Lavinia 164, Lucy 50,
  Nancy 130, Peninah 58,
  Sarah 89, Susan 31
Mulkey, Philip 216
Mullen, Fran. 66, Mary
  50
Mumford, Peninah 31,
  Sophia 239,
Myrick, Chas. 297, Jas.
  297, John 297, Moses
  297

- N -

Nadal, Sarah 113
Nairney, Elsie 163
Neal, Char. 32-259,
  Polly 35
Nelson, Albena 28,
  Cinderella 96-263,
  Fannie 155, Jonas
  263, Judith 132
Nettle, Eliz. 60-258,
  John 202-206-279,
Mary 42, Oliff 206,
  Polly 202, Russia
  38-246-261, Sally 279
Newsome, Lucy 76,
  Nancy 3, Patty 194,
  Susa. 98, Thos. 194
Nicholson, Eliz. 222,
  John 199, Letitia 199
  Nancy 193, Penelope
  193-212-222-227-236
  (2), Pheriba 227, Polly
  212, Sarah 297
Nixon, Eliz. 240, Peter
  260
Nolly, Berthana 105
  Drucilla 88, Fran. 106
Nobleland, John 198,
  Mary 198
Norcom, Mary 168
Norfleet, Christian 218,
  Emily 84-213-243-
  253, Jas. 264, John
  253, Isaac 263, Isham
  218, Marg. 107-218,
  Marmaduke 289-291,
  Nancy 83, Pheribe 289,
  Sally 264, Sarah 291,
  Thos. 289
Norman, Mary 16, Polly
  255
Norris, Charity 216,
  Eliz. 216, Jacky 111,
  John 226, Peggy 106,
  Rebecca 82, Silvah
  226
Norville, Norvil, Arrena
  222, Chapman 222,
  Eliz. 158, Raney 122,
  Sally 179
Norwood, Betty 289,
  Sam. 289
Nowell, Darky Ann 27

- O -

O'Berry, Anne 156,
  Mary 110-248
O'Brien, Lawrence 240
O'Day, Polly 136
Odom, Abraham 229,
  Ann 115, Cath 129,
  Lavina 160, Mary
  103, Nancy 93, Rebecca 26, Sally 35,
  Sealy 229
O'Neal, O Neil, O'Neel,
  Edmund, 205, Isham
  224, Molly 51-205,
  Nancy 80, Nannie
  112, Penny 86,
  Polly 224, Susan
  104, Vicey 168
Owens, Amanda 26,
  Anna 116, Betsy 117,
  Caroline 51, Celia
  30-94, Delpha 61,
  Dicey 26, Easter 44,
  Eliza 107, Eliz. 31,
  Kath. 13-69, Laura
  70, Martha 117, Mary

313

118, Milly 168, Naomi 43, Obedience 61, Penny 116, Phereby 154, Sally 94, Sarah 50-61, Rev. Thos. 260, Zoan 26
Outlaw, Fran. 71

- P -

Pace, Amey 150, Ann 86
Page, Amanda 64, Eliz. 104-116, John 296-280, Letha 162, Martha 104, Mary 87, Nancy 65-179, Patty 296, Sally 116, Sarah 280-296
Pallomountain, Emily 15
Parish, Angelina 223
Parker, Amanda 41, Ann 252, Arcena 47, Caroline 67-208-245-258, Casanda 153, Cath. 210, Charity 195, Cinderella 18, Conzada 35, Cornelia 151, Ed. 245-259, Eliza 15-193, Eliz. 29-122-124-130-206-246, Elvira 115, Emily 107, Fannie 145, Fran. 195, Francis 206-210, Hardy 193-203, Henrietta 11-255, Mrs. Jas. 2, Joan 65, John 243-247-252, Marg. 11-192-243-253-268, Martha 126-128-177, Mary 6-46-52-73-89-191-208-246-261, M. W. 67, Nancy 36-45-203, Sally 103, Sidney 142, Simmons 259, Tempie 9-191, Thos. 208-240-258-261-262, Weeks 192-239-253-255-259-268-297, Wm. 191, Virginia 111
Passmore, Eliz. 226, John 226
Patience, Cynthia 247
Patterson, Eliza 50, Peggy 56, Polly 3
Payne, Ann 291, Mourning 291
Peacock, Sally 49
Peal, Lydia 165, Nancy 94, Rebecca 147, Tabitha 3
Pearce, Patsy 93
Peebles, Eliz. 98, Mary 269, Susan 269, Thos. 269, Wm. 270

Peele, Peel, Cath. 203-205-222-231, Char. 6, Easter 219, Eliz. 104-201-205-299, Fereby 210, Hillary 201-219-229-233-299, John 299-287, Louisa 30, Marg. 221, Martha 163-203, Mary 148-201-229-276-299, Patsy 53, Pennetta 164, Robt. 201-210-221-276, Sally 178-299, Sarah 287, Wm. Ann 5, Winnefred 100
Pelt, Nancy 108, Polly 13
Pender, Amarilla 246-263, Andrew 261, Cath. 273, Cullen 257, Eliza 86, Eliz. 31-120-139-210, Evelina 153, Jas. 120-273, Janis 222, John 210-242-257, Jos. 258-272, Joshua 259, Josiah 120-232-234, Julia 61-252, Kate 120-184, Laura 99-120-249, L. C. 120, L. D. 247, Lewis 260, Louisiana 252, L. R. 26, Lucinda 143-151-242-248-250-284, Martha 97-142-143, Mary 17-134-165, Nancy 48-125-272, Polly 140-195, Rhoda 143, Robt. 246-249-263, Rose 158-185, Sarah 182-232 Selah 234, Sol. 232-250-251-234-284, Thos. 245-257, Wm. 222-263, Wm. Ann 63
Peoples, Louisa 186, Mary 80-116, Nancy 136
Permenter, Betsy 59, Jas. 195-230 (2), John 278, Lydia 230, Martha 150-230-278, Mary 195, Susa. 282
Pernton, Martha 82
Perritt, Ann 224, John 224
Perry, B. L. 121, Nancy 174, Bytha 21, Sol. 267
Pettaway, Petway, Anna 152, Cath. 133, Carolina 170, Eliz. 44, Marg. 14, Martha 84, Micaj. 242-251-297, Susan 94-295, Wm. 297
Philips, Amanda 49-137, Arthur 188-208-217, Caroline 136, Celia 82, Dr. Chas. 265-268, Char. 212, David 282, Eliza 118-247, Eliz. 224, Fred. 259, Dr. Jas. 298, Jos. 222-264-266, Leah 282, Lucy 188, Malvina 48, Martha 162, Mary 73-137-208, Nancy 127, Patience 217, Peninah 77, Prudence 47, Sarah 6-34-118-202, Susan 11-88, Winny 282
Pierson, Berona 292
Pinnell, Sarah 90
Pippen, Pippin, Bethia 256, Bethinae 195, Cath. 165-233-244-256, Eliz. 30-199, Emeliza 78, Harriett 217, J. J. 256 (2), Jos. 190-195-199-217-223-229-233 (2)-251-297-298 (2), Kinchen 298, Lavinia 229, Lucrecia 25, Lydia 190, Martha 78-223-296, Mary 43-116-195, Matilda 23-91, Nancy 149-233-297-298, Peninah 55, Spicey 105, Talitha 95-185-299, Temp. 201-223
Pitt, Ann 91-190 (2)-222-229, Anna 119, Caroline 139, Cath. 103-115, Char. 56-182-282, Drucilla 106-184, Eliz. 78-85-148-177-250-281, Emily 103, Esther 107, Etheld. 190-229, Gatsey 156-284, Jas. 56-190-195-212-222-229-273-279, John Ella 182, Jos. 282, Joab 262 (2)-284, Judidah 9-273, Keziah 274-279, Lussetta 68, Mary 6-144-150-170, Mollie 229, Nancy 125, Nathan 262, Penelope 128, Pernetta 21-195, Polly 43, Ralph 281, Rebecca 212-262-279, Robt. 279, Sally 163-284-285, Sarah 51-126-178-222, Susan 176, Thos. 285, West 190, Winnifred 43
Pittman, Pitman, Amy 220, Ann 246, Avery 11, Benj. 194-205, Eliza. 56, Eliz. 50-56-85-106-108-148-151, Emeliza 31,

Emily 161, Georgiana 28, Ginsey 8, Harriett 84, Harrison 258, Julia 65, Lucinda 164, Lucy 12, Lusetta 68, Malissa 5, Marg. 162, Martha 43-78-79, Mary 86-126-138-185-194-231, Millie 29, Melbry 169, Nancy 231, Dr. Newsom 269, Patience 205, Patsy 50-120, Peggy 169, Penelope 9-101-124-245-258, Peninah 164, Polly 43-54, Prisc. 159, Rebecca 14, Redding 254, Sally 220, Sarah 3-82, Susan 57, Wm. 262

Phelps, Rhoda 102
Poland, Ann 13, Charity 79
Pond, Emily 39
Pope, Betsey 262, Eliza 83, Emily 6, Jacob 278-230-237, John 261, Julian 220, Lucretia 15-259, Marg. 247, Martha 44-88-90-115-232-266, Mary 180-230-232, Mourning 237-278, Nancy 169, Rebecca 230, Wm. 220
Porie, Eliza 239
Porter, Benj. 255, Chas. 199, Eli 211-256, Elisha 282, Eliz. 199-120, Fran. 42, Jos. 247-258, Martha 79-190-211-223-233-256, Mary 173, Moody 255, Nancy 45-255, Penelopy 19, Peninah 282, Sarah 85, Susan 186
Portis, Eliza 159, Lucy 6, Mary 128
Potts, Dr. John 244
Powell, Charity 269, Christian 225, Cinta 127, Cotten 296, Cuita 185, Eliza 138, Eliz. 25-77-206-225, Fran. 269, Isabella 127, Jesse 241-248-269-270-298, John 274, Marg. 299, Mary 123-130-213, Nancy 206, Patty 291, Rich. 291, Sally 7-110, Sarah 200-274, Wm. 200-213-225 (2)-298, Winnefred 295, Winny 55
Power, Sarah 295
Poyner, Mary 298
Price, Ann 207, Betsey 211, Mrs. Celia 245-259, Charity 195, Elijah 241, Eliz. 77-90-205, Henrietta 43, Jesse 195, Jos. 211, Kesiah 32-199, Louisa 128, Lydia 157, Martha 109, Mary 65-116, Mourning 4-189, Nanny 206, Patience 195, Patsy 38, Penny 156, Prisc. 22-206, Rachel 188, Rhoda 94, Robt. 292, Sarah 70-160, Temp. 93, Thos. 188-189-199-207, Wm. 205-206
Pridgen, Mary 234, Wm. 234
Prince, Thos. 243
Proctor, Aaron 280-285-286, Betty 232, Celia 295, Cittury 74, Eliz. 37-63-118-132-136-180, Fran. 81, Fred. 295, Gatsey 126, John 213, Joice 174, Joshua 190, Louisiana 173, Lovey 48, Lucinda 20, Lucy 241-265, Martha 73-93-100-170-183-295, Mary 131-154-157-208-286, Murphy 104, Nancy 285, Nanny 190, Patience 213, Patsey 280, Piety 55, Polly 109, Rhoda 62-75, Robenia 16, Susan 186, Virginia 105, Wm. 208-232, Winnefred 279, Zana 74
Pugh, Harriett 180, Maria 242, Rachel 81
Pullen, Blake 298, Lem. 298
Purvis, Eliza 36, Eliz. 68, Emily 37, Hannah 200, Isabella 154, Lewis 198-200, Julia 33-198, Sally 294-299

- Q -

Quinn, Nancy 226, Patty 213, Wm. 213-226

- R -

Randall, Alex 279, Mary 279
Randolph, Martha 79
Rascoe, Thos. 255
Ratterford, Nancy 20
Rawls, Rachel 19, Prisc. 173
Ray, John 298
Raynor, Rainer, Anna 68, Mary 118, Polly 121, Sallie 249
Read, Reed, Reid, Betsy 63, Elder Jesse 278, Kath. 290, Louisa 133, Lydia 278, Martha 72-108-244-254, Penny 62, Phereby 12, Polly 4, Sally 66, Susa. 290, Willis 133
Reasons, Delphia 31-136, Nancy 70, Susan 139
Reddick, Perlina 183
Redding, Lawrence 262
Redmond, Alice 156, Alicia 255, Ann 133, Dan. 239, Jas. 260
Revel, Delilah 97
Revis, Eliz. 27
Rey (Ray?), Anna 275
Rhoades, Abraham 235, Polly 235
Rhymes, Jesse 289, Mony 289
Rice, Mary 273
Richards, Danford 244-255

Ricks, Rix, Ann 210-278-289, Benj. 293 (2), Charity 207-265-277-295, Cornelia 183, Drucilla 8, Fran. 130, Isaac 223-225-298, Jas. 189-192-207-210-219-265-277-278-295, John 289, Judy 219, Laura 150, Lewis 293-298, Malany 294, Mary 70-85-185-223, Mourning 189-293, Nancy 99-278, Patience 293, Phoebe 128-207-295, Piety 62, Rhoda 192, Sally 134, Sarah 225-293-298, Temp. 81-242-251, Wm. 298

Riddick (Reddick?), Sally 145,
Ridley, John 253
Ritter, Amanda 169, Ansy 33, Lucinda 58, Polly 167
Robards, Wm. 251
Robbins, Robins, Barsheba 153, Betsey 41, Charity 152-195-227, Christiana 89-154, Christina 183-Eliz. 9-21-58-221-237, Evelina 84, Jacob 260, John 189-221, Ledy 225, Lousana 20, Luraney 210, Martha 28-52-159, Matilda 177, Milly 225, Nancy 38-50-

87-189, Obedience 10, Polly 174, Rachel 136, Rebecca 137, Sarah 158-225 (2), Simon 191, Wm. 89-195-210-227-237
Roberson, Archelaus 212-279, Kittrena 92, Kittura 183, Joshua 92, Mary 212-279, Susa. 22, Winnie 25
Roberts, Sarah 137, Wm. 255
Robertson, Betsey 234, Elijah 261, Hardy 207-221-234, Henry 234, Lavina 61, Patsy 221, Peter 223-234, Phereby 207, Polly 160, Rebecca 169, 253, Rhoda 223, Temp. 234, Wm. 202
Robinson, Dicey 132, Esther 71, Mary 168, Milly 29, Rhoda 72
Rogers, Rodgers, Asenith 13-112, Eliz. 94-215-250, Emanuel 289, Josiah 209, Martha 166, Mary 285-289, Prisc. 232, Rachel 283, Sally 177-209, Sarah 238, Stephen 250, Thos. 285, Tristram 236, winnefred 236
Rose, Adaline 93, Eliz. 232, Keddy 160, Mary 124, Nancy 132, Piety 101, Robt. 197-232, Sarah 197
Ross, Andrew 223-229-232, Ann 225, Charity 75, Dan 267, Eliz. 115, Esther 134, Jude 225, Kallum 225 (2), Margaret 147-244-254, Mary 76
Rountree, Clarenda 103, Delphia 275-287, Eliza 37-300, Eliz. 118, Emily 79, Harriett 204, John 276, Lewis 200-204-214, Marg. 113, Martha 52, Mary 88, Nancy 8-271, Nathan 255, Obedience 277, Penelope 98-276, Sarah 10-214-284, Treacy 10, Wiley 287, Willie 271-277-284-287
Routh, Ruth, Cath. 254, Eliz. 273, Fran. 173, Marg. 262, Mary 273-297-294, Nancy 297, Robt. 273-294-298, Sally 281, Wm. 273-281-297-298
Rud, Rudd, Betha 2
Ruffin, Benj. 202, Bethane 77, Cecelia 295, Celia 77, Charity 37-237, Eliza 232 (2), Eliz. 59-176-231-237, Esther 159-232-285-293-299, Fran. 9, Jacky 132-282, John 298, Julian 141, Lucy 183, Marg. 10-175-254-272, Martha 96-129-139-157-252, Mary 16-75-84-118-209-257-278, Meduvia 182, Milicent 298, Nancy 54-96, Olivia 266, Ona 39, Penelope 39, Polly 231, Prisc. 101, Prudence 285, Rachel 22, Sally 141-209, Sarah 273, Sam. 232-254-271-272-278-282-285 (2)-295-298-299, Wm. 283-298, Winnefred 202
Rutland, Randolph 264

- S -

Sanders, Sarah 190, Thos. 190
Sasnett, Sassnett, Eliz. 158, Esther 172-236, Fannie 99, Henrietta 216, Joshua 202-236, Martha 216, Mary 43-202, Sally 60, Sarah 241-250
Saul, Mary 227, Abraham 227
Sauls, Lydia 141
Saunders, Sarah 105
Sawyer, Isaac 253
Savage, Savadge, Savedge, Savidge, Absalom 214-218, Angelina 139, Betsey 66, Brittania 42, Chas. 212, Char. 170, Cinderella 85, Eliz. 143-218-227, Ellen 59, Emeliza 149, Emily 33, Fran. 29-227, Harriett 140, Jack Eliza 87, Jas. 190-224-257-257-263, Jane 3, Jennie 78, Keziah 198-204, Lem. 255, Lovelace 188-198, Lovey 30, Lucy 23, Martha 14, Mary 188, Nancy 8-178, Peninah 140, Sarah 40-87, Sabra 104, Sally 132-140-214, Susan 22, Wealtha 106

Scarborough, David 298, Jas. 203 (2), 276, Maj. Jas. 298, Martha 294, Mary 59, Polly 203-276
Scott, Tempy 49
Screw, Anna 139
Scutchins, Mary 107
Seabrook, Eliz. 63
Sellers, Penelope 136, Sarah 41-180
Sessums, Sessoms, Ann 95-203-275, Cath. 150, Char. 200 (2)-269, Eliz. 200 (2)-202-241-296, Emeliza 74, Emily 61-111, Lavinia 87, Martha 128, Mary 140-174, Nicholas 202-203-217 (2)-221-275, Patience 199, Peninah 139-145, Rich. 199, Roderic 239, Sol. 200 (2)-212, Wm. Delha 99, Wilson 244-256
Shallington, Dr. Wm. 246-263, Winnefred 66
Sharpe, Abraham 286, Mrs. A. S. 263, Benj. 253, Col. Benj. 259, Eliz. 176, Emily 142, Jane 13, John P. 191-252-263, Mahala 9-191-253, Malzina 29, Marg. 12, Mary 7, Mrs. Mary 246, Nancy 150-157-285, Queen Esther 49, Sarah 38
Sheals, Ann 240
Shelton, Ameliza 66, Burwell 252, Caroline 143, Evelina 183, Emily 183, Harriett 211, Maria 105-256, Marg. 73-129, Martha 31-75, Penelope 50, Pennina 182, Wm. 211
Sheppard, Pamela 184-249,
Sherrod, Sherod, Amanda 39, Bethia 297, Cath. 230-296, Eliz. 23, Franky 147, Harriett 143, John 296-297, J. Wm 230-11, Keddy 50, Manisia 242-251, Marg. 59, Mary 296 Pheraby 86, Rhoda 53
Shingleton, Eliz. 51, Sally 70
Ship, Mary 76-210, Rich. 210-233, Sukey 233, Susa. 163
Shirley, Shurly, Shearly, Courtney 42, Delilah 234, Eliza. 39-203, Elsie 217, Geraldus

246-261-279, Henry 192-203-211-254-256, Julia 7-254, Marg. 79 279, Martha 13-192-263, Mary 44-124, Murphey 234, Nancy 204, Peninah 8-256, Rich 204-217, Susan 129
Short, Sally Turner 269
Sikes, Bazel 254, Harriett 59, Letitia 2 Letitia 2
Simmons, Edward 210 (2), Eliz. 210, Mrs. Harrison 260, Jane 210, Mary 260, Thos. 240
Simms, Asenath 279, Barnes 287 (2), Benj. 190-191-218-271-278, Diana 278, Eliz. 190-191-272-287, Jacob 278, Jas. 191-201-272-275, Jos. 202-207, Maria 73, Martha 39 (2)-274-275-201 (2), Mary 63-277-278-287, Patience 22-179, Patsey 10-191, Patty 207, Penelope 278, Polly 207-218, Rachel 221, Robt. 274-276, Sally 15-190, Sarah 210-278, Senah 202, Simon 279, Theresa 271, Wm. 207-210, Zelia 49, Zilla 190-191-201 (2)
Simpson, Emeliza 133, Tempy 19
Skinner, Andrew 261, Annie 9, Eliza 251, Eliz. 190-242-259-297, Felicia 158, Frances 135, Henry 227, Lydia 53, Mary 10-69, Peggy 119, Wm. 252-297
Slade, Ann 241
Smith, Amelia 4, Ann 46-86, Arabella 90, Cherry 7, Bithia 298, Drew 289-292, Georgiana 167, Jas. 291, Lucy 291, Marg. 57, Mary 46-51-289-290-291-292, Nancy 88, Nicholas 292 (2), Parmetta 70, Robt. 290, Sarah 70-291-292, Wm. 242-251-257-291 (2), Zylpha 164
Snead, Caroline 244
Snow, Emma 246
Soary, Sorey, Andrew 195-231, Eli 260, Eliza 108, Eliz. 116-160, Lucinda 110, Lucy 195-219-231, Mary 62, Nancy 99-108, Polly 162-195-262, Sally 231, Sol. 216-219
Somerville, Johanna 249
Sorrell, Celia 178
Southall, Mattie 181
Southerland, Dan. 299, Eliz. 297, Janette 17, Mary 294-298-299, Dr. Sam 243-253
Spain, Jenny 23
Sparkman, Cynthia 4, Letha 53, Silpha (Zylpha) 65
Sparks, Eliz. 21
Sparrow, Annie 56
Spath (Speight?), Marg. 115
Spaw, Ann 86
Speight, Mrs. Jesse 247, Rev. John 246, Dr. Rich. 299
Speight, Mrs. Jesse 247, Rev. John 246-261, Dr. Rich 299
Spell, Ann 225, Dolly 86, Selvent 17, Thos. 225
Spelling, Brittania 180
Spicer, Emeliza 180, Keziah 190, Marg. 213, Mary 213, Moses 299, Nancy 15, Sally 223, Wm. 213 (2)-223
Spivey, Mary 125
Spruill, Benj. 244-254, Geo. 240, Mary 5,
Stafford, Ann 242, Nancy 16
Stakes (Stokes?), Sally 62
Stallings, Stalings, Stallin, Stallions, Absala 194, Amanda 24, Cath. 140, Celia 99, Eliz. 158-277, Fran. 158, Greg. 194-204-213-220, Hannah 204, Jas. 202-223-225-299, Jane 140, Louisa 33-61, Marg. 45, Marinah 16, Martha 202-225, Mary 43-67-72-115-220, Milly 98, Nancy 44-123, Penelope 98-156, Rachel 213, Sarah 220, Temp. 38
Stancil, Stancell, Harriet 181-294, Jane 123, Jesse 256, Louisa 156, Sallie 76,
Standard, Rachel 162
Stanton, Eliz. 39-148-276, Jas. 276
Starke, Dr. Lucien 299
Staton, Annie 216,
Arthur 211-219-296, Baker 242-251, Bytha 213, Bythal 251-262, Char. 296, Cherry 8, Eliz. 39-148 (2)-190, Ezekiel 210-211-213-216-236, Finella 74, Fran. 102-241-250, Grace 250, Gracie 67-95-211, Hannah 82, Harriett 15-296, Hettie 140, Jesse 189-217, Llewelling 258, Lovey 3-189, Lucinda 80, Martha 75, Mary 85-180-262, Nancy 67-171-236-262, Nehemiah 190-202, Nerva 90, Nicey 211, Penelope 1, Phenetta 257, Sabra 210, Sarah 217, Simmons 257. Susa. 219, Talitha 202, Virginia 87-161, W. A. 24, Wm. 250, Willie 249, Winfield 262 (2)
Stephenson, Mary 184, Sarah 138, Susa. 32
Stewart, Stuart, Robt. 240, Wm. 254-293
Stillman, Cath. 133-260
Stokes, Betty 232, Evelina 65, Gatsy 105, John 232, Mary 101, Nancy 84, Lurana 111
Story, Sarah 32
Strautidge (Daughtridge?), Nancy 149
Strawther (Strother?), Sarah 112
Strickland, Stricklin, Amanda 97, Cath. 97 97, David 252, Luerelia 73, Martha 12, Mary 113, Nelly 125, Sarah 113
Stringer, Anselana 286, Wm. 286
Sugg, Acquilla 266(2), 279, Esther 279, Euphemia 230, Fran. 145-236-298, Lem. 266-297-299, Lucy 60, Marg. 102, Mary 59-297, Noah 222, Dr. Pheasanton 250, Redding 236-254-298-299, Sarah 265-266, Wm. 230
Summertin, Summerton, Peninah 61
Summerlin, Sumlin, Angelina 181, Barnes 223-234, Betsy 48-151, Jinnetta 61, Louiza 76, Mary 111,

Millie 169, Polly 223, Susan 106
Sumner, Eliz. 264, Sylvania 65
Surginer, Hannah 227, Olive 127-223, Robt. 223-227
Sutton, Jane 139, Martha 31-261, Wm. 253.
Swales, Ann 228, Mary 209-228, Susa. 209,
Swanner, Lucy 40
Swinney, Molly 110
Swinson, Ann 196

- T -

Talbert, Tolbert, Eliz. 125, Mary 32, Penelope 152, Pripa (Prissa?) 184, Prissa 115, Torq. 115
Tannabil, Wm. 254
Tanner, Sarah 104, Susan 146
Tartt, Cath. 281-284, Eliz. 276-234-285, Elnathan 273-283, Enos 284, Fereby 205, Jonathan 205-234-276-281-282-285, Martha 1-118-243-252-276-299, Mary 254-283-293, Obedience 273, Sarah 143-282, Theresa 57-241
Taylor, Allen 261, Ann 211, Annie 269, Annis 142, Arthur 201, Barzada 175, Blaney 25, Casandra 170, Celia 5-130, Char. 33-259, Eliza 126, Eliz. 20-142-155-213-227-258-261-286, Ellen 193, Faithy 106, Ford 299, Frankey 29, Gracy 209, Harriett 160, Jas. 188-213, Jane 109, John 193-222-296, Johnson 254, Kiddy 118, Kinchen 299, Kindred 256, Lavina 72, Letha 176, Lovey 135, Lucinda 143, Lucy 24, Marg. 40-71-142-252-253, Maria 171, Marina 81-155-262, Martha 23-178-201, Mary 37-57-76-113-171-182-272, Milbry 236-286, Nancy 3-4-222-233, Patsey 233, Polly 161, Rachel 236, Rebecca 92-167, Robt. 211, Sally 29, Sarah 25-128-153-232, Stephen 227-232-233 (2)-236-252-286,

Susan 177, Susa. 188, Tabitha 100-171-209, Thos. 250-259-262-263, Wm. 258-272, Zelpha 296
Teak, Mary 66
Teal, Sevesta 83
Teat, Nancy 129, Louisa Louisa 32
Tedder, Jas. 72, Wm. Ann 16, Sarah 87
Telfair, Marg. 243, Mary 279, O. W. 248,
Terrell, Alley 270, Ann 32, Nath. 245-255
Thigpen, Anna 138, Delphia 116, Edney 156, Eliza 55, Eliz. 106-166-245-233-257, Fannie 216, Finetta 145-257, Gilliard 203-207, Harriett 172, Howell 256, Lem. 228-233-257, Littleberry 251, Lydia 97-199, Jas. 199-216-256, Mary 30-44-117-262, Penetta 228, Sally 68-207-256, Tamsey 69, Wm. 262, Vicey 203
Thomas, Ann 272, Charity 12-177-234, Delphia 144, Eason 273, Eliza 90-132, Eliz. 25-191-199-273, Gatsey 12, Harriett 131, Hilliard 299, Ichabod 282, Jacob 273-254, Jonathan 275 (2)-282, John 209-210-218-228-282, Elder John 278, Jos. 275-294, Lively 199, Marg. 10-55, Martha 93-105-159, Mary 10-11-21-77-158-191-195 (2)-196-199-201-228 (2)-231-234-236-273, Micajah 299 (2), Milicent 210-278, Molly 195, Mourning 40-129-236-275-294, Nancy 275, Obedience 196-284, Patsey 133, Peninah 27, Pheraby 133 Philip 272, Polly 195, Prisc. 35-294, Sally 201, Sarah 218-275, Susa. 282, Tabitha 228-283, Temp. 241-282, Theophilus 228 (2)-231-283-284-(2), Theresa 52-75-282-284, Treasy 209-231, Wade 242-250, Wm. 299, Dr. Wm. 246-263, Wm. Ann

60, Zypha 50
Thompson, Ann 72, Jacque 189, Mary 189-240-285, Noah 254-259, Susan 28.
Thorne, Thorn, Eliz. 11-117, Jane 25, Marg. 9, Nancy 128, Polly 22, Sarah 131
Thornell, Benj. 195-214, Dolly 195, Sally 214
Thorpe, Fran. 279, Henry 279, Mary 194, Sol. 194
Thurston, Lucy 40-256
Tillery, Georgeanna 95, Sarah 147
Tisdal, Eliz. 221, Mary 214, Oney 10-191, Renison 191-210-214-221-224, Tabitha 214,
Titus, Marg. 87
Todd, Elsie 54, Mary 50, Nancy 142
Tolson, Chacy 54, Eliz. 98, Letha 123-124, Lydia 151, Mary 224, Talitha 222, Winder 222-224
Tomlinson, Temp. 135, Treacy 171
Toole, Amelia 225-253, Ann 109-134-251, Arabella 239, Caroline 180, Eliza 225, Geraldous 225 (2)-251-253, Henry 243, Jean 194, Mary 240-244, Susan 245
Trevathan, Cath. 19, Celia 137, Eliz. 84, Harriett 81, Joanna 64, Martha 20, Mary 42, Nannie 183, Rosa 137
Tucker, Nancy 87
Tunnell, Char. 147, Martha 261
Turnage, Nancy 75
Turner, Alfred 263, Henrietta 124, Henry 209, Jacob 263, Mary 21, Matt. 255, Sallie 249, Sarah 157-285, Susan 14-255, Winny 209
Tyler, Celestia 39, Lorenza 177, Louisa 26-181, Lucy 165, Susan 177-186, Wm. 26

Tyson, Aaron 277, Esther 6-254-271, Jerusha 277, Marg. 78, Nancy 141, Wm. 232-293-299

- V -

Vainwright, Edie 183
Valentine, Gilbert 252
Vann, Van, Martha 51, Sally 146
Varb, Louisa 104, Marg. 14
Varnell, Barsheba 53, Eliz. 54
Vasser, Dolly 83, Sally 74, Susan 50
Vaughan, Vaughn, Laura 158, Mary 170
Veal, Eliz. 285-299
Vettel, Sally 82
Vick, Celia 6, Eliza 58-152, Fran. 8-58, Jas. 262, Josiah 274, Lucy A. 184, Malvina 137, Marg. 22, Nancy 116, Sarah 274
Vickers, Eliz. 235, John 209-219-230-235, Martha 71-209, Mary 190-219, Patience 230, Rachel 227-283, Ralph 190-227-283
Vines. Chas. 220-247, Eliz. 227, Emily 273, Latetia 113, Lucy 220, Mary 151, Olivia 9, Sam. 240-273, Sophia 84

- W -

Walker, Ann 243, Dan. 279, Eliza 66, Fannie 268, Mary 96, Polly 65, Sarah 157, Winifred 279, Vestia 25
Walke, Rhoda 121
Wall, Ann 175, Faithy 64, John 214, Phebe 2, Selah 214, Thena (Pheby) 188
Waller, Ann 15-243-254, Cath. 97, Jas. 211-219-231, Jenny 64-219, Marg. 186-207, Martha 151, Mary 231-267, Nancy 211, Sally 114-126, Susan 65
Walls, Elsie 163, Sally 181
Walston, Betsey 14, Eliza 128, John 259, Mary 2, Nancy 7, Sarah 97
Walton, Christian 280, John 280-281, Marg. 71, Martha 3-283, Mary 40, Sarah 281
Warbelton, Wabbleton, Lenora 147, Mary 40
Warbritton, Fran. 3
Ward, Amanda 65, Char. 194-211, Eliza 97, Eliz 122, Harmon 244-256, Harriett 216, Henrietta 72, Dr. John 257, Louisa 10, Luke 256, Lydia 126, Marg. 168-257, Mary 61-109-121, Nancy 216, Sally 28-125, Willie 258
Warren, Ama 67, Eliz. 122-129, Jane 288, John 285, Lovey 166, Marg. 23, Mary 134, 150, Milicent 288, Nancy 150-285, Penelope 147, Prisc. 215-232-238, Rich. 245-257, Robt. 288 (3)-291, Sarah 288-291, Winnefred 262
Wasdon, Eliza 72, Olive 137
Washington, Dolly 118
Watkins, Jas. 253
Watson, Dolly 251, Fereby 25, Jordan 297, Mullion 292, Polly 297, Sally 167, Thos. 251, Viney 57
Watts, Eliz. 289, Jos. 289 289
Weathersbee, Jos. 299,
Weaver, Benj. 215-231, Charity 186, Eliza 195, Emily 124-145-262, Evelina 135, Jonathan 195-227, Malvina 74, Martha 54, Mourning 101-231, Nancy 88, Obedience 144-227, Piety 215, Rich. 262, Sally 101
Webb, Amanda 69, Annie 53, Bedy 186, Betsey 68, Celia 69, Char. 144-208, Christiana 168, Cynthia 85, Cypy 228, Edy 161, Eliz. 69, Ellen 181, Emily 69, Gatsey 151, Jacky 68, John 208-213-228-234, Junetta 145, Litha 68, Louisiana 168, Marinda 29, Matilda 14-61, Mary 54-55-159-162-213, Mourning 89, Polly 234, Rebecca 179, Rissa 49, Sealy 167, Susan 145, Treacy 26, Vicey 69, Viney 164 Weltha 163
Weddell, Jas. 257
Weeks, Amanda 104-262, Ann 221, Betsey 66, Celia 269, Cely 196-208-214-222, Char. 154, Eliza 90, Eliz. 214, Jas. 196-208-214-222 (2), Lucy 18, Malissa 4, Martha 65-128-196-207, Mary 118-221-222, Patsey 93, Sally 108, Sarah 207-208-221-232, Selah 222, Silas 262, Susan 4-41, Tabitha 47

Welch, Charity 32
Wells, Betty 229, Eliz. 5-150, Harriett 31, Honor 219, Jane 13, Kiddy 1, Lydia 80, Maizie 142, Martha 75-103, Mary 109-129-225, Matt. 219, Nancy 168, Piety 17, Prisc. 3- 223, Rachel 213, Sally 31, Sarah 200, Stephen 223 (2)-225-229, Susan 131, Thos. 200-213-234, Winnefred 44, Winnie 223
Wember (Wimberly?), Prisc. 41,
West, Eliz. 289, Henry, 253-291, Israel 289, Mary 236-291, Susa. 291, Wm. 236-291
Wester, Ann 234, Sarah 11
Weston, Amos 223, Nancy 233
Westry, Celestia 65, Sally 241-269, Sam. 269
Whichard, Jennett 184,
Whitaker, Eliz. 199, Jas. 242-251, John 250, Lydia 91, Mourning 204
White, Ann 214, Edith 201, John 201-208, Nancy 276, Sarah 208-214, Talitha 136, Treacy 138
Whitehead, Augustine 215, Char. 244, Chloe 35, Eliz. 58-175-200, Henry 258, Jacob 292, Laz. 264, Marg. 157-207, Martha 43, Mary 119-174-293, Matt. 207-232, Nancy 157-235, Piety 171, Prisc. 290, Prudence 215, Rhoda 264, Sally 264, Sarah 191 (2)-200-225, Susa. 225, Thaney 135-157-232, Wm. 191-200-225-235-264-290, Wm. Ann 142
Whitehouse, Mary 180
Whitehurst, Caroline 172, Eliz. 27, Jas. 262

Whitfield, Albena 113, Marg. 299
Whitley, Cath. 65, Caroline 5, Eliz. 63-75-163, Teruthy 117, Julia 54, Keziah 43, Lucinda 117, Nancy 58 58, Sarah 125, Temp. 58, Wm. 236
Whitney, Caroline 5
Whittonton, Jenny 147
Wiggins, Ann 146, Cath. 36-235-296, Delphia 173, E. 172, Eliz. 125, Maria 132, Martha 239-296, Nancy 146-180-199, Polly 36-240, Prisc. 258, Robt. 199-235, Sarah 76-167-299, Wm. 299, Winnefred 58
Wilder, Caroline 247
Wilkins, Jacky 73, Jas. 278, Jane 10-256, Lisby 161, Lukins 120, Martha 33, Mary 108-122-298, Nancy 13-70-204, Sarah 57, Susan 241-258-278, Wells 256-258, Wm. 204-225-298, Wm. Ann 114

Wilkinson, Abner 245-257-261, Alvana 13, Anetta 145, Annaliza 147, Ansey (Anselana) 20-273, Belinda 173, Benoni 261, Edith 214, Eliza 105-261, Eliz. 45-111, Fran. 45, John 273, Joshua 203-214-219-275, Julia 141, Mary 203-275, Melinda 258, Nancy 172, Sally 12-112-252, Sarah 6-219, Susan 30-179, Treacy 5, Wm. 258, Winney 96
Willard, Sara 68

Williams, Absolam 224, Ann 212-292, Anna 224-282, Arthur 235-282, Axcy 109, Benj. 243-260, Betsey 13-131, Burwell 292, Cath. 7-85-256, Celia 119-297, Charity 209-224-282, Creasy 96, Crissy 80, Dancy 8, Dan. 289, Col. David 254, Dellah 60, Delphia 22, Dorcas 267-279-295, Egbert 256, Elisha 197, Eliz. 54-64-100-200-272-289, Ellen 8, Emily 13-57, Esther 17, Fran. 172, Henrietta 60,
Jas. 209, Jane 24-169, Jileen (Julian) 290, Joel 292, John 193-215-224-243-252-267-272-279-290-297, Joshua 243-252, Julia 297, Louisa 183, Louisiana 181, Lucinda 181, Lucy 193, Malvina 121, Marg. 114, Maria 222, Martha 7-147-236-247-271, Mary 20-175-197-212-215-235-260-290-296, Milbrey 88, Nancy 1-5-54-92-144-174-183, Oney 100, Patience 285, Patsey 174, Penelope 7, Penny 13, Phebe 165, Polly 52-135-203, Rhoda 224, Rich. 267, Dr. Robt. 267-299, Sally 63-81-83-136-160, Sarah 92, Susan 175, Thos. 224-282, Visa 130, Wealthy 275, Winnefred 42-203-236
Williamson, Chloe 113
Williford, Willaford, Amanda 37, Eliz. 81-272, Harmon 176, Hartwell 272, Lucinda 130, Mahala 134, Mary 55-51-110-176-245-258, Meedie 258, Peninah 37, Zany 130
Willingham, A. B. 268
Willis, Ann 189, Rhoda 192, Wm. 189-192
Wilson, Eliz. 269, Isaac 269, John 256, Nancy 269, Susa. 269, Wm. 269
Wimberley, Creecy 254, Geo. 198-251, Zilpha 198
Winborne, Jos. 177
Windham, Gracy 259
Wingate, Isabella 268
Winstead, Arcady 1, Chaney 237, Charity 237-286, Christana 49, David 271, Jeremiah 292, Martha 174, Mary 12, Mourning 138, Sally 154-200-237 (2), Temp. 271, Zylphia 200
Womack (Wammock), Louisa 111, Mary 39-129, Olivia 126
Womble, Celia 146, Enos 259, Finetta 96
Wood, Ann 137, Benj. 288, Eliz. 86, Martha 288, Mary 97, Milly 135, Nancy 61-99, Susan 79

Woodard, Ann 215, David 299, Delanah 189, Elisha 189-200-252-272-280-281-284-299, Eliz. 2-148-281, Jas. 261-272-276-299, John 210-215-216, Judith 2, Marg. 12-272, Martha 189-272-280, Mary 200-216-275-276-299 (2), Patience 53-277, Patsey 12, Pilgrim 275, Sarah 210, Susan 165, Treacy 159, Wm. 277, Zypha 284-299
Woolard, Patsey 72, Selecta 112
Wooten, Absalom 198-199-204, Charity 47, Delphia 179, Drucilla 155, Eliza 107, Eliz. 37-204, Fanny 179, Jas. 231, Letha 146, Milly 198, Nancy 146-204, Polly 117, Prissy 46, Sally 231, Tresina 53, Vina 33, Winnie 199
Worrell, Betsey 10, Louisa 159, Martha 165, Polly 122, Sally 10, Sarah A. 182
Worsley, Amanda 69, Caroline 119, Eliz. 132, Jennie 38, Leona 186, Laura 31-153, Littleberry 254, Lizina 24, Marina 95, Martha 126, Mayo 262, Redding 262, Sally 147
Wright Anna 261, Eliz. 34, Harriett 158-259, Mary 148, Susan 175
Wyatt, Eliz. 27
Wynn, Elmyra 175

- Y -

Yates, Rich. 264
Young, Jennett 149-242-251, Rutha 291, Sally 77, Thos. 291

- Z -

Zoeller, Amelia 141

www.ingramcontent.com/pod-product-compliance
Lightning Source LLC
Chambersburg PA
CBHW020639300426
44112CB00007B/176